CHINA AND AFRICA

CHINA
AND
AFRICA

A CENTURY OF ENGAGEMENT

DAVID H. SHINN
AND
JOSHUA EISENMAN

PENN

UNIVERSITY OF PENNSYLVANIA PRESS

PHILADELPHIA

Published by
University of Pennsylvania Press
Philadelphia, Pennsylvania 19104-4112

Printed in the United States of America
on acid-free paper
10 9 8 7 6 5 4 3 2 1

Library of Congress Cataloging-in-Publication Data

Shinn, David Hamilton.
    China and Africa : a century of engagement / David H.
Shinn and Joshua Eisenman. — 1st ed.
        p.   cm.
    Includes bibliographical references and index.
    ISBN 978-0-8122-4419-9 (hardcover : alk. paper)
    1. China—Foreign relations—20th century—Africa.
2. Africa—Foreign relations—20th century—China.
3. China—Foreign economic relations—20th century—
Africa.   4. Africa—Foreign economic relations—20th
century—China.   I. Eisenman, Joshua, 1977–   II. Title.
DS740.5.A34S55   2012
327.5106—dc23   2012006237

To our wives, Judy and Iris,
for their support and patience.

CONTENTS

FOREWORD

George T. Yu

"Let China sleep, for when she awakes, she will shake the world," was Napoleon's response to those who asked about the quiescent China of the eighteenth and nineteenth centuries. Today, China has indeed awakened, and she is shaking the world. As Mao Zedong declared in October 1949, upon the founding of the People's Republic of China, "China has stood up!"

One measurement of how "China has stood up" is its emergence as a global economic and political power, extending its presence to nearly all corners of the world. As the second-largest global economy and the world's factory floor, Chinese merchandise floods global markets. And as a permanent member of the United Nations Security Council, China is vested with worldwide decision-making power and responsibility. Some even call China a superpower, notwithstanding Beijing's strenuous rejection of the title.

Whether China is a superpower or a rising power with worldwide influence, there can be no disputing that China's interests are wide-ranging, quickly expanding, and on a global scale. In an era of globalization, China has established enduring relationships on all continents and with numerous partners, both major and minor. However, with the exception of Asia, no other continent can rival the extent, the intensity, the speed, and the impact of China's relations in Africa.

China's relationship with Africa has evolved in stages over six decades and has included ideological, economic, political, and security interests. In the years following the founding of the People's Republic of China in 1949, Beijing was repressive politically, weak militarily, and backward economically. It also faced challenges to its legitimacy and sovereignty. Subsequent ideological battles with the Soviet Union over leadership over the world communist movement catalyzed Beijing's early political outreach in Africa. China's weakness constrained its Africa policy, which first focused on cultural and political exchanges to extend ties with African countries. Later, commerce became the central driving force as China sought African energy and other commodities and markets for its products and infrastructure projects.

Chinese leaders have long viewed their movement in global terms. China's original decision to reach out to Africa was a necessary part of a foreign policy dedicated to spreading Maoist ideology around the world. China joined in common cause to assist the oppressed peoples of the world, support wars of national liberation, and provide aid to developing nations in what China labeled the Third World. Although China's resources were limited until its economic reforms began, Beijing's objectives and the immediate beginnings of China's African policy used revolutionary rhetoric in the service of cold pragmatism.

As Chinese officials and scholars regularly note, China's foreign policy is founded on three foundations: relations with major powers (the United States and European nations), neighboring states (South and Southeast Asia), and developing nations in Africa, Asia and Latin America. Depending on China's interests, its relations with these blocs have ranged from cooperative to confrontational and provided both challenges and opportunities. Beijing's ability to juggle these three sets of relationships is a hallmark of contemporary Chinese foreign policy and Africa has remained a part of China's broader global engagement since the early 1950s.

China's African foreign policy began in the context of its challenges and response to these three blocs: defending against political and military encirclement and seeking new allies in distant developing lands like Africa. Africa represented China's first major independent foreign policy outreach outside Asia, designed to defend Beijing's tenuous sovereignty and fragile security. China's efforts to build common cause with likeminded African revolutionaries were, at base, pragmatic: a response to U.S.-led economic isolation and later the Soviet military threat. How China was able to weather the domestic and foreign political, economic, and security issues that cropped up as it worked to develop relations with the countries of Africa—and did so with little or no experience and from a position of relative economic and military weakness—is one of the great sagas of modern foreign relations.

Two Distinct Periods in Policy Orientation

Two major periods divide China's Africa policy. From the early 1950s to mid-1970s, China's Africa policy had three primary objectives: breaking out of international isolation, battling the former Soviet Union for primacy in the world communist movement, and displacing Taiwan as the internationally recognized government of China. To that end, the People's Republic cooperated with African countries and revolutionary groups by supporting national liberation movements, assisting independent African governments economically and rhetorically, and seeking African support for its membership in the United Nations and other international organizations. It was during this period that China announced the "Eight Principles on Economic and Technical Aid" in 1964, which included this well-known provision governing relations with African nations: "the Chinese Government never asks for any privileges or attaches any conditions."

During this initial period, China interacted with independent African governments and revolutionary groups almost entirely through official government and party channels. Although constrained by economic weakness, China provided loans and grants as the principal instruments of economic relations with African countries. The $500 million Tanzania-Zambia Railway, the flagship project of Chinese assistance in Africa, was completed in 1975. China also provided limited military equipment and training to African allies and some national liberation groups. China made effective use of its limited, but sizeable economic base to establish and develop an operational infrastructure to support a growing network of relationships in Africa.

In the 1980s, a sea change occurred in China's Africa policy. Developments with roots dating back to 1971 helped bring about this change, including Beijing's wresting control of China's UN seat from Taipei, the opening of diplomatic exchanges with Washington in 1972, and the weakening and later dissolution of the Soviet Union. These changes freed China's policy makers from the Cold War's most pressing political and military stresses, thus permitting China to interact openly with all African states and groups, regardless of ideological leanings. These developments allowed African states to more openly conduct and deepen relations with China.

Second, the "reform and opening" policy that China initiated in the 1980s transformed the country economically. Through the adaptation and use of domestic and foreign capital, management skills, and technology, China became a global manufacturing center, the world's second-largest economy, and a regional and global power—all within only thirty years.

The impact of China's economic transformation on its African policy cannot be overstated. China-Africa commerce was forever altered along with African states' geostrategic importance to China. They became a growing market for China's products and other business ventures, a region for Chinese private and state investments, a source of energy and other commodities for China's industries, and allies in China's efforts to craft a more favorable global environment and institutions. This new era in Chinese-African relations continues.

Today, China's state-run companies and its burgeoning private sector firms have supplemented the state's activities and resources in Africa in areas including trade, investment, and infrastructure construction projects. Large-scale Chinese investment in Africa and the flow of Chinese migration to the continent are key indicators of this change.

Since the 1950s, Chinese military assistance to Africa has never ceased, although it has taken different forms. China is now the largest contributor among Security Council members to United Nations peacekeeping forces in Africa (albeit noncombat forces), and supplies select African states with military equipment and training. A gradual deepening of military relations has included numerous high-level military exchanges and the appointment of military attachés by Chinese and African governments to their respective embassies.

The Libyan crisis in 2011 illustrated, not atypically, the extent of Chinese involvement in one African country. As Libyan rebel forces and NATO warplanes worked to oust Muammar Qaddafi from power, China mobilized civilian and military aircraft along with foreign planes and ships to rescue 36,000 Chinese workers and return them safely to China. To protect ships ferrying Chinese workers from Libya Beijing also dispatched naval ships to the Mediterranean Sea off the Libyan coast for temporary assignment from their antipiracy deployment off the Somali coast in the Gulf of Aden. Clearly, this was a demonstration of China's new power projection capabilities. The crisis also revealed the intensity of China's economic presence and the risks and responsibilities its government now must assume thanks to its fast growing engagement. China had over 50 large-scale Chinese-funded enterprises involving $18.8 billion in Libya.

The Economic Turn

In the twenty-first century, China's economic impact on African development has demonstrated its newly acquired economic power and global reach. Two sectors, trade and investment, have been especially significant. As trade has grown, the substance of that trade has changed. During the 1980s and 1990s, Chinese exports to Africa were mainly food and light industrial products, but by 2000 the lion's share of China's exports consisted of electronics and machinery. Until the beginning of the twenty-first century, China was barely relevant as a trading partner for Africa. Over the last decade, however, to support China's economic growth, Africa has become a primary supplier of energy and mineral resources. Angola and South Africa are among China's most important African trading partners. Angola is one of China's largest foreign oil suppliers and South Africa sells China a variety of minerals, agricultural and manufactured goods.

Chinese direct investment overseas is a relatively new phenomenon and direct investment in Africa became formalized only in 2000, yet the growth of Chinese investment in Africa was extraordinary between 2000 and 2011. China has been attractive to African suppliers both as a potential market and for a source of investment capital in mineral prospecting and construction projects. Angola, Sudan, Nigeria, South Africa, and Zambia, for instance, have become major centers of Chinese investment.

China's developing relations with Africa have also aroused doubts and reservations, including concerns about neocolonialism, exploitation, China's policy of noninterference, labor rights, social and cultural tensions, elite versus local interaction, and trade competitiveness. At first these misgivings were voiced primarily in the Western press, but by decade's end they had become a common refrain in African countries as well.

China's policy of noninterference in the internal affairs of other countries, a principle that reflects the strong priority its leaders have placed on the primacy of state sovereignty in foreign relations, has become an important area of disquietude. China's lack of "strings attached"—compared to Western political and economic conditionality—has led to charges that China supports African dictators, disregards acts of violence and genocide (for example, Darfur), and contributes to Africa's continued political instability in some areas through indiscriminate small arms sales. Additional concerns include questions about hiring and the treatment of African labor by Chinese firms, the negative impact of Chinese trade competitiveness on an African country's ability to develop indigenous industry, large numbers of Chinese migrants and traders moving to Africa, and the cozy ties between African and Chinese elites versus the often competitive and strained relationships between Chinese traders and local African merchants.

A Century of China-Africa Relations

David H. Shinn and Joshua Eisenman's study of China-Africa relations is a much-needed contribution to an often neglected and controversial subject. Written jointly by a seasoned senior American foreign service officer experienced in African politics and foreign relations, David H. Shinn, and a rising China scholar, Joshua Eisenman, and based on extensive research, including fieldwork and hundreds of interviews, the authors have produced a work of remarkable proportions. Not since Bruce D. Larkin's *China and Africa, 1949–1970: The Foreign Policy of the People's Republic of China*, published in 1971, has there been an overall study of the progression of China-Africa relations of this caliber. This new study focuses on contemporary China-Africa relations, but its historical arc stretches back to Zheng He's journeys to East Africa during the fifteenth century.

As scholars, policymakers, and journalists will recognize, the study of China's Africa policy is both demanding and contentious. In 2011, China maintained relations with all but four African countries—including democracies and dictatorships, low and middle-income countries, and those rich with natural resources and those without. Securing data on China's economic activities to examine its activities would be difficult enough for fifty-four countries, even without the lack of transparency and consistent and reliable data that plague both Chinese and African statistics. In addition, studying China's foreign policy requires the authors to meet the challenge of presenting a balanced analysis based on available data without succumbing to either the "optimist" or "pessimist" schools of thought. That too was a truly challenging task for the authors to accomplish.

The authors have combined historical, topical, and geographic approaches to reveal accurately and completely China's activities in Africa. The book begins by examining the continuities and changes in China's diplomacy, politics, trade, aid and investment, military, and interpersonal policies toward Africa. The regional studies that make up the latter half of the volume are a unique description of China's relations with all fifty-four African countries. These chapters offer vivid country-by-country accounts of both the extent and the intensity of China's reach and relationship with the nations of Africa. The individual country accounts comprehensively document the PRC's experiences and reactions to African political changes in each African country over sixty years. Taken together these two sections make this book essential for both scholars and policymakers working on the subject.

China's rise is exemplified by its changing policies in Africa. But looking forward, what issues will determine China's relations with Africa? What future modes of statecraft, cooperative and conflictual, will China initiate? How sustainable is China's approach to Africa, economic, political and otherwise? How will Africa react to the commercial opportunities and challenges China represents? How will the United States and Europe respond to China's rising influence? And how will Brazil, India, and other rapidly developing countries advance their interests in Africa vis-à-vis China? It may be too early to answer many of these questions, but this work will certainly provide the background and context to helps shape the answers.

China's relationship with African countries remains a work in progress and future interactions will depend as much on Chinese and African interests as the global economic and political environment. Shinn and Eisenman's study provides a precious guide to the past and present that is critical to predicting the future of these relationships. The authors have written a thorough, balanced, and much-needed analytical and foundational study of the subject, advancing our awareness and knowledge of the impact of China's relations with individual African countries and on Africa as a continent.

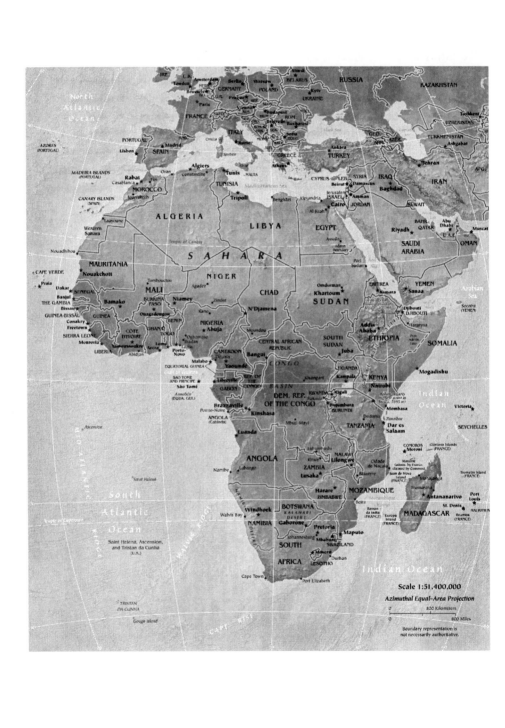

1

Introduction

Unity and cooperation with African countries remains a
cornerstone of China's foreign policy.
—China President Hu Jintao, comments to South African
President Jacob Zuma, 22 September 2009

Political leaders in Beijing regularly refer to China as the world's "largest
developing country" and Africa as "the continent with the most developing
countries." Yet China is hardly a typical developing country and Africa is
hardly a cohesive political entity. China's growing economic and political
clout over the last decade is a fact, but its remarkable rise remains incomplete and the global implications uncertain. Meanwhile, rising commodity
prices have given African elites newfound wealth and in many countries
"stability" has become the motto of autocrats. Although China's influence
on global affairs is growing, its actions to safeguard its interests are increasingly affecting the interests of the international community. Beyond its
neighbors perhaps nowhere has China's political and economic relations
with developing countries received more attention than in Africa. Going
forward this trend is set to continue as China's expanding engagement will
influence both the international system and the continent's prosperity and
stability for decades to come.

This volume explores the development of China-Africa relations during
the era of modern China, 1911–2011, but focuses the lion's share of its
attention on the post-1949 period. It pays particular consideration to the
People's Republic of China's objectives and methods vis-à-vis African
countries on a wide range of issues, from arms sales to education exchanges.

In this book we have sought to provide academics, journalists, practitioners, and policymakers with a comprehensive analysis of China's relations with all fifty-four African countries. Indeed, the toughest hurdle in
writing on this topic is that any attempt to generalize is treacherous, particularly in diverse Africa; there are always exceptions and unique circumstances that beg for closer examination. It is for this reason that our book
uses a continent-wide approach that examines each country's relationship
with China individually, while covering each subtopic in intricate detail.
We hope this book will serve as a researcher's desk reference, a university
textbook, a guide for government, private sector, and nongovernmental
organization (NGO) practitioners and an engaging read for nonspecialists
and long-time watchers alike.

This book is the product of an extensive five-year research project
designed to gain a more complete understanding of the phenomenon of
China and African states' relations and their rapid expansion. The initial
goal was to investigate the political, economic, military, and social aspects of
China's relations with African countries over the last decade. But it quickly
became clear that a complete examination of the relationships that dominate
contemporary news reports and polemical accounts would require an explanation of the historical basis of China's relations with African states.

To dig into this history we relied on the work of a previous generation
of senior China-Africa researchers, including George T. Yu, Bruce Larkin,
and Alaba Ogunsanwo. We also included a full array of newspaper coverage, government reports, academic journal articles, declassified documents,
think tank reports, NGO studies, and onsite interviews.

During the course of our examination, we traveled to nine African
countries,[1] visited China a half dozen times, and conducted more than 400
interviews with a panoply of Chinese and Africans from across the social
spectrum, including Chinese ditch diggers in Sudan, West African textile
traders in Guangzhou, China's ambassadors to several African countries,
Taiwan's Ambassador to Swaziland, and African ambassadors to China.
Examples of third country national interviews include Africa-based oil
executives, the U.S. deputy assistant secretary of state for African affairs,
Japan's ambassador to Egypt, the chief of staff to Portugal's prime minister,
as well as Members of the European Parliament and senior officials in the
European Commission. During many of these interviews we used our combined Chinese and French language skills to great advantage and also refer-
enced documents in both languages.

Key Themes and Historical Trends in China-Africa Relations

While we were writing this volume, nine key themes and historical trends in China's relations with African countries stood out. To make them more accessible to the reader they are briefly summarized below in no particular order.

China Initiates the Relationship: From the first voyages of Admiral Zheng He in the Ming Dynasty until today, China has largely determined the agenda in its relations with African countries.[2] China's relative national strength has grown over time along with Beijing's ability to chart the course of the relationship. Behind the rhetoric of equality in China's commercial deals with African states, China's GDP ($10.1 trillion in 2010) dwarfs every African country, even South Africa ($524 billion in 2010).[3] As a single country representing over 1.3 billion people, China interacts with fifty-four African countries whose combined population is 1 billion. The most populous country, Nigeria, numbers about 150 million people. By 2008 China's total foreign trade by dollar value was two and a half times larger than that of all fifty-four African countries combined. China's ability to guide the course of China-Africa relations also depends on its coordinated continent-wide approach, anchored by the Forum on China-Africa Cooperation (FOCAC) framework begun in 2000.

China's overwhelming economy and its comparative advantage in most labor and capital intensive production has resulted in some pushback against the large quantity of low-cost Chinese imports available in most African markets. Each African country's ability to derive long-term benefit from its own unique bilateral relationship with China is the result of its leverage or lack thereof on contentious trade issues and the level of coordination in its response to China's superior economic and political strength.

China's "Package" Strategy: Since the founding of the People's Republic of China (PRC), Beijing has used a state-run packaged approach to relations with African countries. In the early years, China offered modest foreign aid, had little trade with Africa and provided almost no direct investment. During that period there was a greater emphasis on high level visits, cultural exchanges, student scholarships, and less expensive technical assistance. Although far smaller at their inception, these exchange programs remain just as state-controlled today. Beginning in the mid- to late 1990s, however,

Beijing's growing need for raw materials resulted in increased aid, trade, and investment with most African states. As China's state-directed assistance and commerce grew, so did the presence of state-run firms in African countries, building bridges, dams, roads, and railroads. With China's assistance some African countries are building special economic zones (SEZs) that offer Chinese firms preferential tax and investment terms.

China is now engaged at all levels and competing successfully in most areas with Western countries. The fruits of China's multipronged engagement strategy in Africa have already been tasted. In 2009, China became Africa's largest trading partner, surpassing the United States; China's arms makers are an increasingly important supplier of military assistance; Xinhua has more bureaus in Africa than any other news service; every year Chinese universities and training centers teach thousands of Africans; there are twenty-eight Confucius Institutes in Africa and the Chinese equivalent of the U.S. Peace Corps program, albeit on a much smaller scale.[4] Even Chinese foreign direct investment (FDI), which still lags that of Western countries, is growing rapidly. Those who question whether China has a "package" strategy in Africa would do well to read Beijing's official 2006 Africa white paper.

No "China Development Model": Although China has a strategy toward Africa, this does not mean it is promoting any particular development model. Impressed by China's official 10 percent annual GDP growth rate over three decades, some African leaders envisage a similar result in their own country. Although there may be individual aspects of China's model that can be replicated in some African countries, the goal of importing the Chinese development model is unrealistic and Chinese growth rates remain little more than a campaign promise. Idealists in Africa and the West regularly depict China's modernization in romantic terms—the so-called "Beijing Consensus"—without fully appreciating the vast differences between Africa and China. Omitted variables include population size, political system, colonial history, state coercive power, religious beliefs, savings rate, role of the Chinese overseas community, and so on. By contrast, the Chinese themselves often scoff at the idea of a one size fits all "China Model," and suggest an experimental approach that takes each country's national conditions into account.

The Taiwan Issue: From the establishment of the PRC in 1949 until today Beijing has invested enormous energy and financial resources to end African countries' diplomatic recognition of Taipei. For African countries (as it was for the United States, Japan, and other countries), diplomatic recognition of the PRC is acceptable only if that country is willing to end official ties with the Republic of China (ROC) on Taiwan. In the past several African countries have taken advantage of Chinese determination and strategically switched their recognition between Beijing and Taipei in an effort to obtain increasing amounts of largesse from both sides. At the end of 2007, Malawi was the latest country to switch recognition from Taipei to Beijing. Soon after the election in late 2008 of Taiwan President Ma Ying-jeou, Beijing and Taipei initiated an unofficial diplomatic truce, leaving only four African countries that officially recognize the Republic of China (Taiwan)—Burkina Faso, Swaziland, Gambia, and São Tomé and Principe.

Over the years much of the PRC's efforts have been quiet and behind the scenes, some public and overt. While Beijing is determined to end Taipei's official diplomatic presence, it is far less concerned about Taiwan's commercial presence in Africa. But when Taipei's commerce and trade offices are located in capital cities as in the case of its office in Abuja, Nigeria, this implies a more official connection than Beijing is prepared to accept. Instead, China's diplomatic demarches to Nigeria's government calling for the office to be moved to Lagos or any other city suggest that in the case of important African countries Beijing is prepared to tolerate Taipei's semi-official presence in commercial hubs.

Closer Political Relations: Some African countries have multiparty systems of government and meaningful opposition parties, relatively strong labor unions, significant numbers of NGOs, and an outspoken civil society. These features generally do not exist in China, which has struggled to understand their role and counter African criticism about Chinese policies and labor relations both at home and abroad. In recent years, however, China has made an effort to overcome these differences through the development of exchanges with African political parties, parliamentary delegations, cadres, and cultural and educational groups. More recently, China's political outreach has even been extended to carefully selected opposition political parties, NGOs, and, increasingly, civil society. African labor unions and human rights activists remain a serious challenge for Beijing, largely because their interests generally conflict with those of China's state-run firms.

From Support for Revolutions to Pragmatism: China's approach to Africa shifted from a focus on support for wars of national liberation and revolutionary movements in the 1950s and 1960s to a more pragmatic approach from the mid-1970s onward. The escalating Sino-Soviet split coupled with the U.S.-China rapprochement gradually refocused Beijing's objectives in Africa: first to counter the Soviet Union, then later in support of China's post-1978 economic reform efforts. This shift was evolutionary. As a new crop of independent African nations emerged from colonialism in the 1950s and early 1960s, China engaged them using Zhou Enlai's "Five Principles of Peaceful Coexistence." During China's Cultural Revolution of the late 1960s and early 1970s, however, leftists on both sides pushed a more revolutionary agenda. When Deng Xiaoping gained power in the late 1970s, this signaled a new age of stability and predictability in China-Africa relations. To some extent it is also possible to date this change between pre- and post-Mao policies, but the movement toward pragmatism evolved gradually, apace with both Chinese and African countries' domestic political and economic conditions and the Soviet threat.

By the 1990s, pragmatism had overwhelmingly prevailed, particularly in the economic relationship. Since its inception in 2000, a wide range of China-Africa political and economic interaction has occurred under the FOCAC framework. In addition to African government actors, there are scores of Chinese agencies and firms at the central and provincial levels that continue to influence the trajectory of contemporary bilateral relations between China and African countries under the banner of the "Going Out Policy" initiated under Jiang Zemin.

Quick Succession: Although during its Maoist period China was well known for close ties to African revolutionary movements, it also developed ties with some more right-leaning independent African countries. China established relations with Morocco's conservative monarchy in 1958, Kenya's moderate government in 1963, Tunisia's conservative government in 1964, and tried hard to establish relations with Ethiopia's Emperor Haile Selassie throughout the 1960s, finally succeeding in 1970. Since the mid-1970s, however, Beijing has proved particularly adept at cultivating ties with various types of African governments to advance China's interests, and above all to squeeze Taiwan out. China has maintained a consistent policy of supporting the status quo regime in nearly all African countries regardless whether that government is a democracy, monarchy, dictatorship, or under military or Islamist rule. China will try to maintain cordial relations with any government in control of the levers of state power. As regimes change in Africa, China has proven itself adept at moving quickly to establish cordial relations with the successor government.

Unencumbered by domestic pressure groups and an activist parliament, China's one-party state allows it to quickly establish relations with new African regimes. China has even made this transition when it had close ties with the preceding ruling party. Beijing had backed several losing liberation groups in southern Africa, but after their defeat quickly reached out to their victorious rivals. In the case of Zambia, Beijing skillfully switched from the United National Independence Party to the Movement for Multi-Party Democracy after the latter's victory in the 1991 elections. It had to make another transfer of allegiance when the Zambian opposition presidential candidate won in 2011. As China's economic power has increased in recent years, both its commercial carrots and sticks for new African regimes have increased, making it easier and faster to move from one regime to another. New African leaders, faced with the problems of governing, are in desperate need of Chinese assistance, and are rarely distressed that China once supported their former political enemies.

China's Growing Military Presence: China has no military alliances with African countries and no bases in Africa and claims it will never pursue either of these goals. Meanwhile, since the earliest days of the PRC's engagement with Africa it has sold or given small arms to select nationalist and revolutionary groups. As China's policies became increasingly pragmatic, the People's Liberation Army (PLA) and its state-run arms suppliers have taken advantage of increased opportunities in Africa. During the Ethiopia and Eritrea war in the late 1990s, for instance, Beijing sold military equipment to both sides. China also provided helicopter gunships to the Khartoum government to suppress opposition in Southern Sudan and Darfur, sold millions in weapons and ammunition to Robert Mugabe's repressive regime in Zimbabwe, and in 2011 offered the Qadhafi regime in Libya arms worth $200 million to fight NATO and rebel forces. China is now a global manufacturing and regional military power, and it is safe to say that vast quantities of cheap, lightweight Chinese-made weapons continue to make their way into the hands of African armed forces and rebels alike.

The PLA navy has already begun efforts to protect the sea-lanes through which China's ships transport fuel, minerals, and raw materials from Africa and the Middle East. This raises questions about the PLA navy's access to

African ports. As more Chinese engage in Africa they find themselves caught in local conflicts and occasionally specifically targeted—as has occurred in Algeria, Nigeria, Sudan, Ethiopia, and Libya. Over the last decade safety concerns have forced China to rethink military cooperation with African countries. China has become a major participant in UN peacekeeping operations in Africa and contributed naval forces to combat piracy in the Gulf of Aden.

The Growth of Chinese Communities in Africa: There are three kinds of Chinese communities in Africa today. The first group consists of Chinese professionals who staff the embassies, aid missions, and large Chinese companies and serve as project managers. They often come with families, usually speak one of the local languages and blend in well with the international community. Nearly all return to China or go to another foreign posting at the conclusion of their assignment. The second category is the tens of thousands of contract Chinese laborers who arrive without families, rarely speak one of the local languages and tend to live on compounds with other Chinese. They return to China at the end of their contracts. The third group is the small traders or business persons. Some of them migrated to South Africa, Madagascar, and Mauritius more than a century ago. Most mainland Chinese traders are relatively recent arrivals and many bring families. They tend to live in small communities among Africans and learn enough of the local language to do business. Some will not return to China. They move around the continent based on profit, security conditions, and family and business connections.

There is growing resentment among some Africans toward Chinese workers who are perceived to be taking jobs from local African labor. Some local traders and business persons also harbor resentment toward Chinese traders. This is especially true in southern Africa, where their cheaper products, direct relationships with Chinese factories, and willingness to work longer hours are forcing local traders and manufacturers out of business. African consumers, on the other hand, often welcome the Chinese competition and affordable products.

The Academic Study of China-Africa Relations

Beyond its immediate neighborhood, China's relationship with Africa stands as China's most important in the developing world. Yet, while academic literature on Chinese relations with Asia and the West has grown significantly over the last decade, work on Beijing's interests in and policies toward Africa remains sparse, with only a few dozen or so researchers regularly publishing on the topic. Of that group only a handful of scholars have become what might be called China-Africa specialists, and most of them reside outside the United States. By contrast, the previous generation of specialists included several senior American political scientists. With rare exception, the U.S. academic community abandoned the field of China-Africa studies for nearly three decades. We hope this book will mark the beginning of a renaissance in the study of Sino-African relations in American academic institutions. It is the first full-length account on this subject in an American academic press since Bruce D. Larkin's, *China and Africa 1949–1970*.[5]

The decline in American attention over the years, from a historical standpoint, is understandable. During the 1960s and 1970s, when the United States was engaged in a strategic and ideological struggle for influence in what Mao Zedong called the Third World, the subject was well covered in Western surveys of Chinese foreign policy.[6] In 1963–1966 alone at least four books were written on China's foreign policy toward Africa, all touting what one author titled *Red China's African Offensive*.[7] Between 1974 and 1976, no fewer than five books, as well as countless articles, focused on China's relations with the African continent alone.[8] Other works addressed Beijing's role in Latin America, the Middle East, and Southeast Asia.[9] During the 1980s and much of the 1990s as China looked inward and its role in Africa was perceived as less confrontational toward the United States, American literature and expertise on Sino-African relations diminished.

The Contemporary Literature

Despite broad acknowledgment of China's resource-related objectives, there is little agreement about their relative importance and, in a larger sense, what all this suggests about China's long-term aspirations or intentions in Africa.

Among Africanists, China's emergence as an economic and political partner has become intertwined with the already robust development literature sparking comparisons between the "Washington Consensus" and the so-called "Beijing Consensus." Is China's model of illiberal, authoritarian capitalism transferable to African countries? And, if so, is it more suitable to African conditions than free-market, liberal democracy? Africanist discussions on China regularly revolve around such questions, although the Chinese themselves shrug off any notion of a "Beijing Consensus."

Meanwhile, among Sinologists the ongoing debate about China's strategic intentions has spilled over into the China-Africa literature. Is China "recolonizing" Africa? Is China a rogue donor? Is Chinese illiberalism inimical to liberal Western values? Is China seeking to challenge U.S. dominance over the international system and, if so, what role does Africa play? Collectively, the discussions Africanists and Sinologists have been having for nearly three decades have become part of a sub-debate about the strategic objectives of Chinese involvement and its influence on African development.

Instead of being divided among Africanists and Sinologists, much of the contemporary literature on China-Africa relations is framed by a vigorous debate between relative optimists and pessimists. Optimistic researchers see China as a benign business partner supporting Africa's progressive political elements and loyal to "old friendships" on the continent. They see little immediate cause for concern regarding China's relations with African countries and a number of positive signs regarding recent trends in its diplomacy and economic opportunities for Africans.

On the other side are more pessimistic observers who believe China supports political illiberalism and African governments outside the influence of Western development institutions. They see an authoritarian China as inherently hostile to liberal democracy and believe there are few limitations on its ambitions.[10] Still others argue that regime type matters little, but that China, as a rising power, and the United States, as the hegemon, are nevertheless likely to clash in Africa and elsewhere.[11] Some Sinologists, however, counter that Beijing's freedom to maneuver is constrained by its domestic weaknesses and membership in international organizations, making it unlikely to initiate conflict so far from its shores.[12]

Optimists

Optimistic interpretations of China's involvement in Africa reference its emphasis on engagement with multilateral institutions, confidence building, and improved (if still rudimentary) transparency.[13] These developments represent a trend toward economic relations with African countries based on political principles such as equality, mutual respect, and support for localized solutions. Proponents argue that China's business elite and policymakers' worldview is evolving as they internalize the values associated with international organizations and their own constructive rhetoric toward Africans. They point to a long list of accomplishments, including political pressure on Sudan and deployment of peacekeeping troops in Africa, and to its claims to support fairer global trade, increased foreign aid, stronger African representation on the UN Security Council, and with African multilateral organizations such as the African Union, African Development Bank, and the New Partnership for Africa's Development.

These arguments depict China as both a welcome business partner and political counter-weight that helps Africans gain leverage over an exploitative West. China's involvement is portrayed as a good economic opportunity and a source of political support for progressive forces in African and other developing countries. Joshua Cooper Ramo's well-known publication "The Beijing Consensus" summarized one such viewpoint:

> To the degree China's development is changing China it is important; but what is far more important is that China's new ideas are having a gigantic effect outside of China. China is marking a path for other nations around the world who are trying to figure out not simply how to develop their countries, but also how to fit into the international order in a way that allows them to be truly independent, to protect their way of life and political choices in a world with a single massively powerful centre of gravity. I call this new physics of power and development the Beijing Consensus.[14]

The Beijing Consensus, according to Ramo, "replaces the widely discredited Washington Consensus, an economic theory made famous in the 1990s for its prescriptive, Washington-knows-best approach to telling other nations how to run themselves."[15] Ramo argues that China is taking its place on the global stage through a willingness to innovate, take into account quality of life as well as economic growth, provide enough equality to avoid unrest, and value national self-determination.[16]

Deborah Brautigam also stresses the benefits of African countries' relations with China and believes "the fears about Chinese aid and engagement are misinformed, the alarm is out of proportion."[17] Her book, *The Dragon's Gift: The Real Story of China in Africa*, concludes:

At the end of the day, we should remember this: China's own experiments have raised hundreds of millions of Chinese out of poverty, largely without foreign aid. They believe in investment, trade, and technology as levers for development, and they are applying these same tools in their African engagement, not out of altruism but because of what they learned at home. They learned that natural resources could be assets for modernization and prosperity [and] that a central government commitment to capitalist business development could rapidly reduce poverty.[18]

Barry Sautman and Yan Hairong agree that China provides Africans an attractive set of economic opportunities and political options. They argue that "China, unlike Western states, is not obstructing the development in the world's poorer countries."[19] As does Jing Men who suggests that China and Africa "help each other politically, economically as well in many other fields based on the principle of mutual benefit."[20] Men, Ramo, Brautigam, Sautman, and Yan are among those authors who argue that alongside the new commercial opportunities that have emerged for both Chinese and African businesses and consumers, China also provides Africans critical leverage over Western countries that have traditionally dominated and exploited them.[21]

Chinese and African researchers and policymakers also tend to be optimistic about the prospects for China-Africa economic relations.[22] They regularly adopt a path-dependent argument, affirming the important role of historical friendship as a driver in the economic and political relationship. In February 2009, for instance, before China's President Hu Jintao left for a five-nation African tour, Professor Xu Wenzhong, director of African studies at the Beijing-based China Institutes of Contemporary International Relations, said, "Hu's Africa visit will indicate that Beijing values the importance of Africa [based] on friendship and from a long-term view."[23]

Official reports of meetings between Chinese and African leaders regularly result in the affirmation of "friendship" as an important driver of the relationship. During one such gathering between Hu and several African leaders in November 2006, for instance, the Chinese president explained the connection between Sino-African friendship and economic development: "China attaches great importance to the traditional friendship and is ready to work to maintain high level friendly exchanges, deepen economic and trade cooperation of mutual benefits." One long-serving former African leader, oil-and-iron rich Gabon's Omar Bongo, responded that "China is a sincere friend and the two peoples share a profound friendship," then promptly called for the continued expansion of bilateral economic relations.[24]

Pessimists

In juxtaposition to these arguments are those who insist that China-Africa economic relations are linked to political illiberalism or tend to be with African countries outside the influence of Western development institutions. Advocates of such arguments take a dimmer, more pessimistic view of the politics they associate with China's involvement on the African continent, even if they remain divided over whether these results stem from Beijing policymakers' design, coincidence, or are a natural component of great power rivalries.

Some American and European policymakers and researchers are dubious of an authoritarian China that actively works to "seduce illiberal regimes" and describe it as a "formidable ideological challenge" to the West. They contend that although China may be weak today its illiberal tendencies have become evident and are likely to present an even greater challenge as it grows stronger in the future. Naazneen Barma and Ely Ratner, for instance, argue that "through a wide array of bilateral and multilateral arrangements, the Chinese government has begun to build an alternative international structure anchored by illiberal norms" and that, "nowhere is this trend more evident than in Africa." They contend that "Chinese illiberalism presents the real long-term geopolitical challenge: It is easily exportable, and it is dangerously appealing to a disaffected world." Furthermore, they link China's political illiberalism with its economic relations by arguing that Beijing leverages its "mercantilist strength in the international system" to attain its national interests.[25]

More hawkish critics, such as Peter Brookes and Ji Hye Shin, link Western development assistance with liberalism and depict China's commercial competition in Africa as part of a zero-sum game that presents an inevitable threat to both liberalism and Western predominance. They argue that "Chinese support for political and economic repression in Africa counters the liberalizing influences of Africa's traditional European and American partners."[26]

Those who link the West with liberalism also regularly argue that China's economic relations tend to be with African countries outside the influence of traditional development institutions, including Western countries' national development agencies (e.g., USAID and the United Kingdom's Department for International Development) and multilateral development institutions (e.g., the World Bank and the International Monetary Fund, IMF). Princeton Lyman, for instance, noted in his Congressional testimony that China's economic involvement in Africa "comes with no conditionality related to governance, fiscal probity or other of the concerns that now drive western donors." This view was echoed in a Council on Foreign Relations report in June 2008:

> The way China does business—particularly its willingness to pay bribes, as documented by Transparency International—undermines local efforts to increase good governance and international efforts at macroeconomic reform by institutions like the World Bank and the International Monetary Fund.[27]

Two prominent researchers, Denis M. Tull and Ian Taylor, suggest political illiberalism is a component of China's relations with African countries, but are unsure whether to attribute this to China's indifference or its design. They agree that: "There is virtually no way around the conclusion that China's massive return to Africa presents a negative political development that 'almost certainly does not contribute to the promotion of peace, prosperity and democracy on the continent.'"[28] In the "Illiberal regimes" section of his 2007 book, *China in Africa*, Chris Alden explained why he believes China's demand for African resource commodities instinctively increases the tendency to do business with illiberal regimes:

> From the Chinese perspective, these economies are generally closely tied to African elites' interests, and there are fewer obstacles to rapid investment in the resource sector than they might experience in a state with stronger institutions and commitment to constitutional law.[29]

In 2010 Eric Kiss and Kate Zhou concluded that China's "acquiescence in corrupt and brutal neopatrimonial regimes . . . will be increasingly pitted against an emerging narrative of resistance [in Africa]."[30]

A Broad-Based Perspective

This volume adopts a "thick description" approach to examining patterns and implications of China-Africa relations. Following the introduction we trace the history of China-Africa relations. The next five chapters examine China-Africa relations from a specific issue area: political, trade, investment and foreign assistance, military, and media and social relations. Chapters 8–11 detail the individual bilateral relationships throughout the last six decades of China-Africa relations, 1949 to 2011. The Conclusion makes predictions based on our research.

In the pages that follow we seek to present the broadest and most comprehensive examination of China-Africa relations. China's continent-wide relationship, regional and state targeted initiatives, are traced back to their inception and discussed as part of the historical development of the relationship. We begin even before China's imperial voyages to East Africa, discuss the relationship's relative neglect during the Qing Dynasty until 1911, the Nationalist Period until 1949, PRC relations with African liberation movements in the 1950s, 1960s, and 1970s, and the emergence of economic and political partnership in the contemporary period.

The book traces the PRC's quest to gain African countries' diplomatic recognition, the Communist Party of China's (CPC) use of "people's organizations" to build political relationships in Africa and the establishment of formal party-to-party political outreach after 1977. It catalogues the extent and nature of China's extensive political and military relationships in African countries from China's early arms provisions to African liberation groups to current arms transfers to Africa, and training and high level military exchanges.

Next we examine Chinese trade, investment, and foreign assistance with Africa. After looking at the historical development of investment and aid, we highlight the difficulty in accurately measuring each of them. China has become an important part of African countries' trade portfolio—particularly its consumer product imports and resource purchases—but Africa still remains a tiny part of China's global trade. As such, we developed the first published dataset tracing China-Africa trade in 1938 and from 1948 to 2010 using only those figures published by the IMF and the UN. We conclude our topical examination with a discussion of the extensive outreach from China's official Xinhua News Agency, China-Africa educational and vocational training initiatives, cultural and language exchanges, Confucius Institutes, and the growth of Chinese communities in Africa and African communities in China. Increasing interpersonal relations, especially among elites, will provide an important framework for long-term Sino-African cooperation for decades to come.

The four regional chapters trace the PRC's relations with each of Africa's fifty-four countries since 1949, review the historical ties, but emphasize the current relationship. This is the only account of China-Africa relations that has looked at each African country's bilateral relationship individually. It is designed as a reference guide for students, practitioners, and researchers looking for background on a particular bilateral relationship.

In the conclusion we go beyond our analysis of the past and present and project some of the principal trends in China-Africa relations into the future. As the relationship matures, how will it develop? What opportunities and problems are likely to emerge over time? It includes eight broad predictions about the future of China-Africa relations based on the facts and analyses offered throughout the volume. The goal of this book is to trace the continuities and changes in China-Africa relations over the last century from the broadest possible perspective.

2

A Historical Overview of China-Africa Relations

Africa and Imperial China: It Started with Trade

Trade was the first link between Africa and China. Chinese scholar Gao Jinyuan noted that Queen Cleopatra of Egypt, who reigned between 51 and 30 BCE, reportedly wore silks that likely came from China. In about 166 CE the Han emperor received gifts, some of which originated in northeast Africa, from the Roman emperor, who ruled Egypt at the time.[1] Former Chinese ambassador to Kenya, An Yongu, stated that Chinese goods dating to the Han Dynasty (206 BCE–220 CE) have been found in Africa.[2] British scholar Basil Davidson agreed that Chinese products reached the Red Sea, Mediterranean, and even Meroë in present-day northern Sudan by the beginning of the Christian era.[3]

British businessman, traveler, and writer Philip Snow's popular account of China-Africa contact acknowledged that Chinese scholars date the trade relationship from the Han Dynasty.[4] Based on available research as of 1930, East African expert W. H. Ingrams argued that Chinese trade with the east coast of Africa took place during a later period, probably beginning in the Tang Dynasty (618–907).[5] As more evidence becomes available, we are learning that the trade began earlier than many scholars believed.

Largely confined in the beginning to northeast Africa, the eastern coastal areas, and African islands in the western Indian Ocean, trade now dominates China's relationship with most of Africa's fifty-four countries (fifty-five if you include the disputed Western Sahara). Although trade statistics for this early period are nonexistent, anecdotal information and archaeological evidence strongly support the existence of commerce between Africa and China. Before the arrival of Chinese military commander Zheng He's fleet on the East African coast in the early fifteenth century, the evidence suggests that intermediaries, usually Arab seafarers, conducted trade in both directions.[6] Imperial China did not consider these transactions with Africa or any other foreign region as trade, which Confucian doctrine looked upon with disdain. Rather, they were seen as tribute, homage from remote barbarian peoples to the Son of Heaven or Emperor, and an indication of his generosity to them.[7]

There is widespread agreement on what articles constituted the early trade between China and the limited geography of Africa where it occurred. Archaeological excavations have turned up Tang Dynasty Chinese porcelain and coins in Egypt, Kenya, and Zanzibar. Chinese coins and porcelain from the Song Dynasty (960–1279) and porcelain from the Yuan Dynasty (1279–1368) have been found from the Somali coast to the southern coast of Tanzania and even inland to Zimbabwe. Chinese porcelain of the Ming Dynasty (1368–1644) has been recovered from an even wider area that includes Madagascar, the port of Suakin in Sudan, the Eritrean coast, and the Transvaal in South Africa.[8] Many Chinese trade goods did not withstand the passage of time and, as a result, left no archaeological evidence. Chinese records indicate that rice was an important export to the Somali and Swahili coasts while textiles, especially colored satins and taffetas, were popular items throughout eastern Africa. China also exported sandalwood, pepper, beans, ivory boxes, lacquer ware, fine art objects, white and red cotton cloth, gold, silver, and copper to much of the eastern side of Africa.[9]

African exports to China were more exotic and included elephant tusks, which the Chinese considered superior to Asian ivory, rhinoceros horn, frankincense, myrrh, tortoiseshell, aloes, precious stones, and rare woods. China also imported oil of storax, the aromatic balsam exuded by liquidambar trees and used in medicine and perfume. Perhaps the most unusual export from Africa was ambergris, at the time thought by the Chinese to be solidified dragon spittle. Used in making perfume, ambergris is the waxy substance found floating in tropical waters from the intestines of sperm whales. It appeared frequently along the Somali coast. Occasional African giraffes, zebras, ostriches, and other animals also found their way to China.[10]

Although there was an active slave trade in eastern Africa conducted by the Arabs, it appears that relatively few slaves reached China. According to one account, an Arab ambassador took an African slave to the Chinese court in 976.[11] Sinologist J. J. L. Duyvendak stated categorically that some African slaves found their way to China.[12] American scholar and civil rights leader W. E. Burghardt Du Bois and Columbia University professor Graham W. Irwin agreed that African slaves were sent to China.[13] Although acknowledging the presence of black slaves in China, geographer Paul Wheatley was less certain they had come from Africa. He thought they might have originated in Papua or Melanesia but was inclined to believe that Arab slave traders had brought some from Africa.[14] Snow offered one of the most extensive accounts of African slaves in China, suggesting that they may have come from Madagascar and the Comoro Islands. Assuming they were part of the Arab slave trade, they more likely originated in eastern Africa. The slaves appear to have been concentrated in Canton (now Guangzhou) and were kept by rich people according to a record dated in 1119. They did not necessarily belong to Chinese and were probably indentured by members of the Islamic trading colony in Canton. Snow said the Portuguese subsequently brought African slaves to Macao.[15]

Face-to-Face Contact

There is no agreement on the first face-to-face contact between Chinese and African people. There is one report that the king of the ancient Persian Arsacid Dynasty sent an Egyptian magician and acrobat, "the Alexandrian good string," to Xi'an in 112 BCE. This would constitute the earliest recorded Sino-African cultural exchange and possibly the first Chinese-African personal contact.[16] Some scholars believe the Chinese first reached Alexandria in Egypt by traveling overland in the early first to early third centuries.[17] The evidence is thin. Gao Jinyuan wrote that a Chinese officer named Du Huan, following his capture and release by the Arabs, traveled in Africa during the Tang Dynasty and eventually reached a malaria-infested region inhabited by black people that he called Mo-lin. Some scholars believe this was Malindi on the present Kenya coast while others said it was along the west coast of the Red Sea, eastern coast of Egypt or Morocco.[18] Snow argued that Du Huan ended up in the Ethiopian Kingdom of Axum in the Red Sea coastal area of present-day Eritrea. In any event, Du Huan left behind the first significant Chinese descriptions of some undetermined parts of Africa.[19]

Russian Sinologist Viktor Velgus hypothesized that the Chinese could have sailed to East Africa as early as the eighth century, but acknowledged there is no proof they reached the continent by sea that early.[20] Between 1071 and 1083 an envoy from Zanzibar visited Guangzhou twice where the Northern Song emperor entertained him.[21] The earliest accounts of Africa in Chinese literature appear during the Tang Dynasty. Between the tenth and fourteenth centuries, Chinese geographers and chroniclers increased their knowledge about eastern Africa and the western Indian Ocean islands. The Chinese almost certainly obtained most of this information second-hand from foreigners who made their way to China. The famous Moroccan traveler, Ibn Battúta, traveled in China in 1347, visiting Quanzhou, Guang-zhou, Hangzhou, and Beijing among other locations.[22]

One Chinese seafarer, Wang Dayuan, claimed to have made two voyages across the Indian Ocean in the first half of the fourteenth century and is thought by many Chinese to have reached the East African coast. It is clear, however, that China made little effort to reach Africa until Zheng He made his famous voyages early in the Ming Dynasty.[23]

The first Ming Emperor, Hung-wu, appreciated the importance of naval power. He passed to his son, Yung-lo, a strong navy that Yung-lo used to explore regions far beyond China's borders. Both Hung-wu and Yung-lo encouraged foreign countries and city states to engage in commercial rela-tions with China.[24] This brings us to the most important event so far in China-Africa relations—the naval expeditions of Zheng He, a Muslim and a eunuch in the court of Ming Dynasty Emperor Yongle. His Chinese fleet, which was comparable in size to the Spanish Armada, made seven voyages well beyond the shores of China. The fifth voyage (1417–1419) reached the Somali coast (Mogadishu, Brava, and Kismayu), probably Malindi on the Kenyan coast and possibly Mombasa farther down the Kenyan coast and Mafia Island off Tanzania. Brava and Mogadishu sent four tribute missions to China between 1416 and 1423 and Malindi sent a final mission in 1416. A squadron from Zheng He's sixth voyage (1421–1422) made a return visit to the Somali coast.[25]

China's heightened engagement with Africa's eastern coast declined precipitously at the end of the Zheng He era. China again turned inward. Emperor Cheng-t'ung in 1436 prohibited the construction of ships for overseas voyages and ended the building of warships. Imperial Chinese sea power never regained the position it had during the late Song, Yuan, and early Ming Dynasties. Unlike most other early visitors to the African coast, the Chinese were neither conquerors nor immigrants; they were navigators and merchants. They left virtually no trace of their culture or genetic heritage.[26] Making an invidious comparison with the subsequent arrival of the Europeans, Snow suggested that the Chinese treated the Africans with courtesy and restraint. Most important, they left, turning their backs on Africa abruptly and completely.[27]

Chinese leaders today refer nostalgically to the Zheng He era, suggesting that its current "going out" policy is nonthreatening. State councilor Dai Bingguo told the head of the Association of Southeast Asian Nations in 2010 that "Zheng He is still remembered as an envoy of friendship and peace" and "China is not to be feared."[28] Chinese archaeologists arrived in Kenya in 2010 to begin excavation of a sunken ship believed to have been part of Zheng's armada. Historian Geoff Wade of the Institute of Southeast Asian Studies in Singapore, a translator of Ming documents relating to Zheng's voyages, disputes the portrayal of Zheng as a benign adventurer. Wade argued that historical records show the Chinese fleets carried sophisticated weaponry and participated in at least three major military actions in Java, Sumatra, and Sri Lanka.[29]

The interruption of China-Africa contact can be attributed to a power struggle in the Ming court between the eunuch class, grown powerful during the period of maritime exploration, and the official class, which feared the power of the eunuchs. The official class disparaged maritime trade as extravagant and dependent on contact with barbarians. The official class won. In addition, while the Chinese rulers prohibited ship building and sea-going trade, the Europeans moved into Africa and Asia at the end of the fifteenth and beginning of the sixteenth centuries. Even if Africans had wanted to continue to send missions to China, the Europeans stood in their way.[30]

Following a review of relevant Chinese materials, Asian scholar Wang Gungwu agreed with those who said that Chinese ruling classes determined the voyages were unnecessary, wasteful, and could be ended without any serious consequences for China's economy or political position. He concluded they illustrated that advanced Chinese maritime techniques and China's early awareness of Africa played no part in the growth of Chinese trade with the western reaches of the Indian Ocean. The accomplishments and acknowledged maritime skills of Zheng He also played a relatively small role in the decisions of subsequent ruling classes about future voyages for exploration or even profitable trade.[31]

Chinese Laborers and Traders Come to Africa

Following a long hiatus in China-Africa contact, except for the continua-
tion of trade conducted by intermediaries and visits to Egypt by Chinese
Muslims making the pilgrimage to Mecca, the next significant development
began with the migration of Chinese laborers and traders to Africa. The
regions geographically closest to China—Africa's western Indian Ocean
islands—and South Africa were the first to experience modest Chinese
immigration. Snow wrote that a Frenchman, Comte d'Estaing, abducted
three hundred Chinese from Sumatra in 1760 to work in the fields of Mauritius. Traders by tradition, the Chinese objected to field work and d'Estaing
sent them back to Sumatra. English, French, and Danish ships transported
more than three thousand Chinese to Mauritius in 1783. The British, who
subsequently seized Mauritius from the French, imported a group of Chinese in 1829 to work on the sugar plantations. The European sugar planters
worked them like slaves; the Chinese revolted and the effort failed. By 1846
an estimated fifty Chinese were arriving in Mauritius each year. Under pressure from foreign governments, Imperial China finally recognized the right
of Chinese to leave the country in 1860.[32]

Merchants from Fujian Province and Canton brought Mauritius into
the China trade soon after 1750. Two Chinese started a tea plantation in
1770 and by 1817 there was a small Chinatown on the island. By one
account in the mid-1840s, Chinese dominated the market in the principal
city, Port Louis, and by the mid-1880s they numbered several thousand.
The first Chinese-language newspaper published in the western Indian
Ocean, the *Mauritius Chinese Gazette*, appeared in 1895. The Chinese, then
numbering about 3,000, established some of the earliest factories on the
island. By the turn of the century, more than 80 percent of them were
traders and in 1909 they organized a Chamber of Commerce. It was
entrusted with controlling the arrival of Chinese immigrants to Mauritius
and performed functions normally assigned to consulates. By the early
twentieth century, there were some twenty-five to thirty Chinese clans in
Mauritius, mainly Hakka (people who trekked historically from the north
of China to the southeast coast and then continued on to create Chinese
communities in Southeast Asia) and Cantonese. The Chinese population in
Mauritius was just over 3,500 in 1901 and just under 3,700 in 1911.[33]

According to Leon Slawecki, one of the leading authorities on the Chinese
in Madagascar, there is no evidence that Chinese arrived in Madagascar

before the middle of the nineteenth century. The first recorded sighting of a Chinese national on Madagascar occurred in 1862 in the village of Toamasina (then called Tamatave) on the east coast. There were six Chinese at Nossi Bé on the northwest coast in 1866; others reached Toamasina during the 1870s. A small group of Chinese laborers temporarily came to Antsiranana (then called Diego Suarez) on the north end of the island in the late 1880s. Permanent immigrants eventually arrived from Fujian Province followed soon thereafter by Cantonese. By 1893 there were an estimated forty Chinese in Madagascar. By the end of the century there was considerable coming and going by the Chinese, especially to and from Mauritius and the French Indian Ocean territories of Réunion and the Comoro Islands. Following the French conquest of Madagascar in 1896, more Chinese were attracted to the island. The first group of 1,025 Chinese coolies arrived in that year to help build the road from the interior capital, Antananarivo, to Toamasina. Eventually more than 3,000 coolies worked on the road, a railroad between Antananarivo and Toamasina that began in 1901, public works projects, and in agricultural services. The coolies are not, however, the ancestors of the current Chinese community on Madagascar. The French required that the coolies leave at the end of their contracts and nearly all of those who deserted were rounded up by French authorities and deported. The 1904 census for the island identified 452 Chinese, including 3 women and 6 children. The 1910 estimate rose to 540 with eleven women and seventeen children. Most of the early Chinese immigrants came from Mauritius or Réunion. A permanent Chinese community had begun to develop in Madagascar.[34]

The Seychelles were inhabited much later than Mauritius and Madagascar and even today the island chain has a population of only about 100,000. The early Chinese community was correspondingly small. According to one account, the first Chinese traders came to the Seychelles in 1863.[35] The 1871 census made, however, no mention of Chinese. In 1886, 23 Chinese traders arrived in the islands. Census reports listed 45 Chinese in 1891, 110 in 1901, and 81 in 1911.[36] In a study of the islands published in 1907, a British geographer said there were only "a few" Chinese shopkeepers whom he described as recent immigrants.[37] In the waning years of Imperial China, the Chinese community in the Seychelles was less significant than its counterparts in Mauritius and Madagascar.

Perhaps the most intriguing and certainly most thoroughly documented early presence of Chinese in Africa occurred in South Africa. Beginning in 1658, the Dutch East India Company imported slaves to the Cape of Good

Hope, which the company used as a penal colony for criminals and political exiles from Batavia in the East Indies. Small numbers of Chinese, believed to be primarily from Fujian Province, were part of this movement. Never numbering more than fifty to one hundred at any time, the Chinese convicts worked as basket makers, fishermen, and masons. After they completed their sentence or received a pardon, the Chinese either returned to Batavia or remained in the Cape as "free blacks," a term that included persons wholly or partially of African and Asian descent. By the 1740s, a dozen or so free Chinese operated restaurants or served as traders, chandlers, and craftsmen. The number of free Chinese declined in the latter part of the eighteenth century. During the nineteenth century, the various South African administrative jurisdictions adopted varying policies toward Chinese immigration. The net result was only modest growth in their numbers, although there was a significant increase following the discovery of diamonds in South Africa in 1867 and gold in 1886.[38]

South African historian Karen Harris, who has studied Chinese labor, suggested there were fewer than 5,000 Chinese in the country at the beginning of the twentieth century. This situation changed dramatically in 1904 when the Anglo-Chinese Labour Convention and the Transvaal Labour Importation Ordinance permitted the introduction of indentured labor to work in the gold mines. As an expression of its racial concerns, South Africa passed the same year a Chinese Exclusion Act aimed at preventing Chinese from remaining permanently in the country. The European mining companies recruited 63,695 Chinese indentured laborers to work in the Transvaal gold mines under a contract that limited their stay to three years. At the end of the contract, which was renewable, the regulation required that they return to China. While the small numbers of free Chinese who arrived in South Africa as independent immigrants were primarily from the southeastern regions of China, the indentured laborers were from the northern provinces.[39] At the beginning of 1907, there were nearly 54,000 Chinese in the Witwatersrand fields. They constituted almost 35 percent of the total unskilled work force.[40] By 1910, when the four self-governing British colonies—Cape, Natal, Transvaal, and Orange River—amalgamated to form the Union of South Africa, only 2,000 of these workers remained in the Transvaal fields. The others had been repatriated to China.[41]

The rights and racial status of Chinese in white-ruled South Africa was a contentious issue from the beginning. The relatively small Chinese community joined the larger Indian community, led by Mahatma Gandhi who lived in South Africa from 1893 until he returned to India in 1915, to achieve racial acceptance. The Indians claimed to be British subjects with the right to be treated the same as whites in South Africa. Leung Quinn, chairman of the Cantonese Club in South Africa, petitioned the Chinese embassy in London to inform the South African government that Chinese should not be subject to South Africa's Asiatic Registration Act. South African legislation in the early twentieth century disappointed the entire Asian community. South African authorities deported or arrested a number of Chinese near the end of the Imperial era.[42]

The sizeable Chinese community in South Africa led to what was Imperial China's first and probably only diplomatic/consular representative in Africa. South African journalist Melanie Yap and librarian Dianne Leong Man, in a detailed account of the Chinese consulate-general in South Africa, documented that the first person to hold this position was Lew Yuk Lin, who arrived in Johannesburg in 1905. He remained until 1907 when his secretary, Liu Ngai, became acting consul-general. On the eve of the Chinese Revolution of 1911, China recalled Liu Ngai and the American consul in Johannesburg assumed responsibility for China's affairs.[43]

The use of Chinese labor in Africa during the Imperial period was not confined to the Indian Ocean islands and South Africa. The British colonial government in the Gold Coast (now Ghana) recruited small numbers of Chinese laborers to work in the gold fields. Newspaper accounts reported that sixteen to thirty Chinese arrived in 1897 but only remained for a month. A few more Chinese came in 1902 and about thirty joined the workforce in 1914. Africans in the Gold Coast generally opposed the use of Chinese labor and the colonial government stopped recruiting them.[44]

The Portuguese brought several thousand Chinese laborers from Canton to build the first railway in the southern part of Portuguese East Africa (Mozambique). At the beginning of the twentieth century, Mozambique also permitted the entry of Chinese traders. By 1912, there were some three hundred Chinese in Lourenço Marques (now Maputo) and smaller numbers in other coastal towns.[45] Germany brought about 2,000 Chinese laborers from Shandong, Shanghai, Fujian and Guangdong to colonial Tanganyika to build railways. Together with local workers, they built the railway from Dar es Salaam to Mwanza. When completed in 1914, only six hundred Chinese laborers had survived, and most of them returned to China. Local residents thought the Chinese were the most industrious and honest people they had ever met. There is a village along the line called

"Shanghai," where many of the laborers once lived.[46] The Germans concluded Chinese coolies were also the best choice to work on the coffee and
tobacco plantations in colonial Tanganyika.[47]

In the late 1800s, Belgium undertook to build a railway from Matadi
on the Congo's Atlantic coast to the future capital of Léopoldville (now
Kinshasa). Unable to locate enough African labor, the Belgians recruited
550 Chinese from Macao to work alongside the Africans. Conditions were
harsh and most died or abandoned the project. Some of the Chinese reportedly settled permanently in the Congo. In 1898, the administrators of the
Congo Free State established by King Leopold II of the Belgians concluded
a treaty of commerce and friendship in Peking with the Qing government.
It gave Chinese the right to settle in the Congo, buy fixed and moveable
assets, practice their professions, and change jobs. According to Snow, this
was the first formal Sino-African treaty, albeit with the colonial power. The
French also deployed Chinese workers to build a rail line from the town of
Kayès to the Niger River in West Africa.[48]

Links between Africa and Imperial China, although not substantial,
were more extensive than the oft-cited trade and the fifteenth-century
voyages to eastern Africa by Zheng He. There was widespread use of Chinese labor in Africa on major infrastructure projects although very few of
the laborers remained permanently on the continent. This is a tradition
that continues with more recent Chinese laborers brought to Africa for
construction projects. There is also a long tradition of Chinese traders,
merchants, and service providers immigrating to Mauritius, Madagascar,
Seychelles, South Africa, and Mozambique. Some of these Chinese became permanent residents and eventually citizens of those countries.
Some became thoroughly integrated with the local population, as in the
case of the Seychelles, while others tended to retain their identity, as in
South Africa. There is every reason to believe that many of the recently
arrived and similarly employed Chinese will become part of new permanent communities.

Africa and the Republic of China, 1912–1949

A new National Government of China (referred to hereafter in this section
as the Republic of China or ROC) begun by Sun Yat Sen and later led by
Chiang Kai-shek replaced the Qing or Manchu Dynasty (1644–1911) on 1

January 1912. It was preoccupied with maintaining control over the country and often failed. Two world wars, rampant warlordism, an internal communist challenge and the Japanese occupation combined to thwart the ROC's leaders. These challenges left virtually no time for interaction with faraway Africa. In any event, only three African countries—Ethiopia, Liberia, and white-ruled South Africa—were independent throughout the period until 1949 when the communists pushed the ROC off the mainland to Taiwan. Egypt received partial independence from the United Kingdom in 1922, but did not obtain full sovereignty until the overthrow of the British-backed Egyptian monarchy in 1952.

The ROC maintained limited contact with Africa from 1912 through 1949 and gave more attention to countries such as South Africa and French-ruled Madagascar that had sizeable Chinese communities. Curiously, the ROC seems to have taken less interest in the British-controlled Indian Ocean island of Mauritius, which had the largest permanent Chinese community in Africa. The two agreements that the ROC signed with African countries were also surprising. The first one was an exchange of notes on most-favored nation treatment of goods traded between semi-independent Egypt and the ROC. Signed in 1930, it remained in effect for less than a year.[49] The second was a treaty of friendship between independent Liberia and the ROC. Signed in Paris in 1937 by their respective diplomatic representatives to France, it entered into force in 1941. It constituted China's first treaty with a fully independent African country. Liberia did not, however, establish diplomatic relations with the ROC until 1957.[50] Until then, there was virtually no interaction between the ROC and Liberia.

China maintained a special interest in the Arab world and Egypt in particular because of China's own minority Muslim community. Chinese Muslims studied at Al-Azhar, the center of Islamic learning in Egypt.[51] In 1931, Al-Azhar appointed the first Chinese Sheikh, Mohammad Ibrahim Shao Kuo-chen, to its faculty. Chinese interest in Islam led to the establishment of diplomatic relations between the Egyptian monarchy and the ROC in 1942, when Tang Wu became China's first diplomatic representative resident in Cairo.[52] Egypt established an office in China in 1944.[53]

Following its defeat on the mainland in 1949, the ROC's diplomatic relations were a shambles as it transferred the government to Taiwan. Only seven nations, none of them African, initially established permanent diplomatic missions on Taiwan.[54] The ROC did not take a strong political interest in Africa until a number of years later, when the African colonies began to achieve independence. Fierce competition with the People's Republic of China for acceptance and diplomatic recognition by the new African states inspired this attention by ROC leaders.

The most significant Chinese diplomatic contact with independent Africa during the republican era occurred with South Africa because it was home to one of the largest Chinese communities. After the recall of Chinese consul-general Liu Ngai in 1911, the United States retained responsibility for Chinese affairs until 1919, when Liu returned to South Africa and reopened the consulate-general. The British government also recognized Liu as the consul-general for Basutoland (now Lesotho), Swaziland, Bechuanaland Protectorate (now Botswana), and Southern Rhodesia (now Zimbabwe). An activist, he established contacts with Chinese throughout South Africa, solicited funds from them to pay the cost of operating the consulate-general, and outspokenly advocated on their behalf vis-à-vis the South African government. In the process, he ran afoul of the white South African leaders. He remained until 1930, when a succession of ROC government representatives served as consul-general until 1948. None of them remained more than three years. South Africa occasionally allowed the appointment of local Chinese leaders as honorary consuls in key cities. At no time during the ROC period did South Africa assign diplomatic or consular personnel to China.[55]

The Chinese community in South Africa grew slowly during the republican era, rising from 1,905 in 1911 to 2,944 in 1936 and 4,340 in 1946. Most lived in the Cape and Transvaal and most were small traders. Many of them retained a strong allegiance with China and supported the Chinese Nationalist Party, the Kuomintang (KMT). Beginning in 1920, Chinese communities established KMT branches in South Africa's larger cities. The Second Sino-Japanese War (1937–1945) united the Chinese community in South Africa with China and led to fund-raising campaigns in support of the ROC. When South Africa entered World War II as an ally of China, white South African liberals began to condemn the long-standing discrimination against the Chinese. After the KMT fled to Taiwan, however, Chinese in South Africa again found themselves facing racial hostility and with no prospect their situation would improve in the racially divided country.[56]

There was considerable Chinese support in Madagascar for the KMT, which had some 1,500 members and twenty-seven cells by 1947. France had permitted the ROC to open a consulate in Antananarivo the previous year. The first Chinese consul, Kou Chao-fen, sensing a communist victory in China, helped organize a Communist Party of China branch and subsequently defected to the PRC. Kou and his staff left Madagascar for the PRC in mid-1950, leaving behind a politically divided Chinese community.[57]

On Mauritius, the China Society, also known as the Harmony Society, supported the republican revolution. Eventually the Chinese Chamber of Commerce became the official headquarters of the KMT. Following the death of Sun Yat Sen in 1925, most Chinese in Mauritius shifted their allegiance to Chiang Kai-shek. At the same time, they did not initially perceive communism as a threat to Confucian values. In addition, Chiang Kai-shek's strategy to take the communist threat more seriously than the Japanese one confused them. Although the ROC opened its first consulate in 1945, support in the Chinese community for the KMT began to waver.[58]

During the time the ROC ruled from the Chinese mainland, its engagement with Africa was never significant. The ROC was preoccupied with the Japanese occupation and Mao Zedong's communist insurgency. Whatever concerns it had about relations with African countries, they were generally negotiated in colonial capitals such as Paris and London, where the ROC had diplomatic representation. To the extent it had any interest in Africa, it tended to focus on modest trade links and maintained contact with the small Chinese communities in a few countries on the African continent and islands in the western Indian Ocean. The ROC became considerably more interested in Africa once the communists seized power on the mainland. It then began to press the African countries for recognition as the sole representative of China.

The PRC and the Role of Exogenous Events

Many scholars have analyzed PRC-Africa relations over different chronological periods. Some were unusually nuanced and included events that spanned only a few years while others preferred sweeping generalizations that covered a decade or more for each stage. There is little consistency in the way they chronologically grouped the policy changes that occurred in the China-Africa relationship after 1949.[59] The chronology in this chapter is equally arbitrary, but offers, we believe, a reasonable way to categorize the interaction between the PRC and Africa. China-Africa relations tended to be dictated by Chinese foreign policy ideology, at least in the first two decades, Chinese internal developments, and other events that were exogenous to Africa.[60] This is not surprising for several reasons. While the PRC has the luxury of speaking with one voice, African countries have never been in this position. The Organization of African Unity and its successor, the African Union, do not speak for all members when they deal with China or any other non-African country; differences among individual African states remain considerable. Countries such as South Africa, Egypt, and Nigeria because of their large populations and economic power inevitably receive more attention from China than smaller and economically weak ones such as Togo, Lesotho, and the Central African Republic. Until recently, when Africa became a major exporter of oil, even collectively Africans had little influence on international politics or global markets.

The major exogenous developments that affected China-Africa relations include the Cold War, which continued from the beginning of the relationship in 1949 until about 1990. It accounted for many of the PRC's differences about Africa with the West and especially the United States. The existence of colonial rule and white-ruled regimes in Africa worked to the advantage of China's communist ideology. The PRC supported the Africans in their efforts to end Western colonialism. Although the Africans themselves were instrumental in removing colonialism, the colonial powers played a significant role in determining the timing of African independence and the structure of most of the first African governments. Seventeen African states became independent in 1960 alone, offering a major opportunity for Chinese diplomacy.

Another important development for Africa was the Sino-Soviet conflict that began in the late 1950s and continued until the mid-1980s. This dispute became highly public by 1960 when Soviet technical advisers left the PRC, Chinese students returned from the USSR, and Soviet assistance to China dried up. A combination of the Cold War and the Sino-Soviet split essentially dictated the PRC's political/strategic approach to Africa until the mid-1980s, when only the Cold War remained as an issue. China's Great Leap Forward from 1958 to 1960 or 1961 affected PRC activities in Africa. Designed to transform China from an agrarian to a modern industrial economy, it was largely an economic failure, which limited China's ability to assist Africa.

The Great Proletarian Cultural Revolution began in 1966 and remained intense through 1969; it continued in a milder form until 1976. Launched by Mao Zedong to rid the country of its liberal bourgeoisie and revitalize the revolutionary class struggle, it resulted in carefully controlled chaos and violence. The Cultural Revolution, which the CPC subsequently deemed a serious policy error, had the effect of diminishing contact with Africa during the late 1960s. On 25 October 1971, the PRC, after a long diplomatic struggle, replaced the ROC on the UN Security Council. A significant majority of African states voted in favor of the PRC, a development Beijing continues to highlight in its relations with African countries. This change put the PRC in a position to assist its African friends on controversial issues before the Council.

The 1989 Tiananmen Square crackdown and its aftermath indirectly affected relations with Africa because of the harsh criticism expressed by the West about China's human rights practices. The end of the Cold War had important implications for China-Africa ties by allowing China to refocus its economic priorities on industrialization, trade, and competing in the global economy. It even offered the possibility of collaboration with the West in Africa. At the same time, it raised Chinese concerns about the role in Africa of the world's only remaining superpower—the United States. It is not yet clear how the newest exogenous factors—counterterrorism, climate change, global financial challenges, and growing interest in Africa by countries such as India and Brazil—will affect China-Africa relations. Even if they do not reach the importance of earlier developments, they are already influencing the relationship. New issues will certainly come into play; a global food crisis and China's goal of achieving increased sea lane security may be among them.

Taking Power Until the Eve of Bandung

Mao Zedong's "long march" and the CPC removal of the KMT from the Chinese mainland in October 1949 was followed by a period of relative disinterest in Africa and much of the rest of the world. As the PRC consolidated its power, it focused on domestic issues. The PRC did send troops to Korea in support of the communist government in Pyongyang and participated in the 1951–1953 negotiations at Panmunjom that eventually led to an armistice. In 1954, it had representatives at the Geneva Conference that ended French colonial rule in Indochina. The communist government also used this period to sign a mutual defense treaty with the Soviet Union and to strengthen relations with North Korea and the countries of Eastern

Europe.[61] During these years, to the extent that the PRC engaged in external affairs, there were no differences with the Soviet Union concerning policy toward Africa.[62] Africa did not become a serious part of Beijing's foreign policy agenda until the historic Bandung Conference in 1955.

In any event, there were few independent African states in the years immediately after the communists seized power in China. In addition to Ethiopia, Liberia, South Africa, and Egypt, only Libya became independent in 1951 before the Bandung Conference. Liberia had close ties to the United States while white-ruled South Africa envisaged its future with the West and particularly the United Kingdom. Ethiopia and Libya were developing strong security relationships with the United States. Ethiopia even sent two battalions to Korea to fight alongside the U.S.-led UN force supporting South Korea. Following the 1952 coup in Egypt, this left only Gamal Abdel Nasser as a potential partner for China's communist government.

The PRC did not completely absent itself from African affairs during the six years before the Bandung Conference. There were a few meetings between CPC officials and African delegates attending Soviet-financed international meetings. A small number of Africans went to China during this period. Walter Sisulu, Secretary General of South Africa's African National Congress (ANC), visited in 1953.[63] The ANC eventually received most of its support from the Soviet Union and the PRC aided the ANC's major rival, the Pan Africanist Congress. Félix Moumié, one of the leaders of Cameroon's Union des Populations du Cameroon (UPC), visited the PRC the same year. The UPC refusal to collaborate with the French colonial government in Cameroon caught the attention of Beijing.[64] These early contacts with an opponent of the white-ruled government in South Africa and a leader of a group in Cameroon that was unwilling to cooperate with French colonialists were harbingers of PRC policy in support of African liberation movements and several revolutionary groups. To some extent, Africa served as an entry point into Europe and a way to pursue goals that impacted Europe.

The PRC began to turn its attention to Africa in the second half of 1954. Zhou Enlai, in a report to the First National People's Congress, expressed the desire to promote business relations with Middle Eastern and African countries to improve understanding and create favorable conditions for the establishment of normal relations. He did not, however, consider Africa a likely ally at that time. By the end of 1954, the PRC showed increased appreciation for the importance of Africa following the communiqué from the Bogor (Indonesia) Conference, which served as a preparatory session for the Bandung Conference. The PRC realized it had concerns in common with Africa. Commenting on the Bogor communiqué, which proposed an Afro-Asian conference, *People's Daily* noted that much of Africa has long been subjected to oppression and enslavement by colonialism and most Africans have suffered the scourge or threats of war by imperialist aggressors. It added that a new dawn is breaking over the African continent.[65]

The Afro-Asian Period: From Bandung to Winneba

The 1955 Asian-African conference at Bandung, Indonesia, attracted representatives from twenty-nine Asian and African states. It marked an important change in the PRC's relations with Africa. Premier Zhou Enlai led the Chinese delegation. There were representatives from six African countries—Egypt, Ethiopia, Liberia, Libya, and soon to be independent Sudan and Ghana. The Chinese delegates had an opportunity to meet personally with the Africans. They developed a particularly good relationship with the Egyptians and began a dialogue on trade. Two Egyptians visited China after Bandung to continue the trade talks. The Chinese also met with representatives of several African liberation movements who attended as observers. It provided a forum for Zhou Enlai to speak out against colonialism and imperialism in Africa and to support independence movements in Algeria, Morocco, and Tunisia. He also upheld Egypt's claim to the Suez Canal as a new crisis over its control approached.[66]

The Bandung Conference, which eventually led to the creation of the Non-Aligned Movement, incorporated the PRC's "Five Principles of Peaceful Coexistence" into the "Ten Principles of Bandung." The original five principles remain as an essential part of China's policy toward Africa. Zhou Enlai initially proposed the five principles in 1953 as the preamble for the Indian-Chinese Trading Treaty in Tibet. Known as the Panchsheel, China and India agreed to them in 1954. The principles include mutual respect for sovereignty and territorial integrity, mutual nonaggression, noninterference in each other's internal affairs, equality, and mutual benefit and peaceful coexistence. Bandung was a personal triumph for Zhou Enlai and a watershed for Chinese diplomacy, including its relations with Africa.[67]

Building on its success at Bandung and the Conference of Asian Countries that took place several days earlier in New Delhi, the PRC decided to expand its engagement with the Afro-Asian world in an effort to mold its thinking and actions in a fashion that accorded with Chinese ideology. Following Bandung, this effort began to meet some resistance from the USSR, which had not been invited to the conference, and from some other nonaligned countries. China sent a delegation to the first Afro-Asian People's Solidarity Organization (AAPSO) Conference in Cairo, which began in late 1957 and continued into early 1958. China took note of the growing role of Africans in this movement. Even before the Conference opened, China held a rally in Beijing where the head of the delegation expressed support for several African national liberation movements, including those in Algeria, Kenya, Cameroon, and Uganda. Early in 1958, the CPC acknowledged the growing importance of Africa in world politics.[68]

By early 1960, Afro-Asian solidarity had become an essential component of China's foreign policy. In a key speech, China's Chairman of the Committee for Afro-Asian Solidarity, Liao Cheng-chih, pledged support for Africa's struggle against colonialism and reaffirmed adherence to the "Five Principles of Peaceful Coexistence." He singled out the United States for criticism, arguing that Washington intended to supplant the colonial powers in Africa. He described "U.S. imperialism" as the most dangerous enemy of African independence. The answer to America's "imperialist aggression" was Afro-Asian solidarity. Liao Cheng-chih pledged that China would uphold sovereignty and territorial integrity, adding that China regarded as its international duty the backing of "national liberation struggles of all oppressed nations."[69]

The second AAPSO conference took place in Conakry, Guinea, in 1960 with representatives from more than fifty countries. It was an opportunity to solidify relations with a growing number of independent African countries. It also became clear there was increasing friction between China and the USSR.[70] After Conakry, AAPSO became a venue for Sino-Soviet hostility. By 1961, China concluded that the Soviet Union should not be eligible to take part in the organization. AAPSO members were generally reluctant to take sides in the Sino-Soviet dispute, which dominated the third AAPSO conference in Moshi, Tanzania, in 1963. The PRC sought to portray itself as more revolutionary than the Soviet Union. It urged the creation of an international united front that included itself and the independent and colonized countries of Africa, Asia, and Latin America to destroy capitalism and imperialism. The conference in Moshi and its Sino-Soviet conflict overtones alarmed many African representatives. The 1962 Sino-Indian border war emerged as an issue at Moshi. Most African countries remained silent after the outbreak of conflict while some of the more militant African countries expressed concern about the damage it was doing to Afro-Asian solidarity. Among the African participants, however, only Niger condemned Chinese aggression against India; several others spoke out elsewhere. At a meeting of the AAPSO Council in 1964, the Chinese representative criticized the Soviet position on peaceful coexistence, disarmament, and solving territorial disputes by peaceful means. The Africans concluded that the rupture between the USSR and China was complete. In 1965, the fourth AAPSO conference in Winneba, Ghana, again demonstrated the corrosive effect of the Sino-Soviet conflict on Afro-Asian solidarity. The Afro-Asian organization never recovered. Winneba was the last large gathering limited to Afro-Asian states.[71]

China used AAPSO conferences to announce policies and encourage their acceptance by African and Asian nations. Chinese representatives also established contact during these meetings with leaders of African governments and African nationalist leaders, some of whom would later lead independence movements in their countries.[72] At the same time, the PRC worked hard in Africa to achieve diplomatic recognition and political support. The fact that the ROC continued to hold China's seat in the UN Security Council drove much of this diplomatic effort. After an agreement in 1955 to purchase Egyptian cotton and an exchange of trade offices in their respective capitals, Egypt became the first African country to recognize the PRC. Cairo was the center of the Arab world, headquarters for AAPSO, and host to several African liberation groups. Beijing established an important embassy in Cairo and used it to considerable advantage to expand its diplomacy in the Arab world, including North Africa, and eventually in Sub-Saharan Africa. Following the outbreak of the Suez Canal crisis in 1956, China strongly backed Egypt. It offered Cairo a $5 million credit, another Chinese first for Africa, and called on the UK and France to end their aggression. China restrained itself, however, by urging an end to the conflict by peaceful negotiations.[73]

An important component of China's early policy toward Africa was rhetorical and material support for independence movements and revolutionary groups that opposed several established African governments. The PRC eventually ended its practice of supporting revolutionary organizations committed to overthrowing existing African governments. Chinese support for liberation movements began with Algeria's Front de Libération

Nationale (FLN), established in 1954. China offered rhetorical support the following year and then stepped up contact with Algerian revolutionaries. The PRC promptly recognized Algeria's Provisional Government in 1958 followed by a credit for the purchase of arms and training of Algerian fighters in China. The FLN, for its part, agreed to a communiqué in 1960 that fully supported the PRC's control over Taiwan. Beijing subsequently insisted that the "One China" policy be part of any agreement on diplomatic recognition. The FLN, which achieved victory over France in 1962, was one of the relatively few revolutionary groups in Africa supported by the PRC that took over the reins of government. Throughout its support, China appeared primarily interested in the fact that the FLN remained anti-imperialist, which it saw as a way to confront its main enemy—the United States—in these early years. The PRC also perceived Algeria's struggle as similar to its own war for liberation.[74]

In the early 1960s, the failure of China's Great Leap Forward severely limited assistance the PRC could provide to the newly independent African countries.[75] As a result, Beijing sought influence on the cheap. One tactic was the establishment of numerous front organizations. Two examples were the China Peace Committee or the Chinese branch of the World Peace Council and the Chinese Committee for Afro-Asian Solidarity, which served as the Chinese branch of AAPSO. The PRC also relied on people-to-people organizations such as the Chinese-African People's Friendship Association established in 1960 as an umbrella organization to oversee a plethora of such groups. Following the establishment of diplomatic relations with an African country, China created a separate friendship association under the control of the Chinese People's Association for Cultural Relations with Foreign Countries.[76] The success of this effort varied widely from country to country, often depending on the closeness of the official relationship and amount of tangible support China offered the country.

China's diplomatic breakthrough in Egypt opened the door for other successes in both North and Sub-Saharan Africa. One important diplomatic development was Zhou Enlai's historic ten-country visit to Africa at the end of 1963 and beginning of 1964. Although it was not the first high level Chinese delegation to visit Africa, it was the most dramatic. It also signaled the beginning of a Chinese policy to emphasize the importance of regular, senior, face-to-face contact with African leaders.[77] This practice continues to the present day. Zhou Enlai used the African tour to unveil the five principles guiding China's relations with African and Arab countries. They continue to be widely quoted by Chinese officials and scholars, although China's 2006 African policy statement updated, modified, and expanded the five principles. When he announced the principles in Accra, Ghana, Zhou emphasized that they were in accord with the previously mentioned "Five Principles of Peaceful Coexistence" and the "Ten Principles of Bandung." Zhou Enlai also presented during his African tour eight principles governing China's foreign aid. They are cited in the chapter on assistance. The five principles concerning relations with African and Arab countries were[78]

- China supports the African and Arab peoples in their struggle to oppose imperialism and old and new colonialism and to win and safeguard national independence;
- It supports the pursuance of a policy of peace, neutrality and non-alignment by the governments of the African and Arab countries;
- It supports the desire of the African and Arab peoples to achieve unity and solidarity in the manner of their own choice;
- It supports the African and Arab states in their efforts to settle their disputes through peaceful consultation; and
- It holds that the sovereignty of the African and Arab countries should be respected by all other countries and that encroachment and interference from any quarter should be opposed.

These principles are sufficiently general that they have withstood the test of time. China did not, however, always adhere to them. Chinese support in the 1960s for several African revolutionary movements committed to the overthrow of independent governments violated the principles of noninterference, settling disputes through peaceful consultation, and respect for sovereignty of African countries.[79] Nevertheless, this was the public face of China's African and Arab policy after 1963; the principles became a litany in official rhetoric.

The economic relationship with Africa was not very important through the mid-1960s. Although China was quick to sign trade agreements with African countries, the volume of trade was small and roughly in balance.[80] It was not until the 1990s that trade became a significant part of the relationship. China was not in a position to offer much economic aid until the 1990s. It did begin to send more Chinese technicians to Africa after 1960.[81] For example, the first Chinese medical team arrived in Algeria in 1963.

Chinese direct investment in African economies, an important effort later, was not part of the Maoist agenda.

From the Cultural Revolution to UN Admission

Beginning in August 1966, the Great Proletarian Cultural Revolution marked a new phase in the China-Africa relationship. There was considerable debate in China about the Cultural Revolution before Mao Zedong formally launched it at the Eleventh Plenum of the Eighth Central Committee. In terms of China-Africa relations, the Cultural Revolution was also an attempt by Mao to move the center of world revolution from Moscow to Beijing. Influential Defense Minister Lin Biao, a strong supporter of the Cultural Revolution, wrote in 1965 that Asia, Africa, and Latin America were the main battlefields in the struggle against American imperialism and its lackeys. He called for world revolution and the promotion of wars of national liberation. The most damaging internal phase of the Cultural Revolution, which included attacks by the Red Guards on perceived counter-revolutionaries and "capitalist-roaders," occurred from 1966 through 1969. It continued in a milder form until Mao's death in September 1976 and the purge of the Gang of Four in October. The Cultural Revolution set back modernization and production, disrupted education and science, and isolated China from the rest of the world.[82]

The impact of the Cultural Revolution on Africa was significant and its beginning coincided with the overthrow of governments in Dahomey (now Benin) and the Central African Republic. The new governments in both countries expelled PRC embassy personnel. In 1966, President Kwame Nkrumah of Ghana, who allowed the PRC to train African revolutionaries in his country, was removed from power while visiting China. The new government in Accra immediately sent 430 Chinese staff, including thirteen guerrilla warfare instructors, back to China and significantly reduced the size of the embassy. Beijing accepted this setback even as it endured the worst abuses of the Cultural Revolution and chose to keep open its mission in Accra in order to wait for a more favorable political situation. This early demonstration of patience and pragmatism became a hallmark of later PRC policy in Africa. By the end of the year, Accra charged that China was supporting an attempt by Nkrumah to return to power; Beijing then closed its embassy. China also experienced serious difficulties in its relations with Kenya, although the two countries maintained diplomatic relations.[83]

In 1967 China recalled its ambassadors worldwide, except for the one in Cairo, to answer charges brought against the Foreign Ministry and its senior personnel. Ambassador Huang Hua remained in Cairo to coordinate policy toward Africa and the Middle East in the absence of other ambassadors. During the Cultural Revolution there was a sharp drop in high level African visits to China and senior Chinese to Africa. By 1969, four fewer African countries recognized the PRC than in 1965, trade was down moderately, and new PRC loans to Africa had dried up. China did not terminate cooperative initiatives in Africa, but tended to focus on countries such as Tanzania, Zambia, Mali, Guinea, Congo-Brazzaville, and Algeria, with which it had especially close relations. China continued to support African liberation movements throughout the Cultural Revolution, but its preoccupation with internal developments diminished its ability and willingness to engage as actively as before. These unsettling events in China caused anxiety among China's African friends. Although some militant Chinese embassy personnel in Africa tried to encourage Africans to follow a similar revolutionary model, very few African countries showed any interest. Tanzania created its own half-hearted version of the Cultural Revolution known as "Operation Vijaana," complete with "Green Guards." It was a poor copy. In spite of all the turmoil in China, Beijing generally handled its relations with Africa competently and Chinese officials maintained their long-term foreign policy objectives toward the continent. For example, in 1967 China made the final decision to move forward with financing the Tanzania-Zambia railroad project. Nevertheless, the Cultural Revolution was a setback for China's relations with Africa.[84]

China adopted a pragmatic policy designed to accommodate the African countries as it competed with Taiwan for diplomatic recognition. Zhou Enlai demanded patience and understanding from China's diplomats in the establishment of diplomatic relations. (See Appendix 1 for the order and dates that African countries established diplomatic relations with the PRC.) Faced with African skepticism and suspicion of China, Zhou told Chinese diplomats to wait as long as necessary for the right moment and even agreed to sign cultural agreements and set up trade offices in countries with diplomatic relations with Taiwan. China operated in these early years in Africa on the basis of the Chinese phrase "when water flows, a channel is formed."[85]

As dismally as this stage of China-Africa relations began, it ended in October 1971 with one of Beijing's crowning achievements—admission to the UN and replacement of the ROC on the Security Council. The tactic for keeping the PRC out of the UN was a U.S.-inspired procedural vote in the General Assembly that allowed admission of the PRC only if it received a two-thirds majority. This ploy failed for the first time in 1971. The General Assembly then admitted the PRC by a vote of 76-35 with 17 abstentions. The PRC received 34 percent of its votes from African countries. Beijing received the support of twenty-six African states; only fifteen voted with Taipei. Ten of the fifteen countries that supported Taipei recognized Beijing in the next few years.[86]

China repaired with surprising speed the damage to its relations with Africa during the Cultural Revolution. It began returning experienced career ambassadors to African capitals in 1969. By 1970, China increased significantly the number of friendship, cultural, technical, and governmental delegations visiting the continent. For the first time, China became the largest provider of foreign aid to Africa by a communist country. The PRC launched a diplomatic offensive that helped achieve its successful result at the UN. Some outside developments also worked to its advantage. U.S. president Richard Nixon announced in 1971 that national security adviser Henry Kissinger had made a secret visit to China and that Nixon had agreed to visit within a year. In view of long-standing U.S. opposition to the PRC holding a seat on the Security Council, this clearly sent mixed signals to Africans and the rest of the world. In addition, many Africans had become disappointed with apparent American indifference to the continent. For its part, the Soviet Union's 1968 invasion of Czechoslovakia disillusioned many Africans.[87] China took advantage of these developments. This fast reversal of fortune is a reminder that China is capable of making colossal mistakes, for example, the Cultural Revolution, but once it puts its collective mind to repairing the damage, it can achieve quick and impressive success.

China emerged from the Cultural Revolution pursuing less extreme policies toward Africa. Not only had relative moderates in China prevailed, but some of the most radical African leaders including Ahmed Ben Bella in Algeria, Kwame Nkrumah in Ghana, and Modibo Keita in Mali had been replaced by Africans who exercised more restraint. As a result, China ended support for revolutionary groups in Africa whose goal was the overthrow of established governments. Rather, it limited its material assistance to those liberation movements engaged in the removal of colonial and white-ruled governments.[88] At the same time, it recognized and worked closely with governments of all kinds irrespective of their political and economic ideology. This policy has prevailed to the present day.

Stirrings of Pragmatism and Third World Focus in the 1970s

China was unusually active in Africa in the early 1970s. Following its political success at the UN, it began a campaign to secure additional diplomatic recognition. China significantly increased its assistance commitments to Africa and invited sixteen African heads of government to visit Beijing by the end of 1975.[89] By 1971, for example, China had replaced Great Britain as Tanzania's principal trade partner and by the middle of the decade China was fully engaged in constructing the Tanzania-Zambia railway.[90] It continued to support African liberation groups, but found it difficult to compete with a Soviet Union that had deeper pockets. From 1970 to 1976, however, China actually provided more aid (mostly loans) to Africa than the Soviet Union—$1.8 billion to twenty-eight African countries compared to the USSR's $1 billion to twenty states. After 1976 Chinese aid commitments fell sharply.[91]

Although trade with Africa grew in the 1970s, China accounted for only about 1 percent of total African exports by the end of the decade.[92] Snow wrote that beginning in the late 1970s, Chinese diplomats were telling their African interlocutors that socialist governments should privatize their economies, offer material incentives to motivate their workers and encourage investment from other countries.[93] China's revolutionary rhetoric continued, but its policy in Africa became more pragmatic.

Alan Hutchison, a British journalist with extensive African experience, asserted in the mid-1970s that although China's stated aims were revolutionary, its policy toward Africa, except during the Cultural Revolution, was evolutionary and eventually pragmatic. It evolved toward accommodation with conservative governments such as Emperor Haile Selassie's Ethiopia and Mobutu Sese Seko's Zaire (now Democratic Republic of the Congo). China had little in common ideologically with either country.[94] Sudan offers an especially telling example. A failed coup in 1971 by army officers sympathetic to the Sudanese Communist Party (SCP), a surprisingly strong organization, resulted in the imprisonment and execution of SCP members. China remained silent about the executions. Furthermore,

Zhou Enlai subsequently commented that the Sudanese government "victoriously smashed a foreign subversive plot." China concluded that it preferred an anti-Soviet, reactionary Sudanese government to one dominated by the SCP, which was sympathetic to the Soviet Union.[95]

An American expert on China-Africa relations, George Yu, identified three major components of China's policy in Africa during the 1970s. First, China saw itself as an alternative development model to the Western liberal model implicitly encouraged by the former colonial powers and the United States. African governments became increasingly dissatisfied with the Western model at a time when African socialism resonated in much of the continent. China perceived that its approach to development would appeal to Africans. Although Tanzania adopted, with notable lack of success, some key tenets of Chinese social and economic theory, few other African countries offered more than lip service.[96] Mali tried to launch a Chinese-style class struggle in 1968 and the Comoro Islands did likewise in the mid-1970s. Both regimes soon fell from power. Although it is not surprising that Africans had little interest in adopting wholesale the Chinese version of communism, China was equally disinterested in trying to teach it to them.[97] Second, China emphasized the struggle against the two super powers—the Soviet Union and the United States. During the 1970s, China perceived the USSR as a greater threat to its interests in Africa than the United States. Beijing believed that Moscow pursued a policy of world domination and set out to prevent a Soviet success.[98] Washington's recognition of Beijing at the beginning of 1979 helped ameliorate China's concern about American activities in Africa, although other contentious issues prevented a significant improvement in the relationship. Third, China attached extraordinary importance during the 1970s to the role of the Third World, of which Africa was an important part. This component of China's strategy requires elaboration.

Beginning with the Ninth CPC Congress in 1969 and continuing until 1979, in accordance with Mao's so-called Three Worlds Theory, Beijing underscored that the Third World was the principal force for confronting the two superpowers. In its effort to unite the Third World against the superpowers, China improved its state-to-state relations, especially in Africa.[99] Deng Xiaoping, in his capacity as chairman of Beijing's UN delegation in 1974, summarized China's Third World policy before the General Assembly. He proposed that "the world today actually consists of three parts, or three worlds, that are both interconnected and in contradiction to one another. The United States and the Soviet Union make up the First World. The developing countries in Asia, Africa, Latin America and other regions make up the Third World. The developed countries between the two make up the Second World."[100]

The Three Worlds Theory held that the two superpowers sought world hegemony, were the biggest international exploiters and oppressors of the day, and were the source of a new world war. Real power, Beijing argued, resided in a united Third World that avoids the plunder of its natural resources by the superpowers. To this end, in his 1974 speech Deng pledged China's support to developing countries for improving the terms of trade for their raw materials. He emphasized that China is a socialist and developing country that belongs to the Third World, adding that "China is not a superpower, nor will she ever seek to be one."[101] Ironically, the concerns that Deng expressed in 1974 about the Soviet Union and the United States concerning African natural resources are heard today in connection with China's policy toward Africa.

The 1980s: More Pragmatism But Less Interest in Africa

China's policy toward Africa in the early 1980s did not change significantly from the late 1970s. During 1979–1982, there was a modest reduction in economic aid, a decline in trade and a drop in the number of medical teams sent to Africa.[102] The Twelfth National Congress of the CPC in 1982 marked a shift in global Chinese policy from "war and revolution" to "peace and development." The new policy reaffirmed, however, the "Five Principles of Peaceful Coexistence." Two elements of the new policy had important implications for China's approach to Africa. China set a course that emphasized domestic economic development and said that it would pursue a peaceful and "independent" foreign policy. On the one hand, this served warning that China would make fewer resources available for aiding other countries. China also signaled that it was not prepared to align itself with any major power. This underscored support for its goal aimed at enhancing the role of the Third World. These policy adaptations also led to the development of relations between the CPC and ruling political parties in African countries.[103]

Premier Zhao Ziyang visited eleven African countries in late 1982 and early 1983. This tour recalled Zhou Enlai's in 1963–1964. The visit was an effort to reaffirm China's interest in Africa. Zhao repeated Beijing's support for African liberation struggles, the consolidation of African independence and South-South economic cooperation. Importantly, he indicated that China was ready to normalize relations with the Soviet Union and that Africa no longer had to choose between China and the USSR. He also announced China's "Four Principles on Sino-African Economic and Technical Cooperation." These are discussed in Chapter 5. Zhao's visit emphasized China's continuing interest in Africa and provided a foundation for China's current relations with Africa. It set the stage for a different kind of economic cooperation in view of China's focus on domestic modernization. Zhao also encouraged Africans to resist influence from the USSR and the United States. Finally, Zhao used his stops in three North African countries to reiterate Beijing's support for the "just struggle" of the Arab people, Israel's right to exist so long as it withdrew from occupied Arab lands, and Palestine's right to exist.[104]

British scholar Ian Taylor has been writing about China-Africa relations for two decades. He concludes that Africa became less important to China in the 1980s, especially during the second half of the decade, as China focused on economic modernization and the Cold War began to diminish as a policy factor toward Africa. Preoccupied with its economy, China provided less aid to Africa and Sino-African trade grew slowly in the 1980s. Beginning in the mid-1980s, there were fewer high level visits from China to Africa, although they increased to other parts of the world. Following an improvement in China's relations with the Soviet Union in the mid-1980s, China no longer considered Africa an area of contention between them. Beijing became increasingly skeptical about Africa's requests for assistance and even began warning visiting African leaders of the dangers of uncritically embracing socialism as a developmental model. By the late 1980s, China's policy toward Africa was one of relative disinterest.[105]

One of China's leading Africanists, He Wenping, although she made every effort to emphasize the positive, described China-Africa relations in the 1980s in a circumspect manner. She said the guiding principle of Chinese diplomacy changed from "ideological idealism to pragmatic idealism and from unconditional internationalism to a priority of national interest."[106] He Wenping wrote that China no longer developed relations with African countries based on their ideology or their policies toward the United States and USSR. She pointed out the number of African countries recognizing Beijing increased from forty-four in the 1970s to forty-eight in the 1980s and that fifty-five African presidents visited China from 1981 to 1989. At the same time, He Wenping acknowledged that China's economic modernization left the country short of capital and unable to provide Africa the same level of economic assistance as before. China also moved away from loans and emphasized other forms of development cooperation such as signing commercial contracts, engaging in joint ventures, and providing technical services. In sum, China's relations with Africa shifted increasingly from the political to the economic arena.[107]

The decade ended with a setback for China following its harsh repression of the protests in Tiananmen Square in the spring of 1989. The 1980s reaffirmed that China largely structured the China-Africa relationship. China was almost always in the position of taking the initiative. African countries found themselves reacting to developments in China and decisions taken by Beijing. Of even greater concern to many Africans, there was no coordinated African response to China's policies and actions.

Post-Cold War Relations During the 1990s

Two significant developments exogenous to Africa affected Sino-African relations at the dawn of the last decade of the twentieth century. The most important was the end of the Cold War. This event had positive implications in that it ended East-West competition in Africa and, theoretically, offered the possibility of a peace dividend. The downside, however, was decreased interest in and commitment to Africa by the West and, especially, by the former Soviet Union and its East European allies. The end of the Cold War roughly coincided with another event that had the potential for a negative impact on Sino-African relations—the military crackdown on the protestors in Tiananmen Square. While Beijing's response to the crisis elicited a sharp condemnation from Western countries, most African countries were indifferent and a few supported Beijing's actions.

The end of the Cold War provided an opportunity for China to take advantage of the relative disinterest in Africa by traditional donor countries and to initiate a more normal relationship based on economic interaction. Although concerned about the African reaction to Tiananmen Square, Beijing was relieved by the response. Angola's foreign minister, Namibia's president, and Burkina Faso's president, who now recognizes Taipei, publicly supported the government of China.[108] In the aftermath of Tiananmen

Square, Botswana opened its first Asian embassy in Beijing in 1991.[109] The prevailing reaction in North Africa suggested the crackdown was a necessary and understandable response by a legitimate government that felt threatened.[110]

Leaders in China and many African countries had long believed that Western countries unfairly criticized their human rights practices. This was an issue where many African governments and China could support each other. Looking to control the damage, China began a campaign to improve its contacts with Africa. Between June 1989 and June 1992, Foreign Minister Qian Qichen visited seventeen Sub-Saharan African countries and Vice Premier Wu Xueqian went to another three. During a 1989 visit to six countries in southern Africa, Qian Qichen pointed out that most African countries considered events at Tiananmen Square an internal Chinese issue. During the same period, Beijing invited sixteen Sub-Saharan African heads of state or government and twenty-three other senior officials to China. Beijing welcomed the support, or at least silence, from Africa. As a result, its assistance to the continent increased in the period immediately following Tiananmen.[111]

Taiwan has always been a critical consideration for the PRC's policy in Africa. Beijing routinely insisted that diplomatic recognition include acceptance of its "One China" policy. When Taiwan officially abandoned its claim in 1991 to represent all of China, the leaders in Taipei sought to create a special status that seemed to be a prelude to a declaration of independence. The PRC vigorously opposed any Taiwan independence movement and Taiwan's efforts to obtain diplomatic recognition. This message was pervasive in China's dialogue with African leaders. The return of Hong Kong to Chinese control in 1997 underscored that Taiwan remained free of Beijing's reach and reinvigorated PRC efforts to rule in Taiwan.[112]

Chinese president Yang Shangkun visited Africa in 1992, when he set forth the following as China's African policy:

- Support for African sovereignty, national independence and economic development;
- Opposition to foreign intervention;
- Respect for different political systems and development paths;
- Support for African unity, cooperation and the Organization of African Unity; and

- Belief that African states should participate actively in the international system as equal members.[113]

There is nothing particularly new in this policy except that it shed the revolutionary rhetoric of earlier statements. It also highlighted China's opposition to foreign (read Western) intervention in Africa.

President Jiang Zemin made his first visit to Africa in 1996. In a speech at the headquarters of the Organization of African Unity in Addis Ababa he announced a five-point proposal for long-term cooperation with Africa during the twenty-first century. The five points were anodyne and in keeping with previous policy statements:[114]

- To foster a sincere friendship and become each other's "all weather friend";
- To treat each other as equals, respect each other's sovereignty and refrain from interfering in each other's internal affairs;
- To seek common development on the basis of mutual benefit;
- To increase consultation and cooperation in international affairs; and
- To look into the future and create a more splendid world.

In 1993, China became for the first time a net importer of petroleum. During the 1990s, imports of energy and raw materials from Africa were increasingly important to sustaining China's booming economy and its export of ever-larger quantities of consumer and industrial products. In addition to oil, China sought iron ore, titanium, cobalt, copper, uranium, aluminum, manganese, and timber.[115] China downplays the importance of Africa's raw materials as one of its interests in the continent. Sino-African trade grew impressively during the 1990s, from about $1 billion at the end of the 1980s to well over $6 billion by the end of the 1990s. Chinese investment in Africa also began to feature as a significant part of the relationship, reaching almost $4 billion by the turn of the century.[116] The 1990s established the base for phenomenal expansion of China-Africa relations in the twenty-first century.

China never abandoned its focus on the Third World. The end of the Cold War and its bipolar international system, the fact that the United States remained as the world's only superpower, and China's interest in becoming a global economic power led to its self-identification as leader of developing countries. As a result, China began increasingly to refer in policy statements to developing countries rather than the Third World. More important, before the end of the last century it began to encourage a multi-polar world aimed at diluting American power. China continued to strengthen cooperation with developing nations "in their common struggle against power politics so as to promote the establishment of a multipolar world."[117]

The Development of Chinese Policy in the Twenty-First Century

In view of the rapidly growing ties between the PRC and African countries, Beijing concluded that it needed a multilateral, consultative mechanism to help coordinate the relationship. As a result, eighty ministerial-level officials from China and more than forty African countries attended the first FOCAC conference in Beijing in 2000. It focused on strengthening coopera-tion between China and Africa. Premier Wen Jiabao then joined thirteen African leaders and more than seventy ministers from China and forty-four African nations at the second FOCAC conference in Addis Ababa in 2003. The third conference returned to Beijing in 2006 when nearly every African head of state or government that recognized Beijing participated.[118] Wen Jiabao headed the Chinese delegation to the fourth FOCAC conference at Sharm el-Sheikh, Egypt, in 2009. FOCAC has proven to be a useful tool in improving coordination between China and Africa. The initiative began with China and decisions largely remain in the hands of China.

One of the first foreign policy changes introduced publicly under Hu Jintao was the "peaceful rise" concept in 2003. Following meetings with American officials in Washington in 2002, Zheng Bijian, former CPC offi-cial, proposed the idea, which grew out of Deng Xiaoping's "peace and development" concept. Zheng argued that if China achieves economic devel-opment and raises the standard of living of the Chinese people over the next half century, China will not destabilize the international order or oppress its neighbors. In other words, China's rise will not seek external expansion, but will uphold peace, mutual cooperation, and common development. Although senior Chinese leaders publicly embraced the new theory, within a year, apparently in response to concerns that the term "rise" was seen as threatening, Hu Jintao stopped using it and substituted "peaceful develop-ment." Since late 2005, the official mantra has been peaceful development, although "peaceful rise" still appears in Chinese academic journals. This debate has more relevance for China's neighbors and the United States; nevertheless, it is also intended to reassure the rest of the developing world. It has implications for China's involvement in global security, including UN peacekeeping operations in Africa.[119]

China presented at the 1997 ASEAN Summit the idea of a New Security Concept, which it refined in subsequent years. Known as "The Four No's," Hu Jintao publicly endorsed the doctrine during a speech in April 2004. "The Four No's" consisted of no hegemonism, no power politics, no military alliances, and no arms races. Although not aimed at Africa, many developing countries concluded that "The Four No's" encouraged mutual confidence and international cooperation while avoiding Cold War conflict and confrontation.[120]

Another policy debate focused on the concept of "harmonious society" and its foreign policy alter ego "harmonious world." It first appeared in the international arena in 2005 when Hu Jintao proposed at the Asia-Africa Summit that Asian and African countries "promote friendly coexistence, equality-based dialogues, and common development and prosperity of different civilizations, in order to create a harmonious world."[121] The concept marks a shift in the leadership's understanding of China's position in the world and has become a guidepost for foreign affairs. "Harmonious world" suggests that China is moving to a new stage of development and is more willing to engage in international activities such as UN peacekeeping operations. It is based on the assumption that China's economic well-being is its highest priority and this will only be possible in a benign international environment. It is also an invitation for the outside world to participate in China's development. These concepts have important implications for Africa where China supports the status quo and African peacekeeping operations, and where it depends increasingly on African raw materials to fuel its economy. African countries are even encouraged to invest in China as South Africa, Mauritius, and several others are doing.[122]

The State Council issued a white paper in 2005 that outlined a foreign policy strategy for China. Called "China's Peaceful Development Road," it stressed that achieving peaceful development has been the "unremitting pursuit" of the Chinese people and administration for almost thirty years. The strategy aims to sustain a peaceful international environment that helps Chinese development while allowing China to contribute to the building of a harmonious world. The white paper pledged increased aid to developing countries, especially those in Africa.[123] Sinologist Robert G. Sutter explained the strategy is recognition that China is prepared to accept the world as it is and to avoid disruptive initiatives characteristic of the Maoist period. China is also ready to work with international and regional organizations in a variety of fields.[124]

China issued a widely publicized white paper titled "China's African Policy" in 2006 as part of the run-up to the FOCAC conference in Beijing at the end of the year. It set forth the general principles and objectives of China's policy:[125]

- Sincerity, friendship and equality. China adheres to the Five Principles of Peaceful Coexistence, respects African countries' independent choice of the road to development and supports African countries' efforts to grow stronger through unity.
- Mutual benefit, reciprocity and common prosperity. China supports African countries' endeavors for economic development and nation building, carries out cooperation in various forms in economic and social development, and promotes common prosperity of China and Africa.
- Mutual support and close coordination. China will strengthen cooperation with Africa in the UN and other multilateral systems by supporting each other's just demands and reasonable propositions and continue to appeal to the international community to give more attention to questions concerning peace and development in Africa.
- Learning from each other and seeking common development. China and Africa will learn from and draw upon each other's experience in governance and development, strengthen exchange and cooperation in education, science, culture and health. Supporting African countries' efforts to enhance capacity building, China will work together with Africa in the exploration of the road to sustainable development.

The 2006 white paper concluded with a strong reiteration of the PRC's policy on Taiwan, emphasizing that China stood ready to establish diplomatic relations with any country that was willing to accept the "One China" principle.

Hu Jintao made his sixth trip to Africa early in 2009, visiting Mali, Senegal, Tanzania, and Mauritius. He used the stop in Dar es Salaam to make a key speech on China's policy toward Africa in view of the growing global financial crisis. He set out a new six-point strategic partnership:

- China will implement its promises of assistance to Africa made at the 2006 Beijing summit and even increase its aid "within its capacity." It will also continue to reduce or cancel debt.
- China will try to increase high level contact, strengthen communication and participate actively in UN peacekeeping operations in Africa.
- China will implement preferential measures to increase imports from Africa and transfer technology to the continent.
- China will increase educational and cultural cooperation.
- China will work closely with African countries in multilateral organizations such as the United Nations and the WTO to address climate change, food security, poverty alleviation and development.
- China will strengthen FOCAC so that it can improve China-Africa cooperation.[126]

Late in 2009, China's *Outlook Weekly*, which reflects the views of the CPC, discussed a significant foreign policy initiative known as "Hu Jintao's Viewpoints About the Times." The five viewpoints provide a theoretical guide for China's future participation in global affairs. They deal with profound changes in the world situation, constructing a harmonious world, joint development, shared responsibilities, and enthusiastic participation in the world situation. Several of these views reflect earlier principles. The emphasis on shared responsibility and enthusiastic participation suggest, however, that Beijing is now prepared to assume more global responsibility because of China's growing economic and political power. In Africa, this has resulted in increasing troop commitments to UN peacekeeping operations, engaging in efforts to resolve the crisis in Sudan's Darfur region, contributing ships to the anti-piracy operation in the Gulf of Aden, and aligning more closely with African positions on global climate change. China has also learned to adapt quickly to political change in Africa even when its interests are challenged by a potentially unfriendly new regime. Beijing reacts with restraint, avoids becoming entangled in international sanctions, maintains its focus on sovereignty, and does not allow regime change to threaten its economic interests in the country.[127]

At the 2009 FOCAC conference in Egypt, Wen Jiabao announced a series of measures for strengthening ties with Africa. Half of them reiterated earlier promises. Several of them suggested a new emphasis in Chinese policy. Wen Jiabao called for partnership with the Africans on climate change and agreed to increase cooperation in science and technology, including the creation of one hundred joint demonstration projects with Africa. He announced a special loan of $1 billion for small and medium-sized African businesses and said China will offer zero tariff treatment to 95 percent of the products from Africa's least developed countries with which it has diplomatic relations.[128]

China is a major force in Africa, rivaling the United States in some countries. In 2009, China became Africa's largest trading partner, passing the United States. Sino-African trade reached $128.5 billion in 2010. Chinese investment in Africa, although still modest compared with European investment, is growing faster than Western investment. Total aid to Africa is still small compared to that of Western countries—averaging perhaps $2 billion annually in the last few years. By comparison, assistance to Africa from Development Assistance Committee countries is running at about $30 billion annually. On the other hand, China is offering huge low-interest loans, often tied to infrastructure projects built by Chinese companies and paid for in natural resources shipped to China. In some countries, these loans surpass the total of all loans from other countries or international banks.[129]

Between 1956 and 2006, there were more than 800 high level visits between African countries and China. Chinese leaders and foreign ministers made more than 160 visits to Africa while 524 Africans of ministerial rank or higher made 676 visits to China. Many African countries helped defeat eleven anti-China resolutions in the UN Commission on Human Rights and thirteen attempts by Taiwan to return to the UN General Assembly, and they supported China's successful bid for the 2008 Olympic Games and the 2010 Shanghai World Expo.[130]

China's increasingly pragmatic approach to Africa makes every effort to appear nonthreatening. China is sensitive that its enormous economic power and growing military strength has the potential to worry mostly small, poor, and weak African countries. Hence, it constantly describes its trade, aid, and investment activities in Africa as "win-win" for both China and Africa. Its twenty-first-century policy rhetoric of "peaceful development," "The Four No's," and "harmonious world" all underscore themes of noninterference, nonconfrontation, and cooperation. In 2009, Chinese State Councilor Dai Bingguo described China's "strategic partnership" with

African countries as based on political equality and mutual trust, economic win-win cooperation, and cultural exchange.[131] Put bluntly, China is trying hard to increase its global economic and political power while not scaring the rest of the world, including Africa.[132]

China as a Development Model for Africa

The literature on China-Africa relations is replete with commentary on China as a development model for Africa.[133] Many scholars and African leaders argue that China, or the "Beijing Consensus," as it is now often called, serves as a model for Africa.[134] China's officials have been careful, however, to avoid this idea; some have even publicly warned African countries away from following China's experience.[135] A billion people live in Africa compared to China's more than 1.3 billion. Making the argument that China serves as a developmental model often overlooks the fact that Africa consists of fifty-four highly diverse countries, the largest of which has a population of about 150 million. A number of African countries have fewer than a million people. Suggesting that China is a model for Africa strains credulity. On the other hand, some of China's more successful policies may be appropriate for some African countries.[136]

In recent years, the debate has centered on the "Washington Consensus" versus the "Beijing Consensus," a term coined by American Joshua Cooper Ramo. He based the term on China's "Four No's," discussed above. Ramo described the "Beijing Consensus" as similar to the Monroe Doctrine.[137] He sees it less as a development model and more as a broader security concept. Nevertheless, the "Beijing Consensus" has become a catchword for China's development model. Chinese scholar Wei-Wei Zhang suggested that it is inaccurate to describe the Chinese model as the Beijing Consensus. He argued that China's experience is unique because it adapted some foreign ideas to its own cultural and policy background.[138]

The development implications of the "Beijing Consensus" include a high national savings rate, a huge pool of cheap and compliant labor, state-targeted capital investments, a coherent continent-wide market with a single currency, internal market integration, a relatively well-educated and highly motivated workforce with a common language, investment from the Chinese diaspora, developed state institutions, and political unity within a single ruling party to implement large-scale economic reform policies. No African country has even half these attributes.

In addition, there are downsides to China's development: growing income inequality between urban and rural areas and among regions, devastating pollution problems, and willingness to sacrifice human rights and democratic governance for national development. In fact, there is no single development model in China. The industrial, export-dominated model in the urban areas along the Chinese coast is quite different from that in much of rural China. This entire debate is largely polemical, many Chinese and some Africans acknowledge.[139] Chinese scholar Pang Zhongying argued that because the "Beijing Consensus" is nothing more than a revised U.S. neoliberal model, its success or failure in Africa is also the success or failure of the "Washington Consensus."[140]

African leaders can benefit from studying China's approach to development and adapt piecemeal policies that benefit their own countries. African attempts to adopt Chinese economic policies without modifying them to fit local conditions will result in failures and disappointments similar to those that accompanied attempts to follow the "Washington Consensus."[141] David Shambaugh concluded "that while there are some individual elements of China's development experience that are unique, they do not constitute a comprehensive and coherent 'model'—nor are they easily transferred abroad."[142]

Two Chinese programs that have attracted considerable interest in Africa are poverty reduction and Special Economic Zones, which are now appearing in Africa.[143] In an extensive analysis of China as a development model, Edward Friedman concluded that many African governments will treat China as a model for their own economic success.[144] In 2010, China established the China-Africa Economic and Technology Cooperation Committee of the China Economic and Social Council to share its development experience with African countries. It promotes exchanges and cooperation between Chinese businesses and African countries.

China has positioned itself as a country that can help Africa on the basis of mutual benefit, nonconditionality, and demonstration by example.[145] But the relationship between China and Africa is asymmetric, especially in trade, where African countries export natural resources and primary products to China while China exports labor and capital intensive goods to Africa. Total Chinese trade by dollar value is almost three times that for all fifty-four African countries combined. No single African economy can compete on an equal basis with China or adopt its policies wholesale.[146] Foreign Minister Yang Jiechi, reflecting growing Chinese confidence, commented in 2011 that China had greater relative success in weathering the 2008 global financial crisis. As a result, China has become more inclined to tout its development model, not suggesting it is exportable, but that China is on the right path.[147]

3

Political Relations

Political ties are, of course, inextricably linked to the China-Africa government-to-government relationships described in Chapter 2. This chapter, however, traces the development of party-to-party relations, which in the early years of the PRC, were dominated by numerous united front, solidarity, and friendship organizations.

Party-to-party contacts were established during the 1950s and 1960s, but conducted through less formal subordinate CPC-led groups known as "mass organizations" (*qunzhong zuzhi*), "united front groups" (*tongzhan tuanti*), and "people's organizations" (*mingjian tuanti*). Before the establishment of the CPC's International Department (CPC-ID) in 1977, the international liaison offices of these organizations were charged with maintenance of CPC links to African political groups. Generally speaking, CPC-controlled mass organizations (e.g., the All-China Youth Federation) appointed the personnel of united front groups (e.g., the Union of Chinese Writers) who, in turn, administered people's organizations (e.g., the Liaison Committee with the Permanent Bureau of the Afro-Asian Writers Conference). Although the political outreach of China's party and state organs sometimes overlapped, CPC cadres were generally given greater latitude to build ties with African revolutionary groups than their diplomatic colleagues. Between 1955 and 1978 the CPC's objectives in Africa gradually shifted from anti-colonialism to anti-U.S. imperialism and finally to anti-Soviet revisionism. Although Sino-African political contacts were not as institutionalized as they are today, thanks largely to the CPC they were far more influential and enduring than commercial ties established at the time.

Since China's reform and opening up began in 1978, the CPC has implemented a well-coordinated international outreach campaign to build lasting ties to African political parties and organizations. In pursuit of improved official state-to-state relations and profitable economic opportunities, the CPC-ID and its affiliated organizations have used their deep pockets and diplomatic adroitness to engage African political parties.[1] Parliamentary delegations from the National People's Congress (NPC) have also been a part of these efforts, albeit to a lesser degree.

Over the last three decades CPC-ID and NPC delegations have established teams that work with African counterparts to lay the foundations for commercial and diplomatic cooperation, provide opportunities for interactions among Chinese and African political elites, and follow up to ensure policies are implemented in accordance with the CPC's strategic objectives. Despite the success of its political outreach, however, the CPC-ID remains among the "least well understood organs of China's foreign policy system."[2]

Four sensitive policy issues—Taiwan, Islam, Tibet, and human rights—play a role in China's political relations with foreign parties, not just those in Africa. Each is tied to sovereignty, a Chinese sore spot inflamed by national resentment over Western and Japanese domination in the nineteenth and early twentieth centuries. Indeed, CPC and NPC meetings with African counterparts regularly include the latter's affirmation of the PRC position on one, several, or all of these four sensitive policy topics. In cases where African states or political parties have contradicted the PRC position on these subjects they have endured a variety of consequences, from diplomatic threats to the removal of investment, public criticism, and Chinese support for their political opponents.

A History of Chinese Ties to African Political Organizations

The Birth of CPC Political Outreach in Africa, 1949–1965

Between 1949 and the lead-up to the First Afro-Asian Conference in Bandung, Indonesia, in April 1955, political outreach in Africa was not a CPC priority. Although the CPC was a strong and cohesive organization it was also domestically oriented; focused mainly on wiping out remaining pockets of KMT resistance, subduing the country's disparate regions, and combating U.S.-led UN forces on the China-North Korea border. In the early 1950s, the small number of independent African countries coupled with the emergence of revolution-minded African political groups led the CPC to establish a variety of political outreach organizations to engage them. But while CPC-led outreach organizations existed in the years following the Chinese civil war, distance, lack of worthy vessels or aircraft, and the country's desperate economic conditions prohibited their interaction with African counterparts. In Africa, the lack of coherent and well-organized anti-colonial resistance groups also reduced opportunities to expand ties with the CPC.

Sino-African political contacts during the second half of the 1950s surpassed economic, military, and official diplomatic relations, which were also negligible in 1949–1954.[3] On 5 October 1954, the CPC magazine *World Culture* published an article titled "Foreign Relations of New China During the Past Five Years," suggesting the CPC was preparing to adopt a more active global approach to anti-imperialism. The article argued that the independence struggles of Asian, African, and Latin American states "share a common interest in the wiping out of colonialism, and there are no basic conflicts of interest among them, for their common aggressors, oppressors and exploiters are the imperialists."[4] This global clarion call for "opposition to the imperialist policy of aggression and war"—first enshrined in the 1949 Common Program of the Chinese People's Political Consultative Congress—became the basis for the CPC's earliest political outreach to Africa.[5]

Some organizations involved in political outreach in Africa during this period were clearly identified as party organs while others were ostensibly public organizations controlled by CPC cadre.[6] The All-China Student Federation, for instance, was bound by its constitution "under the leadership of the CPC to support the struggle against imperialism and colonialism."[7] Party cadres coordinated China's political relations with African groups in this period, although for some groups CPC control was more transparent than others. As Larkin observed: "Prior to the Cultural Revolution, the International Liaison Department of the China Young Communist League was headed by the same persons who lead the International Liaison Office of the All-China Youth Federation; in effect, the departments were identical. Such ties maintained party primacy."

The CPC leadership—rather than diplomats or military officers—were the dominant force in Africa policymaking, according to Larkin: "Most decisive decisions are probably made by members of the Standing Committee of the Political Bureau of the Central Committee, that handful of men—

seven prior to the Cultural Revolution—at the apex of the CCP structure."[8] Before the founding of the Afro-Asian People's Solidarity Organization (AAPSO) in 1957, the CPC created numerous groups to gain access to friendly African political organizations and individuals. Through mass organizations, the CPC controlled the appointment of officers and traveling secretaries to international front groups that, in turn, administered the activities of public organizations in Africa.[9] The CPC used various overlapping front groups and solidarity organizations to issue invitations and host African political parties. For instance, in 1959 and 1960, respectively, Morocco's National Union of Popular Forces and Angola's Movimento de Libertação de Angola(MPLA) visited Beijing upon the invitation of the Chinese People's Institute of Foreign Affairs (identified in Table1).[10]

Beginning in 1955 the CPC initiated a pragmatic strategy that engaged African independence groups almost exclusively on political grounds. The cash-strapped CPC sought to proclaim itself the leader of a global movement of revolutionary communists fighting the European colonialists and U.S. imperialists. By stressing self-reliance, however, the party justified the limited amount of material support provided to African liberation groups. CPC support was, in most cases, largely rhetorical, leading to a notable discrepancy between verbal and actual support.[11]

By mid-1957, Libya, Egypt, Sudan, Tunisia, Morocco, and Ghana had gained independence and the CPC, sensing an opportunity to expand political relations, threw its full support behind anti-colonial independence movements across Africa. To provide assistance to African political organizations via the AAPSO, which was headquartered in Cairo, the CPC established the All-China Afro-Asian Solidarity Committee in Beijing in 1958. With the Committee's help in the late 1950s and early 1960s the AAPSO became the most important vehicle for Sino-African political cooperation, a channel through which the CPC transmitted its rhetorical and material support to African parties. In February 1958, a month after the Afro-Asian Solidarity Conference in Cairo, Zhou Enlai summed up the mood among African delegates in a speech before China's NPC:

> The conference maintains that all peoples are entitled to the sacred rights of freedom, self-determination, sovereignty and independence. These resolutions without a doubt voiced the common will of hundreds of millions of people in Asia and Africa. There is still a long struggle ahead in the national independence movements in

Table 1. CPC Controlled Political Outreach Organizations Active in Africa, 1955–1963

Mass organizations	United front groups	People's organizations with foreign policy mandates	Africa-focused friendship organizations and solidarity groups
All-China Federation of Trade Unions National Women's Federation All China Youth Federation All-China Student Federation	All-China Federation and Art Circles, including Union of Chinese Writers (1949) All-China Athletic Association (1949) Political Science and Law Association of China (1953) Chinese Islamic Association (1953) All-China Federation of Industry and Commerce (1953) All-China Journalists Association (1957) National Red Cross Society of China (1950) All-China Scientific and Technical Association (1958)	China Peace Committee Chinese People's Institute of Foreign Affairs Chinese People's Association for Cultural Relations with Foreign Countries (1958) All China Journalists Association China Council for the Promotion of International Trade China Federation of Industry and Commerce	China-Africa People's Friendship Organization (1960) Chinese Committee for Afro-Asian Solidarity (1958) Asia-Africa Society of China (1962) Chinese Islamic Association (1953) (had African and non-African mandate) China-U.A.R. Friendship Association Chinese People's Committee for Aiding Egypt Against Aggression Liaison Committee with the Permanent Bureau of the Afro-Asian Writers Conference

Note: United front groups include year of founding.
Sources: Bruce Larkin, *China and Africa 1949–1970: The Foreign Policy of the People's Republic of China* (Berkeley: University of California Press, 1971), 219–21; Alaba Ogunsanwo, *China's Policy in Africa 1958–1971* (London: Cambridge University Press, 1974), 97.

Asia and Africa and there will inevitably be more twists and turns in their future development, but the Asian and African peoples have already stood up and will never again be crushed.[12]

The CPC helped to plan the First Afro-Asian Writers Conference in Tashkent, Uzbekistan, in October 1958, which included African delegations from Algeria, Cameroon, Ghana, Sudan, and the United Arab Republic (Egypt). The CPC delegation in Tashkent used the conference as both a staging point for the All-African People's Conference held soon afterward in Accra and to coordinate the subsequent visits to China by Angolan, Ghanaian, Nigerian, Senegalese, Somali, and Ugandan delegations. During the first week of December 1958 in Accra the CPC delegation held meetings with a variety of leftist African leaders including Patrice Lumumba of the Mouvement National Congolais, Félix-Roland Moumié of the Union des Populations du Cameroun, and Holden Roberto then of the Angolan People's Union.[13]

China's Ministry of Foreign Affairs (MOFA) established an African section in 1960 to handle official relations with the seventeen African nations that gained independence that year and the half dozen more that did so the following year.[14] But, while PRC diplomats competed with their rivals from the Republic of China (ROC or Taiwan) to build and maintain official ties with the growing number of independent states, various CPC-controlled groups worked to cultivate political relations in those states still under colonial rule. Thus, as English and French colonial rule largely came to an end in the early 1960s, the CPC shifted its support toward revolutionary groups in countries still under Portuguese control (Angola, Cape Verde, Guinea-Bissau, Mozambique, São Tomé) or under repressive white minority groups (Rhodesia, Namibia, South Africa). Through its outreach groups the CPC provided limited aid for revolutionary groups in these countries while training their guerrillas and cadres in independent neighboring countries and sometimes China.

In 1960, the CPC Central Committee created a Special Committee in Charge of African Affairs and the China African People's Friendship Association (CAPFA); an umbrella group to administer the numerous Africa-focused people's organizations.[15] Although they appeared separate, there was substantial overlap in personnel among these organizations. Eight of CAPFA's original founding members, for instance, were associated with the CPC's youth arm, the China Young Communist League.[16] It was through this web of interwoven political groups and overlapping membership that CPC largesse, however limited, was transmitted to African counterparts.

Between January 1958 and August 1964 the CPC's political outreach in Africa achieved some impressive results. Beijing sent 144 missions (including individuals) to various African countries and received 405 African missions. These contacts grew over time, culminating in 1963, just before Premier Zhou Enlai's historic Africa tour, when fifty-five CPC missions visited Africa and 131 African missions reportedly touched down in Beijing. By 1964, CPC political outreach paid diplomatic dividends with fifteen of thirty-five independent African countries choosing to recognize the CPC, rather than the KMT, as China's legal ruling party, up from only seven in 1960.[17] The CPC also targeted African liberation groups in states that had yet to gain independence. One of these delegations met with Mao Zedong in late 1963. A CPC member, Sidney Rittenberg (aka Li Dunbai), attended this meeting and later recounted the proceedings:

> The African guests were assembled in the hall, standing just inside the open door. There were about twenty people, none from an independent African state. They were all from various nationalist organizations or guerrilla movements. More than half were in traditional African dress, long loose gowns with gorgeous purple and gold and green fabric billowing around them. Some wore headdresses to match. I knew a few of them were receiving military training in China. I recognized a cherubic young student who had once told me he was learning from the People's Liberation Army how to use small arms, hand grenades, land mines, and booby traps.[18]

During the meeting, which came just before Zhou Enlai's visit to Africa, Mao Zedong welcomed the "friends and comrades in arms from Africa," and said: "I know you are having a very difficult struggle in Africa, and you've already made big successes. Many battles remain to be fought, but Africa is coming alive." Rittenberg also recounts an exchange between Mao and one African revolutionary from Southern Rhodesia:

> African visitor: The Soviets used to help us, and then the red star went out and they don't help us anymore. On the contrary they sell arms to our oppressors. What I worry about is: Will the red star over Tiananmen Square in China go out? Will you abandon us and sell arms to our oppressors as well? If that happens we will be alone.
>   Mao Zedong: I understand your question. It is that the USSR has turned revisionist and has betrayed the revolution. Can I guarantee to you that China won't betray the revolution? Right now I can't give you that guarantee. We are searching very hard to find the way to keep China from becoming corrupt, bureaucratic, and revisionist. We are afraid that we will stop being a revolutionary country and will become a revisionist one. When that happens in a socialist country, they become worse than a capitalist country. A

communist party can turn into a fascist party. We've seen that happen in the Soviet Union. We understand the seriousness of this problem, but we don't know how to handle it yet.[19]

Zhou's Africa tour from December 1963 to February 1964 can be seen as both the climax of the honeymoon period of Sino-African political relations and a turning point toward an unabashedly anti-Soviet approach. Zhou had long nurtured the idea that Africa was engulfed in a wave of Chinese-style revolutionary zeal and he distrusted the Soviets. At the November 1960 Moscow summit of communist parties, for instance, China's state-run press reported that African parties were "studying Mao's works and using Chinese guerrilla methods."[20] In October 1961, Zhou took the podium at the Twenty-Second Communist Party Congress in Moscow and publicly chided the Communist Party of the Soviet Union (CPSU) leadership for its open attack on the Communist Party of Albania: "To openly display in the enemy's presence disputes between brother countries cannot be regarded as a serious Marxist-Leninist approach, and can only distress friends and delight our enemies."[21]

In 1962, what had been an ideological argument among political leaders and parties was expanded to nation-states when the Soviet Union supported India during the Sino-Indian border war. The dispute intensified throughout 1962–1963 with both sides offering tit-for-tat accusations and condemnations of each other. On 14 June 1963, just months before Zhou left for Africa, the CPC issued its Proposal Concerning the General Line of the International Communist Movement in which it openly criticized the CPSU for "denying the great international significance of the anti-imperialist revolutionary struggles of the Asian, African and Latin American peoples, catering to the needs of imperialism and the promotion of its policies of old and new colonialism."[22] By contrast, the CPC called for all communists to "study the revolutionary experience of the peoples of Asia, Africa and Latin America, firmly support their revolutionary actions and regard the cause of their liberation as a most dependable support for itself."[23]

The expansion of the Sino-Soviet dispute infused Zhou's Africa trip with a mandate that was both fervently anti-Soviet and anti-colonial. Zhou depicted the CPC as the true guardian of communist orthodoxy and the CPSU as the revisionist patsies of imperialism. In this way CPC ties to African political groups first based on anti-colonial, pro-revolutionary and anti-U.S. ideology were gradually altered to counter the threat of Soviet hegemony.

The Maoists' "People's Diplomacy" (1966–1971)

As the 1960s progressed the lingering influence of the colonial powers, domestic turmoil in China, and the extension of Cold War tensions in Africa preoccupied the CPC and limited its engagement almost entirely to militant revolutionary ideology and targeted arms shipments.

During the most tumultuous years of the Cultural Revolution (1966–1971) the CPC, weakened by purges of senior members, came to be dominated by younger, more ideological, left-leaning Maoists. In their effort to guide African political opposition groups toward conceptions of action closely akin to their own, these revolution-minded CPC cadres channeled support toward those African revolutionary forces fighting guerrilla wars—a hallmark of Maoism.[24] Maoists began replacing members of China's diplomatic service in its African embassies with younger, radical, and less experienced cadres more interested in advocating and reporting the proper ideological perspective than with objectivity or accuracy. Some were even accused of subversion and expelled from African countries.[25] In 1968, the Maoist radicals, seeking to implement "people's diplomacy" and "re-educate" China's senior diplomats, recalled all ambassadors from Africa, except its ambassador in Egypt, back to Beijing.[26]

Under Maoist leadership the CPC-led people's organizations including the Bureau of Afro-Asian Writers, the Afro-Asian Journalists Association, and the Afro-Asian Solidarity Organization remained prominent in Sino-African political relations. In 1966, for example, Beijing released the first and only postage stamps commemorating the contribution of an Africa-focused people's organization: the Afro-Asian Writers Conference. One stamp, titled "Wind and Thunder," underscored the group's importance, depicting it as the vanguard of the global revolutionary struggle.[27]

During this period CPC propaganda stressed the role of "Mao Zedong Thought" and the scope of armed struggles; portraying the CPC as shepherd of a flock of African parties moving toward a new democratic revolution.[28] According to *People's Daily*, "More and more of the oppressed African nations are recognizing that Mao Zedong Thought is their strongest weapon for gaining true independence, and armed struggle is their road to gaining liberation in Congo, Mozambique, Angola and 'Portuguese' Guinea."[29] By asserting that anti-colonial conflicts in Africa and elsewhere were proletarian revolutions, the CPC exaggerated its influence among African revolutionary groups. Calls for armed struggle did not cost much, so if an indigenous group chose rebellion, the CPC might support it with subversive rhetoric and modest arms shipments.[30] Yet while many African leaders were steeped in Maoist revolutionary thought and liberation politics, the tumult of the Cultural Revolution limited their direct contacts with the CPC.[31] Generally speaking, the Maoists' "people's diplomacy" turned the CPC's political relations in Africa from zealous public support, but limited arms supplies, for mainstream revolutionary groups during the late 1950s and early 1960s, to targeted support for smaller, more revolutionary splinter groups.[32]

Return to Pragmatism (1972–1977)

Although throughout the late 1960s Zhou was challenged by anti-American hardliners like Defense Minister Lin Biao, he continued to believe the Soviet threat to China was greater than the one presented by the United States. In practice this meant that although China's propaganda continued to condemn U.S. imperialism throughout the late 1960s and early 1970s the CPC's ideology of a continuous proletarian revolution was gradually reoriented to counter Soviet hegemony. This change paralleled the gradual reinstatement of party leaders intent on restoring pragmatism to the CPC's political relations in Africa, a domestic development that was catalyzed by widespread cynicism as the Cultural Revolution's most turbulent days subsided. The largely disillusioned CPC leadership—weary of ideological fervor and fearful of the Soviet forces on their northern border—turned away from ideology in favor of self-preservation.

The CPC began to support only those revolutionary movements that fought against revisionist or social-imperialist forces—terms synonymous with groups supported by the CPSU. During the 1970s the CPC's willingness to place geopolitical objectives before ideological consistency grew apace with the growing Soviet threat and the expansion of Sino-U.S. rapprochement. The result was a strategy designed to preoccupy Soviet resources in far off conflicts, particularly in Africa.[33] In Angola, for instance, China's cooperation with the United States and the South African white supremacist regime to aid the opposition União Nacional para a Indepen-dência Total de Angola (UNITA) and Frente de Libertação de Angola (FNLA) rebels against the Soviet and Cuban backed MPLA succeeded in attracting Soviet resources away from the China-Russia border. Yet, it did so at the expense of alienating those Africans who could not understand how China could condemn the American imperialists and the apartheid regime in Pretoria while cooperating with them against socialists in Angola. In this way the CPC's rapid return to pragmatism risked overcompensating and undermining China's image among Africans.

The CPC move from ideology to pragmatism reflected the organiza-tion's gradual transformation from a revolutionary to a ruling party. The resulting changes in institutions and priorities also altered CPC outreach to African political parties. The CPC became willing "to grant ideological autonomy, and when African countries seemed to embark on a policy closely akin to Chinese thinking, Peking refrained from claiming that the Africans were following a Maoist path."[34] The gradual removal of ideology from China's foreign policy cleared the way for the CPC to build ties to African ruling parties across the entire political spectrum. In 1977, the CPC formally began to work toward this goal and undertook a full reconstruc-tion of its Africa-related political outreach activities.[35]

China's Reform-Era Political Outreach in Africa (1978–1999)

Since the Third Plenary Session of the Eleventh CPC Central Committee in 1978, the CPC-ID has emerged as the department primarily "responsible for the party's international exchanges and communications with foreign political parties and organizations."[36] Deng Xiaoping, the CPC party boss, supported a new CPC-ID strategy to cultivate contacts with various parties on the basis of "four principles of party-to-party relations: independence, complete equality, mutual respect, and non-interference in each other's internal affairs."[37] The CPC-ID was also given four responsibilities: imple-menting CPC Central Committee principles and policies, researching for-eign developments and key global issues, providing briefings and policy proposals to the Central Committee, and carrying out CPC exchanges with foreign political parties and organizations.[38]

From these four principles and four responsibilities, the CPC-ID derived seven guidelines to govern its interaction with foreign political parties. These were laid out in 2001 in a speech by the CPC-ID Vice Minister Cai Wu:

- Establish a new type of relations between parties—new, sound and friendly relations.
- Every party should decide its own country's affairs independently.
- No party should judge the achievements and mistakes of foreign parties on the basis of its own experience.
- All parties should be completely equal; they should respect each other and not interfere in each other's internal affairs.
- Ideological differences should not be obstacles to establishing a new type of party-to-party relations. When developing exchanges and cooperation with foreign parties, parties in the various countries should proceed from the spirit of seeking common ground while reserving differences.
- The purpose of exchanges and cooperation with foreign parties should be to promote the development of state-to-state relations.
- In their relations with foreign parties, all parties should look to the future and forget old scores.[39]

This "complete concept for establishing a new type of party-to-party relations" served to operationalize CPC strategy and stands as a useful guide to understanding CPC political outreach in the modern era. Over time it has gradually been developed to engage African ruling parties and cultivate long-standing and stable relationships that underpin and augment official ties, regardless of ideological differences in accordance with the fifth guideline listed above.

Between 1978 and 1990, the CPC-ID successfully established ties with dozens of African political parties. The vast majority, more than thirty parties, were governing parties (*guozhengdang*), while only two were opposition parties (*fanduidang*). The CPC-ID conducted more than three hundred exchanges with these political parties, underwrote travel costs for dozens of African delegations, and helped facilitate their meetings with CPC cadres, executives from Chinese state-run companies, and government officials.[40] This period was a new beginning in the PRC's political outreach, when Sino-African commercial ties were still at low levels.

Between 1991 and 1996, the growing number of African political parties (approximately 1,800 by 1997), political power-sharing in some countries, and turnover in older African parties undermined CPC efforts.[41] In 1992, Deng Xiaoping visited and praised the bustling Special Economic Zones in southern China, thereby quashing a conservative backlash and giving market reforms the blessing of the CPC leadership. Economic development was now unquestionably the priority and Chinese people were told to get rich, leading many to turn to trade with the extensive Chinese communities in East Asia and the West. As a result, attention was drawn away from Africa, and prestige, funding, and personnel at African programs at China's state-run research institutions played subordinate roles to their counterparts in American, European, and Asian studies.[42]

Led by CPC Chairman Jiang Zemin, the so-called third generation of the CPC leadership gave international political outreach a strategic and methodological makeover in the mid- to late 1990s. The CPC's increasingly technocratic elite continued Deng's efforts to address economic challenges. Reforms were designed to foster economic growth and integrate the country into the global economy, and this objective required the CPC to build political relationships to support these goals. These new international efforts coupled with Moscow's receding influence gave the CPC an opportunity to extend cooperation with African political parties. Meanwhile, the durability of ruling parties in key African states, such as Egypt, Ethiopia, South Africa, Sudan, Zambia, and Zimbabwe, provided a group of long-term CPC political partners.

Beginning in the 1990s China's growing demand for African raw materials and consumer markets gave new purpose to party-to-party outreach. Growing economic ties pushed Sino-African political ties toward a new era of cooperation: the FOCAC framework established in 2000.[43] In his keynote address at the first FOCAC ministerial conference in Beijing on 10 October 2000, President Jiang said the event was "the first of its kind in the history of Sino-African relationship" and ushered in a new era of relations that "should form the political basis for the new international order."[44]

Methods of PRC Political Outreach
with African Political Parties, 2000–2011

In the 1990s, China's grants, loans, and low-cost infrastructure projects came largely in response to its growing need for African trade, Taiwan's dollar diplomacy victories, and China's need for African countries' support on human rights at the UN. Over the last decade, however, their expansion and refinement suggests a long-term strategy to court African political elites, which has yielded impressive results. Between 1997 and 2006, there were more than two hundred exchanges with political parties in forty Sub-Saharan African countries. As of 2006, the CPC had established ties to at least sixty Sub-Saharan African political parties and continues to expand ties with African ruling parties, parties included in ruling coalitions, and, occasionally, opposition parties.[45]

Although the details of the CPC's relationship with each African political party are unique, there are some consistencies in its approach. Our examination suggests the CPC uses five primary tactics: party exchanges, material support, cadre training, opposition party outreach, and interparliamentary exchanges.

Party Exchanges

The CPC seeks to improve its image and influence public sentiment through its exchanges with African political parties. The CPC's expanding political outreach occurs in terms of frequency of visits and the level of the visitor. Between 1997 and 2006, for instance, the CPC-ID feted over sixty African party chiefs. During these meetings, African party leaders and their Chinese counterparts looked to translate party ties into long-term bilateral cooperation on issues of mutual interest and concern. The meetings themselves provided a forum for exchange of views, coordination of policies, provision of economic assistance, and voicing of grievances. Leaders of China's state-controlled firms depend on the CPC-ID and related liaison organizations such as the Chinese Association for International Understanding (CAFIU) to arrange meetings and social activities with African delegations. On the other side, African party leaders rely on their CPC-ID hosts to ensure access to relevant Chinese political and business leaders.[46]

Visits from African political party delegations give the CPC-ID an opportunity to practice its intoxicating mix of contemporary and traditional hospitality. CPC-ID hosting techniques are derived from centuries of Chinese tradition and can be traced back to the teachings of Confucius.[47] According to Richard H. Solomon, "The most distinctive characteristic of Chinese negotiating behavior is an effort to develop and manipulate strong interpersonal relationships with foreign officials [and] feelings of good will, obligation, guilt or dependence to achieve their negotiating objectives." Hosting, according to Solomon, allows the Chinese "to carry out negotiations on their own turf and by their own rules while maximizing [the visitor's] sense of gratitude, awe and helplessness."[48]

The CPC's rhetoric of equality, mutual respect, and noninterference, coupled with first-class hospitality, has won over African elites from across the political spectrum. The PRC has simplified procedures and supported delegations led by African political leaders. One former African ambassador who served in China recounted his own experience:

> When I was arriving at my post, I was scheduled for a brief meeting and photo with President and CPC Chairman Jiang Zemin. Instead, we spoke for nearly an hour. President Jiang not only had a broad continental view of Africa, but I was also very impressed with his detailed knowledge of African issues and how close they were to his heart.[49]

CPC delegations provide "facts" (*shishi*), "statistics" (*xuju*), and "materials" (*cailiao*) designed to "help African parties better understand CPC policies and China's national condition."[50] One such publication, *China and Africa*, released in September 2006 for distribution by PRC embassies, contains a variety of Chinese government statistics, as well as a chapter, "Cooperation and Support between China and Africa in the Political Arena." *China and Africa* promotes the "frequent association between the Chinese National People's Congress and its counterparts in African countries, as well as contacts between political parties."[51]

CPC-ID personnel attached to China's embassies in Africa also transmit information back to China about African host countries. These efforts range from normal embassy functions and general reporting about domestic politics to covert information collection. Even determining if a particular African embassy has a CPC-ID envoy can be a difficult task. Chinese diplomatic personnel "do not openly identify themselves as such, usually identifying themselves simply as Foreign Ministry personnel."[52] For instance, one CPC-ID official posted to an African embassy carried three business cards: one from his CPC-ID bureau, another as PRC embassy staff, and yet another as a research fellow at CAFIU.[53] Another CPC-ID attaché posted to a different African embassy identified himself as an embassy official until further enquiries clarified his CPC-ID affiliation. Informational obstacles make it uniquely difficult to identify confidently those African countries that have CPC-ID personnel and those that do not.[54] Generally speaking, however, the CPC-ID tends to be more active in developing states dominated by one party; yet, it also works to keep options open for relations with opposition parties in case they achieve political power.

Anecdotal information suggests that there is also a more nefarious side to the CPC-ID's exchanges with African parties. David Shambaugh notes that it is assumed, although hard evidence is lacking, "that ID attachés work closely with Ministry of State Security (undercover) personnel abroad for the purpose of intelligence collection and agent recruitment."[55] Hostesses can be employed to entertain foreign visitors and solidify relationships and agreements with African elites. In the long term, however, evidence of such liaisons can be leveraged. The latter scenario, often called a "honey trap," is a common method utilized by clandestine Chinese operatives. According to Philip Idro, Uganda's ambassador to China from 1999 to 2005, these methods are common, although, he said, differing attitudes toward sexuality and monogamy within Chinese and some African cultures may undermine this strategy's effectiveness.[56]

Material Support

Under Chairman Hu Jintao and the CPC's fourth generation leadership, China's surging need for energy and minerals to power its economy increased the value of political capital with resource-rich African states and, in turn, the importance the CPC attaches to its political outreach efforts on the continent. The CPC's willingness to provide material support for African counterparts has also helped to improve party-to-party ties. Chinese largesse, including trade incentives, investment, debt forgiveness, and direct aid, is most often transmitted through state-channels, but in some cases the CPC has provided funds and materials directly to African parties or supported pet projects at the ruling party's behest. Although in the 1980s and 1990s Xinhua's reports discussed CPC material support for some African parties more openly, today it is nearly impossible to track CPC largesse to African political parties. In some cases, such as Zambia and Zimbabwe, there is enough evidence to strongly suggest that the ruling party receives CPC material support.

During the 1980s the CPC worked to build close relations with Zambia's United National Independence Party (UNIP), then the ruling party. CPC material support to UNIP appears to have begun in 1979 when it sponsored a three-week tour for a six-man UNIP delegation led by Kaspasa Makasa, a member of UNIP's Central Committee and Clement Mwananshiku, Minister of Lands and Natural Resources.[57] Relations developed slowly at first and material support was largely symbolic. In 1984, for instance, the CPC-ID donated over 140 books on Chinese politics and economic development to UNIP.[58] Between 1984 and 1988, at least one CPC delegation a year visited Lusaka and they signed a bilateral protocol on party-to-party cooperation in 1987. That agreement called for both sides to "exchange delegations, publications and other materials."[59] In practice, however, the CPC was more generous. In 1986, the Chinese party gave UNIP a generous "contribution towards the construction of the new party headquarters [and] pledged an undisclosed sum of money to use for the purchase of furniture, equipment and sport material."[60] Then again in 1990 the CPC gave the Zambian party a second larger gift "towards the ongoing construction of its UNIP HQ in Lusaka."[61]

In 1990 the Movement for Multiparty Democracy (MMD), which began as a coalition party aimed at ousting UNIP, assembled an impressive group of prominent Zambians, including several top UNIP defectors. In 1991, thanks largely to UNIP's boycott of national elections, the MMD won a landslide victory and soon after began exchanges with the CPC. In 1992, a CPC-ID delegation led by Zhu Liang visited Lusaka and was welcomed by senior MMD cadre Vernon Mwaanga who said his organization "cherishes the traditional bonds of friendship with China despite the changes of government in Zambia."[62] Levy Mwanawasa, MMD vice-president, echoed those sentiments to another senior CPC-ID delegation in 1994.[63] Unlike Xinhua's reporting about CPC material support for UNIP, however, the CPC and MMD do not release such information to the press. Instead, the fruits of CPC-MMD cooperation in Zambia are nearly always expressed publically in terms of benefits to the country and the people—not the MMD, making direct references to CPC aid hard to come by.

The MMD cadre's public statements suggest substantial CPC financial support. In the 2000s, the parties continued to exchange delegations regularly and in the run-up to Zambia's 2006 presidential elections the CPC publically supported the MMD. In 2005, a CPC delegation lead by Tan Jialin, assistant head of the CPC-ID, met with MMD leaders at their party's headquarters in Lusaka. At the meeting, Mwaanga, who was then MMD national secretary, said his party "regards the CPC as a very dependable ally of Zambia" and he hoped "that more cooperative opportunities would swarm into the country from China." Meanwhile, MMD National Chairman Boniface Kawimbe told his Chinese guests that they "should take full advantage of the new economic environment of Zambia for increased cooperation."[64] Similar language was used again the following September when another high level CPC delegation visited Lusaka.[65] As it had done prior to previous elections, the Chinese side also gave the MMD FM transmitters to help get out the vote in the rural areas.[66]

In 2006, Michael Sata, head of the Patriotic Front (PF) and the leading opposition candidate, launched a series of scathing anti-Chinese attacks in an effort to build anti-MMD sentiment before the elections. Provoked, China's Ambassador Li Baodong gave the ruling MMD strong diplomatic support and threatened that Beijing would "have nothing to do with Zambia if Sata wins the elections."[67] Sata responded by accusing Li of acting as a "MMD cadre" and "openly campaigning for the MMD."[68] To which Ambassador Li replied: "Chinese investors in mining, construction and tourism have put on hold further investment until uncertainty surrounding our bilateral relations with Zambia is cleared." Fearing Sata would upset bilateral relations, Mwanawasa, then the sitting president and MMD candidate opposing Sata, was contrite: "We value the friendship of the Chinese people and will continue to cherish their assistance." Meanwhile, to soften China's image and bolster Mwanawasa and his fellow MMD candidates before the election, the CPC promised several aid projects, including a water system for Lusaka's impoverished townships and a $14.5 million bridge across the Luapula River linking Zambia to the Democratic Republic of Congo.[69]

After the MMD success in the 2006 election, increased competition from Chinese imports, traders, and farmers left many Zambians deeply distrustful.[70] Despite grassroots criticism, however, the CPC-MMD relationship has flourished. In July 2008, for instance, a visiting CPC delegation was greeted by Kabinga Pande, MMD national vice chairman, who "expressed gratitude to the CPC for its assistance and support since the two parties established communication in the 1990s."[71]

In 2009, China signed an agreement to build government buildings in Zambia.[72] This was followed the same year by a CPC-ID delegation that visited Lusaka and met with President and MMD Chairman Rupiah Banda who told delegates that "the MMD had greatly benefited from the CPC which was now the world's strongest political party."[73] In 2010, Banda visited China for nine days and held extensive meetings with CPC interlocutors. When Wynter Kabimba, secretary general of the opposition PF party, denounced the president's trip as a wasteful "tourist stint,"[74] the president's spokesman fired back that the criticism was "part of the PF's orchestrated anti-China campaign to undermine the positive accomplishments being made."[75]

Although the details of CPC material support for the MMD remain unknown, its numerous exchanges with the CPC, threats to remove investment if PF had won the 2006 elections, MMD cadre's public statements, and CPC support for timely public infrastructure projects and government facilities that bolstered MMD candidates, are all strong indicators of the close relationship between the two parties. The CPC's direct material support for UNIP during its time as Zambia's ruling party in the 1980s and 1990s also hints at the type of largesse that the MMD and PF are likely to have received. See Chapter 11 (Zambia) for the 2011 PF victory.

In Zimbabwe, the parties' relationship with the CPC followed a somewhat different pattern. In Zambia, the MMD's takeover from UNIP and PF's victory over MMD witnessed a speedy transfer of CPC support from one ruling party to the next. In Zimbabwe, by contrast, one ruling party has dominated politics from independence until 2011: the Zimbabwe African National Union-Patriotic Front (ZANU-PF). The first contacts between ZANU-PF and the CPC occurred between 1962 and 1964.[76] In the year following the country's founding in 1980, Party Secretary and President Robert Mugabe visited China twice to receive CPC material support.[77] "After independence in 1980, Zimbabwe got a lot of valuable assistance from China in defending national independence and reconstruction," Mugabe told Huang Ju, a member of the CPC political bureau, years later in Harare. At that 1998 meeting Mugabe also said "friendship between the CPC and ZANU-PF will be further developed and cooperation areas continuously expanded."[78] CPC support for ZANU-PF has continued, although like the MMD, ZANU-PF does not publicly disclose the details of the material support it receives from the CPC and instead reports CPC contributions in the context of the official bilateral relationship. In March 2011, for instance, Chinese firms began construction of a large electronic surveillance complex just outside Harare for Zimbabwe's ZANU-PF dominated security services, which, among other things, will be used to monitor Internet use and telephone calls of opposition party leaders.[79]

Like the projects used to bolster the MMD before Zambia's 2006 elections, some projects have been targeted to meet ZANU-PF's political needs or reward loyal constituencies. In 2010, for instance, China's government agreed to contribute $1 million to build a school in Bindra, Central Mashonaland, a ZANU-PF stronghold that has seen ample political violence against supporters of the opposition party, the Movement for Democratic Change (MDC).[80] China built another school in Highfield, a Harare suburb dominated by ZANU-PF where Mugabe once lived and taught.[81] In fact, in 2006 after Mugabe seized 6,000 hectares of farmland for personal use, he renamed it Highfield Estate to commemorate his old home.[82] Construction on the 25-room mansion on the property was completed in 2009 with Chinese and Malaysian funds.[83] "It has Chinese roofing material which makes it very beautiful, but it was donated to us—the Chinese are our good friends, you see," President Mugabe said in an interview.[84]

Unlike in Zambia, where the opposition PF had directly criticized the CPC, the MDC has shied away from attacking the Chinese party. In 2008, even as 77 tons of Chinese-made weapons valued at $1.25 million were on their way to ZANU-PF militiamen, MDC leaders still held their tongues.[85] As of 2011, the CPC has yet to directly criticize the MDC, but despite a power sharing deal between MDC and ZANU-PF, it has not begun direct exchanges with the opposition party as it did under national unity governments in Sudan and South Africa. For ZANU-PF, however, CPC material support continues, as Mugabe told reporters at his eighty-sixth birthday in February 2010: "assistance from China continues to come. We will always remember not only what China has done in the past but what continues to be done."[86] In May 2011 Mugabe reiterated his gratitude to Chief Air Marshal Xu Qiliang, a member of China's Senior Military Commission. "China is a great friend of us in many ways. They have assisted us in our struggle to free ourselves from colonialism," he said.[87] These sentiments were echoed by Zimbabwe's former ambassador to China, Chris Mutsvangwa, who in July 2011 said the ZANU-PF–CPC relationship remains "the savior of Zimbabwe."[88]

Cadre Training

China has sponsored the training of thousands of African personnel in areas of diplomacy, economic management, national defense, agriculture, science, technology, and medical treatment.[89] Among these programs are CPC initiatives to educate African party officials through political cadre training sessions on diverse topics from internal party governance to CPC Chairman Jiang Zemin's theory of the "Three Represents." In 1998–2006, the CPC brought party officials from more than ten African governing parties to China for political training. Senior CPC cadres and specialists in areas such as party development and structure teach two-week training programs and encourage African political parties to coordinate international policies with the CPC. Some parties have also received CPC support to establish their own party schools. According to Li Chengwen, China's ambassador to the Sudan, CPC cadre training courses can contain about twenty participants from one African country or several.[90]

According to one CPC-ID official attached to an embassy in Africa, CPC-ID cadre training programs are based on "equality" and "mutual respect."[91] The increasingly influential CPC uses rhetoric to invoke the relative equality of the past and to avoid directly confronting growing power asymmetries in the bilateral relationship. This rhetoric is used in contrast to what CPC and African party officials perceived as the more heavy-handed and unequal Soviet political training of the past. For this reason, according to the official, "CPC-ID cadre training programs are conducted only at the request of African political parties, which are asked to submit specific requests about their party's particular needs. African political parties' demands for CPC-ID cadre training programs have enhanced the understanding, friendship, and cooperation between these parties and CPC."[92]

The CPC naturally seeks to partner with like-minded African parties and uses cadre training and party management courses to develop interpersonal ties and influence future generations of African political leaders. CPC cadre training, however, varies dramatically among African political parties. Where long-standing CPC relationships exist, as with Tanzania's ruling Party of the Revolution (Chama Cha Mapinduzi or CCM), Namibia's South West Africa People's Organization (SWAPO), and Zimbabwe's ZANU-PF, CPC instructors quickly established bilateral political education exchanges. In Zambia, for instance, a 1987 protocol on cooperation between UNIP and the CPC enshrined cadre training whereby "the two sides will send teaching staff and researchers to lecture at each other's party institutions or engage in study tours on chosen topics concerning party and national construction."[93] When working with those African political parties with little prior relationship with the CPC, however, the Chinese side may send instructors or bring a representative or delegation to train at one of its CPC training academies in China. There are exceptions. In Angola, despite a relationship with the CPC dating back to the 1960s, the strong party structure and decades of Soviet training of the MPLA make CPC cadre training unnecessary.[94]

The CPC's domestic cadre training system now consists of the Central Party School (CPS), the Chinese Academy of Governance (known as the National School of Administration until 2009) in Beijing, and three executive leadership academies and the senior managers training school in Dalian.[95] The Central Party School, which "remains the most important institution in the whole mid-career training system," hosts high level African party leaders interested in cadre training programs.[96] In 2009, for instance, the CPC Central Party School hosted Cyril Ramaphosa, member of the national executive committee of South Africa's ruling ANC, during a two-week, eighteen-member "study tour" under the theme "From Revolution to Governance: Theories and Practice."[97] According to an ANC report published after the delegation's return, while in China the ANC delegation met with CPC-ID minister Wang Jiarui and focused on topics including "the theoretical basis for 'socialism with Chinese characteristics,' the party-building experience, experiences in political education, party discipline and combating corruption."[98] Also in 2009, after attending meetings at the Central Party School, Pius Msekwa, Vice Chairman of Tanzania's CCM, said his party "would like to learn successful experience from the Chinese Communist Party in the areas of cadre training, discipline and anti-corruption, [and] further push forward exchanges between the two parties."[99]

The responsibilities of the Chinese Academy of Governance include "promoting exchanges and cooperation with relevant international organizations," but like the CPS, it does not appear to train Africans on site.[100] Instead, African party delegations that visit these two institutions are relatively high level and generally interested in expanding future exchanges and CPC cadre training for their subordinates. For example, in 2009 Liberia's minister of the interior, Ambullai Johnson, was briefed on the CPC training programs held at the Academy.[101]

The CPC's three executive leadership academies—China Executive Leadership Academy Pudong (CELAP), Jinggangshan Executive Leadership Academy, and Ya'nan Executive Leadership Academy—were established in 2005 to improve the party's governing capacity.[102] The brainchild of Politburo Member and Central Party School President Zeng Qinghong, they aim to "educate CPC officials through experience-based courses and motivate them.''[103] Each plays its role. CELAP emphasizes innovation in system reform, human resource management, and leadership methods, while Jingganshan and Ya'nan focus on CPC revolutionary history, China's "national situation," and the interior provinces.[104] Although each academy maintains an office for international exchanges, CELAP hosts the most Africans, followed by Jingganshan academy, leaving Ya'nan academy to focus almost exclusively on training domestic CPC cadres.

CELAP in Shanghai conducts multilateral training programs for African participants and has established bilateral programs with several African ruling parties. In late 2006 and again in mid-2007 CELAP's Department of International Exchanges and Program Development held multilateral training programs for forty-two Africans from twenty-six countries and twenty Africans from fifteen countries.[105] "Through the training program," CELAP's website reports, "the participants obtained better understanding of China, China's vision of constructing harmonious society and promoting world peace."[106] China's Ministry of Commerce sponsored the second training program, which included participants from Angola, Burundi, Central African Republic, Congo, Equatorial Guinea, Gabon, Guinea, Madagascar, Mali, Mauritania, and Senegal.[107]

CELAP has also developed bilateral exchanges and training programs with African parties and training academies. As of May 2008, it had contacts with the University of the Western Cape in South Africa, Egypt's Sadat Academy for Management Sciences, Suez Canal University, and its Senegalese counterpart, the Ecole Nationale d'Administration.[108] In the first four years following its founding, CELAP's relationship with Senegal expanded faster than with any other African country. The two sides exchanged five delegations beginning at the aforementioned 2006 multilateral African training session and culminating with a visit from the West African country's foreign minister to CELAP in 2007.[109] Uganda's National Resistance Organization (NRO) has used CELAP to learn cadre training from the CPC, and under CPC instruction a number of African ruling parties are building their own training academies.[110]

In 2006, after returning from a CPC-hosted delegation study tour in China, Aggrey Mwanri, the CCM's national secretary for ideology and publicity, announced that with the CPC's "financial and technical assistance" the CCM would build two cadre training centers in Iringa and Tunguu, Zanzibar. Mwanri said "the CCM cadres learnt from the Chinese how to build and strengthen a political party."[111] Two years later, the CPC-ID organized and accompanied another fifteen senior CCM cadres to a training program at the Jingganshan academy. The Tanzanian visitors met with Jingganshan officials and trainers for talks on "cadre training, organization setups, curriculum development and internal operation, etc."[112]

CPC Chairman Hu Jintao and ANC Chairman Jacob Zuma also signed an agreement in 2008 that included cadre training. In accordance with this agreement in 2010 ANC National Chairperson Baleka Mbete led a twenty-one-member senior delegation to participate in two weeks of training at CELAP. At the end of the workshop, which included lectures on socialism with Chinese characteristics, theories and practice of strengthening CPC governing capability, and the relationship between governments and media, the CPC agreed to provide training materials and instructors for the development of the ANC's own party school in South Africa.[113]

Like the CCM and ANC, ZANU-PF held talks with the CPC on the establishment of a "political school to train cadres along the model of the CPC school."[114] In Harare in 2006, ZANU-PF's national political commissar Elliot Manyika announced to a visiting delegation of CPC party historians and instructors that ZANU-PF would "draw on experiences from the CPC and the good bilateral relations between the two parties to set up the school."[115] Meanwhile in Windhoek, Namibia, a CPC delegation from the Central Party School and CPC-ID conducted a three-day training workshop for fifty SWAPO cadres on party building. Netumbo Nanda-Ndaitwah, then SWAPO's information and mobilization secretary, vowed "to start a SWAPO party school to teach members the history of their party and conduct research."[116]

By the start of 2009, the Jingganshan academy had hosted delegations from the Democratic Republic of Congo's People's Party for Reconstruction and Democracy, the Democratic Party of Equatorial Guinea, Mauritius' Labor Party, and Seychelles National Party, among others. Moreover, the academy's official website reports that in 2007 it hosted a three-country, twelve-member "cadre commission" from African ruling party newspapers to build their "understanding of our Party leadership training and Party publicity."[117]

Opposition Party Outreach

Information collection is expanded through the CPC's increased outreach to opposition parties. David Shambaugh describes this practice: "By maintaining ties with nonruling parties, the ID has been able to keep track of domestic politics in various nations and to establish contacts with a wide range of politicians and experts who subsequently staff governments after they come to power."[118] Opposition party outreach, however, remains a secondary priority in Africa and is not appropriate in all cases. Ties to opposition political figures in one-party-dominated African states, in particular, could open the CPC to accusations of interference in internal affairs.[119] In Angola, Ethiopia, and Zimbabwe, among China's most important African partners, the CPC maintains ties only with ruling parties.

Political outreach to African opposition parties remains in its infancy and is regularly subordinated if it jeopardizes CPC relations with the ruling party. However, Africa expert Liu Naiya and others see opposition party outreach as an important growth area for the CPC-ID in Africa.[120] Because CPC-ID opposition outreach is still relatively new and can be politically sensitive, links have been quite limited and are particularly hard to trace. However, two relationships—with Sudan and South Africa—reveal the increasingly flexible nature of the CPC-ID's political outreach to opposition groups.

Since 2002, the CPC has developed a close party-to-party relationship with the Sudan's Islamist National Congress Party (NCP), and until 2005 it had no contacts with opposition political parties, including the Communist Party of Sudan.[121] After the signing of the Comprehensive Peace Agreement (CPA) between the NCP and the opposition Sudan People's Liberation Movement (SPLM) in 2005, the two joined to form a tenuous government of national unity. The CPA legitimized the SPLM and opened the door for the gradual expansion of SPLM-CPC political relations. The first outreach took place in March 2005, when SPLM chief commander Salva Kiir Mayardit was delegated by party leader John Garang to head a SPLM delegation to China to "hold talks on economic cooperation between the two parties."[122]

After the untimely death of Garang in July 2005, the CPC and SPLM did not hold meetings in 2006. In 2007, however, CPC and SPLM party-to-party relations expanded considerably. In February, while visiting Khartoum, President Hu Jintao met again with Kiir, Sudan's first vice president, and invited him to return to China. Six months later, Kiir touched down in Beijing. After meeting again with President Hu, Kiir held a press conference where he said that they "discussed the cooperation between the SPLM and the Chinese Communist Party."[123] CPC-SPLM party-to-party ties were again raised when Kiir held talks with Wang Jiarui, head of the CPC-ID. Notably, the CPC-ID's website posting about this meeting reflects the sensitivity of gatherings with African opposition party leaders. It mentioned China's support for the Sudan's "peace, unification and development," but unlike most official CPC-ID announcements, the name of Kiir's party, the SPLM, was not mentioned.[124]

Before conducting opposition party outreach, the CPC-ID must pay particular attention to domestic political tensions in each African capital. In the case of Khartoum, any expansion of CPC-SPLM ties prior to South Sudan's independence in 2011 took place within the framework of Sudan's government of national unity and the CPA. For this reason, during his July 2007 China trip, Kiir was also obliged to affirm the "strength of the partnership between the National Congress and the Sudan People's Liberation Movement (SPLM)."[125] With the independence of SPLM-led South Sudan, however, there are no longer restrictions on CPC-SPLM contacts.

The CPC's ties to the SPLM, and to opposition parties in general, are also part of a hedging strategy. In the case of Sudan, the CPC developed extensive and public ties with the NCP, while taking advantage of opportunities to ensure its influence in South Sudan through expanding ties to the SPLM. To this end, in August 2007, an official Chinese delegation, invited by Kiir, arrived in Juba, the capital of South Sudan, to gather "more information about southern Sudan."[126] Between 2008 and 2011, as Sudan moved toward its first multiparty elections in over two decades and a referendum on the independence of South Sudan, the CPC's relationship with the SPLM grew. In 2008, Assistant Foreign Minister Zhai Jun visited Juba, the capital of South Sudan, met with Kiir and numerous senior SPLM cadre, and attended the inauguration ceremony of the Consulate General of China in Juba with Riek Machar, deputy chairman of the SPLM and vice president of the Government of South Sudan.[127] A year later, Zhou Yongkang, a member of the Standing Committee of the CPC Central Committee Political Bureau, greeted Machar's delegation in Beijing and discussed strengthening cooperation between the CPC and SPLM.[128]

After the 2011 referendum both sides wasted little time expanding ties. In April Antipas Nyok, SPLM secretary for political affairs, led an SPLM delegation to China for bilateral talks with the CPC-ID aimed at expanding cooperation, establishing regular cross-party exchanges, and acquiring CPC's experiences in party building, party organization, economic development, and other issues relevant to the transition from a revolutionary to a ruling party. This meeting, not mentioned on the CPC-ID website, took place in Zhengzhou, Henan, rather than Beijing, and with the CPC-ID deputy director-general, a relatively low-ranking cadre.[129] The PRC officially recognized South Sudan's independence in July, and in October the CPC vowed to "cement" relations with the SPLM. "Under the new circumstances, it is of vital significance for both parties to further consolidate and develop their relations," senior CPC official Li Changchun told SPLM secretary-general Pagan Amum during their meeting in Beijing.[130]

As the case of Sudan suggests, the CPC does conduct exchanges with opposition parties, but those contacts are subjugated to ties with the ruling party and are conducted in a less public fashion or behind a veil of state-to-state relations. Before the independence of South Sudan, CPC-SPLM ties remained in the framework of the CPA so, for instance, before visiting Juba in 2008 Zhai also visited NCP leaders in Khartoum. Sudan's Vice President Ali Osman Mohamed Taha of the NCP accompanied Machar on his November 2009 visit to Beijing.[131]

Similarly, in South Africa the CPC has been able to maintain its relations with the South African Communist Party (SACP) as part of the ANC's ruling coalition. In 2007, for instance, Wang Dongming, deputy head of the Department of Organization and member of the CPC Central Committee, led a CPC delegation to South Africa to address the SACP's Twelfth National Party Congress.[132] In South Africa, however, the CPC has also reached out to the opposition Democratic Alliance (DA) and the Inkatha Freedom Party (IFP). In April 2005, CAFIU hosted a week-long visit to Beijing, Shanghai, and the Three Gorges Dam for a DA delegation headed by then-party leader Tony Leon.[133] In 2008 (as detailed below) IFP leader Mangosuthu Buthelezi headed a delegation to Beijing, Xian, and Shanghai and met with CPC-ID Vice Minister Li Jinjun.[134] These contacts with genuine opposition parties in South Africa suggest that in democracies that permit freedom of association the CPC is willing to expand its outreach beyond those parties represented in the ruling collation.

NPC Interparliamentary Exchanges

Although the CPC-ID conducts the lion's share of PRC political outreach in Africa, interparliamentary exchanges via the NPC are also part of this effort. NPC delegations have become increasingly important tools for aiding CPC outreach to nonruling parties. The NPC works at "strengthening and improving the mechanism for regular exchanges with other parliaments and congresses."[135] But because foreign relations are only one of NPC officials' responsibilities, it remains an important, but junior partner compared to the CPC-ID, which is specifically dedicated to the task.

To develop relations with opposition parties in South Africa the CPC-ID and the NPC work together to conduct Beijing's political outreach. In 2006, the NPC was the first national legislature to sign a memorandum of understanding establishing a regular mechanism for exchanges with the parliament of South Africa.[136] As part of this mechanism, Fu Zhihuan, chairman of the NPC's Finance and Economic Committee, led a delegation to South Africa in 2007 to strengthen cooperation between the NPC and South African parliament.[137] Wang Zhaoguo's 2009 NPC delegation to South Africa, which included meetings with Max Sisulu, speaker of the National Assembly, also came at the South African parliament's invitation.[138]

Using bilateral friendship groups, the NPC conducts exchanges with over a dozen African parliaments.[139] As is the case with the CPC-ID, the NPC's current political outreach strategy was defined in the post-1977 period. In the intervening years, "the NPC has proactively developed exchanges and cooperation with foreign parliaments and international parliamentary organizations."[140] In 2006, the NPC received a total of ninety delegations from fifty-six countries, and NPC delegations visited thirty countries and regions. This political outreach, like that of the CPC-ID, is intended to "inject fresh vitality into the development of state-to-state relations" and "strengthen mutual trust in the political arena and promote mutually beneficial cooperation."[141]

Unlike the CPC-ID, however, which is purely a party organ, the NPC nominally includes a mix of government and political party influence. Nearly all countries' top legislative bodies include a combination of political parties but unlike in democratic countries, one party—the CPC—dominates China's legislative body. Thus, while the NPC's Foreign Affairs Committee and bilateral friendship groups are officially state organizations, like the friendship groups of the 1950s and 1960s, they are dominated by and accountable to the CPC. Wu Bangguo, chairman of the Standing Committee of the NPC, explained this relationship:

We must uphold the Party's leadership. The CPC is the leadership
core for the cause of socialism with Chinese characteristics. Uphold-
ing the Party's leadership is a basic prerequisite and fundamental
guarantee for success in the work of people's congresses. All the
work of people's congresses must contribute to improving the Party's leadership, consolidating the Party's position as the governing
party and ensuring implementation of the Party's line, principles
and policies.[142]

The NPC's international outreach efforts serve to complement the work of
the CPC-ID. This cooperation is not surprising since the two organizations
not only share policy objectives, they also share tactics and sometimes leaders. Wu Bangguo, for instance, is also a member of the Standing Committee
of the Political Bureau of the CPC; CPC-ID Vice Minister Ma Wenpu is
also a vice chairman of the NPC's Foreign Affairs Committee; and between
1998 and 2002, Jiang Enzhu, the NPC Foreign Affairs Committee chairman,
served simultaneously as the Foreign Affairs Committee's vice chairman
and as a member of the CPC Central Committee.[143]

Tactically, the NPC and CPC-ID work in tandem to balance Beijing's
international political outreach. While the CPC-ID's mandate to increase
exchanges with ruling African parties is quite clearly defined, the NPC's
international exchanges in Africa are fewer in number but can be more
diverse in character. NPC leaders can take on a range of commercial and
ceremonial roles, from leading a delegation of Chinese businessmen to
Cairo, to representing President Hu at the inauguration of the Senegalese
President.

The political outreach efforts of the NPC and CPC-ID can overlap during visits by African party leaders who are also legislators. In African states,
whose legislatures (like China's) are controlled by a single ruling party,
the NPC sometimes assists the CPC-ID in hosting African political party
delegations. In 2007, for instance, a ZANU-PF party delegation led by
Kumbirai Manyika Kangai, secretary for external relations for the political
bureau of Zimbabwe's ruling party as well as deputy speaker of Zimbabwe's
House of Assembly, was hosted in Beijing by the CPC-ID to meet with
NPC interlocutors led by He Luli, vice chairwoman of the NPC Standing
Committee.[144] A reciprocal visit occurred in 2010 when a delegation from
the NPC Standing Committee met with Mugabe and Vice President John
Nkomo, national ZANU-PF chairman, in Harare.[145]

In the Sudan case, party-to-party and NPC political outreach efforts also overlap considerably. In 2007, for instance, Nafi Ali Nafi, deputy president of Sudan's ruling NCP, arrived in Beijing as a CPC-ID guest.[146] He met with Wu Bangguo who, in his NPC capacity as "China's top legislator," said the "CPC would like to expand exchanges and cooperation with the NCP."[147] This statement underscores the tandem efforts of the CPC-ID and the NPC.

Taiwan, Islam, Tibet, Human Rights

Taiwan

Taiwan (the ROC) remains the most sensitive political subject for China. Unlike Tibet or Xinjiang—also sensitive topics—the ROC maintains an independent government, autonomous foreign policy, Ministry of Foreign Affairs, and diplomatic corps.

ROC diplomats have long competed with counterparts in Beijing for the recognition of African countries. They work to represent Taipei's interests on the continent through official embassies in a handful of countries—Burkina Faso, Swaziland, São Tomé and Principe, and Gambia—and trade offices in Nigeria and South Africa. By contrast, Beijing enjoys the support of fifty of the fifty-four African nations as it works to isolate Taipei from the international community.

The PRC rivalry with the ROC stems from the Chinese Civil War, which ended in 1949 when Chiang Kai-shek's Nationalists lost to Mao Zedong's Communists and fled to the island of Taiwan. Between 1949 and 1991, both Taipei and Beijing claimed to be the sole legal authority of all China and sought diplomatic recognition to support their claims. Although in 1991 Taiwan's President Lee Deng-hui admitted Taipei does not actually control the mainland, ROC diplomats have nonetheless continued to work to expand official diplomatic ties around the world based on the fig leaf of "rightful" ROC sovereignty. Beijing has sought to thwart these efforts. Until the election of Taiwan's President Ma Ying-jeou in 2008, when an unofficial "diplomatic truce" appears to have gone into effect, Africa remained a key battleground for this competitive "dollar diplomacy," as both sides vied to establish relations with as many African countries as possible.

Despite the unofficial diplomatic truce, during meetings with their Chinese counterparts African leaders are regularly expected to publicly reaffirm their support for China's national unification strategy, known as the One China Principle. Support for the One China Principle is Beijing's foremost requirement for collaboration and diplomatic recognition. Many African nations see affirmation of Beijing's sovereignty over Taiwan as a necessary part of their diplomacy with China, an easy concession that costs them nothing but can pay dividends.

In the early 1990s, Taipei's financial incentives and astute diplomacy helped it to establish formal relations with several African countries at Beijing's expense. Senegal, a long-time ally of Beijing and one of West Africa's most important states, switched sides. For nearly thirty years, the PRC had cooperated with Senegal, helping to build hospitals and a huge national stadium. Taipei also used its financial resources to woo Gambia and Niger, providing the former with roughly $35 million in assistance and helping the latter pay civil service salaries with a $50 million loan. In 1997, Taipei's economic assistance also extended to Chad and Sâo Tomé and Principe, which received $125 million and $30 million loans respectively. Unfortunately for Taipei, in nearly all cases the fruits of dollar diplomacy were short-lived.[148]

Taipei's diplomatic problems in Africa increased in 1996 when Niger severed ties, but its biggest loss came in 1998, when South Africa, Africa's wealthiest country, exchanged ambassadors with Beijing. In late 2005 Beijing lured Senegal back to its camp, and in 2006 Chad also ended its official diplomatic relations with Taipei after Beijing agreed to stop supporting the country's rebels, Taipei officials said.[149] At the end of 2007, just prior to the 2008 unofficial diplomatic truce, Malawian government officials announced that after its forty-one-year diplomatic relationship with Taipei it had agreed to recognize Beijing.[150] In 2008, a memorandum of understanding covering trade and investment was signed between the two countries committing China to help increase Malawi's productive capacity in agriculture, mining, forestry, fertilizer production, and in processing hides and skins. Between 2007 and 2011 bilateral trade grew exponentially and Beijing provided $260 million in concessionary loans, grants, and aid to Lilongwe.[151]

For the PRC, gaining international support for its claims to Taiwan remains a top priority and Beijing's prerequisite for official recognition. In 2003, for instance, after nearly twenty years as an ally of Taiwan under dictator Charles Taylor, Liberia reestablished relations with the PRC. Liberia's new leaders, whose priority was reconstruction following years of civil war, were swayed by Beijing's combination of economic and diplomatic clout. A spokesman for the Liberian president said switching to Beijing would help with Liberia's reconstruction efforts.[152] He was referring to the aid package Beijing leveraged to sway the embattled nation. China agreed to support a UN resolution to budget $250 million for 15,000 peacekeepers to stabilize Liberia and offered Monrovia assistance and training in energy development, infrastructure, agriculture, and manufacturing.[153] Beijing had the power to veto the resolution had Liberia's government not acquiesced, providing a powerful incentive for Monrovia to recognize Beijing. Later China contributed peacekeepers to the UN mission in Liberia.

This strategy was again on display in 2006 when Chad, desperately seeking support on the UN Security Council and in its dealings with the World Bank, switched recognition to Beijing. Chad had seen 200,000 refugees arrive on its soil and faced internal strife stemming from the conflict in the Darfur region of western Sudan. This had inflamed tensions with Khartoum, which, with Beijing's support, had complicated the process of UN force deployments in the region. According to one Chadian diplomat, "As China has a veto [on the UN Security Council] we have to have it by our side so the draft [UN resolution] on the presence of UN forces [in Darfur] goes through without difficulty."[154] According to one anonymous Chinese official, as of 2011 Beijing's inducements to N'Djamena included over $10 billion in economic and infrastructure investment. These methods are consistent with China's use of political and financial carrots and sticks to convince African nations to cut ties with Taipei.

Disagreements in Abuja over Taiwan's status have benefited Nigerians. From 1991 to 2001, the ROC offices were located in Lagos before being relocated to the capital Abuja. During a meeting at the ROC trade offices in the Nigerian capital in 2007, the island's top representative, Ming Chang, proudly displayed a copy of the 21 November 1990 agreement with Nigeria's Ministry of Commerce that awards the ROC representative the right to remain in Abuja. Yet, this document contradicts statements from the president's office, thus providing ample wiggle room for the Nigerian authorities. Ming, for instance, is permitted a diplomatic car but cannot fly the ROC flag as is common practice among ambassadors. He told of one incident in 2004 when Nigerian police closed the ROC office in Abuja before allowing it to reopen, for a price.[155] For its part, Beijing regularly requests that the office be relocated to Lagos, the country's trade hub, or any city other than the capital. Entreaties like this, recalled Nigeria's former ambassador to China, Jonathan Oluwole Coker, were often made in the NPC "Taiwan Room" and included efforts to solicit Nigeria to press West African holdouts like Gambia and Burkina Faso to switch recognition to Beijing.[156]

Although in public statements Abuja does not waver on Taiwan's status as a part of China, it does maintain ample relations with Taipei. In practice this means that while Nigeria maintains trade offices in Taipei it also issued a joint communiqué with Beijing in 2005 supporting "China's efforts to reunify the nation, including the formulation of the Anti-Secession Law" and reaffirmed that Beijing is "the only legitimate government representing the whole China and Taiwan is an inalienable part of China's territory."[157] In addition to Nigeria, twenty-two other African countries including Egypt, Ethiopia, Zimbabwe, Libya, South Africa, as well as the African Union, issued statements or formal declarations in support of the NPC's 2005 Anti-Secession Law.[158]

Taipei's four remaining diplomatic partners in Africa along with its Nigeria and South Africa trade offices have joined the ROC to establish the Africa Taiwan Economic Forum (ATEF). ATEF, according to Executive Director Richard Lin, was established in 2003 to help Africans "enhance economic relationships with the ROC."[159] ATEF prioritizes "human resource development, health, wealth, people-to-people co-operation (cultural exchange) and sustainable development" with the objective to "promote Africa's values and interests in Taiwan."[160] In practical terms ATEF seeks to coordinate Taiwan's policies in much the same way that China does with FOCAC, albeit on a much smaller scale.

At the ROC's 16 June 2006 Africa Day celebrations in Taipei, ROC President Chen Shuibian described the value Taiwan attached to its African allies: "On behalf of the government and people of Taiwan, I would like to take this opportunity to express our gratitude to our African diplomatic allies for once again speaking out in support of Taiwan."[161] A year later at the Taiwan-Africa Heads of State Summit in Taipei on 9–10 September 2007, Chen was joined by the leaders of Swaziland, Burkina Faso, São Tomé and Principe, Malawi, and the vice president of Gambia. They identified five core areas of cooperation: information and communications technologies, economic development, medical assistance, the environment, and peace and security, while affirming that "as a sovereign country, Taiwan should not be deprived of its right to participate in the United Nations" or other international forums.[162] Since Ma Ying-jeou became president in 2008, however, Taipei has shied away from high profile events that flaunt its remaining diplomatic relationships on the continent. Instead, lower profile events such as the 2010 Taiwan and Africa Environmental Leader Meeting in Taipei have provided a venue for officials from MOFA and their counterparts from Taiwan's African allies "to explore opportunities for exchange and cooperation."[163]

The Taiwan-Swaziland relationship remains the closest of any Taiwan has in Africa, if not the world. Swaziland, a tiny mountainous country, is the continent's only remaining kingdom. Taiwanese investment in the textile industry has helped the country take advantage of the African Growth and Opportunity Act (AGOA), which permits some 6,000 items to enter the United States duty free, and by 2008, according to ROC Vice President Vincent Siew, it had helped create 100,000 Swazi jobs.[164] Siew gushed at a press conference held during his 2008 visit to Mbabane to mark king Mswati III's birthday and forty years of Taiwan-Swaziland relations: "Taiwan and Swaziland enjoy good relations, which continue to grow from strength to strength. There is commitment and dedication from both countries to improve relations." Siew also attended the launch of the Taipei-funded Taiwan Medical Mission.[165] As of 2010, the Mission had a dozen staff including a neurosurgeon, general surgeon, oral surgeon, infectious disease specialist, neurologist, registered nurse, and assistants.[166] It also has pediatric facilities, a tuberculosis clinic, and a HIV/AIDS clinic.[167]

There is an opaque side to ROC support for Swaziland. Statistics on funds for the king and royal family are not publicly available and during interviews with officials in August 2007 they would not, or could not, estimate total Taiwanese investment or gifts to the royal family.[168]

As of 2011 Taiwan's four African allies represent about one-quarter of all Taiwan's formal diplomatic partners. Taiwan continues to provide these nations with material support, but also hopes that increased cooperation in developing communications technology, democratization, and good governance will entice other African nations. Unfortunately for Taipei, over the last decade these tactics were increasingly undermined by China's rapid economic growth and political power, leading many African leaders to conclude that their historic ties to the ROC were no longer as valuable as

relations with the mainland. Yet some faithful holdouts, like longtime partner Swaziland, believe that as Taiwan's diplomatic partners dwindle, more
opportunities will come their way.[169]

Islam

During the 1950s and early 1960s the China Islamic Association served as
the first Islam-based connection between China and Africa, a critical part
of CPC outreach to African Muslims. In 1951 Mohammed Makin, a graduate of Al Azhar University in Cairo teaching Arabic in Beijing, addressed the
Chinese People's Institute for Foreign Affairs on how to enhance political
relations with the Arab world.[170] Makin and seven others began the China
Islamic Association in July 1952 with the selection of a forty-member preparatory committee headed by a Chinese Uighur and CPC member Burhan
Shahidi and formally launched the organization in 1953. Although at first
domestically oriented, after contacts with Egypt began in 1955 the association became an important conduit for the CPC's political outreach to the
Muslim world.[171] Shahidi and other leaders were particularly proactive,
leading numerous delegations to Africa and the Middle East and sharing
the CPC's positions with countless visitors from Muslim countries.[172]

The China Islamic Association paid particular concern to the sacred
pilgrimage to Mecca, Saudi Arabia, known as the hajj, and beginning in
1955 sent at least one Chinese group every year until 1964.[173] Pilgrimage
trips usually included visits to Egypt, Tunisia, Morocco, or Sudan, but
could range as far as Guinea, Senegal, Mali, Mauritania, Niger, and Northern Nigeria. But, as Ogunsanwo explains, "The long detour from Saudi
Arabia to Guinea and Senegal would hardly have been justified had there
been no political motivation."[174] After departing Mecca, Chinese Muslims
would spend two or three months visiting African brethren telling them
about the religious freedoms enjoyed under the CPC. To achieve this objective at home, African Muslims were invited to China for Muslim festivals
or to worship in Chinese mosques. For China, Islam became a valuable
instrument not only to foster its relations with the countries of the Muslim
world, but also to spread Mao's thought to the millions of Muslims in Asia
and Africa.[175]

In accordance with its mandate to "support the Chinese Communist
Party's leadership," the work of the China Islamic Association was and

remains political: seeking to use China's Muslims as an entrée to talks with political parties in the Muslim world.[176] This was particularly important in North Africa, the only African region in which multiple countries successfully achieved independence during the 1950s.[177] Whereas the litany of political outreach organizations—mass organizations, front groups, friendship and solidarity associations—took the lead in most Sub-Saharan African states, in North Africa the presence of both independent postcolonial governments and Islam allowed the Foreign Ministry and China Islamic Association to work together to make important inroads. The latter also worked closely with other CPC mass organizations and front groups to expand CPC political outreach. In 1958, for instance, Radio Peking announced that as a token of solidarity the China Islamic Association, All-China Federation of Trade Unions, and Asian Solidarity Committee of China would provide a sizable grant to the Algerian National Liberation Front via the AAPSO Secretariat in Cairo.[178]

The China Islamic Association also helped compile and distribute CPC propaganda in North Africa via official publishing houses and its exchanges with Arabic experts. A number of picture books were published in the late 1950s and early 1960s, including "Chinese Muslims' Life," "Muslims in China," "The Holy Qur'an and Women's Rights and Status," and "Chinese Muslims' Religious Life," with captions in Chinese, Arabic, English, and French. The PRC's constitution was translated into Arabic and distributed along with a picture book, "Beijing Muslims' Life," in Chinese, Arabic, and English.[179]

Chinese Muslims suffered during the Cultural Revolution. Starting in 1966 with the "Four Olds" political campaign to destroy Old Customs, Old Culture, Old Habits, and Old Ideas, countless mosques and schools were shut down or destroyed, along with Korans and holy manuscripts. Muslims who resisted were imprisoned or killed and nearly all in government were purged. In 1968 all PRC ambassadors in Africa were recalled, except in Egypt, where Zhou Enlai's skilled deputy, Ambassador Huang Hua, remained in place.[180] On 25 September 1969, a week before the twentieth anniversary of the PRC and at the lowest point in the country's foreign relations since its founding, the First Islamic Summit opened in Rabat, Morocco. The Summit, which focused almost entirely on Israel, neglected to mention CPC repression of millions of Chinese Muslims.[181]

China's relations with Africa's Muslim nations were strongly anti-Soviet throughout the late 1960s and early 1970s. After attending the Second

Islamic Summit in Lahore, Pakistan, in February 1974, Algerian President Houari Boumediene flew to Beijing where he met with Zhou Enlai. At a welcoming banquet Zhou said the summit's participants represented the "strong desire of the third world countries to support one another and line up against the enemy." In his usual adroit manner, Zhou connected China's primary adversary, Soviet (and to a lesser degree U.S.) hegemony, with Israel, the focus of Muslim anger at that time:

> The crux of the Middle East question is the fierce rivalry between the two superpowers for hegemony there. Driven by their respective selfish interests, they have, for a long time, supported and connived at Israeli aggression and done their utmost to maintain a state of "no war, no peace" to the great detriment of the Arab people including the Palestinian people.[182]

In this way Zhou tied North African countries' united stand against Israel with China's united front against Soviet hegemonism. For Boumedienne, who flew to Washington the following month for meetings with President Nixon and Henry Kissinger and reestablished diplomatic relations with the United States later that year, Beijing's rapprochement with Washington, not Tel Aviv, was the top priority.[183] "We are gratified at the evolution of East-West relations towards détente, which is registered as an appreciable factor for strengthening peace in certain parts of the world," said the Algerian leader.[184]

The struggle against Soviet hegemony remained an element in China's relations with North African states in the years after the Cultural Revolution. Although China never failed to send a letter of congratulations to the Islamic Summit Conferences (held in 1974, 1981, 1987, and 1991), the international outreach of the China Islamic Association fell precipitously during the 1980s and early 1990s.[185] In 1993, however, Hamid Algabid, secretary-general of the Organization of the Islamic Conference (OIC) and former prime minister of Niger, wrote a letter to Foreign Minister Qian Qichen regarding the Serbian threat to Bosnian Muslims in Bosnia-Herzegovina. This was followed a month later by another letter from Abdou Diouf, president of Senegal and then executive chairman of the Organization of the Islamic Conference. These letters prompted the China Islamic Association to again issue invitations to OIC delegations to visit China, which began in 1994 and continued throughout the decade.[186] Yet, the China Islamic Association would never again regain its prominence as the leading political liaison group between Chinese and North African Muslims.

More recently, the issue of Islamist terrorism and tightening of restrictions on Uighurs have entered China's relations with Islamic states in Africa. To avenge state suppression of Uighur Muslims after the July 2009 Urumqi riots, al-Qaeda's North African wing, al-Qaeda in the Islamic Maghreb (AQIM), killed twenty-four Algerians when they ambushed a convoy of Chinese engineers guarded by Algerian security forces.[187] This was the first time an African terrorist network targeted Chinese in Africa in direct response to Beijing's domestic repression of Muslims.

Tibet

The Tibet issue has become an increasingly important topic in Sino-African relations, particularly after anti-Chinese riots erupted there in March 2008. Although many African countries had previously made remarks supporting China's sovereignty over Tibet, after the riots they were strongly encouraged to reiterate, even strengthen their support for Beijing's position and the CPC.

While visiting Morocco less than two weeks after the Tibet riots, Li Changchun, a member of the Standing Committee of the Political Bureau of the Central Committee of the CPC, stressed PRC claims over Tibet. Xinhua, the *People's Daily*, and China Radio International were among the official Chinese news outlets that filed a report titled "Morocco Supports China's Tibet Policy, Beijing Olympics," reflecting the primacy of the Tibet issue at the time. After Prime Minister Abbas Al Fassi reiterated that "Morocco firmly believes that the affairs concerning Tibet are China's internal affairs," Li signed a bilateral agreement on economic and technological cooperation and agreed that "the CPC is ready to enrich the cooperation with the Independence Party of Morocco."[188] It is noteworthy, however, that a report on the meeting carried in Morocco's official news agency Maroc did not mention Tibet.[189]

Similarly, in 2008, a senior CPC delegation visited Addis Ababa, Ethiopia, at the invitation of Prime Minister Meles Zenawi's Ethiopian People's Revolutionary Democratic Front. Xinhua reported that during the meeting Meles said Tibet was an internal Chinese affair, and his CPC guests thanked him.[190] By contrast, the official Ethiopian News Agency reported the meeting but made no mention of Tibet.[191] In addition to Ethiopia and Morocco in the wake of the 2008 Tibet riots, China elicited and received diplomatic support from the political leaders of African countries including Algeria, Zambia, Sierra Leone, Benin, Eritrea, Central African Republic, Comoros, Congo (Brazzaville), Côte d'Ivoire, Lesotho, and Mauritania.[192] CPC-ID and NPC delegations obtained similar statements during their exchanges with African political parties and parliaments.

Unlike Taiwan, the issue of Tibet has generally not been politically contentious in Africa. Under the Dalai Lama's leadership until 2011 the official Tibetan government in exile, known as the Central Tibetan Administration (CTA), did not seek African states' formal recognition of Tibetan independence. Yet, the CTA has reached out to a few sympathetic Africans for support to expand Tibetan political and religious autonomy. Since 1997 the group has maintained a Representative for Africa in Pretoria responsible for all African countries except Morocco, Algeria, Tunisia, and Libya, which come under the jurisdiction of the Brussels office.[193] The CTA's Information Division also disseminates Tibet-related information to Arabic-speaking people.

Kenya and South Africa are the only African countries with a local Tibet Support Group.[194] To counter its influence and persuade Kenyan lawmakers not to be "influenced by western media on the Tibetan issue due to their British-style education" in 2009 Beijing sent a delegation to introduce "the basic facts of Tibet [and] the origin of the 'Tibetan issue.'"[195] Kenya and China also discussed establishing a Tibetan cultural research center at a Kenyan university with links to China's Tibetan Research Center.[196] In nearly all African states Tibet remains an insignificant issue. This is not the case in South Africa, where the Tibetan cause has stirred the passions of citizens in a fashion akin to Europe or the United States.

In South Africa the Free Tibet Movement has developed its strongest political bonds. South Africa has three organizations dedicated to the cause of increased Tibetan autonomy: Tibet Society of South Africa, South African Friends of Tibet, and Tibet African Rainbow Alliance.[197] In 2008 and 2009 the circumstances surrounding the Dalai Lama's invitation to attend the 2010 World Cup in South Africa provoked controversy. In 2008 the opposition IFP president, Mangosuthu Buthelezi, published an open letter calling for China to increase autonomy in Tibet and hold a "meeting between the Chinese government and the Dalai Lama." Two months later he led an IFP delegation to China to meet with CPC-ID counterparts led by Vice Minister Li Jinjun. In another open letter from China to his "fellow South Africans" Buthelezi recalled his unusual exchange about Tibet with the CPC:

> I decided to take the "bull by the horns" and discard diplomatic niceties. I emphatically stated that His Holiness the Dalai Lama had made it clear to me that neither he or his supporters were seeking independence for Tibet, but sought cultural and religious autonomy, and that Tibet be transformed into a region of non-violence and peace. I also said that the Dalai Lama should be commended for unequivocally stating that countries should not boycott the Beijing Olympics. In responding, the Minister, in essence, accused the Dalai Lama of double speak when I pressed the above points. The Minister said that the Dalai Lama had it in his power to restrain his supporters, but chose not to. I crisply pointed out that unless the Dalai Lama could return to Tibet there was little more he could to do to restrain his Tibetan protestors.[198]

In March 2009, CPC relations with South Africa's opposition parties grew even more strained when, responding to CPC pressure, the ANC-dominated government denied a visa for the Dalai Lama to visit South Africa. The DA said the decision "flies in the face of all logic" since the Dalai Lama had already visited the country in 1999 and 2004.[199] The opposition Independent Democrats' President Patricia de Lille agreed: "By giving in to China the [South African] Government is saying to the world that we do not afford other people the same rights we are afforded in our own Constitution."[200]

The Chinese consul general in Durban also sent a letter warning that IFP attendance at The Fifth World Parliamentarians' Convention on Tibet in Rome in November 2009 would "interfere in China's internal affairs and hurt Chinese people's feelings" and said that "although Inkatha Freedom Party is an opposition party, it should also cherish the China-South African friendship."[201] In November 2009, the DA's parliamentary leader, Athol Trollip, met a CPC delegation in Cape Town led by Wang Zhaoguo to discuss the Convention.[202] Yet, both opposition party leaders refused to acquiesce and attended the Conference despite CPC entreaties. IFP leader

Buthelezi also published the consul's letter and continued to publicly support the Tibetan cause.[203]

By contrast, those South African political parties with close ties to the CPC, namely the ruling ANC and the SACP, supported the decision not to provide a visa for the Tibetan leader. ANC Finance Minister Trevor Manuel was unapologetic. He said the reason the Dalai Lama wants to visit South Africa "is to make a big global, political statement about the secession of Tibet from China."[204] This was a view supported by the SACP, the ANC's coalition partner, in a public statement.[205] But not all high-ranking ANC members agreed. Barbara Hogan, South Africa's Health Minister, for instance, argued that "the very fact that this [ANC] government has refused entry to the Dalai Lama is an example of a government [that] is dismissive of human rights."[206]

In October 2011 a similar row erupted when the Dalai Lama was denied a visa to attend the birthday of Archbishop Desmond Tutu and give several public talks. The decision coincided with South African Vice President Kgalema Motlanthe's visit to China, where he signed multiple trade and development agreements. In response, Archbishop Tutu lashed out at the South African government, President Jacob Zuma, and the ANC: "Mr. Zuma, you and your government don't represent me. You represent your own interests." Tony Ehrenreich, the leader of COSATU, a coalition of trade unions, also criticized the ANC for allowing China to influence South Africa's foreign policy: "Even though China is our biggest trading partner we should not exchange our morality for dollars or yuan."[207]

Human Rights

Beginning in the mid-1990s African countries' political support played a key role in Beijing's successful eleven-year campaign to avoid censure for its human rights record by the UN Commission on Human Rights (UNCHR). Human rights became a source of great concern for CPC leaders during this time. They fought relentlessly to prevent their domestic policies towards dissent from being scrutinized by outsiders. Although the reasons behind China's increased engagement in Africa were overwhelmingly economic, solidarity on human rights issues helped influence this renewed interest.

Beijing began focusing on the UNCHR in March 1995, when it lost a motion to quash a vote on a resolution supported by Western nations to condemn China's human rights practices. Although China and its supporters won the actual vote on the resolution, it was close, leading Beijing to begin a campaign to influence the African voting members of the organization.[208] As a part of this effort, Vice Premier Li Lanqing visited six African countries including UNCHR members Mali, Guinea, Gabon, Cameroon, and Côte d'Ivoire. After China won the 1996 UNCHR vote, all fifteen African members held high level talks with China and signed at least twenty-three agreements and protocols on Sino-African cooperation.[209] In this way the issue of human rights provided another catalyst for Sino-African political cooperation.

In 2004, China again put forth a motion designed to avoid censure for human rights abuses, which passed with the support of every African nation on the UNCHR. Of the twenty-seven countries that supported China's motion, over half were African, including nations with questionable human rights records such as Sudan, Eritrea, and Zimbabwe, each of which had its membership supported by Beijing. The UNCHR was replaced in 2006 with the UN Human Rights Council. For Beijing, the Council provides a safe environment. While Zimbabwe and Sudan have been removed from the 47-member Council, China remains along with thirteen African countries, many with extensive commercial and political ties to Beijing.[210] This ensures that China will continue to exert influence and that the Council cannot take actions contrary to Beijing's interests. It also allows African nations to continue to leverage their votes as political capital in their bilateral negotiations with Beijing, albeit to a lesser degree than in the past.

Conclusion

The CPC-ID and the NPC have collaborated to extend PRC relations with political parties and parliaments throughout Africa. In the mid-1950s the CPC began its political outreach in Africa; in the 1960s and 1970s these efforts were intended to spread revolutionary ideology; in the 1980s they were altered to oppose Soviet hegemony; in the 1990s they countered Taiwan's well-funded dollar diplomacy, and in the 2000s they largely supported China's trade, economic, and industrial development.

Today, PRC political outreach activities are well funded, targeted at political elites, and, to a much lesser degree, engage opposition parties. They include a menu of well-developed techniques including hospitality, party cadre training, information management, opposition party outreach, and interparliamentary exchanges. Taken together, these elements constitute a unique approach to developing relations with African political elites that remains largely unexplored by Western experts. The CPC's international political outreach strategy in Africa has been generally successful in cultivating the personal relationships intended to open new opportunities for Chinese foreign policymakers and state-run firms.

Taiwan remains the most sensitive topic for China because Taipei's diplomats have long competed with those from Beijing for the recognition of African countries. After decades of dollar diplomacy, an unofficial diplomatic truce initiated in 2008 leaves Taiwan with four diplomatic partners in Africa—Burkina Faso, Swaziland, Sâo Tomé and Principe, and Gambia. Islam, first a basis for CPC outreach through the China Islamic Association, has taken on new and complex political dimensions amid the growth of Uighur separatism and Islamist activity in Africa. Despite becoming a short-lived source of contention within the South Africa-China relationship, Tibet, a topic of much debate in the West, has remained largely unimportant in China-Africa political relations. Human rights remains a source of China-Africa solidarity on the official level, yet as Sino-African interaction increases, African civil society groups are beginning to question Chinese human rights practices, particularly in Africa.

4

Trade Relations

Driven by Chinese resource purchases and African demand for affordable consumer products, trade is now the largest feature of the China-Africa economic relationship. China-Africa trade deals concluded before China's economic reform and opening up in the late 1970s were politically expedient, but rarely amounted to much trade. Although trade with Africa was briefly, and marginally, important to China at the height of its international isolation during the active period of the Cultural Revolution, 1967–1971, it did not become a sizable portion of Africa's total world trade until the second half of the decade 2005–2010.

Together, China's increasing demand for raw materials and ability to produce affordable consumer goods and capital equipment has become the dual catalyst for the sharp growth in China-Africa trade. As of 2011 multi-million-dollar trade deals between China and African countries are commonplace. The dollar value of China-Africa trade has risen twenty-fold over the last decade—from $6.3 billion in 1999 to $128.5 billion in 2010—when it represented about 13.5 percent of Africa's total world trade and 4.3 percent of China's. This chapter traces the China-Africa trade relationship from the establishment of the PRC in 1949 until 2011 and concludes with an examination of China's relations with African regional organizations.

China-Africa Trade Data

The largest problem we confronted in researching China-Africa trade is the lack of reliable and consistent data. Despite the attention China-Africa trade has received over the last decade and the numerous publications on the topic, none since Larkin (1971) has included a year-by-year dataset. Generally speaking, those trade numbers cited in journalistic accounts are from China Customs data that do not reflect African figures, which can be quite different. We found good reason for this lack of contemporary trade data and that even after compiling a "complete" China-Africa dataset important questions still remained. Such questions forced difficult choices; for instance, according to African countries' trade data, China has run a trade surplus of varying sizes since 1978. By contrast, China reported that Africa had a surplus in some years and China in others. This was just one of the many inconsistencies we were forced to reconcile.

Unless otherwise noted, all graphical displays in this chapter that indicate levels of China-Africa trade as a nominal figure or in percentage terms were calculated based on the International Monetary Fund Direction of Trade Statistics (IMF DOTS) and UN trade statistics, with preference always afforded to the former when available. Three principles guided this effort: accuracy, comprehensiveness, and repeatability. To best approximate the true level of China-Africa trade we included data from both the IMF DOTS China pages and African countries pages. The trade statistics used in this chapter are a combination of African countries' reporting on imports from China and China's reporting on imports from Africa. We used the same system for individual country trade figures in the four regional chapters. Since tariffs are extracted from imports, customs officials, the logic goes, tend to keep closer tabs on them than on exports, which can be difficult to trace. After much deliberation we concluded that these numbers are the most accurate available.

To achieve comprehensiveness nearly every year of IMF or UN data back to 1948 was used to ensure that whenever possible the most recent published statistics were selected. Also, China's trade relations with those states (Algeria, 1969–1977; Egypt, 1949–1950, 1956–present; Libya, 1982–present; Nigeria, 1969–1977, South Africa, 1948–1968), which at times have been counted apart from Africa as a whole, were sought out and included whenever necessary. A complete China-Africa trade dataset for each year including both imports and exports from the China and Africa pages is available in Appendix 2.

Following is a series of graphical displays based on our China-Africa dataset. Each display is intended to add another layer of specificity to our presentation of the data. The first set of displays (Figure 1) presents the breadth of China-Africa trade beginning with the data available tracing

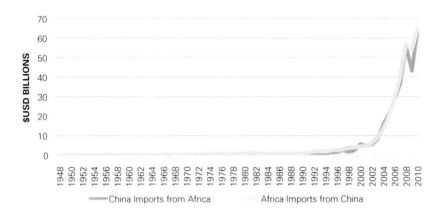

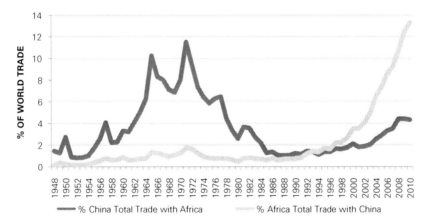

Figure 1. China-Africa trade, 1948–2010.

uninterrupted from 1948 to 2010. The second set (Figure 2) breaks down the data into three periods: 1948–1977, 1978–1989, and 1990–2010. The third set (Figure 3) places China-Africa trade in the context of both sides' total world trade. Additionally, each historical section includes a graphical display focused on the particular group of years under examination.

African Colonialism Meets New China, 1948–1954

"Profit is not the first consideration, friendship is," Premier Zhou Enlai once told the Kuwaiti Trade Minister.[1] The use of trade deals primarily as

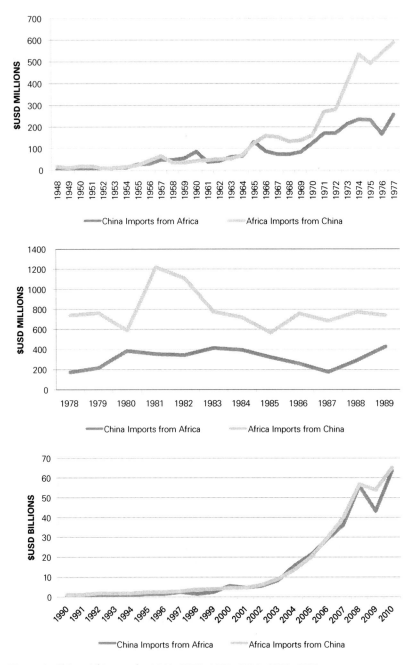

Figure 2. China-Africa trade, 1948–1977, 1978–1990, 1978–2010.

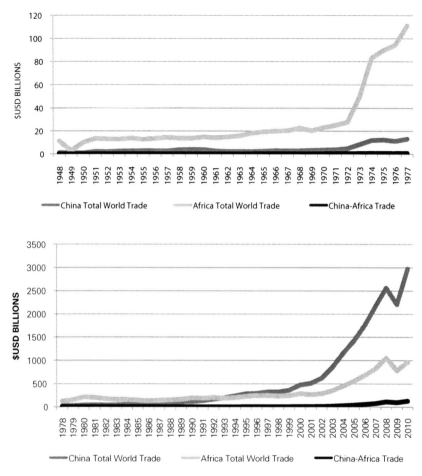

Figure 3. China-Africa trade as a portion of both sides' total world trade, 1948–1977, 1978–2010.

"a weapon for the international political struggle" started in the 1950s.[2] Although China-Africa trade before 1955 was limited—only $27 million in 1954—China began to use trade to facilitate CPC foreign relations in 1952 when the China Council for the Promotion of International Trade (CCPIT) was established. Since its creation this organization has continued to expand and administer China's international trade policies in accordance with CPC directives.[3] Throughout the 1950s the activities of the CCPIT and the All-China Federation of Industry and Commerce (ACFIC) were

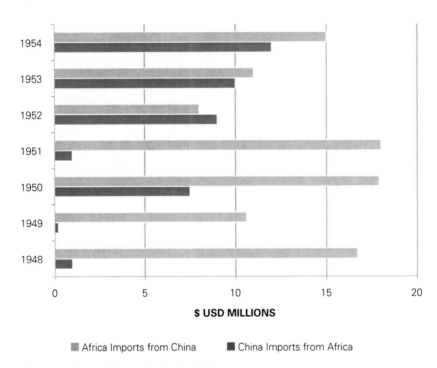

$ USD MILLIONS

■ Africa Imports from China   ■ China Imports from Africa

Figure 4. China-Africa trade, 1948–1954.

overwhelmingly political in character, as were PRC displays at international trade fairs, which touted the success of China's state-planned socialist economy.[4]

European colonial dominance over African economies, China's post-civil war political consolidation, the distance between China and Africa, and lack of commercial shipping between them combined to hinder the growth of China-Africa trade in this period. Before 1955 China's largest African export was green tea to North Africa. Although trade was small, China enjoyed trade surpluses with Africa in every year between 1948 and 1954 except 1952. In 1955 one Xinhua report touting the size of China's potential market suggests trade with Africa during this period was at least somewhat market-driven: "China, which has a population of 600,000,000, is devoting itself to peaceful construction. It has a big and growing market. It needs cotton produced by Egypt [and] China's silk goods, paper, tea, cotton and woolen textiles have traditional markets in Asia and Africa."[5]

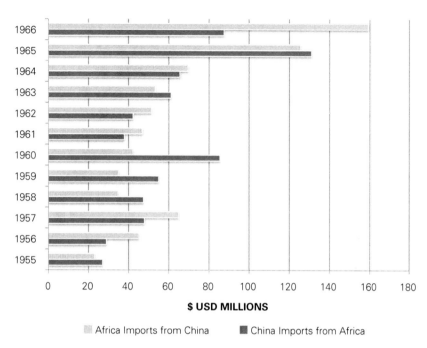

Figure 5. China-Africa trade, 1955–1966.

Emerging from Revolution, 1955–1966

During the mid- to late 1950s China-Africa trade expanded primarily as an extension of political relations. In 1955, surplus Egyptian cotton and slow demand in Western markets allowed China to purchase 15,000 tons. Later that year a trade delegation from Cairo visited Beijing and negotiated a three-year trade agreement whereby both sides established trade offices in each other's capitals.[6] In this way trade became the first foundation of China-Egypt political relations, and China-Africa relations more broadly. In January 1956, China opened its Cairo trade office, which became the center of CPC political outreach to African liberation movements detailed in Chapters 2 and 3. For Beijing, purchases from Egypt, rather than meeting actual market demand, served to build goodwill and help expand China's relations with other newly independent African countries such as Morocco, Algeria, Tunisia, and Sudan.[7]

For Cairo there was a strong commercial component to the China trade agreement. While Egypt had increased its production from 616,000 cotton spindles in 1954 to 657,000 in 1955 to over 800,000 in 1956, the area used for growing cotton in the Middle East rose 10 percent.[8] Faced with excess domestic supplies and growing foreign competition, the Egyptian government needed China's cotton purchases to stabilize its economy.[9] Between 1956 and 1960, China-Egypt trade totaled $284 million, $81.5 million more than China's trade with all other African countries combined. In 1960, for instance, China's trade with Egypt totaled $68.5 million and China's trade with all other African countries was $59.2 million.

Between 1955 and 1966, China-Africa trade remained at low levels but grew rapidly. In 1955, just as China-Egypt trade began in earnest, China's exports to Africa were $23 million and its imports were $27 million, for a total of $50 million. A decade later, by 1966, China's exports were worth $159.2 million and its African imports cost $87.5 million; the total, $246.7 million, represented a nearly five-fold increase over 1955 levels. Africa became a surprisingly important part of China's overall trade portfolio during this period. In 1955 only 1.7 percent of China's trade was with Africa. By 1965 and 1966, however, the African percentage of China's foreign trade had steadily grown to over 10 percent and 8 percent respectively. This increase reflected the fruits of China's political outreach to North Africa in the late 1950s, when European colonialism still dominated Sub-Saharan African trade. Largely for this reason China remained an almost insignificant trade partner for Africa, representing less than 0.5 percent of Africa's total trade in 1955 and just over one percent in 1965 and 1966.

China's domestic policies also influenced trade with Africa. In 1960, amid the worst days of the famine wrought by the Great Leap Forward's disastrous agricultural policies, China purchased large shipments of African grain, pushing its imports up to $85.4 million while exports fell to $42.3 million. But after more moderate Chinese economic policies were reinstated in 1961 and African states proved unable to continue supplying large quantities of grain, China's imports fell to $37.9 million in 1961, $17.1 million below 1959 levels.[10]

As early as 1961, Beijing's state-run press recognized that "Africa possesses very rich mineral deposits and agricultural resources, especially diamonds, petroleum, gold, cobalt, uranium, lithium and other rare metals of great strategic importance."[11] Yet, it took decades before China's economy required considerable amounts of these resource inputs. China's economy at the time—like that of most of its African trading partners—was essentially poor, agrarian, and closed to trade. The lack of tradable items did not prevent China from signing trade agreements with African countries, however. China signed at least two trade deals with African countries in 1955–1957, eight in 1960–1965, and fifteen in 1970–1974. At the time, the growing number of independent Sub-Saharan African countries provided new opportunities for the expansion of China-Africa commerce, particularly for China's exports.

During the early-1960s, as China's economy recovered, so did its exports to Africa, which jumped from $34.9 million in 1959 to $159.2 million in 1965. China emphasized its trade with political allies and played down, denied, or ignored completely inexpedient trade relationships with countries outside the socialist camp. Behind the scenes, however, business continued as Chinese negotiators reportedly drove hard commercial bargains and tactically interpreted clauses in trade agreements to their advantage.[12] In Kenya, for instance, even after signing a bilateral trade agreement with China in 1963 and an agreement to import Chinese products in 1965, political differences resulted in a downgrading of Kenya-China relations to the chargé d'affaires level. These problems were exacerbated when Kenya expelled a third secretary at China's embassy on suspicion of plotting subversion in 1966.[13] Yet, while this interruption appears to have hurt Kenya's exports to China, which fell from $1.9 million in 1965 to $1.3 in 1968, Chinese exports rose from $2.5 million to $4.1 million over the same period.[14]

South Africa's trade figures with China are available only until 1964, when the apartheid regime reported exporting a total of $5 million to China and did not disclose its imports. In 1963, Pretoria reported $6 million in South African exports to China and Chinese imports worth $2.5 million. This number represented a fall from 1960, when South Africa exported $9.3 million (mostly maize) to China and imported $2.3 million. Even after official data reporting stopped in 1965 and despite Beijing's relentless propaganda attacks on the apartheid regime, trading with China continued. In 1964 when a South African minister was asked the value of total trade with China he replied he "did not consider it to be in the national interest to disclose these figures."[15]

The Great Proletarian Cultural Revolution, 1967–1971

In 1965, the year before the Cultural Revolution officially began, China was exporting $125.4 million to Africa and importing $130.9 million. Beginning in 1966, however, China-Africa trade fell for four years in a row. After

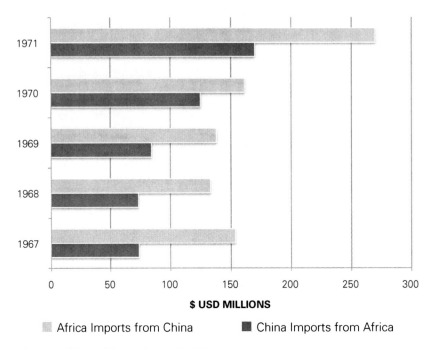

Figure 6. China-Africa trade, 1967–1971.

Maoist political campaigns began interrupting production and exerting influence over foreign affairs, exports to Africa fell from $159.2 million in 1966 to $133.2 million in 1968. During the most turbulent years of the Cultural Revolution only two trade agreements were signed with African states, one with Mauritania in 1967 and the other with Ethiopia in 1970. None was signed in 1968 or 1969.[16]

Despite the fall in China-Africa trade between 1966 and 1968, trade with Africa continued to represent about 7–8 percent of China's total foreign trade. In 1969, Africa's total foreign trade was $20.3 billion, six-fold greater than China's $3.2 billion total foreign trade. That year Africa represented 6.9 percent of China's world trade, but China represented barely 1 percent of Africa's world trade. By 1971, however, China-Africa trade was $440.1 million and 11.5 percent of China's total foreign trade. These figures reflect China's isolation from both the West and the Soviet bloc during the Cultural Revolution. Even after the value of China-Africa trade jumped in 1971, China still represented only 1.7 percent of Africa's total world trade.

In addition to politics, some scholars argue that a profit motive drove early China-Africa trade. Even amid Mao's radical Cultural Revolution, Bruce Larkin identified "expanded markets and economic advantage" as among China's reasons for increasing African trade. In 1971, he wrote that "improved access to Zambian copper" and petroleum imports from Algeria were economic drivers of China-Africa trade and surmised that:

> In large measure China's economic aims appear to be simply those of normal commerce. Cotton and cobalt might have been bought elsewhere, but it was convenient to buy them from Africans. If China purchased maize from South Africa, as is widely believed, it was done for economic reasons; the political cost was high.[17]

In hindsight, however, although some profit-minded Chinese entertained an interest in African resources in the early and mid-1960s, by the end of the decade these so-called "Capitalist Roaders" were almost certainly in grave trouble or desperately hiding such tendencies. China's nominal dollar denominated world trade (aided by a falling dollar) increased only modestly during the active phase of the Cultural Revolution, from almost $3 billion in 1966 to $3.8 billion in 1971. During the 1960s and 1970s oil and minerals did not figure prominently in China-Africa trade relations and one Sinologist correctly estimated that such "strategic materials" would not become important for some time.[18]

The Pre-Reform Period, 1972–1977

Although China-Africa trade rose rapidly in the pre-reform era, it still grew slower than China's total global trade and thus fell as a percentage of China's world trade. From $3.8 billion in 1971, China's total trade rose sharply to $11.9 billion in 1974 and $13.1 billion in 1977. The large increase in China's total foreign trade (measured in U.S. dollars) during this period was mainly driven by three factors unrelated to Africa: increased domestic stability at the end of the Cultural Revolution's active phase, rapprochement with the West, and U.S. dollar depreciation throughout the early 1970s. Even after taking inflation into account, however, China's trade in 1974 was roughly 75 percent higher than four years earlier.[19] A surge of capital imports from the West reduced the importance of Africa as a trading

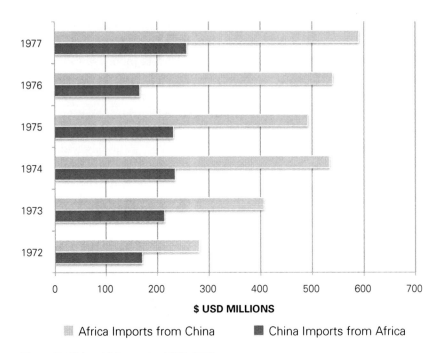

Figure 7. China-Africa trade, 1972–1977.

partner for China in the early reform period. China-Africa trade fell from
$769 million in 1974, to $724 million in 1975, and $707 million in 1976.
As a result, from 1974 to 1977 African trade made up an average of about
6.5 percent of China's total world trade, compared to an average of 9 percent from 1970 to 1973.

During this period Chinese trade went from scarcely important to Africans to even less so. In 1972, Africa's trade with China made up 1.6 percent
of its total world trade and that fell to below 1 percent in 1974, 0.8 percent
in 1975, and 0.75 percent in both 1976 and 1977. At the time, Africa was a
much larger part of the global economy than China. In 1974, bolstered by
high commodity prices, Africa's foreign trade totaled over $83 billion, seven
times more than China's $11.9 billion. By 1977 the gulf had widened; Afri-
ca's total trade was $111.2 billion while China's lagged at only $13.1 billion.

China's focus on importing capital goods from the West, including
whole factories, overwhelmed China-Africa trade during the pre-reform
period. In 1973, Beijing began what one U.S. government publication called

its "Great Leap in Machinery and Equipment Imports." Amid the relative calm and stability of the pre-reform period, China sought to improve its capital stocks through increases in state-directed foreign trade. During the Cultural Revolution, capital had been neglected or destroyed and now the country was rebuilding. China's imports of machinery and equipment jumped from $860 million in 1973, a fifth of total imports, to $1.6 billion in 1974, a quarter of total imports, to $2.2 billion in 1975, a third of imports.[20] In 1976, for instance, China's imports from Africa totaled $167 million, far less than one $200 million deal with Rolls Royce for fifty jet engines and a plant to produce them. China's citizens were poor and its economy was undeveloped, making it unable to absorb imports from Africa or elsewhere. Although Africa ran trade deficits with China throughout this period, China's large capital purchases from the West produced trade deficits with the rest of the world totaling $224 million in 1973 and $1.3 billion in 1974.[21]

In the mid-1970s, China's leaders viewed the West's resource purchases from Africa with scorn. Although by this time nearly all African countries were independent, France, England, Germany, and the United States still dominated Africa's foreign trade.[22] China's response came in Vice Premier Deng Xiaoping's 1974 speech before the UN General Assembly in which he condemned Western nations for working to "exploit other countries economically, plundering their wealth and grabbing their resources."[23] Beijing's position on the resource trade would gradually change during China's Reform Era.

The Reform Era, 1978–1999

In the late 1970s, two decades of economic stagnation, widespread rural poverty, and public disenchantment required a reorientation of China's economic priorities. Development was prioritized in the 1980s and 1990s and Chinese people were told to get rich, leading many to turn to networks in Hong Kong, Southeast Asia, and the West, or to new entrepreneurial opportunities at home. Between 1978, when China officially started its economic reform and opening-up policies, and 2000, the country's foreign trade grew 23-fold, from $20.7 billion to $474.4 billion. By contrast, over the same period Africa's total trade grew at a much slower pace, going from $122 billion to $287 billion. This pattern was particularly apparent as

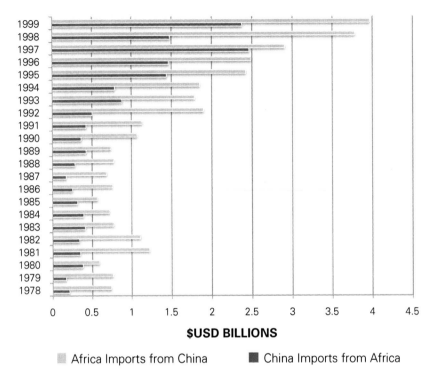

Figure 8. China-Africa trade, 1978–1999.

commodity prices fell during the 1980s. While Africa's world trade fell from
$213 billion in 1980 to $197 billion in 1990, China's expanded from $37
billion to $117 billion, a 316 percent increase.

Trade with Africa was deemphasized while China built commercial links
with overseas Chinese communities in Asia and the West. Large government investments in transportation and communications infrastructure
during this period required technology and know-how so China's new
"open door" policies facilitated growing trade ties with the capital-rich
West, not capital-poor Africa.[24] China-Africa trade, in turn, remained
unimportant for both Chinese and Africans in this period. In 1978, China-
Africa trade was $914 million and, buoyed by a surge in Chinese exports,
rose to about $1.5 billion in both 1981 and 1982. But after peaking in
1981–1982, China-Africa trade fell throughout the mid- to late 1980s and
only regained nominal 1983 levels in 1989. Trade also fell as a percentage

of both sides' total world trade. In 1977, Africa represented 6.5 percent of China's total foreign trade; by 1980, African trade accounted for only 2.6 percent and that percentage continued to fall steadily until bottoming out at about 1 percent in 1987 and 1988. China-Africa trade remained between 1 and 2 percent of China's total trade until 2000. Similarly, trade with China made up less than 1 percent of Africa's total trade through the 1980s and remained below 3 percent until 2000.

One major reason for the decline of China-Africa trade both in nominal and percentage terms during the 1980s was the reorientation of China's economic development strategy. Throughout the decade China built its state-coordinated approach to international trade. China's leadership focused on gradually introducing market forces into the domestic economy. The oft-repeated mantra "liberate the productive forces," notes Richard Baum, "was used to justify the gradual dismantling of China's centrally planned economy." The state was trying to get out of its own way and to give firm managers enough room to make profitable business decisions without giving up the power to determine a company's strategic objectives or, when deemed necessary, direct its behavior.[25] Local authorities retained day-to-day control over provincial and municipal level enterprises, while the Ministry of Commerce maintained regulatory authority over their overseas business transactions.[26] Administrative decentralization, liberalization of the state material allocation system, corporate profit retention, and the creation of both private and mixed-ownership companies with foreign firms were among the policies designed to both increase accountability among firm managers and identify foreign markets. One U.S. Commerce Department report published in 1982 summarized these trade policies:

> As a developing economy, the need to import is China's main reason for expanding its foreign trade. China will continue to import technology and equipment, however, the Chinese now consider the importation of turnkey projects an inefficient, costly way of acquiring technology. Complete plant imports, therefore, are likely to be kept to a minimum.[27]

In strategic material sectors like minerals and petroleum, China sought to both improve competiveness and reassert state authority. State-run corporations dealing in essential products were restructured to improve their access to world markets. However incomplete, these changes gave company managers more control over purchasing decisions, which, in turn, allowed them to trade more freely than ever before. More market forces were introduced into these sectors in the 1990s, yet the state retained final authority.

In the 1990s, China became a manufacturing powerhouse and developed its multipronged, state-driven approach to strategic resource acquisition in Africa. China-Africa trade grew quickly from $1.4 billion in 1990 to almost $10 billion in 2000. Despite this sizable nominal increase, however, China went from representing less than .75 percent of all African foreign trade in 1990 to only 3.5 percent in 2000, making it still a minor trade partner for most African countries. China's domestic investments in manufacturing capacity, new industries, and infrastructure during the 1990s demanded sizeable raw material imports. To get at them, China's "going out policy" (*zuo chuqu zhengci*) encouraged resource-related companies and exporters to find profitable investment opportunities and new markets in Africa and elsewhere.[28] Meanwhile, China's expanding manufacturing capacity and economies of scale allowed its exporters to begin supplying a steady stream of affordable consumer goods to African markets. These exports allowed China to enjoy trade surpluses with Africa every year from 1978 to 1999, despite its growing imports. Together, China's increasing demand for raw materials and ability to produce affordable consumer and capital goods became the dual catalyst for the unprecedented rise in China-Africa trade in the following decade.

The FOCAC Decade, 2000–2010

Almost every year since the FOCAC framework's adoption, China-Africa trade, although relatively small, has grown. Yet, unlike during the Cultural Revolution (when China's international isolation and U.S. dollar devaluations inflated the relative value of African trade to China), this rise reflects increases in China-Africa trade even amid a vast expansion of China's global trade and a generally stable Yuan to dollar exchange rate. The numbers are extraordinary: China-Africa total trade grew from $6.3 billion in 1999 to $128.5 billion in 2010, a 20-fold increase. This steep rise in nominal U.S. dollar terms was temporarily reversed as commodity prices fell in 2008 and 2009, but returned apace in 2010. As a percentage of China's total trade, Africa has gone from 1.8 percent in 1999 to more than 4.3 percent in 2010. While over the same period as a percentage of Africa's total world

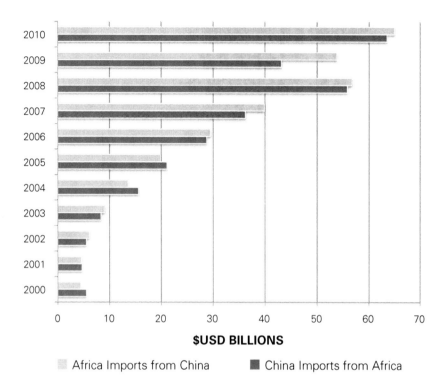

Figure 9. China-Africa trade, 2000–2010.

trade China has gone from 2.6 percent to almost 13.3 percent, its highest level ever. Even as China-Africa trade fell in 2008 and 2009, it continued to rise as a percentage of Africa's total world trade from 10.7 to 12.4 percent respectively.

The seeds of this unprecedented surge in China-Africa trade—China's demand for raw material inputs and export markets for its products—that were planted in the Chinese economy in the 1980s and 1990s thrived during the FOCAC era. During this period, China's exporters have rapidly expanded access to African markets and purchased increasing supplies of critical raw materials from Africa. China continues to create powerful economies of scale that attract capital and large pools of skilled and unskilled labor. The combination of top-quality capital stocks, cheap labor costs, and government incentives and infrastructure construction resulted in heretofore unseen economies of scale that granted China's industries a

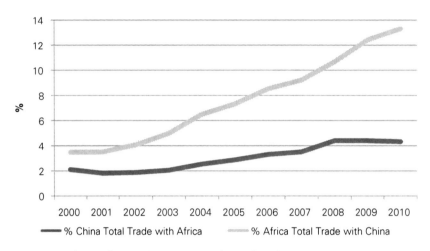

Figure 10. China-Africa trade as percent of overall trade, 2000–2010.

comparative advantage over those of nearly all African countries in both capital and labor intensive production. Massive round-the-clock production kept costs down and allowed razor-thin profit margins to sustain entire export industries. African markets have become awash in China's cheap, mass-produced textiles and consumer electronic goods. One IMF working paper described the trade pattern: "Strong growth of the Chinese and African economies, together with the complementary trade pattern—China imports fuel and other commodities, Africa purchases investment and manufactured products from China—largely explains their surging trade in recent years."[29]

Relative factor endowments of labor, capital, and resources substantially determine China-Africa trade patterns as well as the unique patterns of each African country's trade with China. The result is a generally balanced China-Africa trade relationship when all fifty-four are taken together, but important differences emerge when the data are disaggregated. On a country-by-country basis, the balance of trade between China and resource exporters tends to favor the African country, meanwhile, China's exports dominate its commerce with nonresource-exporting African trade partners. Comparing China's trade with Egypt and its trade with Libya—both tightly controlled autocracies until 2011—helps illustrate the role factor endowments play in determining China-Africa trade patterns. In both cases, China's comparative advantage in consumer goods and capital equipment

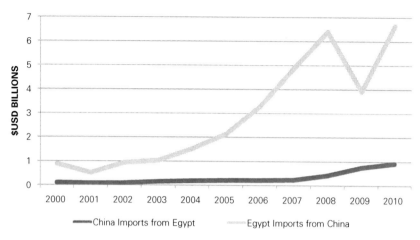

Figure 11. China-Egypt trade, 2000–2010.

drives steep growth in exports. Yet, the presence of oil in Libya resulted in a Libyan trade surplus, while the lack of resources in Egypt has led to a severely imbalanced trade relationship in China's favor. These graphical displays are indicative of the stark split in China's balance of trade generally observed between resource-exporting and non-resource-exporting African countries.

African countries with few resources usually endure large trade deficits with China (e.g., Benin, Egypt, Ethiopia, and Liberia) while resource exporters enjoy surpluses (e.g., Angola, Republic of Congo, the Democratic Republic of Congo, Libya, and Gabon). This pattern reflects the dichotomous nature of China-Africa trade. China's exports are diversified, that is, each category accounts for a small piece of total trade; by contrast, African exports to China are generally concentrated in a narrow band of primary products. Since 2005, China's top four import categories from Sub-Saharan Africa—mineral products, base metals (including oil), precious stones and metals, wood products—make up 90 percent of its total purchases. By 2009, nearly 80 percent of China's exports from Africa were metals and petroleum products. Since 2000, crude oil has made up over two-thirds of Africa's total export value to China. Iron ore and platinum are also important African exports to China.[30] Responding to this structure, Alhaji Babamanga Tukur, president of the African Business Roundtable and chairman of the NEPAD Business Group, told a visiting Chinese delegation in June 2008

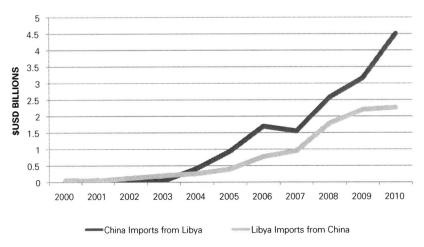

Figure 12. China-Libya trade, 2000–2010.

"that China does not have a proper trade structure in Africa" and expressed concern for "raw materials being removed from the continent for factories in Asia."[31]

China is the world's largest copper consumer, and has made sizable purchases from African producers such as Zambia and the Democratic Republic of Congo. In Zambia, for instance, Chinese copper investors provided the lion's share of the $100 million invested there between 2001 and 2005 and continued to be very active throughout the decade (see Zambia country section).[32] By 2005, China consumed roughly one-third of the total global production of steel, 40 percent of cement, and 26 percent of copper.[33] Between 2000 and 2005 China was also one of Africa's primary markets for illicit timber and ivory exports. In the wake of the deadly 1998 Yangtze River floods, China imposed new domestic logging restrictions, pushing Chinese firms to increase imports from African timber suppliers. Between 1998 and 2005 Chinese timber imports from African nations such as Liberia and Gabon grew and with them China's role in the black market timber trade. The secretive nature of black market timber and illegal ivory imports make them impossible to accurately calculate, but the availability of both resources on the Chinese market and expert testimony confirmed a robust trade in the first half of the decade.[34] In the last half of the decade, however, China appears to have significantly reduced its black market timber imports from Africa.

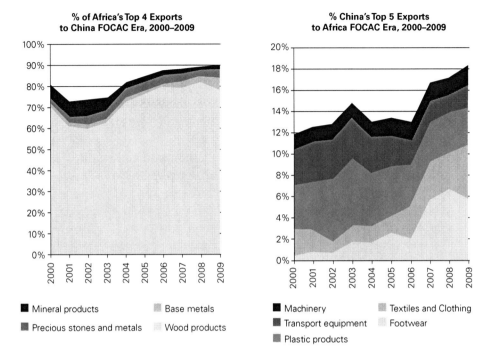

% of Africa's Top 4 Exports to China FOCAC Era, 2000–2009

Mineral products
Precious stones and metals
Base metals
Wood products

% China's Top 5 Exports to Africa FOCAC Era, 2000–2009

Machinery
Transport equipment
Plastic products
Textiles and Clothing
Footwear

Figure 13. Structure of China-Africa trade in the FOCAC era. Based on a study of detailed PRC trade data conducted by the Trade Law Centre for Southern Africa, TRALAC, Stellenbosch, South Africa.

Oil producers Angola, Nigeria, and Sudan were three of China's top five African trading partners in 2008, 2009, and 2010, and each is also a large market for Chinese exports. The BP Statistical Review of World Energy 2011 reports that from 2009 to 2010 alone China's oil consumption increased 10.4 percent, 860,000 barrels per day. "China's growth is spectacular," said one BP executive. "It is now the world's largest energy user as well as the largest producer of energy and the largest emitter of carbon dioxide."[35]

China's economies of scale and subsidies to manufacturers for power, fuel, garbage collection, and other materials and social services have made it nearly impossible for African manufactured products to enter its markets. China's manufacturing capacity and economies of scale supply a steady stream of affordable Chinese consumer and capital goods for the domestic market and for export to African markets. This trend looks set to continue as African consumers, businesses, and governments snap up Chinese products. Since 2000, China's exports of textiles to Sub-Saharan Africa have increased considerably, although a large portion of these imports are smuggled in and thus remain unaccounted for in official trade statistics.[36] Chinese sales to African countries were also highly diversified in the consumer goods sector, ranging from cell phones to T-shirts. African imports from China include a range of consumer and industrial products, transportation equipment, and machinery. The top twenty products China exported to Africa in 2009 were only 36 percent of its total exports to Africa, and its top five accounted for only 18 percent of total exports to African countries.[37] The prior year, the top twenty exports from China to Africa represented 35 percent of its total exports and the top five export products from China (machinery 10 percent; textiles and clothing 4 percent; transport equipment 4 percent; footwear 2 percent; and plastic products 2 percent) represented 21 percent of Africa's Chinese imports.[38]

China's financing and construction of rail and road networks both at home and in Africa allow Beijing to exert influence over the destination of exports and the location of its suppliers. Throughout the 1990s and 2000s, China invested heavily in shipping and port construction for supersized cargo shipping fleets. In 2011, Dar es Salaam, Tanzania, became the first port of call for the world's biggest car and truck megaship, which docked on its way from Dalian, China. The vessel can carry 8,000 vehicles per voyage and make the trip from China to East Africa in two weeks, shaving one-third off the previous shipping time.[39] Like countless other megaships, this one now makes monthly voyages from China to and from African ports. This shipping capacity and speed has catalyzed the growth of China-Africa trade over the last decade. However, as with other parts of the world, the rapid inroads made by Chinese producers and merchants have increased tensions. In some African countries there is growing concern about trade deficits, export competition, intellectual property rights infringement, and poor quality Chinese goods.[40]

Although a boon for Chinese producers and African traders and consumers, the patterns of China-Africa trade also inhibit African countries from getting a foothold in labor-intensive manufacturing, the first rung of the development ladder. "It is possible to build an unequal relationship (between China and Africa), the kind of relationship that has developed between African countries as colonies. The African continent exports raw material and imports manufactured goods, condemning (it) to underdevelopment," South African President Thabo Mbeki said in 2006.

China's Relations with African Regional Organizations

Africa has several regional organizations each with its own unique economic or political mandate. China works closely with some while minimizing interaction with others. Over the last decade China has preferred to engage those regional African organizations whose mandates include a significant economic and trade component. China has emphasized relations with the Common Market for Eastern and Southern Africa (COMESA), the Southern African Development Community (SADC), and the Economic Community of West African States (ECOWAS).

China's fast-growing interaction with these three organizations remains an underexamined aspect of the China-Africa trade relationship. Compared to case studies of China's bilateral trade relations with large African countries such as South Africa, Nigeria, and Angola, relatively little has been written about China relations with African regional organizations. The prevalence of widespread multinational production and trans-shipping in Africa, however, argues for a regional approach to examining contemporary China-Africa trade. In 2007, about two-thirds of world trade involved multinational corporations, whether intrafirm trade or transactions in intermediate goods; the latter has risen more rapidly than trade in final goods.[41] This is also true in the resource sector. COMESA, for instance, recognizes that "arrangements for importation of copper into China are such that the country of origin may be masked due to third country importation transactions."[42]

Regional organizations offer competition and scale effects, but sometimes red tape and corruption undermine their effectiveness. African organizations with a mandate for regional trade promotion remain limited due to their small economic size relative to their large geographic area. They are also inefficient because some African countries are members of more than one organization, resulting in overlapping and inconsistent rules of origin, tariff schedules, and implementation periods. According to Harry Broadman, they sometimes hinder China-Africa trade because they "engender complications of customs administration and delays in customs processing, eventually driving up the cost of trade."[43]

COMESA

China's relationship with COMESA is longer and better established than its relations with any other regional African organization. COMESA began in 1978 when the ministers of trade, finance, and planning from its prospective member countries adopted the Lusaka Declaration of Intent and Commitment to the Establishment of a Preferential Trade Area for Eastern and Southern Africa (PTA). COMESA established the PTA to take advantage of a larger market size with the ultimate objective to create an economic community. The agreement created a subregional preferential trade area among nineteen eastern and southern African countries, which, in 1993, became a common market.[44] COMESA's objectives are to "create a fully integrated and internationally competitive region where goods, services, capital, labour and persons move freely," "create an enabling environment for foreign, cross border and domestic investments business," and "contribute towards realization of the African Economic community by 2025."[45]

Beginning in the late 1990s, COMESA's business-first approach to regional integration helped China's trade with member states grow steadily. In 1999, China was one of only four non-COMESA countries to book space at the COMESA trade exhibition in Kenya.[46] That year, the China Import and Export Bank signed an export credit agreement with COMESA's Trade and Development Bank of Eastern and Southern Africa (PTA Bank) and in 2000 the People's Bank of China joined the PTA Bank's leadership. This deal made China the PTA Bank's biggest shareholder outside the region and gave it a representative on its board of directors. A COMESA delegation followed up with trade talks in Beijing in 2001.[47]

China-COMESA trade grew quickly over the last decade as China worked to secure more predictable market access to the trade bloc's members.[48] In 2005, China's newly appointed special representative to COMESA met with the organization's Secretary General Erastus J. O. Mwench in Zambia, who described the relationship's underpinnings: "China is a major consumer of some raw materials we found in COMESA, like copper and oil. And we believe China has got the technology that we could be looking at, like in telecommunications, industry and agribusiness."[49]

On behalf of COMESA, Mwench called for a "trade agreement where we can identify specific products" that COMESA members can trade with China.[50] In response to this and similar requests from other African officials to expand African countries' higher value added imports, China's Ministry of Commerce granted special preferential tariff treatment to select goods in 2005. Under this program, China's General Administration of Customs cut tariff rates for Africa's poorest twenty-five countries on 190 products to zero and established rules of origin and operational procedures of certification and verification; the initial list was later expanded to 454 products.[51] Deborah Brautigam—noting that about three-quarters of the products on the list are low-value manufacturing goods (e.g., vehicle spare parts, bicycles, soap, plastic products, leather wallets, cotton fabric, T-shirts, umbrellas, ball-point pens, and table lamps)—wrote in 2009: "There is a clear correspondence between these items, and China's domestic restructuring plans. China's government wants its companies at home to move up the value-chain."[52]

A 2007 report on the effects of China's tariff-free entry program by COMESA's statistics bureau found that in 2005 China's tariff-free imports from COMESA stood at $474 million, an impressive 470 percent increase since 2001. Yet only twenty of the 454 products identified under China's program in 2006 accounted for over 97 percent of China's tariff-free imports from COMESA. Copper from Zambia alone made up 32 percent of China's tariff-free imports, the largest single share that year, while cobalt, also from Zambia, accounted for 6 percent. Both metals were also sourced from Zambia's neighbor, the DRC. China's tariff-free commodity imports included Egyptian marble, 5 percent, and sesame seed from Ethiopia and Sudan, which accounted for 23 percent and 12 percent, respectively. Although COMESA claims its members have a comparative advantage over China in several additional product groups (e.g., cotton, salt, sulfur, skins, coffee, tea, fish, and crustaceans), they could not gain a foothold in China's markets. Rather than manufactured goods, China's tariff-free program has attracted more resource exports from COMESA member countries.[53]

In 2009, responding to this problem, COMESA Secretary-General Sindiso Ngwenya called for China to expand economic activity beyond raw materials to diversify trade with COMESA countries and build domestic production to "take advantage of COMESA's access to the European market."[54] China, however, seems satisfied with the current trajectory of its trade with COMESA. On the heels of COMESA's 2009 summit, Li Qiangmin, special representative to COMESA and ambassador to Zambia, called COMESA "the largest economic institution in Africa" and said efforts to harmonize member countries' customs duties "will promote the bilateral trade between China and Eastern and Southern African countries. There is a great potential to expand the trade." Yet, Li also cautioned COMESA countries to avoid over-enthusiasm and identified several constraints that limited their trade with China, including their relatively lower development level, smaller market shares, limited purchasing power, and absence of a leading economy like South Africa.[55] To overcome these problems in 2011, Special Representative to COMESA Zhou Yuxiao vowed "China's continuous contribution to the building of the Great COMESA-SADC-EAC Free Trade Zone."[56]

SADC

China-SADC trade has developed a pattern akin to China-COMESA trade. SADC, like COMESA, also traces its roots to the early 1980s but was formally established in the early 1990s.[57] The China-SADC relationship began in 2002 at the SADC Consultative Conference when China's Vice Minister of Foreign Trade and Economic Cooperation, Wei Jianguo, succeeded in lobbying the organization to pass a vote that "stressed the need to strengthen the relations between China and SADC." The Communiqué of the 2002 SADC Consultative Conference also noted that China had lent its "support to SADC in its pursuit of economic development agenda." The 2002 Communiqué also encouraged Chinese companies and enterprises to take part in the development of the economies of SADC countries.[58]

The China-SADC relationship accelerated in 2004 when newly elected SADC Chairman Paul Berenger (then prime minister of Mauritius) declared: "it is my intention during my tenure as chair to give a new dimension to relations between SADC and China."[59] A year later, Premier Wen Jiabao also called for the continuous strengthening of China's relations with SADC.[60] This statement was quickly followed by an article in the *People's Daily* touting SADC as "the most promising regional organization in Africa." The CPC mouthpiece applauded SADC for "providing for cross-border investment and trade, and freer movement of factors of production, goods and services across national boundaries."[61] In 2007, China appointed Ding Xiaowen, China's ambassador to Botswana, as "permanent representative to SADC." In a statement SADC welcomed Ding and called for "enhancing cooperation between China and SADC."[62]

Between December 2007 and December 2008, there was a 65 percent increase in SADC exports to China and a 34 percent increase in SADC imports from China.[63] The dollar value of China-SADC trade fell in 2009, dragged down by falling commodity prices, although both rebounded in 2010. In 2011, the SADC-China Trade Fair and Investment Forum was scheduled for Johannesburg, South Africa, but was canceled on short notice "due to the unexpected withdrawal of previously committed support" forcing Chinese participants, including twenty-one Chinese mining firms, to cancel their trips.[64] Soon afterward, however, China hosted the China-SADC Business Forum in Beijing with over two hundred entrepreneurs from China and SADC countries. At the opening ceremony, Vice Premier Wang Qishan said: "China has become an important trading partner and a source of investment in the SADC region. We are ready to further expand imports from SADC countries, and encourage Chinese enterprises to invest there." SADC President Hifikepunye Pohamba and China's President Hu Jintao also agreed to increase trade during their 2011 meeting.[65]

ECOWAS

In 1975, fifteen West African leaders assembled in Nigeria to sign the ECOWAS Treaty and to accelerate economic integration.[66] A revised ECOWAS Treaty in 1993 made "the achievement of a common market" an ECOWAS objective. China, however, has regularly balked on engaging ECOWAS on trade, preferring, instead, to focus talks on investment and address trade issues directly with ECOWAS member states. China's access to ECOWAS members' markets may well have improved by working directly through member states rather than ECOWAS, which suffers from inadequate coordination of trade policies and tariff and nontariff barriers among its member states. In 2010, for instance, *People's Daily* reported the bloc's "deliberate breaching of the full implementation of the sub-region's protocol on free movement of persons, goods and services."[67]

ECOWAS, like COMESA and SADC, seeks to increase economic integration among its members, however, China's relationship with ECOWAS has developed slower than its relationship with the other two.[68] Although China recognizes that ECOWAS contributes to regional peace and development, the bloc has done little to contribute to the expansion of Chinese exports to ECOWAS countries.[69] Before 2004, Beijing engaged with ECOWAS only on political issues. No major China-ECOWAS meetings took place in 2005 or 2006, although this did not appear to harm China's exports to ECOWAS member countries, which continued to rise steadily during this period.[70] During the run-up to the 2006 China-Africa FOCAC Summit, Mamadou Tandja, then chairman of ECOWAS and Niger's president, called on China to "find and acknowledge the existing deficiencies in the trade relationship."[71] Support for the expansion of the China-ECOWAS trade talks also came from Mohamed Ibn Chambas, president of the ECOWAS Commission, who said that West Africa had a lot to gain from expanded trade with China and called for the elimination of ECOWAS trade barriers on Chinese products.[72] At the 2006 FOCAC Summit, both sides agreed to hold a China-ECOWAS Business Forum, which they did in 2008. That "forum focused on investments in infrastructure, exploitation of natural resources, agriculture, banking and other services," but did not mention trade.[73]

In the run-up to the 2008 China-ECOWAS Business Forum, trade topped ECOWAS member states' concerns. Christian Adovelande, president of the ECOWAS Bank for Investment and Development, signed a Memorandum of Understanding with the secretary general of the little-known China Optimization Society of Capital Construction "for the establishment of an ECOWAS Purchasing Centre in China as well as a Chinese Wholesale Market in the various countries of the ECOWAS region." Although ECOWAS called the project "the first step towards promoting ECOWAS-Chinese trade cooperation," China's press appeared to ignore it. It appears that little came of the agreement since ECOWAS later issued a press release calling for another MoU on "the establishment of an ECOWAS official market in China and a Chinese wholesale market in West Africa [to] facilitate access to products from West Africa in China and Chinese products in the region."[74] Nigeria's *This Day* newspaper echoed this sentiment when it reported that the China-ECOWAS forum "came amidst fears by some stakeholders over cheap and inferior Chinese products."[75]

At the 2008 China-ECOWAS Business Forum, Chambas, who led the ECOWAS delegation, called for regular trade meetings to boost collaboration between China and ECOWAS, but that idea, and the idea of establishing an ECOWAS market in China, were not approved. Discussions about market access for ECOWAS' trade goods were entirely absent from Chinese reports on the forum.[76] Other than an agreement to hold the forum annually, which does not appear to have been upheld in 2009 or 2010, the China-ECOWAS summit's constructive outcomes were largely investment related.[77] They included a "comprehensive" set of MoUs between ECOWAS and CCPIT to "provide the linchpin for attracting Chinese private sector investment into strategic sectors of the West African economy." Sectors singled out for investment included agriculture, livestock, forestry, food processing, training, real estate, engineering, and infrastructure development.[78]

In 2011, a delegation led by ECOWAS Commission President James Victor Gbeho met with CCPIT and Ministry of Commerce officials, among others, in Beijing. The talks focused on infrastructure investment rather than trade, although Gbeho did invite China to become the first non-ECOWAS member state to participate in the ECOWAS Trade Fair; he did not receive an answer.[79]

5

Investment and Assistance

China's Investment Strategy, Tactics and Goals

Chinese overseas investment is a relatively new phenomenon. Beginning in 1979 and continuing until 1985, only state-owned corporations and provincial and municipal international economic and technological cooperation enterprises could invest outside China. Beijing had a strict approval system for outward investment projects. China liberalized the system between 1986 and 1991, allowing more enterprises to apply for permission to establish subsidiaries in other countries. From 1992 to 1998, there was a major expansion in overseas investment by local and provincial enterprises. In the early 1990s, China identified Africa as a key market for development and began establishing trade and investment centers in a number of African countries. The precursor organization to the Ministry of Commerce issued in 1993 a four-part strategy to help Chinese companies strengthen Sino-African trade and investment. First, China identified Africa's natural resources as vital to the development of China's economy. Second, China saw Africa's large population as an important potential market for Chinese consumer goods. Third, African countries had become increasingly attractive to China for mineral prospecting, construction projects, and use of Chinese labor. Fourth, China identified several African countries as key targets for profitable long-term investments.[1]

China consolidated its "going out" strategy beginning in 1999, when it encouraged its firms to expand abroad. China offered as incentives easy access to bank loans, simplified travel procedures, and preferential policies for taxation, imports, and exports.[2] In 2000, China formalized its support for investment in Africa in its Programme for China-Africa Co-Operation in Economic and Social Development, which encouraged guarantees for investment and an improved investment environment.[3] China's 2006 African Policy Statement emphasized support for investment by Chinese enterprises in Africa while it welcomed African investment in China. Beijing agreed to facilitate investment protection agreements and those that avoid double taxation.[4] The Beijing Action Plan reiterated these points, noted the holding of the Second Conference of Chinese and African Entrepreneurs during the 2006 Beijing summit and the establishment of the China-Africa Joint Chamber of Commerce and Industry. China also announced creation of the China-Africa Development Fund (CADF).[5]

Companies that have majority government ownership, known as state-owned enterprises (SOEs), undertake most Chinese investment in Africa by dollar value. They tend to engage in the resource sector, infrastructure, and construction. Companies run by Chinese provincial and local jurisdictions also invest in Africa, with the province often twinned with one or more African countries.[6] As much as one-quarter of Chinese investment in Africa originates from companies in Chinese provinces, many of them SOEs at the provincial or local level.[7]

In 2006, China's Export Import Bank said there were about 800 Chinese companies in Africa, approximately 85 percent privately owned. By the end of 2009, the number had increased to 2,000; in 2011 China's vice minister of commerce reported 4,600.[8] Most private Chinese firms are small and medium enterprises (SMEs). They tend to work with the Chinese diaspora in Africa and usually have weak links with local African firms. They are fiercely competitive among each other but often co-locate in industrial parks for mutual support and coordinated production. Their head offices are highly concentrated in the coastal provinces of Zhejiang, Guangdong, Fujian, Jiangsu, and Shandong.[9] A few companies such as Huawei Technologies are technically private but have close ties to the government. Huawei, active throughout Africa, is a designated "national champion" that works closely with the military and other state actors and their research institutes. It receives lines of credit from state banks and funding for research and development.[10] Huawei employs more than 2,500 people in about forty African countries.

When Chinese firms enter new markets in Africa, they often build new facilities, create businesses that are vertically integrated, buy supplies from China rather than locally, and tend to sell to government entities.[11] Much of the investment is in the form of joint ventures; Chinese firms generally hold a majority equity stake in order to control the operation. China invests in any country, even those considered as pariahs by the West. China's bidding strategy also benefits from lower costs for labor and capital equipment, fewer managerial expenses, and slimmer profit margins compared to Western companies. Many Chinese companies are willing to take losses and support prestige projects to gain market entry or share and to support government policies.[12] Chinese companies have traditionally been willing to take more risk than Western companies by operating in conflict areas such as southeastern Nigeria, the DRC, Ogaden region of Ethiopia, and Darfur and Kordofan provinces in Sudan.[13] Most African governments welcome Chinese investment, especially following the decline in Western investment after the end of the Cold War. Chinese companies also invest in infrastructure, manufacturing, and agriculture, areas that have been avoided in recent years by private Western companies.

There are numerous motives behind Chinese investment in Africa. Profit maximization, even in the case of SOEs, is probably most important. Market saturation in China and the availability of idle equipment have caused some companies to go abroad. The government encourages companies to open new markets and to use foreign market access to circumvent trade barriers by foreign countries. China did this in the case of textile production in Africa in order to enter U.S. markets after passage of the Africa Growth and Opportunity Act. Investments in Africa may also permit Chinese companies to take advantage of regional or international trade agreements. Although rarely acknowledged by Beijing, China often uses investment to secure access to raw materials and natural resources. Chinese investment may be a way to obtain advanced Western technology and modern manufacturing techniques. China's investment in BP's deep water block off Angola is a case in point. Risk diversification and government incentives are additional reasons for investing in Africa. There is a strong connection between Chinese investment in Africa, its efforts to expand exports, and its foreign assistance program.[14]

Chinese companies have learned that the most important factor for success is linking up with a suitable local partner. They prefer an investment environment where the government plays a significant role in investment activities. In identifying potential projects, a major Chinese consideration is market demand and business orientation. Chinese technology, although not the most advanced, is frequently appropriate and adaptable to African countries. In some African countries, Chinese companies have encountered problems such as political instability, limited market size, a shortage of skilled workers, rigid foreign exchange regimes, and unfavorable tax treatment. Chinese companies have worked closely with Chinese communities in those African countries where they exist such as South Africa, Mauritius, and Madagascar.[15]

Companies from Hong Kong and Macau play important investment roles in certain countries. This has been thoroughly documented in the case of Hong Kong's investment in Angola.[16] Hong Kong investors are particularly active in Madagascar and Mozambique. Guinea's controversial military government, in an effort to demonstrate international support, announced in 2009 a $7 billion Chinese investment in exchange for minerals. The deal originated with the Chinese International Fund, a joint Chinese-Angolan venture based in Hong Kong. China's Commerce Ministry claimed to know nothing about the arrangement.[17]

Although Chinese companies in Africa are working to improve their corporate behavior and social responsibility, this is an area that Africans continue to criticize. The complaints include inadequate attention to worker safety, failure to comply with minimum wage laws, minimal attention to environmental concerns, unwillingness to train African workers, and unfair investment practices.[18] Chinese investment in the copper fields of Zambia, for example, caused enough complaints that the opposition political party used them as a campaign issue against the government party in national elections. China has learned, however, to adapt to legitimate criticism. As the global financial crisis resulted in the laying off of workers in Zambia, for example, China's special representative on African affairs, Liu Giujin, urged Chinese companies in Zambia to avoid layoffs. In 2008, researchers with the Chinese Academy of Social Sciences (CASS) assessed corporate social responsibility (CSR) conditions at Chinese firms in Mali, Ethiopia, and Sudan. The report recommended more attention by the Chinese government to a variety of problems.[19] CSR has become a higher priority in China and was part of the agenda at the 2009 FOCAC in Egypt.[20]

Measuring Chinese Investment in Africa

Measuring China's foreign direct investment (FDI) is an art rather than a science. The two official sources of China's FDI are the Ministry of Commerce and the State Administration of Foreign Exchange; neither publishes data on Chinese financial institutions' FDI in Africa. Official Chinese statistics do not fully capture China's FDI. The distinction between trade credits, development cooperation, project financing by Chinese financial institutions, and direct investment by Chinese enterprises is rarely clear. China's companies rely heavily on retained earnings and informal arrangements rather than capital markets and bank borrowing to finance investments.[21] These reasons help explain the wide disparity between official FDI statistics and larger figures cited by Chinese scholars and even some officials. China's FDI to Africa remained modest until 2004, when it increased significantly and has been growing rapidly ever since.

Drawing on China's official statistics, UNCTAD calculated China's cumulative FDI to Africa in 1990 at $49 million. By the end of the 1990s, China had invested $820 million in forty-seven African countries. By the end of 2005, UNCTAD placed China's cumulative investment at $1.6 billion.[22] Premier Wen Jiabao stated that China's total investment in Africa reached $6.27 billion by the end of 2005. Vice Minister of Commerce Wei Jianguo and the *China Commerce Yearbook for 2007* increased the FDI figure at the end of 2006 to $11.7 billion. The Ministry of Commerce put the figure at $13.5 billion at the beginning of 2007. Wen Jiabao stated, however, that total direct investment in Africa totaled only $7.8 billion at the end of 2008. Hong Kong accounted for another $5.3 billion. While China's official FDI figure for Africa at the end of 2009 was $9.33 billion, senior CPC official Li Changchun said it was more than $30 billion.[23] To put China's figure in context, global FDI flows to Africa peaked in 2008 at $72 billion before declining in 2009 to $59 billion, with developed countries providing most of the investment.[24]

There are no obvious explanations for the discrepancies in Chinese FDI figures. The figures may be based on different definitions of FDI or reflect a gap between commitment and disbursement of funds. In recent years, for example, Chinese companies announced investments of $2.7 billion in Nigerian oil blocks and $2.4 billion in Angolan blocks, and the Industrial and Commercial Bank of China purchased a 20 percent stake of South Africa's Standard Bank for $5.5 billion.[25] The larger cumulative FDI figures reflect more accurately the state of China's FDI in Africa.[26] While recent Chinese FDI is impressive, an estimated $1.3 billion in 2009 alone, it falls well behind that of the United States and major European countries. China accounted in 2007 for about 3 percent of total FDI in Africa, up from less than 1 percent in 2003. About 4 percent of China's global FDI went to

Africa in 2008. China's global outward FDI increased significantly in 2009, while the figure for Africa fell back to less than 3 percent as compared to 13 percent for Latin America and more than 70 percent to Asia.[27] While these percentages are based on China's overly conservative official FDI totals for Africa, they do reflect the small portion of China's total FDI.

China has provided FDI to forty-nine of fifty-four African countries. It is common for companies from a particular Chinese province or municipality to focus their FDI in specific African countries. Guangdong has been the largest source of FDI to Africa, followed by Shanghai, Shandong, Beijing, Jiangsu, and Zhejiang. By the end of 2009, the largest amounts of Chinese FDI according to official statistics had gone in descending order to South Africa, Nigeria, Zambia, Sudan, Algeria, and Egypt. All these countries except Egypt are major energy or mineral producers while Egypt is a gateway to North Africa and the Middle East. By 2010, China had signed bilateral investment treaties with thirty-three African countries and agreements on avoiding double taxation with eleven countries.[28]

Chinese Investment Promotion Institutions

China has created a variety of investment promotion institutions. Most of them operate globally; a few focus exclusively on Africa. They are of relatively recent origin and varying effectiveness. Collectively, however, they underscore a serious commitment by the government of China to encourage investment throughout the world and specifically in Africa. Chinese investors in Africa have traditionally relied on low-interest loans from state-owned banks. With the sharp increase in Chinese private sector investment in Africa, state financial institutions are beginning to be stretched and are urging companies to seek commercial lending.[29]

Beijing established the China Development Bank (CDB) in 1994 primarily to promote development within China. Although the percentage of loans going outside China is growing slowly, it remained below 5 percent in 2008. In 2009, the CDB issued a $1.2 billion line of credit to Angola for agricultural development over four years. By late 2009, the CDB had financed twenty-seven projects in eighteen African countries totaling $2.15 billion. It also opened an office in Cairo. The CDB is the principal source of funding behind the CADF.[30]

Created in 2007, CADF encourages Chinese enterprises to conduct trade and economic activities in Africa. It began with investment equity of $1 billion; it is scheduled to rise to $5 billion. CADF has a fifty-year mandate limited to Chinese companies and African joint venture partners. This effectively ties the investment to Chinese enterprises. CADF does not hold controlling stakes in any project and limits holdings to between 10 and 50 percent. It operates on market economy principles and assumes sole responsibility for profit and loss. It can make investments in any manner permitted under Chinese state policy and can invest a proportion of its capital in other funds that invest in Africa. CADF provides management, consulting, and financial advisory services for Chinese enterprises. Targeted industries include agriculture, manufacturing, infrastructure, natural resources, and industrial parks.[31]

CADF investments include a ferrochrome plant in Zimbabwe (with Sinosteel), a glass factory in Ethiopia (with CGC Overseas Construction), a power station in Ghana (with Shenzhen Energy Investment), and a cotton project in Malawi, Mozambique, and Zambia. CADF signed a deal in 2010 with the China National Nuclear Group to examine and exploit uranium resources throughout Africa. Most of the investments have been in the range of $5 to $25 million. As of 2010, the CADF agreed to invest about $800 million in thirty projects in Africa and disbursed between $300 and $400 million. CADF opened offices in South Africa, Ghana, and Ethiopia; it plans to open others. CADF is one of the first Chinese funds to insist on an environmental assessment for its investment projects. It emphasizes entrepreneurial opportunities in a wide range of sectors where Africans in the private sector can engage with their Chinese counterparts. It cooperates with Ecobank and Standard Bank of South Africa and is in discussion with the World Bank and African Development Bank. CADF also supports the principles of the New Partnership for African Development (NEPAD).[32]

China's sovereign wealth fund, the China Investment Corporation (CIC), offers the potential for investment in Africa. Launched in 2007 with $200 billion in capital, its assets grew to about $300 billion by the end of 2008. Jesse Wang, CIC vice president, noted that the corporation will move cautiously into Africa because of concerns about political risks and an immature legal system. World Bank President Robert Zoellick has encouraged the CIC to invest in the World Bank's new asset management company, which invests private sector funds in Africa. This could result in investments in debt restructuring, equity investment, health care, and the financial sector. Zoellick said the CIC has expressed interest in investing in a new International Finance Corporation program to acquire and restructure distressed debt in developing nations. The World Bank welcomes China's investment in Sub-Saharan Africa because it has the potential to build infrastructure, create jobs, and increase opportunities in the manufacturing sector.[33]

The China Export and Credit Insurance Corporation (SINOSURE) began operations in 2001. It supports Chinese exports and investment abroad by insuring against buyer and country risks such as foreign exchange restrictions, expropriation, nationalization, and war. Its business volume reached $30 billion in 2006, although Africa received only 3 percent of its short-term insurance. Africa accounted for 29 percent of its medium- and long-term business, second only to Asia.[34] The China-Africa Business Council (CABC) began operations in 2005 with support from the United Nations Development Programme (UNDP), China's Ministry of Commerce, and the China Society for Promotion of the Guangcai Program, which links the CPC and the private sector and has more than 16,500 member private companies. The CABC encourages these companies to pursue the "going-out" strategy in Africa. It organizes business missions to Africa and receives African commercial delegations. It provides information on establishing joint ventures and research for trade and investment. It remains to be seen how effective it will be in promoting private sector investment in Africa.[35] The CCPIT and the Union of African Chambers of Commerce, Industry, Agriculture and Professions established the China-Africa Joint Chamber of Commerce and Industry in 2006. It is intended to strengthen investment promotion, information sharing, technology transfer, legal consultation, and business publishing between Africa and China.[36] This organization does not appear to have been particularly effective so far.

China promotes SMEs in overseas markets through the Small-Medium Enterprises International Market Development Fund. China has more than forty million SMEs, which account for 99 percent of Chinese companies and 60 percent of Chinese exports. SMEs with export volume below $15 million are entitled to apply to this fund for up to a maximum of $100,000. Support is linked to the size of the investment and is generally limited to about $10,000.[37] It is not clear if this fund has been useful to Chinese companies investing in Africa. In 2010, the Ministry of Commerce launched the China-Africa Research Center, a think tank designed to increase trade and investment with Africa. The think tank is under the auspices of the Chinese

Academy of International Trade and Economic Cooperation, a subsidiary of the ministry. It opened with ten senior researchers and is expected to double that number in the next two years.[38]

Distribution of Chinese FDI by Sector

Allowing for enormous discrepancies in the cumulative total of Chinese FDI to Africa, a comprehensive UNCTAD study provided the most detailed information on where most of this investment has gone by sector. By dollar value between 1979 and 2000, 46 percent went to manufacturing (mainly textiles, light industry, home appliances, and machinery), 28 percent to resource extraction, 18 percent to services (mainly construction), 7 percent to agriculture, and 1 percent to miscellaneous.[39] There has been no subsequent Africa-wide study on the sector distribution of Chinese FDI. There are, however, many subsequent country investment case studies and much anecdotal information. By most accounts, there has been a major shift during the twenty-first century of Chinese FDI toward resource extraction, especially oil and minerals, telecommunications, and banking.[40]

While there has been a move away from Chinese investment in manufacturing and toward resource extraction, manufacturing remains the predominant investment sector in a number of countries. According to a summary of case studies, 90 percent of Chinese investment in Côte d'Ivoire in 2000–2007 went into manufacturing, 66 percent in Ethiopia, 92 percent in Ghana, 50 percent in Sudan, 63 percent in Uganda and 87 percent in Zambia.[41] China's large investment in petroleum in Sudan and copper in Zambia raises doubts about some percentages.

One important and potentially significant Chinese effort for encouraging investment and trade in Africa has been the development of Special Economic Zones (SEZs), also known as free trade zones, export processing zones, industrial zones and free ports. Originally proposed by Deng Xiaoping in 1978 as a way to develop China, they have become part of China's investment program in Africa.[42] The zones are private initiatives based on profit calculations. The Chinese government provides guidance and support but private developers manage the projects. China agreed at the 2006 FOCAC in Beijing to establish three to five of these zones in Africa and announced the first SEZ for Chambishi at the center of Zambia's Copperbelt region. China committed $800 million in investment credit for its companies to join the project. The key investment is a $250 million copper smelter. China agreed to a second SEZ in Mauritius in order to consolidate its trade and investment in the Indian Ocean area. This project is under construction and expected to attract $750 million in Chinese FDI over five years.

China is supporting two zones in Nigeria—the Guangdong Ogun Economic and Trade Cooperation Zone and the Lekki Free Trade Zone. Construction is underway on the Suez Economic and Trade Cooperation Zone in Egypt. Scheduled for completion in 2018, its goal is to attract $293 million from more than fifty companies over the next ten years. China is establishing the Eastern Industrial Park in Ethiopia and a second zone in Zambia. It agreed to locate an economic and trade cooperation zone in Algeria, which has been suspended due to changes in Algeria's foreign investment laws. China understands that SEZs in Africa will look different than those in China and even vary significantly in concept from one location in Africa to another. One similarity will be the introduction of competition, international cooperation, and incentives from local government. Africans look to the SEZs to help redress growing trade deficits with China. The Director General of Tanzania's Export Processing Zones Authority, Adelhelm Meru, explained that "instead of just mining and bringing its domestic laborers, Chinese investors need to add value and make more efforts to train local residents to create jobs."[43] SEZs in Africa have encountered some challenges and early evaluations are mixed. While it is too early to judge their success, SEZs have attracted considerable interest in Africa.[44]

The World Bank estimated the 2001–2007 Chinese investment in the oil sector for Sub-Saharan Africa at about $7.5 billion with Nigeria accounting for $4.8 billion and Angola $2.4 billion. This study showed zero investment in Sudan; the head of Sudan's investment office told the authors it is estimated at $5 billion. World Bank investment figures for oil alone in Sub-Saharan Africa nearly equal Wen Jiabao's total of $7.8 billion for all Africa at the end of 2008. The World Bank estimated China invested an additional $3.1 billion in the mineral sector during the same period, mainly for chromium, copper, bauxite, cobalt, iron, diamonds, coal, and nickel. The primary recipients were South Africa, Zambia, Zimbabwe, DRC, Nigeria, and Eritrea.[45]

The major Chinese investors in Africa's oil sector are the China National Petroleum Corporation (CNPC), the China National Offshore Oil Company (CNOOC), and China Petrochemical Corporation (Sinopec). As of 2006, CNPC had invested in nine African countries, Sinopec in six, and

CNOOC in three.[46] The web of ties among multinational companies complicates the task of explaining China-Africa investment relationships. For example, Sinopec International Petroleum Exploration and Production Corporation (SIPC), a wholly owned subsidiary of Sinopec, acquired Addax Petroleum in 2009 for $7.2 billion. This constituted the largest takeover so far of a foreign company by a Chinese company. The acquisition of Addax Petroleum provided China with producing oil assets and reserves of undetermined value in Nigeria, Cameroon, and Gabon.

Chinese investment in Africa's agricultural sector has received more attention than it deserves because of charges, usually inaccurate, that China is grabbing land in Africa to feed its own people. To some extent, China created this problem for itself. There were discussions several years ago with countries like Mozambique for leasing large tracts of land. For the most part, these discussions did not reach agreement or China realized these deals were politically explosive and abandoned the proposals. In 2007, China's Export Import Bank head Li Ruogu commented that many African countries had plenty of land and urged Chinese farmers to move to Africa. Li added there is no harm in allowing Chinese farmers to become farm owners in Africa, and he said the bank would fully support such migration.[47] Such comments added to African concerns about China's intentions.

China has a long history of agricultural aid projects in Africa; investment in agriculture is a more recent development. Some of the media attention devoted to this subject fails to distinguish between China's agricultural cooperation and its less frequent investments in agriculture. In 2008, the China State Farm Agribusiness Corporation operated at least eleven agricultural projects on about 40,000 acres in Zambia, Mali, Guinea, Ghana, Mauritania, Tanzania, Togo, Gabon, and South Africa. Some of these qualified as aid projects. Zambia has at least twenty-three Chinese farms representing an investment of $10 million. They all provide food for the local market. In 2007, ZTE signed an agreement with the DRC for a 247,000 acre palm biofuels project.[48] In 2010, Sudan granted ZTE about 25,000 acres to cultivate wheat and maize. Ethiopia allowed China to grow sesame seed, a major Ethiopian export to China. This may be a rare case where production goes to China.[49] There are villages that employ equal numbers of Chinese and Africans in Nigeria, Kenya, Zambia, Uganda, Senegal, and Sudan that host between 400 and 2,000 Chinese farmers.[50]

China grows about 95 percent of the food it consumes and feeds 20 percent of the earth's population on only about 8 percent of the world's arable land. Looking forward, this is cause for concern. In the context of a global food crisis and serious food price inflation in China, the Ministry of Agriculture in 2008 prepared a document that argued China would not be able to maintain its own food security, and that it should secure land acquisitions overseas. This resulted in a sharp response from some officials that land acquisition overseas was not a feasible food security strategy due to logistics and political risk. By the end of 2008, the National Development and Reform Commission announced a twenty-year food security strategy that explicitly stated foreign land acquisitions would not be part of the strategy.[51]

A number of Chinese officials subsequently discouraged the idea that China has any interest in acquiring land in Africa to grow food for Chinese. Xue Guoli, a senior official in the Ministry of Agriculture trade promotion center, said it is neither realistic nor politically acceptable for China to grow grain in Africa for shipment back to China.[52] Qian Keming, director for market economics in the Ministry of Agriculture, noted that China will continue to meet its food shortages by importing from major agricultural exporters such as the United States rather than buy farmland outside China. He emphasized the political and economic downsides of foreign land purchases.[53]

While China will face an increasing food security dilemma in the coming decades, stated government policy is to minimize leasing of land in Africa or elsewhere to feed Chinese. China's investors, however, will almost certainly pursue attractive agricultural investments in Africa as a business for satisfying local demand.[54] An example of what may be increasingly China's approach to agriculture in Africa was the five-year agreement signed by Tanzania and China in 2010 whereby China will encourage its firms to invest in aquaculture and livestock projects.

As Chinese trade and investment have increased in Africa, so has China's need for an improved understanding of African markets and access to more financing options. Chinese corporate customers prefer to deal with Chinese banks in Africa or African banks that have partnered with Chinese banks. The growth of China's SMEs in Africa has been an added incentive for Chinese banks to expand their operations. The global financial crisis has also caused China to play a more assertive role in international finance by suggesting alternatives to the U.S. dollar in international trade transactions.[55]

Direct Chinese involvement in African banking is a relatively new phenomenon, although the Hong Kong and Shanghai Banking Corporation established a presence in Africa in 1981 through acquisition of a controlling interest in Equator Bank, which focuses primarily on trade finance.[56] In 2007, the CDB signed a purchase agreement and cooperation memorandum with Barclays Bank. It paid $3 billion for a 3.1 percent stake in Barclays' existing share capital. Barclays has a strong presence in African trade finance.[57] It is also a majority shareholder in South Africa's Absa Bank. Both banks teamed with China's Export Import Bank to advise clients about African investment opportunities by Chinese SOEs.[58]

The 2007 decision by the Industrial and Commercial Bank of China (ICBC) to purchase 20 percent of South Africa's Standard Bank for $5.5 billion made China an important player in African banking. This was the largest foreign investment ever in South Africa and ICBC's biggest investment outside China. Standard Bank is Africa's largest in terms of assets and has offices in seventeen African countries and twenty-one countries outside Africa, including China. The deal gives Standard Bank access to capital from Chinese investors and deposits from Chinese retail and corporate customers. ICBC gains access to information about local credit conditions, defaults, and retail consumer behavior.[59] ICBC did not demand a portion of financial control or require pledges for financial change. One Western banking expert said the deal was a sign that Chinese bankers are willing to treat Africans as peers.[60] Standard Bank CEO Jacko Maree commented in 2010 that ICBC involvement is "overwhelmingly positive" and the Chinese bank has been an extremely good partner.[61] ICBC and Standard announced in 2008 creation of a $1 billion resource fund primarily for investing in the mining and energy sectors in China and Africa; sixty deals in Africa were under discussion by the end of 2009.[62]

The China Construction Bank (CCB) and the Bank of China (BOC) opened branches in Johannesburg in 2000. The CCB primarily offers merchant, wholesale, and investment banking products and services to the South African business community. Its operations are expanding rapidly. In 2009, the CCB signed an agreement with FirstRand Bank that permits both banks to identify new investment opportunities. The immediate goal is to provide joint advisory and structuring services to the CCB's clients looking to expand in Africa. The BOC focuses on trade, energy, mining, real estate development, and telecommunications.[63] The BOC established a single branch in Zambia in 1997. Ten years later, it had become the eighth largest bank in Zambia.[64] Nigeria's United Bank of Africa (UBA) announced in 2007 a partnership with the CDB. Ecobank and the BOC signed an agreement in 2010 that provides for the establishment of a China desk in one or more of Ecobank's subsidiaries permitting Chinese staff to assist BOC customers in Africa.[65] China Union Pay, the only domestic credit card organization in China, has established agent relationships with banks in South Africa, Mauritius, and Kenya, increasing the number of ATM outlets.[66]

China has a banking connection with Lusophone Africa through Geocapital, an investment company based in Macau. Geocapital has a small bank in Guinea-Bissau and holds 49 percent of the shares of Moza Banco in Mozambique. The bank opened in 2008 with an initial capitalization of $10 million and a focus on investment banking. Chinese financial institutions have not yet penetrated French-speaking Africa.[67]

One area where China has been slow to invest is the development of airline service from China to Africa. As of 2011, at least five African airlines had regular flights to China, but Air China had no service to Africa. Dragonair code shares with China Southern Airways on service to Lagos. Hainan Airlines provides service to Khartoum, Cairo, and Luanda.[68]

An Evaluation of Chinese Investment in Africa

The movement of Chinese corporations into Africa is a relatively recent development. There were fewer than 80 in 1988. The number has increased exponentially. The companies tend to be young and employ more staff than their competitors. Chinese SOEs have a longer term perspective than their Western counterparts. China encourages strategic investment and emphasizes long-term over short-term profitability. The government provides cheap credit and has established a number of institutions to support the flow of FDI to Africa.[69] China is even beginning to take advantage of the World Bank's private sector arm, the International Finance Corporation (IFC), to finance projects. In 2010, the IFC for the first time agreed to finance a Chinese investment in Tanzania.[70]

A mutual learning process is underway for the Chinese SOEs and private companies and for governments in China and Africa. African governments and private individuals are still coming to terms with the different practices and approaches to business that diverse Chinese companies bring to the table.[71] It is important to distinguish between the corporate nature of the company and the amount of support it receives from the Chinese government as it invests overseas. It is not surprising, for example, that a senior official with ZTE, a large SOE that sells telecommunications equipment and has offices throughout Africa, told African journalists that the success of Chinese companies was due in large part to the strong support of the Chinese government and financial institutions.[72] China is also more focused on country risk assessment and has developed a global guide that provides detailed descriptions of African investment environments.[73]

The African Center for Economic Transformation (ACET) in Accra, Ghana, in an analysis of Chinese FDI in Africa concluded that Chinese investment has the potential to assist economic transformation through technology transfer. As evidence it cited the impact of telecommunications projects by ZTE and Huawei. ACET documented the actual and potential for employment creation as a result of Chinese FDI and noted that it is going to nontraditional sectors such as agriculture, manufacturing, and infrastructure. Chinese investment has also helped African manufacturing integrate economies into global supply chains and diversify African exports. On the negative side, ACET argued that Chinese FDI emphasizes projects that do not build local capacity or expertise, and investment in manufacturing has been erratic. Chinese investment emphasizes retail, general trading, and textiles, which has led to the displacement of African companies. Cheaper Chinese imports make domestic substitutes relatively more expensive. Finally, Chinese investors are often accused of unfair labor practices and harsh working conditions.[74] On the other hand, China is paying increasing attention to meeting some of the principles of corporate social responsibility.

African Investment in China

As of 2011, there was far more Chinese FDI in Africa than there was African FDI in China. We feel confident in making this claim despite China's State Council figures that said as of the end of 2009 African countries had $9.93 billion of FDI in China compared to $9.33 billion of Chinese FDI in Africa. Mauritius, South Africa, Seychelles, Nigeria, and Tunisia are the principal African investors in China. Mauritius has traditionally accounted for most African investment in China; it exceeded $1.3 billion as of 2007. Mauritius has a double taxation agreement with China and permits outsiders to invest in a Mauritian wholly owned foreign enterprise that can, in turn, invest in

China. South African investors account for the single largest amount of African FDI in China. China's official statistics almost certainly do not capture all of it. In 2007, China recorded $654 million in cumulative South African FDI.[75] In 2008, South Africa's Deputy Minister of Foreign Affairs estimated South Africa's investment in China at $700 million, close to the official Chinese figure.[76] In 2007, however, South African specialist on China-South Africa relations, Martyn Davies, suggested the figure was closer to $2 billion.[77] Individual African countries tend to concentrate investment in a single province or municipality, suggesting there is an effort to pair African countries with Chinese regions and municipalities.[78]

Little research has been done on African investment in China and most of it deals with South Africa. SABMiller has invested more than $400 million in the Chinese consumer goods sector since 1994 through China Resources Breweries. The joint venture, known as CR Snow, is the largest brewer in China by sales volume and brewing capacity with a 19 percent market share. By 2014, China will account for 45 percent of SABMiller's growth.[79] Kumba Resources invested in a zinc smelter in China. South African mining companies, Gold Fields and Anglo Gold Ashanti, purchased shares in Chinese gold companies. Anglo American holds $150 million worth of shares in China Shenhua Energy, China's largest coal producer. Standard Bank has an East Asian operation based in Hong Kong. South African paper producer, Sappi, and a number of other companies have investments in China. Tunisian and Chinese investors established a joint venture to produce fertilizer in China. One particularly interesting project is a 2004 letter of intent between South Africa's Sasol, the world's largest producer of synthetic fuels, and a consortium of Chinese companies to develop a coal-to-fuel conversion program. It has the potential to be a multibillion dollar project.[80]

Assistance: The Principles and Evolution of China's Aid to Africa

The PRC view of development during the Maoist period emphasized the need to get rid of colonial control and to implement national construction. The unjust and inequitable international economic order was the main cause for underdevelopment, according to the PRC, and had to be eradicated. During the development process, a country needed to consolidate its national independence and safeguard its sovereignty. The new order should be rebuilt on the basis of sovereignty and self-reliance.[81] The PRC linked its foreign aid policy to the "Five Principles of Peaceful Coexistence" discussed in Chapter 2. China charged that severe conditions and demands for a variety of privileges characterized aid from the "imperialist" countries. The PRC claimed it never provided assistance in its self-interest nor did it regard recipient countries as markets for Chinese commodities.[82] Premier Zhou Enlai spelled out China's "Eight Principles" of foreign aid during a visit to Ghana in 1964.[83] China continues to cite these principles as an integral part of its aid policy.

China put the most altruistic face possible on its assistance to Africa. Like the major donor countries, however, China's aid was primarily an important foreign policy tool. It used the aid to counter both the influence of Western countries in Africa and, during the Sino-Soviet conflict, the Soviet Union's growing involvement on the continent. It was also used to convince African countries to recognize diplomatically Beijing rather than Taipei. This continues to be a rationale for Chinese aid to Africa even though only four African countries recognize Taiwan. Much early assistance, especially military aid, went to African liberation movements, which supported China's worldview and desire to change the superpower-dominated world order.[84]

There have been various analyses of the evolution in China's assistance to Africa. It is instructive to look at three of them, all of which identify three phases in Chinese aid policy. The "official" Chinese account prepared by Yuan Wu for the 2006 FOCAC in Beijing dated the first phase from 1956 to 1978. China's assistance to Africa began with Egypt in 1956. Yuan described this period as one in which China designed and planned the aid project, shipped and assembled the equipment, sent experts to explain its use, and provided follow-up. African countries then took control of the completed project. The most famous project during this period was the Tanzania-Zambia railway.[85] Li Xiaoyun at the China Agricultural University said the first phase occurred from 1950 to 1974. He described it as a period of "ideology exportation" whereby aid went largely to socialist African countries.[86] Deborah Bräutigam, who confined her analysis to Sub-Saharan Africa, identified 1960 to 1976 as the first phase, which she called the Maoist period. Guinea was the first Sub-Saharan recipient of Chinese aid. The most important factor was a country's willingness to recognize Beijing rather than Taipei.[87]

Although China's view of development and its foreign assistance principles evolved over time, strong elements of its early philosophy permeated subsequent phases. China's outspoken criticism of Western aid began to disappear as Western countries normalized relations with China. In 1983, at the end of a visit to eleven African countries, Premier Zhao Ziyang made an important statement on foreign assistance in Tanzania, at the time Africa's largest recipient of Chinese aid. Zhao announced "Four Principles on Sino-African Economic and Technical Co-operation." Zhao's "Four Principles" emphasized mutual benefit and no political conditions, practical results, diversity in form, and common development. He said China would stress cooperative projects, joint ventures, and Chinese bidding on projects funded by African governments, third party foreign donors, or international organizations.[88]

China's Vice Foreign Minister for African Affairs Gong Dafei accompanied Zhao to Africa when he enunciated his "Four Principles." Gong added that the PRC would no longer repeat big projects like the Tanzania-Zambia railway or the Nouakchott port in Mauritania. It would favor instead smaller agricultural projects, small processing industries, textile mills, road construction, stadiums, and people's palaces. As China reduced its assistance to Africa and focused on its own economy, Gong insisted that African leaders would understand Beijing's position. He promised that China would gradually increase economic assistance to Africa.[89]

In a study of PRC foreign assistance published in 1984, Law Yu Fai explained that the aim of China's aid was to help Third World countries develop their national economies independently and self-reliantly. China designed aid projects that encouraged autonomy and self-reliance of the state. China's goal was to provide self-sustaining or turn-key projects and encouraged low-cost and easily operated projects that benefited the poorest people. China emphasized basic health services, self-sufficiency in food production, relatively simple technology, and proposals that usually included a training component. China usually monitored the projects after completion.[90]

The "official" analysis placed the second phase of China's aid policy between 1978 and 1995 when China claimed to combine aid with mutually beneficial cooperation for common advancement. Examples were a cement factory in Rwanda and textile plants in Burundi and Benin that brought profits and taxes to the recipient governments. Li Xiaoyun described phase two as a period of adjustment and transformation between 1974 and 1990 when aid to Africa declined and China attended to internal modernization. Deborah Bräutigam identified 1977 to 1989 as the reform phase, noting that China had begun to establish a market economy. China's decentralized economic development strategy empowered officials at the provincial and municipal levels. While Chinese aid levels declined, SOEs became more common and active in Africa. This was the "diversity in form" that Premier Zhao Ziyang mentioned in 1983.[91]

The third phase of China's aid policy, according to the "official" version, began in 1995 and continues to the present. China retained grant aid and concessional loans but introduced promissory loans with interest paid by the Chinese government and stepped up joint ventures. China combined aid with investment and foreign trade to facilitate the entry of Chinese companies in Africa. Examples were loans for oil prospecting in Sudan, forest development in Equatorial Guinea, and a farm machinery assembly factory in Côte d'Ivoire. Li Xiaoyun dated this phase from 1991 and called it financial aid and technical assistance with integrated objectives. Chinese aid increased globally, especially to Africa, and emphasized mutual and economic benefits, integration of political interests, and the new obligations of a "big country."[92]

Bräutigam chose 1990 as the beginning of phase three and called it economic cooperation for mutual benefit. She noted that the 1989 Tiananmen Square crisis and reinvigorated "checkbook diplomacy" in Africa by Taiwan caused China to reassess its aid policy. China also became concerned about the deterioration of some previous aid projects that had been turned over to African governments. Providing subsidies for Chinese exports and the need to access natural resources became part of the assistance strategy. China looked to its Development Bank, Export Import Bank, and Agriculture Bank as government tools to engage in projects where Chinese commercial banks were reluctant to go. In visits to Africa in the last half of the 1990s, Premier Jiang Zemin and Premier Li Peng explained that China's policy had moved from providing aid to economic cooperation for mutual benefit.[93]

In 2000, China issued a white paper on development assistance. The document contained a few remnants of Maoist era ideology, for example, a reference to the "present unjust and inequitable world order." It urged a new strategic partnership for sustainable development in the twenty-first century and listed five principles of cooperation: equality and mutual benefit, diversity in form and content, emphasis on practical results, pursuit of common progress, and amicable settlement of differences. The first four were a repetition of Zhao's "Four Principles"; the last one was new to China's aid policy. Increasingly, however, China's policy began to reflect African concerns. Beijing claimed it was promoting local industries, sourcing local materials, and creating local employment. China announced it would increase grant aid while continuing concessional and interest-free loans and increase support for the African Development Bank and other multilateral financial institutions in Africa. China agreed to provide debt relief and cooperate in agriculture, natural resources, public health, and education.[94]

China's 2006 white paper on African policy and its Beijing Action Plan addressed all aspects of China-Africa relations, including development assistance. Both documents offered similar guidelines and policy prescriptions concerning China's assistance relationship with Africa. Both stressed that China would increase support for African agriculture, infrastructure, public health, science and technology, professional training, and scholarship aid. China also agreed to cancel more debt and cooperate on environmental protection and disaster relief.[95]

Wen Jiabao announced at the 2009 FOCAC eight "new" measures China would take to strengthen China-Africa cooperation in the next three years. Most of the eight were a reiteration of past assistance policy. Two, however, qualified as a new focus by China: working with African countries to tackle the challenges of the global financial crisis and climate change.

In evaluating the reasons for China's aid to Africa, it is important to remember that China still faces enormous developmental challenges, including rural poverty where nearly 500 million Chinese live on less than $2 a day. Chinese officials regularly stress to African interlocutors that China is a developing country and that its ability to provide assistance should not be compared to that of traditional donor nations. At the same time, if China's GNP continues to grow at about 9 percent annually while growth rates of the major donor countries remain stagnant, China can be expected to offer an increasingly higher percentage of assistance, including grants, to African nations. China now views its assistance, investment, and preferential trade arrangements as a way to gain access to Africa's natural resources and to build stronger political ties with Africa's fifty-four countries. China's aid is also part of a package to help its companies expand export markets and develop business in Africa.[96]

Measuring China's Aid to Africa

China does not publish annual country aid disbursement figures, which are treated as a state secret.[97] Most statistical information on the value of Chinese aid comes from African governments; there is no consistency to Chinese announcements. Information from African and Chinese sources is not only spotty but often does not distinguish between aid commitments and disbursements. China has a history, at least in earlier years, of announcing aid commitments that were not always disbursed. All Chinese aid figures, especially disbursements, for an individual country over a lengthy period of time are subject to question. There are several continent-wide, country-by-country estimates covering different periods between 1954 and 1996.[98] Since 1996, there has been no individual country account of China's aid to Africa. There are more recent estimated annual totals for Africa, but the data vary considerably.

It is difficult to determine what properly constitutes foreign aid in the Chinese context and how China calculates foreign aid figures. According to the Development Assistance Committee (DAC) of the OECD, grants or concessional loans extended to developing countries constitute Overseas Development Assistance (ODA) when governments use them to promote economic development. China has no official definition of aid and seems to follow a broad interpretation. China may, for example, include trade concessions and the provision of commercial loans to companies that assist a country's development as foreign aid even though they do not involve any donation of funds to another government. On the other hand, the DAC counts the value of debt relief as official aid while China does not. The Chinese Ministry of Commerce has primary responsibility for foreign aid, but the Ministries of Foreign Affairs and Finance play important roles. The Ministry of Social Welfare administers humanitarian aid following natural disasters. The Ministry of Health is responsible for medical teams while the Ministry of Education administers the scholarship program. These ministries do not effectively coordinate foreign aid statistics.[99]

China provides three kinds of aid: grants (in-kind transfers of agricultural products and tangible goods, especially machinery, and occasionally cash), interest-free loans, and concessional loans with subsidized interest rates.[100] China's Export Import Bank manages concessional loans, also known as preferential or low-interest loans. These have accounted in recent years for large loans to a number of African countries. By the end of 2007, the Export Import Bank had approved some 300 loans for African nations valued at nearly $24 billion.[101] In 2007, the Export Import Bank said that it provided concessional loans to Africa with a total outstanding balance of about $8–9 billion.[102] The interest rate is 2–3 percent; the period of repayment is usually fifteen to twenty years, with a grace period of five to seven years.[103] The Bank has a regional office in Johannesburg that covers southern and eastern Africa, one in Khartoum for northern Africa, and one in Paris for Francophone Africa.[104]

Angola has been Africa's major recipient of Export Import Bank loans. Repaid in oil deliveries to China, Angola's first loan of $2 billion had an interest rate of London Inter-Bank Offered Rate (LIBOR) plus 1.75 percent with a maturity date of fifteen years and six months. The second $2 billion loan, also reimbursable in oil, had an interest rate of LIBOR plus 1.5 percent and a maturity date of eighteen years and six months. As of mid-2007, Angola and China had agreed to another $9 billion loan on the same terms as the first loan.[105] While these rates are attractive when compared to commercial loans, they are not concessional.[106]

In 2006, Premier Wen Jiabao stated that China had provided $5.6 billion to African countries since the beginning of its aid program. Many scholars believe this figure is excessively low, especially if the concessionary component of Export Import Bank loans is included. China announced it provided $1.05 billion worth of assistance globally in 2006. Sub-Saharan Africa traditionally received about 44 percent of China's aid and North Africa about 6 percent. This suggests that Chinese aid to Africa in 2006, according to official Chinese statistics, was about $500 million. This figure includes only the concessional part of the interest rate, not the face value of loans extended by the Export Import Bank.[107] Scholars who follow this issue believe global Chinese aid is higher, which means the amount for Africa would be greater than China's announced $500 million in 2006.[108] China's State Council said that 45.7 percent of its global assistance, for which it did not offer a total figure, went to fifty-one African countries in 2009.

One analyst who has studied this issue estimated that by 2009 total Chinese aid to Sub-Saharan Africa had reached $2 billion annually.[109] Another specialist put the total for 2009, including debt relief, at almost $2.5 billion for the entire continent.[110] The African Development Bank concluded in 2009 that China's annual aid to Africa is between $1.4 billion and $2.7 billion, while loans had reached about $8.5 billion.[111] Wen Jiabao announced at the 2009 FOCAC that China would provide $10 billion in concessional loans to African countries and help Chinese financial institutions establish a $1 billion loan fund for African SMEs. Until China is more transparent with its aid figures and the way it calculates the numbers, we are limited to estimates by experts who follow this subject.

Types of Chinese Aid Projects

Over the years China has provided assistance for a wide range of projects in Africa. The four regional chapters illustrate the variety of projects. Areas of engagement have included light industry and manufacturing, mining and natural resource development, transportation infrastructure, power stations, public buildings and stadiums, housing projects, irrigation and water supply, broadcasting stations, agriculture, medical teams, and specialized training in both China and Africa.[112] This section highlights two of the oldest programs—medical and agricultural assistance; the current largest effort—infrastructure; and China's newest initiative—volunteers to Africa.

China began sending basic medical teams to Africa in 1963 with the first one going to Algeria. By 2009, China had sent more than 20,000 medical specialists to forty-four African countries and claimed to have treated up to 240 million patients. In 2009, about nine hundred medical personnel were assigned to about one hundred African hospitals and health centers. The teams typically range in size from twenty to fifty persons. They normally remain for two years and are replaced by a new group. For purposes of recruiting the teams, China has twinned one of its provinces with one or more African countries. The province is responsible for replacing the teams in the countries with which it is paired. They conduct surgical operations, acupuncture therapy, basic health care, and conduct herbal research. Traditional Chinese medicine is often well suited to a continent that has its own form of traditional treatment. They organize long-term and short-term training courses for African medical personnel. After China established diplomatic relations with an African country, sending a medical team was one of the first agreements reached. By all accounts, Chinese medical teams have been highly successful.[113]

Chinese medical assistance goes well beyond the sending of medical teams and reflects China's own experience in establishing a basic health care system in rural areas. China builds hospitals, clinics, and pharmaceutical plants in Africa. It donates medicine, especially antimalaria drugs, and medical supplies. In recent years there has been an emphasis on workshops and training aimed at preventing and treating infectious diseases such as malaria, HIV/AIDS, and avian influenza. China's own problems with Severe Acute Respiratory Syndrome and avian influenza underscore cross-border diseases' impact on political stability. China agreed at the 2009 FOCAC to build thirty hospitals, provide $38 million in free antimalaria medicine, and construct thirty demonstration centers for the prevention and treatment of malaria.

Agriculture has been a staple of China-Africa cooperation beginning with Guinea in 1959.[114] By 2006, China had undertaken about two hundred projects and sent some 10,000 technicians to the continent. Until the late 1970s, most of China's aid to Africa went into turnkey, grant agricultural projects. Some of these projects encountered management problems that resulted in a policy reassessment. From the late 1970s until the mid-1990s, China and Africa emphasized mutually beneficial cooperation and continuing Chinese involvement rather than turning projects over to the recipient country. China also began in the mid-1980s to cooperate on agricultural projects with international multilateral organizations. From the mid-1990s until the present, China has encouraged large Chinese businesses such as China's General Farming Group Company, China's Fishing Company, and China's Animal Husbandry Company to invest in Africa. The projects were either solely owned or joint ventures. Many of the aid projects over the years have consisted of paddy-rice plantations and experimental farms. China has also undertaken cotton, sugar, tea, soy bean, fruit, fish, pig, and chicken farming.[115] As African nations switched diplomatic recognition between China and Taiwan, Beijing and Taipei found themselves inheriting responsibility for an agricultural project, often a rice paddy, initiated by the other country.

Chinese agricultural cooperation in Africa has had a mixed record.[116] While China's more basic agricultural technology generally worked well, African governments often did not maintain the turnkey projects properly and some failed. This caused China to change its approach toward agricultural cooperation with Africa. But even the more businesslike approach has not been a complete success. Beginning in the 1990s, the China State Farms Agribusiness Corporation established projects in five countries—Gabon, Ghana, Guinea, Zambia, and Tanzania. The projects in West Africa involved a bilateral agreement with the host government while those in East Africa consisted of independent investment with no government agreement. As of 2007, the sisal farm in Tanzania failed, although it may be possible to revive the project. Two of the three farms in Zambia were making a profit. Two chicken farms in Guinea had not turned a profit and the project became a big aid project. The animal husbandry operation in Gabon was not a success. The joint venture to grow cocoa in Ghana became politicized by Ghanaians and remained plagued with problems.[117]

Past failures have not dampened Chinese enthusiasm to assist African agriculture. China agreed between 2006 and 2009 to send one hundred senior experts in agricultural technology to Africa, set up ten demonstration centers for agricultural technology, expand agricultural investment, and strengthen cooperation with the Special Program for Food Security of the Food and Agricultural Organization.[118] Senior Chinese officials routinely tout the importance of agricultural cooperation with Africa and their plans to continue this collaboration. Increasingly, however, it involves training, technology transfer, and investment rather than state-to-state aid projects.[119] Wen Jiabao announced at the 2009 FOCAC that China would increase the number of agricultural demonstration centers to twenty, send fifty agricultural technology teams to Africa, and train 2,000 African agricultural technology personnel.[120] Since 2004, China has sent more than nine hundred agricultural experts and technicians to Africa to train 4,200 management officials and technicians and completed fourteen of the agricultural demonstration centers.[121]

Most of China's current assistance to Africa is in the form of infrastructure development. According to one Chinese estimate, infrastructure constitutes 70 percent of all assistance.[122] When analyzing Chinese aid and investment, however, statistics can be misleading. Most Chinese infrastructure projects in Africa are commercial deals with construction done by Chinese companies, usually SOEs. Nevertheless, there often is an aid component when the project is based on a low-interest Chinese loan or the debt for the project is eventually canceled by China. A French government study in 2007 concluded that Chinese companies control over half of the African market for major construction and civil engineering projects.[123]

The World Bank did a survey of Chinese infrastructure projects in Sub-Saharan Africa covering the period 2001–2007. It estimated that Chinese financial commitments for infrastructure projects averaged about $500 million annually in the early 2000s, increased after 2003 to between $1.3 and

$1.7 billion annually, reached $7 billion in 2006, and fell back to about $4.5 billion in 2007. Nigeria, Angola, Ethiopia, and Sudan accounted for about 70 percent of the financing while Guinea, Ghana, and Mauritania were also major recipients.[124]

About 33 percent of these projects involved power, mainly hydro-power.[125] By 2008, China had committed to building twenty-seven dams in nineteen African countries. The projects ranged in cost from a few million dollars to well over $1 billion.[126] Most were noncontroversial, although the recently completed Merowe dam on the Nile's fourth cataract in Sudan has been criticized for possible environmental damage and the displacement of local residents. China's Export Import Bank suspended a loan for the Belinga dam in Gabon after a local environmental group complained that the project would be built in a national park without a public environmental assessment. China recently agreed to build the Gibe 3 dam on the Omo River in Ethiopia. Scientists have expressed concern that the dam will curtail the annual floods and impact negatively the fragile ecosystems of the Lower Omo Valley and Lake Turkana in Kenya. Most Chinese hydro projects have been praised by recipient governments, however, and China has increasingly demonstrated that it is aware of and concerned about their environmental impacts.[127]

Transportation projects, especially railroads and roads, accounted for another 33 percent of infrastructure projects from 2001 through 2007. China's long history of building railroads extended to Africa with the Tanzania-Zambia railway in the 1970s (see Chapter 9). China agreed in 2009 to lend Tanzania and Zambia money to upgrade the system and has committed to massive new railway projects in Nigeria, Gabon, and Mauritania. The other major transportation sector has been road building. In countries such as Botswana, Ethiopia, and Sudan, China nearly has a monopoly on road construction. The most active company has been the China Road and Bridge Corporation.[128]

The information and telecommunications sector was the third most important sector, attracting 17 percent of Chinese financing. Most of this activity represented equipment sales to Africa; only a small component qualifies as foreign aid. Increasingly Chinese institutions such as the Export Import Bank and China Development Bank financed IT projects tied to the purchase of Chinese equipment. ZTE, Huawei, and the French-Chinese joint venture Alcatel Shanghai Bell are the most active Chinese communications companies in Africa. Huawei and ZTE each received a $500 million export credit from the Export Import Bank. Huawei also obtained $10 billion in credit from the China Development Bank.[129] Of the remaining funding for infrastructure, about 17 percent went to general projects. African subregional organizations such as the SADC and East African Community are increasingly interested in attracting financing for regional infrastructure projects. China has begun discussion on some of these requests.[130]

China's newest assistance program, Chinese Young Volunteers Serving Africa, began in 2005 with the assignment of twelve volunteers to Ethiopia. It is an expansion of China's young volunteer overseas service program launched jointly in 2002 by the Central Committee of the Communist Youth League of China and the Chinese Young Volunteer Association. Somewhat similar to the U.S. Peace Corps, volunteers assigned to Ethiopia helped to develop the use of marsh gas, improve physical education, expand information technology, and upgrade medical technology. China sent fifty more volunteers to Ethiopia in 2006 to teach Chinese, assist in public health, engage in rural construction, and teach industrial techniques and cultural development.[131]

Ten volunteers arrived in Seychelles in 2007 where they provided medical assistance and taught music and tourism skills. Zimbabwe received fifteen volunteers the same year. They offered assistance in the fields of medicine, animal husbandry, sports, computer technology, and teaching Chinese. In 2009, Liberia received twelve volunteers. As in the case of the Chinese medical teams, the central government sometimes asks a province, municipality, or organization to provide volunteers for a particular country in Africa. The volunteers for Seychelles came from the Guangzhou Youth Volunteers Association. China also sent a few volunteers to Mauritius and Tunisia. In 2009, the Shenzhen City government began recruiting twenty volunteers for Togo.[132] At the end of 2009, China had 312 youth volunteers in Africa.[133]

Aid Conditionality

Much has been written about China's "no strings" policy of providing aid. It is true that, unlike Western donors and international financial institutions, China does not attach political conditions to assistance, with the reasonable exception that a country maintaining diplomatic relations with Taiwan cannot expect aid from China. China does not link aid to issues such as good governance, human rights practices, and the need for economic policy reform. In fact, drawing on its basic belief in national sovereignty, it expressly opposes such conditions.[134]

It is less clear whether there are more subtle links between China's aid and the policies of African governments toward China. How would China react, for example, if an African country receiving Chinese assistance made critical comments about its policy toward Tibet or its handling of ethnic clashes in Xinjiang Uygur Autonomous Region? African countries, even those that have a good record on human rights, are notoriously silent about any questionable human rights practices in China. There has been no case in recent years where the government of an African country has criticized the human rights situation in China. Some African governments such as Sudan and Zimbabwe are publicly supportive of China's human rights polices just as China supports their policies.[135] As one Chinese official said, "no African aid recipient has ever asked China to impose conditions."[136]

As in the case of most other major donors, Chinese aid to Africa is driven largely by strategic and political objectives, including stronger links with resource rich countries. Chinese aid, in turn, helps to strengthen the position of African governments. This may explain why China emphasizes, among other projects, the construction of government buildings, presidential palaces, parliaments, police headquarters, military facilities, political party offices, and public stadiums. Such a policy does not constitute conditionality, but it is a reminder to the ruling elite that China is helping to keep them in power. It will be a long time before China adopts lending rules similar to those in the West. Ding Xueliang believes China will "always be guided by the strategic importance of the countries seeking loans."[137]

While Chinese aid conditionality may be subtle and subject to interpretation, there is no doubt that most Chinese aid is tied to the purchase of Chinese goods and services. In fact, the only component of China's aid that may be untied is debt relief. Western aid donors follow similar practices. China stated in 1987 that 69 percent of its aid funds were spent on Chinese equipment.[138] An article in a 2004 edition of *Market Daily*, which is associated with *People's Daily*, advised Chinese firms to purchase and import from China as much equipment, technology, and services as possible in connection with concessional loan agreements.[139]

The most controversial aspect of some Chinese-financed projects is the use of Chinese labor in African countries where unemployment is usually high. While China's labor input is sometimes significant, it is important not to generalize about this practice throughout the continent.[140] Angolan law requires that 70 percent of the labor on Chinese-financed projects be performed by Angolans although the percentage has occasionally slipped to 60 percent.[141] One study of four African countries concluded that Chinese companies used local labor for 85–95 percent of the total workforce.[142] In any event, African governments welcome projects implemented by Chinese companies because they are almost always cheaper than those performed by other countries. China offers low labor costs and profit margins. Most Western firms expect a 15–25 percent profit return. Most Chinese firms are willing to accept less than 10 percent and many accept 3 to 5 percent.[143]

Debt Cancellation

Precise figures on Chinese loans are not available, so it is not possible to determine with any precision the percentage of debt that China has canceled. It is also difficult to compare Chinese debt statistics with the Heavily Indebted Poor Country (HIPC) initiative because there is no breakdown by country, maturity, and concessionality of the original debt.[144] Historically, China has not contributed significantly to Africa's debt problem. Many Chinese loans have been interest-free and have had long and even extended repayment periods. China has a history of debt forgiveness to the poorest countries, effectively converting loans to grant aid. African debt to China is a relatively small percentage of its global debt. Chinese debt cancellation comes without policy conditionality associated with the HIPC initiative. As China increases its loans to Africa, however, there are new concerns about the ability of African countries to repay the loans.[145] Many are tied to the shipment of natural resources to China. So long as the price of oil and minerals remains reasonably high, these arrangements should pose no debt repayment problem.

China has a view of debt sustainability that is different from other donors. It considers the economic potential of African countries over the long-term rather than their immediate ability to repay loans, which is the criterion followed by Western donors and international financial institutions. The huge loan to the DRC is a case in point. While the Chinese consider debt sustainability as important, they are more interested in "development sustainability." Chinese loans probably have a positive impact on debt sustainability by stimulating African exports and GNP, but a negative impact by reducing diversification. Some argue that Chinese loan practices lower standards, undermine democratic institutions, and increase corruption, especially in oil rich countries. Assuming this occurs, it would tend to undermine debt tolerance.[146] On the other hand, there is the competition factor of Chinese loans vis-à-vis loans from traditional donors, and the positive impact competition has on promoting African development.[147] China has not canceled the debt of three countries—Gambia, Burkina Faso, and São Tomé and Principe—that switched their recognition from Beijing to Taipei.

From 2000 to 2009, China canceled 312 debts of thirty-five African countries totaling $2.8 billion.[148] In 2006, Assistant Foreign Minister Zhai Jun pointed out that China's loans were a small proportion of the $284 billion dollars Africa owed globally. China said that it intends to cancel interest-free loans that became due by the end of 2005 with all HIPC and lower-developed countries in Africa. In addition, China promised to take an active part in debt relief efforts for Africa within the international multilateral framework. By 2008, China had signed debt cancellation protocols with thirty-two of thirty-three HIPC countries in Africa that maintained diplomatic relations with China, effectively canceling debt that matured at the end of 2005.[149] China offers debt relief on a case-by-case basis rather than on a set of established principles. So far, there is no clear evidence that China is adding significantly to the debt of Africa's poorest countries.[150]

Engagement with Multilateral Aid Organizations

It is estimated that as much as 95 percent of China's assistance is provided directly to recipient governments.[151] As China has become a more important source of foreign assistance, it has engaged more actively with African and international aid organizations, which tend to designate a high proportion of their funding to Africa. China uses its influence in these organizations to encourage a new international political and economic order that emphasizes its view of justice, rationality, equality, mutual benefit, and the rights and interests of developing countries. Reflecting a priority within China, poverty reduction is a major goal of Chinese aid.

The PRC took China's seat at the UN in 1971 and began contributing modestly to some of its specialized agencies as early as 1980. China's annual contribution to the UNDP in the early 1980s was just over $1 million. By

2008, it grew to $28 million. At the same time, China has received far more assistance from the UNDP.[152] Since the early 1980s, China has consistently made small donations to the UN Capital Development Fund, UN High Commissioner for Refugees (UNHCR), and the UN Population Fund. Annual contributions to UNHCR have remained under $1 million.[153] By 1980, China began making small contributions, reaching $1.6 million in 2008, to the UN Industrial Development Program.[154] China has been a modest donor to UNICEF since 1981, but it is also a major beneficiary.[155] China initiated donations to the World Food Program in 1981; they grew to about $1 million in 1998 and almost $10 million in 2008.[156] China joined the International Fund for Agricultural Development (IFAD) in 1980 and began making small donations. It remains a modest donor but is also a recipient of IFAD assistance.[157] China has periodically made limited donations to the Food and Agricultural Organization (FAO). In 2009, it signed an agreement with FAO to establish a $30 million trust fund over three years to help developing countries improve agricultural productivity.[158]

The Republic of China joined the IMF in 1945; the PRC subsequently assumed its membership. China now holds one of the twenty-four director positions. By 2012, its voting share is scheduled to reach 6.1 percent compared to 16.5 percent for the United States.[159] China agreed to invest up to $50 billion in notes issued by the Fund. The IMF's managing director expressed appreciation for China's assistance to help weather the global economic financial crisis, particularly in developing and emerging market countries.[160] This growing engagement by China will diminish the tendency of the IMF to criticize huge Chinese loans to African countries and provide it with greater policy influence over the organization.

China joined the World Bank in 1980, paying initially $136 million for shares in the Bank's capital.[161] By 2009, its subscription reached about $4.5 billion. In 2010, the World Bank agreed to increase China's voting rights to 4.42 percent compared to 15.85 percent for the United States, giving China the third highest voting share. In addition, China held 1.88 percent voting power in the IDA and 1.02 percent in the Bank's private investment arm, the IFC.[162] China was once the World Bank's biggest borrower, mainly to finance rural development. It continues to seek Bank financing, and the Bank wants to remain in China. As China becomes wealthier and a significant donor itself, the Bank is recasting its relationship with China. China's Export Import Bank, for example, has agreed to fund joint projects in Africa with the World Bank.[163] In 2010, the IFC agreed to make its first loan to a Chinese company doing business in Sub-Saharan Africa: $10 million to a joint venture of China Railway Jianchang Engineering Company and a Tanzanian NGO to help finance retail and office building in Dar es Salaam.[164]

China is a founding board member of the Global Fund to Fight AIDS, Tuberculosis and Malaria, which dedicates a significant part of its budget to Africa. As of 2010, China pledged $16 million to the Fund and paid in $14 million. On the other hand, China has benefited significantly from it. China has a commitment from the Fund for $659 million and a funding request that totals almost $2 billion.[165] It is the fourth largest recipient of money from the Fund behind Ethiopia, India, and Tanzania and has received about sixty times more than it has contributed. By comparison, the United States has committed $5.5 billion to the Fund.[166] In 2011, the Fund suspended payments to China on charges of mismanagement by the Chinese Center for Disease Control and Prevention.

China joined the African Development Bank (ADB) and African Development Fund (ADF) in 1985. Following token donations in the early years, China contributed almost $15 million in 1996. By 2009, China had participated in eight replenishments for a total contribution of $486 million. It controlled 1.119 percent of the voting rights compared to 6.498 percent for the United States. In 2007, China hosted the 42nd annual meeting of the ADB Board of Governors and the 33rd annual meeting of the Board of Governors of the ADF in Shanghai. This was only the second time that the ADB convened outside Africa and the first time in Asia. It marked a new stage in China's role as a donor to Africa. China also holds one of the ADB executive director positions.[167]

With the strong support of South Africa, Nigeria, Senegal, and Algeria, the African countries launched NEPAD in 2001. It advanced a comprehensive agenda for a new development partnership with the donor community based on the promotion of peace, development, human rights, and sound economic management for the continent. Although initially aimed at Western donors, China embraced NEPAD at the 2003 FOCAC in Addis Ababa. China signed a memorandum of understanding with the NEPAD Secretariat and agreed to provide long-term training assistance. While the United States and most Western countries have paid lip service to NEPAD, China has more actively supported this concept, whose core assumption is that development is impossible in the absence of true democracy, respect for human rights, peace, and good governance.[168] China decided to accept this

African initiative, which does not reflect priority Chinese development interests, and mold it more to its liking. In 2010, the African Union assumed control of NEPAD by creating the NEPAD Planning and Coordination Agency (NPCA). Whatever the success of the NPCA, China gets credit at very little cost for supporting NEPAD from the beginning.

Evaluation of Chinese Assistance to Africa

China has moved from a minor to an important aid donor in Africa.[169] China puts a premium on support for development because it leads to stability.[170] African governments are particularly pleased with Chinese assistance that supports infrastructure, a sector largely abandoned by Western donors a couple of decades ago, and prestige projects like government ministries, presidential palaces, and stadiums, which the West always avoided. African leaders have long praised China's medical teams. African governments also welcome the absence of political conditionality and have shown no inclination to criticize Chinese assistance to authoritarian governments such as those in the Central African Republic, Equatorial Guinea, Zimbabwe, and Sudan. Even democratic African governments have not criticized Chinese aid that makes no effort to improve governance and human rights. Civil society groups, labor unions, and opposition political parties have been more critical of Chinese aid. Because most Chinese grant aid is in kind rather than in cash, it probably contributes less to corruption. In part for this reason, China seems to prefer project and in-kind assistance.

China, along with other donors, has had its share of marginal and failed projects in Africa. It is, nevertheless, proud of its record and anxious to avoid future mistakes. Although lacking transparency, the Ministry of Commerce says that it has a program for evaluating completed projects. Beijing has established a good record on debt cancellation for Africa's poorest countries. China normally avoids cooperation with multinational donor groups in individual countries unless asked to participate by the host country's government. It has no interest in becoming linked to political conditionality often pursued by other donors. To the extent that China cooperates with other donors, it prefers to do so within the UN system rather than the OECD's DAC.[171] China believes there is more room for influencing UN agencies than the DAC. It has also shown some recent willingness to collaborate with UK and Canadian aid agencies on assistance to Africa. China is reluctant to acknowledge that its assistance is usually tied to Chinese companies and sources of supply and there seems to be no plan to untie this aid. In a study of Chinese economic relations with Africa, World Bank economist Ali Zafar concluded, "Aid is being used principally to facilitate trade and improve access to natural resources."[172]

6

Military and Security Ties
and Peacekeeping Missions

Global and African Security Issues

China's security relationship with select African countries dates back to the 1950s and now extends in some fashion to all fifty African countries that recognize Beijing. It began with Chinese support for African independence movements and several revolutionary groups that opposed conservative African governments. This was part of Mao Zedong and Vice Premier and Defense Minister Lin Biao's doctrine of revolutionary warfare and promoting wars of national liberation around the world.[1] As the African countries gained independence and China's policy became more pragmatic and less ideological, it shifted to arms transfers, contracts for military construction, increased training, and high level military exchange visits. Since the late 1990s, support for UN and African Union peacekeeping operations has become an important part of the relationship. More recently, combating Somali piracy and protecting Chinese personnel and workers in Africa have been added.[2]

China's 2010 white paper on national defense states it "will never seek hegemony, nor will it adopt the approach of military expansion now or in the future, no matter how its economy develops."[3] China has no bases in Africa and insists that it has no intention to establish any, and it has not entered into any formal military alliance with an African country. On the other hand, there is strong evidence that China is seeking to extend its naval reach into the Indian Ocean, including the east coast of Africa, so that it does not have to rely on the U.S. navy to protect the sea lanes that transport so much of its imported oil and minerals from Africa and the Middle East. There is a loose correlation between those African countries that are the main beneficiaries of Chinese military cooperation and those that are major suppliers of oil and minerals to China.

China's security priorities are perpetuating CPC rule, sustaining economic growth and development, maintaining domestic political stability, defending China's national sovereignty and territorial integrity, and securing China's status as a great power.[4] China increasingly emphasizes military operations other than war. It also participates in international security cooperation, encourages military exchanges, and promotes the establishment of military confidence-building mechanisms. China is concerned about risks posed to the global economy by terrorism, energy shortages, environmental disasters, climate change, epidemics, transnational crime, and piracy. China, because of its growing economic and military power, may be pushed by Africans to become more engaged in African security issues. The African Union has urged China to play a more active role. Its ability to maintain a low military profile in Africa is diminishing.[5]

China has applied these global security concerns and policies to Africa. In its 2006 Africa policy statement, China pledged to promote high level military exchanges and to continue training African military personnel. It said it will support efforts by the UN, African Union, and African regional organizations to settle conflicts and participate in peacekeeping operations. China also agreed to work with African law enforcement organizations to combat transnational organized crime, terrorism, small arms smuggling, drug trafficking, and illegal migration.[6] The 2006 paper did not mention Chinese arms sales to Africa. The security component of its follow-up to FOCAC summit meetings has emphasized support for UN peacekeeping, conflict resolution, combating Somali piracy, and cooperation in dealing with natural disasters.[7]

The People's Liberation Army (PLA) is not an independent actor. It must coordinate with the CPC and state bureaucracy, depending on the type of military initiative contemplated and the country with which it is interacting. The PLA's conduct of foreign military relations is a strategic activity by the Chinese leadership. It supports the larger diplomatic, political, economic, and security agenda determined by the CPC leadership and state. The political and military aspects are inseparable. Both the PLA and China's civilian leadership view the PLA overseas military activities as a political undertaking using military means for strategic reasons, not a freestanding set of military initiatives conducted by military professionals for explicitly military reasons.[8]

It is important not to overstate the significance of China's security and military relationship with Africa. China's national security interests rest primarily on its periphery: South Asia, Southeast Asia, Central Asia, West Asia (including the Middle East), Russia, Japan, Mongolia, and the Koreas. China is also focused on the ability of the United States and Europe to project power into Asia, especially in connection with a possible defense of Taiwan.[9] Africa is a security concern only to the extent there might be interruptions in the flow of critical raw materials that help support China's industrial economy or threats to the growing Chinese presence in Africa. These concerns translate into a Chinese strategy that puts a premium on strengthening stability of African countries, irrespective of political ideology, especially those that are major exporters of key raw materials.

Support for African Liberation and Revolutionary Movements

China's military cooperation with Africa began in the late 1950s with assistance to Algeria's Front de Libération Nationale (FLN) as it fought for independence from France.[10] Chinese training for rebels from Guinea-Bissau followed in 1960 as the rebels tried to end Portuguese rule. China significantly expanded its military assistance to liberation movements in the 1960s. Some of these organizations, such as Robert Mugabe's Zimbabwe African National Union (ZANU), are still in power. Early Chinese support for ZANU and Mugabe accounts to a large degree for China's policy toward Zimbabwe today. The Sino-Soviet split had an increasingly significant impact on which African liberation groups China agreed to supply with military training and assistance. For example, when the Soviet Union backed South Africa's ANC, China agreed to support the opposition Pan Africanist Congress. The ANC prevailed and China found itself scrambling to normalize relations with and supply military equipment to the ANC.[11]

Tanzania, Ghana, and Congo-Brazzaville allowed China to train freedom fighters and revolutionaries on their territory. The training in Tanzania focused on Eduardo Mondlane's Frente de Libertação de Moçambique (FRELIMO), whose fighters received weapons from China and adopted Chinese tactics of guerrilla warfare. In the early 1960s, FRELIMO began sending delegations to China. China trained ZANU forces in Tanzania, assisted the Resistência Nacional Moçambicana (RENAMO) in Zambia, and Chinese arms experts trained nationalists from the Portuguese territories in Ghana. The first group of five Chinese guerrilla warfare experts arrived in 1964. The Chinese instructors remained until Ghana experienced a coup early in 1966, which ended the program.[12] China also coordinated its military training for liberation groups with the Organization of African Unity, providing the organization's liberation committee with 75 percent of all the military aid that it received from countries outside Africa during 1971 and 1972.[13] China trained and supplied arms to a number of losing opposition and revolutionary groups in Africa. Its early involvement in Angola and the Congo, now the Democratic Republic of the Congo (DRC), were particularly unsuccessful.

China found African liberation groups difficult to deal with and often politically unreliable and militarily feckless. Beijing gradually adopted a tougher, more selective approach. The Chinese began to concentrate on providing instructors for guerrilla training camps, supplying modest quantities of arms and accepting small groups for training in China. They concluded that African liberation movements were primarily national movements that sought foreign support but rejected foreign domination. China's support for radical dissidents in Kenya, Uganda, Zanzibar, Senegal, Cameroon, Niger, and the Congo had a disastrous impact on early China-Africa relations. Several nations broke off relations and ousted the Chinese while others became distrustful of Chinese intentions. China's support for such groups diminished significantly after 1965 as China's leaders realized that revolution was not about to sweep across Africa, and they also became preoccupied with domestic concerns. A CIA National Intelligence Estimate in 1971 concluded that China was not actively trying to overthrow any independent African regime with the possible exception of Ethiopia.[14] A 1974 Department of the Army study added that because the Chinese spread their military assistance thinly over a broad area of the Third World, it "appeared that their program was greater than it was."[15]

Military Assistance to African Governments
in the 1960s, 1970s, and 1980s

Africa obtained only $42 million worth of Chinese arms from 1961 to 1971, according to the U.S. Arms Control and Disarmament Agency. This placed

China seventh as an arms supplier to Africa (excluding Egypt) after the Soviet Union, France, the United States, United Kingdom, West Germany, and Czechoslovakia. China concentrated its military assistance in Tanzania, which received 83 percent of the total. Algeria, Congo-Brazzaville, and Guinea obtained modest amounts, about 2.4 percent of Africa's military acquisitions. In 1967–1971, China supplied Africa (excluding Egypt) with 245 major weapons systems: 50 tanks and self-propelled guns, 160 artillery pieces, 20 armored personnel carriers, and 15 patrol boats. This was, however, only about 5 percent of Africa's major weapons imports. Deliveries by Moscow far exceeded those from Beijing. Chinese arms deliveries surpassed those of all other countries only in Tanzania.[16]

There was a significant increase in Chinese military assistance to Africa in the early 1970s. From 1967 through 1976, China transferred $142 million worth of arms to fifteen African countries. The major recipients were Tanzania ($75 million), DRC ($21 million), Congo-Brazzaville ($10 million), and Cameroon, Egypt, Guinea, Sudan, Tunisia, and Zambia ($5 million each). Burundi, Gambia, Malawi, Mali, Mozambique, and Rwanda received $1 million each. Africa obtained only about 7 percent of the PRC's arms exports to the developing world. While China's share of the African arms market during this period was only about 2.8 percent, it represented Beijing's principal military investment outside its immediate geostrategic periphery.[17] Training African military personnel was an important component of China's program. From 1955 through 1979, China trained 2,720 African military personnel from at least thirteen countries. Tanzania headed the list with 1,025, followed by Congo-Brazzaville, 515; Guinea, 360; Sudan, 200; DRC, 175; Sierra Leone, 150; Cameroon, 125; Zambia, 60; Togo, 55; Mali and Mozambique, 50 each; and Algeria and Somalia, less than 30 each.[18] In 1979, there were 305 Chinese military technicians assigned to African countries.[19]

Chinese arms transfers to Africa from 1966 through 1977 included fighter aircraft (MiG-17s, 19s, and 21s), patrol boats, and tanks to Tanzania; MiG-17s and tanks to Sudan; tanks to the DRC; and gunboats to Cameroon, Congo-Brazzaville, Equatorial Guinea, Guinea, and Tunisia. In 1977, Beijing delivered small arms, ammunition, and antiaircraft guns to Botswana after Western countries refused to arm Botswana's defense force. China airlifted military equipment and field artillery to the DRC during the 1977 emergency in the Shaba region.[20] Beijing also put itself in a potentially compromising position by arming anti-MPLA forces in Angola in the

1970s, arming the DRC against anti-Mobutu invaders from Angola in 1977–1978 and arming Somalia against Ethiopia after 1978.[21] Through the 1970s, China's military aid had little impact on local military or strategic balances with the exception of Tanzania. Beijing was able to supplement Western and Soviet-bloc sources, but rarely to offer an effective alternative.[22] The CIA concluded in 1980 that Beijing was not able to match Soviet arms deliveries to Sub-Saharan Africa in quantity or sophistication of weaponry.[23]

Mao's death and the reforms put in place by Deng Xiaoping changed China's arms transfer policy to one focused on earning hard currency from the sale of arms.[24] Beijing also shifted its arms transfers beginning in the late 1970s, emphasizing sales to new customers such as Bangladesh, Burma, Iran, Iraq, and Thailand. Transfers to African countries, other than Egypt, declined.[25] China's new arms transfer commitments to Sub-Saharan Africa from 1980 through 1984 totaled $161 million with Zimbabwe, Sudan, Somalia, the DRC, Nigeria, and Tanzania designated for most of the arms. Actual deliveries to Sub-Saharan Africa during this period reached $237 million. The major recipients were Sudan ($85 million), Somalia ($48 million), DRC ($34 million), Tanzania ($29 million), and Zimbabwe ($15 million).[26] Most weapons were relatively low-tech, primarily Chinese copies of Soviet systems from the 1950s and 1960s.

During the 1980s, China became a major supplier of military equipment to Egypt, which received eighty F-7 fighters, ninety-six Hai Ying-2 surface-to-surface missiles, seven Hainan-class and six Huangfen-class fast attack craft, three Jianghu-class frigates, and six Romeo-class submarines. China transferred twenty T-55 armored personnel carriers to Guinea-Bissau.[27] From Algeria in North Africa to Zimbabwe in Southern Africa, China delivered an assortment of military equipment, including fighter aircraft, artillery, patrol craft, and tanks. China also trained Zimbabwean pilots and Congolese soldiers.[28]

Military Assistance in the 1990s

China's arms supplies to Africa increased in the 1990s, but remained well behind those supplied by Russia. The Congressional Research Service, which has tracked conventional arms transfers to developing nations since 1992, ranked Russia first in deliveries to Sub-Saharan Africa from 1992 through 1999. During the 1992–1995 timeframe, China tied with the United Kingdom for third place with 5.5 percent ($200 million) of total deliveries. During 1996–1999, China was in second place with 15.6 percent ($500 million). In addition, China delivered $100 million worth of weapons to Algeria in North Africa. These deliveries included artillery pieces, aircraft, tanks, self-propelled guns, armored personnel carriers, and patrol craft. The United States provided less than 4 percent of deliveries for both periods. These statistics do not include small arms and ammunition, for which China was a major supplier, although the dollar value was not high.[29]

The U.S. Department of State recorded $1.3 billion in Chinese weapons deliveries and agreements to Africa from 1989 through 1999. Of this total, $200 million went to North, $600 million to Central, and $500 million to Southern Africa. Deliveries to North Africa included ten ships and 100 anti-ship missiles; deliveries to Central Africa consisted of 100 tanks, 1,270 artillery pieces, 40 armored personnel carriers, 13 ships, 20 supersonic combat aircraft, 30 other military aircraft and 30 surface-to-air missiles; and deliveries to Southern Africa included 40 tanks, two ships, and 20 supersonic combat aircraft. It is important to put Chinese military transfers into perspective. From 1989 through 1999, U.S. military transfers to and agreements with Africa totaled $2 billion (mainly to Egypt) while Russian transfers and agreements totaled $7.6 billion.[30]

Chinese conventional weapons transfers, mostly sales, in the 1990s went to a variety of countries and included patrol craft, fighter aircraft, an increasing number of transport aircraft, and artillery.[31] Small arms and light weapons (SALW) were also an important part of Chinese transfers to Africa in the 1990s. While information on deliveries is incomplete, they ranged in value from $29 million for the DRC to a few thousand dollars for Rwanda. Other recipients were Algeria, Cameroon, Djibouti, Egypt, Ethiopia, Morocco, Nigeria, Sudan, and Tanzania.[32]

A major attraction of Chinese military equipment is its low price. Chinese weapons are rugged and simple to operate and maintain. During the Ethiopia-Eritrea war from 1998–2000, both countries purchased significant quantities of equipment from China. Ethiopia obtained ammunition, light mortars, AK-47s, and vehicles. The quality of the Chinese equipment is adequate. The ammunition cost about one-third that of Russian ammunition and the quality was equal. The mortars were light and easily deployed by two persons in a mountainous environment. They were more appropriate than equivalent U.S. mortars. Although the Chinese vehicles were not high quality, their low price still made them attractive.[33] Chinese equipment is similar to Soviet/Russian stock, which formed the basis of many African countries' arsenals. China had a significant store of old weapons; some of this stock ended up in Africa.

Military Attachés and High Level Exchange Visits

Although African chiefs of state personally negotiate some of their country's military cooperation agreements with China, most of the negotiation takes place during high level military exchange visits. Chinese defense attachés in Africa and African attachés in Beijing normally monitor implementation of the programs. In 1988, there were only nine African defense attachés in Beijing: Algeria, Congo-Brazzaville, Egypt, Somalia, Sudan, Tanzania, DRC, Zambia, and Zimbabwe. By 1998, the number increased to thirteen. Guinea, Côte d'Ivoire, Kenya, Mali, and Nigeria joined the African defense attachés in Beijing but the DRC removed its representative.[34] In 2007, eighteen African countries had a defense attaché in Beijing; the number jumped to twenty-eight by 2010. Angola, Botswana, Burundi, Central African Republic, Equatorial Guinea, Ethiopia, Ghana, Mauritania, Morocco, Mozambique, Namibia, Niger, Rwanda, Senegal, and South Africa established defense attaché offices after 1998.[35]

It is difficult to document the number of Chinese defense attachés who are career intelligence officers assigned to Africa. From 1985 until 2006, China almost doubled the number of its defense attaché offices worldwide to 107. In Africa, however, the number grew modestly during that period from nine to fourteen.[36] By the end of 2007, the number had increased to sixteen: Egypt, Libya, Tunisia, Algeria, Sudan, Congo-Brazzaville, DRC, Nigeria, Zambia, Mozambique, Zimbabwe, Ethiopia, South Africa, Morocco, Namibia, and Liberia.[37] China accredited some of these attachés to other African countries on a nonresident basis. It is, nevertheless, surprising that China has so few defense attaché offices in Africa and none in Tanzania, one of its major military assistance partners. By comparison, in 2009 there were thirty-four U.S. attaché/security assistance offices in Africa with some accredited to additional countries.[38]

China routinely announces high level military exchange visits involving both Chinese and African military personnel and includes a list of them as an appendix in its biannual national defense white paper. The public announcements almost never offer, however, any substantive information about the discussions; they simply reaffirm existing cordial military relations or say they reached agreements to enhance cooperation. African media accounts occasionally offer some details on the results of the visits. The regional chapters reflect available information.

In 2000, high level Chinese military delegations visited eighteen African countries.[39] While there has been a significant increase in high level Chinese military visits to many countries outside Africa, the numbers for visits involving Africa have remained fairly stable since 2000.[40] In 2005, six high level Chinese military delegations visited eleven African countries while thirteen African delegations went to China. In 2006, eleven Chinese delegations went to eighteen African countries while sixteen African delegations visited China. In 2007, only six Chinese military delegations visited nine African countries, but twenty-two African delegations went to China. In 2008, probably because of competition from the Beijing Olympic Games, there were seven high level Chinese military visits to thirteen African countries but only eight African delegations to China.[41]

The African countries visited by high level Chinese delegations from 2005 through 2008 offer useful insights on the importance China attaches to the military relationship. Egypt led the list with eight visits from China, followed by six for Tanzania, five for South Africa, four for Tunisia, three for Kenya, and two each for Ethiopia, Sudan, Algeria, Zambia, Namibia, and Uganda. The countries receiving one high level visit during this period were Eritrea, Cameroon, Togo, Benin, Zimbabwe, Rwanda, Madagascar, Botswana, Lesotho, and Morocco. A longer list of African countries sent high level military delegations to China. South Africa and Gabon led the list at four each while Tanzania and the Comoro Islands each sent three delegations. Kenya, Liberia, Mozambique, Mali, Central African Republic, Namibia, Sudan, Cape Verde, Zimbabwe, and Morocco all sent two delegations. Many other African countries had only one high level military delegation visit China during these four years.[42]

The limited number of visits involving China, on the one hand, and Sudan and Zimbabwe, on the other, is surprising in view of their important military relationship. China may have underreported visits involving both countries. The fact that Egypt sent only one high level military delegation to China during these four years is also notable, particularly since it received more high level Chinese delegations than any other African country. South Africa is the only African country to engage in formal, biannual, bilateral defense related talks with China, although China has established a mechanism for defense cooperation meetings with Egypt. No African countries have been included in joint military exercises with China, although there have been a few cases of specialized joint training exercises noted below.[43]

China's Policy on Arms Deliveries

In 1996, China suspended its annual submission of data to the UN Register of Conventional Arms to protest U.S. reporting on exports to "China's Taiwan Province." When the United States ended this reporting in 2007, China resumed submitting data annually to the Register on imports and exports of conventional arms.[44] Although China gives lip service to small arms export controls, its systems leave much to be desired. The 2000 Beijing Declaration stated that China would cooperate in stopping the illegal production, circulation, and trafficking of SALW in Africa.[45] Chinese Vice Foreign Minister Qiao Zonghuai stated at the 2005 opening ceremony for the UN workshop on SALW that "China has constantly intensified cooperation with Africa against illicit proliferation, transfer and trafficking of SALW."[46]

Assistant Foreign Minister Zhai Jun said in 2006 that China always takes a cautious and accountable attitude toward the export of military equipment to Africa. He said that China exports military hardware only to the governments of sovereign states and never exports weapons to any non-state entity or individual. China requires that the recipient government certify the end user and the ultimate purpose. The recipient must promise not to transfer the weapons to any third party. Zhai added that China strictly observes UN resolutions and does not export military equipment to countries and regions where the Security Council has imposed arms sanctions.[47] Foreign ministry spokesperson Jiang Yu added that "China only exports military products to sovereign countries and requests the commitment of relevant countries not to transfer China's weapons to a third party."[48]

China says that it does not sell arms to countries in conflict zones, although some officials acknowledge privately that Chinese weapons, as well as those from other countries, do appear in those areas.[49] China argues that any Chinese weapons that show up in conflict zones were purchased on the international arms market. The officials add that China tries to monitor these transfers and insist that it would fine violators. They point out, for example, that after conflict broke out between Cameroon and Nigeria, China stopped providing arms to both sides. China says that it controls all exports of conventional military items, including small arms in accordance with the Regulations on Control of Military Product Exports. Despite these assertions and the fact that state-run companies manufacture all Chinese weapons, serious questions remain about the control of exported military equipment, especially SALW.[50]

Chinese officials say the country is not in the arms business to make money. However, during a discussion with the authors in Beijing, one African ambassador to China whose country has purchased substantial quantities of Chinese weapons begged to differ with this assertion. He said China "will sell to anyone if it will make money."[51] Contrary to its willingness to sell or give weapons in the 1950s and 1960s to certain African revolutionary groups that opposed established governments, there is little evidence to suggest that China knowingly allows its arms to reach the hands of rebel groups today. On the other hand, China seems willing to sell military equipment to any African government when it serves Beijing's interests.

China issued its first publicly available export control regulations covering military equipment in 1997. It codified China's export principles and adopted some international export control standards. It failed to include, however, a list of specific military items controlled under the regulations. China revised these regulations in 2002 but again did not list specific military items. The regulations remained vague.[52] The 2005 Chinese white paper on arms control stated that international mechanisms for arms control should be maintained, further strengthened, and improved. It added that firmly combating illegal activities in the field of SALW is of great importance to maintaining regional peace, stability, and development, fighting terrorism and cracking down on transnational organized crimes such as drug trafficking and smuggling.[53]

The Current State of Chinese Arms Transfers to Africa

China reformed its defense industry in 1999 by moving from military to civilian production. It converted all military/industrial ministries into industrial corporations as economic bodies and industrial groupings. The enterprises pay the state both taxes and a percentage of their profits. The companies now seek increased profits primarily by increasing exports.[54]

This includes selling greater quantities of more sophisticated military hardware to Africa in competition with Western countries, Russia, and several former Soviet republics. Its largest client for the K-8 trainer jet is Egypt, which is coproducing 120 with China. Other K-8 customers include Ghana, Sudan, Zambia, Namibia, and Zimbabwe. Namibia and Nigeria have received the F-7MG fighter jet and Sudan the A-5C Fantan ground attack aircraft. Algeria has purchased C-802 missile boats complete with ship-to-ship missiles. Gabon, Kenya, Sudan, Congo-Brazzaville, Zambia, and Tanzania have the WZ-551 armored personnel carrier. Gabon is a customer for the T-63 and T-90 multiple rocket launcher; Mali and Mauritania for the Panther helicopter; Sudan for the T-85 HAP tank; and Nigeria for the PL-9 short range anti-air missile. China has exported the Y-7, Y-8, Y-12, and MA-60 military transport aircraft to numerous African countries. China's Norinco has delivered the 155 mm howitzer to Algeria, Sudan, and Egypt.[55] During 2007, for example, China acknowledged that it exported two armored combat vehicles to Tanzania, thirty-two to Kenya and ten to Chad; six large caliber artillery systems to Rwanda; and four combat aircraft to Ghana.[56]

The Congressional Research Service evaluated conventional arms transfers to developing countries from 2002 through 2009. These transfers do not include SALW. During this period, China supplied $1.1 billion in conventional weapons to Sub-Saharan Africa and another $1.4 billion to North Africa. The weapons transferred to Sub-Saharan Africa constituted about 14 percent of China's global arms transfers and almost 20 percent of arms transferred to Sub-Saharan Africa by all suppliers. China is an important supplier to Sub-Saharan Africa, but provided fewer conventional weapons by dollar value than Russia and Germany from 2002 through 2005. From 2006 through 2009, China tied with Germany for the top position. From 2002 through 2009, China transferred the following military equipment to all of Africa: 390 artillery pieces, 590 armored personnel carriers and armored cars, 56 minor surface combatants, 220 aircraft, 130 anti-ship missiles, and 20 tanks and self-propelled guns.[57]

On a global basis, China is a modest exporter of conventional weapons, especially compared to the United States and Russia. Its role in Africa is proportionally greater, but still less than many accounts would lead one to believe. China remains a key source of SALW, which provides limited revenue earnings. China may view the SALW transfers as a way to enhance its status as an international political power and to increase its ability to obtain access to important natural resources, especially oil.[58] In 2006, for example, French Defense Minister Michele Alliot-Marie told the upper house of parliament that too many Chinese weapons are turning up in Africa as part of Beijing's effort to gain mineral wealth and political influence.[59]

Training remains important to China's military cooperation with African countries. The PLA sends many military experts to Africa to help with military education, training, equipment maintenance, and health care.[60] Angola's defense minister commented that China provided without charge training for Angolan soldiers in Chinese military training centers.[61] Zimbabwean officers at the major and lieutenant colonel level have received training in Nanjing at a regimental commander course. China trained personnel in connection with an air defense system it provided to Zimbabwe. China generally provides pilot training linked to its aircraft sales. Most Zimbabwe pilots have trained in China and China trained Sudanese pilots for the A-5C Fantan ground attack fighters.[62] China has sent teams of three to ten instructors to maintain military equipment in Sudan, Zimbabwe, Cameroon, and Gabon. Chinese military trainers instructed troops in Equatorial Guinea on the use of heavy weaponry, perhaps as part of an effort to sell military hardware. The Chinese navy held a joint maritime training exercise with South Africa. In 2009, China conducted a military medical exercise in Gabon, the first of its kind. China eschews direct combat training for African ground forces, but its pilot, naval, and ground equipment training qualify as such.

Western countries criticize China for its close military relationship with Zimbabwe, which is subject to Western sanctions and includes an arms embargo related to its undermining of democratic institutions and practices. China flatly disagrees with the sanctions and continues to transfer significant quantities of military equipment to Zimbabwe.[63]

In April 2008, a shipment of Chinese arms arrived in Durban, South Africa, aboard the Chinese ship, *An Yue Jiang*, for onward transport to landlocked Zimbabwe. The arrival of the arms followed Zimbabwe's highly controversial 29 March presidential election and preceded the 27 June runoff; South African dockworkers in Durban refused to offload the seventy-seven tons of small arms valued at $1.2 million. The shipment included more than three million rounds of ammunition, AK-47 assault rifles, mortars, and rocket propelled grenades.[64] This led to a drama known as China's "ship of shame" that received unprecedented, negative press coverage as it sought an African port where it could offload the arms. Authorities in

South Africa, Namibia, and Mozambique refused. Angolan officials allowed the ship to offload its nonmilitary cargo, but not the weapons for Zimbabwe. China's Foreign Ministry spokesperson, Jiang Yu, protested that the shipment "was perfectly normal trade in military goods between China and Zimbabwe."[65] China's ambassador to Kenya subsequently explained that the Chinese shipping company agreed in 2007 to deliver the arms, long before the political tension in Zimbabwe.[66] Although the Zimbabwe government claimed the arms eventually reached Harare, the U.S. Office of the Secretary of Defense stated that China "off-loaded non-military cargo in Angola, after which the ship returned to China with its remaining cargo."[67]

Arms Transfers and African Conflict Areas

Chinese arms transfers to Africa that end up in African conflicts have become controversial. In any given conflict, SALW are being used that have been manufactured in a variety of countries. In recent years, there is no evidence China has provided these arms directly to rebel groups. They appear to have been transferred to African governments, which in some cases allowed them to reach rebel or militia groups in neighboring countries or parts of their own country out of government control. Alternatively, they originated from the international arms market. It is very difficult to track the movement of SALW and ammunition. Because China is playing a growing role in transferring SALW to African governments, however, there seem to be more Chinese weapons turning up in African conflicts.

Between 2001 and 2003, Liberia's Oriental Timber Company allegedly played a central role in facilitating the transfer of assault rifles, machine guns, rocket propelled grenades, and ammunition to Charles Taylor's forces from the China National Aero-Technology Import and Export Corporation. These transfers occurred while Liberian sanctions were in place. Ignoring sanctions, China also imported timber from Liberia until 2003. The rebel group, Liberians United for Reconciliation and Democracy (LURD), used weapons from many countries including China. The government of Guinea reportedly provided the Chinese weapons, which included Type-56 AKM rifles, heavy machine guns, and ammunition.[68]

The horrific conflict in Sierra Leone attracted SALW from several countries, including China. China provided SALW to the Republic of Sierra Leone Military Forces (RSLMF), the National Provisional Ruling

Council (NPRC) military junta, and the Ahmed Tejan Kabbah government. There is no evidence that the insurgent Revolutionary United Front (RUF), which committed most of the atrocities, used Chinese weapons. China reportedly provided AK-type assault rifles and antitank rocket launchers to the NPRC before sanctions went into effect. These purchases may have been funded by illicit diamond smuggling, money-laundering, and the misuse of loans for development and emergency aid. Chinese versions of the AK-47 and antitank rocket launchers also appeared in the inventory of Kabbah's forces. Together with a number of European governments, China continued to transfer SALW to the Kabbah government after the imposition of sanctions.[69]

Chinese arms played an especially suspicious role in Chad. In April 2006, rebel forces with the support of neighboring Sudan nearly toppled Chad's Idriss Déby government. France intervened in support of Déby. China is one of the major sources of weapons for Sudan, and it was widely believed that Sudan diverted Chinese weapons to the rebel forces for use in Chad. At the time, the Déby government had diplomatic relations with Taiwan. Following the failure of the rebel attack, Déby concluded that he could not always depend on France and decided to ensure good future relations with China. In August, Chad ended its recognition of Taiwan and recognized Beijing. By 2007, China and Chad agreed to increase military cooperation and Chad signed an agreement with China to construct an oil refinery. China sent ten light armored vehicles to Chad the same year. In 2008, a Chinese shipment of armored vehicles and fifty containers of arms and ammunition arrived in Cameroon for delivery to Chad. Chadian rebels continued their efforts to topple the Déby government, but without the blessing of China. Following another attack in 2008, Chad's foreign minister, Ahmad Allam-Mi, urged China to put pressure on Sudan to end any support for the rebels, adding that "China was a friendly country to both Sudan and Chad."[70]

Chinese weapons, together with those from other nations, are in widespread use in the Somali conflict. The Chinese Type-56 assault rifle is among the most common in Somalia and China's RPG-69 anti-tank weapon is well adapted to battlefield conditions. The al-Shabaab extremist organization uses the B10 recoilless rifle and Chinese versions of the heavy machine gun are in use by all parties. Somali armed forces and rebel groups use the Type-55 anti-aircraft gun.[71] There is no indication that China supplies the arms to any party in the conflict; all weaponry is widely available on the Somali and international arms markets.

Chinese arms played a role during and after the 1994 genocide in Rwanda and the toppling of the Hutu-led government by the Tutsi-led Rwandan Patriotic Front (RPF). Chinese weapons used by the RPF came from Ugandan stocks. The Hutu government's Forces Armées du Rwanda (FAR) probably purchased Chinese rifles and hand grenades from independent arms dealers. Before the Hutu regime fled to the neighboring DRC, however, it secured arms from companies in a number of countries, including China. Beijing honored a $5 million contract with the FAR in 1994 for assault rifles, grenades, and rocket-propelled grenades. A Chinese official justified the sale by stating that there was no embargo in place against the DRC. Independent Hutu militias operating out of the DRC also obtained some Chinese weapons.[72]

Self-proclaimed Congolese patriots known as Mäi-Mäi received Chinese weapons primarily from the DRC government. Chinese landmines, Kalashnikov rifles and parts for MAG machine guns arrived from Tanzania while M-1 rifles and M-2 machine guns apparently came from Uganda. Rwandan political, military and business leaders provided most of the arms, including those of Chinese origin, to the Rassemblement Congolais pour la Démocratie-Goma (RCD-Goma).[73] Chinese versions of the AK-47 assault rifle were in widespread use in the DRC as determined by the number "56" stamped as a suffix to the serial number. The DRC and governments in several other countries transferred the weapons to rebel groups in the DRC.[74]

Following the outbreak of conflict between Ethiopia and Eritrea in 1998, the UN Security Council passed a resolution urging that countries not supply arms to either party. UN Security Council members China and Russia and several other countries ignored the recommendation and continued to supply both countries. The UNSC then passed an arms embargo in May 2000 that remained in place for one year. It is not clear if China ceased its supply after the embargo.[75] In any event, the total value of Chinese military sales to both Ethiopia and Eritrea may have reached a half billion dollars.[76]

The most controversial use of Chinese weapons in Africa occurred in Sudan following the outbreak of conflict in Darfur in 2003. Rebel groups in Darfur, the western region that borders Chad, challenged Khartoum's authority. Sudan responded harshly with its national military forces but also armed the Darfur-based Arab Janjaweed militia, who were responsible for major atrocities in the region. China was and remains one of the major arms suppliers to Sudan. Government forces used some of these Chinese

arms against rebel forces and civilians and transferred others to the Janjaweed. The Darfur conflict has spawned a cottage industry of books, journal articles, and reports; some give substantial attention to the role of
China.[77]

Since the early 1990s, Sudan has received most of its conventional weapons from China, Russia, and Belarus. Chinese, Iranian, and Russian companies also supported the development of Sudan's industry for assembling
and producing small arms, artillery, and armored vehicles.[78] China and Iran
together accounted for more than 90 percent of Sudan's self-reported
SALW and ammunition imports from 2001 through 2008.[79] The UN Security Council in 2004 imposed an embargo only on transfers of weapons to
nongovernment armed forces and individuals operating in Darfur. It
excluded the Sudan government from the embargo at the insistence of
China and Russia. The Council expanded the arms embargo in 2005 by
covering all parties, including the Sudanese government, in the dispute.
China and Russia abstained on the vote. In any event, the new arms
embargo did not apply to deliveries of weapons to the Sudanese government that would not be used in Darfur. A UN Panel of Experts subsequently concluded that Sudan continued to supply the Janjaweed with arms
well after the embargo took effect.[80] Although some of the arms sent to the
Janjaweed may have been received by Sudan before passage of the embargo,
there is evidence that Khartoum also transferred arms received after the
embargo. The Panel identified ammunition in use by belligerent parties in
Darfur supplied by China that was manufactured in 2006 and 2007. The
Panel concluded that some items of Chinese origin "have been imported
into Darfur in violation of Security Council sanctions."[81]

Suppliers of arms argued that they did not violate the Security Council
arms embargo because they only transferred weapons and ammunition to
the Sudan government for use outside Darfur. At the same time, those
states, including China that continued to supply arms to Sudan had a
responsibility to prevent them from being used in Darfur in contravention
of the embargo on the movement of weapons to Darfur. One of the rebel
leaders, Abdelwahid al-Nur of the Sudan Liberation Movement, declared
that China was part of the problem because of its military relationship with
Khartoum. China trained Sudanese pilots on Chinese Fantan fighter planes
used in Darfur. International lawyers say this also constituted a violation of
the Security Council arms embargo.[82] China, Belarus, and Russia made no
effort to restrain arms deliveries to the Sudanese government following the

arms embargo. There was a lack of political will on the part of permanent Security Council members China and Russia to pressure the Sudanese government to comply with the embargo. Eventually, China played a helpful role in restraining Sudan in Darfur and pressured Khartoum to accept the hybrid African Union/UN peacekeeping operation.[83]

At one point, China's special envoy to Africa, Liu Guijin, defended China's arms sales to Sudan by arguing that Chinese sales accounted for just 8 percent of total arms sales to Sudan. He suggested Western countries were putting pressure on China as part of a campaign to undermine the upcoming Olympic Games in Beijing.[84] Chinese Foreign Ministry spokesperson Qin Gang declared that a carefully documented Human Rights First report on China's military relationship with Sudan was "groundless" and based on "ulterior motives." He denied that China had broken the Security Council arms embargo, adding that China never exported arms to a country or region under an embargo.[85] This was clearly a case where China's close economic relationship, mainly oil, with Sudan and its overriding belief in national sovereignty caused it to pursue a course of action that was impossible to defend in the West.

Security Threats to Chinese Nationals in Africa

As China expands its presence in Africa and the number of Chinese increases, it is not surprising they have become increasingly exposed to security threats in conflict zones and occasionally even in nonconflict areas.[86] While China may have once assumed that its citizens would not attract the same hostile attention that Westerners have confronted, it has been disabused of the idea. In recent years, Chinese workers, business representatives, and investors have located in risky areas such as the Niger Delta in Nigeria, Kordofan region in Sudan, and the Ogaden in Ethiopia. Westerners have generally avoided these areas as they became more dangerous. This risk-taking has resulted in attacks on Chinese nationals.

The Movement for the Emancipation of the Niger Delta (MEND) in Nigeria has been conducting attacks against the Nigerian government for years arguing that residents of the oil producing Delta do not receive a fair share of the revenue. China has oil interests in the Delta and supplied high-speed patrol boats to the Nigerian government to counter the rebels. In 2006, MEND warned "the Chinese government and its oil companies to steer well clear of the Niger Delta."[87] Subsequently MEND or other rebel organizations kidnapped more than twenty Chinese nationals working in the Delta for the Sichuan Telecommunication Corporation, China Civil Engineering Construction Corporation, and China National Petroleum Corporation. The kidnappers eventually released all of the Chinese. Although China never acknowledged payment of ransom, it likely did so as other kidnapped foreigners have been required to do.[88] In 2009, a MEND spokesperson commented that the Chinese are "locusts who will ravage any farmland in minutes," although he added that existing oil companies operating in the Delta "are no better except that they adhere to standards under the right conditions."[89]

Sudan's Kordofan region borders Darfur, the location of a major conflict where Chinese arms have played a large role. In 2007, the rebel Justice and Equality Movement (JEM) attacked the Defra oilfield operation in Kordofan and seized five non-Chinese personnel as a warning to China, which leads the oil consortium, to cease its military and political support of Khartoum. JEM spokespersons said all of the weapons seized in the attack were Chinese and demanded that China, India, and Malaysia end their energy cooperation with Sudan "because Khartoum is using the oil money to buy arms and kill the people in Darfur. This is our country and they must go."[90] Later in 2007, the JEM attacked a Sudanese army garrison protecting the Rahaw oilfield facility in the Heglig production area under the jurisdiction of the Great Wall Drilling Company. The JEM's leader, Khalil Ibrahim, said that "we are doing these attacks because China is trading petroleum for our blood."[91] The Chinese Foreign Ministry issued a statement that any threats or attacks on Chinese are unacceptable and "the safety of Chinese personnel in Sudan must be effectively guaranteed."[92] The most serious incident occurred in 2008 when an unknown group, but probably the JEM, carried out a third attack in South Kordofan against an oil facility where the CNPC is part of the consortium. The attackers captured three Chinese engineers and six other Chinese workers employed by the CNPC. During a rescue attempt, four of the Chinese died, four were rescued, and one remained missing.[93] China's Foreign Ministry called the incident an "inhumane terrorist deed."[94]

The Somali-inhabited Ogaden region of Ethiopia was the location of the heaviest loss of Chinese lives. There has been a long-standing conflict between Ethiopian government forces and the Ogaden National Liberation Front (ONLF), which seeks self-determination for the region. The Ogaden is rich in gas reserves and may have oil. The ONLF had warned foreign companies to stay out of the Ogaden. In 2007, the ONLF attacked the heavily guarded Chinese operating base, killing nine Chinese employees and sixty-five Ethiopian soldiers. The Chinese worked for the Zhongyuan Petroleum Exploration Bureau, a subsidiary of Sinopec. After the attack, the ONLF announced that it would not allow resources from the region to be exploited by the Ethiopian government or "any firm that enters into an illegal contract."[95] China subsequently abandoned the project and has not returned.[96]

China's 2009 crackdown on the Muslim Uighurs in Xinjiang Uygur Autonomous Region of western China resulted in threats against Chinese nationals from al-Qaeda in the Islamic Maghreb (AQIM), which vowed to target Chinese workers in Algeria and elsewhere. There are as many as 50,000 Chinese in Algeria alone. AQIM ambushed Algerian security forces protecting Chinese workers building the highway between the Algerian capital and Borj Bouaririj, killing twenty-four Algerians. The AQIM threat is the first time that al-Qaeda or an al-Qaeda affiliate has directly threatened Chinese interests in Africa.[97]

Somali piracy has become a serious threat to Chinese shipping in the Gulf of Aden and the Indian Ocean. In 2007, Somali pirates captured a Taiwanese fishing vessel northeast of Mogadishu. The ship had two Taiwanese and twelve Chinese crew members who were eventually released after payment of a ransom.[98] The same year, pirates captured a pair of South Korean vessels with a crew of South Koreans, Indonesians, Vietnamese, Indians, and ten Chinese. In 2008, pirates attacked seven of the 1,265 Chinese commercial vessels passing through the Gulf. Pirates captured the Chinese fishing vessel, *Tianyu 8*, off the coast of Kenya with fifteen Chinese crew members and a chemical tanker from Hong Kong in the Gulf of Aden. In 2009, Somali pirates captured another Taiwanese fishing vessel with five Chinese crew members. Pirates seized a Chinese bulk carrier, *De Xin Hai*, with twenty-five Chinese sailors 550 nautical miles from Seychelles. The pirates said they collected $3.5 million in ransom before releasing the vessel. In 2010, Somali pirates hijacked a St. Vincent and Grenadines flagged cargo ship with twenty-three Chinese crew members, a Singaporean flagged vessel with seventeen Chinese sailors, and a Panamanian flagged ship with twenty-nine Chinese crewmembers. In 2011, Somali pirates seized the Chinese ship *Full City* and twenty-four of the crewmembers. The international naval force quickly rescued the vessel.

Chinese nationals have also fallen victim to more routine security threats in Africa. In 2007, Tuareg rebels in Niger kidnapped and released several days later a Chinese uranium executive as a warning to China for disregarding the environment and signing an unacceptable agreement with the Niger government. The rebels also attacked an armed convoy heading to a CNPC exploration camp in Niger. In 2008, renewed fighting in the eastern DRC led to the death of one Chinese national in Lubumbashi. A strike by one hundred Chinese workers in Equatorial Guinea resulted in a face off with local police, who claimed the strike violated the law. The police killed two Chinese and wounded four others in the confrontation.

China's first evacuation experience in Africa occurred in 1991 during a civil war in Somalia when the PLA navy (PLAN) was not able to remove Chinese embassy personnel from Mogadishu.[99] China diverted a ship from the state-owned China Ocean Shipping Company to evacuate Chinese nationals. Chinese embassies in Africa have become more proactive in issuing security alerts and organizing evacuations of Chinese citizens. China's Foreign Ministry established in 2006 a consular protection department to improve security for Chinese living overseas, although Chinese embassies continue to rely primarily on the cooperation of host governments. When rebels pushed toward the capital of Chad in 2008, China successfully evacuated its embassy personnel from N'djamena. In its greatest security challenge in Africa, China evacuated without any fatalities 36,000 workers from Libya in 2011. Although most Chinese left Libya on commercial vessels, China diverted a frigate from the anti-piracy operation in the Gulf of Aden to the Mediterranean and sent four IL-76 transport aircraft to Tripoli via Khartoum. The unprecedented evacuation has important implications for Chinese defense procurement and security policy.[100]

He Wenping, head of African studies at the Chinese Academy of Social Sciences, acknowledged that protection of Chinese in Africa has become a sensitive issue, and public opinion is demanding the government do more. She admitted that Chinese companies are evaluating the local security situation more closely before starting projects.[101] The concern has become even more pronounced since the massive evacuation of Chinese workers from Libya.[102]

The one area where China has responded militarily in Africa is the threat of Somali piracy to Chinese ships and crew. China made an unprecedented decision late in 2008 to send two destroyers and a supply ship to the Gulf of Aden to help the international force deter Somali piracy. It has continued to rotate three PLAN vessels in and out of the Gulf of Aden. Li Wei, director of the anti-terrorism research center at the China Institute of Contemporary International Relations, described the decision as "a huge breakthrough in China's concepts about security."[103] He added that it alters how China is dealing with perceived threats and signals a change in China's concept of security from the traditional to the nontraditional.

Support for Peacekeeping in Africa

One security area where China receives positive marks from nearly everyone is its contribution to UN and African Union peacekeeping efforts. A study prepared by the Stockholm International Peace Research Institute (SIPRI) said that by sending engineers, transport battalions, and medical units, China provides critically needed material assets at a time when multilateral peacekeeping is severely overstretched.[104] The report added: "Chinese peacekeepers are consistently rated among the most professional, well-trained, effective and disciplined in UN peacekeeping operations."[105] In 2008, in remarks about China's peacekeeping role before students at Beijing's Foreign Affairs University, UN Secretary General Ban Ki-Moon said, "this is an area where China stands tall."[106] Prior to the 2007 arrival of Hu Jintao to Liberia, President Ellen Johnson Sirleaf praised the help of Chinese peacekeepers, adding "Liberians will never forget the friendship of Chinese peacekeeping soldiers."[107]

When China took its place on the UN Security Council in 1971, it opposed peacekeeping operations, which it considered interventions in sovereign countries manipulated by superpowers.[108] It underwent a gradual change in attitude between 1981 and 1987 after which it began to cooperate in some UN peacekeeping operations. In 1989, for the first time, China deployed personnel to a UN peacekeeping operation, when twenty Chinese military observers took part in the UN Transition Assistance Group monitoring elections in Namibia. Beginning in the early 1990s, China sent small numbers of peacekeepers to several UN operations in Africa: the Western Sahara beginning in 1991, Mozambique from 1993 to 1994, Liberia from 1993 to 1997, and Sierra Leone from 1998 to 1999. While China did not contribute troops to the two UN missions in Somalia from 1992 through 1995 or the U.S.-led operation from late 1992 until early 1993 that separated the UN missions, China supported all three operations in the Security Council because of their "exceptional" humanitarian mission.[109]

Beginning in 2000, China contributed ten observers to the UN mission along the Ethiopia-Eritrea border.[110] In 2003, China expanded significantly its engagement in UN peacekeeping in Africa by sending a 175-person engineering company and 43-person medical unit to the DRC, where it had earlier assigned a small number of military observers. In announcing the troop contribution, Senior Colonel Dai Shaoan, director general of the peacekeeping affairs office in the Defense Ministry, said China is now ready to play a more prominent role in peacekeeping operations and planned to set up a peacekeeping training center.[111] Several months later, China sent a 275-person engineering company, 240-person transportation company, and 43-person field hospital to Liberia. This engagement by China quickly followed the decision by Liberia to end recognition of Taiwan and reestablish relations with Beijing. Until mid-2003, China was also a major buyer of Liberian timber from the Charles Taylor regime in violation of UN sanctions. In 2004, China sent a small number of military observers to Burundi and Côte d'Ivoire, where they continue to be assigned.

China now considers peacekeeping a core activity of the UN, and this is reflected in its policy documents.[112] China's 2008 white paper on defense states that it "has consistently supported and actively participated in the peacekeeping operations consonant with the spirit of the UN Charter."[113] While that statement overlooks earlier history, it certainly is true since about 2000. The various papers prepared by China and Africa on the FOCAC summits have increasingly stressed the role of peacekeeping. The action plan prepared after the 2003 FOCAC in Addis Ababa called on China to intensify its participation in peacekeeping. Following the 2006 Beijing FOCAC, China promised to take an active part in UN peacekeeping operations in Africa. China agreed at the 2009 FOCAC in Egypt to continue to support and participate in UN peacekeeping missions in Africa and intensify cooperation with African countries in peacekeeping theory research, peacekeeping training and exchanges, and in supporting the building of peacekeeping capacity in Africa.[114]

As of mid-2011, China had 1,550 troops, 40 police, and 42 military experts for a total of 1,632 personnel assigned to the six UN peacekeeping operations in Africa. This was far more than any other permanent member of the Security Council and compares with twenty-eight for the United States, although Washington provides about 26 percent of the global UN peacekeeping budget and Beijing only 3 percent. The largest number of personnel was in Liberia (564 troops, 18 police, 2 military experts); followed by Southern Sudan (444 troops, 22 police, 12 military experts); Darfur (324 troops); and the DRC (218 troops, 15 military experts). China also had three military experts in Côte d'Ivoire and ten in the Western Sahara. In 2007, Ban Ki-Moon appointed a Chinese general as commanding officer of the peacekeeping mission in the Western Sahara, a position China continues to hold. This was the first time that a Chinese national led a UN peacekeeping mission.[115]

As an indication of its commitment to global peacekeeping, China now has three facilities engaged in some aspect of peacekeeping training. There is the International Relations Academy in Nanjing and the China Police Peacekeeping Training Center at Langfang in Hebei Province, which is designed for police officers deployed to UN missions. In 2009, the Defense Ministry opened the first military peacekeeping training center at Huairou in suburban Beijing. It offers English-language training, simulated UN peacekeeping camps, demining training areas, swimming, and diving. It is also the primary location for international peacekeeping exchanges.

China's most controversial deployment of peacekeeping forces has been in Darfur because of Beijing's close ties with Khartoum and the fact that about 6 percent of its imported oil comes from Sudan. China also has peacekeeping forces in South Sudan, but there has been a ceasefire since 2003 and the Chinese troops have not come under criticism. Even in Darfur, the Chinese force has acted professionally and taken no sides politically. In 2007, China agreed to send 315 troops comprising three engineer platoons, one well-digging platoon, and one field hospital. The UN asked the Chinese to build roads and bridges and dig wells ahead of the arrival of an enhanced hybrid African Union/UN peacekeeping force. The deployment followed criticism of China by human rights groups and some governments over Beijing's reluctance to support a more robust international force in Darfur.

A commander of one of the Darfur rebel groups, the Sudan Liberation Movement (SLM), said that Beijing is an "accomplice" of Khartoum in Darfur and "we can't trust them or cooperate with them."[116] The leader of the other major rebel group at the time, the JEM, said that the people of Darfur do not welcome the Chinese troops but "we will not target the Chinese peacekeepers."[117] China's Foreign Ministry spokesperson Qin Gang responded that China could not tolerate criticism from any party for its

participation in the peacekeeping mission in Darfur and promised unremitting efforts to promote the peace process.[118] The SLM and JEM and human
rights activists, particularly in the United States, continued their criticism
of the Chinese peacekeeping presence. Meanwhile, China and the commander of the African Union/UN force touted the good deeds performed
by the Chinese engineers and medical teams. While rebel groups in Darfur
apparently have never targeted Chinese peacekeepers, the JEM carried out
three attacks on Chinese oilfield operations in the Kordofan region.

China has provided diplomatic support and modest funding for African
Union and African subregional peacekeeping efforts. China considers African regional organizations well situated to make judgments on issues that
impact the sovereignty and internal affairs of their members. China agreed
to support an arms embargo on Côte d'Ivoire in 2004 because of strong
agreement within the African Union. In 2009, however, when the African
Union asked the UN to impose sanctions on Eritrea for supporting extrem-
ists in Somalia, China objected but eventually abstained on the UN resolution. China provides financial assistance on an ad hoc basis. It made its
largest donation to the African Union's peacekeeping mission in Darfur. In
2006, it provided $1 million in budgetary support to the African Union
mission and $2.5 million in humanitarian assistance for the people of
Darfur. In 2008, China provided $300,000 to the African Union's peace-
keeping mission in Somalia and another $400,000 in 2009. These are small
donations in view of the huge expense of the operations.[119] China is still
working out its security cooperation with the African Union and subregional organizations. Because it represents fifty-four countries, the African
Union has not always been a coordinated and easy interlocutor.[120]

Africa, Western countries, and the UN all welcome China's participation in peacekeeping operations generally and in Africa particularly. The
UN is always looking for more troop contributing countries and Western
nations, especially the United States, are not anxious to send troops to
African conflicts. But peacekeeping generally and in Africa particularly has
benefits for China. It allows China to respond to African requests and build
confidence with both African governments and African regional organizations. Increasingly, China wants to be seen as a "responsible great power."
Peacekeeping is a relatively low cost way to help achieve this goal in a
nonthreatening way. This positive role for the PLA also contributes to
efforts by the CPC leadership to improve its position in the international
community. China gains practical policy benefits from its peacekeeping

presence in Africa. It is not coincidental that its four large peacekeeping efforts occur in three countries where China has or once had significant interest in natural resources: oil in South Sudan and Sudan, minerals in the DRC, and, in an earlier period, hardwood timber in Liberia.

Finally, there are important operational considerations for the PLA. U.S. Marine Colonel Philippe Rogers explained that UN peacekeeping operations provide an opportunity for distant operational experience. The PLA gains insights about operational logistics, multinational operations, combat, and civil engineering. It learns valuable knowledge about logistics, ports of debarkation, lines of communication, lines of operations, operational intelligence, and the best way to sustain forces in Africa over prolonged periods. At the tactical level, there is nothing like lessons learned on the ground. The experience of traveling across the Sahara Desert under harsh conditions using GPS cannot be replicated in the classroom. Repeated deployments to UN missions in Africa permit the PLA to build an extensive information base.[121] Rogers concluded that China's "effort is outpacing Washington's efforts dedicated to operations in Africa by a considerable margin. Conceivably, the United States will one day turn to the Chinese military for help and expertise in missions in Africa."[122]

The Return of Zheng He Naval Diplomacy to Africa

As noted in Chapter 2, Zheng He was the first Chinese navigator to reach Africa. He made voyages during the Ming Dynasty to some thirty countries in West Asia and East Africa in 1405–1433, predating Christopher Columbus, Vasco da Gama, and Ferdinand Magellan. In 2005, the 600th anniversary of Zheng's voyages, China's Vice Premier Huang Ju called on the Chinese people to carry forward Zheng's spirit of scientific exploration and the expansion of friendly cooperation with peoples of other countries.[123] Chinese diplomacy in Africa today frequently cites the "peaceful" voyages of Zheng He. In the past several years there has been a lively discussion concerning China's intentions on extending naval power into the Indian Ocean and even as far as the East African coast. Increasingly, China specialists and naval analysts see this as an integral part of Chinese strategy. As early as 1979, American Sinologist George T. Yu flagged this as an issue to watch.[124]

China's 2006 white paper on defense said that the navy "aims at gradual extension of the strategic depth for off-shore defensive operations" and must guard not only coastal areas but also nearby oceans.[125] China acknowledged that the PLAN is undergoing a "strategic transformation" and subtly suggested this includes the ability to deploy well beyond its shores. The 2008 defense white paper said the navy is striving "to gradually develop its capabilities of conducting cooperation in distant waters and countering non-traditional security threats, so as to push forward the overall transformation of the service."[126] An analysis by the U.S. Office of Naval Intelligence was less subtle. It argued that China is economically dependent on sea lanes, which transport more than 90 percent by volume and 80 percent by value of China's foreign trade. The CPC has made protection of these lanes a key mission of the PLAN because China's continued prosperity depends upon a reliable flow of resources from foreign suppliers.[127] A related concern is the lack of oil tankers under China's control. As a result, Chinese shipping companies have begun a major acquisition of very large crude carriers, accounting for 20 percent of all new vessels built in 2008.

China's statistics report an average annual GDP growth rate of about 9 percent over the last three decades. China's economic planners hope to sustain an average annual GDP growth rate of about 7–8 percent. Some of this growth depends on the importation of oil and minerals from Africa. While oil and gas account for only 20 percent of China's energy requirement (coal, most of it available locally, provides the preponderance of China's energy needs), the importance of imported gas and oil is growing rapidly. China currently imports more than 40 percent of its oil, and this could rise to 75 percent by 2025.[128] China now obtains almost one-third of its imported oil from Africa, and that percentage may rise. Africa currently holds about 10 percent of the world's proven petroleum reserves and remains largely unexplored. More oil finds are anticipated in Africa than in any other part of the world.[129] About 90 percent of China's imported oil from the Middle East and Africa passes through the Straits of Malacca, and China is building a pair of oil and gas pipelines through Burma to ensure the safety of those supplies. Zhang Wenmu, professor in the Centre for Strategic Studies at the Beijing University of Aeronautics and Astronautics, wrote in 2006: "The more developed China becomes the greater its dependence grows not only on foreign trade but also on the resources to fuel the economy."[130] For the most part, the United States and, to some extent, India, control the sea lanes from the African coast to the Straits of Malacca.

This situation is not tenable over the long term for a China with global aspirations.[131]

The PLAN surface force as of 2010 had about 25 destroyers, 49 frigates, 85 missile-armed patrol craft, and 55 amphibious ships. Since the mid-1990s, the PLAN has emphasized the submarine force in its modernization effort. It has fifty-four diesel attack submarines and six nuclear attack submarines. Its most capable submarines are probably used for patrol operations of longer duration and distances in the Pacific and possibly Indian Ocean.[132] China now has the second largest navy after the United States.[133]

Until 2011, China was the only permanent member of the UN Security Council without a functioning aircraft carrier. In 1998, China purchased from Ukraine an incomplete Soviet-era carrier and started to renovate it in 2002. In 2008, fifty Chinese students began training at the PLAN Dalian Naval Academy as China's first naval pilots capable of operating fixed-wing aircraft from an aircraft carrier. The carrier began its first sea trial in mid-2011 but will not be operational until 2013. The addition of a carrier signals that China intends to expand its naval presence into distant waters, almost certainly to include the Indian Ocean. At the 2009 National People's Congress, former PLAN political commissar Admiral Hu Yanlin stated that China is capable of building aircraft carriers, and increasing security demands require them. Research and development for carrier construction is underway. Retired PLAN Rear Admiral Yin Zhou commented in 2011 that it will take China at least ten years to build a carrier group. The U.S. Office of Naval Intelligence believes China will have an operational, domestically produced carrier sometime after 2015. The U.S. Department of Defense says PLAN is considering building multiple carriers by 2020.[134]

The modern Chinese navy sent its first-ever naval fleet formation to Africa in 2000, with port calls in Tanzania and South Africa. Rear Admiral Huang Jiang, chief of the general staff of the South China Sea Fleet, joined the *Shenzhen 167* guided missile destroyer, the *Nancang 953* supply ship, and 480 officers and sailors during stops at Dar es Salaam and the Simonstown naval dock near Cape Town. The Commander of the North China Sea Fleet, Ding Yiping, accompanied the *Qingdao 113* guided missile destroyer, the *Taicang 575* supply ship, and 500 crew members on China's first world cruise in 2002. After passing through the Suez Canal, the ships called at Alexandria, Egypt. Eight years passed until the next Chinese ships visited Africa; the guided missile frigate *Ma'anshan*, part of China's anti-piracy effort in the Gulf of Aden, made a port call at Djibouti early in 2010 to take on supplies. This began a series of calls at Djibouti by Chinese ships assigned to the anti-piracy patrol. After completing their mission in the Gulf of Aden in 2011, China's two frigates called at Dar es Salaam, Tanzania, Durban, South Africa, and the Seychelles before returning to their home port.

Late in 2010, the new PLAN hospital ship *Peace Ark* made port calls in Djibouti, Kenya, Tanzania, and the Seychelles where it provided medical services for local nationals and personnel conducting anti-piracy activities in the Gulf of Aden. The *Peace Ark*, central to China's new emphasis on humanitarian and disaster assistance, served as a goodwill mission.

Robert D. Kaplan, senior fellow at the Center for a New American Security and correspondent for the *Atlantic*, has written extensively and persuasively on China's naval plans for the Indian Ocean. He argued that China has adopted a "string of pearls" strategy for the Indian Ocean, which consists of establishing a series of ports in friendly countries along the ocean's northern rim. It is building a large naval base and listening post in Gwadar, Pakistan; a port in Pasni, Pakistan, seventy-five miles east of Gwadar, which is to be joined to the Gwadar facility by a new highway; a fueling station on the southern coast of Sri Lanka; and a container facility with extensive naval and commercial access in Chittagong, Bangladesh; and plans to use Burma's ports on the Indian Ocean for logistical support for its shipping lanes.[135] These facilities are being developed for commercial rather than military purposes.[136] Nevertheless, they permit China to establish a special relationship that will likely permit the PLAN to parlay into regular port calls and fulfill resupply requirements. The father of the modern Chinese navy, Liu Huaqing, proposed a three-phase maritime strategy that by 2050 would create a blue water navy capable of exercising global influence.[137]

China is in discussion with Kenya on building a major port facility north of Mombasa and has significant interests in two container facilities in Port Said, Egypt. Li Jie, a strategist at the PLA Naval Research Institute, commented in China's official press that China should consider establishing a supply and support base in East Africa, perhaps in Djibouti.[138] Rear Admiral Yin Zhou, then a senior official at the PLAN's Equipment Research Center, subsequently echoed the need for a permanent naval base to resupply Chinese ships contributing to the anti-piracy campaign in the Gulf of Aden.[139] China's Defense Ministry quickly clarified that its ships in the Gulf of Aden would continue to be supplied at sea supplemented by access to the French base in Djibouti. China's English-language television then said "an overseas supply base might be an option in the future, but it's not being considered at this time."[140] China is probably planning not for traditional military bases, but for facilities that can support expanded PLAN engagement in nontraditional missions such as anti-piracy and disaster relief operations.[141]

The most important Chinese naval development in African waters since Zheng He's early fifteenth-century voyages has been China's participation in the anti-piracy effort in the Gulf of Aden. China has rotated on a continuing basis two frigates and a supply ship in support of the effort. This represents the PLAN's first series of operational deployments beyond the immediate western Pacific region. Beijing emphasized at the beginning of the deployment that it does not constitute a commitment to further blue water operations. China skillfully prepared both the domestic and international audiences for this historic new engagement.[142] China has been reluctant to join any of the formal naval coalitions operating in the Gulf of Aden; the stated purpose of its operation is "safeguarding and providing security for Chinese vessels and personnel sailing through the region."[143] The PLAN has, however, cooperated with other naval units, expressed a willingness to strengthen intelligence and information exchange and to take part in humanitarian relief operations. In 2010, it took an important step when the PLAN agreed to head the monthly meetings of the anti-piracy coordination group. Because of long-standing mistrust of NATO, however, the PLA imposed conditions. Tang Yinchu, a senior consultant at the China Institute of International Strategic Studies, said China will emphasize independence and sovereignty in overseas operations. He added that "we won't tell other countries what to do, or be told what to do, and that principle will never change in our future anti-piracy operations."[144]

The deployment has provided China and the PLAN with a unique opportunity. Professor Pang Zhongying at the People's University of China said, "China's image as a responsible sovereign nation will improve by participating in such missions."[145] Li Jie added that another key goal is to register the presence of the Chinese navy.[146] Professor Yan Xuetong, director of the International Studies Institute at Tsinghua University, commented that China's foreign policy is entering a new stage reflecting China's relations with the world.[147] Zhuang Congyong, a researcher with the Naval

Command Academy, said the operation reflects a transformation in Chinese military strategy, and the PLAN "will conduct more long-distance missions in the future."[148] The mission illustrates China's growing military capabilities and its willingness to help enforce global security. It allows the PLAN to improve its tactics, techniques, and procedures by operating in close proximity with more experienced navies. It provides the PLAN an opportunity to refine doctrine for blue water operations and helps justify China's defense buildup to foreign audiences. Finally, the operation showcases vessels designed and manufactured by Chinese shipbuilders.[149]

By all accounts, the Chinese contribution has been welcome and its naval forces have acted professionally. The piracy challenge offered China the ideal occasion to test its navy far from its shores and ease concerns about its traditional doctrine of nonintervention. Chinese lives and interests were at risk. The UN blessed the international intervention and Somalia's Transitional Federal Government invited China. Beijing also protects Hong Kong and Macau-registered ships and offered to assist Taiwan-flagged vessels, putting Taipei in a difficult position, and underscoring the dependency on the PLAN of ships from Macau and Hong Kong. China used its engagement in the Gulf of Aden to refine its policy toward the larger Somali conflict. Li Baoding, China's permanent UN representative, emphasized the need to deal with the root causes of the Somali problem and spelled out a three-point program. He argued the international community should promote dialogue among the different parties in Somalia, accelerate economic and social development, and support the arms embargo and freezing of assets of those persons aiding Somali pirates.[150] General Chen Bingde, chief of the PLA general staff, during a visit to Washington in 2011 took a much harder line when he suggested "we should probably move beyond the ocean and crash their [pirate] bases on the land."[151]

China's recent activity in the Indian Ocean raises the question of potential conflict with the U.S. navy's presence in the region. While this could become an issue in the long-term, the more immediate concern comes from India, which sees itself as the principal regional power.[152] Some Indian strategists argue that China's naval capability is growing rapidly and is part of a plan for "strategic encirclement" of India.[153] China and India currently have good relations and have even held joint naval maneuvers, but this situation could change. China's continued support for Pakistan's military and close political ties with Islamabad could pose a problem. Likewise, India's alignment with the United States may give China some pause. The

PLAN is superior to the Indian navy in quality and quantity. As a result, India has signed cooperation agreements with the Indian Ocean island countries and signed a port access agreement with Seychelles. India has a high-tech monitoring station on the north end of Madagascar. It has engaged in naval collaboration with Mauritius, Kenya, Tanzania, Mozambique, and South Africa.[154] India will not let China forget that it is, after all, the Indian Ocean.

7

Media, Education, and Cultural Relations and Ties with Chinese Communities in Africa

The state-controlled media are China's most effective conduit for information collection and distribution in Africa. Xinhua News Agency (Xinhua), China Radio International (CRI), and China Central Television's (CCTV) coverage of China-Africa relations have grown apace with China's engagement on the continent. At the same time, China's universities have become the choice for increasing numbers of elite African students. They, along with vocational training and Confucius Institutes in African countries, have spread knowledge about China and Chinese language to African youth. Since the 1950s, youth conferences, film festivals, and delegations of artists and writers have been part of Sino-African cultural exchanges. Direct interaction between communities—a consequence of unprecedented numbers of Chinese in Africa and growing numbers of Africans in China—is a largely new element of interpersonal relations. Together, media, education, culture, and community represent the lion's share of social interaction.

Media

China's officials have long felt that their policies toward Africa receive unfair treatment in the Western press and that a disparity exists between China's growing economic strength and its media's relatively weak influence in Africa. As these concerns have grown, so has the government's financial support for the expansion of state-owned overseas media outlets led by Xinhua and to a lesser degree CRI and CCTV. Over the last decade these media outlets have sought to project a softer, more cooperative image of China to Africans.

Xinhua, which has the longest history and the most outlets of any Chinese or Western news agency in Africa, effectively functions as Beijing's eyes, ears, and mouth on the continent. According to Xin Xin of Westminster University, Xinhua, the CPC's most loyal mouthpiece, "is responsible for setting the official tone that other Chinese media outlets follow [and] has also been active in promoting China's Africa policy and China-Africa relations."[1] This section examines Xinhua and its radio-based sister agency CRI's information collection and distribution activities in Africa.

Xinhua's Expanding International Presence

Xinhua is the world's largest news agency. In 2005, it had 8,400 employees (compared to Agence France-Presse's 2,000) including 1,900 journalists and editors, and released more than 4,500 news items in seven languages every day.[2] Between 2005 and 2010, these numbers have swelled, particularly in Africa, due to Xinhua's investments on the continent. The official news agency has reporters in more than 100 countries and five regional offices, including the African regional office in Nairobi, and the North Africa and Middle East regional office in Cairo.[3] Xinhua is a publisher as well as a news agency; it prints some forty different newspapers and magazines and supplies reports to publications in more than 130 countries.[4]

Xinhua "maintains the historical mission of 'publicizing China and reporting on the world.'"[5] The agency adopted its current name in 1937 and after the founding of the PRC in 1949 became a ministerial-level state agency.[6] In the 1960s and 1970s Xinhua published only a few regular periodicals for foreign readers but then propaganda workers were encouraged to build China's image outside the country. During China's reform and opening up period, considerable quantities of Xinhua propaganda materials were translated from Chinese into Western languages and "broadcast worldwide more than ever before and picked up by other news agencies."[7] The reason for expanded foreign content according to Zhao Qizheng, head of Renmin University's School of Journalism, is that "foreigners differ from Chinese in both languages and ways of thinking." Zhao adds that to

> let foreigners understand thoughts, behaviors and values of Chinese people, both the language and culture should be "translated." That

is to say, to tell Chinese stories to the outside world, languages and manners that are understandable and acceptable to foreign audience should be employed. [SIC][8]

Since 2000, Xinhua's Leading Party Group, the agency's top decision-making body, has worked to make the agency "more influential and bigger as soon as possible."[9] Xinhua and other state media outlets expanded rapidly and by decade's end had strengthened their "international cross-cultural communication" capabilities through enhanced cooperation with foreign counterparts in news coverage, human resources, and information technology.[10]

Xinhua in Africa

In 1963, political scientist June Teufel Dreyer identified "disseminating Chinese propaganda" and aiding "African leaders sympathetic to the Chinese cause" as China's two chief policy objectives in Africa.[11] Xinhua journalists were deeply involved in both efforts, reporting and acting on behalf of the Chinese state to support revolutionary groups.[12] Emmanuel John Hevi, an African student disaffected by his time in China, observed in 1966, "As a matter of policy, correspondents of the New China News Agency [Xinhua] are expected to devote part of their time and talents to such gentle pastimes as spying on and subverting their host (African) countries."[13]

In the 1960s, China's state correspondents distributed pamphlets encouraging African countries to recognize the PRC, explaining its international positions and spreading CPC revolutionary slogans.[14] These materials appeared in African bookstores along with cheap paperbound editions of the works of Mao Zedong.[15] Between January and May 1960, Xinhua reported that one bookstore in Conakry, Guinea, alone had sold 395 copies of Mao's works.[16] As early as 1961, Xinhua maintained offices in Accra, Ghana; Dakar, Senegal; Conakry, Guinea; Dar es Salaam, Tanzania; and Rabat, Morocco.[17] Generally speaking, early Xinhua reports centered on five major themes: African repression under colonialism; the anticolonial struggle in Africa; Beijing's support for African peoples' struggle against colonialism; China as a model for oppressed nations; peaceful and friendly relations between China and African countries.[18] A *People's Daily* article in 1961 gives a taste of propaganda in this era:

All oppressed nations and peoples will sooner or later rise in revolution, and this is precisely why revolutionary experience and theories
will naturally gain currency among these nations and peoples and
go deep to their hearts. That is why pamphlets introducing guerrilla
warfare in China have such a wide circulation in Africa . . . and are
looked upon as precious things even after they are worn and come
apart and the print has become illegible through rubbing. The
influence of ideas knows no state boundaries. No one can prevent
the dissemination among the people of what they need.[19]

Xinhua's earliest claims that "colonial rule in Africa [was] approaching
total collapse" and that African revolutionaries were Maoists exaggerated
the scope of resistance in some African countries, distorted the nature of
armed struggle in others, and generally overemphasized Beijing's influence
on the continent.[20] Some Africans did not advocate armed struggle, others
disagreed with China's depiction of their conflict, still others were disappointed when the revolutionary results Xinhua was promising did not
materialize. In Rwanda, for instance, Xinhua Correspondent Gao Liang
arranged for Chinese largesse to reach the Tutsi rebels in Burundi seeking
to overthrow the Hutu-led Bahutu Republic of Rwanda in 1963. One would
have expected that having condemned feudalism, China would support the
long-oppressed Hutu against the reestablishment of Tutsi dominance. But
Xinhua distorted the root of the ill-fated Tutsi invasion for China's own
ends: at that time Rwanda had an anti-communist clause in its constitution
and had diplomatic relations with Taipei.[21]

    In the late 1960s, amid growing African hostility toward its increasingly
radical rhetoric, Xinhua recalled its journalists (along with its diplomats)
for reeducation in China. As a result Xinhua's reporting on Africa diminished during the Cultural Revolution and its broadcasts became
increasingly extreme. These broadcasts' vehement condemnation of U.S.
imperialism and South African apartheid were contradicted, however, by
the U.S.-China rapprochement in 1972 and China's collaboration with
Pretoria in Angola two years later. After the Cultural Revolution most of
Xinhua's preexisting Africa bureaus were reestablished and its reporters
adopted a softer, more cooperative line. In the 1980s Africa received more
of Xinhua's attention, not as a breeding ground for communist revolutions,
but as a potential source of untapped news. However, its foreign coverage
at this time prioritized Europe, North America, and Asia in order to help

cultivate commercial links with the West and neighboring countries. Moreover, Africa was relatively unimportant to Beijing; China was not a force in
African markets, a consumer of African petroleum and minerals, or an
international pariah in need of diplomatic partners as it was during the
Cultural Revolution and after the 1989 Tiananmen crackdown.[22]

Xinhua lacked the necessary government financing during China's early
reform era and its journalists in Africa fell from seventy-two in 1979 to
forty-eight in 1984. Difficult working conditions in Africa made talented
young journalists hard to attract and constrained the revival of Xinhua's
bureaus. Throughout the 1980s, chronic neglect and understaffing resulted
in superficial reports on limited topics from Xinhua's African operations.
To redress these problems in 1986, Xinhua established an Africa regional
bureau in Nairobi to coordinate its reporting and English and Swahili programming in Sub-Saharan Africa.[23]

In the 1980s, Xinhua's news wires were free for all Africans and as of
2011 they remained free for those who cannot afford to pay. In 1995, however, to underwrite its expansion, Xinhua began to charge media outlets a
fee in some African countries (e.g., Egypt, Nigeria, and Kenya).[24] By combining government and private funds, Xinhua created one of the most complete information transmission systems in Africa, a premier "global news
and information gathering network."[25] Guo Chaoren, Xinhua's former
president, worked to increase the number of Xinhua domestic and international subscribers from 1,876 in 1994 to 3,400 in 1998 and 16,969 in 2002.[26]
In 2010, the agency maintained twenty-three overseas offices in Africa
(eighteen in Sub-Saharan Africa and five in North Africa).[27] Since local
Chinese newspapers do not have Africa bureaus, Xinhua's international
reports are distributed in China through the agency's extensive domestic
distribution network, which by 2005 included 306 radio stations, 369 TV
stations, 2,119 newspapers, and 9,038 periodicals.[28]

Many African capitals and provincial cities receive scant attention in
major Western news services unless there is a crisis. This information gap
adds value to Xinhua's internal reports for China's state agencies and companies in Africa as well as its open source materials for private clients. To
obtain information Xinhua reporters are often transferred around Africa
allowing them to build extensive regional contact networks. Senior correspondent Dai Adi, for instance, who was serving as Xinhua's correspondent
in Luanda in 2007, previously served as correspondent in Lagos, Nigeria,

while Shao Jie, a Chinese Hui Muslim working as Xinhua's correspondent in Khartoum, previously served in Lebanon, Jordan, Algeria, and Iraq.[29]

In 2006, the Nairobi regional bureau took over the production and dissemination of French-language reports on the continent from the Paris bureau, added eight journalists, and hired two local Kenyans. The expansion of the Nairobi bureau into Xinhua's multilingual Africa media hub eased the problem of understaffing, quickened the pace of English and French translations, and increased coordination with the Cairo regional bureau, which administers Arabic content from the five North African bureaus.[30] Portuguese-language reports go through Xinhua's Beijing headquarters.

To ensure Chinese policymakers and propagandists' messages are carried to an ever-larger African audience, Xinhua purchases space in African newspapers. For instance, in 2009 Malawi's *Daily Times* ran a twelve-page supplement titled "50 years of Democratic Reform in Tibet." This "advertisement" was a reprint of a white paper issued by the Information Office of the State Council and published by Xinhua the month before.[31]

Xinhua's activities in Africa today are in sharp contrast to those in the pre-Cultural Revolution era. Africans' suspicion toward Xinhua's early revolutionary style helped shape the agency's contemporary approach to reporting and information dissemination in Africa. At the historic 2006 FOCAC ministerial summit in Beijing, for instance, the agency added 177 new African subscribers and according to a Xinhua survey that year the agency was the source of 31 percent of African stories on China, followed by Reuters 29 percent, AFP 7 percent, and AP 2 percent.[32] Xinhua's results in Africa appear to be quite successful.

Editorial Policy

Xinhua continues to face difficulties reconciling its role as a loyal CPC mouthpiece and as a trusted news source that covers all topics—even negative ones—for its subscribers. Xinhua journalists are instructed to analyze African problems through the prism of its colonial past. According to Xin Xin, to ease "African concerns over the 'China threat'," Xinhua uses three techniques: stressing China as a peace-loving country, using per capita figures to down play China's economic successes, and highlighting China's developing country status.[33]

Xinhua produces both public news and "internal reference" reports. The former are released as one of Xinhua's thousands of daily news items through Xinhua's conduits in China or to its 4,200 overseas subscribers in some 130 countries.[34] The latter "provide proprietary information and in-depth analyses for senior government officials, business executives and media leaders."[35] The classification of news and distribution of information within the CPC according to category began during the Chinese civil war and continued after the PRC was established in 1949. Sidney Rittenberg (aka Li Dunbai), an American CPC member who polished Xinhua's English broadcasts from the CPC's base in Yanan during the Chinese civil war and for Radio Peking until 1963 explained how the process worked in his autobiography:

> I was one of the few who had access to the real news, which came in secret, restricted-circulation documents. The lowest level was the *Cankao Xiaoshi,* or Reference News, which contained digests of foreign news—from *Le Monde* and *La Prensa* to *The New York Times* and *The Wall Street Journal*—that was considered safe for the average low-level cadre to read. The next higher level, *Cankao Ziliao,* or the Reference Materials, came out twice a day, one thick magazine of forty pages or more, along with one thinner one, and was circulated among higher-ranking officials, like central department heads and provincial party secretaries, and those of us in the propaganda organizations. The more important, and possibly explosive, international news, like political attacks on China by foreign leaders and writers, went in there. The real harsh truth about domestic and world events went in the *Neibu Cankao,* or Internal Reference, a flimsy magazine about the size and thickness of *Readers Digest,* which was published by the ministry of propaganda and distributed selectively on a need-to-know basis. And then there were the secret cables that only selected high-ranking party officials were cleared to read.[36]

The process of classifying some stories as *Neibu Cankao,* while releasing others for public consumption, remains highly political. The Propaganda Department of the CPC Central Committee monitors which reports are selected for internal consumption and which are released by Xinhua's wire service.[37] Reports on sensitive topics such as Taiwan, Islam, Tibet, or human rights and those portraying Chinese interests or firms in an unfavorable light are unlikely to be released. Instead, they are labeled "internal reference," kept only in Chinese, and sent to the relevant leaders, agencies, or state-run firms.[38] Xinhua editors in Beijing sort and classify correspondents' field reports, a structure that insures that reporters freely cover both sensitive and public topics.[39] A report on Xinhua produced by Reporters Without Borders describes the agency's contemporary classification process: "Heads of sections select the stories, the editor-translators translate them, the foreign experts correct them, then they go back to the heads of section, who decide to put them on the wire, after checking, according to the criteria laid down by the Propaganda department."[40]

Working with African Media

Xinhua reporters regularly cooperate with counterparts in African governments' official news agencies, an approach that makes them among the most well-connected and informed foreigners on the continent. Working with African news outlets helps Xinhua write reports more palatable for African readers and extends the agency's reach into countries that often receive minimal or primarily negative attention in the Western press. According to Liu Yunshan, director of the CPC Central Propaganda Department, these collaborations can help Xinhua collect information on "the ways overseas viewers customarily receive information [to] constantly enhance the appeal and affinity of overseas propaganda."[41] Shao Jie, for instance, works closely with the official Sudanese News Agency, although he has virtually no contacts with Sudan's private press.[42]

To promote exchanges between Xinhua and African media, China hosts delegations that include heads of African official news agencies. In 2007, for instance, the heads of the official news agencies of Senegal, Togo, and Benin visited China. They met with Xinhua President Tian Congming, signed "news exchange agreements" and expressed their hopes to "learn from Xinhua experiences and strengthen cooperation with the Chinese state media."[43] One of the participants, Beninese News Agency (ABP) director general Yaovi Hounkponou, described the experience in a Xinhua interview after his return to Cotonou. He fondly recounted the delegation's visits to

Beijing, Tianjin, Shenzhen, and Guangzhou and, in a statement revealing the effectiveness of Xinhua's approach, described ABP-Xinhua ties as "win-win cooperation," a moniker used frequently by China's state media.

In 2005, Xinhua's vice president, Ma Shengrong, officially announced that "Xinhua will further exchanges and cooperation with African news agencies."[44] Afterward the agency expanded cooperation and information sharing with at least a dozen African news agencies.[45] Examples include "enhanced exchanges in the areas of news stories, telecommunications technology, information, and data" with the Tunisia Africa News Agency, "cooperation on human resource training, technology and management" with a variety of media organizations in Sierra Leone, and the donation of computer systems for Zimbabwe's state-run *Herald* in 2007.[46] Kenya's state-run media has a cooperation agreement with China, and in 2010 Xinhua granted the *Kenya Times* unlimited use of its pictures and stories.[47] These agreements help develop long-term relationships among Xinhua reporters and their African counterparts that facilitate both information collection and distribution.

Relations between Xinhua and Zimbabwe's official news agency, New Ziana, have grown steadily; in 2009, the two signed an agreement to strengthen cooperation in technology and personnel training. Under the agreement eight Zimbabwe state-controlled community newspapers will run international pages carrying Xinhua stories and pictures.[48] Xinhua has also published collaborative stories with South Africa's official Bua News Agency. Those stories, labeled BuaNews-Xinhua, often include China-related content intended for South African readers and articles on international topics of interest to both Chinese and South African audiences.[49] Xinhua's Johannesburg correspondents' reports also run in local Chinese-language newspapers that cater to South Africa's Chinese communities.[50]

Sino-African media exchanges have not always gone smoothly, however. In 2006, Xinhua hosted Patrick Jabani, head of the Zambia News Agency, in China for a weeklong visit together with his counterparts from the Ethiopian News Agency and Tanzania's Guardian News Group.[51] Several months later, during a banquet welcoming President Hu Jintao to Lusaka, Jabani and fellow Zambian journalists were "isolated in a small room preventing them from observing the proceedings" while Xinhua journalists were allowed to cover the event. After Jabani's efforts to persuade protocol officers to allow Zambian journalists to gain access were rebuffed, one frustrated Zambian reporter exclaimed: "This is an insult to the profession. It is unacceptable for journalists to be quarantined."[52] By contrast, Chinese experts, like Zhao Shu-lan, who conducted an eight-month study on Zambia's media, blame such disagreements on Western influence and call for China's government news outlets "to propagandize China's work in Zambia as much as possible" and "utilize media resources reasonably to enlarge the influence [*SIC*]." According to Zhao, Zambia's international news is almost entirely "reprinted from BBC or CNN and other Western major media." Zambia's "elite class," Zhao argues, "is completely under western countries' control from economic development to knowledge about the outside world" resulting in an anti-China "bias" among Zambians.[53]

One way China has assuaged independent-minded African journalists' frustration with the Chinese media's steadfast subservience to the CPC has been to court them.[54] In 2006, for instance, the Foreign Ministry Information Department hosted twenty-four journalists from French-speaking African countries to help them "gain a comprehensive understanding of China," as assistant foreign minister Zhai Jun told the group.[55] African journalists also participate in tours that include participants from Asian and Latin American countries. In 2008, Xinhua organized a five-day "whirlwind visit" sponsored by the Beijing International Media Center that brought fifty-seven journalists from sixteen African countries to Beijing and Tianjin to "tour the Olympic media centers [and] scenic spots."[56] Short junkets like these supplement the more formal bilateral cooperation agreements and multilateral African journalist training sessions under the FOCAC framework.

Journalist Training

China conducts both bilateral and multilateral training sessions for African journalists intended to generate positive reporting about China in the African press and increase the number of media outlets that carry Xinhua reports. Xinhua says that during the symposiums "participants gain a thorough and deep understanding of the ongoing changes taking place in China through two weeks of lectures, seminars and tours." Journalist training workshops are "one of the key components of China-Africa human resource cooperation and will help enhance the exchange between [the] press of China and Africa," Li Qiangmin, deputy director general of the African Department of the Foreign Ministry, told African participants at a

2006 workshop in Beijing.[57] Xinhua's historical mission includes "publicizing China," and in Africa that requires cultivating sympathetic journalists
to spread the word. To this end, and in accordance with its FOCAC commitments, China hosts journalism training seminars for African media
personnel.

China's earliest media training sessions were technical support programs aimed mostly at teaching African reporters how to use Chinese
equipment. They included some instruction on the practice of journalism,
but not much.[58] Today, by contrast, bilateral media training programs are
conducted at Xinhua's journalist training centers in Beijing.[59] According to
Shen Ang, Xinhua's Khartoum bureau sends a small contingent of press
officials and journalists from the Sudan News Agency to Beijing annually
for a two-week training program.[60] Xinhua's bureau in Addis Ababa has a
similar program, as does its bureau in Lagos.[61] According to the chief of
Xinhua's Lagos bureau, bilateral training programs for Nigerian media
include both private and official news agencies and are intended to help
participants improve reporting skills while learning the "Xinhua style."
These bilateral training sessions also give Xinhua the opportunity to coordinate fact-checking and reporting with its often better informed African
counterparts.[62]

According to Dai Adi, Xinhua's Luanda bureau chief, during his five-
year appointment in Lagos he trained two Nigerian reporters who later
served as Nigerian News Agency's deputy chief editor and head of the Delta
regional office. These Nigerian journalists began their training at the local
Xinhua bureau in Lagos and completed it in Beijing, a process Dai said was
common.[63] Xinhua's Lagos bureau also provides Chinese-language content
for local newspapers that target the city's Chinese community.[64] Similarly,
South Africa's Bua and Xinhua host alternating delegations that last seven
to ten days; one year Xinhua news writers will visit Bua and the next year
Bua staff will travel to Xinhua headquarters. These efforts continue to
expand Xinhua's readership among South Africans and Chinese living in
South Africa.

In recent years, Xinhua's multilateral training sessions and workshops
for African media have increased with China's overall outreach on the continent. These workshops are the most public examples of increasingly regu-
larized journalist training initiatives conducted with the support of Xinhua,
State Council Information Office, Foreign Ministry, Ministry of Commerce,
and Chinese universities. The 2010–2012 FOCAC Action Plan agreed on in

Egypt described the ongoing nature of Sino-African media cooperation and reiterated both sides' commitment:

> The two sides will promote mutual visits between Chinese and African press department officials, editors and journalists, support the posting of journalists to each other's country by news organizations of the two sides, and encourage news media of the two sides to step up objective and fair coverage on China and Africa.[65]

In accordance with these FOCAC commitments, China held eight training workshops for African media between 2004 and 2011. Over this time Beijing sponsored training for about three hundred African media officials from forty-eight African countries in China.[66]

2004: Twenty African journalists from nineteen countries attended the first African Journalists' workshop in Beijing. They heard presentations from Foreign Ministry personal and the deputy editor-in-chief of Xinhua.[67] Participants toured information distribution and overseas propaganda related agencies including Xinhua and CCTV. Vice Minister of Foreign Affairs Dai Bingguo urged the participants to "write more stories about China and Africa and the trade opportunities that exist in both China and Africa."[68]

2005: China's State Council Information Office hosted the second workshop, which included press officials from more than twenty African countries. They attended a meeting with Xinhua vice president who pledged to boost "exchanges and cooperation with African news agencies."[69] They also met Li Changchun, a senior member of the Standing Committee of the CPC Central Committee Political Bureau, who "appealed to Chinese and African media organizations to enhance cooperation."[70]

2006: The FOCAC Secretariat hosted the Third Workshop for African Journalists in the run-up to the 2006 FOCAC in Beijing. The journalists attended instructional courses on topics including "China-Africa Relations and China's African Policy," "China's Experience and Achievements on Economic Reform and National Development," "Taiwan Question," and "China's Journalistic View and the Operation of Chinese Press." The delegation also visited the headquarters of Xinhua, CCTV, and China Radio International.[71] At the concluding ceremony Vice Foreign Minister Lu Guozeng awarded certificates to the forty-two African journalists from twenty-three English-speaking African countries.[72]

2008: The China Foreign Affairs University sponsored the fourth training program for twenty-two African journalists.[73] This program included training seminars and lectures on "China's National Conditions," "Relations Between China and African Countries," and China's news system. African participants also attended "study tours" at CCTV and CRI.[74]

The Information Office of China's State Council hosted the fifth training seminar for African press officials including thirty-two officials from eighteen African countries. According to Xinhua, during the two-week training program "the African press officials and media heads attend lectures and discuss with Chinese press officials, journalists and experts."[75] They also met with key propaganda officials including Wang Chen, the Information Office head, who called for "enhanced exchanges and cooperation between Chinese and African press departments"[76] and the head of the Publicity Department of the Central Committee of CPC.[77] African participants included the head of Togo's national TV station and Mali's presidential communication advisor.[78]

2009: The Information Office of China's State Council and the Ministry of Foreign Affairs jointly hosted the sixth training seminar for African press officials in Beijing. The workshop included seventy African media officials from twenty-seven African countries. Wang Chen again addressed the group, as did Zhai Jun, Assistant Foreign Minister.[79]

2010: The Information Office of China's State Council hosted the seventh training seminar for African press officials including thirty-six press officials from nineteen countries. African participants who visited Beijing and Chongqing, "were informed of the real situation in China through taking lectures, seminars, tours and other activities." They met with senior officials including the deputy director of the State Council Information Office and the director general of Chongqing's Propaganda Department.[80]

2011: The Ministry of Commerce and the State Council Information
  Office jointly hosted the eighth symposium for forty-two African
  government media officials, spokesmen, and senior managers of
  mainstream media organizations. Officials from seventeen
  African countries attended "two weeks of lectures, seminars and
  tours."[81]

After returning home from the June 2008 African journalist training program, Gideon Nkala of Botswana's *The Reporter* newspaper published his
firsthand account providing a rare glimpse into China's multilateral journalist training programs through African eyes. He notes that the African
journalists were all looking forward to the lecture on Tibet, during which,
the CPC instructor said, "Tibet has always been a part of China and greater
Tibet is a media creation that never existed." The Chinese people "see all
the lies and fabrications of the West, [which] tells of the atrocities committed by the Chinese and says nothing when the monks in Tibet kill and
maim people." The instructor also "brought pictures to show that even
pictures are cropped to cover the atrocities committed by the monks and
their supporters." Nkala reports that: "He made the whole class burst into
laughter when he said, with a straight face, that a new entrant into Chinese
street lingua for anything that is untrue and fabricated is now called CNN.
'If someone is telling a lie in China, we now say you are CNN.'"[82]

China Radio International (CRI)/Radio Peking in Africa

Radio Peking began transmissions to Africa in 1956, and prior to the Cultural Revolution, worked closely with Xinhua to magnify the CPC's voice
on the continent. Although its first broadcasts were weak and in Morse
code, only two years later Radio Peking began broadcasting a daily program
in Cantonese for Chinese communities in southern Africa and the Indian
Ocean. Surprisingly, these broadcasts contained little propaganda; they
were probably used to gauge listener response and to experiment with new
broadcast technology. In 1959, Radio Peking launched its first two-hour
English language radio broadcasts for Africans, and thereafter expanded its
Africa service.[83]

By 1961 Radio Peking's African audience was receiving more than
thirty-five hours of weekly programming in English, seven in Cantonese,

seven in Portuguese, seven in Swahili, four in French and additional broadcasts in Arabic in North Africa.[84] Teufel wrote in 1961, however, that Radio Peking's Africa service was broadcasting more than 100 total hours per week.[85] In 1963, China began broadcasting in Hausa, a West African language prevalent in Nigeria. To snare listeners from its competitors, Radio Peking broadcast in both American and British English; the latter mimicked the BBC both in radio frequency and its opening jingle.[86]

In 1964, Radio Peking began broadcasting more field reports illustrating the similarity in political, economic, and cultural conditions between African countries and China. Broadcasts to Africa provided "incitement and encouragement" for revolutionaries from their home countries. That year Radio Peking reported that there was "no prospect for a peaceful solution" in South Africa. Its Africa programming applauded the establishment of a Zimbabwe government-in-exile in Zambia, and its French-language African service reported that Moroccan guerillas had been fighting heroically "against modern arms furnished by the clique of imperialists with the United States at their head."[87] In nearly all cases, Radio Peking stressed the need for violent anti-colonial and anti-imperialist revolution. In 1965, journalist John K. Cooley said of Radio Peking:

> Every day, in all major tongues of Africa, Radio Peking broadcasts the rigid message of the Chinese Communists: "Only through violent revolution and armed struggle will the colonialists, the white men, be thrown out. Only through violence and fighting will real freedom come to Africa. Only by fighting for it will oppressed peoples of Africa, Asia, and Latin America defeat their worst enemy: American imperialism."[88]

Radio Peking and Xinhua correspondents in Beijing regularly asked Africans visiting China to give their impressions of various issues for African listeners.[89] In 1963, for example, Radio Peking covered the visit of a delegation from Zanzibar, hailed the "glorious traditions of heroic struggle against colonialism and imperialism" and reported a message from the delegation's leader, Sheikh Ali Mushin, thanking China for its "moral and material support" in the fight for independence.[90]

Through its donation of radio equipment China expanded the number of African listeners. In 1964, for instance, China provided the Republic of Congo with transmitters to broadcast shortwave signals.[91] By 1965, Radio

Peking had expanded its African service to nearly 100 hours a week, making it "the best-known and most effective propaganda channel of Red China in Africa."[92] When the Cultural Revolution began in 1966, radio journalists in Africa suffered the same fate as their Xinhua counterparts. Chinese diplomats and press correspondents were recalled, and by 1967, Radio Peking's English transmissions in East Africa had fallen to twenty-one hours a week, with transmissions only between six and nine o'clock in the evening.[93]

After the Cultural Revolution, Beijing reenergized Radio Peking's broadcasts and expanded its mission to include "providing listeners inside China with timely news and reports." Radio Peking was on the air for another decade until changing its name to Radio Beijing in 1983, and then again in 1993 to China Radio International. In the 1980s, as China's reform and opening up continued, Radio Beijing began to broadcast international topics including Africa into China. Throughout the 1990s international news broadcasts were gradually expanded to dozens of Chinese cities and in 1997, thanks to a 40 million RMB investment from the Chinese government and a $3.2 million loan from Austria, CRI switched from traditional analog broadcasts to digital ones.[94] CRI's digital facilities, provided by Siemens, include a data storage bank, a central control, live broadcast systems, and recording workstations, giving CRI the world's largest digital broadcasting system. According to its website CRI "serves the entire globe with 211 hours of broadcasts every day in forty-three foreign languages and Chinese dialects."[95]

CRI's Contemporary Activities in Africa

CRI's African offices are located in Cairo, Lagos, Nairobi, and Harare, and it broadcasts and hosts websites in Arabic, Hausa, Swahili, and English.[96] Although Xinhua remains the premier conduit of Chinese news and propaganda to Africans, CRI broadcasts via media including shortwave radio, satellite, webcast, and Internet pictures and stories. In 2000, there were an estimated one hundred million CRI listeners in Africa.[97] To expand this number over the last decade China has provided radio equipment to African countries including Comoro Islands, the DRC, the Congo, Equatorial Guinea, Lesotho, Malawi, Mali, Togo, Zambia, and Zimbabwe.

CRI has numerous AM and FM relays and in 2006 launched its first overseas-based FM radio station, 91.9 FM Nairobi. This station, a cooperative venture between the Chinese and Kenyan governments, provides nineteen hours of programming daily in English, Swahili, and Chinese to about two million listeners. Unlike its revolutionary forebear, CRI now includes a large amount of nonpolitical, cross-cultural content intended to bridge gaps between Chinese and Africans. In 2009, for instance, 91.9 FM Nairobi's schedule included programs such as *Music Safari* and *The Hot Pot Show* staggered between hourly news coverage in both Chinese and Swahili.[98]

In 2010, Togolese authorities and CRI and CCTV officials agreed that Radio Lome and Togolese Television would broadcast China's French-language reports. The agreement also provides technical and material assistance for modernization of Togo's state-owned radio and TV stations.[99]

Education

African elites generally do not have detailed and timely information about China. This is due to a lack of interest, historical contact, a common language, and formal mechanisms for Africans to pool their knowledge and develop coordinated policies toward China. Although a few African think tanks and universities have a small number of African experts devoted to understanding China, Stellenbosch University in South Africa hosts the only center for Chinese studies on the continent. Nevertheless, increasing numbers of African diplomats, students, and businessmen are returning from assignments and visits to China with a better understanding of Chinese politics and a continuing interest in China.

China has noticed this gap and taken measures to promote its image and influence among young Africans through educational programs. Like journalist training, educational and vocational training initiatives also develop person-to-person links and cultivate a group of African interlocutors who feel comfortable working with Chinese. Education also brings together African and Chinese elites and allows China to pass on both technical and political information. Although it often receives less attention than economics, foreign aid, and strategic topics, Chinese scholars and policymakers consistently emphasize education cooperation in publications and public statements. Through the FOCAC framework, Sino-African education initiatives continue to grow.

China-Africa Educational Exchanges (1960–2000)

China's educational and training programs began in the 1950s and early 1960s but were seriously damaged during the Cultural Revolution.[100] They were reconstituted between 1973 and 1978, but only fully reemerged during China's early reform period. In the 1990s, thanks to Chinese funding, the number of African students in China, Chinese instructors in Africa, and educational delegation exchanges in both directions grew exponentially. Since 2000 educational exchanges have been included in the FOCAC framework and expanded at an unprecedented rate.

Educational exchanges date to 1958, when the Prague-based International Union of Students began operating an African students' medical clinic in Beijing. In 1961, after many African countries gained independence, an estimated 500 African students from Algeria, Sudan, Somalia, Kenya, Egypt, Zanzibar, Cameroon, Chad, Ghana, and Uganda were studying at China's Institute of Foreign Languages in Beijing.[101] By 1963, the number of African students in China fell to approximately 380.[102] By 1966 it had slipped to 190 from fourteen countries, yet educational outreach efforts to Africa continued. That year China provided Tanzania and Somalia with teaching facilities, and sent Chinese students to Egypt, Morocco, and Algeria and five Chinese educational delegations to Egypt, Algeria, Mali, Guinea, Tanzania, Morocco, and the Central African Republic.[103]

When the Cultural Revolution began in earnest, however, Beijing cut off all African educational exchanges, recalled its teachers, and expelled all foreign students. All China-Africa educational programs were suspended until 1970–1971, when China again began sending language, mathematics, physics, and chemistry teachers to the Congo. China started readmitting foreign students in 1973, and by 1978 almost 500 students from twenty-five African countries attended Chinese universities. While China reduced the number of educational delegations to Africa, it increased the number of delegations it received from Africa. In the 1970s, the education ministers of Benin, Algeria, Tanzania, and Zambia visited China while Sudan, Somalia, DRC, Rwanda, Guinea, and Ethiopia each sent at least one educational delegation to Beijing.[104]

Between 1979 and 1989 few Chinese studied in Africa, but 2,271 African students from forty-three countries studied in China. Beijing continued to send teachers and teaching equipment to Africa. In 1990, a policy termed "high level, short term, high benefit" shifted the focus from African undergraduates to graduate students and vocational training programs. Between 1990 and 1996, China hosted 1,500 African students from forty-five countries, sent nearly 100 Chinese students to nine African countries, and sponsored twenty-four onsite training programs in eighteen African countries. China's vocational training initiatives for Africans included courses in computers, food processing, civil engineering, construction, land surveying, and Chinese language. Like journalist training, however, educational and vocational training initiatives were small compared to programs begun under the FOCAC framework in 2000.[105]

FOCAC and the Development of China-Africa Education Cooperation (2000–2011)

FOCAC Summit #1, Beijing, October 2000: At the inaugural FOCAC meeting a new framework for China-Africa education cooperation was established and "unleashed a new level of interaction in education, in many different modalities." Several mechanisms to expand education were introduced including the African Human Resources Development Fund, the Program for China-Africa Cooperation in Economic and Social Development, and an agreement to work toward country-specific education plans. Scholarships for long-term degrees, posting Chinese teachers in Africa, and the development of relations between Chinese and African universities were approved, although no specific targets were set.[106]

FOCAC Summit #2, Addis Ababa, October 2003:[107] At this meeting China agreed to sponsor over 300 courses for 10,000 African professionals in areas such as economic management, agriculture, education, science, technology, and medical treatment between 2004 and 2006.[108] African countries selected participants and agreed to provide logistical support for the establishment of Chinese schools for technical and vocational education in Africa.[109] China also offered new scholarship opportunities for African students to study in China. In 2003, 1,793 Africans studied in China, representing about one-third of total foreign students.[110]

Sino-Africa Education Minister Forum, Beijing, November 2005: This meeting pulled together and evaluated the China-Africa educational programs before the 2006 FOCAC. African education ministers emphasized vocational and technical education, university-level education, and cultural diversity. These concepts were reiterated in China's 2006 Africa Policy White Paper. In 2005, China offered 1,200 annual scholarships to African students and about sixty education projects in twenty-five African countries.[111] Between 2000 and 2005 the total number of African students studying in China rose from 1,388 to 2,757.[112]

FOCAC Summit #3, Beijing, November 2006: The Beijing Action Plan approved at this meeting included pledges for educational scholarships and vocational training. Between 2006 and 2009 China agreed to train 15,000 African professionals, double the number of scholarships for Africans to study in China from 2,000 a year to 4,000, send 300 "Chinese Young Volunteers" to African countries, and set up 100 rural schools and thirty hospitals.[113] These pledges and the establishment of the African Visiting Scholars Program set ambitious targets. In 2007, there were about 2,700 African students in China pursuing higher education in areas including agriculture, medicine, linguistics, education, economy, and management; 57.3 percent of them were working on MA and PhD degrees.[114]

FOCAC Summit #4, Sharm el-Sheikh, November 2009: In the Sharm el-Sheikh Action Plan approved at this meeting China again provided specific guarantees to African countries on "human resources development and education."[115] By 2012, China promised to train another 20,000 professionals, offer 5,500 Chinese government scholarships to African students, build fifty schools, and train 1,500 African principals and teachers.[116] After the announcement, Premier Wen Jiabao declared: "The ultimate goal of cooperation with Africa is to build up the self-development capacity of African countries. We paid great importance to better living conditions and human resources training in Africa."[117] Both the Egyptian and Sudanese representatives agreed and, according to Xinhua, thanked China for narrowing the "gap in technological know-how" through its joint training and education programs.[118] The Fifth FOCAC Ministerial meeting, scheduled to be held in Beijing in 2012, promises further development of Sino-African educational cooperation.

Professional Training

Africans studying in China can select from a variety of short-term professional and technical training programs. China's Ministry of Education

(MOE) supports courses for Africans at several second-tier Chinese universities including Jilin University, Northeastern Normal University, and China Agricultural University, each of which trained more than two hundred Africans between 2002 and 2006. Each year since 2002, the MOE has held a workshop to coordinate its educational assistance for developing countries, Africa in particular. The fifth such gathering, held in Chengdu, Sichuan, in 2007, included participants from the MOE, Ministry of Commerce, and Ministry of Foreign Affairs, as well as representatives from more than twenty Chinese universities.[119]

Zhejiang Normal University has probably trained the most Africans and in 2006 had relationships with more than twenty universities in over a dozen African countries. In 1996, the university set up a Chinese Language Training Center in Cameroon and in 2003 with support from the MOE established China's first Center for African Education Studies. Zhejiang Normal University's professional training focuses on African university presidents and administrators. In 2006, for instance, the university held the China-Africa University President Forum, including over thirty presidents and education officials from fourteen African countries.[120] In 2009, Institute director Liu Hongwu and Yang Jiemian of the Shanghai Institute of International Studies published a comprehensive book in English titled, *Fifty Years of Sino-African Cooperation: Background, Progress & Significance*. This volume includes thirty-three essays on China-Africa relations, each from a different Chinese expert.

Tianjin University of Technology and Education was designated in 2003 as an official base for African professional training. In 2005, after the Sino-African Education Minister's Forum, the university upgraded its facilities into a Center for African Vocational Educational Studies for training African midcareer professionals. In 2006, China's Ministry of Education sponsored a symposium titled "Principals' Seminar on Asian African Vocational Education" at the Center, trained more than two hundred African students, and sent eighty-four teachers to administer vocational training programs in Africa.[121]

Confucius Institutes

Since there are few Africans with an extensive knowledge of China, Beijing hopes that by educating a new generation in Chinese language and culture it will facilitate economic and political relations with African countries. To this end, China's Office of Chinese Language Council International (Hanban) has expanded its worldwide Confucius Institutes Program to African universities, offering startup grants of $100,000 to $150,000 per center.[122] Confucius Institutes provide Chinese-language programs, train Chinese teachers, administer Chinese exams and tutoring services, and organize Chinese language competitions. Some offer services for African students interested in studying in China and provide commercial and cultural information regarding China.[123] According to the Hanban program director in Beijing, these activities are conducted to fulfill three primary objectives: teach Chinese, promote cultural exchange, and promote business.[124]

The Hanban began establishing Chinese-learning institutions overseas in 2002 and in 2004 linked them together as Confucius Institutes.[125] China christened its first Confucius Institute in Seoul, South Korea, and two years later held the first Confucius Institute Conference in Beijing with over two hundred representatives from thirty-eight countries worldwide to discuss their charter and facilitate its global expansion.[126]

China spends about $12 million a year on Confucius Institutes plus $25 million to support Chinese as a foreign language. Although this expenditure is small, the Institutes have largely been a public relations success. This has been due, in part, to the cooperative nature of the programs, for which China supplies teachers, materials, and start-up money, while the African host institution houses the institute.[127] Although generous with support, the Hanban is tightfisted on Institutes' teaching content. According to its "2007 Standard Model for Confucius Institutes," the Hanban only grants a "license to operate Confucius Institutes to qualified educational organizations that accept Confucius Institutes' unified curriculum and management model."[128]

The activities of each Confucius Institute in Africa and its effectiveness depends on the agency of the Chinese university partner and the local capacity and needs of the African host country. In a sign of high level support for Africa's Confucius Institutes, senior Chinese officials often inaugurate or visit them on trips to Africa.[129] The Nairobi University Confucius Institute was established in 2005 and began its activities with a dumpling making activity for Kenyan students to celebrate Chinese New Year.[130] In 2006, the Institute began with forty students in two classes; within two years it had expanded to 260 students in nine classes. In 2009, one of the Kenyan administrators announced that within three years the

Institute would have independent facilities for a full research center for Chinese studies.[131] The Institute's deputy dean responded with a plan to "root the Institute into African soil by means of integrating it into [the] Kenyan educational system." He praised the establishment of a "research center for Chinese studies to diversify the function of the Institute" and described its functions to CRI:

> We have established Bachelor's Degree in Chinese language and we're ready to recruit students from this school year. The degree lasts four years with 44 credits. The Confucius Institute will enlarge its recruitment to the whole society instead of just university students. We are going to launch a training class for Kenyan primary and secondary school teachers so as to make sure Kenyans can get to know about Chinese at a younger age. Meanwhile, we will strengthen cultural exchanges between China and Kenya. For example, we are planning to hold ten seminars concerning Chinese culture and development in the past thirty years.[132]

Kenyatta University's Confucius Institute opened in 2009 with Chinese language and culture instructors provided by Shandong Normal University. The Hanban provided $150,000 startup funds plus books, equipment, and in-service training and smaller targeted grants for four years, although the Institute is expected to be self-sustaining after that. The Institute began with six students the first semester; the second group numbered seventy (of the university's 28,000 students). To attract more Kenyans, the Institute, which in 2010 was temporarily housed in a former residence but will have a specially designed center, hosted summer courses for eighteen students from other Kenyan universities. That year five Kenyatta University students had year-long scholarships at Shandong Normal University to learn Chinese.[133]

Of course, not all the twenty-eight or so Confucius Institutes in eighteen African countries have come together as quickly as Kenya's.[134] In 2006, Egypt's Cairo University signed an agreement with Peking University to establish a Confucius Institute.[135] Although scheduled to begin operation in 2007, classes did not begin until 2008, after China had donated some 3,000 books.[136]

Egypt's second Confucius Institute at Suez Canal University appears to have developed at a similar pace. In 2007, the university joined with China's

little-known Hubei Electric Power University to open a Chinese department and sent five instructors to China to develop curricula.[137] In 2008,
the Institute was unveiled, and by 2009, it was providing elementary and
professional Chinese language courses for Egyptian employees of Chinese-
owned enterprises operating in Egypt.[138] In 2010, it began offering Chinese
courses for personnel from the Chinese-owned Zhigao Electrical Appliance
Industry Co., Ltd. Thirteen Egyptian employees underwent a two-month
elementary Chinese training course at the Institute followed by three
months of training in specialized vocabulary for the air conditioning
industry.[139]

As of 2011, South Africa alone had four Confucius Institutes, initiated
in 2007 at Rhodes University, University of Cape Town, Tshwane University of Technology, and University of Stellenbosch.[140] The latter has been
the most active in South Africa, if not the entire continent. Xiamen University established the Confucius Institute at the University of Stellenbosch in South Africa.[141] For its first two years under the stewardship of
Stellenbosch's Centre for Chinese Studies the relationship bolstered the
Centre's already robust research capacity and underwrote several high
quality publications, China-related events, and student scholarships to
China.[142] In 2009, however, after key staff departed, the Institute moved
to the University's Postgraduate and International Office for reorganiza-
tion and development.[143]

In an attempt to set standards and create "best practices in the operation of Confucius Institutes," Beijing has hosted several conferences bringing together current and potential hosts from around the world. In 2008,
for instance, the Hanban hosted representatives from Africa's Confucius
Institutes for a conference in Beijing on the establishment and operation of
Confucius Institutes in Africa.[144] Africa-based Confucius Institutes' staff are
also invited to discuss their activities and operations with counterparts from
around the world in larger gatherings such as the World Forum on Confucius Institutes held in 2007 at *Ritsumeikan* University in Kyoto, Japan.
Beijing now hosts the Confucius Institute Conference every December; the
fifth annual Conference was held there in 2010.[145]

Student Grievances

Given the linguistic and cultural differences between Chinese and African
ethnicities it is not surprising that many Africans studying in China have

returned home feeling lonely and disillusioned.[146] During the 1960s, African students regularly returned from China's universities complaining about state surveillance and censored mail. Dozens were expelled in the early 1960s for violating prohibitions on fraternization with Chinese women. Four of five Sudanese students left China and twenty-two of forty-two Somalis who went in 1960 had returned by mid-1961.[147] In 1962, thirty Cameroonian students were expelled after they reacted openly to racial discrimination.[148]

Intercultural conflicts whereby linguistic, racial, or interpersonal relations have resulted in arguments and even violent clashes between African and Chinese students have been reported over the years. The earliest recorded clash came in 1962 when a scuffle between an African student and a Chinese outside a Beijing hotel became a riot. Several people were hospitalized and the Africans arrested were released only after the intervention of Guinea's ambassador and Ghana's chargé d'affaires. Chinese authorities eventually apologized to the African students.[149]

The most infamous incident occurred in Nanjing in December 1988 when a mob of Chinese students and residents attacked African students at Hohai University after rumors spread they were hosting Chinese women in their dormitories. No doubt jealousy over living conditions also played a part; African students had heat and lived two to a room compared with their Chinese classmates who had no heat and slept six to a room. Regardless of the reason, African students were detained for five days at a guesthouse where they were stripped and tortured by Chinese police with electric batons on their genitals.[150]

Large-scale confrontations between Chinese and African students and Chinese authorities have become less common over the years, yet discrimination by cab drivers, merchants, and average Chinese toward African students remains a source of anxiety for Africans in Chinese cities.[151] In 2010, for instance, Muslim Africans at Zhejiang Normal University were angered after they, unlike their Christian compatriots, were denied a place to worship.[152]

One way China and African countries have sought to mitigate intercultural conflicts and attract Africans to study in China is through China-Africa youth gatherings. Although they have existed for decades, in 2004 the Communist Youth League of China and All-China Youth Federation expanded this concept by sponsoring the first China-Africa Youth Festival, including 132 "youth organizations, statesmen and entrepreneurs" from forty-four African countries.[153] The second Festival was held in 2006 and by 2009, it had attracted over 750 participants, including youth representatives of forty-nine African countries. In his keynote address to participants, Premier Wen Jiabao encouraged them to "contribute to the building of a China-Africa strategic partnership."[154]

Culture

Cultural exchanges, a feature of China-Africa social relations for over half a century, have helped lay the groundwork for political, economic, media, and education cooperation. Whereas cultural links had once been the first and sometimes only ties between China and African countries, today they have given way to a diverse array of interpersonal links.

Unlike highly asymmetric media and educational cooperative programs where China funds the exchanges and provides the lion's share of content, cultural activities facilitate an equal exchange. Cultural exchange was often the first area of cooperation for countries beginning to open relations with China.[155] For Africa these activities began when Egypt signed Africa's first cultural agreement with China in 1955; a seventy-six-member Chinese Cultural and Art Ensemble delegation visited Egypt and Sudan in 1956.[156] In 1958, twenty Chinese cultural delegations visited Africa, forty-five African delegations visited China, and China established cultural exchanges with Morocco, Ghana, Nigeria, Somaliland, Uganda, and Angola. The next year, ten Chinese cultural delegations visited Africa and fifty African delegations went to China. These delegations, as they do today, included a variety of people such as acrobats, sports teams, youth delegations, and theater groups. In the 1950s and 1960s African delegations often attended rallies with thousands of Chinese to celebrate such occasions as "Algeria Day" and "Congo Week." CPC Front Groups organized these events making them inherently political.[157]

Early cultural delegations under the joint supervision of the China-Africa People's Friendship Association and the State Council's Commission for Cultural Relations with Foreign Countries provided an important first outreach to African countries reluctant to engage in political relations with the PRC. Under their umbrella numerous front organizations—including the Chinese People's Association for Cultural Relations with Foreign Countries established in 1954 and the Chinese People's Institute for Foreign

Affairs established in 1949—worked to develop cultural ties with Africans. In 1957, the former published the *China Handbook* in which it explained the role of Chinese cultural exchanges:

> [China] sponsors the exchange of cultural delegations, and visits of writers, artists and scientists, the holding of exhibitions and commemoration meetings of outstanding cultural figures of different ages and different countries, and the staging of theatrical performances. Through these and other channels, Chinese cultural achievements are introduced to the peoples of other countries whilst those of other peoples are introduced into China.[158]

In the 1950s African delegations hosted by groups including the All China Journalists Association and the All China Students Federation officially came under the framework of China-Africa cultural exchanges. They also expanded opportunities for Sino-African media and educational exchanges. In 1958, for instance, eight African journalists from Senegal, Angola, Nigeria, Somalia, Uganda, and Ghana visited China and their "satisfaction with China's astonishing progress" was broadcast in Africa via Radio Beijing and published in the official *People's Daily*. That year an Egyptian teachers' delegation led by the country's assistant minister of education also visited China for three weeks.[159] In 1960, however, these initiatives were placed under the Chinese African People's Friendship Association (CAPFA), which has remained an important vehicle for Sino-African cultural cooperation ever since.[160]

In the 1980s China-Africa cultural cooperation expanded on the city and provincial levels. These initiatives began in 1982 when the Foreign Affairs Office of the Hunan Provincial People's Government agreed to allow Changsha to establish the first China-Africa sister-city friendship agreement with Brazzaville.[161] Between 1982 and 2006, sixty-nine such agreements were established between Chinese provinces and cities and African counterparts. According to CAPFA, through "consolidating and strengthening friendship-city and province relations Sino-African friendship has extended to the grass-roots level and entered the households of common people."[162]

Cultural Exchanges Under FOCAC

Under the FOCAC framework cultural exchanges became more formalized. In the 2003 Addis Ababa Action plan, for instance, China initiated an annual international art festival featuring African arts and established "bilateral cultural exchange programs" to host "government cultural delegations from Africa."[163] An official government website titled "Cultural Exchange Between China and Africa" identified a half-dozen "main features" of contemporary China-Africa cultural exchange: high level exchanges, performances and art exhibitions, expanding the content of cultural exhibitions, cooperative training of arts and performers, establishment of China cultural centers in Benin and Mauritius, and "special theme activities," for example, "Moroccan Culture Week," and "Algerian Movie Week" in China and "Chinese Culture Month" in African countries.[164]

Between 2007 and 2009, five Chinese cultural delegations visited ten African countries, and African delegations from fifteen countries toured China.[165] One such delegation visited Nigeria in 2008 when the Chinese embassy, in collaboration with the Nigerian Film Corporation (NFC), sponsored "Chinese Movie Week 2008." The Chinese side financed the venture, provided the film projectors, and trained Nigerians to use them. The embassy also established a scholarship for NFC staff to pursue graduate degrees in film studies at Chinese universities.[166]

In 2009, China reaffirmed the importance of cultural exchanges with African countries. That year China signed sixteen new bilateral cultural agreements with African countries, adding to the existing twenty cultural agreements with African countries since 2006. China's National Cultural Bureau, National Radio Television Film Bureau, and Press and Publication Administration hosted the "2009 Chinese Culture Focus," which broadcast Chinese tradition and culture into twenty African countries. This programming was the corollary of the "2008 African Culture Focus" held in Shenzhen. In 2009, 734 Chinese artists from twenty provinces attended twenty-seven festivals and celebrations in African countries while 370 African artists from twenty-one African countries performed at the International Art Show in China.[167]

These contemporary cultural exchanges between Chinese and Africans still carry political overtones. In 2009, for instance, China hosted sixty-one delegations from African countries to participate in discussions on titles such as "Cultural Policy Discussion," "Idea Exchanging on Managing State Affairs," and "Creative Thinking in Painting." For China, crafting a favorable national image remains a key component of all cultural exchange with African countries.[168]

Community

Chinese in Africa

Over the last decade Chinese communities have grown throughout Africa, and in 2007, Xinhua estimated that at least 750,000 Chinese were working or living on the continent.[169] Although no one knows the exact number, we judge it is now closer to a million. These growing numbers of Chinese often live together in Chinatowns or company-owned compounds for laborers rather than interspersed throughout society. There are, however, important distinctions among Chinese of different classes, professions, regions, and generations. These divisions limit contacts among some Chinese with Africans. Broadly speaking, Chinese communities in Africa consist of three different groups: professionals, unskilled laborers, and traders and businesspersons.

The first category, professionals, includes Chinese embassy personnel, government specialists, representatives of large Chinese companies, and project managers. Chinese in this group usually speak one of the local languages and interact well with Africans. After completing their assignment, most return to China or move to another posting within their firm or agency. The second and probably largest category is the minimally skilled or unskilled Chinese workers sent for a fixed period to work on a particular project. They rarely speak a local language, tend to live in compounds, seldom interact socially with Africans, and leave their families in China. They come because of higher salaries and are anxious to return to China when their contract ends. They frequently have unkind words about their experiences and interaction with Africans.

The third category includes Chinese traders and small businesspersons. They come seeking business opportunities, often bringing their families, speak a little of the local language, live modestly, and tend to remain longer. So long as business is good and personal security remains satisfactory, larger numbers are likely to become permanent residents in Africa. Many of them have become part of permanent Chinese communities in Africa and some live among Africans. They sell affordable products sometimes supplied by a vertically integrated supply chain that links family producers and distributors in China (predominantly Fujian and Zhejiang) to African retailers and consumers. Through hard work and avoiding tariffs, these traders have undercut the price of local producers and businesses in some African countries.

Although there appears to be ample understanding on the official level, cultural clashes do occur. In particular, intercultural conflicts have occurred during on-site training sessions in Africa, in which Africans have not been receptive to Chinese training methods, leading to hostility on both sides. Chinese trainers from the state-controlled Huawei and the provincial-level Hunan Development Corporation complained in separate interviews that efforts to train Ethiopians had been difficult. "You teach them one day and they forget or are gone the next. Training Africans is a waste of time," said one disgruntled Huawei trainer in 2007.[170] Representatives of the Hunan Development Corporation in Addis Ababa also expressed frustrations with their training programs and local hires. Some Chinese instructors called Ethiopians "low-quality persons" (*suzhi hen di*), "lazy" (*lan*), and "black devil" (*heigui*). "All these people are born with their hand out. They even eat with their hands like dogs!" said one Chinese in a thick Hunan accent over lunch in Addis Ababa. They told of bad blood created by a brawl between Ethiopians and Chinese at the local Chinese restaurant a few months prior.[171]

Labor protests have sometimes been a problem. In 2008, for instance, in Equatorial Guinea four hundred Chinese workers were summarily deported for protesting against their employer, a Chinese construction company. Protesting is illegal under Equatorial Guinea's repressive laws. Compensation probably triggered the dispute since Chinese workers often work on one- to two-year contracts with salaries in U.S. dollars, and the value of the dollar had fallen sharply against the local currency.[172] Chinese firms' labor contracts for both Chinese and African workers are written in accordance with local labor laws to avoid compensating employees who are dismissed or injured.[173] In 2007, China's Non-Ferrous Metals Mining Company labor practices sparked violent protests at Zambia's Chambishi copper mine after forty-nine miners died in an accident.[174] On the eve of President Hu Jintao's 2007 visit to Zambia, workers' sentiments were running high: "I hope their president will use this trip to educate his people on how to treat workers properly," said Joyce Nonde, president of the Federation of Free Trade Unions in Zambia. "We are fed up with them."[175]

The spread of anti-Chinese narratives in Africa need not have coherent or predictable consequences. For instance, in 2010 soccer fans chanting, "Chinese go home" rioted and attacked Chinese businesses in Lubumbashi,

DRC, after their side lost to Inter Milan. Congolese fans mistook the Japanese referee for a Chinese, and were angered by some of his decisions in the match.[176] Incidents like this one suggest that simmering anti-Chinese sentiment at the grassroots level is an increasingly powerful force that can be activated by spontaneous, unforeseen events.

South Africa's Chinese Community. South Africa's 200,000–300,000 Chinese residents represent Africa's largest and oldest Chinese immigrant community, yet they are starkly divided.[177] Relations among the older generations of Chinese immigrants, which tend to be from Hong Kong or Taiwan, and the more recently arrived mainland Chinese can be tense. The first wave of Chinese immigrants came to South Africa as convicts in the early eighteenth century, the second came as Britain took over the colony in the early nineteenth century, the third came from Taiwan (which maintained diplomatic relations with South Africa during apartheid), and the fourth, from the mainland, began with the establishment of diplomatic relations between Beijing and South Africa in 1998.[178] The latest group of Chinese immigrants, which represents a large majority of today's Chinese population, is made up mostly of men who either migrated illegally to South Africa or overstayed their visas. Although the largest group of these new Chinese immigrants appears to be from Fujian province, there are thirty-four Chinese community organizations divided by province. In 2007, there were at least three local Chinese language newspapers in South Africa and a variety of radio programs.[179]

While South Africa's mainland community has flourished over the last decade, the Taiwanese community (which had once benefited under the apartheid regime by being classified as "White" unlike their mainland cousins who were indentified as "Colored") has dwindled from about 50,000 to about 5,000–10,000 in 2007. Thousands chose to return to Taiwan rather than cope with increased crime and competition from new immigrant traders with better supply chains on the mainland. Many Hong Kong Chinese have also returned home or moved to Australia, Canada, or the United States.[180]

Although the Chinese community—like those in Western nations—tends to refrain from active involvement in politics (only about 3 percent have voting rights) some Chinese, like Huang Shiaan-Bin, have embraced South Africa's postapartheid democracy.[181] Huang was elected city senator and vice mayor of New Castle in the 1990s before joining the ANC in 2000 and winning a seat in Parliament in 2004. He holds both South African and

Taiwan passports, maintains his family home in Taipei, and visited main-land China in 2004 and 2005 in his official capacity as a South African MP.[182] In 2010, Chen Sherry Su-Huei of the opposition Democratic Alliance was the only other ethnic Chinese serving with MP Huang in the South African parliament.[183] Although she is also of Taiwanese descent, they are members of opposing political parties and, according to Huang, rarely agree on South African politics.

Disagreements among Chinese communities go beyond the official realm in South Africa. Beginning in the late 1970s and early 1980s, intra-communal conflicts extended to the criminal world. In 2001, seven major Chinese organized criminal groups were identified in Cape Town and Johannesburg. Four were Cantonese-speaking and originated from Hong Kong and southern China, and the other three, mainly Mandarin-speaking, have links to Taiwan's triads.[184] According to a 2000 report on gang violence in Cape Town these groups were involved in drugs, prostitution, gambling, import of counterfeit goods, and the illegal export of abalone and shark fins. Some Chinese-owned import/export companies participate in both the legal and illicit export of abalone to China.[185]

Nigeria's Chinese Traders. In Lagos, Nigeria, the Chinese trader community lives and works in a large red fortress resembling the Great Wall of China and adorned with a sign in both English and Chinese that reads: "Long Live Nigeria-China Friendship!" During interviews conducted in 2007, residents of the Chinese trader community in Lagos were most concerned about security. Many of Nigeria's at least 30,000 Chinese are undocumented and their cash businesses and poor English makes them targets for local thieves.[186] One Lagos-based Chinese language paper, *West Africa United Business Weekly*, carried a cover story in 2007 warning Chinese residents not to provoke robbers by "looking them in the eye" or "fighting back." The article noted that China's consulate in Lagos was working with local police to improve security and solve several robberies of Chinese businesses and restaurants.[187] To inform residents of the Chinese community the Lagos consulate also provided each household with a Chinese language pamphlet detailing relevant Nigerian laws and providing emergency instructions.[188]

Chinese merchants in Lagos depend on a steady supply of imports from China. The Nigerian government has imposed import duties designed to curtail Chinese imports in favor of Nigerian producers and in 2004 police targeting counterfeit and smuggled goods raided the Chinatown market in central Lagos.[189] With the support of Nigerian merchants, customs officials confiscated Chinese goods before destroying their shops and leaving Chinese merchants and their families little choice but to move to the new complex.

Corruption among Nigerian customs officials fed by Chinese merchants allows for a steady stream of smuggled Chinese textile goods. Once these items arrive in the wholesale China market, Nigerian traders purchase them in bulk for resale at marked-up prices to local residents in shops inside the city's center. Yet, Lagos's Chinatown has its advantages. It offers increased personal security, convenient and spacious living quarters, ample parking, wholesale and retail sales venues, and is close to the highway. Facilities include a pub, karaoke parlor, and medical clinic for Chinese residents.[190]

Africans in China

Between 2000 and 2011, in addition to students, the number of Africans working in China grew rapidly. Nearly all Africans live in major Chinese cities including Beijing, Shanghai, Hong Kong, Guangzhou, Nanjing, and Tianjin. In Hong Kong, Chongking Mansion is a center for the African trader community. Although Africans from around the continent congregate there, the majority are West African—mainly Nigerian. One center of African community activity in Guangzhou is the Tianshi Building complex, which includes a multitiered market for Chinese products aimed at both local African residents and exporters.[191]

Some African communities in Guangzhou, like the Ghanaians and the Senegalese, have developed community-based civic organizations. Estimates vary on Guangzhou's African population. Huang Shiding, a city management expert at the Guangzhou Academy of Social Sciences, estimated there are about 20,000 Africans in the city, but in 2007, the *Guangzhou Daily* reported there could be as many as 100,000. That year police complained about the African drug-trafficking network that they said could turn Guangzhou into a narcotics hub.[192]

To stem the growing number of Africans in Guangzhou, after the 2008 Beijing Olympics, police cracked down on those who overstayed their visas. In 2009, a Nigerian trader shattered his leg attempting to escape visa inspection and six months later another died after jumping from a window to avoid Chinese immigration agents.[193] In response, more than one hundred Africans carrying the man's body surrounded a Guangzhou police station demanding justice. One Nigerian embassy official in Beijing accused authorities of "heavy-handedness" and pursuing "to the point of death."[194] A Nigerian trader in Guangzhou summed up the Africans' gripe: "The Chinese make money from Africa, but they want to stop us doing the same here. To me, it doesn't make sense."[195]

Large numbers of African diplomats and students live in Beijing. In 2007, accusations of drug dealing led to the roundup and beating of at least twenty Africans.[196] Where there are concentrations of Africans, there can be a tension between them and local citizens. Despite anti-African sentiments, however, some African businesses in China—particularly restaurants, coffee shops, and bars catering to the expatriate community—have found success. In Nanjing, a local magazine reported on Oscar Mbeben, a Cameroonian student-turned-businessman. In 1995 Mbeben arrived in Nanjing to study electronics at Nanjing Normal University. He confronted much of the racism and xenophobia of previous generations of Africans. Some Chinese would get off the elevator if he was inside, comment about his "dirty skin," or cross the street to avoid him. These experiences hardened Mbeben's resolve to introduce "black culture" to Nanjing and precipitated his establishment of two hip-hop clubs, a clothing store, and an album entitled "Nanjing Love." Mbeben explained that "when he first came to China [he] encountered ignorance and fear toward people of his race. Now things are different in Nanjing but that same ignorance does still exist."[197]

8

China's Relations with North Africa and the Sahel

In the mid-1950s, the PRC began its African diplomatic offensive in North Africa for very practical reasons. It was the region of Africa that had the largest number of independent states; Beijing believed it could persuade several to recognize the PRC. China began with Egypt, and followed success there two years later in Morocco and with the provisional government in Algeria, which was in a war for independence with France. Although conservative Tunisia did not recognize Taiwan, it required more persuasion. The Kingdom of Libya established relations with Taiwan in 1959 and the socialist government that seized power in 1969 continued that relationship until it agreed to recognize only Beijing in 1978. This gave the PRC a monopoly on diplomatic relations with the five countries of North Africa.

China's relations with Egypt and Algeria are close and both are strategic partners of the PRC, a relationship that survived the 2011 Arab Spring. Ties with Morocco and Tunisia are good but not as developed as with Egypt and Algeria. Their relationship depends primarily on trade. Libya continues to pose challenges for Beijing, although China seems willing to suffer an occasional indignity because of Libya's significant oil resources in which China has shown increasing interest.

The five Sahel countries located immediately south of North Africa initially presented a combination of opportunity and challenge for Beijing. Soon after independence, then left-leaning Mali quickly recognized the PRC. Mauritania opted for relations with Taiwan after independence but switched five years later to the PRC. Chad began by recognizing Taipei two years after independence, switched back and forth and now recognizes Beijing. Niger followed a similar path but reestablished ties with Beijing sooner than Chad. Burkina Faso, which recognized the PRC from 1973 to 1994, is one of only four African countries that currently recognize Taiwan.

Of the Sahel countries, Beijing has consistently had the warmest relationship with Mauritania. Although Beijing has maintained cordial ties with Mali, they have not lived up to their early potential. This may be a result of Mali's lack of important natural resources and its more recent pursuit of democratic governance. Beijing's interest in Niger has increased notably in recent years because of its oil and uranium deposits. China's relations with Chad, which has significant oil reserves, were complicated by China's more important relationship with neighboring Sudan, which periodically has been in conflict with Chad. Except for Burkina Faso, China has been successful in developing good relations with the Sahel countries. The region has, however, presented challenges for Chinese diplomacy and will continue to do so.

Egypt

The PRC identified Egypt as the most likely independent African country to be receptive to diplomatic recognition. Although Egypt established relations with the ROC in 1942, Gamal Abdel Nasser and a group of "free officers" overthrew the Egyptian monarchy in 1952. Nasser instituted left-wing rule and a policy of Arab socialism. The PRC initially reacted negatively to the Nasser revolution, calling it a product of U.S. imperialism. China's attitude changed in 1954 when Egypt pursued a more neutral foreign policy and Beijing decided to cooperate with the global national bourgeoisie. The PRC concluded that Egypt could be enticed to switch recognition from Taipei to Beijing and worked hard beginning at the Bandung Conference to cultivate the Egyptians. In 1955, a number of Egyptian government delegations visited China and the two countries signed a trade agreement. Egypt even suggested that the Arab League recognize the PRC. Beijing's efforts paid off; in 1956, Egypt became the first African country to establish formal relations with the PRC[1] (see Appendix 1 for dates when PRC and African countries established diplomatic relations). China initiated a modest economic assistance program the same year.[2] Beijing opened its first African Xinhua office in Cairo in 1958. Today, Xinhua's Cairo bureau serves as its headquarters for North Africa and the Middle East.

Compared to other African countries, Sino-Egyptian relations have been more equal from the beginning. Like China, Egypt has a long and proud history. China initially needed Egypt more than Egypt needed China as it sought to establish a diplomatic foothold on the African continent. Egypt appreciated the PRC's moral support during the Suez Canal crisis in 1956 but subsequently navigated carefully between a desire for good relations with both the Soviet Union and the PRC and the challenges of the Sino-Soviet conflict. The union of Egypt and Syria, known as the United Arab Republic from 1958 to 1961, further complicated the Sino-Egyptian relationship, especially when Beijing supported the communists in Syria and Iraq in 1959. Nasser criticized China's aggressive actions in Tibet, worried about China's growing influence in Yemen, which he viewed as within Egypt's sphere of influence, and failed to take China's side in its 1962 border dispute with India. Nasser's harsh treatment of the weak Egyptian Communist Party resulted in protests from the PRC.[3] Throughout these contentious periods, however, Egypt strongly supported the PRC's effort to replace Taiwan in the UN. Beijing provided in 1964 an interest-free loan of $80 million to cover the cost of Chinese goods and services. The following year it renewed an agreement on technical and scientific cooperation.[4]

Beijing assigned one of its most experienced diplomats, Chen Jiakang, to the new embassy in Cairo. From there, he negotiated the establishment of diplomatic relations with Yemen, Somalia, and Sudan. The PRC embassy in Cairo became China's field headquarters for developing relations with countries in Africa and the Middle East.[5] China supported the Arab countries during the 1967 war with Israel but encountered disagreements with Nasser concerning support for Palestinian commandos after the war. China and Egypt were working out their differences when Nasser died in 1970.[6]

Sino-Egyptian relations developed steadily over the decades in spite of the fact that Egypt did not have surplus oil or minerals to fuel China's economy. The two countries developed close military relations although the United States has in more recent years met most of Egypt's armament needs. China and Egypt established a strategic partnership in 1999 covering investment, tourism, technology development, manufacturing, research and development, nuclear power, and cooperation in petroleum, gas, mining, and transportation. This included production of Egypt's third satellite with Chinese technology.[7] Mubarak visited China in 2002 when he signed an agreement making Egypt the first African country officially designated for Chinese tourists. The first tour groups visited Egypt the same year; two

Egyptian airlines launched flights to China. A Chinese guided missile destroyer and supply ship passed through the Suez Canal and called at the port of Alexandria as part of China's first world cruise. The following year, the two countries signed an agreement to establish a Sino-Egyptian TV school where Chinese instructors teach Egyptians in Chinese and Egyptians teach Chinese in Arabic.[8]

Egypt is one of China's more important recipients of arms. The two countries signed a contract valued at $347 million in 1999 to export and coproduce K-8E jet aircraft and provide pilot training for the Egyptian air force. China delivered the eightieth and final aircraft in 2005 before coproduction began in Egypt. The PLA navy has provided training to the Egyptian navy. Egypt received thirty multiple rocket launchers from China in 2004. China has virtually replaced Russia as a supplier of military equipment. Egypt was one of only two African countries to observe a PLA military exercise in 2005. That same year, the PLA's Institute of Science invited cadets from Egypt to participate in activities at the military academy in Nanjing. High level exchange military visits are a common feature of the relationship.[9]

Premier Wen Jiabao visited Egypt in 2006 when he signed an agreement for implementing the strategic partnership.[10] At the 2006 FOCAC in Beijing, President Hosni Mubarak said the strategic partnership "is both the shared desire and independent choice of China and Africa, serves our common interests, and will help enhance solidarity, mutual support and assistance and unity of the developing countries and contribute to durable peace and harmonious development of the world."[11] Egypt hosted the 2009 FOCAC at Sharm el-Sheikh.

Although Egyptian presidents Nasser and Sadat never visited China, Mubarak made three visits to China while serving as vice president and another six visits as president.[12] Cairo is no longer in a position to deal with China and its immense economic power as an equal, but even today Egypt is not intimidated by the PRC. A professor at Cairo University told the authors that China is more interested in relations with Egypt than Egypt is with China.[13] A senior Egyptian government official added that China understands Egypt is the gateway to the Middle East and Africa. In addition, Egypt leverages its strong ties with the United States and Israel to its advantage as it interacts with China.[14]

By 2006, Egypt had become a major destination for Chinese FDI and the two countries had joint ventures worth $2.7 billion. By 2007, about 150 Chinese companies had invested in Egypt. Chinese investment declined significantly in 2009 and Egyptian officials began complaining in 2010 at the modest investment flowing from China to Egypt. China's total investment over the past ten years reached an estimated $800 million. The two governments have signed eleven trade and business cooperation agreements that included manufacturing, communications equipment, cooperation in hydrocarbons, and simplification of investment procedures. China agreed to build Egypt's first marble waste recycling plant and to establish technological service centers targeting Egypt's building materials and textile industries. China is especially interested in developing a container port. Its international shipping company, Cosco, has a 20 percent share in Maersk's container facility in Port Said. The Chinese Harbor State Company is building a second facility for $220 million to be shared by Cosco, Maersk, the Suez Canal Authority, and Egypt's Ministry of Transportation. Egypt is becoming a growing tourist destination for Chinese, some 90,000 in 2009, although very few Egyptian tourists visit China.[15]

In the past several years, China has been Egypt's third or fourth largest global trading partner. Within Africa, Egypt is China's fifth largest trade partner. In 2010, Egypt imported $6.6 billion of Chinese goods while China imported only $918 million worth of Egyptian products. The flood of cheap Chinese goods into Egypt has resulted in criticism about local job losses. To help offset this trade imbalance, China is constructing the Suez Economic Zone that is designed to attract fifty Chinese-owned factories employing 10,000 Egyptians and 1,000 Chinese.[16]

The 2011 revolution in Egypt posed a challenge for China's diplomacy. China provided minimal media coverage of developments in Egypt. As the protests expanded, China said it supported Egypt's efforts to maintain social stability and restore normal order. Vice Foreign Minister Zhai Jun visited Cairo and called for stability and development while Egyptian officials said the relationship with China remains solid. Several hundred of the 2,000 Chinese nationals living in Egypt did leave the country.[17] Foreign Minister Yang Jiechi subsequently visited Cairo and emphasized that China respects the will of the Egyptian people. Nevertheless, events dampened confidence and led to a sharp decline in 2011 of Chinese investment and trade.

Algeria

Algeria was the second country in Africa identified by the PRC as a candidate for recognition. Engaged in a violent war of independence with France beginning in 1954, Algeria provided the PRC an opportunity to demonstrate its strong support for African revolutionary movements. China supported the Algerian revolution diplomatically, politically, and militarily.[18] It recognized the Algerian Provisional Revolutionary Government (PRG) when it formed in 1958 and established full diplomatic relations within three months. China took this step two years before the Soviet Union gave Algeria de facto recognition. The Algerian struggle for independence contributed to serious differences between China and the Soviet Union. The PRC trained Algerian fighters. A representative of the PRG took up residence in Beijing in 1960, and China's first ambassador, Zeng Tao, arrived in Algiers in 1962; there were frequent high level visits between Algeria and China. The head of the PRG made a state visit to Beijing in 1960 while senior Chinese officials went to Algeria in the first half of the 1960s, culminating with one by Premier Zhou Enlai in 1964 and another in 1965. China began its economic aid program in 1963 with a $50 million interest-free loan, a cultural agreement, and its first ever medical team. In 1965, China gave Algeria a 13,000-ton freighter from its own merchant fleet.[19]

China took the position that Algeria's war was one of national liberation that could only be won through armed struggle. Ambassador Zeng, who had served in Cuba, believed the Algerian revolution was a progressive socialist liberation movement. Deceived by his own commitment to national liberation ideology, Zeng did not consider an explanation that involved nationalism, rejection of French rule, and a desire for reform. China also lagged well behind France, the United States, and the Soviet Union in total assistance to Algeria. A military coup in 1965 surprised the Chinese embassy and undermined ambassador Zeng's argument that Algeria was undergoing national liberation. Although China was one of only three governments to announce immediately support for the coup led by Houari Boumediene, political changes in Algeria drew it closer to the USSR.[20]

In spite of China's misreading of the situation, Algeria-China relations remained good although Algeria carefully balanced its policy toward Beijing and Moscow during the Sino-Soviet conflict. A 1971 U.S. National Intelligence Estimate described the Algerian-Chinese relationship as one of "long distance cordiality." It added that China provided virtually no economic or military aid and the level of trade was low.[21] Algerian President Boumediene visited Beijing in 1974 and he praised the PRC for its military support during the struggle for independence. He also spoke in favor of détente, a concept important at the time to the USSR, noting that it was inseparable from peaceful coexistence, a notion being pushed by China. Premier Zhou Enlai underscored the necessity of revolution throughout the world, describing it as the irresistible trend of history.[22]

Algeria and China have long had important military relations. Algerian military officers have trained in China for many years. While Russia remains Algeria's largest source of arms, China is expanding its arms exports to Algeria. It was the first country in Africa to import China's C-85 missile boats fitted with C-802 ship-to-ship missiles and a 5,550 ton training ship. Algeria has also purchased Chinese artillery, including 155mm howitzers.[23]

As Algeria became an important producer and exporter of gas and oil, China became increasingly interested in the country. The CNPC built a $350 million refinery at Adrar in southwestern Algeria. Chinese companies have a number of agreements for oil exploration and related projects in the energy sector. China was late to engage in Algeria's energy sector, however, and lags well behind Western countries in development of energy resources and as an importer of Algerian gas and oil. Algeria has awarded about fifty Chinese firms $20 billion in government construction contracts. The China Civil Engineering and Construction Corporation is building two-thirds of Algeria's 745-mile east-west highway, one of the biggest construction projects in the world. Algiers also awarded three contracts worth $2.1 billion to the China Civil Engineering and Construction Corporation to build railway networks. Chinese firms use largely Chinese labor, and estimates of Chinese living and working in Algeria run as high as 50,000. There is now a Chinatown in a suburb of Algiers.[24]

Unlike countries such as Angola and the Democratic Republic of the Congo, Algeria does not seek Chinese loan and aid packages in exchange for granting access to its natural resources and its markets to Chinese companies. Algerian banks also finance major projects undertaken by Chinese companies in the country. This arrangement is unusual in the Sino-African relationship. Algerian-Chinese ties have not been free of problems. In 2009, a minor incident involving a Chinese trader in the capital resulted in the first anti-Chinese riot in Algeria. The Algeria-based AQIM, following unrest in 2009 by the Muslim Uighur minority in western China, killed twenty-four Algerian paramilitary police officers escorting Chinese workers near a highway construction site. AQIM, which also has a presence in Mauritania, Niger, and Mali, announced it would target Chinese workers in North

Africa. Two extremist Islamic websites affiliated with al-Qaeda called for the killing of Han working in Algeria.[25]

China established a strategic partnership with Algeria during a visit to Algiers by Hu Jintao in 2004. While visiting China in 2006, Algerian President Abdelaziz Bouteflika signed a communiqué that consolidated the strategic partnership.[26] China and Algeria subsequently signed two agreements concerning cooperation in the development of civilian nuclear power. Chinese companies are seeking access to Algeria's mineral resources, including uranium. Between 2000 and 2007, China and Algeria signed twenty-one investment projects valued at $387 million. Algeria looks to China as an important supplier of technology whose companies can execute projects at a lower cost than Western countries. China is a major importer of Algerian goods ($4.4 billion in 2010) while Algeria imported only $1.2 billion worth of goods from China.[27] Algeria is China's seventh largest trading partner in Africa and Air Algerie has direct flights to Beijing.

China refrained from commenting on the 2011 Arab Spring protests in Algeria. Vice Foreign Minister Zhai Jun assured President Bouteflika in Algiers that China wants to strengthen relations. So long as Bouteflika is in power, China-Algeria relations are likely to remain strong.[28]

Morocco

Morocco was a monarchy when it obtained independence in 1956. Before Morocco recognized China, Moroccan trade union, parliamentary, and trade delegations visited China and a Chinese trade delegation came to Rabat in 1958 to sign an agreement. China opened its campaign for recognition in Morocco by using the Casablanca international trade fair as a political opportunity. China's exhibits, although unimposing by Western standards, fascinated North Africans. China sent numerous technical and cultural missions to Morocco and had no qualms about establishing diplomatic relations in 1958 with the government led by King Mohammed V. It offered to train Moroccan military pilots, deliver military equipment, and build a light-arms factory, offers that Morocco did not pursue.[29]

When Morocco proscribed the activities of the Moroccan Communist Party in 1959, China severed all relations with the organization and never criticized, at least publicly, the anticommunist actions taken by Morocco. This was one of several occasions when Mao Zedong's China sacrificed principle for necessity in its African policy.[30] Morocco's important commercial ties with China and the Chinese presence there enabled Beijing to support revolutionaries in neighboring Algeria. China opened a consulate at Ouida along the Algerian border. It also opened a Xinhua office.[31]

There have been numerous high level visits in both directions, including one by Moroccan King Mohammed VI to China in 2002 and Hu Jintao to Morocco in 2006. During a visit to Beijing in 2006 by Moroccan Prime Minister Driss Jettou, Premier Wen Jiabao called for expanded cooperation in the fields of agriculture, fisheries, telecommunications, personnel training, and labor contracts. By 2006, at least thirty Chinese companies were operating in Morocco, about 90 percent of them engaged in maritime fishing. Wen Jiabao also addressed Morocco's most important and contentious political issue—control over the disputed Western Sahara. He urged a political solution and hoped that all parties would resolve the dispute in the framework of UN resolutions. A senior Chinese military officer heads the UN peacekeeping mission in the Western Sahara. Wen Jiabao offered China's help in ending the dispute. In 2007, Morocco and China initiated a political consultation mechanism.[32]

During a visit in 2008 to Rabat by a senior CPC official, Moroccan Prime Minister Abbas El Fassi voiced support for China's Tibet policy, adding that other countries should not interfere in China's internal affairs.[33] Morocco's Minister of Foreign Affairs and Cooperation, Taleb Fassi Fihri, praised China's African policy during a visit to Rabat in 2009 by China's special envoy on African affairs, Liu Guijin. According to Xinhua, Fihri said that the riots in China's Xinjiang Uighur Autonomous Region were an internal issue and no country or organization should interfere under the pretext of religion.[34] In 2010, Prime Minister El Fassi received Chinese Foreign Minister Yang Jiechi in Rabat. Morocco expressed appreciation for China's new measures for working with Africa and expressed a willingness to increase cooperation with China. They signed a joint communiqué on Morocco's recognition of China's market economy status and acknowledged they share "identical and similar" views on international and regional issues.[35] Moroccan support for controversial Chinese internal policies such as Tibet and the Uighurs is probably linked to China's unwillingness to recognize the Western Sahara, which Morocco claims.

Trade has always been the priority in the China-Morocco relationship, although it totaled only about $300 million as recently as the beginning of the twenty-first century. Cheap Chinese textile exports also harmed the

Moroccan textile industry early in the twenty-first century. In 2010, China's imports, mostly phosphate and cobalt, totaled $450 million while Morocco imported $2.7 billion from China.

Tunisia

Tunisia became independent in 1956. It sent a cultural delegation to Beijing in 1957 and the two countries established Tunisia-China associations in their respective capitals. Tunisia and China signed trade agreements in 1958 and 1960. A delegation from the New Destour party of Tunisia attended the celebration of China's eleventh anniversary in 1960.[36] Nevertheless, Tunisia did not recognize the PRC until 1964. Disagreements over the "one China" policy and Tunisia's arrest of a Chinese table tennis coach and embassy staff member resulted in suspension of relations between 1967 and 1971.[37] This was a case where China initially pursued its principles rather than a more pragmatic approach. At no point did Tunisia recognize Taiwan, but even consideration of a "two China" policy was sufficient to convince Beijing that the relationship was not worth the price until 1972, when China offered $40 million in credits for canal and transportation projects. After it added another $57 million in 1977, China became the largest communist donor in Tunisia, accounting for one-fourth of total communist economic aid. The first of many Chinese medical teams arrived in 1973. China began sending students to Tunisia in 2008 to study language.[38]

High level Chinese visitors to Tunisia have included Premier Zhou Enlai in 1964, Premier Zhao Ziyang in 1986, President Yang Shangkun in 1992, and President Jiang Zemin in 2002. Vice President Zeng Qinghong signed eight cooperation agreements in Tunis in 2004. China has also relied on senior PLA officials to cement the relationship. For example, General Jing Zhiyua, member of the Central Military Commission and commander of the Second Artillery Force, visited Tunisia in 2005. Jia Qinglin, chairman of the National Committee for the Chinese People's Political Consultative Conference, arrived in 2007, and high level CPC officials regularly visit. Since 1975, only three Tunisian prime ministers or presidents have visited China. In 1966, the two countries created a mechanism for periodic political consultation.[39] In 2010, during a visit to Tunisia, Chinese Foreign Minister Yang Jiechi met with President Zine al-Abidine Ben Ali, who said that political trust has deepened and economic, trade, and cultural ties have

intensified. Yang Jiechi expressed appreciation for Tunisia's support on Taiwan, Tibet, and the Xinjiang Uighur Autonomous Region.[40]

Chinese investment in Tunisia remains modest; there are only six Chinese companies among 3,000 foreign enterprises operating in the country.
Trade has grown impressively in recent years, but remains well below that
of key European countries and heavily favors China. In 2010, China
imported $125 million of products from Tunisia while Tunisia imported
$1.1 billion from China. Cheap Chinese textile exports cut deeply into
Tunisia's export of textiles to Europe early in the twenty-first century. Tunisia is especially interested in attracting Chinese tourists, a theme it emphasized in its exhibit at the 2010 Universal Exhibition in Shanghai. Although
the two countries have signed twenty-three economic, technical, diplomatic, scientific, and financial agreements since 1993, China seems to be
trying harder to consolidate the relationship than Tunisia.[41] Tunisia sees its
future linked more closely to the European Union than to China.

The 2011 revolution that deposed President Ben Ali presented a
dilemma for China, which initially remained silent on this internal crisis.
Once Ben Ali went into exile, China called for return of stability in Tunisia
and sent Vice Foreign Minister Zhai Jun to Tunis to reaffirm close ties with
the new government. Zhai Jun also announced a $6 million donation for a
development project. China made a successful transition from the Ben Ali
government to the new one.[42]

Libya

Libya, which became independent in 1951 under a monarchy led by King
Idris, was hostile to communism. Taiwan, which then held a seat on the
UN Security Council, strongly supported Libya's 1955 application for UN
membership, although Libya did not recognize Taiwan until 1959. Perhaps
influenced by President Nasser in neighboring Egypt, Libya began following
a more neutral foreign policy in 1960.[43]

Mu'ammar al-Qadhafi seized power in 1969. He announced Libya's
unilateral recognition of the PRC in 1971, while there was still an ambassador in Tripoli representing Taiwan. Libya did not formally break ties with
Taiwan until 1978, when Tripoli and Beijing established diplomatic relations. Although there have been numerous exchange visits, rarely have they
involved the most senior leaders of either country. Al-Qadhafi visited

Beijing in 1982. Chinese vice premiers and senior CPC officials have visited Libya, but neither the president nor the premier has done so. The Taiwan issue periodically complicated the relationship. Although Libya regularly stated that it accepts Beijing's "one-China" policy, in January 2006 al-Qadhafi's son met with President Chen Shui-bian in Taiwan, who stopped in Tripoli four months later on return from an overseas trip. The Chinese Foreign Ministry fired a warning that China was "strongly dissatisfied with Libya" and demanded "that Libya live up to its commitment and immediately cease all official exchanges with Taiwan."[44] Libya sent a low-ranking representative to the 2006 FOCAC in Beijing. Taiwan opened a commercial office in Tripoli in 2008 and announced that its deputy representative resident in Saudi Arabia would serve as its deputy representative to Libya.[45]

Addressing Oxford University students via satellite in 2007, al-Qadhafi warned of the emerging conflict between China and the United States over Africa. He was especially critical of the United States, noting that at least China does not lecture African countries about their system of government, human rights, freedom of expression, and good governance. Al-Qadhafi said that because of this soft approach, Africans welcome China; the Chinese will eventually win in Africa and Libya will take its side. An equal opportunity critic, he went on to say, "however, China must know that we are aware that it could turn into an imperialist power. If it wishes to settle in Africa or to plunder Africa's resources at a low price and sell its manufactured products at an exorbitant one, it will turn into a colonial power."[46]

Libyan Foreign Minister Musa Kusa, in a 2009 interview with an influential Egyptian daily, criticized China's Africa policy. Although Kusa praised China's support for African liberation movements, he urged that China not send thousands of Chinese workers to Africa under the pretext of employment. While he welcomed China's training and employment of Africans, he emphasized it does not mean Africans want Chinese to settle in Africa, suggesting that it revives memories of colonialism. Noting Africa's strong support for China's successful campaign to replace Taiwan on the UN Security Council, he also chided Beijing for opposing a seat for an African country. He asked rhetorically: "What is the difference between them and the imperialists?"[47]

Chinese oil companies have worked hard to penetrate Libya's petroleum sector. In 2009, Libya blocked a CNPC bid to buy a Canadian oil-producing company that controlled Libyan oil assets. A year later, the director of the

Libyan National Oil Company assured China that Libya would take steps to improve oil trade ties. As of early 2011, seventy-five Chinese companies held fifty construction contracts valued at $18 billion, primarily in oil, railroads, housing, and telecommunications, with 36,000 Chinese workers implementing the projects. Trade has also become an important part of the relationship, especially rapidly growing Chinese imports of Libyan petroleum that reached $4.5 billion in 2010, 3 percent of its oil imports. Libya imported $2.3 billion from China that year, making it China's sixth largest trading partner in Africa.[48]

Efforts by Libyan rebels to topple al-Qadhafi in 2011 posed a major challenge for China's extensive economic interests in Libya. China voted in the UN Security Council to impose an arms embargo, travel ban, and asset freeze on Libya, but abstained on a resolution authorizing member states to take all necessary measures to protect Libyan civilians and was subsequently highly critical of the NATO no fly zone. China successfully evacuated all 36,000 of its workers but incurred significant financial losses as well as looting of facilities and injuries to a few personnel. China initially maintained a neutral policy and avoided contact with rebel forces. It subsequently contracted for one of the few oil shipments from rebel-held territory, met with Libya's opposition leader in a third country, and then hosted him in Beijing as "an important dialogue participant."[49]

By mid-2011, China's policy on Libya was in flux as the rebels increased their control but al-Qadhafi stubbornly refused to yield power. Libyan documents show that an al-Qadhafi delegation visited three companies—China North, China Precision Machinery, and China Xinxing Import and Export Corporation—to discuss a $200 million arms deal at a time when the UN had imposed arms sanctions on Libya. China's Ministry of Foreign Affairs denied that any arms were shipped and claimed the visit took place without the knowledge of the government.[50] At a minimum, this embarrassing incident illustrated confusion if not outright duplicity in China's government.

Following the overthrow of al-Qadhafi, interim leader Mustafa Abdel Jalil called in mid-September for forgiveness and reconciliation. China announced recognition of Libya's new National Transitional Council (NTC) as the legitimate representative of the Libyan people and returned its ambassador to Tripoli. China, the last permanent member of the UN Security Council to accept the NTC, then called on the Council to play a leading role in postwar reconstruction.[51]

Mali

Mali became independent in 1960 and recognized China the same year. Beijing signed an economic and cooperation agreement in 1961 and sent agricultural specialists to Mali the following year. From the beginning, China has provided a regular flow of assistance for projects, including a textile mill, leather processing factory, sports stadiums, conference buildings, housing, and an oil refinery. China initiated fifteen projects by 1965 and sent its first shipment of arms that year. It made a special effort to cultivate youth, women's groups, and the media. Mali began receiving Chinese medical teams in 1968. Mali also had close relations with the Soviet Union, which equipped the army and air force, and walked a careful line between Soviet and Chinese influence. When Mali publicly supported the Soviet invasion of Czechoslovakia in 1968, opposing China's position, Beijing continued its close ties with Bamako. By 1968, China had dispersed $35 million in economic aid to Mali and had almost nine hundred technicians in the country. A military coup that year resulted in a more moderate Malian government. This development set back relations with China and resulted in a termination of discussions for a major railroad project between Mali and Guinea. Cultural exchanges and high level visits have been a constant in the relationship. Mali's presidents have visited Beijing ten times since 1964. Although Premier Zhou Enlai went to Bamako in 1964, subsequent Chinese visitors did not rise above the vice premier level until Hu Jintao visited in 2009. In 2010, President Amadou Toumany Touré attended the Shanghai World Expo, where he met with Hu Jintao.[52]

China emphasized support for the agricultural sector in Mali. It began with a tea plantation in 1962 and a sugar plantation in 1966. Ten years later, China added another sugar plantation and refinery. China began developing rice fields in the early 1960s and completed two rice mills by the mid-1970s. China also assisted the cotton sector. China received high marks for the success of this cooperation. By the late 1970s, China had disbursed most of its $100 million commitment for agricultural and light industrial projects. In the mid-1980s, it turned increasingly to joint ventures using private capital and developed two more sugar plantations and two refineries in Mali.[53]

In 2006, Chinese direct investment in Mali represented about 10 percent of total foreign investment. Mali is the eighth largest recipient of Chinese aid to countries in Africa. Between 1966 and 2003, it received $30 million in grants and $133 million in interest-free loans. China canceled $80 million of Mali's debt in 2006. In 2005, however, China's aid represented just over 3 percent of Mali's total foreign assistance. China has provided technical assistance to help maintain military helicopters it provided to Mali. During his 2009 visit, Hu Jintao inaugurated a $75 million grant aid project known as the Sino-Malian Friendship Bridge across the Niger River. China also established a Confucius classroom at a middle school in Mali and sends about fifty students annually to study in China. About 2,000 Chinese reside in Mali, mostly workers on Chinese projects and owners of small businesses.[54]

Trade remains modest, but is growing. In 2010, Mali imported from China goods valued at $253 million and China only $70 million worth from Mali. Mali has had a significant trade deficit with China since 2006. It is somewhat surprising that this relationship, uninterrupted since 1960, has not developed to a higher level. Mali's lack of exportable resources, except for cotton, and its small market for Chinese products has limited trade.

Mauritania

The day it became independent in 1960, Mauritania established diplomatic relations with Taiwan. Beijing sent an agricultural mission to Mauritania in 1965 and established diplomatic relations a month later. Mauritania signed trade, economic and technical cooperation, and cultural agreements with China in 1967 and President Moktar ould Daddah then visited Beijing. China offered an interest-free $5 million loan and sent two hundred tons of agricultural machinery to Mauritania. Additional loans and aid projects followed in quick succession. China began sending medical teams in 1968 and has sent them consistently ever since. Ould Daddah returned to China in 1974 and signed an agreement for $37 million to build the deep water harbor at Nouakchott, complete a road project begun by another financier, and build a sports stadium. When completed in 1986, Nouakchott harbor was China's most ambitious aid project in Africa since the Tanzania-Zambia railway. The CIA concluded in 1977 that except for France, China had become the most influential non-Arab country in Mauritania. Chinese prestige resulted from a combination of Beijing's neutrality on the disputed Western Sahara, part of which Mauritania once claimed, and its involvement in Mauritanian development. Other projects included construction of the presidential palace, a water source for Nouakchott, and cultural, youth, and health centers. Mauritanian chiefs of state made visits to China in 1977, 1980, 1986, and 1993.[55]

Cooperation in fisheries began in 1991, and by 2004 there were eight hundred Chinese working in the fishing sector. In 2005, China signed a loan for $136 million to build the international airport in Nouakchott. The following year, head of state Ely ould Mohamed Vall represented Mauritania at the FOCAC summit in Beijing. In 2007, a Sudanese company and China's Transtech Engineering won the $686 million contract financed by the Export Import Bank of China to build a 290-mile rail line from Nouakchott to the phosphate deposits at Boffal in southern Mauritania. In 2009, China established a Chinese-language multimedia classroom at the University of Mauritania.[56]

In 2007, Mauritania signed a deal with one of China's major steel mills to sell about one million tons of iron ore annually for seven years. Mauritania is a recent exporter of oil; the CNPC is drilling offshore. China's imports (iron ore, copper, and oil) from Mauritania jumped from $4 million in 2005 to $968 million in 2010, while Mauritania's imports from China increased from $82 million to $313 million in the same period.

A senior CPC delegation visited Nouakchott in 2008 and thanked Mauritania for its support on Tibet. China's relations with Mauritania have been uninterrupted and untroubled. China managed to avoid becoming embroiled in hostility between Mauritania and Morocco in the 1960s and Mauritania and Algeria in the 1970s, both over the Western Sahara issue. The PRC maintained good relations with all three countries throughout these bilateral conflicts.

Chad

Chad became independent in 1960 and recognized Taiwan at the beginning of 1962. In the early 1960s, the PRC supported the Chadian National Union (CNU), a revolutionary group opposed to the pro-French government.[57] The CNU joined with another revolutionary group in 1966 to form the Front de Libération Nationale du Tchad (FROLINAT). By this time, France had recognized Beijing, which caused the PRC to reconsider the way it treated pro-French regimes in Africa. There is no indication that China ever supported FROLINAT.[58]

China donated cholera vaccine and $2.5 million to Chad during a cholera outbreak in 1971. This helped prepare for recognition of Beijing in 1972, when Chad's president said it was no longer possible to ignore a country with more than eight hundred million people. The two countries signed economic and technical cooperation and trade agreements in 1973. China offered a $10 million loan the same year. The PRC provided another loan of $50 million in 1974 and agreed in 1976 to build a bridge across the Chari River linking Chad with Cameroon.[59] Chad is another reminder that "dollar diplomacy" applies to the PRC just as it does Taiwan.

China signed a protocol with Chad in 1978 for sending medical teams to Chad. The two countries agreed to additional economic and technical protocols in 1983 that included a loan for $50 million and a cultural agreement in 1989. President Hissène Habré visited Beijing in 1990 and signed agreements covering economic, cultural, and agricultural cooperation and another loan.[60] In 1997, however, Chad restored relations with Taiwan, resulting in Beijing's decision to break ties.[61]

Although oil exploration in Chad began in the early 1970s and discoveries followed soon thereafter, it was only in the late 1990s that a largely Western consortium began to build the infrastructure to bring the oil on line.[62] This development increased China's desire to resume relations with Chad. Chadian rebels nearly overthrew the government of Idriss Deby in April 2006. Sudan backed the rebels, who denied that they had any direct link to China, a strong supporter of Sudan. Nevertheless, the rebels used some weapons supplied by China to Sudan. Taiwan's foreign minister said Deby told Taiwanese officials that China had armed rebels in eastern Chad. Taiwan charged publicly that the PRC offered Deby a deal that promised an end to the rebel threat in exchange for recognition of Beijing. Whatever was agreed upon behind closed doors, China and Chad resumed diplomatic relations in August 2006 and Beijing promised to "safeguard" Chad's sovereignty and promote its economic development.[63]

Within months of the resumption in relations, the Chadian defense minister met in Beijing with his counterpart, who said that the relationship between the armed forces of the two countries is an important part of the overall bilateral relationship. China announced plans to build Chad's first oil refinery, new roads, irrigation projects, and a mobile telephone network. The CNPC first invested in Chad in 2003, three years before the two countries reestablished diplomatic relations. Deby visited China in 2007 when the two countries agreed to expand cooperation in the fields of agriculture, infrastructure construction, and energy. When Chadian rebels again tried with Sudanese support early in 2008 to overthrow Deby, there was no indication of involvement by China, which suffered a $1 billion loss in its projects and investments due mainly to theft. Chad's prime minister visited China in 2008 when Premier Wen Jiabao said China supported efforts to safeguard its sovereignty. China's close relations with Sudan have periodically strained relations with Chad. In 2009, Deby criticized China for failing during a UN Security Council meeting to support it unconditionally when Chadian rebels, assisted by Sudan, again attacked Chad. Sudan-Chad relations subsequently improved, making it easier for China to strengthen its ties with Chad. By 2009, the CNPC began construction of the pipeline from oil fields 190 miles south of N'djamena to the refinery north of the capital. By 2011, Chinese investments in energy, manufacturing, and electric power may have reached $10 billion and about 5,000 Chinese worked in Chad. Chad signed a $7.5 billion contract with China's Civil Engineering Construction Corporation to build 840 miles of railway in the oil producing areas.[64]

While the China-Chad political relationship has occasionally been hostage to the vicissitudes of Sudan-Chad ties and competition from Taiwan, trade links between China and Chad expanded rapidly through 2006. They fell back for three years and then increased dramatically in 2010 when Chad imported $353 million from China and China imported $496 million worth of oil from Chad.

Niger

Niger became independent in 1960 but did not recognize Taiwan until 1963, after which it became one of Taipei's strongest supporters during the 1960s. An antigovernment group known as Sawaba (Freedom party), based in Ghana and Mali, tried to overthrow the conservative Niger government in 1964. President Hamani Diori charged that the PRC organized and financed the effort. The Ghana government subsequently released compelling evidence of PRC involvement with Sawaba. Good relations with Taiwan continued until Niger's military overthrew Diori in April 1974.[65]

A Nigerien delegation visited Beijing in July 1974, established diplomatic relations, signed an economic and technical cooperation agreement, and received an interest-free loan of about $50 million to finance cement works, an agro-industrial complex, a fruit plant, and a farm implement factory. China sent its first medical team in 1976 and began to offer scholarships in 1978. The two countries signed a trade agreement in 1982, a protocol on agricultural cooperation in 1985, and another loan agreement in 1990. The leader of Niger visited Beijing in 1977 and 1984. Cordial relations continued until 1992, when Niger again recognized Taiwan. The PRC charged that Taiwan engaged in "dollar diplomacy." The relationship with Taiwan lasted only until 1996, when Niamey renewed relations with Beijing.[66]

China-Niger relations since 1996 have been good. The president of Niger visited China in 1997, 2001, and 2006, and the prime minister went to Beijing in 2003. China engaged in various aid projects including the development of a water supply system, renovating the stadium it had built years earlier, adding classrooms at Niamey University, and building agricultural implement workshops. The towns of Zinder in Niger and Nanning in China have a sister city relationship. Exchange visits between senior military personnel and those from the CPC and Niger's ruling party have become an important part of the relationship. For example, Wang Gang, a member of the CPC Political Bureau, expressed appreciation to Niger's visiting chairman of the Economic, Social and Cultural Council for Niamey's support on issues related to Tibet and Taiwan.[67] In 2009, China assigned fifteen of its youth volunteers to Niger.

China is looking to Niger as a supplier of uranium and oil. In 2008, a Chinese company as part of a joint venture signed a $140 million uranium mining deal with Niger. China's state-owned SINO-U invested $300 million to develop a new uranium mine at Azelik. China is the second largest investor in Niger's uranium sector. The CNPC invested $5 billion over three years to develop oil reserves in eastern Niger, to build a refinery with a capacity of 20,000 barrels per day and a 1,200-mile oil pipeline. This deal, which Niger accepted over an offer by a Mobil-Petronas consortium, quickly became subject to criticism by a coalition of organizations, including the mining union, for lack of transparency. The coalition called for a parliamentary investigation of the transaction and an examination on how the funds will be spent. Chinese companies also have exploration rights to two additional blocks. In 2009, China Geoengineering Corporation received a contract to build a dam on the Niger River. The World Bank refused to put money into the $240 million project because of environmental impact concerns. The Islamic Investment Bank and Saudi Development

Fund agreed to fund the initial stages and China implied it may finance some of the later sections.[68]

Growing Chinese interests in Niger, a country threatened by a dissident group, have posed some security challenges for China. A Tuareg-led rebel group, Le Movement des Nigeriens pour la Justice (MNJ), wants an end to economic marginalization, environmental degradation, and ethnic discrimination. The rebels have harassed Chinese companies and in 2007 kidnapped a Sino-Uranium executive as a warning to foreign mineral firms that their disregard for the environment and support for Niger's government are not acceptable. The Chinese subsequently pulled out of their field operations. The MNJ accused China of supplying arms for Nigerien military operations in the north in exchange for mineral concessions.[69]

China was close to former autocratic President Mamadou Tandja at a time when the United States and European Union had suspended their aid programs in Niger. Early in 2010, a military junta overthrew Tandja. The new military government announced that the coup d'état did not affect its relations with China. China's ambassador to Niger said on state television that his country's extensive oil and uranium interests in Niger had not been disrupted.[70] Niger then held democratic elections in 2011. China deftly made the transition from an autocratic to a military to an elected government and will almost certainly continue to play a major role.

Chinese imports from Niger have been almost nonexistent through 2010, but Niger's imports from China have been growing impressively and reached $301 million in 2010. As China helps develop the oil and mineral sector in Niger and the country eventually exports uranium and oil to China, its balance of trade should change dramatically.

Burkina Faso

Burkina Faso, known as Upper Volta at independence in 1960, recognized Taiwan at the end of 1961. President Maurice Yameogo was an outspoken critic of the PRC and referred publicly to Chinese subversion in Africa. Although Yameogo lost power in 1966, Upper Volta's anti-communist policy continued.[71] The country experienced a serious famine and measles epidemic in the early 1970s. President Sangoule Lamizana concluded the country needed to reach out for additional sources of assistance. In 1973, Premier Zhou Enlai sent Lamizana a message of sympathy, 300,000 doses of measles vaccine, and $50,000 worth of antibiotics. Five months later a delegation from Upper Volta visited Beijing, signed an economic and technical cooperation agreement, and then recognized Beijing. In 1973, China offered a $48 million credit. At the time, this was Burkina Faso's largest aid pledge from a communist country. In 1978, China completed a second rice project and provided $200,000 cash for drought relief. Chinese assistance followed a familiar pattern in the 1970s and 1980s: agricultural cooperation, medical teams, water well construction, a hospital, cultural agreement, and cooperation between Xinhua and the Burkina Faso Ministry of Information. High level contact during the 1980s took place primarily at the foreign minister level, although President Thomas Sankara visited Beijing in 1984.[72]

President Blaise Compaore, who toppled Sankara in 1987, had the distinction of being the first head of state to visit China after the Tiananmen Square crackdown in 1989. At a banquet for Compaore, Chinese President Yang Shangkun thanked African countries for their understanding and support for "China's quelling of the recent counter-revolutionary rebellion." Compaore said he came to show the world that mutual support exists between China and Burkina Faso and laid a wreath at the Monument to the People's Heroes on Tiananmen Square. Burkina Faso's foreign minister visited Beijing in April 1993, when he proclaimed that all was well with the relationship. Burkina Faso then surprisingly recognized Taiwan in February 1994, precipitating a break with Beijing. Burkina Faso continues to be one of four African countries that recognize Taiwan.[73]

Curiously, China's imports from Burkina Faso, mainly cotton, averaged $133 million from 2004 through 2010, and Burkina's imports from China averaged $37 million. By comparison, Taiwan's imports from Burkina during the same period averaged $10 million and Burkina's imports from Taiwan about $1.5 million. In 2010, China imported $121 million worth of cotton from Burkina and Burkina imported $53 million worth of goods from China. This is one of several examples in Africa where a country's recognition of Taiwan has resulted in a more important trade relationship with the PRC. In addition, many PRC companies are active in Burkina Faso.

9

China's Relations with East Africa,
the Horn, and the Indian Ocean Islands

The nine countries of East Africa and the Horn have had diplomatic relations only with the PRC; they never recognized Taiwan. Sudan was the first to establish relations, albeit three years after independence. Somalia, Tanzania, Uganda, Kenya, and Eritrea recognized Beijing the year they became independent. Djibouti delayed for two years. Ethiopia, under imperial rule for about 2,000 years and never colonized, waited longest before establishing ties in 1970. South Sudan became independent in 2011 and immediately recognized Beijing. Of the nine, China initially had the closest and most intensive links with Tanzania. Somalia ties were also strong, especially as the Soviet Union switched its focus from Somalia to Ethiopia in the 1970s. Relations with Kenya in the early years were strained.

Today, China has solid ties with all nine countries. Because of its huge investment in the oil sector, the most important link is with Sudan, a relationship complicated by the secession of South Sudan. Although relations with Tanzania remain strong, they do not occupy the same relative importance as in the 1960s and 1970s. China has made a special effort to expand ties with Ethiopia, where Addis Ababa serves as headquarters for the African Union and Economic Commission for Africa. It has significantly improved relations with Kenya and made a special effort to work with the Transitional Federal Government in the failed state of Somalia. China is even expanding ties with Somaliland, which in 1991 unilaterally declared independence from Somalia but is not recognized by any country. China can count on all nine countries for political support on most issues important to Beijing.

In the years after their independence, China devoted limited attention to the four Indian Ocean Island countries. Two of them—the Comoro Islands and Seychelles—are tiny and lack natural resources of interest to China. Both did, however, establish relations with the PRC immediately after independence and China took more interest in them than Soviet and Taiwanese rivals did. Madagascar initially had a conservative government that recognized Taiwan after independence in 1960; it switched to Beijing twelve years later. Although it did not recognize Taiwan, Mauritius waited four years before it established ties with the PRC. All these countries except the Comoro Islands had long-standing Chinese communities. After 1949, however, they divided their sympathies between Beijing and Taipei.

China now has close relations with all four countries. Mauritius and Madagascar are important destinations for Chinese exports and investment. Chinese construction companies are making significant inroads, especially in Madagascar. Although their economies are miniscule, the Comoro Islands and Seychelles seem to be of interest for political reasons. All four countries are likely to become increasingly important to China as it expands its naval presence in the Indian Ocean. At a minimum, PLA navy ships will need ports of call for refueling and supply.

Sudan

Sudan obtained independence in 1956 and concluded an economic agreement with China the same year. In 1958, China signed a barter agreement whereby Sudan sent cotton to China in exchange for textiles.[1] Sudan established relations with Beijing in 1959, the fourth African country to do so. There was an early test in the relationship during 1963–1964 when Sudan confiscated Chinese arms destined for Congolese rebels. This incident did not prevent Zhou Enlai from visiting Sudan in 1964 and Sudan's president from traveling to Beijing the same year. In any event, the overthrow of Sudan's military government in October 1964 saved Sudan from any serious diplomatic disagreements with China.[2] The more radical government that followed gave China more room for maneuver. The Sudan Communist Party (SCP) had a small pro-Chinese wing, but was dominated by pro-Soviet elements.[3]

China's relations with Sudan remained at a low level until the early 1970s. China supported the northern Sudan government during the first North-South civil war from 1955 to 1972. Following a visit to Beijing in 1970 by President Gaafar Nimeiri, China provided its first loan to Sudan; it was interest-free and repayable in Sudanese crops. Among other projects, it financed the building of Friendship Hall, which remains a major landmark in Khartoum. Friendship Hall is a reminder that many of these early Chinese structures, especially sports stadiums, that the West has been quick to disparage, continue to be perceived positively by Africans. China's first medical team arrived in 1971. Trade, especially Sudanese cotton to China, increased significantly in the early 1970s.[4]

In 1971, Sudanese army officers sympathetic to the pro-Soviet SCP, at the time the largest communist party in the Middle East and Africa, failed in their attempt to overthrow Nimeiri, who then decimated the SCP. China benefited from the blame put on the USSR and spoke approvingly of Nimeiri's harsh measures; the Soviets, who had helped to build the Sudanese armed forces, protested strongly. To cultivate better relations with Sudan in 1971, China provided another interest-free loan and offered to help train and equip the Sudanese armed forces. This response was intended to cultivate better relations with Sudan. Nimeiri was grateful for China's support and Sino-Sudan relations steadily improved. The West, especially the United States, took even greater advantage of this turn of events and expanded relations with Khartoum. America's Chevron Oil Company had earlier discovered oil in Sudan's North-South border area. Security concerns during the second civil war (1983–2005) forced Chevron to give up its leases by the late 1980s.[5]

The period after the Islamist government of Omar al-Bashir seized power in 1989 offered China an opportunity to extend its influence in Sudan. Political relations between Sudan and the West deteriorated as a result of the policies of the new government, its human rights practices, the brutality of the civil war, and Sudan's links to international terrorist organizations. Sudan supported Saddam Hussein during the 1991 Gulf War, further alienating the United States. These concerns did not deter China. Al-Bashir visited Beijing in 1990, which led the next year to Iranian-funded purchases of Chinese arms. In 1994, Sudan suggested that China develop Sudan's petroleum reserves. Sudan's ambassador to China at the time explained to the authors that growing Chinese oil demand precipitated its interest in developing Sudan's oil. Al-Bashir returned to Beijing in 1995.

This was the beginning of a major investment in Sudan by the CNPC with other foreign partners. China provided major loans for infrastructure projects throughout the country, invested an estimated $6 billion in the petroleum sector, and expanded its military assistance program.[6]

Sudan acquired thirty-four Shenyang jet fighters from China in 2000, three A-5C Fanton FGA aircraft several years later, and twelve K-8 jet trainers in 2006. Sudan also received Dong Feng military trucks, and China trained fifty Sudanese pilots on helicopter gunships. While China is a significant supplier of military hardware to Sudan, by dollar value Russia is more important. China helped Sudan establish industrial facilities, now known as the Military Industrial Corporation, for local production of weapons, ammunition, vehicles, communications equipment, and rockets. As a result, Sudan is today the continent's third most important manufacturer of military equipment after South Africa and Egypt. China and Russia are helping Sudan produce a single-engine propeller-driven observation plane known as the Safat-01.[7]

Chinese influence in Sudan is now closely linked to its massive economic connection, especially its investment in oil. Although Sudan has severed ties with international terrorist groups and ended the North-South civil war, it continues to have a poor human rights record. Its handling of the conflict that broke out in Darfur in 2003 has subjected it to strong criticism from the West. With veto power on the UN Security Council and its huge investment in Sudan, China found itself in the middle of the West's efforts to pressure Sudan to end the conflict in Darfur. China initially supported the government of Sudan but eventually played an instrumental role in convincing Khartoum to accept a hybrid African Union-UN peacekeeping force, to which China contributed forces. China managed to deflect Western criticism of its actions by following closely the positions of most African and Arab countries.[8]

When the International Criminal Court (ICC) issued a warrant in 2009 to arrest al-Bashir for war crimes and crimes against humanity committed in Darfur, China criticized the decision, noting that it would complicate peace efforts in Sudan. When the ICC added the charge of genocide in 2010, China did not directly address the new charge. Foreign Ministry spokesperson Qin Gang said "we hope relevant sides will listen to the African Union, the League of Arab States and countries concerned, and play a constructive role in maintaining peace and stability in Sudan and the region."[9]

China's close ties with Khartoum subjected it to criticism from Darfur rebel groups and its oil operations to occasional attack. In 2007, the rebel JEM briefly seized Chinese oil facilities at Defra in Kordofan Province as a warning to China to cease its military and political support of Khartoum. JEM then attacked the Heglig oil facility run by the Great Wall Drilling Company. The most serious incident occurred in 2008 when an unknown group kidnapped nine Chinese CNPC employees. The rebels killed four of them while security forces rescued four others and one went missing. These incidents led to greater Chinese interest in resolving conflict in Sudan and more active Chinese political engagement.[10]

Sudan's ruling Islamist party, the National Congress Party (NCP), has developed strong ties with the CPC. In 2009, the NCP invited, for example, Zhou Yongkang, a member of the Standing Committee of the CPC Central Committee's Political Bureau, to visit Sudan. He participated in a ceremony for signing three oil and gas cooperation agreements between Sudan and the CNPC. He also attended a ceremony for the first Beijing-Khartoum direct flight and unveiled the first Confucius Institute in Sudan at Khartoum University.[11]

The two countries support each other on controversial issues that come before international forums or attract foreign press attention. China uses its seat in the UN Security Council to prevent sanctions against Sudan based on human rights violations. Both countries, if they are serving on the UN Human Rights Council, vote in unison on issues that affect them. Sudan publicly backed Chinese policy on Tibet and the Chinese response in 2009 to end violence between the Uighur and Han people at Urumqi in the Xinjiang Uygur Autonomous Region. During a visit to Beijing, Sudan's defense minister supported China's measures to deal with the incident.[12] There are limits to China's cooperation. In a 2009 Security Council vote to refer the situation in Darfur to the ICC, China abstained rather than use its veto. This reportedly angered Sudan.[13] On the other hand, Hu Jintao sent al-Bashir a warm message of congratulations following his victory in highly controversial elections in 2010. Hu Jintao added that "Sudan and China are linked to each other with a longstanding friendship which is based on mutual respect, confidence and honest cooperation."[14]

A senior northern opposition political figure commented to the authors that China is Sudan's most important international partner, adding it is good China is able to balance Khartoum's relations with the West even if it is buying its way into Sudan. He welcomed China's strategic relationship with Sudan and Africa. On the other hand, he argued that China is insensitive to human rights issues and the people of Darfur blame China for protecting the al-Bashir regime.[15] A leader of another northern opposition party described the Chinese presence as nonmeddling, cautious, and generally helpful. He emphasized, however, that Sudan needs alternatives. A senior SPLM official, while serving in the central government, warned that "China is crowding the United States out of Sudan and maybe out of Africa" because it is acting strategically while the United States is not.[16]

During a visit to Sudan in 2010, China's special envoy to Africa, Liu Guijin, told reporters that China prefers a united Sudan but would respect the choice of the Sudanese people in the January 2011 referendum on South Sudan's future. He emphasized China did not want to prejudge the outcome. Sudan Foreign Minister Ali Karti responded that Sudan looked forward to a Chinese role during the period leading up to the referendum in support of unity. Liu also called on armed groups in Darfur that have not yet joined the peace process to do so and praised normalization of relations between Sudan and Chad. Following South Sudan's decision to secede, China praised both sides for the peaceful outcome and promised to play a constructive role in supporting the North-South peace process. During a visit by al-Bashir to Beijing in mid-2011, Hu Jintao proposed expanding bilateral cooperation by deepening political links, boosting trade and economic cooperation, increasing exchanges, and cooperating on international issues.[17] During a visit to Beijing later in 2011 by Sudan's defense minister, his Chinese counterpart pledged to develop military cooperation.[18]

China purchases about 60 percent of Sudan's exported oil, which amounts to about 6 percent of China's total oil imports. Sudan is China's third most important trading partner in Africa. In 2010, China imported $6.7 billion, mostly oil, from Sudan while Sudan imported $2.2 billion worth of goods from China. Chinese companies are building most of the roads, railways, bridges, dams, and power projects in the country, including the massive Merowe dam on the Nile in the northern part of Sudan and the El Gaili power station project.[19]

An advisor to al-Bashir explained to the authors that following diplomatic recognition of China in 1959, the relationship "has never been threatened." He attributed this to the fact that China has not interfered in Sudan's internal affairs. He added that China has maintained good relations with whatever Sudanese government is in power: elected democratically, military dictator, or Islamist. Sometimes relations have been warmer and sometimes cooler but since 1989 there has been a significant improvement as Sudan decided to "look East" after relations deteriorated with the United States. As a result, China is Sudan's principal ally today.[20]

South Sudan

South Sudan voted to secede from Sudan early in 2011 and obtained independence on 9 July; it recognized the PRC the same day. About 75 percent of unified Sudan's oil production is in South Sudan near the North-South border. Infrastructure for exporting and refining the oil is located in the North. As the major foreign investor in and importer of this oil, China had an interest in seeing an end to the civil war and peaceful implementation of the 2005 Comprehensive Peace Agreement (CPA) that authorized the referendum on secession.

Well before the referendum on South Sudan's future, China began hedging its bets. Much of its contact with South Sudan occurred at the party-to-party level so as not to offend Khartoum. In 2005, deputy SPLM leader Salva Kiir visited China. He returned in 2007 at the invitation of the CPC as SPLM leader, South Sudan's president, and first vice president of the national government when it operated under the terms of the CPA. The SPLM reported that it planned to establish relations with the CPC to ensure efficient development and management of oil resources to the benefit of its people. In 2008, China opened a consulate in Juba, South Sudan's capital, and began investing heavily in the South.[21]

China has, however, a history to overcome in South Sudan. The leader of an opposition party warned that southerners do not want the Chinese in the South because they supported the northern government that terrorized southerners during the civil war. He acknowledged, however, that the ruling SPLM is more interested in what the Chinese can offer South Sudan than concerned about previous support for the North.[22]

In the period before the referendum, SPLM Secretary General Pagan Amum received a CPC delegation in Juba and declared that ties with Beijing were very good. He gave assurances that South Sudan would protect China's investments in the oil sector.[23] The CNPC then began regular communication with South Sudan officials. Following the referendum, a delegation from China's Foreign Ministry visited Juba and said China is prepared to expand investment in infrastructure, energy, agriculture, education, and health and begin cultural exchanges. China has negotiated successfully this difficult transition by making available to South Sudan huge amounts of new investment. Chinese investors began with construction of a luxury hotel in Juba.

On independence day, China promised to enhance communication and cooperation between Sudan and South Sudan and the economic construction of the two countries, declaring that it "has kept an impartial attitude in dealing with both sides and maintained a focus on their long-term interests and regional peace and stability."[24] China announced training for thirty South Sudanese who are expected to become the core of its petroleum industry and indicated that cooperation in petroleum is central to the relationship. Foreign Minister Yang Jiechi visited Juba in August 2011 and promised to support the peace process with Khartoum. China subsequently announced a grant of $31.5 million for unspecified development projects, and Pan-China Construction Group received the contract to design South Sudan's proposed new capital at Ramciel in the center of the country.[25]

Somalia

Somalia received independence in 1960 and recognized the PRC later the same year. The relationship has never been interrupted, although Beijing removed its embassy from Mogadishu in 1991 after the fall of the Siad Barre government and security conditions precluded a physical presence. Immediately following independence, China, together with other foreign countries, had to cope with Somalia's irredentist claims against neighboring Ethiopia, Kenya, and Djibouti. Support for Somalia resulted in outspoken criticism from one or more of Somalia's neighbors. For its part, Somalia was careful to leave its options open vis-à-vis the West, USSR, and China.

Somali students were early recipients of significant numbers of Chinese scholarships, although many left China before completing their studies. China's early contact with opposition political parties in Somalia was not viewed favorably by the Somali government. Appreciating the importance of Islam in Somalia, China widely distributed copies of the Qur'an translated into Somali. Although China had the largest embassy in Mogadishu after independence, Sino-Somali relations developed slowly. As of 1963, the government-owned newspaper refused to print material supplied by Xinhua. A 1963 visit to Beijing by Somalia's prime minister resulted in a temporary warming of relations supported by a $19 million loan, a $3 million budgetary grant, and possible military assistance. Following the visit, China found itself reassuring Kenya it would not provide arms to Somalia. Although neighboring Ethiopia had not yet recognized the PRC, it supported Beijing's campaign to replace Taiwan in the UN, forcing China to balance carefully its support for Somalia, Ethiopia's traditional enemy.[26]

China focused on economic and technical assistance, especially in agriculture. During the 1960s, however, China provided only 2 percent of Somalia's foreign assistance compared to 20 percent from the Soviet Union and 17 percent from the United States. The Soviet Union remained Somalia's major donor of economic and military assistance in the early 1970s, but switched its support to Ethiopia after the fall of Emperor Haile Selassie in 1974 and the subsequent sharp reduction of U.S. influence in Addis Ababa. As the Soviets began to phase out of Somalia, China offered spare parts for some of Somalia's Soviet weapons.[27]

Chinese credits totaling $130 million between 1963 and 1971 funded most of its early projects in Somalia. Mogadishu favored Chinese economic aid because of its low cost, efficiency, and the fact that China promised to provide technicians for projects abandoned by the USSR.[28] Journalist Alan Hutchison concluded that "Somalia was one of those target countries where Chinese behaviour was impeccable: as far as possible requests were complied with and no known assistance was given to opposition groups."[29]

Chinese economic assistance to Somalia began to change in the 1980s with less focus on loans. A Chinese company built Somalia's north-south road using World Bank funding.[30] Beijing emerged as a major arms supplier to Somalia by the early 1980s, providing fighter aircraft and a variety of equipment for the army. Between 1980 and 1985, China signed military assistance agreements with Somalia totaling about $48 million. The two countries signed an agreement in 1989 that transferred Somalia's territorial fishing rights to China in exchange for armament credits. Beijing provided military assistance until the Siad Barre regime fell.[31]

China did not contribute troops to the international peacekeeping mission in Somalia between 1992 and 1995, although it did support the operation politically in the UN. It also provided small amounts of humanitarian assistance to Somalia after 2000; these contributions increased when a severe famine occurred in south/central Somalia in 2011.[32] In 2003, China served as the UN Security Council coordinator on the Somali issue. It subsequently helped finance the talks that led in 2004 to the establishment of a Somali parliament and the Transitional Federal Government (TFG). In

2006, China was the first nation to ask the UN Security Council to authorize a peacekeeping mission in Somalia. China also provides financial assistance to the African Union Mission in Somalia (AMISOM) in support of the TFG.[33] China continues to support the peace process, TFG, AMISOM, and more UN engagement, and is working with the international community to aid Ugandan and Burundian forces that comprise AMISOM.[34]

Chinese companies signed controversial oil prospecting agreements with the TFG and provincial authorities in semi-autonomous Puntland. TFG President Abdullahi Yusuf favored the deals while his prime minister opposed them; ultimately they failed to materialize. As of late-2011, the authorities in Puntland said they had no contact with the PRC; all contact occurred at the TFG level. China has provided credits to buy cell phone equipment from Chinese companies. Somalia is the only country in Africa with which Beijing has diplomatic relations but no resident embassy, although Somalia has an embassy in Beijing. As security worsened in 2008, China sat on the political sidelines and adopted a "wait and see" approach toward the TFG. In 2009, China canceled $120 million in Somali debts. In 2011, Somalia's deputy prime minister and foreign minister visited Beijing where he signed cooperation agreements with his Chinese counterpart.[35]

In view of continuing conflict, it is not surprising that China imports little from Somalia. From 2003 to 2010, China averaged $3 million of imports annually from Somalia. Somali imports over the same period averaged $36 million and reached $79 million in 2010.

Somaliland declared independence from Somalia in 1991. No state has recognized it, and China avoided interaction with Somaliland until 2010, when Minister of Aviation Waran Adde and the mayor of Somaliland's capital of Hargeisa made an official visit to Beijing. The aviation minister signed a contract with a Chinese company to expand the international airport in Hargeisa. The delegation anticipated signing additional contracts with Chinese companies to rehabilitate roads in the capital city.[36] Somaliland's minister of planning subsequently commented that "the Chinese are coming to Somaliland in droves."[37]

Somaliland President Ahmed Mohamed Silanyo, accompanied by four cabinet ministers and the director of Berbera Port, visited China in mid-2011. Somaliland signed an agreement with Hong Kong-based Petro Trans Company to expand the port. China also agreed to build a road between Berbera and Ethiopia.[38] Although this activity does not suggest that China intends to recognize Somaliland, it underscores that China will engage with all political entities in Africa, especially if it eventually leads to a long-term commercial relationship.

Tanzania

Immediately after independence in 1961, Tanzania (then called Tanganyika) recognized the PRC. Dar es Salaam became the center of Chinese activity in East Africa following the arrival of Xinhua representative Gao Liang in December 1961.[39] Tanzania developed one of the closest and most consistent relationships of all African countries with the PRC. Beijing perceived an opening in Tanganyika from the beginning. In 1962, it assigned the talented ambassador He Ying to Dar es Salaam. From Tanzania, He Ying negotiated PRC recognition in Burundi, Uganda, and Zanzibar, which was independent until its union with Tanganyika in 1964 and the two countries became known as Tanzania.[40] Before Zanzibar joined with Tanganyika, China hosted in Beijing Zanzibari political parties, trade unions, women and youth groups, and student organizations.[41]

Western influence began to decline sharply in the mid-1960s and socialism became the touchstone of Tanzanian politics under President Julius Nyerere. Tanzania's support for African liberation movements, removal of the American satellite tracking station from Zanzibar in 1964, expulsion of several American diplomats, severing of diplomatic relations in 1965 with the United Kingdom over its Rhodesian policy, and opposition to "imperialist aggression" in Vietnam convinced China that Nyerere's Tanzania merited complete support. Zhou Enlai visited Dar es Salaam in 1965. Nyerere's visit to China the same year persuaded him that China's success in national development offered useful lessons for Tanzania. The two countries signed a friendship treaty in 1965 and began one of China's most important aid relationships in Africa.[42]

In the late 1960s, Tanzania terminated its military assistance relationship with Canada and turned to China, which became the principal partner for all branches of the Tanzanian military. During the 1970s, China provided twenty T-59 medium and fourteen T-62 tanks, ten P6 torpedo boats and Swatow gunboats, and twelve MiG-17 fighters. It built a naval base at Dar es Salaam and a military airfield at Ngerengere outside the capital. Chinese instructors trained the Tanzanian army, navy, and air force. This strong military assistance has continued to the present.[43] More than 1,000

Tanzanian military personnel trained in China as of 1978. By the mid-1970s, however, Tanzania began to shift its dependence for military equipment to the USSR.[44]

Growing Chinese influence in Tanzania was not without controversy. From the beginning, Nyerere resented the impact of the Sino-Soviet split on Tanzania and Africa generally. He was especially concerned that independent Zanzibar might become part of the Sino-Soviet battleground. Both the Soviet Union and the PRC immediately recognized Zanzibar after its independence in December 1963. A left-wing, bloody revolution deposed the sultan of Zanzibar in January 1964. China and the USSR then recognized the new Revolutionary Government of the People's Republic of Zanzibar. Although China was accused at the time of playing a role in the revolution, no conclusive evidence supports this claim. In order to forestall growing factionalism on Zanzibar, Nyerere proposed union with the mainland. Moscow opposed the union while China supported it. The union resulted in a stronger position for China with the Nyerere government. China had developed close relations with Nyerere's political rivals in Zanzibar, especially Sheikh Mohammed Abdul Rahman. Following the union, China became a model of propriety and subsequently conducted its relations with Zanzibar through Dar es Salaam. One of Tanzania's new vice presidents from Zanzibar, Rashidi Kawawa, returned from a visit to Beijing in 1964 with $42 million in loans and a $3 million grant. This was the beginning of an impressive Chinese technical assistance program for Tanzania.[45]

China's early interest in Tanzania extended beyond its bilateral relationship. Tanzania's location permitted it to serve as a base for training members of liberation groups throughout southern Africa, especially Mozambique, and for supplying revolutionary movements opposing independent governments in the Congo, Rwanda, and Burundi. By 1965, Tanzania had become the center of Chinese financial assistance and arms supply to African independence movements. Tanzania arranged for delivery to rebels in the Congo and Mozambique of five shipments of Chinese arms totaling about 1,000 tons. With over fifty Chinese assigned to its embassy and ninety economic technicians, Tanzania had the largest PRC presence in East Africa. Dar es Salaam also became a jumping off point for Africans from the region invited to China. Tanzania hosted numerous liberation movements and allowed China to support several groups aimed at regime change in nearby countries. China even built a powerful radio transmitter in Tanzania that liberation movements could use to broadcast to their home countries.[46]

Tanzania had a long-standing interest in helping landlocked Zambia export its copper via the Indian Ocean port of Dar es Salaam. The road system was inadequate for this purpose. In 1963 the World Bank rejected a Zambian and Tanzanian proposal to build a railway between Dar es Salaam and Kapiri Mposhi near the copper fields in central Zambia, arguing that the project was not economically sound. China expressed interest in the railway during Nyerere's first visit to Beijing in 1965. The three parties signed an agreement in 1967 and a final protocol in 1970 for a long-term, interest-free $401 million Chinese loan. An estimated 30,000 to 50,000 Chinese worked on the Tanzania-Zambia railway project. The railroad authority, which officially became known as TAZARA, was China's premier assistance project and attracted global attention. The railway has been in use since 1975 and continues to be cited by all three countries as an important feature of their close relations.[47]

Over the years, TAZARA has experienced controversy and financial problems. In an effort to cut costs, railway management in 1994 closed nineteen stations that had infrequent train stops. This resulted in angry protests by the people served by these stations.[48] By 2009, the deputy managing director said TAZARA faced a serious crisis: debts of $700 million, mostly to China, and only 300 functioning coaches of the 2,000 required. The railroad suffered from poor management, unreliable timetables, inadequate maintenance, and legal suits from suppliers, contractors, and former workers.[49] By the end of 2009, China agreed to discount the original loan and inject another $50 million so TAZARA could purchase six new locomotives and repair 1,200 coaches.[50]

Nyerere made five visits to China as president and another eight after he stepped down in 1985 (but remained as head of the ruling party for another five years). During his 1981 visit to Beijing, Nyerere stated that "China is an inspiration for those younger and smaller countries that want to construct socialist societies."[51] Despite Tanzania's close ties with China, however, Nyerere emphasized his country's commitment to nonalignment.

Tanzania's economy did poorly in the 1980s and China reduced its activity on the continent generally. The 1980s marked the lowest level of interaction between Tanzania and China, which adopted Western-prescribed structural adjustment economic policies.[52] Although China's position was well established in Tanzania, when Nyerere gave up control of the ruling party in 1990 enthusiasm for Tanzanian socialism declined. Tanzania improved relations with the West while China's African policy became increasingly pragmatic. President Benjamin Mkapa, before departing for Beijing in 2000, referred to Tanzania's "special relationship" with China, which dates back to the 1960s. He added that "China is the ideal country to emulate and cooperate with."[53] President Jakaya Kikwete visited Beijing in 2006 and 2008.[54]

China approved Tanzania as a tourist destination country. There are forty-five flights weekly on four airlines between China and East Africa. Although most Chinese visitors are business persons, cultural and education ties are an important part of the relationship. Some 600 Tanzanian students have studied in China since the establishment of bilateral relations. Mandarin is being taught at the University of Dar es Salaam and Mandarin-speaking Tanzanians are increasingly working in Chinese businesses in Tanzania. Civil society representatives complain, however, that they have not managed to establish relationships with the Chinese government or private companies.[55]

Trade relations between the two countries developed slowly. Through the mid-1970s China accounted for only about 4 percent of Tanzania's exports and 6 percent of its imports except in the early 1970s when it imported large amounts of equipment in connection with the building of the railway. China-Tanzania trade has increased significantly in recent years, but it heavily favors China. In 2009, China accounted for about 7 percent of Tanzania's exports and 15 percent of its imports. Tanzanians have begun to complain about the growing number of cheap and counterfeit Chinese products on the market. In 2011, Tanzania ordered foreign traders doing business in Dar es Salaam to close down and leave the country. The edict, although mentioning no nationality, is generally believed to be aimed at the large number of Chinese traders.[56] In 2010, Tanzania imported $1.4 billion worth of products from China while China imported only $400 million worth from Tanzania, almost entirely raw materials. China's zero-tariff policy for products from Africa's poorest countries has had little impact on trade with Tanzania. Nontariff barriers continue to restrict imports. It has been difficult, for example, for Tanzanian coffee to meet Chinese product, health, and packaging standards.[57]

China's direct investment in Tanzania as of 2007 constituted 174 projects valued at $450 million. This placed China among the top ten foreign investors in the country.[58] In 2011, Tanzania's National Development Corporation (NDC) and China's Sichuan Hongda Group signed a $3 billion joint venture to develop the Mchuchuma coal and Liganga iron ore fields. The NDC controls 20 percent and Sichuan Hongda Group 80 percent of the project.[59] China's Ministry of Commerce established a Chinese Center for Investment Promotion in Tanzania. About 90 percent of foreign construction firms operating in Tanzania are Chinese, and they are winning about 70 percent of all public tenders.[60] The presence of Chinese medical teams from Shandong Province dates to 1968 and remains an important part of the relationship. Approximately 1,000 Chinese medical personnel have served in Tanzania; they have taught traditional Chinese medicine to Tanzanian practitioners.[61]

The United States has also retained a strong presence in Tanzania. The Bush administration emphasized ties with Dar es Salaam, including a large Millennium Challenge Corporation grant. The Obama administration continued the close relations. American and Chinese influence appear to be about equal. Tanzania welcomes China as an alternative to Western aid and FDI, but understands the potential risk in a monopoly position for Chinese contractors and unfavorable deals tied to Chinese assistance.[62] In 2009, a research team evaluated the Beijing action plan in Tanzania and concluded that, "despite the long history of engagement between Tanzania and China, interaction generally appears to be extremely formal," with little evidence that personal relations play a role.[63]

Over the years, China and Tanzania have signed an impressive number of agreements. High level visits are frequent and include numerous military exchanges. The modern Chinese navy sent its first naval fleet formation to Africa in 2000, calling at Dar es Salaam.[64] PLA navy vessels made a return visit in 2011. During a visit in 2009, Hu Jintao signed a $17.5 million agreement to finance investments in agriculture, one for $4.4 million to rehabilitate the state radio and television channels on Zanzibar, and another to send Chinese volunteers to Tanzania. He also inaugurated a $56 million sports complex that China largely financed.[65] In 2010, China's Export Import Bank signed concessional loans with Tanzania for $100 million to support Tanzania's broadband infrastructure and $70 million to upgrade the terminal at Zanzibar's international airport.[66]

Uganda

Uganda became independent in 1962 and recognized China days later. China's relationship with Uganda has been correct and uninterrupted, but until recently not particularly close. Uganda denounced China's attack on India in 1962. In 1964, minister of state in the Prime Minister's Office Grace Ibingira repudiated the views of youth leaders who had recently returned from Beijing. With China in mind, Ibingira warned embassies in Kampala not to meddle in local politics. Relations improved when Premier Milton Obote visited Beijing in 1965 and China provided a $3 million grant and $12 million loan.[67] In 1967, Ugandan officers complained that the resident Chinese military mission was "engaging in revolutionary activity" and Obote asked it to leave the country. Others believed that China provided arms to Rwandan Tutsi refugees living in Uganda.[68] There was a further cooling in relations during Idi Amin's rule from 1971 to 1979. The Tanzanian military helped Ugandan dissidents based in Tanzania to overthrow Amin's government in 1979. Amin alleged but never proved Chinese complicity.[69] Following a meeting between President Yoweri Museveni and Chinese leaders in 1989, China agreed to build a food technology center.

Over the decades there have been surprisingly few high level exchange visits and formal agreements between the two countries. Hu Jintao visited Uganda in 2001 when he was a member of the Standing Committee of the Political Bureau of the Central Committee of the CPC and vice president. Premier Wen Jiabao came in 2006. The following year, China canceled $17 million of Uganda's debt. The two countries have a modest military relationship. A Chinese company funded a $4 million renovation of the country's largest military barracks and contracted to build the defense force's first division headquarters. In 2010, Uganda commissioned a Chinese company to construct new barracks. China has a long-standing scholarship program for Ugandan students in China. Thirty to forty students annually receive five-year scholarships and about one hundred students were there in 2009. More than three hundred Ugandans study in China each year for periods ranging from one year to six months. China also built two rural primary schools. It has assigned medical teams to Uganda since 1983 and provided funding for anti-malaria research. China selected Uganda as the location for one of its agricultural demonstration centers, which will focus on fish farming.[70]

In the first decade of the twenty-first century, the two countries concentrated on economic relations, especially Chinese investment, joint ventures, and construction contracts in Uganda. Chinese companies constructed high visibility buildings including the national stadium, Ministry of Foreign Affairs, Bureau of Statistics, and an office block for the president and prime minister, the latter financed by a $7 million grant. China has a $350 million contract to build and manage a toll road from Entebbe airport to Kampala and a 2,000-acre rice farming project in eastern Uganda. China ranks fifth among countries with investments in Uganda, but it had more FDI in the 2009–2010 financial year than any other country, displacing the United Kingdom. There are about thirty registered Chinese companies and 5,000 registered Chinese in Uganda.[71]

Trade is modest and consistently favors China. In 2010, Uganda imported $284 million from China while China imported $27 million of leather goods, agricultural products, timber, and copper from Uganda. Low-quality, cheap Chinese imports are replacing domestic production and causing growing concerns. The Chinese ambassador recognized the problem, but insisted it is not a deliberate policy of the Chinese government to export low-quality goods. Some Ugandans also complain that Chinese workers are replacing Ugandan workers while providing minimal capacity building, skills training, and technology transfer.[72] Perhaps taking this into account, a delegation from the All-China Federation of Trade Unions visited Uganda in 2011. The Chinese union had earlier provided assistance to Uganda's Central Organization of Free Trade Unions for a trade union center.[73]

China's involvement in Uganda increased significantly when the China National Offshore Oil Corporation (CNOOC) took a one-third stake in an oil field discovered by London-based Tullow Oil PLC. Tullow controls the $2.9 billion project, which has estimated oil deposits of at least one billion barrels in Uganda's Lake Albert region. CNOOC will help develop the oil fields and finance a 750-mile pipeline to one of Kenya's ports.[74]

Commenting in New York in 2011, China's deputy permanent representative to the United Nations strongly condemned attacks by the Lord's Resistance Army (LRA) against Uganda and demanded that the LRA lay down its weapons immediately and cease all violence. The representative added that the final solution to the LRA problem requires close cooperation between affected countries and support from regional organizations as well as vigorous assistance from the international community.[75] Interestingly, this statement came just weeks after the United States pledged to send about one hundred special forces to help Ugandan troops track down the LRA in the DRC, Uganda, Central African Republic and South Sudan. China has notably improved its position in Uganda in recent years. Following meetings with a senior British official in 2010, President Museveni commented that Western countries have mismanaged their relationship with

Uganda. On the other hand, he said the "Chinese are clever, they know how to carefully deal with sensitive issues of African countries. The western world is losing out and yet this is not necessary."[76] Nevertheless, the China-Uganda relationship is not free of problems. Ugandan ambassador to China Charles Wagidoso acknowledged in 2010 that fifty Ugandans were being held in China for drug trafficking, twenty of them sentenced to death. Uganda negotiated with China to extradite all fifty to Uganda to serve their sentences. Wagidoso also found himself defending a program initiated by Huawei for providing software systems in Uganda, denying charges of corruption and shoddy work.[77]

Kenya

China cultivated a prominent Kenyan politician, Oginga Odinga, three years before Kenya achieved independence in 1963. Odinga represented the radical wing of the ruling Kenya African National Union (KANU). He visited China in 1960 and eventually became home affairs minister and vice president. He stated in his autobiography that "it was impossible not to be impressed with life in China."[78] While the Chinese pursued Odinga vigorously, they were anxious not to jeopardize their relations with other Kenyan leaders.

Although Kenya had a trade relationship with China before independence and recognized China immediately afterward, KANU moderates led by President Jomo Kenyatta were more skeptical about developing close ties with Beijing. China appreciated Kenya's regional importance, providing a cash grant of nearly $3 million and long-term credit of $18 million in 1964. China financially supported Odinga, who arranged military training for about twenty Kenyans in China. Kenyatta, who saw Odinga as a threat to his leadership, prevailed in the power struggle. China backed the wrong politician and generally overplayed its hand. Kenyatta expelled a Xinhua correspondent in 1965. A pamphlet attributed to China titled *Revolution in Africa*, which called for the overthrow of the Kenyatta government, circulated in East Africa. Kenyan police intercepted a convoy of forty trucks from Tanzania with Chinese arms for Uganda. Kenyatta was furious he had not been advised in advance. Kenya declared the Chinese chargé d'affaires persona non grata in 1967, the fourth Chinese official to be removed from Kenya in two years. In retaliation, Beijing ordered the Kenyan chargé d'affaires out of the country. Bruce Larkin, in his seminal work on China and Africa, described China's support for Odinga and actions in Kenya as a miscalculation but not inconsistent with policy at the time. These developments set back China-Kenya relations for years but never resulted in a formal break.[79]

Relations began to improve after 1978 when Daniel Arap Moi, who in the 1960s had accused China of plotting revolution in Kenya, replaced Kenyatta as president. Moi concluded it was necessary to diversify Kenya's sources of development funding. Between 1980 and 1985, China provided Kenya with $46 million in economic assistance. One of the most visible projects was the Moi International Sports Center outside Nairobi, constructed for the fourth All-Africa Games in 1987. China provided an interest-free loan for more than half the cost. High level visits resumed in 1980 with Moi going to Beijing that year and in 1988 and 1994. Senior Chinese officials began returning to Kenya in 1980. Premier Zhao Ziyang came in 1983, President Jiang Zemin in 1996, and Premier Zhu Rongji in 2002. The two countries signed a number of economic and technical cooperation agreements and by the mid-1990s there was a sharp increase in trade, mainly imports from China. By the time Moi left office in 2002, relations with China were better than they had ever been. Moi's change of attitude and Beijing's pursuit of Kenya, an important regional gateway, accounted for this success.[80]

China-Kenya ties became even stronger after Mwai Kibaki took office in 2003. Kibaki visited Beijing in 2005 with a large delegation interested in trade and investment, which has been the focus of the relationship. In 2006, China held a successful trade exhibition in Nairobi, where it has its largest trade center in eastern Africa. Hu Jintao came to Kenya in 2006, when he visited China's new Confucius Institute at the University of Nairobi. The same year, Kibaki returned to Beijing and Prime Minister Raila Odinga visited in 2009. The following year, Kibaki met with Hu Jintao while attending the Shanghai World Expo. China established a second Confucius Institute in 2009 at Kenyatta University. There is long-standing cooperation in higher education; in 2011, China increased its annual scholarships from thirty-two to sixty-four. There are ongoing exchange visits between the CPC and Kenya's three major parties in the ruling coalition: the Party of National Unity, Orange Democratic Party (ODM), and ODM Kenya. In 2006, China Radio International established in Nairobi a transmitting station that broadcasts nineteen hours per day in Swahili, English, and Chinese.[81]

Kenya has had a trade deficit with China since 1964 and the problem has become serious. In 2010, Kenya imported almost $2 billion of goods from China while China imported only $39 million (mainly scrap metal, tea, textiles, and vegetables) from Kenya. Kenya initiated high level discussions with China to identify ways to redress the trade imbalance. The huge deficit and the closure of Kenyan textile mills due to cheap Chinese and Asian imports are among the negative aspects of the China-Kenya relationship. Kenyan civil society groups have protested Chinese construction and financing of the Gibe 3 dam on the Omo River in neighboring Ethiopia, which may have negative environmental consequences for Kenya's Lake Turkana. Kenya Airways has regular air service from Nairobi to Guangzhou and Hong Kong. As of 2011, an estimated 8,000 Chinese live in Kenya, which hopes to host more Chinese tourists; there were fewer than 25,000 in 2006. China also has military cooperation and cultural exchange programs with Kenya.[82]

By 2005, Chinese investment projects in Kenya numbered almost one hundred with an investment capital of about $53 million. Between 2000 and 2005, China accounted for $32 million of FDI, representing about 7 percent of Kenya's total. Including small trading companies, restaurants, and clinics, some two hundred Chinese firms operated in Kenya by 2010. China is heavily engaged in road construction. The most successful company, the China Road and Bridge Construction Company, entered Kenya in 1985 and completed more than $200 million worth of projects by 2005. By 2006, Chinese construction and engineering companies completed projects worth $870 million. China is competing to build and finance a multibillion dollar port and oil refinery at Lamu on the Kenya coast and connecting transport infrastructure for serving landlocked countries west of Kenya. Kenyan and Western companies complain that it is difficult to compete with Chinese companies for Kenyan contracts.[83] Beijing Tianpu Xianxing Enterprises and Electrogen Technologies entered into a $140 million partnership to build a solar panel factory in Nairobi, the first of its kind in the region. The project reflects China's growing capability in solar power technology and has the potential to expand its sales throughout the region.[84]

China significantly raised its assistance to Kenya after 2002, when its contribution totaled less than 1 percent of total aid. By 2005 it reached $56 million or 13 percent of total foreign aid to Kenya. Most of it financed a rural telecommunications project using equipment tied to Chinese companies. One technique China has used with considerable effectiveness is providing modest grants-in-kind, usually under $100,000. Examples include a gift of computers from the All-China Federation of Trade Unions to its Kenyan counterpart, relief supplies to flood victims, anti-malarial drugs to the government, and office equipment to the Kenyan Parliament. Larger donations include thirty-two transport vehicles to the military and nearly $1 million in drugs to the Ministry of Health. In 2007, China's visiting defense minister provided Kenya's military a $2.3 million grant to improve its operations. Although these donations have little development value, they provide good public relations and sometimes open the door for subsequent equipment sales. China sees Kenya as a gateway to expanding commercial links throughout the region, especially telecommunications equipment and services. Huawei Technologies and ZTE are major players in Kenya.[85]

Ethiopia

Ethiopia, one of the few independent countries in Africa following Mao Zedong's victory, posed a dilemma for the PRC. Emperor Haile Selassie's feudal Ethiopia had not forgotten the public support it received from the ROC during the 1936–1941 Italian fascist occupation. As a result, it sympathized with the Chiang Kai-shek government. Ethiopia sent troops to Korea in the early 1950s in support of Seoul and eventually clashed with Chinese forces there.[86] From the early 1950s, Beijing sought recognition from Haile Selassie's government but had to overcome this legacy, Ethiopia's conservative, anti-communist policies, and close Ethiopian ties with the United States.

Haile Selassie understood the inherent importance of the PRC but saw an advantage in maintaining some ambiguity on recognition. He chose not to recognize Taiwan, but did accept its agricultural assistance. A PRC cultural mission visited Ethiopia in 1956 and Beijing established trade relations in 1957. Ethiopia sent a cultural delegation to the PRC in 1961, signed an agreement to exchange journalists in 1962, and allowed a Xinhua office to open. Zhou Enlai visited Addis Ababa in 1964, when the two countries implied they would establish diplomatic relations and China thought a decision was imminent. Ethiopia supported Taiwan in the UN from 1950 to 1958, abstained in 1959, and supported Beijing thereafter. It did not recognize Beijing, however, until 1970 after twenty other African states had done so.[87]

Several other considerations affected Haile Selassie's position on recognition of the PRC. Ethiopia denounced the "Chinese aggressors" following the 1962 PRC invasion of India and was critical of its position on the nuclear test ban treaty. The Eritrean Liberation Front (ELF) sought Eritrean independence from Ethiopia beginning in the early 1960s. China looked the other way when Syria sent Chinese weapons to the ELF, and subsequently covertly provided the insurgents with weapons. Ethiopia supported African rebels in neighboring southern Sudan against the Arab north while China had good relations with the Arab government in Khartoum, which also allowed the ELF to operate from within its borders against Ethiopia.[88]

The PRC developed close relations with Somalia in 1960. The Somali government had vowed to regain the Ethiopian Ogaden region, inhabited by ethnic Somalis. Dissident "shifta" or bandits from Somalia operated across the border into Ethiopia and Kenya, which also faced Somali irredentist claims. Haile Selassie believed Beijing was aiding the so-called Somali "shifta." It did not help when Zhou Enlai, two days after visiting Ethiopia in 1964, went to Somalia and told a news conference in Mogadishu that "Ethiopia is controlled by foreigners and a foreign land is over her."[89] Convincing evidence is lacking that China aided the Somali "shifta" against Ethiopia, but Ethiopian perception was more important than reality.[90]

In 1971, less than a year after recognizing Beijing, Haile Selassie visited Beijing, where he praised the progress being made in China and Chairman Mao's "outstanding achievements." They signed trade, economic, and technical cooperation agreements. China granted Ethiopia an interest-free loan of $84 million and soon sent several teams to help with Ethiopia's development.[91] Ethiopia is another example where China converted in a relatively short period of time a contentious relationship into a positive one. After a left-wing military junta led by Mengistu Haile Mariam overthrew Haile Selassie in 1974, one might have expected Sino-Ethiopian relations to improve. In fact, this development complicated China's efforts as the Soviet Union, seeing an opening after Ethiopian relations with the United States worsened, changed its focus from Somalia to Ethiopia. China made clear that it was ready to give moral support to the new revolutionary government in Ethiopia, but it was not prepared to compete with the Soviets in providing arms and financing.[92]

The overthrow of Selassie occurred during the height of the Sino-Soviet split. China began to criticize Soviet involvement in Ethiopia. Ethiopian military leaders took umbrage and accused China of cooperating with the reactionary West and Ethiopia's Somali enemies. This led in 1979 to the expulsion of the Xinhua representatives. By 1984, Ethiopia was heavily under Soviet influence and when prompted by Moscow, Mengistu would excoriate China.[93] This difficult period in China-Ethiopia relations did not, however, end cooperation. In 1978, China completed construction of a diesel power station at Bonga. Between 1975 and 1982, it constructed a 185-mile highway between Weldiya and Werota that has famously become known as the China road.

The downturn in Ethiopian-Chinese relations was evident in the sharp decline in high level visits. During the Mengistu period, no senior Ethiopian official visited China until the foreign minister went in 1987, followed by Mengistu in 1989 and 1991, and the deputy prime minister in 1990. These visits, which occurred as the Mengistu government was under siege from Eritrean and internal opposition, reflected the declining power of the Soviets and the desperation of the Ethiopian regime for outside support. There were no senior visitors from China to Ethiopia until the vice premier/foreign minister came in 1989 and again in 1991. The two governments did maintain diplomatic and trade relations. China continued to send medical teams to Ethiopia, a program begun in 1974, and offered ten scholarships annually after 1988. The Mengistu government fell in 1991, opening the door to a return of cordial Ethiopian-Chinese relations.[94]

The new government initiated high level contact in 1992. Ethiopia's chief of the general staff went to Beijing in 1994. Prime Minister Meles Zenawi made his first visit to Beijing in 1995, followed by the deputy prime minister in 1998 and 2002. President Jiang Zemin visited Addis Ababa in 1996. The two countries signed a series of new agreements. Premier Wen Jiabao visited Ethiopia in 1996 and 2003. Xinhua signed a news exchange agreement with the Ethiopian News Agency. Military cooperation became especially important during the 1998–2000 Eritrean-Ethiopian conflict as China sold Ethiopia (and Eritrea) significant quantities of arms. This led to an increase in high level military exchanges that continue on a regular basis.[95] China considers Ethiopia a strategic partner and provides technical assistance and jamming equipment to help Ethiopia's Information Network Security Agency block signals from anti-government radio stations and the Amharic-language programs of the Voice of America and Deutsche Welle.[96]

China provided $12 million to fund a technical and vocational education and training program that assigned two hundred Chinese teachers throughout Ethiopia. By 2008, China had sent one hundred agricultural experts to Ethiopia and trained more than 50,000 Ethiopians in agricultural techniques.[97] Meles returned to Beijing in 2004, when he signed more cooperation agreements, and co-chaired the 2006 FOCAC in Beijing. He also expressed, however, dissatisfaction over the performance of a Chinese company that was constructing the enormous Tekeze hydroelectric power project.[98] This did not discourage Ethiopia from choosing China to participate in subsequent hydro projects. The Industrial and Commercial Bank of China is funding much of the Gibe 3 dam being built on the Omo River by an Italian company. Dongfang Electric Corporation is one of the largest suppliers of generating equipment. Environmental groups have expressed concern about potential damage stemming from dams on the Omo River.[99]

By 2005, China's embassy in Addis Ababa hosted more high level visits than any Western mission and Chinese companies had become a dominant force building highways and bridges, power stations, cell phone networks, schools, and pharmaceutical factories. Ethiopia's trade minister said that "China has become our most reliable partner."[100] A senior official in the Ministry of Foreign Affairs commented that China has become "critical" to Ethiopia for economic reasons. Ethiopia understands, however, that China has its own interests in the country and close relations with China will not make relations with the West "redundant."[101]

China is involved in virtually every aspect of Ethiopia's economy. One agreement in 2006 with three Chinese companies to upgrade telecommunication services is valued at $1.5 billion. A Chinese investment group agreed to provide $713 million to construct the first private industrial zone in Ethiopia. China has been prospecting for oil and has agreed to develop Ethiopia's coal reserves. In 2009, China and Ethiopia signed a $1.9 billion agreement for two hydroelectric dams to be built by Chinese companies. China will finance 85 percent of the deal with preferential buyers' credit and concessionary loans.[102] The two countries agreed on an additional multibillion loan in 2010 to cover the cost of a light rail line in Addis Ababa, a new rail link from Addis Ababa to Djibouti, the purchase of nine vessels for Ethiopian Shipping Lines, and the construction of two hundred buildings for the Ethiopian Housing Corporation.

Ethiopia was the first African country to receive young Chinese volunteers, a program that continues. There is a Confucius Institute in Addis Ababa that provides training for 250 Ethiopians and then sends five of the highest qualified to Tianjing University of Technology and Education. The

Institute also provides Chinese language training for Ethiopian diplomats in the Ministry of Foreign Affairs. China invested about $30 million to establish the Ethio-China Polytechnic College and continues to provide teachers for vocational education.

The trade relationship remains problematic for Ethiopia. In 2010, Ethiopia imported $1.3 billion worth of products from China while China imported $274 million, mostly oil seeds, from Ethiopia. Ethiopia has a preferential trade agreement that covers more than 95 percent of its exports to China, but this has not redressed the trade imbalance.[103] Several government officials expressed concern to the authors about the large trade deficit with China and, while appreciating duty free entry for most Ethiopian products, emphasized it was important to improve the trade relationship. By 2011, Ethiopian Airlines operated twenty-three flights a week to Beijing, Guangzhou, Hangzhou, and Hong Kong.

Chinese commercial activity in Ethiopia has reached the point where it is now more important than that of any other country. Members of the Ethiopian Chamber of Commerce commented that the Chinese approach is different from the American or Western way of doing business. The Chinese seek a local partner with whom to invest. Although some chamber members had reservations about the rapidly expanding Chinese business presence, they concluded there is no alternative because no one else is making significant investments in the country.[104] Ethiopian business persons have raised concerns about substandard Chinese products, dumping by Chinese suppliers, unfair competition, and displacement of small Ethiopian businesses.[105] In one case ZTE communications equipment sat in a warehouse because no government entity wanted it. The more common reaction, however, was a belief that although Chinese products are not the best they are adequate and much cheaper than their competition.[106] There have also been issues concerning Chinese labor displacing Ethiopians, resulting in occasional complaints from members of Parliament. The Chinese embassy has acknowledged there are more than 10,000 Chinese working in Ethiopia. After a 2010 wage dispute at a cement factory in Mekelle, China sent home more than three hundred Chinese employees.

Chinese companies are building about 70 percent of the roads in Ethiopia, including the highly visible Addis Ababa Ring Road. Chinese soft loans often finance the roads at bids below cost and sometimes with no bidding process. Several Ethiopians commented that China builds extensive goodwill with these projects because so many people see or use them. They compared the political impact of China's road building with America's huge effort to ameliorate HIV/AIDS. The roads are tangible; the HIV/AIDS assistance is hidden except for those who benefit directly.[107]

Chinese investment in Ethiopia as of 2007 was modest but growing rapidly. The Chinese embassy put the total figure at $100 million involving 50 larger Chinese companies and 100 small private companies. According to other accounts, it had reached $900 million by 2009 and $1 billion by 2010. Between 2004 and 2008, Chinese companies provided about 7 percent of Ethiopia's total FDI. Most Chinese investment went into manufacturing.[108] The Ministry of Foreign Affairs said that 257 Chinese companies had registered in Ethiopia while only 78 had begun projects.[109] Chinese investment is criticized for lack of attention to environmental issues while the Ethiopian government has tended to look the other way.

The ruling party of Ethiopia, the Ethiopian People's Revolutionary Democratic Front (EPRDF), has also developed a good relationship with the CPC. When the EPRDF held its Seventh Organizational Conference in 2008, the CPC, together with a number of other foreign political parties, sent representatives. A CPC delegation also attended the Eighth Congress in 2010. Meles expressed his country's solidarity with China on the Tibet issue during a visit to Addis Ababa by Fu Sihe, state minister of the Organization Department of the CPC Central Committee. Meles added that Ethiopia strongly opposes any attempt by an external force to destroy China's national unity and create hatred among Chinese nationalities.[110] Ethiopia faces its own challenges from elements of several ethnic groups that prefer secession; Meles's support for China on Tibet and Xinjiang, in part, reflects these concerns.

Meles returned to China in 2011, when he signed loan agreements with the Export Import Bank totaling $500 million for implementing fifteen projects. China also provided $55 million in emergency food aid for Ethiopia and other drought-affected countries in the region.[111] In 2011, the Ethiopian Railway Corporation and the China Railway Group Limited signed a $1.1 billion loan agreement to cover construction of the first phase of the Ethio-Djibouti railway project.[112]

There is a widespread view that Chinese companies are willing to take more political and economic risks in Ethiopia than are their Western counterparts. Chapter 6 describes the 2007 attack on Chinese personnel in the Ogaden Region by the Ogaden National Liberation Front (ONLF). Following the attack, Chinese companies pulled out of the Ogaden. In August

2011, Hong Kong-based Petro Trans Company announced that it had agreed to invest $4 billion over twenty-five years to develop oil and gas reserves in the Ogaden and build oil and gas pipelines to Somaliland's port of Berbera.[113] Days later, the ONLF announced that these deals constitute an act of war against the Ogaden people and vowed to take all necessary measures to prevent their implementation.[114]

One Ethiopian economist suggested that China is looking decades into the future, describing Chinese business as creating a "new dynamism."[115] Meles noted that rising labor costs in China may cause it to begin relocating some manufacturing industries in countries like Ethiopia where wages are lower. Many Ethiopians see China as a more appropriate development partner than Western countries because China is more responsive to the government's requests. There is a widespread belief in Ethiopia that it can learn valuable lessons from China's poverty reduction strategies.[116] In 2010, during a lecture at China's Foreign Affairs University, Ethiopia State Minister of Foreign Affairs Tekeda Alemu stated that "the golden age of Africa-China relations is ahead of us. But this does not preclude, for both, developing real partnerships with others."[117]

China also sees Ethiopia's value as a regional hub. The African Union, which is establishing a FOCAC Secretariat, has its headquarters in Addis Ababa. China is funding and building the huge African Union conference center, which comes complete with a traditional Chinese-style garden. The New Partnership for Africa's Development has moved to Addis Ababa and the UN Economic Commission for Africa has its headquarters there.

Djibouti

Djibouti was a French territory until independence in 1977. A pan-Somali nationalist from Djibouti, Mohammed Harbi Farah, made contact with the Chinese in 1960 and reportedly received a significant amount of money from China following a visit there. The nationalists used some of the money to purchase arms that appeared in the port of Berbera in northern Somalia. About the same time, Farah died in a plane crash, ending China's support for Somali nationalists in Djibouti.[118]

France has had a military base in Djibouti since independence, and the United States located the headquarters of its Combined Joint Task Force-Horn of Africa there in 2003. Although Djibouti recognized Beijing in 1979, it has carefully balanced its relationship between China and the West. The most senior Chinese official to visit Djibouti is a vice premier. On the other hand, Djibouti's most senior officials have made frequent trips to China. President Gouled Aptidon went to China in 1979, 1991, 1994, 1998, and for medical treatment in 1999. The chief of the general staff of the armed forces visited in 1998 and the prime minister in 1999. President Ismail Omar Guelleh went to China in 2001 and 2006 and the prime minister visited in 2005. The chairman of the National Committee of the Chinese People's Consultative Conference, Jia Qinglin, visited Djibouti in 2010 to consolidate relations with Djibouti's Parliament.[119] When asked in 2010 who is Djibouti's principal external partner, President Guelleh responded that in terms of loans, it is China, while Japan is more generous in providing grant aid.[120]

The two countries have signed a number of agreements, including economic and technical cooperation and promotion and protection of investment. Chinese construction companies are active in Djibouti and China financed construction of the People's Palace convention center, a stadium, an outpatient building, housing projects, and the Ministry of Foreign Affairs. In 2009, work began on a Chinese-funded regional hospital in Arta. In 2010, China agreed to finance rehabilitation of the People's Palace for $7 million. State-owned Djibouti Telecom has partnered with Huawei and ZTE. China has a long-standing scholarship program for Djiboutian students and began sending medical teams in 1980. In 2010, Djibouti imported $489 million in goods from China while China imported only $1 million worth from Djibouti.

Late in 2008, China began sending naval vessels to the Gulf of Aden to assist in efforts to combat Somali piracy. As a result, Djibouti took on added importance for China. Early in 2010, the Chinese guided missile frigate *Ma'anshan* made a resupply visit to Djibouti and Chinese ships engaged in the anti-piracy operation continue to call there regularly.

Eritrea

Eritrea became independent in 1993 and recognized Beijing immediately. The PRC gave limited support to the ELF struggle to obtain independence from Ethiopia. Eritrean President Isaias Afwerki was one of the ELF political commissars who received training in China during 1966 and 1967. This assistance ended as a condition for Ethiopian diplomatic recognition of Beijing in 1970. The experience in China reportedly had a profound impact on Isaias. He was attracted to the concept of the people's war, especially after Ethiopia defeated the Eritrean rebels at Massawa. Isaias also liked the model of rural self-sufficiency and role of the peasantry that was a hallmark of early Chinese communism. Isaias still relies on Chinese doctors for his personal medical attention.[121]

Isaias subsequently broke with the ELF and formed the Eritrean People's Liberation Front. After independence, China was quick to engage Eritrea. Isaias visited China in 1994, 1997, 2005, and 2006. China built a hospital in the capital of Asmara and signed trade, economic, technical, and cultural agreements with Eritrea. Beginning in 1996, it sent experts on sports and culture and the following year medical teams started visiting. China built two rural schools, a cement factory, and a social science college. There have been numerous military exchanges. China trained Eritrea's military band and sent a team for removing land mines. Chinese construction companies are active in Eritrea and four Chinese mining companies have received exploration licenses for gold and base metals. In 2010, twenty Chinese youth volunteers arrived.[122]

Relations between Ethiopia and Eritrea were good following the overthrow of Ethiopia's Mengistu government in 1991, until a border conflict between the two countries erupted in 1998. The conflict remains unresolved, complicating the efforts of all countries to maintain cordial relations with both Ethiopia and Eritrea. China has become one of the most influential countries in Ethiopia while maintaining cordial relations with Eritrea and selling large quantities of weapons to both countries. While China sees Ethiopia as the more important partner and has much larger investments there, it has been careful to treat Isaias respectfully. When the UN Security Council agreed in 2009 to impose sanctions against Eritrea for supporting extremist groups in Somalia and threatening neighboring Djibouti, China abstained. China's Permanent Representative to the UN, Zhang Yesui, said the UN should act prudently in imposing sanctions, which should not replace efforts to resolve disputes through dialogue and negotiations.[123] At a presentation of credentials ceremony for a new Chinese ambassador early in 2010, Isaias expressed surprise that China was not more supportive of

Eritrea's position but described his country's relations with Beijing as "strategic" and unaffected by China's abstention.[124]

In a 2007 interview with *China Business Weekly*, Isaias noted that Eritrea is shifting its trade from Europe to China and expects to depend increasingly on Chinese investment for development. He said China produces quality products at low cost; Eritrea now buys almost 90 percent of its equipment and machinery from China. At the same time, he expressed concern that African countries cannot just sell raw materials to China and buy finished products. There must be a partnership. The bilateral trade statistics underscore this point. From 2003 through 2009, Eritrea imported on average each year about $22 million worth of products from China while China imported only $1 million annually from Eritrea.[125]

Mauritius

Mauritius, which became independent in 1968, recognized Beijing in 1972. The Sino-Mauritian community constitutes about 3 percent of the population. Delegations from Mauritius began visiting China in 1959; a Chinese delegation first went to Mauritius in 1968. The All China Federation of Trade Unions was active in these early exchanges and it is likely the small communist party in Mauritius was also involved.[126] Following diplomatic recognition, relations have been steady and cordial. A cultural cooperation agreement signed in 1980 has resulted in well over thirty exchanges. China built a stadium, bridges, and airport terminal building in Mauritius. Since 1981, China has provided scholarships for Mauritian students to study in China. China opened a cultural center in Bell Village in 1988. The two countries signed treaties aimed at avoiding double taxation and tax evasion and in 1996 signed an investment promotion and protection agreement.[127]

Mauritian presidents and prime ministers have visited China nine times since 1972, when China made available a $33 million loan. Between 2004 and 2007 alone, the two countries signed eight agreements. China provided an interest-free $5 million loan during Prime Minister Paul Berenger's 2000 visit to China in 2005. Prime Minister Navinchandra Ramgoolam attended the 2006 FOCAC in Beijing and returned in 2007. Chinese visitors to Mauritius, although fairly frequent, had been of lower rank until Hu Jintao arrived in 2009. Other organizations that have visited are the Chinese People's Association for Friendship with Foreign Countries and the Chinese

People's Consultative Conference, which signed agreements on trade and scientific cooperation in oceanography. It also agreed to twin the Mauritian town of Vieux-Grand Port and Qingdao.[128] There is a strategic element to China's interest in Mauritius. The Indian Ocean is important to China's trade and, as a result, Chinese naval power is increasing in the region.[129]

In 2009, China was Mauritius's second most important supplier after India. The trade balance strongly favors China. In 2010, Mauritius imported $433 million worth of products from China while China imported only $10 million worth from Mauritius. Chinese imports have been static for the past decade. Trade has been a sensitive issue because the Chinese export of cheap textiles cut deeply into the Mauritian textile industry. Wen Jibao acknowledged the problem in a 2006 meeting with his Mauritian counterpart, adding that China was prepared to provide technical and managerial training to help redress the disparity in textile production efficiency.[130]

Investment has become China's most important thrust in Mauritius, which markets itself heavily to China and India as the source of skilled labor and the gateway into eastern and southern Africa. The Chinese privately owned Shanxi Tianli Enterprise Group and the state-controlled Shanxi Coking Coal Group Co. Ltd. and the Taiyuan Iron and Steel Group Co. Ltd. are developing a $750 million project known as Jinfei. This is the largest ever foreign direct investment in Mauritius. The 521-acre project will provide headquarters for these companies, space for high tech manufacturing, housing, and a branch of a private university. The project came to a halt in 2007–2008, but following revisions in the terms is scheduled for completion in 2015. This is the model China has used successfully and is now replicating in several African countries.[131] During his 2009 visit, Hu Jintao announced a $260 million loan to expand the main airport terminal, a $6.5 million interest-free loan, and a grant of $5 million. He explained that the economic and trade zone will serve as China's strategic trade corridor between Asia and Africa.[132]

Madagascar

Taiwan had a consulate general in the capital of Antananarivo when Madagascar became independent in 1960. President Philibert Tsiranana, one of the most anti-communist African leaders, immediately recognized Taiwan.

The PRC regarded members of the small Chinese community in Madagascar as possible allies and had some contact with left-wing Malagasy opposition politicians. It was never able, however, to overcome strong opposition from Tsiranana until left-wing labor unions and students forced him out in 1972. The new military leader, Didier Ratsiraka, visited Beijing later in the year and established diplomatic relations. Anti-Chinese riots followed and some 2,000 left the country. China offered a $12 million loan in 1973 and agreed to finish a hotel that had been abandoned by South Africa. It made an interest-free loan of $60 million in 1975 to build a sugar factory and improved the national match factory among other projects. Ratsiraka returned to Beijing in 1976 when China agreed to undertake a number of infrastructure projects. China was Madagascar's largest communist donor country by the late 1970s, but Beijing began to show its disapproval of Antananarivo's closer ties with the USSR. China also provided limited military aid during the 1970s. In four years, Madagascar went from one of Taipei's closest African partners to one of Beijing's.[133]

The two countries subsequently signed more agreements and China built roads, a sugar refinery, pharmacy, and stadium. China's student scholarship program began in 1973; sixty-three students from Madagascar were studying in China at the end of 2009. China started sending medical teams to Madagascar in 1975; the seventeenth team of thirty personnel arrived in 2009. President Li Xiannian visited Madagascar in 1986 and Vice President Hu Jintao in 1999. Senior CPC officials have tended to represent China in more recent years. President Ratsiraka returned to Beijing in 1985 and successive presidents visited in 1994, 2004, 2006, and 2007. Madagascar's deputy prime minister visited in 2000 and the prime minister in 2005. China agreed in 2007 to establish a Confucius Institute at Antananarivo University. Chinese construction companies, joint ventures, and investment are playing an increasingly important role. Chinese FDI in Madagascar grew from less than 1 percent of the total in 2000 to 11 percent by 2006. Of the 146 foreign companies registered during this period, 32 were Chinese. China provided hurricane relief assistance in 2008.[134]

There have been significant fluctuations in Malagasy imports from China. They averaged $411 million annually from 2003 through 2010, and reached a high of $831 million in 2008. By 2010, they had fallen back to $436 million. By contrast, China's imports from Madagascar from 2003 through 2010 averaged $39 million annually but reached a high in 2010 of $105 million. China's increasing interest in the Indian Ocean is one of the primary reasons China works hard to maintain good relations with Madagascar's troubled government.[135]

Comoro Islands

Three of the four Comoro Islands obtained their independence from France in 1975 and established relations with the PRC the same year. China had made contact a decade earlier with Comoro Islands Liberation Front members, who made occasional visits to Beijing. A Comoro government delegation made its first visit to China in 1976, when it signed an economic and cooperation agreement. China was the first communist country to establish formal economic ties with the Comoro Islands. A Comoro trade delegation followed later in the year. Exchange visits occurred below the most senior levels until the Comorian president went to Beijing in 1988, 1996, and 2000. China began aid projects in 1976 that eventually included a water supply project, People's Palace, government office building, president's mansion, and TV broadcasting building. The two countries signed a cultural agreement in 1985. China offered scholarships to students beginning in 1982 and sent the first in a series of medical teams in 1994.[136]

Activity between the Comoros and China picked up in the twenty-first century. In 2003, the Comorian president visited Guangxi Zhuang Autonomous Region, which provides medical teams for the Comoros. The Chinese foreign minister made his first visit to the Comoros in 2004. He signed agreements to renovate the international airport and enlarge the Ministry of Foreign Affairs. The chief of staff of the Comorian army visited Beijing in 2005 and the president returned in 2006. During a visit to the Comoros in 2008, China's vice minister of commerce said China is prepared to help connect the country to the African mainland by means of the East African Submarine Cable Network System. He stated that some sixty Comorian civil servants had been trained in China and noted that the two countries have similar opinions on Tibet.[137]

China's approach to the Comoros has been similar to the way it dealt with another island nation in the Atlantic—Equatorial Guinea. In both cases, China established a physical presence after independence, consistently maintained its presence, and methodically increased its interaction with these two small and seemingly unimportant nations. In Equatorial

Guinea, the effort resulted in important benefits for China after the discovery of oil there. So far, the modest investment in the Comoros has not had that kind of benefit. But the methodology of China's diplomacy is clear: establish a modest presence everywhere and be patient. By contrast, the United States shut down its embassy in the Comoros in 1993 for the same reason as in Equatorial Guinea—unwillingness to pay the modest cost of maintaining an embassy when there were no short-term benefits. The United States belatedly reestablished an embassy in Equatorial Guinea after the discovery of oil; it has not done so in the Comoros, although the U.S. ambassador resident in Madagascar is accredited to the Comoros and the United States funds several projects there.

From 2003 through 2010, the Comoros imported on average $9 million worth of goods annually from China; imports reached $15 million in 2010. During the same period, China imported nothing from the Comoros.

Seychelles

Seychelles is an Indian Ocean archipelago of about 80,000 people with an estimated 600 citizens of Chinese descent. The Seychelles became independent in 1976 and established relations with Beijing the same year. The following year, China began a series of assistance projects that included the national swimming pool, polytechnic and middle schools, housing projects, and help to cultivate rice. China was the first communist country to provide economic assistance to Seychelles. It began offering scholarships in 1984 and sending medical teams in 1985.[138]

Senior Seychellois officials have made regular visits to China. The president has visited China six times since the first in 1978. The most recent visit occurred in 2010 when President James Alix Michel attended the Shanghai World Expo and met with Hu Jintao. Although numerous senior Chinese officials visited the Seychelles, the first president to do so was Hu Jintao in 2007. On that occasion, the two countries signed five agreements on the economy and technology, education, and promotion and protection of investment. China made a $1.5 million grant for balance of payments support and extended a concessionary loan to upgrade the water supply, sewer system, and power supply for the principal island of Mahe. The CPC maintains a relationship with the ruling political party, the People's Party of the Seychelles. The visit to Victoria, the capital, in 2009 by Zhou Yong-kang, a member of the Standing Committee of the CPC Central Committee Political Bureau, underscored party-to-party ties. The same year, China finished construction of the National Assembly building. Haikou City in Hainan Province established a sister city relationship with Victoria, the Seychellois capital. Chinese State Councilor Dai Bingguo visited Seychelles in 2010 when President Michel commented that Seychelles-China ties are a model for bilateral relations. The Seychelles have hosted several PLA navy visits since 2010. Michel visited China in 2011 when Beijing donated two Y-12 aircraft for anti-piracy surveillance missions. China is training fifty Seychelles People's Defense Forces soldiers and is in discussion with Seychelles for its use as a resupply port for PLAN ships engaged in the Somali anti-piracy operation.[139]

From 2003 to 2010, the Seychelles imported annually an average $9 million worth of goods from China; imports reached $16 million in 2010. During the same period, China has never imported more than $4 million worth from Seychelles, and some years there have been no imports.

10

China's Relations with West and Central Africa

West and Central Africa were the principal diplomatic battlegrounds between Beijing and Taipei. The different political leanings among governments in this region were strong. These countries also experienced a higher frequency of regime change than those in other African regions, which increased the possibility for them to switch recognition between the PRC and Taiwan. During the 1960s, when it considered opposition groups closer to its views, China interfered in the internal affairs of some independent African governments in the region. On several occasions, China armed and trained opposition groups, angering the affected governments.

Of the twenty-one countries in this region, only Guinea, Ghana, Equatorial Guinea, Nigeria, and Cape Verde never established diplomatic relations with Taiwan. Ghana suspended relations with Beijing in the 1960s but did not recognize Taiwan. All the others either recognized Taiwan after independence or switched recognition at least once since independence. The Central African Republic and Liberia recognized the PRC and Taiwan three times each. Today, all the countries except Gambia and São Tomé and Principe recognize Beijing.

China focused its efforts in the 1960s on left-leaning Guinea, Ghana, Burundi, and Congo-Brazzaville. In response to Washington and Moscow's Cold War competition in the Congo, now the DRC, Beijing unsuccessfully supported Congolese groups opposed to both superpowers. In Guinea-Bissau and Cape Verde, China backed liberation wars against Portugal. In the late 1960s and 1970s, many African governments became more left-wing. A few such as Ghana and the DRC became more moderate. In the 1970s, China adopted a more pragmatic approach to relations with African countries. This combination resulted in increasing numbers of these countries recognizing Beijing. For example, Beijing established cordial relations with the DRC's conservative Mobutu Sese Seko government. Increasing pragmatism and greater focus on economic ties have become China's standard practice.

Over time, China emphasized strong relations with countries that have raw materials. While countries such as Guinea, Burundi, and Guinea-Bissau received disproportional attention in the 1960s, they subsequently fell in relative importance. Guinea became important again in 2009 following a large Chinese investment in its bauxite sector. Other countries that became significantly more important to Beijing include the DRC (minerals), Congo-Brazzaville (oil), Equatorial Guinea (oil), Nigeria (oil and political influence), and Gabon (oil and minerals). Ghana's political clout and recent oil discovery have attracted China's attention. Meanwhile, China has not neglected other countries in the region. As China's requirements for imports change, additional African countries develop desirable raw materials, and governmental developments change policy toward China, these relationships will continue to evolve. The large number of countries in West and Central Africa, the growing importance of the Economic Community of West African States, and the role of these countries in international forums provide added incentives for China to cultivate good relations with countries in this region.

Guinea

Guineans voted against a French constitutional referendum in 1958 that resulted in abrupt independence and a strained relationship with France. Most Western countries abandoned Guinea. The Soviet Union stepped in but made a series of blunders.[1] China promptly recognized Guinea. Conakry reciprocated but sought to maintain good relations with the Soviet Union. Not convinced Guinea was a true revolutionary state, Beijing took a year before opening an embassy in Conakry. Eventually concluding that Guinea could serve as a beachhead in West Africa, the PRC increasingly focused efforts there. It opened a Xinhua office in 1960; several months later Guinean President Sékou Touré was the first African leader to visit Beijing. The two counties signed treaties on political and trade relations. Guinea became a large recipient of PRC grants and loans.[2]

In subsequent decades, Guinea benefited significantly from Chinese economic and military aid. In 1967, Sékou Touré praised China's "unpretentious approach" to aid, although Guineans were disappointed with the quality of Chinese goods.[3] Guinea-China relations have been cordial, but did not live up to early expectations. Sékou Touré sought to play East against West and Moscow against Beijing and by 1979 had received $85 million in grants and loans from China.[4] By 1978, China trained about 360 Guinean military personnel in China and that year had thirty military specialists in Guinea. The military cooperation begun in 1961 was suspended in 1982 but resumed in 1992. High level exchange visits have been less frequent than with many other African countries.[5]

Over the years, Chinese grants and loans funded construction of a cigarette factory, Macenta Tea Factory, Dabola Groundnut Oil Factory, Boffa Sugar Cane Factory, Kankan Brickyard, Bordo Agricultural School, Mamou Agricultural Tool Factory, Kaback Water Development Works, Boffa Water Cooperation Project, Kindia Agriculture Extension Works, People's Palace, Sekhoutereya Palace, and headquarters for Guinean radio and television. In 2007, China began construction on a $50 million stadium and the following year a 150-bed hospital and anti-malaria center.[6]

The 2008 global financial crisis, falling commodity prices, and concern about Guinea's political stability delayed Chinese plans for major investment in Guinea. Early in 2009, China backed away from a $1 billion loan agreement with Guinea to construct a hydropower dam in exchange for rights to mine bauxite.[7] By year's end, however, the China International Fund (CIF) agreed to invest $7 billion in Guinea. CIF and Guinea set up a Singapore-based company that holds the rights to Guinea's oil, gas, and mineral deposits not previously under contract. The new joint company, Guinea Development Corporation, committed to build major infrastructure projects, including a railway to transport Guinea's unexploited iron ore reserves to the coast, a deep water port, and three hydroelectric dams.[8]

The leaders of an unpopular military coup in Guinea embarrassed China by announcing the CIF deal when Guinea was under pressure from human rights activists and Western governments. Beijing denied any connection with CIF, stating it is a Hong Kong-based company not linked to the Chinese government. CIF has a murky corporate background but its chairwoman, Lo Fong Hung, is director of Sonangol Sinopec International Ltd., a joint venture of Sinopec and Angola's state-owned oil company, Sonangol.[9] Following Guinea's elections and an improved human rights situation, CIF announced an agreement to provide $2.7 billion for building rail, port, and associated infrastructure for the iron ore project at Kalia, which hopes to produce 50 million tons annually, and about $1.2 billion to fund the mine.[10]

In 2010, mining giant Rio Tinto completed a deal with the Chinese company Chalco and its parent Chinalco, to develop Rio's Simandou iron ore project in Guinea. Chinalco, which has a 9 percent stake in Rio Tinto, invested $1.35 billion in the Simandou project. Chinalco's president said the agreement will help meet China's iron ore demand.[11] In 2011, China Power Investment negotiated a $5.8 billion deal to mine bauxite in exchange for building a coal power plant, alumina refinery, and deep water port.[12] In 2010, China's imports from Guinea were a modest $55 million; Guinea imported $464 million worth from China, Guinea's largest supplier.

Ghana

Ghana's President Kwame Nkrumah recognized China in 1960, three years after independence. Beijing sent one of its most seasoned diplomats, Huang Hua, as ambassador to Accra.[13] Nkrumah had good relations with the USSR and did not want to become embroiled in the Sino-Soviet dispute. After visiting Moscow in 1961, he continued to Beijing where he received a $20 million, interest-free loan repayable in Ghanaian exports or a third-country currency. The terms were better than the loan he negotiated in Moscow. Repayment of loans in exports, especially oil and minerals, subsequently became a feature of Chinese loans in Africa. The two countries signed a friendship treaty and economic and cultural agreements. China also sent technical experts to Ghana. Zhou Enlai included Ghana on his famous 1963–1964 Africa trip, when he pledged a $22 million loan.[14]

In 1964, although still uneasy about China's intentions in Africa, Nkrumah welcomed the first group of five Chinese military advisors to train African dissidents from countries such as Côte d'Ivoire, Niger, Benin, the Congo, and Cameroon in the basics of guerrilla warfare. All these countries were independent and not under white rule. Nkrumah supported revolutionary movements that could replace relatively conservative governments. This effort came to an end at the beginning of 1966 when Ghana's military deposed Nkrumah while he was being feted in Beijing. The new Ghanaian government demanded immediate withdrawal of all Chinese technical experts and a reduction in embassy staff. Ghana accused China of interfering in its internal affairs by helping to train Africans at secret military camps and supporting Nkrumah's effort to return to power. Following charges and countercharges during the remainder of 1966, the two countries suspended diplomatic relations and all Chinese staff departed the embassy in Accra in November.[15]

Journalist Alan Hutchison argued that China had no coherent plan to subvert the continent through revolution. China moved cautiously and pragmatically, stressing the need for revolutionary self-reliance. When it did intervene militarily, as in the Congo, it did so secretly. During the 1960s, China's revolutionary rhetoric, however, allowed African and Western critics to link China to virtually any subversive group in Africa. Hutchison asserted that Chinese-aided dissidents did not overthrow a single independent African government. He added that China's debacle in Ghana led to extensive criticism and caused a reassessment of Chinese policy in Africa.[16] Nigerian scholar Alaba Ogunsanwo offered a less charitable analysis, stating that Beijing took advantage of Ghana's hospitality to advance its revolutionary interests in Africa.[17]

Ghana and China reestablished diplomatic relations in 1972. During the suspension of relations, Ghana never recognized Taiwan. Political relations gradually improved and Ghana's president finally returned to Beijing in 1985 and in 1995, 2002, and 2006.[18] Hu Jintao visited Ghana in 2003. During a visit by Wen Jiabao in 2007, China and Ghana signed six agreements, including one to build an anti-malaria center and primary school and a $66 million loan to expand and upgrade Ghana's telecommunications network.[19]

Chinese investment as a percentage of total investment in Ghana reached almost 9 percent by 2005.[20] Until recently, most Chinese FDI has been in nonresource sectors such as manufacturing, general trading, telecommunications, power generation, construction, tourism, and services. China's 283 investment projects were the most diversified in Ghana. By 2007, China was Ghana's sixth largest investor at $76 million. Another study covering this period listed China's investment at $61 million with an additional $172 million in loans. Most Chinese companies are small or medium-sized although a few large ones have begun to make direct equity investments or join international partnerships. Alcatel Shanghai invested in Ghana Telecom and Shenzhen Energy announced plans to invest in a gas-fired plant.[21] Ecobank Ghana and Bank of China signed a partnership agreement in 2010 to facilitate international trade and investment.

Following Ghana's 2007 oil discovery, China turned its attention to that sector. In 2009, CNOOC offered to buy a $3 billion to $5 billion stake and grant Ghana a $2 billion concessionary loan. While negotiations continue with CNOOC and major non-Chinese oil companies, it is apparent that China's strategy in Ghana includes access to natural resources.[22]

Chinese contracts in Ghana include a $562 million loan to build the Bui hydroelectric project. A mixed credit financing arrangement, 42 percent is a concessionary loan and the rest a supplier's credit. The concessionary loan is payable over twenty years at 2 percent interest annually.[23] More than 700 Ghanaian professionals and officials have participated in Chinese training courses in education, trading, communication, energy, auditing, agriculture, and fisheries. China and Ghana signed an agreement to teach Chinese at the University of Ghana. China also canceled $90 million of Ghana's debt.[24]

China has expanded military cooperation with Ghana and donated computers, camouflage uniforms, forty troop-carrying vehicles, and fifteen pick-up trucks. China provided an interest-free $3.8 million loan to build military-police barracks at Burma Camp and contributed $1.7 million to help finance the Defense Ministry's office complex. In 2007, Ghana received a $30 million loan from China's Export Import Bank to acquire equipment and build communications systems for the police, armed forces, prison service, and other security agencies; ZTE was the contractor. Ghana purchased four Chinese K-8 jet aircraft, and in 2010 China donated $1.5 million worth of troop carriers, trucks, a field ambulance, and a tanker to Ghana's military.[25]

In 2007, Ghana's trade minister said that Africa must seek markets in China and avoid a "colonial" relationship with Beijing that attempts "to suck all the natural resources from Africa to feed their industries."[26] Ghana's President John Kufour warned of the "intimidating presence of China in Ghana and other parts of the world" and urged African countries to develop ways to compete with the Asians.[27] Ghana's fisheries minister expressed concern about the influx of Chinese fishing vessels in its territorial waters.[28] The Trade Union Congress of Ghana complained about poor working conditions at the Chinese construction site for the Bui hydroelectric project.[29] In 2009, Ghana terminated a $10 million agricultural cooperative program managed by the China State Farms Agribusiness Corporation (CSFAC) when the opposition party assumed office. CSFAC's deputy general manager subsequently commented that "now we prefer to talk with government administrations instead of party leaders when it comes to further cooperation."[30]

By 2010, the Ghana-China relationship was back on track. President John Atta Mills visited Beijing when China's Export Import Bank and Ghana signed a twenty-year $10.4 billion concessionary loan for infrastructure projects. Ghana agreed to use $2.85 billion of the loan for roads and $6 billion for railway infrastructure, hiring Chinese companies. The China Development Bank offered another $3 billion to develop Ghana's new oil and gas sector and guaranteed more than $400 million for water and electronic projects. Ghana will repay the loans with exports, presumably oil, to China. Ghana also signed a $1.2 billion agreement with China's Bosai Minerals Group to build a bauxite and aluminum refinery; Bosai agreed to purchase 80 percent of the shares in the Ghana Bauxite Company, Ltd.[31] Ten Chinese volunteers also arrived in Ghana. As part of the 2010 package, Ghana's Parliament approved in 2011 a $3 billion loan to finance energy infrastructure projects. A minority in Parliament argued that the loan violates the terms of an agreement Ghana has with the IMF concerning debt.[32]

In 2010, Ghana imported $2.1 billion in Chinese goods while China imported only $123 million worth of products, mostly manganese and cocoa, from Ghana. One of Ghana's largest imports was textiles, a product that Ghana produces domestically.[33]

Democratic Republic of Congo

One of China's most controversial involvements in Africa during the 1960s occurred in the DRC, known as Congo-Léopoldville (the city of Léopoldville is now Kinshasa) and later as Zaire. The same criticism can be made about American and Soviet policy in the Congo during this era. Unprepared in 1960 for independence from Belgium and located in the heart of Africa with enormous mineral wealth, the Congo was ripe for foreign intervention. The Congo was at the center of Cold War competition and the Sino-Soviet conflict. China sought to establish a radical government and backed left-wing Patrice Lumumba until his arrest and assassination in 1961; it supported his former deputy Antoine Gizenga based at Stanleyville (now Kisangani) in the eastern Congo.[34]

A secret Chinese analysis in 1961 underscored China's support for revolutionaries while acknowledging the challenges. The analysis concluded that "the situation is favorable, but the [Congolese] leadership is weak."[35] Following the death of Lumumba, China established diplomatic relations with the Gizenga government in Stanleyville. Beijing's efforts were thwarted, however, when Gizenga joined the moderate Cyril Adoula government in Léopoldville, which had diplomatic relations with Taiwan. The mission in Stanleyville closed two months after it opened and the PRC suspended relations with the Congo because of its relations with Taiwan.[36]

In the two years Gizenga was part of the Cyrille Adoula government, Beijing continued to seek out ideologically sympathetic Congolese politicians. They focused on Pierre Mulele, a former education minister in Lumumba's government, and Gaston Soumialot, who had been minister of justice for Kivu Province in Gizenga's 1961 government. Mulele, who had visited China, launched a Maoist-style guerrilla operation in Kwilu Province at the end of 1963. The PRC trained guerrillas from the Congo at camps in nearby Tanzania, Burundi, and Congo-Brazzaville.[37] After Congolese authorities and mercenaries crushed Mulele's movement, Gaston Soumialot operating from Burundi and Christophe Gbenye from Congo-Brazzaville launched another rebellion. British scholar Colin Legum wrote that both received Chinese financial and arms support. Government forces and mercenaries defeated Gbenye and Soumialot by early 1965. Soumialot arrived in China in 1965 heading a large delegation of Congolese as a guest of the Chinese People's Institute of Foreign Affairs. Although China denied supporting the Congolese guerrillas, the evidence suggests otherwise. After 1965, when Mobutu Sese Seko seized power, China abandoned the rebels.[38]

American scholar Warren Weinstein argued that Chinese policy in the Congo by the early 1970s shifted from hard-line ideology to more flexible pragmatism. China concluded that the Congolese were not prepared to confront the government and realized ethnicity trumped ideology in the rebellions. President Mobutu, who renamed the country Zaire, declared in 1972 that he could recognize the PRC if it changed its policies toward Zaire. China assured Mobutu it would do so and the two governments established relations in 1972. Improved relations between Washington and Beijing helped convince Mobutu to end his hostility toward China, which provided Zaire with a $100 million credit for agricultural projects. In 1973, Mobutu made a triumphant trip to Beijing, where Mao reportedly confided that China had "lost much money and arms attempting to overthrow" the Zairian leader.[39]

China's warm relationship with Mobutu, who was politically conservative and maintained close ties with the West, was an indication of China's growing pragmatism. During the 1970s, Mobutu emphasized Zaire's links with China while downplaying those with the United States and France. China sent large numbers of technical experts to Zaire and established a major military assistance program.[40] Chinese policy paralleled U.S. policy toward Zaire; it supported Mobutu against the 1977 and 1978 invasions of the Shaba region and provided more than $130 million in economic aid.[41] Beijing capitalized on Mobutu's mistrust of Moscow and was the only communist country to support him against the Katangan secessionists. China rushed small arms and supplies to Mobutu during the invasion and accelerated work on a sugar project.[42]

Premier Zhao Ziyang visited Zaire in 1983 and "froze" $10 million of Zaire's $100 million debt to China. Mobutu praised China and urged Western countries to follow canceling their much larger debt.[43] Between 1980 and 1985, China delivered nearly $34 million worth of artillery and gunboats to Zaire. Mobutu visited Beijing five times before he was overthrown in 1997. New leader Laurent-Desiré Kabila renamed Zaire the Democratic Republic of the Congo and visited China the year he took power. He had attended a military school in China and participated in leftist uprisings in the Congo in the 1960s. Zimbabwe, which intervened in the DRC in 1998 in support of Kabila, said China was the main arms supplier for the intervention. Following Kabila's assassination in 2001, his son Joseph Kabila succeeded him and visited China the following year. Since 2003, China has contributed more than 200 personnel annually to the UN peacekeeping operation in the DRC.[44]

Chinese loans funded construction of the National Parliament, the People's Palace, and the DRC's largest stadium. Aid projects included the Sino-Congolese Friendship Hospital in Kinshasa, an agricultural tool plant, sugar refinery, rice planting demonstration project, trade center, and mail distribution facility in Kinshasa. In 1973, China's Hebei Province began sending rotating medical teams of about eighteen members. In 1985, China started sending five Congolese students annually on scholarship; the number reached thirty-two by 2008. China completed an anti-malaria center and three rural primary schools in 2009.[45]

China has become a major investor in the DRC copper and cobalt sector. Until 2008, small and medium-sized companies carried out most of this activity in Katanga, North Kivu, and South Kivu provinces. Chinese

investors often formed joint ventures with Congolese who held mining permits but lacked money to implement projects. The Chinese companies even
established a chamber of commerce in Lubumbashi. After 2008, the global
economic crisis and falling commodity prices forced many private Chinese
operations to shut down. Most Chinese mining personnel left the DRC by
late 2008; some Chinese managers and Congolese staff remained.[46]

Just before mineral prices began to fall, however, China and the DRC
signed in 2007 the single largest loan/barter agreement that China had
signed until that time in Africa. China's Export Import Bank agreed to
provide Kinshasa a $6.5 billion (pared down from the original $9 billion)
concessional loan to finance roads, railways, education, and health facilities.
The original interest rates were only 0.25 percent with an extended repayment period. The two governments signed a second agreement in 2008 that
specified the way the joint venture between Gécamines and the group of
Chinese enterprises would function. This document abandoned the concessionary features of the first agreement, allowing interest rates of up to 6.1
percent.[47]

These agreements are similar to earlier ones signed with Angola. Chinese companies will draw down the loan to build or rehabilitate 2,200 miles
of tarred roads and 2,000 miles of railways. China will construct thirty-two
hospitals, 145 health centers, two universities, and 5,000 houses. To guarantee repayment, a joint venture with Chinese majority participation extracts
and sells Congolese copper, cobalt, and gold. The agreements affect a significant amount of the DRC's mineral reserves on which China pays no
taxes. The Export Import Bank underwrote another $2 billion loan for the
modernization of the DRC's mining infrastructure.[48]

This deal caused considerable controversy. The World Bank and IMF
expressed concern that it will plunge the DRC deep into debt. The details of
the agreements lack transparency and change periodically. Others expressed
concern about environmental implications.[49] Two scholars, Stefaan Marysse
and Sara Geenen, questioned the far-reaching guarantees to Chinese companies and the extreme fiscal and custom exemptions obtained by China.
They concluded that the DRC "negotiated badly" and while the deal is
likely to have positive results for the DRC in the short run, it is highly
unequal and is "clearly balanced in favour of the Chinese parties."[50]

Chinese companies have built roads, bridges, and the communications
sector. ZTE, Huawei, and China International Telecommunication Construction Corporation all have large projects in the DRC. ZTE makes

mobile telephones, among other products, while Huawei won a contract to supply hundreds of base stations for a local telecommunications company. Another Chinese company has a concession for cutting a large tract of timber.[51] ZTE signed a memorandum of understanding in 2007 to develop a $1 billion oil palm plantation covering more than seven million acres but as of 2011 the two parties had not reached final agreement.[52]

China-DRC trade has risen sharply in recent years. DRC imports from China reached $2.5 billion in 2010 while China imported $521 million, mostly copper and cobalt, from the DRC. China has become the DRC's largest trading partner.[53]

While China has become a major influence in the DRC, it is subject to growing criticism. Some Congolese perceive China as a new exploiter, with goods that are poorly made. Chinese business persons seldom learn local languages and tend to live separately. They employ few Congolese and organize their businesses so that they can leave quickly if profits fall sharply. For their part, Chinese business persons criticize the Congolese as untrustworthy and lazy.[54] One expert on the DRC concluded that "Chinese engagement in the Congo has the possibility of benefiting some Congolese, but also the possibility of perpetuating harmful practices and networks established by European and American forerunners."[55] Congolese have been especially critical of private Chinese mining and smelter operations in Katanga.[56]

Burundi

Burundi became independent in 1962 and recognized the PRC the following year. China either had an inadequate understanding of Burundi's ethnic politics or chose a calculated but misguided gamble to support one ethnic group. Either way, China's ties to the minority Tutsi, who controlled the government, caused Burundi to end relations with China in 1965. The break occurred during bitter Hutu-Tutsi rivalry and followed the moderate Hutu premier's assassination. While Burundi did not implicate China in the assassination, it claimed the Chinese ambassador was sabotaging efforts to unify Hutus and Tutsis. China also financially supported Burundi's trade union movement. It backed Congolese dissidents and Rwandan Tutsi refugees in Burundi who opposed the Hutu government in neighboring Rwanda. This engagement in Burundi internal affairs contributed to concerns about China. Nevertheless, Burundi officials maintained contact, sometimes unauthorized, with China. The two countries restored diplomatic ties in 1971.[57]

After China and Burundi resumed relations, Beijing cooperated with whatever regime controlled the government. The two countries signed economic and technical agreements in 1972 and China sent military advisors and constructed several military bases. Continuing Hutu-Tutsi conflict complicated China's ability to conduct normal relations. These Chinese military advisors and the arms supply to the largely Tutsi army raised new suspicions.[58] The two countries have exchanged high level visits ever since, but generally below the level of president and prime minister on the Chinese side. Burundi President Jean Baptiste Bagaza visited Beijing in 1979, President Pierre Buyoya in 1989 and 1999, and President Pierre Nkurunziza in 2006. China has cultural and sports exchange programs with Burundi and receives modest military and economic assistance. China supported the UN Burundi peace process.[59] In 2006, China agreed to expand the Burundi Senior Normal College in Bujumbura. In 2008, Chinese Foreign Minister Yang Jiechi visited Burundi and signed an economic and technical agreement.[60]

The major problem in the relationship is Burundi's trade deficit with China. Burundi's imports from China from 2003 through 2010 averaged $15 million annually and rose to $37 million in 2010. During the same period, China's imports from Burundi averaged $1 million.

Congo-Brazzaville

Following independence in 1960, Congo-Brazzaville's president Fulbert Youlou recognized Taiwan. Trade union leaders removed Youlou from power in 1963 and the new president, Alphonse Massamba-Debat, recognized Beijing in 1964. Brazzaville had close relations with France at the time; Brazzaville's decision coincided with French recognition of Beijing. The government initially tried to maintain relations with both Beijing and Taipei; that was unacceptable to both and Taiwan severed relations. Close ties developed quickly between Beijing and Brazzaville. The PRC provided a $5 million loan as budgetary support and another $20 million interest-free loan to establish consumer goods industries. A Congolese military delegation visited China and President Massamba-Debat attended national day

celebrations in Beijing in 1964. The countries signed an economic cooperation agreement in 1965.[61] Beijing sent a senior Xinhua official to manage
propaganda efforts in Congo-Brazzaville and neighboring countries. In
1965, the CIA concluded "Brazzaville's dominant leaders have come to
regard Peiping as their principal foreign benefactor; extreme leftists who
preach revolution for revolution's sake and favor Chinese Communist
models have been in the ascendancy."[62]

China wanted Brazzaville as a base for revolutionaries in central Africa. It
began assisting Pierre Mulele's guerrillas in the Congo, anti-Portuguese liberation groups in Angola, and insurgents in independent Cameroon. China
established at least three secret training camps in the country, which became
an important base for subversion. In 1967, China completed a broadcasting
station for programming to the Portuguese territories and white-ruled South
Africa. Massamba-Debat had good relations with both Moscow and Beijing.
Overthrown in a military coup in 1968, his replacement, Marien Ngouabi,
was pro-PRC. At the end of 1969, Ngouabi proclaimed the first "People's
Republic" in Africa ruled by a Marxist-Leninist party. Many high-ranking
Congolese visited China during the 1970s while fewer officials of lower rank
came from China to Brazzaville. Although China stopped supporting revolu-
tionaries in independent African countries, it continued to use Congo-
Brazzaville as a base for supporting African liberation groups in southern and
Portuguese Africa until those countries became independent. China provided
military training to about 415 Congolese by 1978.[63]

Once Brazzaville was no longer necessary for supporting liberation movements, China developed a more normal relationship. In 1985, China was
providing only minimal military assistance to Brazzaville. President Denis
Sassou-Nguesso visited China in 1980, 1987, and 2000, when he signed an
investment accord permitting Chinese traders to open shops in the Congo.
In 2000, China resumed sending medical teams that began in 1966 and continued until 1997 when insecurity caused by the Congolese civil war ended
the program. Sassou-Nguesso returned to Beijing in 2005 and 2006 and
attended the Shanghai World Expo in 2010. Premier Wen Jiabao visited Brazzaville in 2006. China expanded the number of scholarships for Congolese
students, a program that began in 1975. Chinese investment in Brazzaville
between 1995 and 2005 totaled about $115 million, mostly in the energy
sector. In 2009, China completed a stadium, constitutional court building,
and national radio and television station. China provided 85 percent of the
funding for a $377 million hydropower station inaugurated in 2011.[64]

Congo-Brazzaville is a significant oil exporter. In 2010, China imported $3.2 billion of oil from Brazzaville while the Congo imported $389 million of products from China. Only the United States surpasses China as Brazzaville's largest trading partner.

Central African Republic

The Central African Republic (CAR) proved frustrating for both PRC and Taiwan diplomacy. After independence in 1960, Beijing and Taipei recognized Bangui, which finally recognized only Taipei in 1962. Encouraged by Chinese emissaries that the PRC might provide more aid to the CAR, President David Dacko sent a mission to Beijing in 1964 when the two countries agreed to establish diplomatic relations. A PRC delegation visited Bangui in 1964 and signed agreements on trade, cultural, economic, and technical cooperation. Taiwan severed relations two months later. China offered a $4 million interest-free loan and then tried unsuccessfully to enlist CAR support in the Sino-Soviet dispute. A military coup led by Jean-Bedel Bokassa overthrew Dacko in 1996. Bokassa alleged unconvincingly that China intended to depose Dacko, forcing him to take preemptive action to prevent China's interference in CAR affairs. Bokassa then severed relations with the PRC, giving the entire Chinese mission forty-eight hours to leave the country. Bokassa did not restore relations with Taiwan until 1968, which lasted until 1976 when the CAR again recognized Beijing.[65]

China-CAR relations languished from 1976 until 1991, when Bangui again recognized Taiwan and Beijing suspended ties. China and the CAR resumed diplomatic relations in 1998, and they have been good since. CAR President Ange Patasse visited Beijing in 1999. They signed trade, economic, and technical agreements in 2000, renewed the cultural cooperation agreement, and resumed the scholarship program. CAR President François Bozizé visited Beijing in 2004. China made a number of modest grants and loans—a $2.5 million grant and $2.5 million and $2 million interest-free loans in 2003, a $2 million interest-free loan for civil service salaries, and a $4 million grant of equipment in 2004. It resumed military exchanges and discussed exploring the CAR's oil and timber resources.[66] In 2008, CAR Cabinet Director of the Presidential Palace Michel Gbezera-bria said Tibet is an inseparable part of China and that the CAR opposes any attempt to split Tibet from China.[67] President Bozizé returned to Beijing in 2009. China completed two primary schools and inaugurated a hospital and anti-malaria center. The head of the CPC's International Department visited Bangui in 2010. Trade between the CAR and China is modest, but nearly balanced. The CAR imported $26 million of goods from China in 2010 while China imported $25 million from the CAR.

Rwanda

Rwanda became independent in 1962 under an anti-communist government controlled by the majority Hutu and immediately recognized Taiwan. China, pursuing a revolutionary policy, supported the deposed Tutsi king with funds, ammunition, and training for Rwandan Tutsi refugees in neighboring Burundi, Tanzania, Uganda, and the Congo. The minority Tutsi still controlled Burundi, and allowed China to support armed groups known as Inyenzi (cockroaches) at a training camp in eastern Burundi. The Chinese armed, trained, and financed insurgents first attacked Rwanda in 1963 and nearly reached the capital, Kigali, before being repulsed. Rwandan Hutu responded by attacking Tutsi in Rwanda. China continued to support the Inyenzi following the failed attack, but it became difficult after 1965 when Burundi broke relations with the PRC and sent the embassy home. Chinese support for Tutsi dissidents ended before China and Rwanda normalized relations in 1971. In 1972, they signed an economic and technical agreement, and China provided a $22 million interest-free loan. Beijing began several assistance projects. Tutsi-Hutu fighting broke out again in 1972, and a military coup deposed the government a year later. China did not engage in the conflict and there was no further disruption of diplomatic relations.[68]

Except for signing agreements and undertaking several aid projects, relations floundered in the 1970s and 1980s, although China provided $9 million in arms between 1980 and 1985. China signed an interest-free loan for a cement factory that opened in 1984. Relations expanded significantly by the mid-1990s. Vice President Paul Kagame visited Beijing in 1995 and President Pasteur Bizimungu in 1996. President Kagame visited in 2001, 2006, and 2007, when the two countries signed various cooperation agreements. Cultural exchanges and scholarships for Rwandan students are an integral part of the relationship.[69] China opened a Confucius Institute in 2009. A Chinese company built the $8 million Ministry of Foreign Affairs.

China canceled part of Rwanda's debt and began teaching Chinese at the Kigali Institute of Education. Star Africa Media, a Chinese company, invested $20 million to operate pay TV services. China constructed a $60 million five-star hotel owned 75 percent by Chinese and 25 percent by Rwandese interests. A Chinese company built a cell phone assembly plant and a Chinese club. Chinese companies hold contracts valued at $500 million and there are an estimated 700 Chinese in Rwanda. Trade is growing but generally favors China. In 2010, Rwanda imported $55 million worth of products from China while China imported $39 million from Rwanda.[70]

Equatorial Guinea

Equatorial Guinea was unimportant, had a terrible human rights record, was corrupt, and had no known oil when China established diplomatic relations in 1970. Geographically isolated, Equatorial Guinea offered China only a UN vote. By the early 1970s, China ended its support for revolutionaries trying to remove conservative governments in independent African states. Beijing treated Equatorial Guinea like most other small and seemingly insignificant countries. It signed an economic and technical cooperation agreement in 1971 and the next year began sending technicians and medical teams followed by a road building program.[71] By 1978, China had about 100 military specialists working in the country. Beijing also used high level personal contact to enhance relations, inviting Equatorial Guinea's vice president to China in 1974 and its president in 1977. China's military support for President Macias Nguema during a 1979 coup that overthrew him resulted in a five-year interruption of close relations. Equatorial Guinea's new leader, Teodoro Obiang Nguema, visited China in 1984 and returned six times, the last time in 2010 for the World Expo in Shanghai. China expanded aid to include a broadcasting station and hydropower plant, and began cultural cooperation and military exchanges.[72]

Beijing's early outreach in Equatorial Guinea has paid off. Perhaps China planned from the beginning to one day purchase the country's hardwood timber, but it could not have known about the oil discovered in the 1990s and later developed by American companies in the sea off Bioko Island and Rio Muni on the mainland. China stepped up its assistance to Equatorial Guinea in 1996 during the first meeting of the joint commission for economy and trade cooperation. This led to an increase in Chinese immigration to Equatorial Guinea, now estimated at 5,000. The interaction has been particularly important in the field of health where almost every Equatoguinean family has received services of a Chinese doctor either through a medical team assigned to a hospital or a private Chinese clinic. Chinese traders have also opened numerous shops. They have not generated the same antagonism from local shopkeepers found in many other African countries.[73]

After President Obiang returned from a 2005 visit to Beijing, he said China had become the country's main development partner, announced three new cooperation agreements, and added that China had canceled a "large part" of Equatorial Guinea's debt. China followed with a $2 billion line of credit. In 2007, China's foreign minister opened in Malabo, the capital, the new headquarters of Equatorial Guinea's state radio and television, built by a Chinese company. He also announced the cancellation of $75 million in debt. Equatorial Guinea donated one million Euros to Chinese earthquake victims in 2008. Oil and timber exports to China are central to the relationship. While China is significantly increasing its influence, American oil companies continue to dominate the oil sector.[74] In 2010, Equatoguinean imports from China totaled $502 million while China imported $599 million of oil and timber, a sharp drop from $2.3 billion in 2008.

The relationship has not been controversy free. In 2008, some two hundred Chinese construction workers held a strike and clashed with local security officials. The terms under which the Chinese were working in the country required award of at least half the infrastructure contracts to Chinese companies. China pressed for a maximum percentage of Chinese labor rather than hiring Equatoguineans. China's Ministry of Commerce acknowledged that the laborers were in contravention of Equatorial Guinean labor laws. Malabo put a news blackout on the incident while China's Ministry of Foreign Affairs called for an investigation of the deaths of two Chinese workers during the confrontation. The dispute ended when China sent four hundred construction workers home.[75] In spite of this problem, Mario Esteban, the leading authority on China-Equatorial Guinea relations, concluded that "there is a broad and strong consensus among the Equatoguinean people that China has played an important role in the development of their country after independence" and that China has a positive image.[76]

Nigeria

Nigeria, which became independent in 1960, remains a challenge for China's diplomacy. As the most populous country in Africa and the one with the most oil, Nigeria has considerable economic leverage. It also has a strong civil society that supports democratic governance. Nigeria, even under some of its more authoritarian governments, has maintained a close relationship with democratic India, one of China's main competitors in resource-rich African countries. Beginning in 1960, Nigeria either supported the PRC or abstained on the annual UN vote concerning recognition of China. In spite of heavy lobbying by both the PRC and Taiwan, Nigeria did not recognize either one until it exchanged ambassadors with Beijing in 1971. Nigeria was concerned about Chinese interference in neighboring Cameroon and displeased with China's attack on India in 1962. By 1964, however, there was an active Nigeria-China Friendship Association in the Muslim north.[77]

Nigeria might have recognized the PRC earlier except for Beijing's policy during Nigeria's civil war, which began in 1967 over breakaway Biafra. Initially, China remained neutral while the Soviet Union and all African countries supported the Federal Nigerian government. Although Biafra tended to be pro-West, its radical wing sent a delegation to China to solicit support. In 1968 China, caught up in the Sino-Soviet conflict, issued a statement surprisingly supportive of Biafra. Four African countries, including China's friends in Tanzania and Zambia, eventually recognized Biafra. Nigeria accused China of providing financial and military equipment to the rebels. Federal troops captured Chinese weapons in Biafra supplied initially to Tanzania. Alaba Ogunsanwo concluded that even though China never officially recognized Biafra, its support for the breakaway region constituted interference in Nigerian internal affairs.[78]

The Nigerian civil war ended in 1970. China, as it has done so often on other occasions in Africa, managed quickly to overcome controversial and even hostile actions, in this case support of Biafra, and obtained Nigeria's recognition just over a year later. Official recognition resulted in an increase in trade and led to numerous agreements and exchanges in the early 1970s. Xinhua established a bureau in Lagos in 1972. Controversy returned, however, over Nigeria's support for Angola's MPLA government and China's criticism of the Soviet Union and Cuba, which strongly supported the

MPLA. The disagreement became an issue during the second Nigeria-China Dialogue in Beijing in 1979.[79]

Considering the importance of Nigeria, there were surprisingly few visits at the highest level of government in the 1970s and 1980s. Nigerian head of state Yakubu Gowan visited Beijing in 1974. Chief of Staff General Sani Abacha, who became president in 1993, visited Beijing just four months after the 1989 Tiananmen Square crackdown. The two countries formally established a Nigeria-China Friendship Association in 1994. There was, however, a hiatus in presidential level visits until President Olusegun Obasanjo went to Beijing in 1999. A number of Chinese at the ministerial level visited Nigeria beginning in 1978 and Premier Li Peng went in 1997, but only since 2000 did the two countries begian to rely on high level visits to solidify relations. Obasanjo returned to Beijing in 2001, 2005, and 2006. During the 2005 visit, China and Nigeria agreed to upgrade the relationship to a "strategic partnership." President Umaru Musa Yar'Adua visited in 2008. President Jiang Zemin made a trip to Nigeria in 2002 and Hu Jintao in 2006.[80] Coinciding with the 2002 visit, Nigeria established the Nigerian Council for the Promotion of Peaceful Reunification of China. In 2005, President Obasanjo supported China's Anti-Secession Law aimed at pro-independence forces in Taiwan.[81]

As in many other African countries, Xinhua played a significant role in the bilateral relationship. It sponsored a 1984 visit to China for officials of the Nigerian Federal Radio Corporation and signed a 1987 exchange agreement with the News Agency of Nigeria. Xinhua subsequently donated state-of-the-art satellite receiving equipment to the News Agency of Nigeria. CRI located a bureau in Lagos for gathering and transmitting news about Nigeria to Beijing. It also broadcast locally in Hausa.[82] Cultural, sports, and youth ties became an integral part of the relationship by the early 1980s.[83]

Economic relations between China and Nigeria have grown phenomenally in the twenty-first century. During the 1990s, there were frequent reports in the Nigerian press about inferior and counterfeit products imported from China. Nigerian traders contributed to the problem by engaging in fraudulent arrangements with Chinese business persons. These issues have continued with the arrival of larger numbers of Chinese traders. Nigerian consumers generally like low-cost Chinese products, while manufacturers are sometimes not able to compete and Nigeria has insufficient regulatory institutions to keep harmful products out of the country.[84]

New deals, investments, and agreements occur regularly; it is difficult to differentiate between those that reach implementation and those that do not survive the initial announcement.[85] The activity, however, is frenetic. From the beginning of the century until early 2006, Xinhua counted twenty-seven agreements and memoranda of understanding between China and Nigeria in oil, telecommunications, power, transportation, iron and steel, journalism, culture and education, radio-film-television, water conservation, and medical and health care.[86]

In 2006, the CNOOC announced a $2.27 billion deal to buy a 45 percent stake in an offshore oil field. The China National Petroleum Corporation and China National Petrochemical Corporation have separate investments in Nigeria.[87] A $4 billion commitment by China for investment in Nigerian infrastructure in exchange for four oil-drilling licenses may have collapsed because Nigeria was unhappy with the terms.[88] The Nigerian Investment Promotion Commission put total Chinese FDI at more than $5 billion since 2001.[89] In 2009, the president of the National Association of Nigerian Traders reported that Chinese investment in Nigeria had reached about $6 billion and said there were more than thirty solely owned Chinese companies or joint ventures in the country. In 2011, China's minister of industry and information technology announced China's FDI in Nigeria had reached $7 billion.[90]

There have also been setbacks. In 2008, Nigeria suspended an $8.3 billion contract with the China Railway Construction Company for an 817-mile railway linking the northern and southern parts of the country.[91] China's Sinoma International suspended a cement project worth $1.45 billion and reduced the cost of a second $1.81 billion cement project by two-thirds. By the end of 2006, Nigeria was China's fourth most important destination in Africa for investment after Sudan, Zambia. and Algeria. Depending on the source of information, between one hundred and six hundred Chinese companies and joint ventures operate in construction, oil and gas, technology, communications, power generation, manufacturing, services, and education. Chinese construction companies are heavily involved in building infrastructure.[92] Chinese companies have been supportive of Nigeria's free trade zones; some 20 to 30 percent of the investors in the Lekki Free Trade Zone near Lagos are Chinese. A consortium led by Guangdong Province has an 82 percent stake in the Ogun State Free Trade Zone and 100 percent control of management.[93]

China is expanding military cooperation with Nigeria. Nigeria negotiated a $251 million contract in 2005 with the China National Aero-Technology Import and Export Corporation to purchase twelve F-7M

Airguard multipurpose combat aircraft (the Chinese version of the upgraded MiG-21) and three FT-7NI dual-seat fighter trainer aircraft. A separate deal valued at more than $70 million refurbished five Nigerian air force Alenia G-222 transports. Nigeria also purchased Chinese patrol boats to secure the swamps and creeks in the troubled Niger Delta.[94] In 2007, China launched a telecommunications satellite for Nigeria at a cost of at least $340 million. A solar power failure rendered the satellite useless; China agreed to replace it at no cost.[95]

China is actively engaged in nearly every aspect of Nigeria's economy. An estimated 70,000 Chinese live in Nigeria.[96] China opened a Confucius Institute at Nnamdi Azikiwe University in 2008. China and Nigeria signed an agreement whereby China will train fifty Nigerian officials and medical personnel in comprehensive malaria prevention and control. China built an anti-malaria center, drilled wells, and helped develop water supplies. However, Chinese development aid to Nigeria is small.

Nigeria's First Bank established a correspondent banking relationship with the Bank of China in 1979 and the Industrial and Commercial Bank of China (ICBC) in 2009. It signed memoranda of understanding with the China Construction Bank and China Development Bank. In 2010, First Bank opened an office in Beijing and began discussions for an equity stake in a Chinese bank. Nigeria's Stanbic IBTC Bank also has links with ICBC.[97]

In 2010, the Nigerian National Petroleum Corporation and the China State Construction Engineering Corporation signed a memorandum of understanding for $28.5 billion that will seek financing from Chinese banks to build three refineries and a fuel complex in Nigeria. It is aimed at ending Nigerian fuel imports due to the disrepair and mismanagement of its four state-owned refineries. It requires financing before becoming a reality.[98] The China State Construction Engineering Corporation agreed to fund 80 percent of an $8 billion oil refinery in the Lekki Free Trade Zone. The Nigerian National Petroleum Corporation is responsible for the remainder, and Chinese investors will hold a minimum 25 percent stake in the refinery. The director general of Nigeria's Commonwealth Business Council announced in 2010 that a consortium from China has a credit line from the Chinese government to invest about $20 billion on infrastructure and capacity building in Nigeria.[99]

Nigeria is China's fourth most important trading partner in Africa. In 2010, Nigeria's imports from China totaled $7.4 billion while China's imports from Nigeria reached only $1.1 billion. Because of much higher oil imports, the United States is Nigeria's largest trading partner. Nigeria's huge trade deficit with China and Chinese purchases restricted to raw materials are creating some tension in the relationship. Nigeria has criticized Chinese dumping of cheap products, undercutting Nigerian manufacturers, and exporting counterfeit products. Nigeria has threatened to take these abuses to the World Trade Organization, while Nigerian trade unions claim Chinese imports accounted for the loss of 350,000 Nigerian manufacturing jobs. Smuggling Chinese goods into the country is also a problem.[100]

Nigeria has been especially critical of Asian and especially Chinese textile producers for the collapse of the Nigerian textile industry. Asian competition resulted in the closure of more than 170 Nigerian textile companies; the industry is running at about 20 percent capacity with ten remaining companies employing about 18,000 persons. Chinese textiles accounted for about 80 percent of the Nigerian market in 2010. Chinese firms established trading companies in Nigeria to capture the local market and export to the United States under the preferential Africa Growth and Opportunity Act. Chinese entrepreneurs added insult to injury by fraudulently copying Nigerian textile designs and taking them to China for mass production. The fabrics return from China with counterfeit Nigerian labels for sale in Nigeria and re-export.[101]

The magnitude of the China-Nigeria relationship today is impressive, although Nigeria remains a challenge for China's diplomacy. One Nigerian business-person told the authors China is replacing the West as Nigeria's major economic partner.[102] A senior official in the Ministry of Foreign Affairs explained that except for oil, which Western companies dominate, the West has done little in recent years to develop Nigeria. Western countries have been active in public health and combating HIV/AIDS, but have shown little interest in development.[103] A group of Nigerian scholars familiar with both the West and China concluded that Chinese policy in Nigeria and Africa today "is the most strategic of all nations." They previously believed the United States held this title, but concluded Beijing has surpassed Washington.[104]

Cameroon

Cameroon became independent in 1960 and was the first African country where the PRC supported a revolutionary group that opposed the party

that formed the government. China made contact in 1958 with Félix Moumié, leader of the Union des Populations du Cameroon (UPC), which
began an armed struggle in 1959. Moumié, a Marxist, became disillusioned
with Moscow and turned to Beijing, visiting in 1959 and 1960. Playing both
sides, the PRC offered to recognize Cameroon immediately after independence while it supported the UPC. Not surprisingly, Cameroon recognized
Taiwan. The PRC supported the UPC campaign to topple President Ahmadou Ahidjo's government at least until 1965, when it began to show less
enthusiasm for the rebel group. Ahidjo repeatedly accused the PRC of
"supporting terrorism" and interfering in Cameroon's internal affairs.
Alaba Ogunsanwo concluded China's actions could only be described as
subversion.[105]

In 1970, the Ahidjo government crushed the UPC and arrested and
executed its leaders. Cameroon opened talks with the PRC in 1971 and
recognized Beijing within a month. China promised not to interfere in
Cameroon's internal affairs and a Chinese ambassador arrived the same
year.[106] This diplomatic success for the PRC constituted another example
where Chinese policy was able to establish relations quickly with a government that it had earlier tried to subvert.

Cameroon signed economic and technical agreements with China in
1971 and in 1973 received a $75 million loan for a hydroelectric dam. It
initiated a number of smaller aid projects, and began sending medical teams
in 1975 and military delegations in 1979. Ahidjo visited Beijing in 1973 and
1977; his successor Paul Biya visited in 1987 and 1993. Premier Li Peng
visited Cameroon in 1997. There were few high level Chinese visitors, however, until the twenty-first century.[107] China has a long-standing scholarship
program for Cameroonian students; it awarded forty in 2008 and thirty-
two in 2009. In 1997, Zhejiang Normal University and the International
Relations Institute of Cameroon established a Mandarin language teaching
center in Yaoundé. It became a Confucius Institute in 2007 and set up
branches elsewhere in Cameroon.[108]

Biya returned to Beijing in 2003 and 2006 while Hu Jintao went to
Cameroon in 2007 when he pledged $100 million in new grants and soft
loans and canceled $32 million of Cameroon's debt. This followed a $34
million debt cancellation in 2000. China financed and the China International Water and Electric Corporation built the Lagdo dam in northern
Cameroon, 1,000 wells, and a 500-acre rice growing project.[109] In 2009,
China inaugurated an anti-malaria center and began construction on an

agricultural demonstration center. In 2010, China's Export Import Bank extended a $743 million loan for a water distribution project. Cameroon is also the recipient of military cooperation. As of 2007, twelve teams of Chinese military specialists totaling 150 persons had helped maintain military vehicles and other equipment at the Douala naval base and 228 Cameroonian military officers had undertaken studies in China.[110]

In 2009 the Chinese oil company Yan Chang from Shanxi Province signed an agreement for $18 million with the Cameroonian national oil company to explore two onshore blocks in northern Cameroon. Numerous private Chinese companies tender for infrastructure projects not funded by the Chinese government. Zhejiang Geophysical Prospecting specializes, for example, in well-digging. One of the Shanxi Province state farms is developing a $62 million rice and cassava plantation. Independent Chinese timber traders purchase raw timber for export. There are concerns that much of this timber is not certified and constitutes illegal logging. Although Cameroon had a trade deficit with China during most years since 2000, it has not been huge. In 2010, Cameroon imported $595 million in goods from China, while China imported $462 million (largely oil and timber) from Cameroon.

Benin

Benin, known as Dahomey at independence in 1960, recognized Taiwan in 1962. Following a coup in 1964 while the president was visiting Taiwan, the new government allowed Beijing to open an embassy while leaving the Taiwan embassy in place. Beijing's reported offer of a $20 million credit was probably instrumental in Benin's decision to recognize the PRC. The two missions remained in the country until 1965 when Taipei broke relations with Benin. In 1966, after two coups and two pro-Taipei governments, Benin switched again to Taipei and ended ties with Beijing. Following several more coups, a Marxist government came to power and restored relations with Beijing in 1972. The PRC immediately signed an economic and technical cooperation agreement, offered a $44 million interest-free loan and sent agricultural experts to cultivate rice. Benin's president first visited Beijing in 1976.[111] The CIA commented that as late as 1978 China was Benin's only communist aid donor; 225 Chinese were working on a stadium and agricultural projects.[112]

Benin's presidents returned to China in 1986, 1992, and 1998 while
the most senior Chinese officials to visit Benin were at the ministerial
level. Foreign ministers established a political consultation mechanism in
2004. Benin President Thomas Boni Yayi visited China twice in 2006.
While the relationship remains limited, since 1972 China has provided
$200 million in loans and grants for training, fisheries, agriculture, indus-
try, and infrastructure. China has funded students from Benin since 1973
and sent medical teams since 1978. Military exchanges began in 1982.
Benin has earned a reputation in recent years for democratic governance.
It was surprising, therefore, when Benin's government spokesman condemned the policies of the Dalai Lama in Tibet. In 2009, China sent
twenty volunteers to Benin and opened a Confucius Institute at the University of Abomey-Calavi.[113]

Benin's imports (mostly textiles, batteries, wigs, and footwear) from
China grew exponentially from $60 million in 2005 to $2.5 billion in 2010,
while China's imports from Benin totaled only $126 million in 2010. China
is by far Benin's most important trading partner. For a country of nine
million people, these imports are difficult to explain based on internal consumption. The border between Nigeria and Benin is porous; Benin's port
of Cotonou is a center of smuggling. Many goods pass from Benin into
Nigeria's much larger market. At one point, Nigeria banned the import of
Chinese-made shoes, but they continued to appear, probably from Benin.[114]

Sierra Leone

Sierra Leone became independent in 1961 and established relations with
Taiwan in 1963. Nevertheless, it either voted for PRC admission to the UN
or abstained until 1966, when it finally supported Taipei. Influenced by
neighboring, left-leaning Guinea and the promise of Chinese assistance,
Sierra Leone recognized Beijing in 1971. China became Sierra Leone's single
largest source of aid in 1971 following a $40 million interest-free credit for
financing a stadium, two bridges, thirteen agricultural stations, and a sugar
plantation. Beijing has often and accurately accused Taiwan of "checkbook
diplomacy" in Africa. This is one of many cases where the PRC used the
same tactic. In 1972, Chinese agricultural experts took over most of the
projects begun by Taiwan. China began sending medical teams in 1973. As
a result of conflict in Sierra Leone, the teams left in 1994 and did not return

until 2002. China donated two patrol boats in 1973 and trained Sierra Leoneans in China to operate them. China has offered scholarships since 1976 and sent Chinese to study English at Fourah Bay College in the 1970s. Chiefs of state from Sierra Leone visited the PRC nine times between 1973 and 2009, but high level Chinese visitors to Sierra Leone have been rare. The two countries have signed numerous agreements over the years.[115]

By 1996, China had committed $94 million in assistance to Sierra Leone, much of it for agricultural projects. Some projects encountered problems. A state-owned sugar refinery helped subsidize corruption. China built two bridges on roads that connected Sierra Leone to northern Guinea, a stadium and sports complex in Freetown, police headquarters, a government building, and a small hydropower dam, which experienced delays because of corruption by local officials. Several Chinese companies established successful joint ventures, including fishing, palm oil, and agricultural and cattle raising projects. China's aid program is generally well received.[116]

China provided additional patrol boats to the Sierra Leone armed forces and trained personnel to use them. Sierra Leone's vice president told a visiting CPC delegation in 2006 that Sierra Leone convinced Liberia in 2003 to break ties with Taiwan and resume them with Beijing. In 2006, Sierra Leone signed a tripartite agreement with China and the UN Food and Agriculture Organization to improve food security. Two years later, the two countries signed an economic and technology agreement. In 2009, China sent young volunteers to Sierra Leone and opened a malaria prevention center.[117]

In 2010, China Railway Material purchased a 12.5 percent stake in London-based African Minerals Ltd. for $280 million to develop the Tonkolili iron ore project in Sierra Leone. China's Shandong Iron and Steel Group subsequently signed a binding memorandum of understanding to pay African Minerals $1.5 billion for a 25 percent share. The Chinese company secured a long-term supply of 10 million annual tons of iron ore from the mine at a 15 percent discount from the spot price. China may eventually take the entire 75 million ton annual production from the project.[118]

There are occasional contentious issues. In 2008, Sierra Leone banned export of timber following indiscriminate destruction of forests by loggers who sold timber to Chinese and other foreign companies. Sierra Leone's imports from China averaged $72 million between 2006 and 2010 while China's imports from Sierra Leone over the same period averaged $7 million.[119]

Senegal

Senegal established relations with Taipei in 1960, and then recognized the PRC in 1961 without breaking relations with Taiwan. Beijing refused to accept this arrangement. President Léopold Senghor stated in 1964 that he personally was opposed to an exchange of diplomatic missions with the PRC. He reportedly believed the Chinese were supporting subversive elements in Senegal. Other elements of Senegal's government favored relations with Beijing, as did a faction of Senegal's African Independence Party, an illegal communist organization.[120]

In 1968, during the hiatus in relations with Taipei, Senegal expelled two Xinhua representatives for their involvement in student demonstrations. Senegal voted for the PRC's admission to the UN and then recognized it in 1971. In 1973, a PRC agricultural mission arrived and the two countries signed trade, economic, and technical cooperation agreements. Beijing made an interest-free loan of about $50 million to finance agriculture and irrigation projects followed by the arrival of seventy agricultural experts. China built a large stadium and a water conservation project. By 1978, China was Senegal's largest communist aid donor. Senghor visited Beijing in 1974 and President Abdou Diouf in 1984. Numerous Chinese officials at the vice premier level and below visited Senegal until Dakar again tried the "two China" game and resumed relations with Taipei in 1996. China suspended relations. Dakar did not restore ties with Beijing until 2005.[121]

Following the resumption of relations, Senegal and China did not miss an opportunity to expand ties. Senegal's Prime Minister Macky Sall visited Beijing in 2006 when he noted that China's willingness to renew relations "reflected the strategic vision, patience and tolerance of Chinese leaders."[122] President Abdoulaye Wade went to Beijing in 2006 and returned to the FOCAC summit later that year. Senior military officials began discussing cooperation. In 2007, a Chinese medical team arrived and the countries signed cooperation agreements on construction of rural schools and loans for the supply of electricity and construction of a national theater. Chinese construction teams are working on roads, bridges, and other projects. In 2009, China handed over a school, inaugurated a hospital, and stepped up cultural exchanges. Dakar has its own Chinatown with about 160 Chinese shops; 80 percent of the community comes from Henan Province.[123]

President Wade complained at a meeting in Washington that World Bank funding is too slow. As a result, he said, he turned to China to finance and build roads. He noted that China sent a team within fifteen days and completed a road in eight months. Wade added that he was never able to get help from the West in agricultural development; China stepped forward quickly.[124] During a visit to Senegal in 2009, Hu Jintao signed a $23 million loan to renovate public buses, a $49 million loan to establish a government communications system, and a grant of $18 million. From 2006 through 2010, Senegal's imports averaged $349 million annually from China while China imported only $26 million from Senegal.

Togo

Upon independence in 1960, Togo recognized Taiwan. In the early 1960s, a small number of Togolese dissidents received training from Chinese guerrilla warfare experts at the secret camps in Ghana. At least six Togolese delegations visited the PRC between 1958 and 1966 and two PRC delegations came to Togo in 1960 and 1961, but Togo retained ties with Taiwan. The Togolese foreign minister visited Beijing in 1972 and established diplomatic relations. The two countries signed an economic and technical cooperation agreement, and China provided Togo a $45 million interest-free loan for a dam and irrigation complex on the Sio River. This was another example of dollar diplomacy. President Gnassingbe Eyadema visited Beijing in 1974, 1981, 1989, 1995, and 2000. Chinese visitors to Togo were lower ranking. Exchange visits involving the PLA have been important since 1982. China signed educational and cultural protocols with Togo and has been sending medical teams since 1974. It built a sugar refinery, stadium, hospital, and pharmaceutical complex. It signed a variety of additional agreements including one in 1984 on news service cooperation between Xinhua and the Togo News Agency, and provided an interest-free $10 million loan in 1990.[125]

Chinese Vice President Zeng Qinghong visited Togo in 2004 when he signed an agreement to create a joint economic, trade, and technological cooperation commission. China was building a presidential palace at the time of the visit. President Faure Essozimma Gnassingbe visited Beijing twice in 2006; the CPC is also an important part of China's high level exchange visits. Beijing canceled about $20 million of Togo's debt in 2007. In 2009, it inaugurated a hospital, a Confucius Institute at the University of Lomé, and two schools, and launched an agricultural technology demonstration center. In 2010, China provided an $8.6 million grant and a $3.2 million interest-free loan. Togo has huge imports from China, $1.5 billion in 2010, while China's imports from Togo were only $62 million. A significant percentage of Togo's imports consisted of textiles, some of them Togolese designs copied in China. This has upset many in the Togolese textile industry.[126] Togo is a market of only 6.5 million people. Some of the imports are probably smuggled into neighboring countries.

Gabon

Gabon became independent in 1960 under a conservative government that established relations with Taiwan. Although China did not focus on undermining Gabon's government in the early 1960s, Chinese instructors trained a small number of Gabonese dissidents at the guerrilla training camps in Ghana. A delegation from Gabon visited the PRC in 1960 and one from China went to Gabon in 1962. Gabon did not establish relations with Beijing until 1974; President Omar Bongo went to Beijing five months later when he signed trade, economic, and technical cooperation agreements. Gabon received a $26 million interest-free loan for rural development and construction of a textile factory. China started a scholarship program in 1975, which had trained 215 students by 2007. China sent small numbers of teachers to high schools in Gabon and began sending medical teams in 1977. In 1978, China had the only aid presence in Gabon from a communist country. Assistance projects include a health center, primary school, and Senate and National Assembly buildings. China provided concessional financing for the radio and TV headquarters. China has cooperative projects in fisheries, pharmacy, forest development, and timber processing. There have been frequent high level exchange military visits since 1979, including in 2009 a joint military exercise on humanitarian medical rescue.[127]

China and Gabon established a bilateral economic commission in 1982 and signed an investment protection agreement in 1997. Chinese companies are active in mining, oil, agriculture, and forestry.[128] Hu Jintao visited Gabon in 2004 when the two countries agreed to emphasize cooperation on agriculture, infrastructure construction, resource exploitation, and personnel training. When Bongo visited China later in the year, they signed agreements to exploit iron ore at Bélinga in northeastern Gabon, economic and financial support for public finances, and development of forest resources and environmental protection. China purchased Gabon's oil only until 2005, when Sinopec began exploring for oil in Loango national wildlife park. The company's techniques raised the ire of conservationists, temporarily forcing them to shut down the operation. There are concerns China will use similar environmentally unfriendly methods when it develops iron ore deposits at Bélinga. Chinese companies have begun to contract with Western companies to conduct environmental impact assessments in an effort to end these criticisms.[129] In 2009, Sinopec purchased Addax Petroleum and gained access to the Canadian company's oil blocks in Gabon.[130]

President Bongo visited the PRC ten times. At his death in 2009, Vice Premier Zhang Dejiang attended the funeral. Gabon's interim president told Zhang that Gabon would continue to strengthen cooperative ties with China.[131] In 2010, Bongo's son and Gabon's new president, Ali Bongo Ondimba, met with Hu Jintao during a visit to Shanghai World Expo. Both leaders called for strengthening relations. Cooperation between the CPC and Gabon's ruling party have also become important.[132]

In 2007, China and the Food and Agricultural Organization agreed to provide Gabon with forty-four agricultural experts to help small-scale farmers improve crop and animal production, fish farming, and processing of agricultural products. The Association of Overseas Chinese in Gabon has some 2,000 members and twenty to thirty Chinese businesses in Libreville. In 2007, a Chinese company began to develop a $35 million manganese mine in the Bembélé Mountains. In 2008, as part of the $3 billion Bélinga project, China provided Gabon a $83 million loan at 3 percent interest to build a hydropower dam. A Chinese company agreed to build a railroad from the iron ore project to the coast, as part of a plan to tap the ore. Environmental issues are holding up work on the dam and ore development; a drop in the price of iron in 2008 put the project in further doubt.[133]

China's importation of oil, iron ore, manganese, and timber provides Gabon with a large trade surplus. In 2010, China imported $952 million worth of raw materials from Gabon while Gabon imported only $248 million worth of products from China. China is Gabon's third most important trading partner after the United States and France. Gabon imposed a ban on the export of logs in 2009. The seven or eight Chinese timber companies remaining in Gabon hold about 16 percent of the total timber concessions.

Gabon's minister of foreign affairs and cooperation from 1999 until 2008, Jean Ping, has a Chinese father who arrived in Gabon in the 1930s as a trader. Ping is now the chairman, the most senior staff position, of the Commission of the African Union in Addis Ababa.

Gambia

Gambia became independent in 1965 and recognized Taiwan in 1968. Five Gambian delegations visited the PRC in 1964 and 1965; Gambia finally established relations with the PRC in 1974. The two countries signed an agreement on economic and technical cooperation in 1975, and President Dawda Kairaba Jawara visited Beijing later in the year. China offered a $17 million credit, and the two countries subsequently signed a trade agreement. Jawara returned to Beijing in 1987, 1988, and 1991. In 1975, Beijing provided medical assistance and 500 tons of rice for disaster relief. Chinese medical teams began arriving in 1977, and a scholarship program began in 1984. Gambia expressed irritation with slow progress on China's agricultural projects, and criticized the quality of Chinese agricultural equipment, lack of spare parts, and friction between Chinese agricultural technicians and local farmers, largely due to the language barrier. China constructed a stadium, hotel, and health centers, and took over operation of an irrigated rice project abandoned by Taiwan. China also financed the Supreme Court building and police headquarters. After considerable delay, China sent two patrol boats and a team of instructors. By 1991, some five hundred Chinese were participating in Gambian construction, manufacturing, and agro-industry. By 1993, China had committed $36 million in loans to Gambia.[134]

In 1994, the Armed Forces Provisional Ruling Council seized power, deposed Jawara, and recognized Taiwan. Gambia is one of four countries in Africa that still has relations with Taiwan, which provides an estimated $250–300 million of assistance annually.[135] Gambia is, however, a major importer of products from the PRC. Gambia's imports from China reached $206 million in 2010, making China its largest source of imports. By contrast, Gambia's imports from Taiwan have not exceeded $4 million annually. Neither China nor Taiwan has significant imports from Gambia. Taipei occupies the embassy in Banjul, but Beijing is the more important trade partner.

Liberia

Although Liberia signed a treaty of amity with the Republic of China in 1937, Monrovia and Taipei did not establish diplomatic relations until 1957. Liberia was anti-communist and had close relations with the United States. There was little evidence in the period after the communists took power that Liberia entertained the idea of establishing formal relations with the PRC. But in 1977, following an exchange of goodwill visits, Liberia recognized Beijing. The same year, at least 225 Chinese technicians replaced the departing Taiwanese personnel on sugar plantation, refinery, and rice cultivation projects.[136]

President William Tolbert went to Beijing in 1978 when China agreed to provide at least $23 million for three radio transmitters, agricultural products, and a stadium. Samuel Doe, who seized power in 1980, visited China in 1982. Months later China sent twenty military jeeps, two limousines, and four buses to Liberia. China initiated a number of small aid projects, mainly in agriculture, and signed cultural, agricultural, and technical agreements with Liberia. It sent a fifty-person team to determine the feasibility of rehabilitating Taiwan's sugar project, concluding that it was not economically feasible. Funding identified for the project went to other purposes. The centerpiece of China's assistance became the 30,000-seat stadium in Monrovia, financed by an interest-free loan and completed in 1984, the same year that Vice Premier Tian Jiyun visited Liberia. China provided scholarships for Liberians beginning in 1977 and sent three medical teams between 1984 and 1989. By 1988, China initiated joint ventures, some of which had links to its foreign aid program. Chinese aid totaled about $37 million by 1989.[137]

Taiwan, in the meantime, did not give up on Liberia. Some private businessmen remained in the country. In 1981, Taipei established a trade office in Monrovia and the Liberian foreign minister made frequent visits to Taipei. In 1989, Liberia announced reestablishment of diplomatic relations with Taiwan while it continued to recognize Beijing. Based on strict observance of the "one China" policy, the PRC suspended relations with Liberia.

In 1993, China and Liberia resumed diplomatic relations. Beijing did not, however, send high level visitors to Liberia; only two senior Liberian officials traveled to Beijing. China resumed scholarships for Liberian students. In 1997, Liberia again tried to play the "two China" card by recognizing Taiwan, causing Beijing to suspend relations a second time.[138] Liberia recognized Beijing for the third time in 2003, emphasizing on this occasion that Taiwan is an inalienable part of China's territory. As a reward for recognition, China promised up to $3 million in budgetary support. In 2004, China also sent nearly six hundred peacekeepers to the UN peacekeeping mission in Liberia.[139]

By early 2005, China agreed to renovate a sports complex, complete construction of the Ministry of Foreign Affairs, which had been interrupted due to the break in relations, resume its scholarship program, and send medical and agricultural experts as part of a technical assistance package. Private Chinese companies caused a stir in 2005 when they purchased Liberian iron ore at below-market rates in a deal lacking transparency.[140] China provided $600,000 worth of vehicles, computers, and communications equipment to the Ministry of National Defense and $1 million worth of farming tools to the Ministry of Agriculture. In 2006, China canceled all Liberia's debt, about $10 million, as of the end of 2004. When China began training Liberian security, media, and civilian defense personnel, one of the opposition political parties complained the program favored the ruling party. President Ellen Johnson-Sirleaf represented Liberia at the 2006 FOCAC in Beijing where she received promises for additional scholarships, anti-malaria drugs, and two elementary schools.[141]

Hu Jintao visited Liberia in 2007 when he laid out an extensive program for expanding ties with China. The two countries signed seven agreements that included cancellation of Liberia's debt due at the end of 2005, a $1.5 million grant for budgetary support, construction of a building at the University of Liberia and three schools in rural Liberia, special tariff treatment for Liberian goods entering China, upgrading of Liberia's radio and TV station, and $1 million worth of anti-malaria drugs.[142] China and Liberia signed agreements to create a Confucius Institute and $20 million for additional buildings at the University of Liberia. In 2008, China offered $10 million to build a hospital in rural Liberia.[143] It began construction on an agricultural technology demonstration center in 2009. Young volunteers arrived to teach Chinese and physical education and provide medical and agricultural assistance. From the reestablishment of relations in 2003 through 2009, 646 Liberians participated in training programs in China and 106 received Chinese government scholarships.[144]

In 2009, Vice President Joseph Boakai visited Beijing where he signed economic and technological cooperation agreements and expressed support for China's position on Tibet.[145] In 2010, China's vice minister of commerce signed six agreements in Liberia and announced that China had "invested" a total of almost $10 billion. The biggest project is $2.5 billion for development of iron ore mines at Bong by China Union Wuhan Steel; there was little progress on this project as of 2011.

China was the largest importer of Liberian hardwood timber from 2000 through 2003, when UN sanctions against warring factions in the country ended the trade. Corruption, environmental concerns, and the belief that Liberian timber served the interest of conflict groups characterized the trade. The sanctions remain in place and infrastructure for the logging industry deteriorated. China's imports from Liberia have been in decline since the sanctions and totaled only $23 million in 2010. Liberian imports from China, on the other hand, reached a whopping $4.8 billion in 2010. China is Liberia's second most important supplier after South Korea.[146]

Liberia is one of the few countries in Africa where the United States and China have cooperated on assistance projects. They joined forces in efforts to eradicate malaria and supported UN peacekeeping projects, including construction of the barracks at Bonga. In remarks before the Africa-China-United States Trilateral Dialogue Conference on Corporate Social Responsibility, President Ellen Johnson-Sirleaf praised this cooperation. Chinese Ambassador Zhou Yuxiao and American Ambassador Linda Thomas-Greenfield subsequently emphasized collaboration at the same conference.[147]

Côte d'Ivoire

Côte d'Ivoire became independent in 1960 under the leadership of conservative anti-communist President Felix Houphouet-Boigny. In 1960, he said the presence of China on Africa's flank was a source of anxiety. He established relations with Taiwan in 1963 and was one of the few African leaders to criticize French President Charles de Gaulle's decision in 1964 to recognize Beijing.[148] Houphouet-Boigny was highly critical of Chinese support for African revolutionary groups that opposed independent governments, including his own. Chinese based in Ghana trained Ivorian dissidents. Beijing also invited pro-communist labor organizers from Côte d'Ivoire to China.[149] The Ivorian leader said in the mid-1960s that it is China's policy "to maintain permanent revolution in other countries through subversion and assassination of those leaders who refuse to adopt its ideology" and described China as a long-term danger for Africa.[150]

In 1983, Houphouet-Boigny recognized the PRC, one of the last African leaders to do so. Senior Ivorian officials did not begin visiting China until the prime minister went in 1996 and 1999 and Houphouet-Boigny's successors visited in 1997 and 2002. Chinese vice premiers went to Abidjan in 1986 and 1995; President Yang Shangkun visited in 1992 and Vice President Hu Jintao in 1999. There have been extensive military exchange visits dating to the mid-1990s. Cooperative development projects began slowly with construction of a theater and repair of a water conservation project. The two countries signed a trade agreement in 1984, scientific and technical cooperation agreement in 1988, cultural agreement in 1992, and the first of three protocols for cooperation in higher education in 1994. In 1985, China began accepting Ivorian students on scholarship. Beginning in the late 1990s, China and Côte d'Ivoire initiated joint ventures.[151] During a visit to Abidjan by China's defense minister in 2001, Beijing made a 1 million Euro gift to Côte d'Ivoire's armed forces.[152]

The outbreak of Côte d'Ivoire's civil war in 2002 resulted in a deterioration of relations with France, the former colonial power. China opened an imposing new embassy in Abidjan in 2005 and developed a warm but discreet relationship with controversial President Laurent Gbagbo.[153] The Ivorian leader provided an opening for China, but in an environment where Côte d'Ivoire's influence and international standing had diminished. One of the organizations that helped solidify the political relationship is the Chinese People's Association for Friendship with Foreign Countries. The president of Côte d'Ivoire's Economic and Social Council represented the country at the 2006 FOCAC while the prime minister led the delegation to the 2009 FOCAC. In 2007, China canceled 40 percent of Côte d'Ivoire's debt and extended a 10 million Euro gift and a million Euro interest-free loan. Chinese firms built the parliamentary complex, a conference hall for the Ministry of Foreign Affairs, and a cultural center. In 2009, it began a hospital project and opened an anti-malaria center. Laurent Gbagbo lost the election late in 2010, but refused to step down. Following his overthrow in 2011, elected President Alassane Ouattara assumed power. Within months, Vice Foreign Minister Zhai Jun visited Adidjan, met with Ouattara, reaffirmed close Sino-Ivorian relations, and signed new economic and technological agreements.

China imports manganese from a mine it helped to develop and increasing amounts of cocoa; imports totaled $111 million in 2010. Côte d'Ivoire's imports from China in 2010 totaled $603 million. China is Côte d'Ivoire's third most important supplier after Nigeria and France.

Guinea Bissau

China was an early supporter, together with the Soviet Union and East European countries, of the Partido Africano da Independência da Guiné e Cabo Verde (PAIGC), the principal group fighting Portugal for independence of Guinea Bissau and Cape Verde. PAIGC fighters first went to the PRC for training in 1961. Between 1960 and 1962, four nationalist delegations from Guinea Bissau visited China. PAIGC leader Amilcar Cabral praised China during Zhou Enlai's visit to neighboring Guinea in 1964. Cabral was a student of Mao Zedong's writings on guerrilla warfare. Beijing regularly disseminated and glorified PAIGC communiqués while the Chinese Afro-Asian Solidarity Council acknowledged that it collected funds for the organization. In spite of considerable assistance from China, the PAIGC owed its success primarily to assistance from African and other communist countries and its own resourcefulness.[154]

Guinea Bissau declared independence in 1973. Beijing immediately granted recognition but did not establish formal relations until 1974. Guinea Bissau and China signed a technical cooperation agreement and China began sending medical teams in 1976 and initiated a scholarship program in 1977. China built a stadium and hospital and established a rice project. Guinea Bissau's head of state visited Beijing in 1982, when they signed a cultural agreement. In 1984, they signed a cooperative fishing agreement. In 1990, Guinea Bissau recognized Taiwan, becoming the only African country to do so that had ended colonial rule by a military struggle. This situation lasted until Guinea Bissau and the PRC restored relations in 1998.[155]

Relations have been good since 1998. The commander of Guinea Bissau's military commission visited Beijing in 1999 while the president made
trips in 2002 and 2006. The scholarship program and medical teams quickly
resumed. In 2004, China provided $6 million, presumably a grant, to
reconstruct and equip a hospital and reestablish military infrastructure. In
2007, China provided a $4 million grant for budgetary support. A Chinese
company, in cooperation with the Africa Finance Corporation, agreed to
rebuild Guinea Bissau's electric transmission and distribution network. In
2009, the two countries signed an economic and technical cooperation
agreement and China provided emergency food aid and anti-malaria medicine. China imports almost nothing from Guinea Bissau while Guinea Bissau imported $10 million worth of Chinese goods in 2010.[156]

São Tomé and Principe

São Tomé and Principe established relations with Beijing on the same day
this Atlantic Ocean island state obtained independence in 1975. The president of São Tomé and Principe visited China in 1975, 1983, and 1993. They
signed economic, technical cooperation, and cultural agreements. China
provided an interest-free $18 million loan for rice cultivation and hydro-
power development. China also built a People's Palace. By 1978, the CIA
reported that communist aid, especially from China, far exceeded aid from
other sources. Between 1976 and 1997, China received twenty-five students
from São Tomé and Principe and sent 171 medical personnel to the islands.
Foreign Minister Qian Qichen visited São Tomé in January 1997 when he
promised to seek new fields of cooperation. In July 1997, Beijing suspended
relations with São Tomé because it recognized Taiwan. China terminated
all agreements with São Tomé, which still recognizes Taiwan.[157]

In recent years, China returned to São Tomé and Principe through
Nigeria. Sinopec joined other companies to prospect for offshore oil in a
joint development zone owned 60 percent by Nigeria and 40 percent by
São Tomé and Principe. In 2009, Sinopec purchased Addax Petroleum,
which gave the Chinese company control of half of the four blocks in the
São Tomé and Principe-Nigeria joint development zone. With this purchase, Sinopec became the most important player in the São Tomé oil sector, and the company established a presence in the capital.[158]

In 2008, a Chinese business delegation visited São Tomé to research the market for potential investments. Angola, which has close ties to São Tomé, supported the Chinese initiative. São Tomé's Prime Minister Patrice Trovoada told the press on this occasion that "we do not consider China an adversary or an enemy."[159] By some accounts, São Tomé is considering resumption of diplomatic relations with Beijing, although its aid connection with Taiwan remains strong.[160] Neither China nor Taiwan has imports of any significance from São Tomé. While São Tomé's imports from China averaged only $2 million annually from 2007 through 2010, they are substantially higher than imports from Taiwan. This is another case where Taiwan's diplomatic ties have not helped on the trade side.

Cape Verde

China supported the Cape Verde independence movement by assisting Amilcar Cabral, the leader of the PAIGC, which combined the liberation efforts of Cape Verde and Guinea Bissau. China established diplomatic relations with the islands on the day they became independent in 1976. The relationship developed slowly. Foreign Minister Qian Qichen visited Praia in 1997. Cape Verde's president went to China in 1982 and 1995; its prime minister visited in 1986 and 1997. China built a people's conference hall, government office building, housing project, the country's first dam, the national library, and a national monument. The two countries signed economic, trade, technical cooperation, cultural, and investment protection agreements. China began sending medical teams in 1984 and accepting scholarship students in 1996.[161]

Chinese retailers and traders began to settle in Cape Verde in the mid-1990s. Estimates on the size of the community vary between several hundred and as many as 2,000. The Chinese presence has had an important economic impact on these small islands. Macau millionaire David Chaw announced in 2007 a $120 million project to build a large entertainment park and pledged another $300 million for major infrastructure projects. A Chinese state-owned company agreed in 2003 to build a $55 million cement plant.[162] Cape Verde's prime minister visited Beijing in 2004, attended the 2006 FOCAC and returned in 2007 for the African Development Bank meeting in Shanghai. China provided Cape Verde an interest-free $2.5 million loan in 2006 for construction of a hospital and the following year canceled debt due before the end of 2005. In 2007, China's defense minister assured his Cape Verde counterpart that Beijing will continue to promote military cooperation and exchanges. In 2009, China inaugurated two rural schools, provided cash assistance to fight dengue fever, and formalized a sister city tie between Jinan and Praia. A CPC delegation met with the PAIGC in Praia. China imports nothing from Cape Verde while Cape Verde imported on average $24 million of Chinese goods annually in 2006–2010.

11

China's Relations with Southern Africa

Five countries (Zambia, Malawi, Botswana, Lesotho, and Swaziland) of the ten in southern Africa achieved independence peacefully in the 1960s. Four (Zimbabwe, Namibia, Mozambique, and Angola) underwent wars of national liberation while South Africa experienced considerable violence as it moved from white minority rule to majority black control. Mozambique and Angola became independent in 1975, Zimbabwe in 1980, Namibia in 1990; South Africa formally implemented majority rule in 1994. These experiences in achieving independence or majority rule had a significant impact on China's relationship with each country.

Of the five countries that had a peaceful transition to independence, only Zambia immediately recognized the PRC. The other four recognized Taiwan at or soon after independence, although Botswana switched to Beijing in the mid-1970s and Lesotho in the early 1980s. China strongly supported the liberation movements in the other five countries. Three of the five (Zimbabwe, Mozambique, and Namibia) recognized Beijing upon independence. The PRC's complicated relations with Angola and South Africa delayed their recognition of Beijing.

Today nine of the ten countries have diplomatic relations with Beijing. Only the conservative Kingdom of Swaziland maintains ties with Taiwan. The most recent country to switch, Malawi, did so at the end of 2007. Malawi offers a case study as to how China achieves its "one China" goal. Due to its immense oil wealth, Angola became China's largest trading partner in Africa. China's most important relationship in southern and throughout Africa, however, is with South Africa, a country that only recognized Beijing in 1998. It involves highly developed interaction at economic, political, military, social, educational, cultural, and scientific levels. South

Africa is China's second largest trading partner in Africa, but unlike Angola, with which China has a large trade deficit, Beijing had a large surplus with Pretoria until 2010.

Except for Swaziland, China has solid relations with all countries in the region. Opposition to the Robert Mugabe government in Zimbabwe has presented Beijing with some challenges, although they dissipated with the formation in 2009 of a coalition government that included the principal opposition politician as prime minister. China's government-to-government relations in the region range from good to excellent. On the other hand, Beijing faces increasing criticism from African small traders, local manufacturers, and civil society organizations on issues such as flooding markets with cheap Chinese goods, large numbers of Chinese traders and laborers, noncompliance with local labor and safety laws, and insufficient attention to environmental standards. Several governments are concerned about trade deficits.

Zambia

Zambia achieved independence in 1964 through a constitutional process rather than revolution. Consequently, there were relatively few contacts between Zambian leaders and China prior to independence, although Beijing did extend early in 1964 a $500,000 grant.[1] Recognizing the importance of Zambia's strategic location in southern Africa and the influence of its first president, Kenneth Kaunda, China made a special effort to cultivate this mineral-rich country. Soon after independence, Zambia and China established diplomatic relations. Zambia never wavered in its support for Beijing, although Kaunda was initially wary of China's communism and had to be persuaded by Tanzania's President Nyerere that a close relationship was in Zambia's best interest. In 1966, Zambia's vice president signed a cultural agreement in Beijing. China offered a $7 million loan in 1967 followed by a $17 million interest-free loan during a visit to Beijing by Kaunda. By the end of 1967, China, Tanzania, and Zambia agreed to build Beijing's signature aid project in Africa, the Tanzania-Zambia railway. The two countries subsequently signed protocols for road construction and a short-wave radio transmitting station, which encountered delays and concerns about equipment quality. China also helped Zambia establish training bases for fighters supporting southern African independence movements.[2]

Zambia's vice president visited Beijing in 1972. China granted Zambia $10 million in 1973 to help overcome transport problems following the closure of Zambia's frontier with white-ruled Rhodesia. Kaunda revisited Beijing in 1974, when he signed a $20 million loan for road construction and agricultural projects and encouraged China's support for liberation groups in neighboring Angola.[3] In 1978, China began admitting Zambian students on scholarship and sending medical teams to Zambia. China's vice premier visited Zambia in 1979, by which time China had extended $230 million, compared with only $15 million from the Soviet Union. Kaunda was more comfortable with China than with the Soviet Union and made a third visit to Beijing in 1980. He signed new agreements on culture, media, sports, and health. A Zambian military delegation followed, leading to close military cooperation. In the early 1980s, China agreed to build a maize mill, bridge, and new headquarters for Zambia's ruling political party, which signed a cooperative agreement with the CPC in 1987. Premier Zhao Ziyang visited in 1983 and Kaunda returned to Beijing in 1988.[4]

Frederick Chiluba defeated Kaunda in a multiparty election in 1991; China maintained close relations with the new government and donated 3,000 tons of maize the following year. In 1992, it started sending teachers to the University of Zambia. The city of Luzhou in Sichuan Province established a sister city link with Kabwe. Zambia reaffirmed its desire for good relations with Beijing and supported China on human rights issues at the UN. President Chiluba visited Beijing in 1993 and 2000; Zambia's vice president went in 1995 and its defense minister in 1998. Vice Premier Zhu Rongji visited Lusaka in 1995 and Premier Li Peng in 1997.[5]

The state-owned Bank of China opened a branch in Zambia in 1997, the first Chinese bank in Sub-Saharan Africa. It is a strategic investment that minimizes the banking challenges facing Chinese investors.[6] Major Chinese investment in Zambia began in 1998 when the China Non-Ferrous Metal Mining Company purchased the Chambishi copper mine for $20 million. The mine subsequently faced a number of labor and safety complaints. In 2005, an explosion at the mine killed forty-nine people. China significantly increased investment at Chambishi, but continuing problems have left a legacy of ill will. China and Zambia created as part of a joint venture the country's largest textile mill, although it shut down in 2007 due to competition from China and other Asian countries.[7]

Zambia's ruling party maintained close relations with the CPC; its national secretary commented in 2005 that the CPC is "a very dependable ally of Zambia" both in terms of development and international relations.[8] During a visit to Beijing in 2005, Zambia's vice president signed several economic and technology agreements with his Chinese counterpart. In a political misstep, China's ambassador in Lusaka, Li Baodong, became embroiled in the 2006 presidential election. The leading opposition candidate, Patriotic Front (PF) head Michael Sata, criticized Chinese business practices in the country and openly contacted Taiwanese officials. Li Baodong threatened to withdraw Chinese support for Zambia if Sata won. Although Sata lost the election in a three way contest, he won 29 percent of the vote. Li Baodong remained for a face-saving period and then transferred to a senior position in Geneva after only two years in Zambia.[9]

Newly elected President Levy Mwanawasa represented Zambia at the 2006 FOCAC when China agreed to cancel $211 million in debt, including the loan for the Tanzania-Zambia railway. Chinese investors signed an agreement to construct a $220 million copper smelter. In 2007, an embarrassing incident marred Hu Jintao's visit when Zambian workers forced him to cancel a stop at Chambishi where there was lingering unhappiness over safety and working conditions at the mine. Zambian workers continue to complain about low wages and poor health and safety conditions at Chinese companies. Guards fired on workers at a Chinese coal mine in 2010, injuring eleven, and strikes over low pay resumed at Chambishi in 2011. While China experiences periodic problems with the political opposition, labor unions, and civil society, it still views Zambia as important for political collaboration and access to copper, nickel, and cobalt. Chinese companies signed a $243 million contract for engineering, procurement, and construction of the Kariba North Bank hydroelectric project. In 2010, Zambia's state power utility signed an agreement with the China Africa Development Fund to build a $1.5 billion hydro power dam in southern Zambia.[10]

By 2011, Chinese FDI reached an estimated $2 billion mostly in extractive industries, natural resources, and agriculture; more than two hundred Chinese companies had established businesses in Zambia. Chinese companies are obtaining 70–75 percent of all infrastructure contracts. China's FDI is growing at a more rapid rate than that of any other country. The Association of Chinese Corporations in Zambia (ACCZ), established in 2005 by China's Ministry of Commerce, operates like a chamber of commerce and comes under the jurisdiction of the economic counselor in the Chinese embassy. ACCZ works on behalf of Chinese companies, promotes Chinese investment, educates member companies on Zambian rules and regulations, and helps with immigration and labor cases for Chinese companies. The Chinese Centre for Investment Promotion and Trade has an office in Zambia designed to identify investment opportunities, support Chinese companies and facilitate contacts with Zambian authorities for new investors.[11] A study of Chinese investment in Zambia by the African Labour Research Network concluded that it has had modest positive impacts on national development and overall negative implications for the labor market.[12]

Zambia and China established the Economic and Trade Cooperation Zone near the Chinese-owned Chambishi mine in the Zambian Copperbelt. The zone is expected to bring sixty Chinese companies and $900 million in Chinese investment to Zambia. This project includes a branch in Lusaka for light manufacturing and services that may attract another $500 million in Chinese investment.[13] Zambia agreed to exempt Chinese firms from import duties and value-added taxes. In 2009, China's Zhongui Mining Group signed a $3.6 billion Investment Promotion and Protection Agreement to explore for copper and other minerals. In 2010, China Nonferrous Metal Mining announced it planned to invest $600 million in the copper sector. The China Development Bank also agreed to provide $5 billion in loans to companies involved in Zambia's mining sector. China is looking to Zambia as a potential source of food but concerned about the political implications. There are fifteen Chinese farms in Zambia established by six state-owned companies on about 25,000 acres producing food for the local market.[14]

China's imports from Zambia have grown steadily in the twenty-first century and reached $2.5 billion in 2010, mostly copper, cobalt, and tobacco. Zambia is China's seventh most important African supplier. Zambia's imports from China in 2010 totaled a relatively modest $341 million.

President Mwanawasa's untimely death in 2008 resulted in a warm eulogy from China. Acting President Rupiah Banda told visiting Foreign Minister Yang Jeichi, who attended Mwanawasa's funeral, relations with China would remain strong. Opposition leader Sata, Acting President Banda, and a third party candidate, Hakainde Hichilema, contested the 2008 election. China had recently invited Hichilema to Beijing where the Zambian candidate pledged to work with China if elected. Although Sata moderated his criticism of China and acknowledged that Zambia needs Chinese investment, relations with Beijing remained an issue in the election, which Sata lost to Banda by only 35,000 votes. The close election suggested that public attitudes toward Chinese investment in Zambia remained controversial.[15]

In 2009, China inaugurated an anti-malaria center and began construction on a stadium, hospital, and agricultural demonstration center. Zambia is one of China's staunchest supporters in Africa. In 2010, Foreign Minister Kabinga Pande commented at the Fifteenth African Union summit in Kampala that it is unfair to say China's aid leads to corruption and huge debt. He praised Chinese assistance, noting that its loans are soft with "no serious or difficult conditions attached." He added that "China's aid has been great."[16] In 2010, Banda visited China where he signed agreements on mining, geology, road construction, an industrial park, and technical and cultural cooperation, and returned with a $1 billion loan. Meanwhile, Sata continued to be critical of China.

Presidential elections in September 2011 resulted in a victory for Sata's PF, China's occasional nemesis, which has consistently called for stricter enforcement of labor regulations related to foreign investment. During the campaign, Sata moderated his criticism of China and said he would maintain strong economic ties with Beijing.[17] Following his victory, Sata met with the Chinese ambassador to dispel fears about his anti-Chinese statements. He assured the ambassador that Zambia welcomes Chinese investment but expressed concern that China is bringing too many nationals into the country and emphasized that "investment should benefit Zambians and not the Chinese."[18]

Within days of the election, the managers at one Chinese-owned mine gave Zambian workers a pay increase, while the Zambian government ordered another Chinese-owned mine to reinstate 2,000 workers released over a pay dispute.[19] Human Rights Watch subsequently issued a massive report documenting persistent abuses in Chinese-run mines in Zambia, including poor health and safety conditions, long working shifts, and anti-union activities in violation of Zambia's national laws or international labor standards.[20] This issue will not go away anytime soon.

Botswana

Botswana, formerly the British protectorate of Bechuanaland, obtained independence peacefully in 1966. In the prelude to independence, the PRC supported a small revolutionary group known as the Bechuanaland Popular Party. In 1963, China's official media called for revolutionary struggle and Bechuanaland's liberation. In 1965, Bechuanaland's Democratic Party led by a moderate tribal chief, Seretse Khama, won the election, and he became Botswana's first president. In 1966, Botswana established diplomatic relations with Taiwan. In 1971, Botswana followed the African majority and voted in the UN General Assembly for the PRC's admission, although it continued relations with Taiwan. Overruling his senior advisers, Khama concluded that Botswana could no longer ignore the importance of the PRC. In 1974, Botswana recognized the PRC and asked Taiwan to leave the country. The PRC and Botswana formally established relations early in 1975.[21]

President Khama made a state visit to Beijing in 1976 during which he carefully avoided taking sides on the Sino-Soviet conflict. The two countries signed an economic and technical cooperation agreement and initiated an active cultural exchange program. Khama returned to China a year later. Until 1978, the aid relationship consisted of a grant of small arms, ammunition, and anti-aircraft guns, accompanied by a few military advisers. Botswana sought the weapons from China after Western countries refused to provide the equipment. In 1978, China allocated almost $17 million in development credits. President Quett Masire went to Beijing in 1980 and 1983 and Vice Premier Li Peng visited Gaborone in 1986, when the two countries granted each other most favored nation status. Botswana eagerly sought Chinese investment and capital. China agreed in 1980 to send medical teams to Botswana and in 1982 to rehabilitate one of the rail lines. China signed agreements in 1986 on railway construction, provision of farm machinery, extension of a previous loan, and a new interest-free loan. Botswana opened its first embassy in Asia in Beijing following Masire's return to China in 1991. Vice Premier Zhu Rongji went to Botswana in 1995, while Vice President Festus Mogae visited Beijing in 1996 and returned as president in 2000.[22]

In 2000, China and Botswana signed agreements for the promotion and protection of investment. China established construction companies in Botswana that have built structures such as Botswana Airlines headquarters, a computer building at the University of Botswana, and a sewage treatment field for Gaborone. Chinese companies invested heavily in the textile sector.[23] Merchants in Botswana have criticized Chinese small traders. An estimated 5,000 Chinese reside in Botswana. Local authorities accused one of the Chinese textile companies of importing cloth from China that is marked "made in Botswana." Police and customs officials shut down the operation. Consumers, however, welcome the low prices in Chinese shops and the fact that they are located in towns not well served by local companies.[24]

In 2005, Huang Ju, member of the Standing Committee of the Political Bureau of the CPC Central Committee and vice premier of the State Council, visited Botswana and offered a five-point program for enhancing China-Botswana relations. He proposed strengthening high level contacts, expanding exchanges at all levels of government, increasing economic cooperation and trade, promoting cultural, educational, and tourism exchanges, and strengthening consultation on international issues. The two countries signed cooperation agreements for a forty-six-person Chinese medical team, an interest-free $4.5 million loan, and a $22 million concessionary loan.[25] China agreed the following year to designate Botswana a preferred tourist destination. President Mogae represented Botswana at the 2006 FOCAC. One of Gaborone's papers, reporting on the visit, complained that Chinese loans to Botswana favored China and were little different from those offered by former colonial powers.[26]

Most Chinese investment in Botswana is in the construction, retail, textile, and manufacturing sectors.[27] Botswana broke ground in 2009 for construction of an industrial park funded by two Chinese companies. The $52 million project focuses on textiles and clothing and expects to attract sixty-six companies. Standard Bank of South Africa, which is 20 percent owned by ICBC, and ICBC agreed in 2009 to finance expansion of a coal power station in Botswana for $825 million. The two banks also agreed to provide a $140 million bridge loan for a power station in eastern Botswana. This was the first major transaction between Standard Bank and ICBC. The China National Electric Equipment Corporation received a $970 million contract to supply and build part of the power station. The first group of young Chinese volunteers arrived in Botswana. During a 2010 visit, Vice President Xi Jinping signed agreements on infrastructure, energy, and assistance and provided a $6 million grant.[28]

One of the most democratic countries in Africa, Botswana's civil society and press criticize the growing Chinese presence and some of its business practices. The leader of the opposition party, Botsalo Ntuane, complained that Chinese companies are forcing local companies out of business. He called on the government to end awarding contracts to Chinese companies. Chinese shops generally sell goods only from China; this has contributed to criticism about the growing trade deficit. Botswana's principal imports from China are textiles, garments, machinery, and electronic products. In 2009, Botswana imported $166 million worth of goods from China while China imported only $65 million from Botswana.[29]

Botswana faces a challenge as it balances its desire for Chinese financing and investment while not undermining its democratic principles, fair labor practices, and efforts to minimize corruption. So far, China has had considerable success in dealing with Botswana's concerns.

Zimbabwe

China developed ties with both liberation groups opposing white minority rule in Southern Rhodesia (now Zimbabwe). Joshua Nkomo established the Zimbabwe African People's Union (ZAPU) in 1961. A 1963 split in ZAPU resulted in the Zimbabwe African National Union (ZANU) led by Ndabaningi Sithole and Robert Mugabe. Beijing had good relations with ZAPU before the break, which coincided with the beginning of the Sino-Soviet conflict. After the split, China supported ZANU because Nkomo had close ties with the Soviets. Beijing seized the opportunity to support the faction free of Soviet influence. ZANU carried out most of the guerrilla activity against the white-ruled Rhodesian government; China was a major provider of military training and equipment. By the early 1970s, ZANU's close association with China led it to pursue Marxist-Leninist principles. While Robert Mugabe described himself as a Maoist and Marxist-Leninist, he was actually more committed to pragmatism, Zimbabwe nationalism, and even the preservation of the capitalist system he inherited from white Rhodesians.[30]

On the day it achieved independence in 1980, Zimbabwe under Prime Minister Mugabe recognized the PRC, which sent its foreign minister to the ceremony. Beijing had picked a winner in Zimbabwe with ZANU and Mugabe, unlike its support for losing liberation movements in several other African countries. The two countries had similar views on economic development, even if socialist rhetoric initially blurred China's goal of opening Zimbabwe's market for Chinese companies. In 1980, Mugabe made the first of eight visits to Beijing. Premier Zhao Ziyang visited Harare in 1983, Vice Premier Zhu Rongji in 1995, and President Jiang Zemin in 1996. China provided Zimbabwe with a $40 million loan in 1980 and signed trade and cultural agreements during Mugabe's 1981 visit to Beijing. China agreed in 1983 to build a large stadium in Harare and signed a $32 million interest-free loan. It initiated a scholarship program and began sending medical teams on a regular basis. China agreed in 1984 to establish a turnkey garment factory and signed additional economic and technical agreements in 1985. In 1988, China offered an interest-free loan that covered half the cost of a teacher training college. Chinese aid was actually exceedingly modest compared to Western assistance. Since China could not compete with Western aid, it encouraged its companies to win contracts.[31]

Mugabe strongly backed China following the Tiananmen Square crisis, describing the hostile Western response as an anti-China campaign. The two countries have a history of supporting each other on human rights issues. Mugabe expressed praise for China's political system during his 1993 visit to Beijing when he obtained a modest $9.4 million in assistance. Jiang Zemin signed eight agreements during his 1996 visit to Harare covering bilateral trade and economic and technical cooperation. He also provided a $1.2 million grant and $10 million loan. Zimbabwe, long dissatisfied with the amount of aid it received from China, pressed for more but China continued to emphasize trade and engagement by Chinese companies.[32]

The surge in Chinese investment coincided with Zimbabwe's controversial land reform program and the deterioration after 2000 of Zimbabwe's relations with Western countries and international financial institutions. Wen Jiabao even publicly supported Zimbabwe's land reform program. The two countries signed a series of agreements and China saw an opportunity to access Zimbabwe's mineral sector. In 2003, as Mugabe encountered increasingly hostile relations with the West, he instituted his "Look East" policy.[33] China soon became a critical ally.

Chinese investments are concentrated in the extractive sectors such as chrome, platinum, nickel, and copper. In 2006, Zimbabwe signed deals with China for more than $1 billion to construct thermal power stations in exchange for chrome and a $200 million loan to support agriculture. Sinosteel agreed to pay $200 million for a 50 percent stake in Zimbabwe's largest ferrochrome producer. Chinese companies established the Chamber of Chinese Enterprises in Zimbabwe to promote trade and economic and technical cooperation. China became Zimbabwe's single largest investor in 2007 with a portfolio of more than $600 million. China provided equipment for the state railway network. Chinese companies signed two agreements with Zimbabwean phone companies, one valued at $288 million for the expansion of the fixed-line subscriber base, and the other a $40 million deal with Zimbabwe's largest mobile phone operator. At least thirty-five Chinese companies now operate in Zimbabwe, which has also issued numerous business permits to Chinese shopkeepers and street traders.[34] In 2010, the China Development Bank acquired a major share in the Infrastructure Development Bank of Zimbabwe and agreed to extend long-term lines of credit.

China Sonangol and the private Hong Kong-based China International Fund (CIF) have reportedly invested $8 billion in Zimbabwe's diamond fields. Zimbabwe ranks as the world's seventh largest producer of diamonds.[35] Sino-Zimbabwe Diamonds, a joint venture between Chinese investors and the Zimbabwe Mining Development Corporation (ZMDC), has not yet reached profitable production. Anjin Investments (Private) Limited is a joint venture between ZMDC and Anhui Foreign Economic Construction (Group) Corporation, a public construction company under China's Ministry of Construction. It has produced 2.5 to 3 million carats that are awaiting the Kimberley Process Certification.[36]

After Western countries imposed an arms embargo on Zimbabwe in 2002, China became the country of choice for supplying military equipment. There have been numerous high level exchange military visits. Zimbabwe purchased K-8 advanced jet trainers to replace aging British Hawk jet fighters, and has purchased military trucks and a variety of small arms. A PLA team teaches at the Zimbabwe Staff College and Zimbabwe officers regularly train in China. Beijing provided a controversial $98 million loan repayable in diamonds to build the Defence College; the terms and cost resulted in widespread public criticism.[37] For a discussion of the imbroglio surrounding the 2008 shipment of Chinese arms to Zimbabwe, see Chapter 6.

Perhaps sensing that a political transition is approaching, China has begun highlighting soft power linkages with Zimbabwe that are intended to help it survive the Mugabe era. China opened a Confucius Institute at the University of Zimbabwe and launched a Zimbabwe-China Friendship Association. The CPC donated computers to the ZANU-PF and helped it establish a party school. ZANU-PF ties with the CPC have been close for many years.[38] Nevertheless, China faces challenges in convincing Zimbabweans that its engagement is positive. A strong anti-Chinese sentiment exists in some quarters. In 2011, the Zimbabwe Congress of Trade Unions warned about the plunder of resources by foreigners, especially China. An affiliate group, the Construction and Allied Trade Workers Union, complained that Chinese companies operate above the law.[39]

Between 2003 and 2009, China annually imported on average $149 million worth of goods from Zimbabwe; the figure rose to $246 million in 2010. Tobacco, cotton, and minerals account for most imports; China may also receive a significant amount of smuggled gold. China is the largest buyer of Zimbabwe's tobacco and participates in its production and processing by providing local farmers loans for the purchase of Chinese fertilizers and pesticides. Zimbabwe's imports from China grew steadily from $6 million in 2003 to $344 million in 2010. In view of the close Zimbabwe-China link, the volume of trade is surprisingly modest.[40]

China has consistently opposed sanctions against Zimbabwe. In 2005, it prevented an effort by the United States and UK to discuss in the UN Security Council Zimbabwe's controversial slum demolition campaign in the suburbs of Harare and Bulawayo. When Hu Jintao failed to include Harare on his 2007 and 2009 visits to Africa, many Western observers concluded this portended a decision by China to draw back from Zimbabwe. These observers failed to note, however, that the chairman of the National Committee of the Chinese People's Political Consultative Conference visited Harare in 2007 and promised China would maintain exchanges at all levels and enhance relations with Parliament. The deputy head for organization of the CPC Central Committee led a delegation to Harare in 2007. China also backed the efforts of African countries, especially South Africa, to resolve Zimbabwe's internal political crisis following the disputed 2008 election.[41]

While China wants to avoid becoming tied too closely to an aging Mugabe, the risk for Zimbabwe is that it may become overly dependent on China. Opposition presidential candidate Morgan Tsvangirai, who claims to have won the 2008 elections, agreed in 2009 to join a coalition government as prime minister with Mugabe as president. This permitted China to reach out to both major political parties in Harare. In 2009, China's assistant minister of foreign affairs, Zhai Jun, met separately in Harare with Mugabe and Tsvangirai. He signed one $4 million agreement with the coalition government that finances an agricultural demonstration center and another that provides a $5 million cash grant to the government. Zhai expressed confidence in the success of the "inclusive" government. Tsvangirai called for "strengthening" Zimbabwe-China relations. He added that China agreed to renegotiate its financial cooperation program with Zimbabwe.[42] China's departing ambassador argued that China's 2008 veto of UN sanctions against Zimbabwe was essential for the establishment of the inclusive government.[43]

In 2009, China continued repositioning itself for political change in the country. As Zimbabwe's economy deteriorated and Mugabe's longevity remained in question, Beijing realized it must balance carefully its long friendship with the ZANU-PF leadership and its need to pivot quickly when political change comes. Tsvangirai returned in 2009 from visits to Europe and the United States announcing that he had obtained pledges of only $500 million to bail out Zimbabwe's economy. In contrast, he emphasized, Zimbabwe had secured credit lines of almost $950 million from China, the largest sum from a single country since the formation of the unity government. In 2010, during a visit to World Expo in Shanghai, Mugabe reiterated that "China has always stood by Zimbabwe."[44] China wants stability in Zimbabwe and believes the situation has improved under the coalition government. High level visits and aid continue; China's Foreign Ministry official responsible for southern Africa said in 2011 there has been no significant change in the relationship.[45]

Mozambique

In 1961, several Mozambican nationalist organizations arrived in Tanzania and merged the following year as the Frente de Libertação de Moçambique (FRELIMO). In 1963, five FRELIMO delegations visited China, including one headed by President Eduardo Mondlane. A victim of factionalism, one group broke away from FRELIMO in 1965 and formed the Comité Revolucionário de Moçambique (COREMO). While continuing support for FRELIMO, China favored COREMO, which followed a pro-Beijing and anti-Soviet line. COREMO operated out of Zambia, professed Maoist ideas, and received external support apparently only from China. Beijing's official media ran press releases from both COREMO and FRELIMO. COREMO encountered frequent splintering and disappeared in the early 1970s. China successfully transferred its allegiance to FRELIMO, which had pro-Moscow and pro-Beijing factions. In 1971, Beijing began increasing its military assistance to FRELIMO and stepped up training for Mozambican fighters in Tanzania. FRELIMO leader Samora Machel visited China in 1971 and 1975, when Deng Xiaoping warmly greeted him. Mozambique became independent in 1975 and immediately recognized Beijing. China donated 30,000 tons of wheat, signed an interest-free $56 million loan, and agreed to send medical experts. About 6,000 persons of Chinese origin lived in Mozambique at independence; most departed within a year, presumably because they were anti-communist.[46]

Following independence, the Soviets had the upper hand in Mozambique. Machel preferred USSR support because it offered more assistance. There was a brief improvement in Sino-Mozambican relations when Machel visited Beijing in 1978 and about one hundred Chinese military specialists were working in Mozambique. China provided nearly $60 million in credits by 1978, making it one of Mozambique's largest donors. This was followed by a setback, however, when Mozambique criticized China for its border war with Vietnam. China experienced an embarrassment in 1982 when a junior officer at the Chinese embassy in Maputo had a dispute with other staff members and killed nine of them.[47]

A famine in 1983 followed by a flood gave China an opening to offer much needed assistance and improve its standing. Machel returned to Beijing in 1984 and China extended more than $20 million in economic aid. China expanded its assistance program in the 1980s and Mozambique did not criticize Beijing in the wake of the 1989 Tiananmen Square crackdown.[48] China and Mozambique reached numerous economic, cultural, and technical assistance agreements in the 1980s. FRELIMO and the CPC signed a cooperation agreement in 1988 and China agreed the following year to build Mozambique's parliament building.[49] Mozambique's premier visited Beijing in 1987 and President Joaquim Chissano went the following year. During this period, Chinese visitors to Mozambique were at the level of vice premier or below.[50] China-Mozambique relations developed slowly in the 1990s, aided by $20 million to encourage Chinese companies to open businesses in Mozambique.[51]

After the collapse of the Soviet Union, China became a natural partner for Mozambique and increased its economic assistance and trade activity in the 1990s. High level visits became more frequent with Chissano going to Beijing in 1998 and 2004; Mozambique's premier visited in 1993, 1997, and 2002. Chinese Vice Premier Zhu Rongji went to Maputo in 1995 and Premier Li Peng in 1997. China signed new trade agreements in 2001 and 2004, and constructed the Ministry of Foreign Affairs in 2004. In 2006, the two countries began scientific cooperation on medicinal plants and information technology. Mozambican President Armando Guebuza attended the 2006 FOCAC and returned for the 2008 Olympic Games; Hu Jintao visited Maputo in 2007, when he promised assistance for schools, an agricultural technology center (inaugurated in 2011), and a national stadium. He agreed to disburse $155 million from a new soft loan and $40 million from China's Export Import Bank. China canceled $52 million of Mozambican debt. China periodically makes modest grants of money and equipment to the Mozambican military. In 2007, for example, the chiefs of staff of the two countries signed a military assistance protocol and Beijing gave the armed forces $1.5 million in nonmilitary equipment.[52]

There is a Chinese Chamber of Commerce in Maputo, and so many Chinese firms are doing business that the government translated the labor law into Chinese. A third of all roads are being built by Chinese companies, as are the auditor-general's office, Maputo International Airport, national soccer stadium, communications networks, and water supply projects. China began offering five scholarships annually in 1992; more than one hundred students were studying in China by 2011 and Mozambican universities are teaching Mandarin. China has sent medical teams to Mozambique since 1976 and provides anti-malaria medicine. In 2011, a CPC delegation signed agreements to establish a Confucius Institute and a Portuguese-language station for CRI.[53]

The Sino-Mozambique relationship has experienced challenges. In 2007, Mozambique reportedly granted China leases to establish Chinese-run farms and cattle ranches for an initial 3,000 settlers. The report caused such uproar that the government was forced to deny any such agreement. The project is dormant and perhaps dead. Chinese traders, local business persons, and Mozambique officials have colluded to strip precious tropical hardwoods from the country. In 2007, Mozambique seized 531 containers of illegal log exports purchased by eight Chinese companies. Chinese buyers eventually exported the $7 million worth of logs after paying a fine of more than a half million dollars.[54] Environmental groups also accuse Chinese fishing vessels in Mozambican waters of using illegal equipment and large-scale poaching. Some analysts concluded that relations between Beijing and Maputo became inconsistent, with neither side able to maximize past cooperation.[55]

Hu Jintao's visit in 2007 reinvigorated the relationship. The Export Import Bank of China agreed to finance construction of the Mpanda Nkua dam. The $2.3 billion loan package includes funding for a transmission line from the dam to the capital of Maputo. While China's projects are usually constructed by Chinese companies, a Brazilian engineering firm and its Mozambican partner won the construction contract. China signed an agreement in 2009 to provide $3 million in military aid for purchase of logistical equipment and agreed to continue to train Mozambique's military. As of 2010, Chinese investment in Mozambique totaled $607 million. In 2010, Mozambique's government information service announced that China plans to invest nearly $13 billion in industrial, tourism, mining, and energy projects over the next five years, including a Chinatown in Maputo, automobile factory, and hydropower dams.[56]

Mozambique's Prime Minister Aires Ali visited China twice in 2010; he received $165 million in financing commitments from the Export Import Bank and the Chinese Bank for Development to upgrade Maputo International Airport and build cement and cotton processing plants. Wuhan Iron and Steel purchased for $200 million an 8 percent share of Riversdale, an Australian company that has coal field concessions in Mozambique. The Chinese company committed an additional $800 million to develop coal reserves. China intends to import significant quantities of coal, and the deal underscores the growing trend by Chinese companies to purchase minority stakes in non-African resource companies with concessions in Africa. Mozambique has a significant trade deficit with China. In 2010, it imported $574 million in goods from China while China imported only $201 million worth of aluminum, oil seeds, and timber from Mozambique.[57]

During a six-day state visit to China in 2011, President Guebuza signed twelve financial agreements with China. They included $15.8 million for distance education and science and technology programs, half as donations and half as interest-free credit. Other agreements covered support for small and medium-sized enterprises and a bio-gas project. China Kingho Energy Group announced it would provide initial funding of $20 million for construction of a coal terminal at the port of Beira and upgrade the Sena rail line that links the Moatize coal mines in northwest Mozambique.[58]

Loro Horta, an expert on Sino-Lusophone Africa relations, concluded: "China is fast emerging as the most important economic and diplomatic player in Mozambique, bringing billions of dollars in investments and asking no questions."[59]

Angola

China strongly supported Angola's war of national liberation; Radio Peking began broadcasting propaganda programs in Portuguese to Angola in 1960. China had a complicated history of interaction with Angolan liberation groups, primarily because of its effort to counter Soviet influence. At one time, and sometimes concurrently, China supported all three Angolan groups: MPLA, FNLA, and UNITA. China initially provided arms and some training to the MPLA, but expanded support to the other two in 1963 when the OAU recognized them as the legitimate liberation organizations. In 1964, UNITA leader Jonas Savimbi met Mao Zedong and Zhou Enlai in Beijing and received military training in China. He returned the following year and again in 1967 seeking arms. Savimbi subsequently complained that UNITA received little from China. In 1971, following OAU recognition of the MPLA, its leader Agostinho Neto led a delegation to Beijing and China began sending aid. By 1973, China turned its attention to the FNLA, led by Holden Roberto. Unlike the MPLA leadership, Roberto was not influenced by the Soviets. The FNLA operated out of Zaire, where China had significantly improved relations with the Mobutu government. After an early 1973 visit to Beijing by Mobutu, Roberto arrived months later and received a promise of aid.[60]

The 1974 overthrow of Portugal's government caused China to worry that the Soviets would increase their influence in Angola. Beijing sent instructors and a large shipment of arms to the FNLA in Zaire and provided arms to UNITA and a splinter group of the MPLA. China encouraged unification and even organized talks in Beijing for representatives of all three organizations. Moscow responded with massive support to the MPLA; a full-scale Angolan civil war began in 1975. As the MPLA improved its military position with Soviet support, China authorized Zaire to supply the FNLA with Chinese-made weapons. Washington also increased support to the FNLA and UNITA and coordinated this activity with China. South African troops joined the FNLA/UNITA offensive in 1975, which embarrassed the Chinese. China's allies in the region—Zaire, Zambia, and Tanzania—supported respectively the FNLA, UNITA, and MPLA. China's support for the FNLA and UNITA strained relations with Tanzania and caused China to pull back, according to a U.S. intelligence report. President Ford in a 1975 meeting in Beijing with Mao Zedong pressed China to resume support for those groups opposing the MPLA. Beijing tarnished its reputation in Africa as a result of its policy in Angola. To make matters worse, the pro-Soviet MPLA prevailed militarily by early 1976, leaving China in a difficult position.[61]

Near the end of 1975, the MPLA established an independent Angola, which the USSR quickly recognized and China did not. The FNLA and

UNITA opposed the MPLA government. Except for continuing anti-Soviet propaganda because of its support of the MPLA, China largely absented itself from the Angolan conflict. It did provide a large shipment of arms via South African-controlled Namibia to UNITA in 1979.[62] Zaire expelled the FNLA in 1979 and Mobutu reconciled with MPLA leader Neto, removing one of the obstacles to improved China-MPLA relations. China finally established diplomatic relations with Angola in 1983, but only opened an embassy in Luanda later in the decade. Sino-Angolan ties developed cautiously, not surprising in view of China's long-standing support for the MPLA's enemies. The two countries signed trade and loan agreements in 1984 and China offered $25 million in economic aid and 2,000 tons of grain. Xinhua and the Angolan News Agency signed a cooperative agreement in 1986. China began criticizing continuing American support for UNITA, although it once supported the organization. Angola's President Eduardo dos Santos visited Beijing in 1988 when the two leaders signed three agreements. They strengthened friendly MPLA-CPC relations; established a joint committee for cooperation in economics, technology, and trade; and agreed to cooperate in culture, education, science, sanitation, sports, and the press. They also established a Joint Economic and Trade Commission.[63]

Angola did not criticize China's actions after Tiananmen Square and the two countries signed three new agreements at the end of 1989, including a feasibility study for building an MPLA party school. The following year, they signed an implementation accord for cultural and educational cooperation, and China offered a $121 million credit to buy Chinese goods. When fighting resumed between the MPLA and UNITA in 1992, China remained aloof. In desperate need of external financing and in defiance of Beijing's "One China" policy, Angola tried unsuccessfully to establish relations with Taiwan in the early 1990s. Following this failure, high level visits increased with Vice Premier Zhu Rongji visiting Luanda in 1995 and President dos Santos returning to Beijing in 1998. The MPLA general secretary went to China in 1998 and 2000.[64]

Sino-Angolan relations developed exponentially in the twenty-first century as a result of trade. In 2000, China imported about $1.7 billion, almost entirely oil, from Angola. Oil imports increased to $22.8 billion in 2010. Angolan imports from China grew from $37 million in 2000 to $2.2 billion in 2010. Angola is China's largest trading partner in Africa and China is Angola's largest trading partner globally.[65]

In 2004, China's Export Import Bank pledged $2 billion as the first in a series of oil-backed loans to fund infrastructure projects throughout Angola. By 2011, China extended $14.5 billion in credit to Angola to be repaid in oil exports and used largely to fund Chinese-built infrastructure projects. This arrangement became the model for Chinese loans to other resource-rich African countries. Angola welcomed them because they do not contain conditionality as some donors require. In 2006, Premier Wen Jiabao announced one of the $2 billion loans during a visit to Luanda. China also canceled $7 million of Angola's debt.[66]

Most Chinese investment has gone into the oil sector. In 2005, Vice Premier Zeng Peiyang visited Angola and signed nine cooperation agreements, most of them related to energy. China began joint ventures for prospecting and mining diamonds. Not all of China's efforts to expand its presence in the oil sector have worked out. Negotiations broke down in 2007 over a $4 billion Chinese proposal to build a refinery in Lobito. The two sides disagreed on the size of the refinery and the ultimate destination of the refined product. Beijing said the oil should go to China; Angola wanted more flexibility. In 2009, Angola's state oil company, Sonangol, awarded the contract to the U.S. company Kellogg, Brown, and Root to design the refinery and the right to choose companies to build it. This suggested that Angola does not wish to be tied too closely to any country.[67]

China's direct investment in other activities is modest. Angola approved fifty Chinese projects between 2005 and 2007 totaling about $74 million.[68] In 2009, China Petroleum and Chemical Corporation (Sinopec) and CNOOC agreed to buy a 20 percent stake in Angola's offshore deep water block 32 from Marathon Oil Corporation for $1.3 billion.[69] Sonangol subsequently invoked its right of first refusal on the grounds that the Chinese companies had not offered market price. China has had difficulty acquiring control of Angolan fields because it is a latecomer and lacks expertise for ultra-deep-water drilling.[70] Sinopec announced in 2010 that it had agreed to pay $2.46 billion for deep-water oil assets by purchasing a 55 percent stake in Sonangol Sinopec International Ltd.[71] Considerable Chinese investment and commercial activity in Angola has occurred in the name of Hong Kong's shadowy China International Fund, also known as China Sonangol. It has provided about $3 billion in oil-backed loans for construction projects.[72]

In 2006, Chinese companies established a Chamber of Commerce in Luanda; Angola now has more than fifty state-owned and four hundred private Chinese companies. It has consulates in Hong Kong, Macau, and

Shanghai designed primarily to attract investment. In 2008, China's Dong-feng and Japan's Nissan opened an automobile manufacturing plant with a goal of producing 30,000 vehicles annually. During a 2008 visit to Luanda Premier Wen Jiabao signed an agreement for construction of a new international airport and rehabilitation of the Benguela and Namibe rail lines and several roads. The rail line rehabilitation by the China Railway Group is one of several Chinese projects that have experienced embarrassing delays. In 2008, President dos Santos inspected China's largest infrastructure project to date in Angola—the $355 million, 300-mile Malanje-Luanda railway. Huawei, ZTE, and Shanghai Bell are engaged in telecommunications projects, including $100 million for military communications.[73] In 2009, the China Development Bank offered a $1.2 billion line of credit so that Angola could rebuild its agricultural sector destroyed by civil war. China also inaugurated an anti-malaria center.[74]

This activity has resulted in a large Chinese presence of mostly low-skilled and temporary workers and shopkeepers in Angola. The official Angolan count in 2007 was 22,000, although the authors heard figures from 8,000 (Chinese embassy in Luanda) to 100,000 (Chinese owner of a restaurant in Luanda). In 2010, the Angolan government said there were 70,000 Chinese working in the country while a researcher at a Chinese think tank said the number was 80,000–100,000. Both Angola Airlines and China's Hainan Airlines have regularly scheduled service between China and Angola. The large Chinese presence has resulted in growing resentment from Angolans and increasing personal attacks.[75] Crime aimed at Chinese business persons has become a problem. In 2009, the Chinese embassy issued a warning on its website on the mounting security risks faced by its nationals, noting that armed robbers are targeting Chinese.[76]

Although a few of the authors' interlocutors in Angola complained that Chinese products and quality of work were substandard, most insisted the quality was at least satisfactory. They commented that the Chinese work hard, usually finish projects on time, and cost less than competitors. Some Angolans complained that China is not complying with Angolan laws that require at least 70 percent of the workforce be Angolans and 30 percent of subcontracts go to Angolan companies. The Angolan government told us the percentage of Angolan workers was closer to 60 percent because Chinese managers could not find enough skilled Angolans.[77]

Military cooperation has been modest, perhaps because the MPLA relied so heavily on Russian equipment. Chinese assistance consists mostly of training, although China has helped Angola remove land mines through-out the country.[78] Following the 2010 visit to Luanda by the PLA general staff chief, China suggested an increase in high level military exchanges, training, and supply of military equipment.[79] China has stepped up cooper-ation in education and training. Angola did not receive Chinese medical teams until 2009.[80] During 2007 and 2008, some two hundred Angolan officials and professionals underwent training in China. In 2010, Vice Presi-dent Xi Jinping visited Angola, where he signed nineteen protocols and increased to sixty the number of scholarships awarded annually to Angolan students. The Macau Foundation offers another five.[81]

During a visit by the authors to Luanda in 2007, there was unanimity on the reasons for China's sharp increase in influence. When the civil war ended in 2002, the MPLA government requested a major donor conference to rebuild wartorn Angola. The conference never took place and the West showed little interest in rebuilding the country, although large Western oil companies dominated the petroleum sector. China quickly filled the void. One source described China's intervention as tantamount to a Marshall Plan, but emphasized that its intention was not altruistic. It coveted Ango-lan oil.[82]

Angola does not want China to have a monopoly on influence in the country. Western oil companies still control most of the sector and Angola seeks greater involvement in the economy from Europe, North America, and Brazil.[83] Angola transmitted a not so subtle message to this effect dur-ing the 2006 FOCAC in Beijing. Angola's prime minister, not its president, represented the country. Just days before the opening of FOCAC, President dos Santos completed a three-day official visit to Moscow and returned directly to Luanda.[84] Russian Prime Minister Mikhail Efimovich Fradkov then visited Luanda in 2007. As oil prices tanked and the world economy began to deteriorate, however, dos Santos made two trips to Beijing in 2008 to ensure that Angola retained access to Chinese funding.[85] Although Angolan prickliness toward China periodically surfaces, so long as China and Angola need each other, ties between them will remain strong.

South Africa

White-ruled South Africa established relations with the Republic of China in 1931. As part of the UN force in Korea, South Africa sent a fighter squadron in 1950 to fly combat missions against Chinese targets.[86] So long as South Africa was an anti-communist, white minority government, it had no interest in diplomatic relations with the PRC, and the feeling was mutual. There were two principal African nationalist organizations during the struggle for majority rule. The ANC began in 1912. A group of dissidents split from the ANC in 1959 and created the Pan Africanist Congress (PAC). The Soviet Union and the PRC regarded South Africa as a major battleground between communism and capitalism. Beijing initially tried to maintain cordial relations with the ANC and the PAC. The South African Communist Party (SACP), which had close ties to the Soviet Union, had a strong influence on the ANC and gradually pulled it toward Moscow. As the Sino-Soviet dispute deepened, China shifted its support in the mid-1960s until the early 1980s, from the ANC to the largely ineffective PAC. In one respect, this worked to Beijing's advantage. The limitations of the PAC put minimal demands on China, which did not, in any event, have the resources to compete with Soviet support for the ANC. Beijing provided modest financial assistance and training for the PAC guerrilla fighters. Expediency and not ideological conviction dictated China's relationship with the PAC. China also tried to build support among members of the South African Confederation of Trade Unions.[87]

China claimed in 1960 that it had ended all economic and trade ties with white-ruled South Africa. When Western and Soviet authorities widely publicized the facts of continuing Chinese trade, China reiterated in 1963 that it had no economic or trade ties, direct or indirect, with South Africa. In 1964, China tripled its trade with Pretoria, which had a "commissioner for trade with the Chinese People's Republic" assigned to Hong Kong. Allegations of Chinese sanctions-busting, including purchase of uranium, continued until the end of apartheid. South African arms manufacturer Armscor also had representation in Beijing in the early 1980s.[88]

Having decided to back the PAC, China tried to improve its weak position by vigorously supporting the diplomatic effort against the white-ruled regime even while it traded with that regime. In 1973, China was one of four UN Security Council members to vote against Pretoria's credentials. A year later it voted to exclude South Africa's representatives from the UN. As relations improved in the early 1980s between Moscow and Beijing, the ANC signaled a willingness to normalize ties with the PRC. In 1983, China said it would treat all liberation groups in southern Africa equally. The ANC's Oliver Tambo visited Beijing that year, marking a sharp departure in China's policy toward the ANC. The U.S. State Department reported in 1985 that China provided diplomatic support, food aid, and possibly arms and training to the ANC and the PAC. In 1986, Beijing feted the ANC's secretary-general. The PAC lost its special relationship with China and by 1987 Beijing turned to the ANC.[89]

Soon after his release from prison in 1990, ANC leader Nelson Mandela met the PRC ambassador to Zambia and thanked China for its support. The same year, China announced South African nationals could visit China; a delegation from China reportedly came to South Africa to discuss possible joint ventures with the still white minority government. South Africa began dismantling apartheid; Foreign Minister Pik Botha, accompanied by representatives of large South African companies, visited China in 1991. The following year the two countries set up "unofficial offices," with China establishing the Center for South African Studies in Pretoria and South Africa opening the Center for Chinese Studies in Beijing. China's foreign minister met his South African counterpart early in 1992 at the Johannesburg airport while traveling to other countries in Africa. China-South African trade reached $250 million in 1992 and China's Ministry of Foreign Trade and Economic Cooperation opened an office in Johannesburg. While China cultivated ties with the minority government, it did the same with the ANC. Mandela visited China later in 1992 and met with Premier Li Peng and President Jiang Zemin. China was one of the first states to resume "official" trade links with Pretoria after Mandela called in 1993 for the removal of sanctions. Prior to the 1994 elections, China reached out to the ANC, PAC, and SACP. The ANC won 63 percent of the vote and the PAC just over 1 percent.[90]

It was ANC policy to attempt to have relations with both Taiwan and the PRC. Taipei reportedly contributed up to $7 million to Mandela's presidential campaign, and he visited Taiwan in 1993. The ANC announced that whatever its past differences with Taipei for supporting the white-ruled government, it was ready to build a new relationship. The ANC acknowledged support it had received from the PRC. Beijing's growing relationship with South Africa encouraged Taiwan to step up high level contact; by early 1995, as many as two hundred South African public officials had received all-expense paid trips to Taiwan. The PRC urged South Africa to shift diplomatic recognition to Beijing by emphasizing ideological similarities between the ANC and CPC. China invited South African Foreign Minister Alfred Nzo to Beijing early in 1996 in an effort to persuade Pretoria to

recognize China and break with Taiwan. Mandela shocked both Taipei and
Beijing in November 1996 when he announced that South Africa would
switch recognition from Taipei to Beijing effective 1 January 1998. By 1997,
China's trade with South Africa, including goods transshipped through
Hong Kong, which had just come under PRC control, reached $3 billion.
Nzo invited Chinese Foreign Minister Qian Qichen to South Africa at the
end of 1997 when they signed a joint communiqué establishing full diplomatic ties. This effectively ended Pretoria's effort to maintain relations with
both Beijing and Taipei, although Taiwan was permitted to maintain a liaison office in Pretoria and trade offices in several South African cities.[91]

The Sino-Soviet conflict was especially fateful for China's future relations with majority-ruled South Africa. China's support for the PAC jeop-
ardized relations with the far more important ANC. Although China
resumed ties with the ANC in the early 1980s and gave strong public
support for majority rule, the decision to support the PAC probably prolonged Taipei's stay in Pretoria. For its part, Taiwan, after the ANC victory in the 1994 elections, had to overcome its past association with the
apartheid regime. China's ties to the PAC and its trade with the sanctioned white minority government left some lingering doubts about its
political reliability.

Immediately following diplomatic recognition, the two countries began
an intense round of high level visits. In 1998, South African Vice President
Thabo Mbeki visited China, followed months later by Speaker of the South
African National Assembly Frene Ginwala. General Secretary of the SACP
Blade Nzimande met in Beijing with President Jiang Zemin, who thanked
the SACP for its contribution to establishment of diplomatic ties with
China.[92] Vice President Hu Jintao came to South Africa early in 1999, and
President Nelson Mandela made a state visit to China. Vice Premier Qian
Qichen attended the inaugural ceremony of President Thabo Mbeki. Li
Peng, Chairman of the National People's Congress Standing Committee,
arrived months later. In 2000, Jiang Zemin made a state visit to South
Africa, where he signed the Pretoria Declaration on the Partnership
Between the PRC and South Africa and agreed to set up a Binational Commission. The two leaders signed six other agreements. Dai Bingguo, head
of the International Liaison Department of the CPC Central Committee,
headed a delegation to South Africa and Foreign Minister Jacob Zuma
visited China twice in 2000. Jia Qinglin, a member of the Political Bureau
of the CPC Standing Committee, and Tian Jiyun, vice chairman of the

Standing Committee of the National People's Congress, made separate visits. There were numerous visits at the secondary level.[93]

The magnitude of activity in the first three years after the establishment of relations was unprecedented for Chinese engagement with an African country and underscored the importance Beijing attached to South Africa. The frenetic schedule of visits and interaction has continued. President Mbeki visited China in 2001 when he co-chaired the first plenary meeting of the Binational Commission with President Jiang. The Commission established the framework for the enhancement of relations. The chief of the South African National Defense Forces met with his counterpart in Beijing. South Africa established the same year a South Africa-China Friendship Association in Pretoria. The CPC invited the ANC general secretary to China twice in 2001. The fact that the SACP had close ties to the ANC permitted the CPC to develop a collaborative relationship. The SACP general secretary visited Beijing in 2001 and a high level CPC delegation returned the visit. Premier Zhu Rongji visited South Africa in 2002 and Vice Premier Li Lanqing and PLA chief of the general staff in 2003. By the end of 2003, China and South Africa established sixteen pairings of provinces or cities that concluded friendship agreements.[94]

In countries like Sudan, where the local communist party is alienated from the ruling party, the CPC has avoided meaningful contact. China only pursues relationships with opposition parties, including communist parties, when it believes the association will not harm ties with the ruling party. South Africa is an example of China's policy in the latter situation.

Premier Wen Jibao visited South Africa in 2006 when he signed an agreement covering a temporary cap on Chinese textile exports to South Africa, mining of uranium, development of peaceful nuclear reactors, and exchange of personnel in the nuclear field.[95] The same year, President Mbeki represented South Africa at the Beijing FOCAC. He urged that Africa seek "a fair and equitable global trading system that is characterized by transparency, good corporate governance, predictability and poverty alleviation and eradication."[96] In late 2006, Mbeki commented that African states run the risk of getting stuck "in an unequal relationship" with Beijing as had developed with the colonial powers.[97] In 2007, Mbeki backed away from this criticism but gently warned China not to repeat the mistakes of the colonial relationship with Africa. He called on China to participate in Africa's development and not use it just as a source of raw materials.[98] In 2007, Hu Jintao said in South Africa that China is concerned by its trade surplus and signed agreements dealing with mining, energy, and agriculture.[99]

Military exchanges began with a visit to South Africa by China's defense minister in 1998 and one to China in 2000 by South Africa's counterpart. The military relationship has become increasingly important. PLA navy vessels called outside Cape Town in 2000 and at Durban in 2011. In 2008, a South African frigate called at Shanghai, the first port call in China by a naval vessel from an African country. The Sino-South African Defense Committee meets regularly. In 2004, China donated electronic equipment for training South African military personnel. South Africa has marketed some of its military equipment in China; the Denel Group signed a deal for its 35-mm multirole machine gun. China negotiated with Denel for the transfer of African Eagle UAV technologies.[100] In 2010, China and South Africa signed a police cooperation agreement whereby they agreed to exchange intelligence information on drug trafficking, organized crime, illegal immigration, money laundering, arms smuggling, and trafficking in women and children.[101]

Chinese aid to South Africa has been minimal because relations were established only in 1998 and South Africa is more developed than any other African country. China offered in 2006 about $6 million for technical training and promised an additional $25 million in 2007. China has a few small technical assistance projects, one for growing mushrooms and another for teaching rice production. There is no indication that China has offered or South Africa has sought soft loans.[102] China and South Africa have engaged in extensive cultural, scientific, and technological cooperation, including agreements on cooperation in traditional medicine, sports, culture, art, human resources, hygiene, agriculture, and the media.

The history of South African students studying in China is brief. South Africa offers ten scholarships annually; about one hundred South African students now study in China, but the number is increasing.[103] More Chinese students study in South Africa and it receives more Chinese tourists than any other African country. South Africa's Bua News Agency and Xinhua have an agreement on media cooperation and exchanges. As of 2007, Xinhua had not been able to develop a collaborative relationship with the private press.[104] South Africa's Stellenbosch University is the only one in Africa with a Centre for Chinese Studies. A joint undertaking between the governments of South Africa and China, it has a heavy focus on business, investment, and trade issues and includes a Confucius Institute.[105]

Chinese investment in South Africa did not live up to early expectations, although there are now more than eighty Chinese companies in the country. Two factors motivate Chinese investment: South Africa is an attractive market and serves as a springboard for commercial activity in southern Africa and beyond. The cumulative value of Chinese investment in the country as of 2007 was only about $600 million. The Industrial and Commercial Bank of China's purchase near the end of 2007 of 20 percent of South Africa's Standard Bank for $5.5 billion significantly changed the equation. Chinese companies have invested primarily in energy technology, mining and metallurgy, consumer electronics, telecommunications equipment, textiles, apparel, commercial banking, transportation, shipping, light manufacturing, construction, and automobiles.[106] In 2010, Jinchuan Group and the China-Africa Development Fund paid $228 million for a 51 percent stake in Wesizwe Platinum and provided another $650 million in loans to finance its platinum project.[107] In 2011, Citic Group, China's largest state-owned investment company, agreed to pay $469 million for Gold One International Ltd., which has gold mines in South Africa, Mozambique, and Namibia.

In 2008, Sinosteel announced a $440 million investment as part of a joint venture in South Africa to produce ferrochrome and raw chromium ore.[108] Pebble Bed Modular Reactor Ltd. of South Africa is developing a pebble bed nuclear reactor in collaboration with the Institute of Nuclear and New Energy Technology of Tsinghua University and Chinergy Co. Ltd. of China. Based on technology for a research reactor in Beijing, the two sides signed a memorandum of understanding in 2009 to further develop pebble bed technology.[109] China and South Africa began following different pebble bed technology, although the South African design appears to be moving closer to the Chinese model; this may increase collaboration.[110] South Africa is one of the few African countries to have significant direct investments in China; the estimates vary between $1 billion and $2 billion.[111]

While trade between South Africa and China has grown impressively, China imports primarily raw materials from South Africa and South Africa primarily manufactured goods from China.[112] For many years, South Africa ran a trade deficit with China; in 2010, trade was nearly in balance. China imported $11.4 billion of South African goods while South Africa imported $11.9 billion from China. The previous deficits raised serious concerns about the future of a free trade agreement. South Africa is China's second largest trading partner in Africa and China is South Africa's largest trading partner globally. South Africa accounts for almost 20 percent of China's total trade with Africa.[113] In 2009, South Africa opened a tourism office in Beijing to tap into the Chinese travel market; more than 45,000 visited South Africa.

South Africa granted China market economy status in 2004, which effectively prevents South African manufacturers from proving that China gives Chinese producers an unfair advantage.[114] The textile, clothing, and footwear industry is South Africa's sixth largest industry. As a result of production inefficiencies and severe competition from Asian countries, especially China, South African manufacturers lost about one-third of market share while Chinese imports increased significantly. The South African Textile and Clothing Workers Union claimed the industry had lost more than 75,000 jobs since 1996. South African unemployment and severe under-employment are about 50 percent. Labor unions, closely linked to the ANC, are an important factor in South African politics. Labor and management convinced the government to pressure China to restrict textile exports to South Africa. In 2006, China agreed to place voluntary restrictions on thirty-one categories of export products for a two-year period to allow South African industry to become more competitive. This did not solve the problem. Other Asian exporters filled the gap and inefficiencies remained in South Africa's industry. China then offered to train South African workers to build capacity. Nevertheless, China's relations with South African labor unions remain strained.[115] In 2009, China did not renew the voluntary restrictions on textile exports to South Africa.

Of all African countries, South Africa has the highest number of residents of Chinese heritage. Estimates vary widely, but the consensus total is about 300,000. Some 100,000 go back as many as four generations, including 10,000 to 13,000 originally from Taiwan and about 5,000 from Hong Kong. Many others from Taiwan and Hong Kong have departed South Africa. Most Chinese consist of recent arrivals from the PRC. As much as 90 percent of the current community arrived since 1980. The Chinese embassy asserts there are about 80,000 legally registered South African-born Chinese in the country, and acknowledges a total of 150,000 to 200,000. As of 2007, four members of the South African parliament were Chinese, all with Taiwan family connections, although at least one had cordial ties with Beijing. Only about 3 percent of the Chinese community are eligible to vote in South Africa. Larger South African cities such as Johannesburg and Cape

Town have Chinatowns. There are thirty-four Chinese community organizations, three Chinese-language newspapers, one weekly magazine, and one radio station. South Africa's high crime rate and targeting of relatively wealthy Chinese led to the departure of many, especially recent arrivals. There are direct flights between Johannesburg and both Shanghai and Hong Kong.[116]

South Africa has expressed concern about unfair practices in the steel industry, issues of reciprocity, and symmetrical versus asymmetrical tariff reductions. As more Chinese companies enter the construction market, South Africa fears the increased competition will harm the local construction industry. China poses a challenge to the South African automotive industry because many of the global component manufacturers have established operations in China. The role of ubiquitous Chinese traders in South Africa has also caused tension. In 2009, South Africa announced that it would no longer license noncitizens (aimed at Chinese) to sell certain kinds of clothing. In 2011, the president of the ANC Youth League complained about China's policy of extracting Africa's mineral wealth and sending too many workers to Africa. In spite of these concerns, the economic links between South Africa and China are growing rapidly.

South Africa seeks China's support in at least four areas. It wants a restructuring of the UN that results in South African Security Council membership. It seeks reform of the global trading system aimed at improving access of developing countries to developed country markets. It wants enhanced South-South cooperation that leads to collaboration in addressing global injustice, discrimination, and marginalization of developing countries. Finally, it seeks Chinese investment to reduce poverty and underdevelopment.[117] While South Africa believes China offers a great opportunity and that Pretoria is best positioned in Africa to take advantage of relations with China, it does not see these links as a zero-sum game. South African officials insist that they follow an independent foreign policy, not one that takes its cue from China.[118]

Jacob Zuma became South Africa's president in 2009. He visited China as deputy president in 2004 and as president of the ANC in 2008. On both occasions he praised relations with China. In 2008, he commented on the longstanding friendship between the ANC and the CPC, adding that the ANC hoped to learn from the CPC about cadre development and party organization.[119] South Africa under Jacob Zuma has continued its important strategic relationship with China.[120] In 2010, Zuma made his first visit as president to China, accompanied by thirteen cabinet ministers and a 370-strong business delegation. He signed a "comprehensive strategic partnership" that outlined thirty-eight bilateral cooperation agreements. He also called on China to import value-added goods as well as raw materials and to invest in the manufacturing sector instead of focusing solely on projects involving commodities.[121] Vice President Xi Jinping then visited South Africa and signed agreements concerning energy, financial supervision, and trade analysis.

Occasional invitations to the Dalai Lama by nongovernmental groups to visit South Africa have marred the relationship (see Chapter 3). For example, in 2011 Archbishop Desmond Tutu invited the Dalai Lama to attend his eightieth birthday celebration. As the government was debating issuance of a visa, Deputy President Kgalema Motlanthe was in China and Beijing announced $2.5 billion in unspecified investment projects in South Africa. The Dalai Lama did not receive a visa and canceled the trip; Archbishop Tutu was furious and accused the Zuma government of being worse than the apartheid regime.[122] Days later, speaking at the University of Pretoria, Zuma said South Africa's foreign policy is not dictated by any other country.[123]

In 2011, with strong support from China, South Africa became the fifth member of the BRICS (Brazil, Russia, India, China, and South Africa) group. Speaking in Washington in 2011, Deputy President Motlanthe said China takes a long-term approach to Africa. It asks what a country's problems are and how it can help. He added, however, that Africans need to interact with China as a continent, not on a country-by-country basis. Africans seek mutually beneficial terms and do not want to be disadvantaged. The China-Africa relationship is evolving.[124]

Namibia

The League of Nations mandated South West Africa to South Africa in 1920. African nationalists created two organizations—the South West African National Union (SWANU) in 1959 and the South West African People's Organization (SWAPO) a year later. The Organization of African Unity officially recognized SWAPO but not SWANU. Beijing initially treated SWAPO and SWANU equally. The chairman of SWANU visited China in 1960 followed by several SWANU delegations in 1963. SWAPO leader Sam Nujoma went to China in 1964 and reportedly returned to his exile location in Africa with two thousand British pounds and high esteem for the Chinese. By the late 1960s, SWANU had ceased being an important organization. Although SWAPO received strong Soviet support, it was not anti-Chinese and continued to send personnel to China for guerrilla training and obtained limited military assistance. SWAPO's close Soviet ties, however, caused China to also support the failing SWANU through the 1960s.[125]

Beginning in the early 1970s, China strongly backed SWAPO's diplomatic offensive against South Africa in the UN General Assembly. Sam Nujoma returned to China in 1975. The Sino-Soviet conflict restrained Beijing's ability to have a major impact on developments in Namibia as it balanced support for Namibian independence with condemnations of Soviet policy. When Sino-Soviet relations improved, Sam Nujoma visited Beijing in 1983 and received a promise of military assistance. Nujoma praised China's past help and relations with SWAPO became stronger. Nujoma subsequently expressed understanding for China's action in putting down the "counter-revolutionary rebellion" at Tiananmen Square. Namibia recognized Beijing at independence in 1990 and China agreed to provide economic and technical assistance.[126]

Namibian Prime Minister Hage Geingob visited China in 1991, when he signed economic and technical agreements and China agreed to send agricultural experts. In 1992, President Nujoma made his ninth visit to Beijing, his first as president. China increasingly emphasized economic ties and arms sales with Namibia. Vice Premier Zhu Rongji visited Namibia in 1995. The following year, President Jiang Zemin went to Namibia and Nujoma returned to China. Nujoma made additional visits in 1999 and 2000, his last one as president in 2004. In 2003, Namibia received a shipment of 2,600 tons of field guns, mortars, and trucks from China. The CPC established close ties with SWAPO and donated $30,000 to the party. The CPC-SWAPO link remains a central part of the relationship as demonstrated by Namibia's warm reception in 2005 of Li Changchun, member of the Standing Committee of the Political Bureau of the CPC Central Committee. During a visit to China in 2006 by SWAPO leader Nujoma, Hu Jintao underscored the importance of party-to-party ties, adding that the CPC is prepared to expand cooperation with SWAPO. President Hifikepunye Pohamba visited China in 2005 and returned the following year for the FOCAC summit.[127]

The China-Namibia Economic and Trade Mixed Committee held its first session in Beijing in 2005. Chinese construction companies have become increasingly active in Namibia; they built State House and the Supreme Court in Windhoek and magistrate courts in rural towns. China provided a $21.5 million interest-free loan in 2005 for upgrading Namibia's railway system. It then sold Namibia rolling stock valued at about $37 million. Namibia announced that it intended to borrow more than $200 million from China's Export Import Bank to finance sixteen locomotives. Hundreds of Namibian officials and technical personnel have gone to China for training; in 2009, for example, China trained ninety-one technical, management, and professional personnel. Experts from China Central Television came to Windhoek to train Namibian technicians. In 2007, China increased the number of student scholarships to twenty-one and sends each year a small number of Chinese professors and lecturers to teach in Namibia. The Namibian Broadcasting Corporation transmits English-language programs from China. Zhejiang Province began sending medical teams in 1996, and China donated three ambulances to the Ministry of Health and Social Services.[128]

Hu Jintao visited Namibia in 2007 when he proposed a four-point development program that included increasing political exchanges; expanding economic and trade cooperation, including Chinese investment; expanding cooperation in education, public health, culture, tourism, and social development; and coordinating on international affairs. The two presidents signed five documents on economic and technology cooperation, personnel training, education, and tourism. Beijing identified Namibia as a designated tourist location and encouraged Chinese travel agencies to organize group tours. China provided a $4 million grant, $4 million interest-free loan, $14 million credit to build youth training centers, $140 million soft loan, and dozens of scholarships.[129] Since 2001, China has had a space tracking, telemetry, and command station in the coastal town of Swakopmund. Since 2008, eleven Namibians have studied space science and technology in China.[130]

Namibia-China trade has risen sharply in recent years. In 2009, Namibia imported $264 million worth of vehicles, machinery, electrical appliances, textiles, and consumer products from China. China imported $310 million worth of uranium, copper, manganese, and seafood from Namibia. Namibia produces 7.5 percent of the world's uranium and hopes to increase that to 10 percent by 2012. In 2008, China's state-owned Aluminum

Corporation of China acquired a 9.3 percent stake in the Australian-British mining giant Rio Tinto Group. It has a 69 percent interest in Namibia's major uranium mine, Rössing Uranium, which exported more than one hundred tons of uranium to China in both 2004 and 2005.[131]

The presence of many Chinese construction companies and more than five hundred small shops has resulted in criticism from Namibian competitors. There are more than 3,000 Chinese in Namibia; some estimates place the number much higher.[132] Namibia's free press allows persons to express their unhappiness. Namibian construction companies and small traders find it difficult to compete with the Chinese. While they often work harder and with longer hours, they have also been charged with violating Namibian labor laws, paying lower than minimum wage, and doing substandard work. Union leaders question, for example, why Chinese bricklayers come to Namibia when there are unemployed Namibian bricklayers and the unemployment rate exceeds 40 percent.[133] Many local business persons believe the government is going out of its way to protect the Chinese because of close bilateral ties.[134] In 2010, responding to criticism, Namibia banned foreign investment in small and medium-sized transport businesses and hair and beauty salons because of Chinese competition.[135] In 2011, President Pohamba lashed out at Namibian entrepreneurs for condemning the Chinese, saying it was shameful when China "provided us with arms during our liberation struggle."[136]

In 2009, Namibia's anti-corruption investigators alleged that a Chinese company, Nuctech, which manufactures cargo scanners, won a $55 million contract facilitated by $4 million of illegal kickbacks. At the time of the deal, President Hu Jintao's son Hu Haifeng ran the company.[137] At about the same time, China secretly awarded scholarships for study in China to children of nine top Namibian officials, including the president, inspector general of police, and minister of justice. The controversy caused some SWAPO officials to conclude that China is trying to buy influence with the political leadership. Another investigation alleged that a Chinese weapons company funneled $700,000 to the commander of Namibia's defense force. Namibia's president subsequently suspended the general from his post.[138]

Two recent studies—one funded by the Labour Resource and Research Institute and the other conducted by researchers in the Department of Public Management at the Polytechnic of Namibia—were critical of the Chinese presence in Namibia.[139] While Chinese companies make goods more affordable to Namibian consumers and offer some employment and lower construction costs, the studies found many harmful aspects of their presence. The Polytechnic study concluded that local businesses have been squeezed out by Chinese retailers. The Chinese reportedly offer poor-quality products, exploit and disrespect their employees, and take their profits out of the country. One of the studies found that Chinese retail shops offer little benefit for Namibia's development and engage in labor practices that border on colonial mentality.[140]

The small town of Oshikango on the Namibia-Angola border is one of the most vibrant trading centers in Namibia. The first Chinese traders arrived in 1999 and their number reached seventy-five by 2006. The Chinese import their merchandise directly from China. The Chinese business community, which emphasizes its contributions to Namibia's development, arranged to twin Oshikango with a much larger city in China. These positive efforts by the Chinese have not, however, dispelled strong Namibian resentment of the Chinese presence.[141] The government-to-government connection, however, remains strong. Pohamba visited Beijing in 2011 as the rotating president of the Southern African Development Community.

Lesotho

The former British protectorate of Basutoland became independent as the Kingdom of Lesotho in 1966. The PRC began funding the nationalistic Basutoland Congress Party (BCP) in 1964 when the BCP leader sent his brother and the party's secretary-general to Beijing. The PRC tried without success to link the Communist Party of Lesotho, which had close ties to the pro-Soviet SACP, with the BCP.[142] The Basutoland National Party (BNP) led by Chief Leabua Jonathan, who was hostile toward communism, won a contested election. Jonathan became prime minister at independence and recognized Taipei two weeks later. The BNP lost the 1970 elections to the BCP, but Jonathan aborted the result and retained power. As Lesotho's ties with white-ruled South Africa worsened, Jonathan considered establishing ties with Beijing. It was not until 1983, however, that Jonathan visited the PRC and Lesotho finally recognized Beijing. The two countries signed economic and technical cooperation and cultural exchange agreements. King Moshoeshoe II visited Beijing in 1985 and Queen Mamohato in 1987, but

China's official visitors to Lesotho through the mid-1980s were at the ministerial level or below.[143]

In 1986, Pretoria imposed an economic embargo on Lesotho, which is surrounded by South Africa, and encouraged the overthrow of Chief Jonathan. The military government that took power assured the PRC it would continue good relations. Lesotho maintained ties with Beijing until 1990 when Maseru again recognized Taiwan. Very modest assistance from the PRC and more generous offers from Taiwan almost certainly caused Lesotho to switch sides. Elections then replaced pro-Taiwan congressmen by those who favored Beijing. In 1994, Lesotho renewed ties with Beijing. The role of South Africa affected Sino-Lesotho relations negatively during Pretoria's apartheid government and positively since majority rule. In 1997, China sent its first medical team to Lesotho and began a small scholarship program. In 2000, it implemented cultural exchanges. Prime Minister Pakalitha Mosisili visited Beijing in 2001 and 2005 and attended the 2006 FOCAC summit.[144]

Lesotho and China signed fourteen economic and technical assistance agreements between 1983 and 2005. China provided grant funding for the National Convention Center, industrial park, and National Library and Archives building. It agreed to expand the government radio and television facilities and build a new Parliament building. China provided food aid during drought years, offered interest-free loans, and canceled most of Lesotho's debt in 2001. It donated more than $2 million worth of equipment and medicine and provides annual training in China for specialists, forty-eight in 2009 alone. In 2007, the CPC hosted the general secretary of the ruling Lesotho Congress for Democracy (LCD) and agreed to share state administration experiences.[145]

The trade balance highly favors China. From 2002 through 2009, China never imported more than $2 million worth of goods from Lesotho, whereas Lesotho's imports from China averaged $51 million. An estimated 10,000 Chinese, many of them small traders, live in Lesotho and are causing local businesses to close.[146] Anti-Chinese sentiment is rising, driven by the main opposition political party, the All Basotho Convention (ABC), and local radio stations. The ABC has a populist platform based in part on criticizing the success of the Chinese community and accusing the LCD of colluding with Chinese businesses. The Chinese Business Association of Lesotho insists it contributes to the development of the country. Lesotho is another example of a small country with a highly visible Chinese community that competes successfully with local business people. The government is caught balancing a desire for investment and aid from China with alienation of its own business community.[147]

Malawi

The British colony of Nyasaland became independent as Malawi in 1964 under Prime Minister Hastings Banda. Prior to independence, Banda said he would recognize Beijing and support China's request for UN membership. In an effort to avoid the PRC-Taiwan controversy, however, he invited representatives of both to attend independence ceremonies. Beijing, concluding this would give credibility to a two China policy, did not accept the invitation although Zhou Enlai sent a congratulatory telegram. According to Banda, China's ambassador in Dar es Salaam, Ho Ying, subsequently attempted to bribe members of the Malawi government to recognize Beijing. This resulted in a cabinet crisis as some in the government were prepared to do so. When Banda refused to go along with the scheme, all the ministers resigned or Banda forced them out. Banda still favored PRC admission to the UN when he addressed the General Assembly in 1964. After learning the full extent of Beijing's interference in Malawi's affairs, he increasingly turned toward Taiwan and became outspokenly anti-Beijing. At the 1966 ceremony upon becoming a republic, Banda (now president) invited a delegation from Taiwan and announced Malawi would establish diplomatic relations with Taipei.[148]

Banda fell from power in 1994, but Malawi continued to rebuff efforts by China to switch recognition to Beijing. Malawi did, however, send observers to the 2000 FOCAC in Beijing and the 2003 FOCAC in Addis Ababa. The government that assumed power in Malawi in 2004 was less enthusiastic about maintaining ties with Taiwan. Although invited to the 2006 FOCAC in Beijing, Malawi did not send any representatives, probably because of pressure from Taiwan.[149]

In December 2007, Malawi engaged the Chinese firm Huawei Technologies to implement a $23 million project to modernize its telecommunications network. Malawi and China secretly established diplomatic ties on 28 December 2007. The Taiwanese foreign minister, scheduled to visit Malawi at the beginning of January, canceled his trip at the last minute. At the time of the break, Taiwan was providing about $400 million in aid and funding for the ruling political party. Taipei announced it would not try to compete with China's dollar diplomacy.[150]

Malawi and China lost no time solidifying the relationship. Malawi offers a case study on how China responds when it convinces a country to switch recognition from Taipei to Beijing. President Bingu wa Mutharika made a seven-day visit to China in March 2008 when he opened Malawi's embassy and assured China that Malawi will adhere to the one China policy and oppose Taiwan's independence effort. The two countries signed agreements on trade, investment, technology cooperation, and preferential tariff treatment. The defense ministers agreed to strengthen military cooperation.[151] On his return to Lilongwe, Mutharika said the relationship with China opens a new chapter in Malawi's bilateral relations. Malawi received a $288 million aid package including a $192 million five-year concessionary loan for development projects and an $88 million grant for construction of a road and new Parliament building in Lilongwe. The $41 million Parliament building has been completed; other projects underway include a national stadium, international conference center, and a new science university. The Anhui Foreign Economic Construction Corporation built a number of these projects and a $15 million hotel that opened in 2011. China also offered about $3 million for defense cooperation, $1.5 million for construction of two rural schools, and twelve student scholarships. The Shanghai Construction Company is building a $90 million five-star hotel in the capital.[152]

In 2008, Zhou Yongkang, a member of the Standing Committee of the Political Bureau of the CPC Central Committee, welcomed in Beijing the general secretary of the Malawian Democratic Progress Party. The two sides agreed to increase party-to-party cooperation.[153] The two countries signed a memorandum of understanding that allows China's private sector to invest in cotton, tobacco, fertilizer, cement, infrastructure, mining, tourism, and professional services. Malawi offered duty free status for 440 products and China announced forty scholarships for short courses in economic management.[154] China's ambassador to Malawi stated that China had become one of Malawi's most important development partners. During 2008, Beijing invited 105 government officials and 129 journalists, scientists, professors, and business people to visit China and China's first medical team arrived in Malawi. In 2009, China's Communist Youth League sent twenty young volunteers to Malawi.[155]

In 2009, China's state-owned telecommunications company ZTE won the bid for a $25 million project including government security systems used for police dispatching, prison management, identification registration, and presidential elections. ZTE established an office in Malawi in 2003, well before Lilongwe recognized Beijing. By 2011, at least fifty Chinese companies had invested $59 million in Malawi.[156] In 2010, President Mutharika attended the Shanghai World Expo and met with Hu Jintao.

Malawi historically has had a trade deficit with China, although it has narrowed with diplomatic relations. The first year after Malawi switched recognition, its total trade with Beijing was almost five times that with Taipei. In 2010, Malawi imported $88 million worth of products from China and China imported $31 million from Malawi.[157]

Not all Malawians are enthusiastic about China's significant engagement. The Human Rights Consultative Committee in Malawi complained that Chinese aid and investment lack transparency and do not include a rule of law component. The business community called on China to manufacture cigarettes in Malawi rather than just purchase its tobacco.[158] The African Labour Research Network was critical of Chinese labor practices and inadequate attention to worker safety regulations. There are growing press accounts of ivory smuggling by Chinese nationals and complaints about Chinese traders. During violent protests against the Malawi government in mid-2011, demonstrators looted a number of shops owned by Chinese and Indians.[159]

Swaziland

The Kingdom of Swaziland is the only country in Africa that has never established diplomatic relations with Beijing. It became independent in 1968 and recognized Taiwan immediately. Taipei values Swaziland as a diplomatic ally and Swazi leaders, including the king, visit Taipei on a regular basis.[160] In the period before independence, Beijing made half-hearted efforts to reach out to groups in Swaziland such as the Progressive Party of Swaziland and a nascent Swaziland Communist Party.[161] These organizations never became significant and the PRC decided Swaziland was not a likely partner any time soon.

Although China has been unsuccessful at the political and diplomatic level in Swaziland, this has not deterred it from making economic and commercial inroads. Goods made in China are widely available in Swaziland. In 2009, Swaziland imported $18 million worth of products from China and China $15 million from Swaziland. There are more Chinese in Swaziland from China than from Taiwan. Most operate small retail shops and some work in textile factories owned by Taiwanese.[162] Swaziland is a member of the Southern African Customs Union (SACU). All the other members recognize Beijing, so Swaziland engages on trade issues with China in the context of SACU.[163]

As China becomes increasingly engaged in international conferences and African subregional organizations, there are opportunities for interacting with representatives of countries such as Swaziland that recognize Taiwan. A Swazi delegation attended the UN-sponsored 1995 World Conference on Women held in Beijing.[164] Swaziland sent observers to the 2003 FOCAC in Addis Ababa. Although invited to the 2006 FOCAC in Beijing, Swaziland did not participate, probably because of pressure from Taiwan.[165] Two senior Swazi officials attended the 2007 African Development Bank meeting hosted by China in Shanghai.[166]

A number of the authors' Swazi interlocutors, especially those in the business community, questioned the wisdom of maintaining ties with Taiwan. They doubted that Swaziland benefits significantly from the Taiwan connection and assumed that China would offer more. There is a minority group in the Swazi Parliament that favors closer ties with China and has on occasion voiced this view. Although parliamentarians are generally becoming more engaged on foreign issues, the Swazi king controls foreign policy and none of our interlocutors suggested he is inclined to switch to Beijing.

12

Conclusion: Looking Forward

> Too many uncertainties lie ahead to predict how others might
> judge a "Chinese model," but there is little question that China's
> ongoing experience will be observed, assessed, and—where
> successful—drawn upon.
>
> —Bruce Larkin, 1986

In this volume we have examined China-Africa relations with a historical, topical, and geographical approach and through the eyes of the Africanist, Sinologist, and policymaker. China-Africa relations encompass a broad, multilayered set of fifty-four bilateral, political, economic, military, and social relationships, and we have investigated each of them. Bilateral relations require two interlocutors, yet China's size and resources allow it to initiate most of its interaction with African countries. China tends to determine the level of interaction, the types of activities, and the terms of agreements. African states want more international respect and acceptance of their continent as an emerging world player. China's diplomats routinely say they want to expand relations with Africa in a manner that is "win-win" for both Africa and China. Not surprisingly, however, China seeks principally to secure its own interests.

For China, Mao's *Little Red Book* has been replaced with a balance sheet. China is a rising power on the international stage whose primary objectives include expanding its influence in the developing world, in Africa particularly. Beginning in the mid-1990s, Chinese producers' growing need for raw materials and export markets resulted in increased trade and investment between China and Africa. China is now engaged at all levels and competing successfully in most areas with Western countries. As China's political and commercial relationships have grown, so has the presence of its state-run firms, which are building bridges, dams, roads, railroads, ports, and oil infrastructure.

Construction services, telecommunications equipment, and affordable consumer products are now China's most important exports to emerging economies the world over. Scores of state-run companies and government bureaus at both central and provincial levels lead China's economic relationships in Africa. Independent Chinese merchants with vertically integrated *guanxi*-bound supply networks on the mainland now dominate Africa's consumer electronics and textile markets. In 2010, China accounted for over 13 percent of Africa's total foreign trade, higher than at any other time in history. Even Chinese FDI, which still lags that of Western countries, is growing at a more rapid rate than Western investment.

Many African countries see expanded relations with China as a way to gain international prestige and make money. African leaders generally want their countries to join the global supply chain, attract increased investment, and be treated as equals in international diplomacy. For Africans, China offers additional economic and political opportunities that are largely untainted by colonialism and sweetened by the allure of a diplomatic relationship free of political strings and public criticism. African leaders look to China to protect their interests through Beijing's threat to wield its veto on the UN Security Council. In this way, African leaders enjoy the diplomatic fruits born from their predecessors' support for Beijing's campaign in the 1960s and 1970s to obtain its seat on the Council, and their resistance to Western countries' efforts to have the United Nations Commission on Human Rights label the PRC as a human rights abuser in the 1980s and 1990s.

Economically, many Africans welcome the benefits of rising energy and commodity prices driven by China's export industries' growing demand. As a result, new streams of wealth have opened on the continent, enriching some Africans. Meanwhile, despite concerns about worker safety, wages, and environmental issues, Chinese investments provide employment and training for thousands of Africans. In the wake of the 2008 financial crisis, as Western economic strength receded, Africa's economic relations with China became an increasingly important engine for growth and market expansion. In 2010 and 2011, labor unrest among China's workers in export sectors forced Chinese firms to increase wages and consider reducing their dependence on low-cost manufacturing. In the future, as Chinese wages continue to rise, it is likely that a new crop of moneyed Chinese investors will take advantage of increasingly cheap African labor and investment tax breaks available in African SEZs largely financed and built with China's assistance.

The purpose of this chapter is to go beyond our analysis of the past and present and project some of the principal themes of China-Africa relations into the future. As the relationship matures how will it develop? What opportunities and problems are likely to emerge over time? Of course, any attempt to predict the future is fraught with uncertainty; we hope time will show our projections to be accurate and forward thinking. This section offers eight broad predictions about the future of China-Africa relations based on the general themes articulated in the introduction and elaborated throughout the volume.

(1) Closer Relations Between the CPC and African Political Parties
Relations between the CPC and African political parties continue to grow and a number of African ruling parties have become close to the CPC. These parties—including the ruling parties of Zimbabwe, South Africa, Namibia, Tanzania, Ethiopia, and Sudan—have sent their cadre to train in CPC academies and their children to CPC-sponsored youth festivals in China. Behind the rhetoric of equality, vast disparities in resources and intraparty cohesion persist in the CPC's relations with African political parties. This relationship is different from the international outreach normally conducted by Western political parties, whose more limited resources are spent on costly elections and whose mandate does not include high level outreach to foreign political parties. For the Republican and Democratic parties in the United States, for instance, nothing approximates the regularity of CPC delegations to Africa, the diversity of cooperative programs, or their generosity toward African political parties. In 2010, the International Republican Institute conducted programs in nine African countries and the National Democratic Institute had them in twenty-one countries. These programs consist primarily of civic education, voter education, and modest support for training political parties, but almost never involve high level political contact. Operating out of China's embassies, the CPC International Department, by contrast, regularly organizes exchanges at the highest levels and does not disclose the location of cadre posted in Africa.

It remains to be seen if the trend of African democratization witnessed over the past decade and a half will be influenced by an illiberal foreign political party based thousands of miles away. What is known, however, is the role China can play if its national interests result in intervention. Already in Zimbabwe the CPC's financial and material support for the ruling party appears to have changed the course of the 2008 elections, while in Chad and Sudan China's support may have altered the political fortunes of presidents Idriss Deby and Omar al-Bashir. These interventions were done not to support one particular type of regime over another but to ensure that Chinese interests in those countries remained protected. For the same reason, when an African ruling party falls from power the CPC consistently reaches out to its successor with material and political support. In 2011, for instance, China quickly and effectively built relations with new political leaders in South Sudan, Libya, Tunisia, Zambia, and Egypt.

The influence of the CPC in African affairs will extend only as far as African political parties allow it. China's national interests such as access to natural resources, profitable infrastructure construction, and expanded export markets can be a powerful force for development when combined with farsighted African national interests. It is in authoritarian and repressive regimes where the CPC's influence can raise the most concerns since its support will not deter an African party that has already committed human rights abuses from continuing such practices. In some extreme cases, such as Zimbabwe and Guinea, CPC support for the ruling party appears to have emboldened autocracies. But as alarming as these examples are, they involve few African countries, and one lesson of this book is that it is dangerous to generalize about China's relations with fifty-four African countries based on a handful of outlying cases.

(2) China Offers Africa an Alternative Economic Partner, Not a Development Model

In the literature on China-Africa relations and in policy-making circles there is much debate about whether Beijing offers a particular development model in Africa. We believe our book demonstrates that a multipronged, centrally guided strategy, although disjointed at times, exists. China's contemporary package approach has a long history and many of its elements were spelled out in the PRC's 2006 Africa white paper. But China's Africa strategy should not be confused with the promotion of a "Chinese development model" or the so-called "Beijing Consensus." Rather than the new rival paradigm that some have identified, China's contemporary Africa strategy is simply the international component of the country's larger efforts to build its comprehensive national strength.

We expect that China and Africa will continue to expand their economic relations in the absence of a large-scale social and political crisis in China that unseats the CPC. Chinese firms' raw materials imports from African suppliers will grow. When coupled with China's comparative advantage in textile and consumer goods production and the relatively small percentage of Chinese trade conducted with African countries, only about 4 percent in 2010, there is ample potential for continued expansion of Sino-African trade.

But it is the composition of trade that continues to be the most significant. China's massive population and lack of labor rights protections have allowed for a largely cheap and compliant labor force that cannot be matched in Africa today. China's economies of scale, subsidies to holders of capital for power, fuel, garbage collection, and other materials and social services have catalyzed its "Go Global" strategy and made it nearly impossible for African manufactured products to enter the Chinese market. We predict that this trend will continue in the short and medium term and African markets will continue to import large amounts of Chinese consumer products and sell their finite raw materials. Chinese state-run firms will continue to help extract raw materials from African countries for export to China. Under such conditions, some African countries risk falling victim to the so-called Dutch Disease, whereby the economy becomes dominated by a single export commodity enriching a small group of elites who control natural resources at the expense of the larger workforce.

African countries' leaders will continue to request infrastructure projects from their Chinese counterparts. But dams, railroads, roads, and bridges come with substantial costs, initially underwritten by loans with low interest rates. For some African countries, debts with China's state-owned firms and banks stretch into the billions. For countries without vast natural resources—like Ethiopia whose indebtedness to China hovers around $3 billion—we predict a contentious repayment schedule. By contrast, resource exporters such as oil-rich Angola, which has borrowed $14.5 billion from Beijing, will likely pay back their loans over time. Still others, such as the DRC, which is borrowing $6.5 billion from China, have the mineral riches but because of fluctuating copper and cobalt prices and instability in mining regions, may experience repayment troubles.

It is unlikely China's leaders will begin to advocate actively a "China development model" or a "Beijing Consensus." Instead they will do business wherever money can be made, from democratic South Africa to authoritarian Sudan. In the end, however, the burden falls on African governments and producers to ensure the proceeds from the sale of finite resources are spent wisely. Chinese infrastructure projects require skilled Africans to maintain them. To the extent African governments can channel the proceeds of their resource sales and Chinese assistance into their own domestic development (e.g., education and infrastructure development) they will take advantage of China's presence. If corruption is permitted to squander Chinese largesse and investment capital, Africans will surely suffer most.

Looking farther into the future, more opportunities exist for African growth and development thanks to Chinese infrastructure projects, especially if China continues its debt relief policies. The costs of capital and labor for Chinese firms in China have already begun to rise, bringing with them new opportunities for African exporters. In 2011, China remained under international pressure to allow its currency to rise in value; its export sector firms are facing calls from unofficial labor organizations to increase wages and from all Chinese to stem the tide of environmental degradation that eats away at its farmland and rivers. These facts ought to alert African officials and investors who would do well to seek opportunity in industries where they can gain export competitiveness and develop alternative products to capture the profits low-cost Chinese suppliers reap today. Profit-seeking Chinese capital holders may also push this process. A new crop of independently wealthy Chinese investors may use its experience and business contacts in Western and Chinese markets to take advantage of pockets of cheaper African labor. This potential transfer of productive capacity to select African countries could place some on the first link of the global supply chain and target Western markets. Chinese markets, by contrast, are likely to remain difficult for African manufactured products and textiles to penetrate for at least a decade to come.

(3) Issues of Sovereignty, Particularly Taiwan, Will Remain Paramount for China
Sensitive sovereignty-related issues—Taiwan, Xinjiang, and Tibet—play a role in all China's political relations with foreign countries, not just those in Africa. In cases where African states or political parties have contradicted

the PRC's position on these subjects they have endured a variety of negative consequences, from diplomatic threats to the removal of investment, public criticism, and even Chinese military and financial support for rebel groups.

Taiwan remains the most sensitive topic for China because Taipei and Beijing diplomats have long competed for official diplomatic recognition of African countries. After decades of dollar diplomacy competition, a diplomatic truce initiated late in 2008 has left Taiwan with four small diplomatic partners in Africa—Burkina Faso, Swaziland, São Tomé and Principe, and Gambia.

Although Taiwan's commercial presence will remain, within a decade we predict its official diplomatic presence will be gone from Africa. The unofficial diplomatic truce between Beijing and Taipei since the election of Taiwan's China-friendly President Ma Ying-jeou will not ensure Taipei's long-term diplomatic presence on the continent. For the moment, Taiwan's diplomatic partners are under diminished pressure to switch sides and can freely trade with both Taiwan and the mainland. But if a government less friendly to Beijing were to take power in Taipei, China is likely to swiftly resume diplomatic pressure on Taiwan's last four African partners. The last holdout will probably be the landlocked Kingdom of Swaziland, the only African country that has never recognized Beijing. Conversely, if at some future date both sides accept a union or federation including the mainland and Taiwan, the existing unofficial diplomatic truce would become irrelevant. In either case, the days of Taiwan's official recognition in Africa appear numbered.

Islam, first a basis for CPC outreach through the China Islamic Association, has taken on new and complex dimensions amid the growth of Islamist activity in North and East Africa and large-scale Uighur riots in Urumqi, Xinjiang, in July 2009 that left more than two hundred dead. Repression of Islam in China is likely to grow as a source of concern among African countries with large Muslim populations. Already al-Qaeda's North Africa branch, citing mistreatment of Uighurs, has attacked Chinese workers in Algeria, killing Algerian bodyguards. State suppression of Uighur nationalism in China has also backfired, and made global jihad movements more attractive to Uighurs. This risks unintentionally expanding Uighur separatist linkages with Islamists worldwide, including those operating in Africa. As China's international profile grows, its suppression of Islam is likely to increasingly undermine relations with some Muslim groups in Africa.

We are less concerned about Tibet's influence on China-Africa relations. Tibetans lack the global communication and financial networks common to the Islamic world. Tibet has no jihad agenda, and there are no sizeable Tibetan communities in Africa. The only support for Tibet will be found in a few countries such as South Africa where there are strong human rights and civil society movements tied to the West.

(4) China "Soft Outreach" to Africans Will Expand, But Its Impact Is Uncertain
China's educational outreach initiatives have been successful in their efforts to build a network between Chinese and African elites. This effort includes sponsoring training of Africans in China and sending Chinese experts to teach Africans in Africa. Xinhua is one of the fastest growing news services in Africa, and it is developing an increasing number of formal news sharing and journalist training programs with African news agencies and papers. China is also rapidly expanding Confucius Institutes that introduce Chinese culture and offer Chinese language instruction in Africa and there is every indication this will continue. The extension of these programs is a sign China seeks to build its influence in "soft" ways that support a framework for bilateral economic and political cooperation.

Educational outreach programs are often the first opportunity elite Africans have to interact with Chinese. They are administered through official channels at China's Ministry of Education or a university. But the impression is not always good. Some Africans who have been educated in China complain about discrimination and limitations on political and religious activities; many Chinese students consider Africans unruly and resent their better living quarters. Some African journalists have also found Xinhua's journalism training programs come with an unwelcome political veneer.

It is unlikely that Chinese culture will have a strong influence on Africans. Despite Chinese efforts to expand their cultural penetration in Africa through films, festivals, sports, art, and delegation exchanges we found that African youth remain more closely tied to Western cultural imports such as African American hip-hop music and fashion and European football (i.e., soccer). These remain more popular in Africa than any Chinese cultural import. Few Africans display outward signs of envy toward Chinese culture, quality of life, or social institutions and Africans we interviewed appeared uninterested in Chinese music, films, and most popular culture.

Most do not aspire to live in China or to gain further exposure to things Chinese.

(5) Some Chinese Will Settle in Africa But Almost All Africans Will Return from China

There are Chinese communities in Africa that date back to the 1800s and the number of Chinese choosing to live in Africa is increasing. Each Chinese has his or her own reasons for moving to Africa; most are economically motivated, a few based on political and personal reasons. Although diplomats and those connected with large Chinese companies and assistance projects almost always return to China, increasing numbers of traders and small-businesspersons have apparently chosen to stay in Africa. In the past, these people were largely from Taiwan. Over the last two decades, however, they have come increasingly from the mainland. Although some express a desire to return someday to China, they will likely stay as long as they can earn a living. If security is adequate and profits are possible, "Chinatowns" will continue to grow throughout Africa.

African communities in China are another story. Although they may still marvel at Chinese acrobats and Kung Fu films, Africans studying and working in China are more likely to bring their culture with them than to adopt Chinese fashion, culinary, musical, or artistic tastes. They tend to confine themselves to large metropolitan areas and do not exhibit the passion to "save China" that motivated many Westerners over the centuries. China maintains strict control over foreigners and the police and immigration authorities in Guangzhou and Beijing have cracked down on Africans who overstay their visas or are involved in illicit activities. Their limited Chinese language skills and lack of cultural understanding can result in misunderstandings and local discrimination. Yet, a small minority of Africans has settled for over a decade or more in major Chinese cities. These exceptions notwithstanding, it is highly unlikely that large numbers of African residents, of the type that has developed in Guangzhou, will form permanent settlements in China.

(6) China's Investments in Africa Will Increase and Most Will Pay Off

China's investment in Africa will increase and help Beijing to shape its relations with African countries. In 2011, China had $3.2 trillion in foreign exchange reserves and is establishing the financial networks in African countries necessary to expand investments and better assess their profitability. In the banking sector, for instance, China will expand its interests through purchasing shares in or partnering with African and international banks that already have a presence in African markets and knowledge of borrowers' creditworthiness.

Most of China's investment in extractive industries will likely turn a profit and, to the extent that China continues to require oil and minerals, attract even more investment in these sectors. Although Africans prefer Chinese invest in small and medium-sized firms that tend to create longer-term job opportunities for locals, returns in these sectors are the most uncertain. Chinese investors have shown over the past decade that they have been willing to take risks, but usually only to obtain natural resources, as occurred in unstable regions such as Ethiopia's Ogaden, Sudan's southern Kordofan, and Nigeria's Niger Delta. Some private Chinese companies that invested in copper mining and smelting in the DRC pulled out when copper prices collapsed. Chinese firms are likely to make many of the same mistakes Western companies did before they gained an adequate appreciation for difficulties on the ground in Africa. Chinese investment will also remain dependent on the volatility of international commodity prices. Despite these concerns, however, we predict that the lion's share of Chinese investments will be profitable.

In an effort to mitigate the political risk associated with investments in many African countries, China's state-owned enterprises will expand joint venture partnerships with African countries' state-run corporations, other foreign countries' state-run firms, and multinational corporations. This has already occurred in the case of China's Sinopec, BP, and Sonangol in Angola; India's Oil and Natural Gas Company, Ltd., Malaysia's Petronas, China's CNPC, and Sudapet in Sudan; CNPC's joint oil project with Total and Tullow in Uganda; and Chinalco and Rio Tinto's joint iron ore venture in Guinea. Chinese companies will increasingly look for joint venture partners to share information and risk and expand economies of scale in Africa's resource sector.

(7) China Will Slowly and Cautiously Expand Its Security Presence in Africa

The PLA has been assiduous at maintaining high level military contacts with all the African countries that recognize Beijing. China's arms producers sell considerable quantities of small arms in Africa, which are praised by Africans for their low cost and reasonable quality. From a security point of view, China's military ties with African countries have not directly threatened African or U.S. interests in the post-Mao period. But as China moves from a regional power to a global power it will become more difficult to continue a benign security relationship with African countries. Meanwhile, African countries are likely to increase pressure on China to provide security in areas where China has made large commercial investments.

China's close military ties to Sudan and Zimbabwe and the fact that its small arms and light weapons have increasingly found their way into African conflict zones have drawn criticism from human rights groups and Western governments. With these exceptions, however, China's military activities in Africa have been largely noncontroversial. The PLA has avoided building bases and establishing formal military alliances in Africa, while its contribution to international efforts in African peacekeeping and countering piracy have been lauded around the world. China has every intention of continuing its participation in the anti-piracy operation in the Gulf of Aden. In fact, this engagement is forcing the PLA to identify land-based facilities in Africa to support the operation that do not conflict with its policy of no bases. China has a special interest in this operation. Chinese shipping has been directly threatened and the international community, including the United States, welcomes China's participation.

China has demonstrated willingness to participate in peacekeeping operations in Africa, although Beijing restricts PLA personnel to noncombat assignments. There is no indication that China intends to increase significantly participation in African peacekeeping operations or put its soldiers in the line of fire. For example, both China and the United States called for a UN peacekeeping force in Somalia, but neither expressed willingness to contribute combat troops.

All signs suggest that China's naval expansion in the Indian Ocean will reach eastern Africa. A PLA navy hospital ship visited ports in northeast Africa in 2010 and PLA ships attached to the anti-piracy operation made port calls in eastern and southern Africa in 2011; these are harbingers of the future. A growing number of port calls in Africa is an indicator of China's expanding security relationship in Africa. While there is no obvious reason for African countries to deny China access to their ports, the sight of PLA navy vessels might begin to raise questions among Africans about China's intentions and could enhance tension with the U.S., Indian, and

European countries' navies. China has already bumped up against the Indian navy, which shadowed its ships in the Indian Ocean on their way to join the anti-piracy mission off the Somali coast.

Africa's natural resources, particularly oil and minerals, will continue to influence China's security relations with individual African countries. Those countries that have the most to offer China will tend to be the recipient of greater military collaboration. We have seen this in the cases of Angola, South Africa, Zimbabwe, Sudan, Nigeria, Gabon, Chad, Algeria, and the DRC. All have resources sought by Chinese firms and all have benefited from close security ties with Beijing. At the same time, there are exceptions. Tanzania and Egypt, which do not sell large quantities of natural resources to China, also have strong military ties with China. In fact, China has been careful to develop at least a modest security relationship with every African country with which it maintains diplomatic relations. This will continue.

As the numbers of Chinese in Africa increase so do the chances that they will come into harm's way. Historically, China has relied on host governments to protect its nationals. China's firms operating in Africa have generally demonstrated willingness to accept higher security risks for their workers than their Western counterparts. As attacks on Chinese nationals increase, Beijing will have to decide when risks are acceptable, and when it wants to expand security to ensure its citizens' safety or recall them from areas or countries where security is questionable. The evacuation in 2011 of 36,000 Chinese from Libya and loss of huge contracts was a wakeup call.

For the time being, China's military and security relations with Africa offer the best of all worlds for China. Unlike the United States, African states do not perceive China as a threatening military power. Its active engagement with militaries in Africa and participation in peacekeeping and anti-piracy operations are viewed favorably. Even its close security ties with countries such as Sudan and Zimbabwe, often condemned by the West, are almost never criticized in African capitals. The question is how long China and Africa can maintain an untroubled security relationship.

(8) Differing Perceptions of China Among Africans and Chinese Will Emerge
Another evolving phenomenon subtly influencing China-Africa relations is the gap between China's own national image and African views of China. This discrepancy was captured in an exchange between a PRC official and

a diplomat from a Southeast Asian country in a Dupont Circle restaurant in 2005. The PRC official explained that China was "assuming its rightful place" and simply "bringing its ship into the international harbor." "Just be sure not to drown us smaller boats when you do!" quipped his interlocutor, who was of Chinese descent.

For many mainland Chinese, party-centric nationalism has become an important part of their identity as Chinese. They perceive criticism of *anything* Chinese, particularly the CPC, as an attack on *everything* Chinese, hence, disapproval of China's state-run corporations and arms sales is readily attributable to Western bullying and American hegemonism. Nationalists' chat rooms and those administered by China's official state-run press regularly stoke jingoistic fears. Such antagonism and strict press censorship often blind millions of Chinese from the harsh truths associated with some of China's state-run firms' activities in Africa. Incidents that have been censored in the Chinese state-run press include Hu Jintao's son Hu Haifeng's corruption scandal, which cost the Namibian Defense Force commander his job, violent riots at China's Chambishi copper mine in Zambia over working conditions and pay, and any reference to China's dealings with apartheid-era South Africa. Chinese are generally completely unaware of smaller countries' perceptions that they are being drowned in the wake of China's rise. For them China remains the champion of the developing world.

Yet, China's central government is well aware of growing resentment toward Beijing abroad, which it has dubbed the "China threat" theory. To cope with this image gap, China has sought to expand its influence over press outlets that control its image including African radio, newspapers, and online sites. The Chinese state-run press, including Xinhua, China Central Television, and China Radio International, work in concert to design China's image abroad. China's state-run press will continue to expand and disseminate information to future generations of Africans through agreements to supply international news to African media outlets as have been inked in Kenya, Togo, and elsewhere. These efforts will be largely successful in building and maintaining a good image of China among millions of Africans. Of course, Africans that interact with Chinese will transmit their own perceptions back to their societies.

The spread of anti-Chinese narratives in Africa need not have coherent or predictable consequences. For example, we cited in Chapter 7 the riots in 2010 against Chinese businesses following a soccer match in the DRC when the local team lost and fans mistook the Japanese referee for Chinese. Incidents like this suggest that simmering anti-Chinese sentiment at the grassroots level is an increasingly powerful force that can be activated by either spontaneous, unforeseen events or ambitious politicians for their own purposes. An even larger concern for China is the increasing antagonism that we documented in the regional chapters toward the growing community of Chinese traders and small shop owners who are forcing Africans out of business and causing some African manufacturers to shut down because they cannot compete.

In the 1950s and 1960s, Beijing's primary motivation in Africa was affirmation of its own brand of communism through domestic propaganda and rhetorical support for national liberation and revolutionary movements. In the years following the turmoil of Mao Zedong's Cultural Revolution and the deepening Sino-Soviet split, an increasingly pragmatic leadership looked to secure China's geopolitical interests by luring the Soviets into costly African conflicts. Today, largely to meet China's growing economic and resource needs, Beijing seeks to bolster its trade and political ties with Africa. As relationships among Chinese and Africans become increasingly mature, the future appears ripe with opportunity for both sides, but of course, with increased interaction, more problems are bound to emerge. As China-Africa relations expand we hope that the number of scholars working on the topic and the application of new and innovative research methods will keep pace.

APPENDIX 1. ESTABLISHMENT OF PRC RELATIONS WITH AFRICAN COUNTRIES

African country	Initial date of establishment of diplomatic relations	Subsequent changes in relations
Egypt	30 May 1956	
Morocco	1 November 1958	
Algeria	20 December 1958	The PRC recognized Algeria's provisional government on this date and Algeria's independent government in 1962.
Sudan	4 February 1959	
Guinea	14 October 1959	
Ghana	5 July 1960	Following a military coup, Ghana precipitated during 1966 the closure of the Chinese embassy, charging that China supported former leader Kwame Nkrumah, who took exile in Guinea. Chinese personnel left in November. Ghana restored ties in January 1972.
Mali	25 October 1960	
Somalia	14 December 1960	
Congo, Dem. Rep.	20 February 1961	The PRC recognized on this date Congo's government headed by Antoine Gizenga. In September 1961, after Gizenga joined the Adula government, which recognized Taiwan, China suspended relations. China established relations with the Mobutu government in November 1972.
Tanzania	9 December 1961	
Uganda	18 October 1962	
Kenya	14 December 1963	
Burundi	21 December 1963	Burundi severed ties with the PRC in January 1965 following hostile Chinese activities in Burundi. The two countries restored ties in October 1971.

African country	Initial date of establishment of diplomatic relations	Subsequent changes in relations
Tunisia	10 January 1964	Disagreement between Tunisian government and Chinese embassy in September 1967 resulted in Chinese suspension of relations. The two countries restored relations in 1971.
Congo, Brazzaville	22 February 1964	
Central African Republic	29 September 1964	The CAR severed relations with the PRC in January 1966 and recognized Taiwan in 1968. The two countries restored relations in August 1976. The CAR again recognized Taiwan in July 1991 and the PRC suspended relations. In January 1998, the PRC and CAR resumed relations for a third time.
Zambia	29 October 1964	
Benin	12 November 1964	Benin severed relations with the PRC in January 1966 and resumed relations with Taiwan in April. The PRC and Benin restored relations in December 1972.
Mauritania	19 July 1965	
Equatorial Guinea	15 October 1970	
Ethiopia	24 November 1970	
Nigeria	10 February 1971	
Cameroon	26 March 1971	
Sierra Leone	29 July 1971	
Rwanda	12 November 1971	
Senegal	7 December 1971	Senegal resumed relations with Taiwan in January 1996 and the PRC suspended ties. The PRC and Senegal restored ties in October 2005.
Mauritius	15 April 1972	
Togo	19 September 1972	
Madagascar	6 November 1972	
Chad	28 November 1972	The PRC suspended relations with Chad in August 1997 when Chad recognized Taiwan. The PRC and Chad restored ties in August 2006.
Burkina Faso	15 September 1973	The PRC suspended relations with Burkina Faso in February 1994 when Burkina Faso recognized Taiwan. Ouagadougou continues to recognize Taiwan.
Guinea Bissau	15 March 1974	The PRC suspended relations with Guinea Bissau in May 1990 when Guinea Bissau recognized Taiwan. The PRC and Guinea restored relations in April 1998.

African country	Initial date of establishment of diplomatic relations	Subsequent changes in relations
Gabon	20 April 1974	
Niger	20 July 1974	The PRC suspended relations with Niger in July 1992 when Niger recognized Taiwan. The PRC and Niger restored ties in August 1996.
Gambia	14 December 1974	The PRC suspended relations with Gambia in July 1995 when Gambia recognized Taiwan. Banjul continues to recognize Taiwan.
Botswana	6 January 1975	
Mozambique	25 June 1975	
São Tomé & Principe	12 July 1975	The PRC suspended relations with São Tomé in July 1997 following São Tomé's announcement of its intention to recognize Taiwan. São Tomé continues to recognize Taiwan.
Comoro Islands	13 November 1975	
Cape Verde	25 April 1976	
Seychelles	30 June 1976	
Liberia	17 February 1977	The PRC suspended relations with Liberia in October 1989 when Liberia recognized Taiwan. The PRC and Liberia restored ties in August 1993. The PRC again suspended ties in September 1997 when Liberia resumed relations with Taiwan. The PRC and Liberia restored ties in October 2003.
Libya	9 August 1978	
Djibouti	8 January 1979	
Zimbabwe	18 April 1980	
Angola	12 January 1983	
Côte d'Ivoire	2 March 1983	
Lesotho	30 April 1983	The PRC suspended relations with Lesotho in April 1990 when Lesotho recognized Taiwan. The PRC and Lesotho restored ties in January 1994.
Namibia	22 March 1990	
Eritrea	24 May 1993	
South Africa	1 January 1998	
Malawi	28 December 2007	
South Sudan	9 July 2011	

African country	Initial date of establishment of diplomatic relations	Subsequent changes in relations
Swaziland		Swaziland is the only country in Africa that has never had diplomatic relations with the PRC. It has maintained diplomatic ties with Taiwan since 1968.

Sources: Most data from country relation fact sheets prepared by PRC foreign ministry and Xinhua press items, www.fmprc.gov.cn/eng/gjhdq/. See also Wei Liang-Tsai, *Peking Versus Taipei in Africa 1960–1978* (Taipei: Asia and World Institute, 1982), 26–27; Bruce D. Larkin, *China and Africa 1949–1970: The Foreign Policy of the People's Republic of China* (Berkeley: University of California Press, 1971), 66–67; George T. Yu, *China's African Policy: A Case Study of Tanzania* (New York: Praeger, 1975), 8; Sithara Fernando, "Chronology of China-Africa Relations," *China Report* 43, 3 (July 2007): 363–73.

APPENDIX 2. TRADE BETWEEN AFRICA AND CHINA, 1938–2010

Year	China imports from Africa	Africa imports from China	Total China-Africa trade	Total China world trade	Total Africa world trade	% China total trade with Africa	% Africa total trade with China
2010	63,495.6	65,045.3	128,540.9	2,974,320	966,036.1	4.3	13.31
2009	43,184	53,851.5	97,035.5	2,207,330	780,737.4	4.4	12.43
2008	55,883	56,743	112,626	2,561,000	1,055,743	4.4	10.67
2007	36,230	39,906	76,136	2,175,000	826,213	3.5	9.22
2006	28,768	29,468	58,236	1,762,000	682,017	3.3	8.54
2005	21,114	19,835	40,949	1,423,000	557,794	2.9	7.34
2004	15,646	13,607	29,253	1,154,000	450,087	2.5	6.50
2003	8,362	9,075	17,437	851,000	349,991	2	4.98
2002	5,522	6,101	11,623	621,000	285,716	1.9	4.07
2001	4,656	4,588	9,244	511,000	263,820	1.8	3.50
2000	5,540	4,434	9,974	474,383	286,826	2.1	3.48
1999	2,375	3,962	6,337	360,654	239,811	1.8	2.64
1998	1,479	3,777	5,256	324,129	232,906	1.6	2.26
1997	2,464	2,904	5,368	325,080	244,585	1.7	2.19
1996	1,464	2,487	3,951	290,114	242,595	1.4	1.63
1995	1,439	2,420	3,859	281,118	226,837	1.4	1.70
1994	788	1,849	2,637	236,570	195,818	1.1	1.35
1993	885	1,789	2,674	195,315	187,690	1.4	1.42
1992	504	1,897	2,401	167,335	201,947	1.4	1.19
1991	427	1,132	1,559	135,795	190,072	1.1	0.82
1990	366	1,071	1,437	116,791	197,442	1.2	0.73
1989	427	740	1,167	112,047	162,052	1	0.72
1988	290	774	1,064	102,990	152,908	1	0.70
1987	175	684	859	82,662	143,518	1	0.60
1986	258	758.3	1,016.3	74,614	131,589.5	1.4	0.77
1985	321	566.2	887.2	69,809	145,334.5	1.3	0.61
1984	394	719.4	1,113.4	50,777	158,263.7	2.2	0.70
1983	413	776.1	1,189.1	43,409	160,833.9	2.7	0.74
1982	343	1,108.4	1,451.4	40,785	174,736.4	3.6	0.83

Year	China imports from Africa	Africa imports from China	Total China-Africa trade	Total China world trade	Total Africa world trade	% China total trade with Africa	% Africa total trade with China
1981	353	1,219.3	1,572.3	43,107	202,514.6	3.6	0.78
1980	384	589.5	973.5	37,644	213,157.8	2.6	0.46
1979	216	762.4	978.4	29,332	150,233.5	3.3	0.65
1978	173	740.8	913.8	20,660	122,360.9	4.4	0.75
1977	258	590.1	848.1	13,133	111,217.8	6.5	0.76
1976	167	540	707.0	11,247	94,255.2	6.3	0.75
1975	232	491.9	723.9	12,382	89,602.9	5.8	0.81
1974	235	534	769.0	11,940	83,025	6.4	0.93
1973	214	406.2	620.2	8,422	49,932.2	7.4	1.24
1972	171.1	281	452.1	4,805	27,752.3	9.4	1.63
1971	170.1	270	440.1	3,830	24,937.9	11.5	1.76
1970	124.8	161.3	286.1	3,575.7	22,963.2	8	1.25
1969	84.2	138	222.2	3,241.8	20,309.9	6.9	1.09
1968	73.4	133.2	206.6	2,900.7	22,601.4	7.1	0.91
1967	73.8	153.8	227.6	2,840.2	20,286	8.0	1.12
1966	87.5	159.2	246.7	2,968	19,956.9	8.3	1.24
1965	130.9	125.4	256.3	2,505.4	19,261.2	10.2	1.33
1964	65.6	69.6	135.2	2,172	18,070.4	6.2	0.75
1963	61.2	53.3	114.5	2,281.4	15,867	5	0.72
1962	42.3	51.3	93.6	2,295.3	14,783.1	4.1	0.63
1961	37.9	46.9	84.8	2,637.5	14,210.5	3.2	0.60
1960	85.4	42.3	127.7	3,876.8	14,775.7	3.3	0.86
1959	55	34.9	89.9	3,959.1	13,713.4	2.3	0.66
1958	47.4	34.6	82	3,674.9	13,730.1	2.2	0.60
1957	47.9	65.0	112.9	2,777.9	14,503.4	4.1	0.78
1956	28.9	45.1	74	2,862.3	13,582.9	2.6	0.54
1955	27	23	50	2,910	12,726.3	1.7	0.39
1954	12	15	27	2,660	13,831.4	1.0	0.20
1953	10	11	21	2,470	12,853.2	0.9	0.16
1952	9	8	17	2,070	13,067.5	0.8	0.13
1951	1	18	19	2,160	13,496.5	0.9	0.14
1950	7.5	17.9	25.4	930.5	9,894.7	2.7	0.26
1949	0.2	10.6	10.8	851.7	2,870.5	1.3	0.38
1948	1	16.7	17.7	1,225	11,112	1.4	0.16
1938	1	6	7	1,045	3,251.3	0.7	0.22

Sources: International Monetary Fund and Direction of Trade Statistics, China and Africa pages; United Nations Trade Statistics. In all cases the most recent available statistics are shown. Trade figures are in U.S.$1 million increments.

NOTES

Chapter 1. Introduction

Epigraph: President Hu Jintao, comments to South African President Jacob Zuma, 22 September 2009, New York, Ministry of Foreign Affairs of the People's Republic of China, http://www.fmprc.gov.cn/eng/.

1. African countries visited include Angola, Egypt, Ethiopia, Kenya, Liberia, Nigeria, South Africa, Sudan, and Swaziland. Chinese cities include Beijing, Guangzhou, Hangzhou, Hong Kong, Jinhua, Nanjing, Qingdao, and Shanghai.

2. In 1405–1433, Zheng He led seven western maritime expeditions reaching as far as East Africa. "Admiral Zheng He (1371–1433)," *Chinaculture.org*, 14 June 2005, http://www.china.org.cn/english/features/zhenhe/131897.htm.

3. "Country Comparison: GDP (purchasing power parity) 2010 est.," CIA World Fact Book official website, undated, https://www.cia.gov/library/publications/the-world-factbook/rankorder/2001.

4. "Africa: China-Africa—an Economic Partnership," FOCAC official website, 14 September 2010, http://www.focac.org/eng/jlydh/xzhd/t752177.htm; Kenneth King, "China-Africa Human Resource Development: Partnership or One-Way?" *Pambazuka News* 497, 23 September 2010, http://pambazuka.org/en/category/comment/67178

5. Bruce D. Larkin, *China and Africa 1949–1970: The Foreign Policy of the People's Republic of China* (Berkeley: University of California Press, 1971).

6. Before 1978 Chinese foreign policy was almost synonymous with its role in the Third World; the topic receives substantial coverage in most treatments of the former. See, for example, G. W. Choudhury, *China in World Affairs: The Foreign Policy of the PRC Since 1970* (Boulder, Colo.: Westview, 1982); King C. Chen, *The Foreign Policy of China* (Miami: East West WHO, 1972); Michael B. Yahuda, *China's Role in World Affairs* (London: Croom Helm, 1978). For works specific to China's relations with the Third World, see W. A. C. Adie, "China, Russia, and the Third World," *China Quarterly* 11 (July–September 1962): 200–213; Wolfgang Bartke, *China's Economic Aid* (London: Hurst, 1975); Janos Horvath, *Chinese Technology Transfer to the Third World: A Grants Economy Analysis* (New York: Praeger, 1976); Alvin Z. Rubinstein, ed., *Soviet and Chinese Influence in the Third World* (New York: Praeger, 1975); Charles Neuhauser, *Third World Politics: China and the Afro-Asian People's Solidarity Organization*

1957–1967, Harvard East Asian Monographs 26 (Cambridge, Mass.: Harvard University Press, 1970); Shen-Yu Dai, *China, the Superpowers and the Third World* (Hong Kong: Chinese University of Hong Kong, 1974); Udo Weiss, "China's Aid to and Trade with the Developing Countries of the Third World," in *China and the Current Era of Détente*, Centre d'Étude du Sud-Est Asiatique et de l'Extrême-Orient (Brussels: Université Libre de Bruxelles, 1974); George T. Yu, "China and the Third World," *Asian Survey* 17, 11 (1977): 1036–48.

7. These include Sven Hamrell and Carl Gosta Widstrand, eds., *The Soviet Bloc, China and Africa* (Uppsala: Scandinavian institute of African Studies, 1964); John C. Cooley, *East Wind over Africa: Red China's African Offensive* (New York: Walker, 1965); Emmanuel John Hevi, *An African Student in China* (New York: Praeger, 1963); Emmanuel John Hevi, *The Dragon's Embrace: The Chinese Communists in Africa* (New York: Praeger, 1966).

8. Books on China-Africa relations published between 1974 and 1976 include Alan Hutchison, *China's African Revolution* (London: Hutchinson, 1975); George T. Yu, *China's Africa Policy: A Study of Tanzania* (New York: Praeger, 1975); Alaba Ogunsanwo, *China's Policy in Africa, 1958–1971* (Cambridge: Cambridge University Press, 1974); Martin Bailey, *Freedom Railway: China and the Tanzania-Zambia Link* (London: Rex Collings, 1976); Richard Hall and Hugh Peyman, *The Great Uhuru Railway: China's Showpiece in Africa* (London: Victor Gollancz, 1976). At least three additional books were written on the subject during the 1970s: Bruce D. Larkin, *China and Africa, 1949–1970: The Foreign Policy of the People's Republic of China* (Berkeley: University of California Press, 1971); Richard Lowenthal, *Model or Ally? The Communist Powers and the Developing Countries* (New York: Oxford University Press, 1977); Warren Weinstein, ed., *Soviet and Chinese Aid to Africa* (New York: Praeger, 1980).

9. Cecil Johnson, *Communist China and Latin America 1959–1967* (New York: Columbia University Press, 1970); Yitzhak Schichor, *The Middle East in China's Foreign Policy* (New York: Cambridge University Press, 1979); Leo Suryadinata, *"Overseas Chinese" in Southeast Asia and China's Foreign Policy: An Interpretative Essay* (Singapore: Institute of Southeast Asian Studies, 1978); Robert G. Sutter, *Chinese Foreign Policy After the Cultural Revolution, 1966–1977* (Boulder, Colo.: Westview, 1978); Melvin Gurtov, *China and Southeast Asia, the Politics of Survival: A Study of Foreign Policy Interaction* (Baltimore: Johns Hopkins University Press, 1975); Joseph Camilleri, *Southeast Asia in China's Foreign Policy* (Singapore: Institute of Southeast Asian Studies, 1975); James C. Hsiung, *Beyond China's Independent Foreign Policy: Challenge for the U.S. and Its Asian Allies* (New York: Praeger, 1985);

10. Richard Bernstein and Ross H. Munro, *The Coming Conflict with China* (New York: Knopf, 1997); Bill Gertz, *The China Threat: How the People's Republic Targets America* (Washington, D.C.: Regnery, 2000); Robert D. Kaplan, "How We Would Fight China," *Atlantic Monthly* (June 2005).

11. For this "structural realist" perspective, see John J. Mearsheimer, *The Tragedy of Great Power Politics* (New York: Norton, 2001); Aaron L. Friedberg, "The Struggle for the Mastery of Asia," *Commentary*, November 2000; Aaron L. Friedberg, "Ripe for

Rivalry: Prospects for Peace in a Multipolar Asia," *International Security* (Winter 1993/94); Ashley Tellis, "A Grand Chessboard," *Foreign Policy* (January/February 2005).

12. On China's economic vulnerabilities and its continuing dependence on openness, see George J. Gilboy, "The Myth Behind China's Miracle," *Foreign Affairs* (July/August 2004); Nicholas R. Lardy, *Integrating China into the Global Economy* (Washington, D.C.: Brookings Institution Press, 2002. On social weaknesses and instability, see Murray Scot Tanner, "China Rethinks Unrest," *Washington Quarterly* (Summer 2004). On how economic and social weakness constrains behavior, see Phillip C. Saunders and Erica Strecker Downs, "Legitimacy and the Limits of Nationalism: China and the Diaoyu Islands," *International Security* (Winter 1998–1999). While somewhat ambivalent about causality, a cautiously optimistic statement is provided in Alastair Iain Johnston, "Is China a Status Quo Power?" *International Security* (Spring 2003).

13. Evan Medeiros and M. Taylor Fravel, "China Takes Off," *Foreign Affairs* (November/December 2003); David Shambaugh, "China Engages Asia: Reshaping the Regional Order," *International Security* (Winter 2004/2005); Rosemary Foot, "Chinese Power and the Idea of a Responsible State," *China Journal*, January 2001; For more descriptive accounts see, for example, Jane Perlez, "The Charm from Beijing: China Strives to Keep Its Backyard Tranquil," *New York Times*, 8 October 2003; Amitav Acharya, "China's Charm Offensive in Southeast Asia," *International Herald Tribune*, 8–9 November 2003; Philip Pan, "China's Improving Image Challenges U.S. in Asia," *Washington Post*, 15 November 2003.

14. Joshua Cooper Ramo, *The Beijing Consensus* (London: Foreign Policy Centre, 18 June 2004), 3–4.

15. Ramo, 4.

16. Alain Gresh, "Understanding the Beijing Consensus," *Le Monde Diplomatique*, 3 November 2008.

17. Deborah Brautigam, *The Dragon's Gift: The Real Story of China in Africa* (London: Oxford University Press, 2009), 307.

18. Brautigam, 311–12.

19. Barry Sautman and Yan Hairong, "Friends and Interests: China's Distinctive Links with Africa," in *China's New Role in Africa and the South: A Search for a New Perspective*, ed. Dorothy-Grace Guerrero and Firoze Manji (Oxford and Bangkok: Fahumu and Chulalongkorn University), 113.

20. Jing Men, "China and Africa: Old Friends, New Partners," in *Dancing with the Dragon?: China's Emergence in the Developing World*, ed. Dennis Hickey and Baogang Guo (New York: Rowman and Littlefield, 2010), 139.

21. Barry Sautman, personal interview, 12 December 2007. The early roots of this argument can be traced to dependency theory; see Patrick J. McGowan, "Economic Dependence and Economic Performance in Black Africa," *Journal of Modern African Studies* 14, 1 (March 1976); Michael B. Dolan and Brian W. Tomlin, "First World-Third World Linkages: External Relations and Economic Development," *International Organization* 34, 1 (Winter 1980); James A. Caporaso, "Dependence, Dependency,

and Power in the Global System: A Structural and Behavioral Analysis," *International Organization* 32, 1 (1978).

22. Notable African experts on China include Ali Abdulla Ali (Khartoum University), Waris Oyesina Ali (Nigerian Institute of International Affairs), Sanusha Naidu (Human Sciences Research Council), Elizabeth Sidiropoulos (South African Institute of International Affairs), and Garth Shelton (University of the Witwatersrand). Notable Chinese experts on Africa include He Wenping (Chinese Academy of Social Sciences, CASS), Li Anshan (Beijing University), Liu Hongwu (Zhejiang Normal University), Wang Duanyong (Shanghai International Affairs University), Wang Hongyi (China Institute of International Studies;), Wang Yingying (CIIS), Xu Wenzhong (China Institutes of Contemporary International Relations), Yang Guang (CASS), and Yang Lihua (CASS).

23. "President Hu to Visit Africa to Consolidate Friendship," *People's Daily*, 4 February 2009, http://english.people.com.cn/90001/90776/90883/6585790.html. This argument is a favorite of Chinese officials visiting African countries. During a trip to Gabon in 2004 President Hu "stressed that China values the traditional friendship between China and Africa and firmly supports the development and rejuvenation of Africa," Ministry of Foreign Affairs of the People's Republic of China official website, 9 September 2004, http://www.fmprc.gov.cn/eng/wjb/zzjg/fzs/gjlb/2989/2991/t156737 .htm. Also see Liu Guijin, "A Peacefully Rising China, New Opportunities for Africa," in *China in Africa: Mercantilist Predator, or Partner in Development?* ed. Garth Le Pere (Johannesburg: South African Institute of International Affairs, 2007), 16; Sautman and Yan, 90–91.

24. "President Hu to Visit Africa to Consolidate Friendship."

25. Naazneen Barma and Ely Ratner, "China's Illiberal Challenge," *Democracy: A Journal of Ideas* 2 (Fall 2006): 57, 61, 63–64.

26. Peter Brookes and Ji Hye Shin, "Backgrounder #1916, China's Influence in Africa: Implications for the United States" (Washington, D.C.: Heritage Foundation, 22 February 2006), http://www.heritage.org/research/asiaandthepacific/bg1916.cfm.

27. Stephanie Hanson, "Backgrounder: China, Africa, and Oil" (Washington, D.C.: Council on Foreign Relations, 6 June 2008).

28. Denis M. Tull, "China's Engagement in Africa: Scope, Significance and Consequences," *Journal of Modern African Studies* 44, 3 (2006): 476. Also see Ian Taylor, "The 'All-Weather Friend'? Sino-African Interaction in the Twenty-First Century," in *Africa in International Politics: External Involvement on the Continent*, ed. Ian Taylor and Paul Williams (London: Routledge, 2004), 99.

29. Chris Alden, *China in Africa* (New York: Zed Books, 2007), 70.

30. Eric Kiss and Kate Zhou, "China's New Burden in Africa," in Hickey and Guo, 156.

Chapter 2. A Historical Overview of China-Africa Relations

1. Gao Jinyuan, "China and Africa: The Development of Relations over Many Centuries," *African Affairs* 83, 331 (April 1984): 242.

2. An Yongyu, "China-Africa Political and Economic Cooperation—Retrospect and Prospect," *Foreign Affairs Journal* 66 (December 2002): 7.

3. Basil Davidson, *Old Africa Rediscovered* (London: Gollancz, 1961), 158.

4. Philip Snow, *The Star Raft: China's Encounter with Africa* (New York: Weidenfeld and Nicolson, 1988), 2.

5. W. H. Ingrams, *Zanzibar: Its History and Its People* (New York: Barnes and Noble, 1931), 88.

6. For the role of Arab seafarers, see George Fadlo Hourani, *Arab Seafaring in the Indian Ocean in Ancient and Early Medieval Times* (Beirut: Khayats, 1963), 51–84.

7. J. J. L. Duyvendak, *China's Discovery of Africa* (London: Arthur Probsthain, 1949), 26; Teobaldo Filesi, *China and Africa in the Middle Ages* (London: Frank Cass, 1972), 27. For a discussion of the Confucian attitude on dealing with non-Chinese, see Lien-sheng Yang, "Historical Notes on the Chinese World Order," in *The Chinese World Order*, ed. John K. Fairbank (Cambridge, Mass.: Harvard University Press, 1968), 24–28. For the relationship between tribute and trade, see Mark Mancall, "The Ch'ing Tribute System: An Interpretive Essay," in *The Chinese World Order*, 75–89.

8. Gao, 243–45; Kuei-Sheng Chang, "The Maritime Scene in China at the Dawn of Great European Discoveries," *Journal of the American Oriental Society* 94, 3 (July–September 1974): 352; Snow, 6–8. For a good discussion of where Chinese porcelain has been found along the East African coast, see Gervase Mathew, "Chinese Porcelain in East Africa and on the Coast of South Arabia," *Oriental Art* n.s. 2, 2 (1956): 50–55.

9. Paul Wheatley, "Analecta Sino-Africana Recensa," in *East Africa and the Orient: Cultural Syntheses in Pre-Colonial Times*, ed. H. Neville Chittick and Robert I. Rotberg (New York: Africana, 1975), 108–9; Snow, 33–35; Louise Levathes, *When China Ruled the Seas: The Treasure Fleet of the Dragon Throne, 1405–1433* (New York: Oxford University Press, 1994), 19.

10. Wheatley, 105–8; Friedrich Hirth, "Chinese Notices of East African Territories," *Journal of the American Oriental Society* 30, 1 (December 1909): 48–49; Raymond A. Dart, "A Chinese Character as a Wall Motive in Rhodesia," *South African Journal of Science* 36 (December 1939): 476; Filesi, 5, 23; Davidson, 158–59; Snow, 21–29; Duvyendak, 14–17.

11. Dart, 475; Filesi, 21.

12. Duvyendak, 23.

13. W. E. Burghardt Du Bois, *The World and Africa* (1947; New York: International Publishers, 1965), 180. Graham W. Irwin provided a more extensive account in *Africans Abroad* (New York: Columbia University Press, 1877), 168–76. He acknowledged that the number of African slaves who reached China "cannot have been large."

14. Wheatley, 109. Filesi also concluded China absorbed a small number of African slaves, 21–22.

15. Snow, 18–19, 38. Maghan Keita concurs with the view that there were African slaves in China during this period. See "Africans and Asians: Historiography and the Long View of Global Interaction," *Journal of World History* 16, 1 (2005): 25–27.

16. Zhang Xiang, "From Sino-African Relations Comes a Steady Stream of Enlightening Guidance," *Contemporary Chinese Thought* 40, 1 (Fall 2008): 12.

17. Filesi, 4.

18. Gao, 243–44; Zhang Xiang, 13.

19. Snow, 3–5. Axumite scholar Stuart Munro-Hay wrote in *Aksum: An African Civilisation of Late Antiquity* (Edinburgh: Edinburgh University Press, 1991), 59, that there is no solid evidence for contacts between China and Axum, though Han Dynasty records include a possible reference.

20. Viktor A. Velgus, "Chinese Voyaging to Africa and to the Persian Gulf: Hypotheses and Sources," *St. Petersburg Journal of African Studies* 1 (1993): 104–12.

21. Zhang Xiang, 13.

22. Ibn Battúta, *Ibn Battúta Travels in Asia and Africa 1325–1354*, trans. H. A. R. Gibb (London: Routledge, 1929), 269–300; Zhang Xiang, 14.

23. Wheatley, 78–87; Filesi, 24; Snow, 11–12; Zhang Xiang, 13–14. One book sanctioned by the PRC states categorically that Wang Dayuan made a trip to Zanzibar in 1311–1350. See Yuan Wu, *China and Africa* (Beijing: China Intercontinental Press, 2006), 22.

24. Filesi, 32–33.

25. Edward L. Dreyer, *Zheng He: China and the Oceans in the Early Ming Dynasty, 1405–1433* (New York: Pearson Longman, 2007), 75–97; Levathes, 149–51; Filesi, 52–55.

26. Filesi, 71–72; Liu Hongwu, "Sino-African Exchanges: The Importance of the History of Civilizations," *Contemporary Chinese Thought* 40, 1 (Fall 2008): 76.

27. Snow, 29–30.

28. Zoe Murphy, "Zheng He: Symbol of China's 'Peaceful Rise'," *BBC News Asia Pacific Service*, 28 July 2010.

29. Ibid.

30. Duyvendak, 27–28; Davidson, 162–63; Gao, 246.

31. Wang Gungwu, "The Chinese and the Countries Across the Indian Ocean," in *Historical Relations Across the Indian Ocean* (Paris: UNESCO, 1980), 63–64. Indian Ocean expert Auguste Toussaint in *History of the Indian Ocean* (Chicago: University of Chicago Press, 1961), 79, described China's withdrawal from maritime exploration as "a curious phenomenon, a real enigma."

32. Mon'im Nasser-Eddine, *Arab-Chinese Relations 1950–1971* (Beirut: Arab Institute for Research and Publishing, 1972), 22; Snow, 43–44; Huguette Ly-Tio-Fane Pineo, *Chinese Diaspora in Western Indian Ocean* (Bell Village, Mauritius: Éditions de l'Océan Indien-Chinese Catholic Mission, 1985), 69–70, 74; Liu Hongwu, 77.

33. Deborah Bräutigam, "Close Encounters: Chinese Business Networks as Industrial Catalysts in Sub-Saharan Africa," *African Affairs* 102, 408 (July 2003): 456–57; A. J. Christopher, "Ethnicity, Community and the Census in Mauritius, 1830–1990," *Geographical Journal* 158, 1 (March 1992): 59; Ly-Tio-Fane Pineo, 44, 47, 97–101.

34. Leon M. S. Slawecki, *French Policy Towards the Chinese in Madagascar* (Hamden, Conn.: Shoe String Press, 1971), 43–49. See also Ly-Tio-Fane Pineo, 182–86, 201–2, for a discussion of the Chinese community in Madagascar.

35. Comment by Philippe Le Gall, first Seychelles resident ambassador to China, *Beijing Review*, 27 September 2007.

36. Ly-Tio-Fane Pineo, 119, 126.

37. J. Stanley Gardiner, "The Seychelles Archipelago," *Geographical Journal* 29, 2 (February 1907): 154.

38. Melanie Yap and Dianne Leong Man, *Colour, Confusion and Concessions: The History of the Chinese in South Africa* (Hong Kong: Hong Kong University Press, 1996), 5–101. This massive and impressive study of the Chinese in South Africa represents nine years of research and writing. Also see Yoon Jung Park, "Sojourners to Settlers: Early Constructions of Chinese Identity in South Africa, 1879–1949," *African Studies* 65, 2 (December 2006): 201–17; Ly-Tio-Fane Pineo, 210–12.

39. Karen L. Harris, "'Not a Chinaman's Chance': Chinese Labour in South Africa and the United States of America," *Historia* 52, 2 (November 2006): 179–84.

40. Peter Richardson, "The Recruiting of Chinese Indentured Labour for the South African Gold-Mines, 1903–1908," *Journal of African History* 18, 1 (1977): 99–100.

41. Thierry Vircoulon, "Chinois d'Afrique, Chinois en Afrique et Afro-Chinois: Les multiples visages de la communauté chinoise d'Afrique du Sud," *Monde Chinois* 8 (Summer/Autumn 2006), 28; Gary Kynoch, "Controlling the Coolies: Chinese Mineworkers and the Struggle for Labor in South Africa, 1904–1910," *International Journal of African Historical Studies* 36, 2 (2003), 309; Gary Kynoch, "'Your Petitioners Are in Mortal Terror': The Violent World of Chinese Mineworkers in South Africa, 1904–1910," *Journal of Southern African Studies* 31, 3 (September 2005): 531–32.

42. Ly-Tio-Fane Pineo, 229–41.

43. Yap and Man, 171–73.

44. Kwabena O. Akurang-Parry, "'We Cast About for a Remedy': Chinese Labor and African Opposition in the Gold Coast, 1874–1914," *International Journal of African Historical Studies* 34, 3 (2001): 365–84.

45. Snow, 46; Sen-Dou Chang, "The Distribution and Occupations of Overseas Chinese," *Geographical Review* 58, 1 (January 1968): 95.

46. Li Baoping, "Sino-Tanzanian Relations and Political Developments," in *Afro-Chinese Relations: Past, Present and Future*, ed. Kwesi Kwaa Prah (Cape Town: CASAS, 2007), 127.

47. Snow, 46.

48. Ibid., 45–46, 57; Republic of China, *China, Treaties, Conventions, Etc., Between China and Foreign States* II, 2nd ed. (Shanghai: Statistical Department of the Inspectorate General of Customs, 1917), 829; Zhang Xiang, 15–16.

49. Republic of China, *Treaties Between the Republic of China and Foreign States (1927–1957)*, (Taipei: Ministry of Foreign Affairs, 1958), 100. Wei Liang-Tsai indicated

that Egypt and the ROC established diplomatic relations in 1942 and maintained the relationship until 1956, when Egypt recognized the PRC. See Wei Liang-Tsai, *Peking Versus Taipei in Africa 1960–1978* (Taipei: Asia and World Institute, 1982), 295.

50. ROC, *Treaties,* 309–10; Wei Liang-Tsai, 332–33.

51. Mohammad El-Sayed Selim, "The Status of China Studies in Egypt," *El Syassa El-Dawliya* 174 (October 2008).

52. Nasser-Eddine, 22–23.

53. Zhang Xiang, 16.

54. Donald Klein, "Formosa's Diplomatic World," *China Quarterly* 15 (July–September 1963): 45.

55. Yap and Man, 173–74, 417.

56. Ibid., 177, 208, 244–45; Park, 220, 224.

57. Slawecki, 161–72.

58. Ly-Tio-Fane Pineo, 47–49, 97, 101.

59. For example, Bruce D. Larkin, who produced one of the first comprehensive analyses of China-Africa relations, identified seven phases covering 1955–1971, "China and Africa: A Prospective on the 1970s," *Africa Today* 18, 3 (July 1971): 7. In discussing the years 1949–1979, Park Sang-Seek grouped the relationship into five stages, "African Policy of the People's Republic of China," *Sino-Soviet Affairs* 6, 3 (Fall 1982): 87–111. One of the earlier experts on China-Africa, W. A. C. Adie, wrote that there were three stages in the relationship, "The Communist Powers in Africa," *Conflict Studies* 10 (December–January 1970/71): 9–10. South African researcher Wim J. Booyse identified six stages between 1955 and 1988, "The People's Republic of China's Role in Africa: 1955–1988," *Southern African Freedom Review* 1, 4 (Fall 1988): 20–22. Chinese scholars took the most sweeping approach in describing China-Africa relations. Xu Jiming of the Institute of West Asian and African Studies, Chinese Academy of Social Sciences, wrote in 2001 that there were four stages: early 1950s, mid-1950s to late 1970s, 1980s, and since 1990, "China's National Interest and Its Relationship with Africa," *Africa Insight* 31, 2 (June 2001): 38–42. Chinese expert on Africa He Wenping, in a 2006 paper, took a similar view, grouping the relationship in periods from the 1950s to the end of the 1970s, the 1980s, and from the end of the 1980s to the present, "Moving Forward with the Time: The Evolution of China's African Policy," paper presented at a workshop in Hong Kong, 11–12 November 2006, www .cctr.ust.hk/china-africa/papers/He,Wengping.pdf. Assistant research fellow Sun Qiaocheng at the China Institute of International Studies, writing in 2000, suggested there were only two stages: from 1949 to the late 1970s and from the end of the 1970s to the beginning of the twentieth century, "Sino-African Relationship at the Turn of the Century," *International Studies* 15, 17 (2000): 19–34. Emma Mawdsley, Department of Geography at Cambridge University, also took a sweeping view in analyzing China-Africa relations. She identified three eras: the Mao years from 1949 to 1976; the first decade under Deng Xiaoping from 1978 to 1989; and the post-Tiananmen Square years since 1989, "China and Africa: Emerging Challenges to the Geographies of Power," *Geography Compass* 1, 3 (May 2007): 408.

60. George T. Yu, an American scholar who did much of the early research on China-Africa relations, seems to disagree with this conclusion. He wrote in 1977 that "while China's policies and behavior have been responsible for whatever successes that have been achieved, the African response to China's policies and behavior have been equally vital." "China's Role in Africa," *Annals of the American Academy of Political and Social Science* 432 (July 1977): 109. The operative words, however, are "African response to China's policies." The initiative has generally remained with China, not Africa.

61. Bruce D. Larkin, *China and Africa, 1949–1970: The Foreign Policy of the People's Republic of China* (Berkeley: University of California Press, 1971), 15–16; Park Sang-Seek, "African Policy of the People's Republic of China," 89–90. Reflecting both this analysis and the PRC view, Xu Jiming of the Institute of West Asian and African Studies wrote that "during this period, conditions both subjective and objective did not allow China to develop a relationship with Africa, apart from a few nongovernmental exchanges." He added that China gave first priority to siding with the Soviet Union and the socialist camp, resisting the United States in Korea and assisting Indochina against France. See "China's National Interest and Its Relationship with Africa," 38.

62. W. A. C. Adie, "China and Africa Today," *Race and Class* 5, 3 (1964): 8.

63. Larkin, 15.

64. Philippe Richer, "Aux origines de la politique chinoise en Afrique Noire (1949–1960)," *Mondes Asiatiques* 15 (Autumn 1978): 165. The PRC subsequently supported the UPC as an opposition party after Cameroon obtained independence in 1960 under a government led by Ahmadou Ahidjo. This eventually resulted in an embarrassing foreign policy setback and put Beijing in direct conflict with an established African government.

65. B. E. Shinde, "China and Afro-Asian Solidarity 1955–65: A Study of China's Policy and Diplomacy (I)," *China Report* 14, 2 (March/April 1978): 51.

66. Nasser-Eddine, 60–104, has a detailed account of Chinese-Egyptian contacts leading up to diplomatic recognition in 1956; see also Larkin, 16–20. For an account of the Bandung Conference, see Richard Wright, *The Color Curtain: A Report on the Bandung Conference* (Jackson, Miss.: Banner Books, 1956).

67. Derek Mitchell and Carola McGiffert, "Expanding the 'Strategic Periphery'," in *China and the Developing World: Beijing's Strategy for the Twenty-First Century*, ed. Joshua Eisenman, Eric Heginbotham, and Derek Mitchell (Armonk, N.Y.: M.E. Sharpe, 2007), 14; He Wenping, "China-Africa Relations Facing the 21st Century," in *Africa Beyond 2000*, ed. Institute of West Asian and African Studies (Beijing: Chinese Academy of Social Sciences, October 1998), 394; Alaba Ogunsanwo, *China's Policy in Africa 1958–1971* (London: Cambridge University Press, 1974), 8. The most recent comprehensive statement of "China's African Policy," 12 January 2006, explicitly reaffirmed that "China adheres to the Five Principles of Peaceful Coexistence," www.fmprc.gov.cn/eng/zxxx/t230615.htm; G. P. Deshpande and H. K. Gupta, *United Front*

Against Imperialism: China's Foreign Policy in Africa (Bombay: Somaiyas, 1986), 24–26; Darryl C. Thomas, "The Impact of the Sino-Soviet Conflict on the Afro-Asian People's Solidarity Organization: Afro-Asianism Versus Non-Alignment, 1955–1966," *Journal of Asian and African Affairs* 3, 2 (Spring 1992): 169; Yitzhak Shichor, *The Middle East in China's Foreign Policy 1949–1977* (Cambridge: Cambridge University Press, 1979), 40. For the text of the Panchsheel Agreement, see www.ignca.nic.in/ks_41062.htm.

68. Larkin, 20, 32–36.

69. Liao Cheng-chih, "Liao Cheng-chih's Speech," *Peking Review* 3, 13 (29 March 1960): 11–13.

70. Richard Lowenthal dates the beginning of the Sino-Soviet conflict to autumn 1959, adding that it had an immediate impact on Moscow's and Beijing's policies in Africa. See "China," in *Africa and the Communist World*, ed. Zbigniew Brzezinski (Stanford, Calif.: Stanford University Press, 1963), 168–69. Mao Zedong told U.S. secretary of state Henry Kissinger during a meeting in Beijing that China's falling out with the Soviet Union began in 1958 when Moscow wanted to control China's seacoast and its naval ports. Mao added that the split became definitive following Khrushchev's visit to China in 1959. See declassified memorandum of conversation between Mao and Kissinger, 12 November 1973.

71. Thomas, 175–79, 184–85, 189; Deshpande and Gupta, 138–39. For a detailed study of China's engagement in the AAPSO movement, see Charles Neuhauser, *Third World Politics: China and the Afro-Asian People's Solidarity Organization 1957–1967* (Cambridge, Mass.: Harvard University Press, 1970). For a useful early analysis of Sino-Soviet differences on their understanding of revolutionary struggle, see R. K. Ramazani, "Russia, China and the Afro-Asian Countries," *Mizan Newsletter* 5, 3 (March 1963): 1–10. The State Department Bureau of Intelligence and Research concluded in a 1964 analysis that the Sino-Soviet conflict caused China and the Soviet Union to compete in Africa not only with the West but with each other. See "An Outline Guide to Communist Activities in Africa," declassified research memorandum, 15 May 1964, 2, Declassified Documents Reference System. A CIA study a year later stated that the Chinese were working in Africa "to eliminate or weaken pro-Western and pro-Soviet influence and to foster the growth of radical nationalist regimes friendly to Communist China." See CIA "Chinese Communist Activities in Africa," 2, declassified research memorandum, 30 April 1965.

72. Mohamed A. El-Khawas, "The Development of China's Foreign Policy Toward Africa, 1955–1972," *Current Bibliography on African Affairs* 6, 2 (Spring 1973), 130.

73. Shichor, 42–51; Larkin, 24–26; Nigel Disney, "China and the Middle East," *MERIP Reports* 63 (December 1977): 4–5; Joseph E. Khalili, "Sino-Arab Relations," *Asian Survey* 8, 8 (August 1968): 681–82.

74. For a good case study of China's support for Algerian revolutionaries, see Deshpande and Gupta, 52–82; Disney, 7; Khalili, 683–85; W. A .C. Adie, "Chinese Policy Towards Africa," in *The Soviet Bloc China and Africa*, ed. Sven Hamrell and Carl Gösta Widstrand (Uppsala: Scandinavian Institute of African Affairs, 1964), 52–53.

75. Larkin, 54–55.

76. For a list of these organizations as of 1970, see Larkin, 219–24. For a list of speeches and editorials by the Chinese-African People's Friendship Association, see *The Chinese People Resolutely Support the Just Struggle of the African People* (Peking: Foreign Languages Press, 1961). See also Alan Hutchison, *China's African Revolution* (London: Hutchinson, 1975), 35–43.

77. Julia C. Strauss, "The Past in the Present: Historical and Rhetorical Lineages in China's Relations with Africa," *China Quarterly* 199 (September 2009): 781–82.

78. This translation comes from Xu Jiming, 39. For a discussion of the principles, see Ogunsanwo, 120.

79. CIA, "What the Chinese Communists Are Up To in Black Africa," declassified secret report, 23 March 1971, 7, www.state.gov/documents/organization/54533.pdf.

80. Ibid., 11.

81. Liang-Tsai, 41–51; Ogunsanwo, 149–53; CIA, "What the Chinese Communists Are Up To," 9–10, 23.

82. Harold C. Hinton, *China's Turbulent Quest: An Analysis of China's Foreign Relations Since 1949* (Bloomington: Indiana University Press, 1973), 137–41; George E. Taylor, "Lin Piao and the Third World," *Virginia Quarterly Review* 42, 1 (Winter 1966): 1–11; Barbara Barnouin and Yu Changgen, *Chinese Foreign Policy During the Cultural Revolution* (London: Kegan Paul, 1998), 6–7, 47.

83. Ogunsanwo, 180–89.

84. For the most thorough analyses of Chinese policy toward Africa during the Cultural Revolution, see Ogunsanwo, 180–240; Hutchison, 133–61. For an account of the Cultural Revolution by a U.S.-educated scholar from Taiwan, see Liang-Tsai, 80–103. For an analysis that looks at North Africa and the Middle East, see Shichor, 125–27, 145–48, 204–5. For a discussion of the importance of the Tanzania-Zambia railroad project on Chinese policy in Africa, see Strauss, 785–89.

85. Xiaohong Liu, *Chinese Ambassadors: The Rise of Diplomatic Professionalism Since 1949* (Seattle: University of Washington Press, 2001), 59–60.

86. Liang-Tsai, 380–96.

87. Hutchison, 162–73. For a similar analysis by an African scholar, see Ogunsanwo, 241–57.

88. El-Khawas, 137. Piet Konings, senior researcher at the African Studies Centre, University of Leiden, dates this policy change from the mid-1960s, "China and Africa," *Journal of Developing Societies* 23, 3 (2007): 345. Although there may be several cases where China began withholding support from such groups in the mid-1960s, it does not appear to have become a general policy until after the Cultural Revolution. Li Anshan, professor at the School of International Studies, Peking University, put it this way: "The end of the Cultural Revolution marked a shift in China's policy toward Africa from one based almost exclusively on ideological alliance to one with a far more pragmatic and diversified approach," "China and Africa: Policy and Challenges," *China Security* 3, 3 (Summer 2007): 72. Writing in 1972, George T. Yu modified

somewhat his earlier analysis of China's objectives in Africa. He said the objectives are (1) establish and maintain revolutionary credibility by supporting African liberation movements and new African states; (2) use Africa as a direct and indirect battleground against the U.S. and USSR; and (3) bolster the Chinese global position by securing support in Africa, especially an African preference for the "Chinese model" of national independence and nation-building, legal recognition, and backing for the PRC, "Peking's African Diplomacy," *Problems of Communism* 21, 2 (March/April 1972): 16–17.

89. George T. Yu, "Africa in Chinese Foreign Policy," *Asian Survey* 28, 8 (August 1988): 855.

90. Gerald Segal, "China and Africa," *Annals of the American Academy of Political and Social Science* 519 (January 1992): 118–20.

91. Philip Snow, "China and Africa: Consensus and Camouflage," in *Chinese Foreign Policy: Theory and Practice*, ed. Thomas W. Robinson and David Shambaugh (Oxford: Clarendon Press, 1994), 295–96, 306.

92. R. A. Akindele, "Africa and the Great Powers, with Particular Reference to the United States, the Soviet Union and China," *Afrika Spectrum* 20, 2 (1985): 142; Mohamed A. El-Khawas, "China's Changing Policies in Africa," *Issue: A Journal of Opinion* 3, 1 (Spring 1973): 26–27.

93. Snow, "China and Africa," 305.

94. Hutchison, 295; V. Sofinsky and A. Khazanov, "PRC Policy in Tropical Africa (1960s–1970s)," *Far Eastern Affairs* 3 (1978): 79–80.

95. Disney, 10–11.

96. Yu, "China's Role in Africa," 98–102; recollections of Shinn while serving at the U.S. embassy in Dar es Salaam, 1971–1973.

97. Snow, "China and Africa," 307–8.

98. Yu, "China's Role in Africa," 102–5.

99. Chang Ya-chün, "Peiping's African Policy in the 1970s," *Issues and Studies* 17, 2 (February 1981): 50–51, and "On Current Chinese Communist Relations with the Third World," *Issues and Studies* 18, 11 (November 1982): 71–82. For a detailed analysis of PRC activities in Africa up to the mid-1970s from the perspective of Taiwan, see Chang Ya-chün, *Chinese Communist Activities in Africa-Policies and Challenges* (Taipei: World Anti-Communist League, April 1981). For a PRC perspective, see He Wenping, "Moving Forward with the Time," 4. For another perspective, see John F. Copper, "The PRC and the Third World: Rhetoric Versus Reality," *Issues and Studies* 22, 3 (March 1986): 110–13. The PRC developed a policy toward the Third World much earlier. See, for example, Philippe Richer, "Doctrine chinoise pour le Tiers Monde," *Politique Étrangère* 1 (1965): 75–97.

100. Deng Xiaoping's 10 April 1974 speech at the UN General Assembly, in *Foreign-Policy Speeches by Chinese Communist Leaders 1963–1975*, ed. Warren Kuo (Taipei: Institute of International Relations, 1976), 50. The "three worlds" theory served as the guiding principle for China's relations with other developing countries

until after the end of the Cold War, when the first and second world ceased to exist. See Zhao Gancheng, "Reform and Opening Up Versus Adjustment of China's Relations with Other Developing Countries," *China International Studies* 13 (Winter 2008): 102–5.

101. Deng Xiaoping, *Foreign Policy Speeches*, 50–58. Much has been written on China's Third World strategy in the 1970s. See, for example, Lillian Craig Harris and Robert L. Worden, eds., *China and the Third World: Champion or Challenger?* (Dover: Mass.: Auburn House, 1986); Sang-Seek, 107–9; George T; Yu, "China and the Third World," *Asian Survey* 17, 11 (November 1977): 1036–48; Stephan Chan, "China's Foreign Policy and Africa: The Rise and Fall of China's Three World's Theory," *Round Table* 296 (1985): 376–84; Michael B. Yahuda, *China's Role in World Affairs* (London: Croom Helm, 1978), 238–60; Peter Van Ness, "China and the Third World: Patterns of Engagement and Indifference," in *China and the World: Chinese Foreign Policy Faces the New Millennium*, ed. Samuel S. Kim (Boulder: Colo.: Westview, 1998), 151–68.

102. Li Anshan, "China and Africa," 72.

103. Ibid.; Booyse, 22–23; Yu, "Africa in Chinese Foreign Policy," 856; Ian Taylor, "China's Relations with Sub-Saharan Africa in the Post-Maoist Era, 1978–1999," in *Politics and Economics of Africa* I, ed. Frank Columbus (Huntington, N.Y.: Nova Science, 2001), 89–90. For a good discussion of China's approach to regions of the Third World in the 1980s, see Xuetong Yan, "Sino-African Relations in the 1990s," *CSIS Africa Notes* 84 (19 April 1988): 1–3.

104. Yu, "Africa in Chinese Foreign Policy," 856–57; Taylor, "China's Relations with Sub-Saharan Africa," 90–91; Xu Jiming, 40–41; Pang Zhongying, "China's Engagement with Africa: Approaches and Challenges," in *China Outside China: China in Africa*, ed. Luca Castellani, Pang Zhongying, and Ian Taylor (Torino: CASCC, 2007), 27. For an analysis of the trip by a scholar from Taiwan, see Chang Ya-chün, "Chao Tzu-yang's Visit to Africa," *Issues and Studies* 19, 1 (January 1983): 10–13 and "An Appraisal of Chao Tzu-yang's Visit to Africa," *Issues and Studies* 19, 2 (February 1983): 8–11. The U.S. embassy in Beijing reported in 1983 that Zhao Ziyang's visit to Africa was China's way of announcing to the world that it had "re-discovered Africa and was ready to work to erode Soviet greater political influence there." The Chinese began courting Soviet-client states, improving relations with Mozambique and establishing relations with Angola. China also reflexively supported the Third World consensus on contentious global and regional issues. See "China's Foreign Policy: A Five-Year Review," from U.S. embassy Beijing, dated 16 December 1983, declassified cable. Over time, China took a more nuanced approach to its harsh criticism of the Soviet Union. The State Department Bureau of Intelligence and Research concluded in 1985 that China had begun to strengthen its Third World image by shifting its focus of criticism from the Soviets to white-ruled South Africa and more generic "superpowers" as the source of Africa's troubles. See "China's Policy Toward Sub-Saharan Africa," 2, 20 August 1985, Digital National Security Archive.

105. Ian Taylor, "China's Foreign Policy Towards Africa in the 1990s," *Journal of Modern African Studies* 36, 3 (September 1998): 443–46. See also Marc Aicardi de

Saint-Paul, "La Chine et l'Afrique," *Mondes et Cultures* 1–4 (2004): 351; Michal Meidan, "China's Africa Policy: Business Now, Politics Later," *Asian Perspective* 30, 4 (2006): 74–76; Mawdsley, 410–11.

106. He Wenping, "Moving Forward with the Time," 7.

107. Ibid., 7–8. See also Xu Jiming, 40. Yung-lo Lin's analysis of Beijing's policy in Africa during the 1980s identified four independent variables in the China-Africa relationship: Chinese internal developments, the China-U.S. relationship, the China-USSR relationship, and internal African considerations. "Peking's African Policy in the 1980s," *Issues and Studies* 25, 4 (April 1989): 83–88.

108. Roland Marchal, "Chine-Afrique: Une histoire ancienne," *Africultures* 66 (January–March 2006): 26.

109. Ian Taylor, "The 'Captive States' of Southern Africa and China: The PRC and Botswana, Lesotho and Swaziland," *Journal of Commonwealth and Comparative Politics* 35, 2 (July 1997): 79–80.

110. Yitzhak Shichor, "China and the Middle East Since Tiananmen," *Annals of the American Academy of Political and Social Science* 519 (January 1992): 89, 92, 96.

111. Weiqun Gu, *Conflicts of Divided Nations: The Cases of China and Korea* (Westport, Conn.: Praeger, 1995), 124–26; Taylor, "China's Relations with Sub-Saharan Africa," 96–100; Chang Qing, "Chinese Foreign Minister Tours Africa," *Beijing Review* 32, 35 (28 August–3 September 1989): 10–11; Taylor, "China's Foreign Policy Towards Africa," 446–49; Chung-lian Jiang, "China's African Policy," *African Geopolitics*, 23 (July–September 2006): 232; Ruchita Beri, "China's Rising Profile in Africa," *China Report* 43, 3 (July 2007): 300.

112. Chris Alden and Ana Cristina Alves, "History and Identity in the Construction of China's Africa Policy," *Review of African Political Economy* 35, 115 (March 2008): 53–54; Richard J. Payne and Cassandra R. Veney, "China's Post-Cold War African Policy," *Asian Survey* 38, 9 (September 1998): 868, 871. For a case study of the PRC's handling of the "Two China" question in South Africa in the 1990s, see Chris Alden and Garth Shelton, "Camarades, parias et hommes d'affaires: Mise en perspective des relations entre l'Afrique du Sud et la Chine," *Politique Africaine* 76 (December 1999): 21–29.

113. Xu Jiming, 41; Taylor, "China's Relations with Sub-Saharan Africa," 102; Chung-lian Jiang, 234.

114. Xu Jiming, 42; Garth Shelton, "China and Africa: Advancing South-South Co-operation," in *China in Africa: Mercantilist Predator or Partner in Development?* ed. Garth le Pere (Midrand, S.A.: Institute for Global Dialogue, 2006), 106–7. Julia Strauss (790) commented that Jiang's framing of the rhetoric on this tour remained as before but the content and tone shifted significantly. Jiang reflected a more confident China convinced by the success of its economic reform policies.

115. Meidan, 76–77.

116. Sun Qiaocheng, 29–30; Taylor, "China's Relations with Sub-Saharan Africa," 101–3.

117. Wu Hongying and Dao Shulin, "China vs. the Third World," *Contemporary International Relations* 11, 9 (September 2001): 8; Chung-lian Jiang, 238.

118. He Wenping, "Moving Forward with the Time," 10–12; "The Balancing Act of China's Africa Policy," *China Security* 3, 3 (Summer 2007): 36–37; He Wenping, "China-Africa Relations Moving into an Era of Rapid Development," *Inside AISA* 3–4 (October/December 2006): 4–5; Mawdsley, 413–16; Chung-lian Jiang, 239–41; Chris Alden, *China in Africa* (London: Zed Books, 2007), 30–31; Yuan Wu, 86–90; Tian Peiliang, "China and Africa in New Period," *Foreign Affairs Journal* 70 (December 2003): 38–39; Strauss, 791–93.

119. Bonnie S. Glaser and Evan S. Medeiros, "The Changing Ecology of Foreign Policy-Making in China: The Ascension and Demise of the Theory of 'Peaceful Rise'," *China Quarterly*, 190 (June 2007): 291–302; Bonnie S. Glaser, "Ensuring the 'Go Abroad' Policy Serves China's Domestic Priorities, *China Brief* 7, 5 (8 March 2007): 4. In a related concept, President Jiang Zemin announced the "Period of Strategic Opportunities" during the Sixteenth National Congress of the Communist Party in 2002. Hu Jintao reiterated the idea at the Tenth National People's Congress in 2003. It subsequently became a refrain within China to suggest that the PRC has a twenty-year period to develop and occupy the global position it merits due to its size, history, and civilization. See Bernt Berger, "Rethinking China's Engagement in Africa," *Sicherheit und Frieden* 25, 3 (2007): 150.

120. Amaury Porto de Oliveira, "A 'Beijing Consensus' Is Emerging," *Panorama* 27 (October/November 2005): 15; Alex E. Fernández Jilberto and Barbara Hogenboom, "Developing Regions, Africa and Indonesia Facing the Rise of China," *Journal of Developing Studies* 23, 3 (2007): 301; Joshua Cooper Ramo, "The Beijing Consensus," Foreign Policy Center, May 2004, 41. The Beijing Consensus provides an alternative to the Washington Consensus that emphasizes economic liberalization, privatization, tax reform, and fiscal discipline.

121. Yuan Peng, "A Harmonious World and China's New Diplomacy," *Contemporary International Relations* 17, 3 (May/June 2007): 3–4.

122. For a thorough analysis of "harmonious society" and "harmonious world," see Yongnian Zheng and Sow Keat Tok, "'Harmonious Society' and 'Harmonious World': China's Policy Discourse Under Hu Jintao," Briefing Series 26, October 2007, China Policy Institute, University of Nottingham.

123. China State Council, "China's Peaceful Development Road," 12 December 2005, www.china.org.cn/english/features/book/152684.htm.

124. Robert G. Sutter, *Chinese Foreign Relations: Power and Policy Since the Cold War* (Lanham, Md.: Rowman and Littlefield, 2008), 4.

125. PRC white paper, "China's African Policy," January 2006.

126. "Hu Jintao Delivers an Important Speech in Dar es Salaam," 16 February 2009.

127. Willy Lam, "Hu Jintao Unveils Major Foreign-Policy Initiative," *China Brief* 9, 24 (3 December 2009): 2–4; Jonathan Holslag, "China and the Coups: Coping with Political Instability in Africa," *African Affairs* 110, 440 (2011): 385–86.

128. He Wenping, "China's Diplomacy in Africa," *African Bulletin*, May 2010, www.african-bulletin.com/doc/wenping.pdf.

129. He Wenping, "The Balancing Act of China's Africa Policy," 33.

130. Ai Fei, "Promoting Friendship, Intensifying Cooperation, and Comprehensively Pushing Forward the New Development of China-Africa Relations," *Renmin Ribao*, 7 July 2006.

131. "Chinese State Councilor Vows to Advance Sino-African Strategic Partnerships," *Xinhua*, 25 May 2009.

132. Chinese Foreign Minister Yang Jiechi commented at Munich early in 2010 that China will undertake more international responsibilities commensurate with its strength and status while never pursuing self-interest at the expense of others, "Chinese FM Highlights Role of 'a Changing China in a Changing World'," *Xinhua*, 5 February 2010. For a good discussion of this increasingly important and delicate balancing act, see Jing Gu, John Humphrey, and Dirk Messner, "Global Governance and Developing Countries: The Implications of the Rise of China," Discussion Paper 18, German Development Institute, 2007, 7–11. Michael Yahuda at the London School of Economics wrote that "Chinese leaders now want their country to be seen as a 'responsible great power' that supports the *status quo*," "China's Foreign Policy Comes of Age," *International Spectator* 42, 3 (September 2007): 341.

133. This debate goes back at least to 1960 when Peter S. H. Tang analyzed the relevance of the Chinese communist model for developing countries in "Communist China as a Developmental Model for Underdeveloped Countries," monograph 1, Research Institute on the Sino-Soviet Bloc Studies, 1960. He quoted a number of African leaders who commented favorably on the Chinese model. President Sekou Touré of Guinea said during a 1960 visit to China: "We have come not only to measure all the progress of your revolution, but to be able to carry away lessons that could be applied to the actual conditions of the African struggle" (105).

134. Ethiopia's Prime Minister Meles Zenawi said that Africa needs to learn from the Chinese "development paradigm," which has provided an alternative for Africa's development, *Ethiopian News Agency*, 22 December 2008. The president of Nigeria's Senate, Ken Nnamani, said in 2006 that "China has become . . . a good model for Nigeria in its quest for an authentic and stable development ideology," quoted in Ndubisi Obiorah, "Who's Afraid of China in Africa? Towards an African Civil Society Perspective on China-Africa Relations," in *African Perspectives on China in Africa*, ed. Firoze Manji and Stephen Marks (Cape Town: Fahamu, 2007), 41. Malagasy President Marc Ravalomanana commented at the African Development Bank meeting in Shanghai: "You are an example of transformation. We in Africa must learn from your success," quoted in Antoaneta Bezlova, "China as Role Model for African Development," *IPS*, 17 May 2007. Not all Africans agree. South African President Thabo Mbeki argued that African countries "could not replicate China, whose massive private capital inflows fuelled rapid export-led growth." He added that South Africa "would not follow the Chinese model of economic development," *Business Day*, 29 July 2005.

135. One of China's leading African specialists, He Wenping, wrote in *People's Daily*, 6 November, 2006, that "China has never promoted its mode of economic development on African soil." Wei-Wei Zhang, who served as English-language interpreter for Deng Xiaoping, recalled, "I well remember Deng telling the visiting president of Ghana, Jerry Rawlings, in September 1985: 'Please don't copy our model. If there is any experience on our part, it is to formulate policies in light of one's own national conditions'"; "China: The New Global Model for Development," *New Perspectives Quarterly* 24, 1 (Winter 2007): 14. African specialist Li Anshan argued that China is reluctant to foist its model on others because as it copied from other models it had some negative experiences. China's development is a process of learning from anyone who can provide a better way for development and the process continues. "Chinese Experiences in Development: Implications for Africa," *Pambazuka News*, 18 June 2009. Chinese scholar Li Zhibiao set forth the positive and negative lessons that Africa can learn from China's development experience. He concluded that African countries should consider their own situation and not mechanically copy the Chinese program, "How Should African Nations Draw Lessons from China's Development Experience?" *Contemporary Chinese Thought* 40, 1 (Fall 2008): 56–72.

136. This is the argument that one African ambassador made to the authors during a meeting in Beijing on 12 January 2007. He added that the entire Chinese model is not appropriate for his country but it might want to adopt certain components such as the system of universal primary education.

137. Ramo, "The Beijing Consensus"; Amaury Porto de Oliveira, "A 'Beijing Consensus' Is Emerging," *Panorama* 27 (October/November 2005): 15; Stefan Halper, *The Beijing Consensus: How China's Authoritarian Model Will Dominate the Twenty-First Century* (New York: Basic Books, 2010), uses the term to refer to the Chinese model of internal development and reform over the last thirty years. The model is "going capitalist and staying autocratic" and demonstrates how to liberalize economically without surrendering one party control. He notes China's unique culture, demography, geography, and governing philosophy, concluding there is no model that can be replicated in Sub-Saharan Africa (32).

138. Wei-Wei Zhang, 13. The term "Beijing Consensus" means different things to different people. It is used widely in the literature because many Africans and a number of scholars like to contrast the Western and Chinese approach to development. See Sautman and Hairong, 81–82, and Chaponnière, 75–76.

139. Joelien Pretorius, "Non-Alignment in the Current World Order: The Impact of the Rise of China," *Strategic Review for Southern Africa* 30, 1 (May 2008): 21–24. Chris Colley, "China's Reforms at 30 and the 'Beijing Consensus'," *Pambazuka News*, 31 January 2009. Chinese sociologist Huang Ping argued there is no such thing as a Beijing Consensus or a Beijing model. See Johan Lagerkvist, "Chinese Eyes on Africa: Authoritarian Flexibility Versus Democratic Governance," *Journal of Contemporary African Studies* 27, 2 (April 2009): 125; Martin Ravallion, "Are There Lessons for Africa from China's Success Against Poverty?" World Bank Policy Research Working Paper

4463 (January 2008): 17–24; Sautman and Hairong, 81–85. African civil society representatives are especially skeptical of the Chinese model. Nigerian human rights activist Ndubisi Obiorah acknowledged that some African leaders have accepted China's alternatives over Western models. He warns, however, that some authoritarian African regimes use China's economic success to avoid "political liberalization and genuine democratization," Obiorah, 44.

140. Pang Zhongying, 49–50. See also Li Anshan, "Chinese Experiences in Development: Implications for Development," *Pambazuka News*, 18 June 2009.

141. Farhana Paruk, "Lessons for Africa from China's Rise," *Institute for Security Study Today* (27 November 2007); Pang Zhongying, 44–46.

142. David Shambaugh, "Is There a Chinese Model?" *China Daily*, 1 March 2010.

143. Martyn Davies, "China's Developmental Model Comes to Africa," *Review of African Political Economy* 35, 115 (March 2008): 134–37.

144. Friedman, 19. World Bank Country Director for China David Dollar laid out the positive and negative lessons that African governments can draw from China's development experience. See "Lessons from China for Africa," World Bank Policy Research Working Paper 4531, February 2008.

145. Julia C. Strauss, "The Past in the Present: Historical and Rhetorical Lineages in China's Relations with Africa," *China Quarterly* 199 (September 2009): 780.

146. Sanusha Naidu and Johanna Jansson, "Africa's Engagement with China: Perpetuating the Class Project?" in *Globalization and Emerging Societies: Development and Inequality*, ed. Jan Nederveen Pieterse and Boike Rehbein (Houndsmills: Palgrave Macmillan, 2009), 203.

147. Comment 2 June 2011 at meeting in Beijing attended by Shinn.

Chapter 3. Political Relations

1. The International Department of the Central Committee of the Communist Party, the functional organ of the Central Committee responsible for the party's outreach work, was originally founded in 1951 as the Liaison Department.

2. The CPC's desire to keep its political outreach activities out of the headlines makes "many things that one would like to know simply not knowable." David Shambaugh, "China's 'Quiet Diplomacy': The International Department of the Chinese Communist Party," *China: An International Journal* 5 (2007): 26–27. But while press reports about CPC political outreach in Africa are scarce, the websites of these organizations provide some of the most useful information about their histories, objectives, activities, strategies, and methods.

3. Y. L. Ying, "The Chinese Communists in Africa," *Free China and Asia* (November 1964): 17. At the end of 1959 only ten African states (Ethiopia, Liberia, South Africa, Libya, Egypt, Sudan, Tunisia, Morocco, Ghana, Guinea) were formally independent.

4. Chu Jungfu, "Xin Zhongguo wu nian lai ti waijiao" (*"Foreign Relations of New China During the Past Five Years"*), *World Culture* (5 October 1954).

5. "Modern History Sourcebook: The Common Program of the Chinese People's Political Consultative Conference, 1949," adopted by First Plenary Session of the Chinese People's Political Consultative Conference, Article 54, 29 September 1949, http://www.fordham.edu/halsall/mod/1949-ccp-program.html.

6. Bruce D. Larkin, *China and Africa, 1949–1970: The Foreign Policy of the People's Republic of China* (Berkeley: University of California Press, 1971), 215, 224–36.

7. "Constitution of the All-China Federation of Students," [102], Appendix H, 238–29, adopted 10 February 1960; see Larkin, 216.

8. Larkin, 216, 214.

9. Ibid., 219, 224.

10. "China, the Arab World and Africa: A Factual Survey 1959–1964," special China issue of *Mizan Newsletter* 6, 5 (May 1964): 6, 25.

11. Daan S. Prinsloo, "China and the Liberation of Portuguese Africa," Foreign Affairs Association Study Report 2 (Pretoria), 2 May 1976, 3.

12. *Xinhua*, February 1958, reporting on Zhou Enlai's speeh to the National People's Congress on the conference; see Ogunsanwo, 40.

13. Larkin, 47.

14. Ying, 17.

15. Ibid.; "Reception Marks Anniversary of Chinese-African People's Friendship Association," *People's Daily*, 22 December 2000.

16. Larkin, 226.

17. Ying, 17–18.

18. Sidney Rittenberg and Amanda Bennett, *The Man Who Stayed Behind* (New York: Simon & Schuster, 1994), 270.

19. Rittenberg and Bennett, 271–72.

20. *Xinhua*, 8 November 1960; see W. A. C. Adie, "Chinese Policy Towards Africa," in *The Soviet Bloc China and Africa*, ed. Sven Hamrell and Carl Gösta Widstrand (Uppsala: Scandinavian Institute of African Affairs, 1964), 53.

21. "Communists: One-Third of the Earth," *Time*, 27 October 1961.

22. *A Proposal Concerning the General Line of the International Communist Movement: The Letter of the Central Committee of the Communist party of China to the Central Committee of the Communist Party of the Soviet Union of 30th March 1963* (Peking: Foreign Language Press, 14 June 1963), 13–14.

23. General Line of the International Communist Movement, 14.

24. Larkin, 157.

25. Steven F. Jackson, "China's Third World Foreign Policy: The Case of Angola and Mozambique," *China Quarterly* 142 (June 1995): 395. In 1967, for instance, a new government in Kenya declared China's chargé d'affaires *ad interim persona non grata* and asked him to leave the country within forty-eight hours. See Sithara Fernando, "Chronology of China-Africa Relations," *China Report* 43, 3 (July 2007): 363–73.

26. Fernando, 364.

27. "C119 Scott 917–918 Afro-Asian Writers' Urgent Conference," *Xabusiness*, 1966. For stamp image see http://www.xabusiness.com/china-stamps-1966/c119.htm.

Although China subsequently issued stamps commemorating the FOCAC summits they did not commemorate people's organizations, as these did.

28. Adie, 53.

29. *People's Daily*, 9 December 1967, 5; see in Jackson, 395.

30. Larkin, 156; Shambaugh, "China's 'Quiet Diplomacy'," 27.

31. Patrick Tyler, *A Great Wall: Six Presidents and China: An Investigative History* (New York: Public Affairs, 2000), 204; Li, 16.

32. Jackson, 395. Also see Bih-jaw Lin, "Communist China's Foreign Policy in Africa: A Historical Review," *Issues and Studies* 17, 2 (February 1982): 40.

33. Richard Lowenthal, "The Sino-Soviet Split and Its Repercussions in Africa," in *The Soviet Bloc China and Africa*, ed. Hamrell and Widstrand, 132.

34. Eugene K. Lawson, "China's Policy in Ethiopia and Angola," in *Soviet and Chinese Aid to African Nations*, ed. Warren Weinstein and Thomas H. Henriksen (New York: Praeger, 1980), 172.

35. Shambaugh, "China's 'Quiet Diplomacy'," 38.

36. "Welcome Message from the Minister," 26 December 2003, CPC-ID official website, www.idcpc.org.cn/english/profile/message.htm. The CPC-ID is divided into fourteen functional offices, of which eight are regional bureaus. Bureau III (West Asian and North African Affairs) and Bureau IV (African Affairs) are relevant to this chapter's examination. "Office Lineup," CPC-ID official website undated.

37. Cai Wu, interview with China Radio International, "A Review of and Reflections on the 80 Years of Foreign Contacts of the Communist Party of China (CPC)," 1 July 2001, CPC-ID official website.

38. "Functional Features," CPC-ID official website.

39. Cai.

40. Li, 17.

41. Ibid.

42. Interview between authors and He Wenping, director of African Studies Section, Institute of West Asian and African Studies, Chinese Academy of Social Sciences, 23 October 2007. Anecdotal information was also mentioned independently during interviews conducted by Joshua Eisenman at the China Institutes of Contemporary International Studies, Chinese Association of Social Sciences, and China Institutes of International Studies, Beijing, January 2007, September 2008, March, December 2009.

43. Li, 17.

44. "Full Text of President Jiang's Speech at China-Africa Forum," PRC Consulate-General in Houston official website, 11 October 2000, http://www.china-houston.org/news/20001010185650.html.

45. Li, 17.

46. Ibid., 17–18.

47. In his *Analects*, Confucius wrote: "It is a pleasure to welcome friends from afar!" This connection between Confucius's teachings and hosting foreign friends was also made by Zhan Tao, president of Shandong University, "Welcome Friends Coming

from Afar," 18 December 2007, http://www.president.sdu.edu.cn/news/news/jqyj/2007-12-18/1197960 071.html.

48. Richard H. Solomon, *Chinese Political Negotiating Behavior: A Briefing Analysis* (Santa Monica, Calif.: Rand, 1985).

49. Interview between the authors and Phillip Idro, former Ugandan ambassador to China, Johannesburg, South Africa, 11 September 2007.

50. Li, 19.

51. This publication was provided by Chinese embassy personnel in South Africa and personnel at China's UN mission in New York. Yuan Wu, *China and Africa, 1956–200* (Beijing: China International Press, 2006), 33.

52. Shambaugh, "China's 'Quiet Diplomacy'," 45.

53. According to CAFIU's constitution (Chapter II: Tasks, article 5), the organization "establishes and develops friendly relations of cooperation with various NGOs, social and political organizations, research institutes and personages of various circles throughout the world," www.cafiu.org.cn/english/Column.asp?ColumnId = 22.

54. According to interviews with embassy staff and CPC-ID members, as of August 2007 there were CPC-ID attachés in Egypt, Ethiopia, South Africa, and Namibia and none in the Sudan, Nigeria, or Angola. The presence of attachés in all other African countries is not known.

55. Shambaugh, "China's 'Quiet Diplomacy'," 45; parentheses in original.

56. Interview with Philip Idro, Johannesburg, 16 September 2007.

57. "Zambia: In Brief; Zambia-PRC Contacts," *BBC* (21 July 1979).

58. "Chinese Communist Party Presents Books to Zambian Ruling Party," *Xinhua*, 11 January 1984.

59. "Zambian-Chinese Party Co-Operation Accord," *Xinhua*, 29 May 1987.

60. "South Africa: In Brief, Donation from PRC for Zambian Party Headquarters," *BBC*, 17 July 1986.

61. "Prime Minister Says China Has Rescheduled Zambian Debt," *Radio Zambia*, 10 August 1990.

62. "Zambia Cherishes Friendly Relations with China, Says Minister," *Xinhua*, 17 January 1992.

63. "Zambian Ruling Party Chief Call for Intercourse with China," *Xinhua*, 14 November 1994.

64. "Zambia to Strengthen Economic Cooperation with China: Official," *People's Daily*, 28 June 2005.

65. In September 2005, for instance, Yu Zhengsheng of the political bureau of the CPC Central Committee led a delegation to Lusaka, Zambia. While there, the delegation met with Information Minister Vernon Mwaanga, Defense Minister Wamundila Muliokela, and MMD National Secretary Katele Kalumba. The latter hailed the growth in the CPC-MMD relationship and assured the delegation that his party was committed to ensuring it won the 2006 elections. "China Lauds State for Economic Gains," *Times of Zambia*, 14 September 2005.

66. Fackson Banda, "China in the African Mediascape," *Rhodes Journalism Review*, 29 September 2009.

67. Dickson Jere, "China Issues Warning over Opposition Leader's Remarks," *Agence France-Presse*, 5 September 2006.

68. "Zambia: Chinese Envoy Is Being Childish—Sata," *Post* (Lusaka), 6 September 2006.

69. Peter Goodspeed, "'King Cobra' Pits Zambia Against China: Presidential Election'," *National Post*, 27 September 2006.

70. Chiwoyu Sinyangwe, "China Is Benefiting More from Trade with Africa," *Post* (Lusaka), 9 March 2010.

71. "Zambian Ruling Party's Senior Official Meets CPC Delegation," *People's Daily*, 24 July 2008.

72. Zhao Shulan, "Reflections of China's Assistance to Zambia," in *Fifty Years of Sino-African Cooperation: Background, Progress & Significance*, ed. Liu Hongwu and Yang Jiemian (Kunming: Yunan University Press, 2009), 383.

73. Among the senior MMD leaders who attended the meeting at State House were Vice President George Kunda, MMD national chairperson Michael Mabenga, MMD chairperson for legal affairs Bwalya Chiti, and party treasurer Suresh Desai. "Zambia: MMD has a lot to learn from CPC," *Times of Zambia* (Lusaka), 16 December 2009.

74. George Chellah and Patson Chilemba, "Rupiah Went to China on a Tourism Stint—Kabimba," *Post* (Lusaka), 8 March 2010.

75. "Kabimba's Utterances Show Arrogance, Says Ronnie," President of the Republic of Zambia official webpage, 9 March 2010, http://www.statehouse.gov.zm/index.php/component/content/article/48-featured-items/351-kabimbas-utterances-show-arrogance-says-ronnie.

76. "Zimbabwe's Zanu-PF, CPC relations visionary: former diplomat," *Xinhua*, 2 July 2011.

77. "Mugabe Begins Visit to China," *New York Times*, 12 May 1981.

78. "Chinese People Are Best Friends of Zimbabwean People, Says Mugabe," *Xinhua*, 17 July 1998.

79. 80 Tichaona Sibanda, "China Helps Build State Intelligence Complex for Mugabe," *SW Radio Africa News*, 3 March 2011.

80. John Dzingi, "Zimbabwe Votes: Mashonaland," *BBC*, 13 March 2002; "China Builds U.S. $1 Million School," *The Herald* (Zimbabwe), 26 February 2010; Retlaw Matatu Matorwa, "Exploit Potential of Township Tourism," *The Herald* (Zimbabwe), 18 August 2009.

81. "China Builds U.S. $1 Million School."

82. Matorwa. Also see "Mugabe Seizes Third Farm for Himself," *The Star* (South Africa), 10 September 2006.

83. Mduduzi Mathuthu, "Mugabe Says China, Malaysia Funded £5 Million Palace," *New Zimbabwe*, 11 December 2009.

84. Chipo Sithole, "Mugabe's £5 Million Palace Complete," *New Zimbabwe*, 11 December 2009.

85. Celia W. Dugger, "Zimbabwe Arms Shipped by China Spark an Uproar," *New York Times*, 19 April 2008.

86. Sydney Kawadza, "Zimbabwe: President Hails Sino-Govt Ties," *The Herald* (Zimbabwe), 22 February 2010.

87. "President Hails China's Military," *The Herald* (Zimbabwe), 30 May 2011.

88. Zimbabwe's Zanu-PF, CPC relations visionary: former diplomat.

89. "Focus Is on Aid and Support for Africa," *Business Day* (South Africa), 1 October 2004.

90. Li, 18. Also, interview between authors and Li Chengwen, Chinese ambassador to the Sudan, Khartoum, Sudan, 8 July 2007.

91. Interview between authors and Zhang Jianwei, first secretary and CPC-ID representative, PRC embassy, Cairo, Egypt, 15 July 2007.

92. Zhang Jianwei interview.

93. "Zambian-Chinese Party Co-Operation Accord," *Xinhua*, 29 May 1987.

94. Interview between authors and Paulo T. Jorge, secretary of the Political Bureau for International Affairs, and Francisca Amelia N'Gonga, chief of the American Division, MPLA Headquarters, and former foreign minister, 15 August 2007.

95. Wu Jiao, "Cadre Training Comes into Focus," *China Daily*, 17 October 2007.

96. David Shambaugh, *China's Communist Party: Atrophy and Adaptation* (Berkeley: University of California Press, 2008), 149.

97. "Director of Education Hao Met African National Congress Executive Seminar Line" (*jiaoyuzhang Hao Shipu huijian nanfei feizhouren guomindahui quanguo zhiwei yanxiuban yixing*), Party School of the Central Committee of CPC official website, 26 November 2009, http://www.ccps.gov.cn/syzblm/sydwjl/14644.htm; "60 Years of the Chinese Revolution, Lessons to Be Learnt," African National Congress official website, undated, http://www.anc.org.za/show.php?doc = ancdocs/pubs/umrabulo/umrabulo32/art13.html.

98. "60 Years of the Chinese Revolution"; "Wang Jiarui Meets South African Guest," CPC-ID official website, 23 November 2009.

99. "Bao-Sheng Chen, Vice President Met with the Tanzanian Revolutionary Party Delegation," Fu xiaozhang Chen Baosheng huijian tansanniya gemingdang daibiaotuan yixing, CPC Central Party School official website, 16 December 2009, http://www.ccps.gov.cn/syzblm/sydwjl/14889.htm; "Africa Says 'NO' to 'China Threat'— Interview with Vice Chairman Msekwa of the Revolutionary Party of Tanzania," Forum on China-Africa Cooperation [FOCAC] official website, 28 December 2009, http://www.focac.org/eng/mtsy/t648396.htm#.

100. "About CNSA," National School of Administration of the People's Republic of China official website, undated, http://www.nsa.gov.cn/cenep/portal/user/anon/page/NSAEnglish_Ab outCNSA.page.

101. Untitled posting, National School of Administration of the People's Republic of China official website, 29 June 2009.

102. Shambaugh, *Atrophy and Adaptation*, 148.

103. Wu Jiao.

104. Shambaugh, *Atrophy and Adaptation*, 148.

105. "Leadership Development Program for Young Senior Officials in Africa," China Executive Leadership Academy Pudong official website, 6 November 2006, http://218.78.215.163:8080/articles/2006/11/06/20071206153246700628.html; "Program of Constructing Economic Zone in Africa." China Executive Leadership Academy Pudong official website, 6 July 2007.

106. "Leadership Development Program for Young Senior Officials in Africa."

107. "Program of Constructing Economic Zone in Africa."

108. "South Africa," "Egypt," 9 December 2007, China Executive Leadership Academy Pudong official website, 14 May 2008; "Egypt," 9 December 2007.

109. "Senegal," China Executive Leadership Academy Pudong official website, 14 May 2008.

110. "Uganda," China Executive Leadership Academy Pudong official website, 14 May 2008; "Tanzania," 14 May 2008; "ANC NEC Workshop II Held at CELAP," 18 October 2010.

111. "CCM to Build Ideological Colleges," *Daily News* (Tanzania), 14 September 2006, http://www.zanzibarhistory.org/2006_news.htm.

112. "Visits-In, Exchanges and Cooperation," China Executive Leadership Academy Jinggangshan official website, undated, http://www.celaj.gov.cn/english/www/12/2008-06/13.html.

113. "ANC NEC Workshop II."

114. "New Political School for Zimbabwe's Ruling Party," *The Citizen* (South Africa), 2 August 2006.

115. "Zimbabwe: Zanu-PT to Set Up Political School—Manyika," *The Herald* (Zimbabwe), 2 August 2006.

116. Brigitte Weidlich, "Swapo to be Schooled Communist Party Way," *The Namibian*, 8 August 2006.

117. "Visits-In, Exchanges and Cooperation."

118. Shambaugh, "China's 'Quiet Diplomacy'," 32.

119. Li Chengwen.

120. Interview with Liu Naiya, party secretary at the Institute of West Asian and African Studies, Chinese Academy of Social Sciences, Los Angeles, 23 October 2007.

121. Li Chengwen. See also "Chinese Communists to Promote Ties with Sudanese Ruling Party," *Xinhua*, 17 May 2006.

122. "Delegation of Sudanese Former Southern Rebels Leaves for China," *Al-Sahafah*, 17 March 2007. Accompanying Kiir on this delegation were SPLM economic section head Akwal Manak, chairman of SPLM External Relations Niyal Dheng, and SPLM spokesmen Samson Kwaje and Pagan Amum. Interestingly, this delegation does not appear on the CPC-ID website or in any Xinhua or other Chinese press report. The delegation is mentioned by the *Sudan Tribune*, "President Hu Invites Sudan's Salva Kiir to Visit China," *Sudan Tribune*, 3 February 2007.

123. "Sudan, China Share Identical Views on Darfur Issue," *Sudanese News Agency SUNA*, 19 July 2007.

124. "Sudan Expects China's Continuous Support," CPC-ID official website, 18 July 2007.

125. "Sudan, China Share Identical Views."

126. "Chinese Delegation Begins Visit to Southern Region," *Sudanese Media Center*, 25 August 2007.

127. "Special Envoy of the Chinese Government and Assistant Foreign Minister Zhai Jun Visits Sudan Successfully," Ministry of Foreign Affairs of the People's Republic of China official website, 4 September 2008, http://www.fmprc.gov.cn/eng/zxxx/t511195.htm; "Special Envoy Opens Chinese Consulate in Juba," *Sudan Tribune*, 2 September 2008.

128. "Senior CPC Official Hails China-Sudan Relations," *Xinhua*, 18 November 2009. Also see Liu Weibing, "Sudan Khartoum SPLM Machar China Zhou Yongkang Meeting, *Finroll News*, 19 November 2009.

129. "SPLM Delegation Visits China," *SPLM Today*, 20 April 2011, http://www .splmtoday.com/index.php?option = com_content&view = article&id = 606:splm-dele gation-visits-china&catid = 1:latest&Itemid = 2

130. "CPC to forge stronger bonds with South Sudan's ruling party, says CPC senior leader," *Xinhua,* 21 October 2011.

131. "Senior CPC Official Hails China-Sudan Relations." Also see Sudan Khartoum SPLM Machar China Zhou Yongkang Meeting.

132. Blade Nzimande, "The SACP 12th National Congress: A Highly Successful Gathering of South African Communists," South African Communist Party official website, 18 July 2007, www.sacp.org.za/main.php?include = pubs/umsebenzi/2007/vol6–13.ht ml. Also see "CPC Delegation Leaves for Three African Countries," *People's Daily*, 9 July 2007. On this trip, Wang's CPC delegation also made stops in Zimbabwe to meet with President Robert Mugabe and Ethiopia to meet with Prime Minister Meles Zenawi. See "China Becomes Zimbabwe's Top Priority Cooperation Partner: President," *Xinhua*, 20 July 2007; International Department Central Committee of CPC, "Ethiopian PM Speaks Highly of China's Peaceful Rise," 20 July 2007.

133. Democratic Alliance, "Leon Leads DA Delegation to China," 17 April 2005, www.da.org.za/da/Site/Eng/News/print-article.asp?id = 5135.

134. Mangosuthu Buthelezi, "Mangosuthu Buthelezi's Weekly Newsletter to the Nation," Inkatha Freedom Party official website, 11 May 2008, http://www.ifp.org.za/Newsletters/080511wn.htm. This meeting does not appear on the CPC-ID website's list of foreign contacts.

135. Wu Bangguo, "Work Report of NPC Standing Committee," *People's Daily*, 12 March 2007.

136. "China's NCP and SA Parliament Strengthen Financial Cooperation," PRC Consulate-General in Cape Town official website, undated, http://capetown.china-consulate.org/eng/xwdt/t306944.htm.

137. "China's NCP and SA Parliament Strengthen Financial Cooperation."

138. "Wang Zhaoguo Meets with South African National Assembly Speaker," National People's Congress of the PRC official website, 4 November 2009, http://www.npc.gov.cn/englishnpc/Special/ViceChairmanWangZhaoguov isitsSouthAfrica/2009-11/04/content_1525734.htm. Also see "Wang Zhaoguo Meets with African National Assembly Opposition leader," 5 November 2009; "Vice Chairman Wang Zhaoguo Leaves for African Visit," 2 November 2009.

139. China's NPC has interparliamentary friendship groups with numerous African countries including Benin, Cameroon, Central African Republic, DR Congo, Côte d'Ivoire, Djibouti, Egypt, Ethiopia, Gabon, Ghana, Guinea-Bissau, Kenya, Madagascar, Mozambique, Togo, Mali, Mauritania, Morocco, Niger, Senegal, South Africa, and Tunisia: "Bilateral Friendship Groups in Africa," NPC official website, undated. These countries were added to the "Untitled List of China-Africa Friendship Groups," undated.

140. "NPC'S Foreign Contacts," NPC official website, undated.. Wu also describes how the NPC uses interparliamentary exchanges to achieve its objectives: "During the exchanges, the two sides conducted a thorough exchange of views on bilateral relations and major international and regional issues of common concern, drew up general plans for multilevel exchanges and cooperation in various areas, and discussed ways and means to promote cooperation in practical matters." Wu, *Work Report of NPC Standing Committee.*

141. Ibid.

142. Ibid.

143. "China's Top Legislator Pledges Friendly Relations with Sudan," *People's Daily*, 16 May 2006. Comparisons were conducted among the members of the Foreign Affairs Committee of the 11th National People's Congress, as listed on the NPC website. See at "Members of the Foreign Affairs Committee of the 11th National People's Congress," undated. See also China Vitae website biographies of Jiang Enzhu and Ma Wenpu, http://chinavitae.com/biography/.

144. "He Luli Meets Zimbabwean Guest," CPC-ID official website, 19 March 2007.

145. "Zimbabwe: Chinese Delegation Calls On President," *The Herald* (Zimbabwe), 17 March 2010.

146. Nafi Ali Nafi, "Sudan and China Sign Agreements," *Sudan Tribune*, 22 May 2006. In a press statement released after his return Nafi mentions the CPC-ID strategy to boost "cooperation in the economic and commercial fields and coordinate political stances" and describes his meetings with "Chinese ministers, leaderships of the Chinese Communist Party and the officials of the Chinese companies operating in Sudan."

147. "China to Expand Friendly Relations with Sudan."

148. Howard French, "Taiwan Competes with China to Win African Hearts," *New York Times*, 24 January 1996. Also see Dan Large and Shiuh-Shen Chien, "China

Rising in Africa: Whither Taiwan?" paper presented at Fifth Conference of the European Association of Taiwan Studies, Charles University, Prague 18–20 April 2008, 5–6, www.soas.ac.uk/taiwanstudies/eats/eats2008/file43256.pdf.

149. "Chad Chooses China over Taiwan," *BBC*, 7 August 2006.

150. Dimitri Bruyas, "Taiwan-Malawi Relations are in Dangerous Tangle: MOFA Head," *China Post*, 9 January 2008. Also see "China: Beijing Ready to Fund Mozambique-Malawi Canal," *Macau Hub*, 31 December 2007.

151. Claire Ngozo, "China Puts Its Mark on Malawi," *The Guardian*, 7 May 2011. Also see Dumbani Mzale, "Malawi-China Trade Jumps 400 percent," *The Nation* (Malawi), 6 May 2011; "Bingu Orders China to Finish Thyolo University by 2014," *Nyasa Times* (Malawi), 23 August 2010; Marcel Chimwala, "Malawi awards Shire river hydropower contract to China Gezuba," *Engineering News Online* (South Africa), 25 February 2011.

152. William Foreman, "Liberia Cuts Diplomatic Ties with Taiwan, Officials Say," *AP*, 12 October 2003.

153. "Taiwan's Foreign Minister Offers Resignation over Liberia Setback," *Deutsche Presse-Agentur*, 13 October 2003; "Chinese Republic Promises 600 Peace-Keeping Force for Liberia," *The Perspective*, 20 January 2004.

154. "Chad Chooses Realism, Cash and China over Taiwan," *Agence France Presse*, 6 August 2006.

155. Interview between authors and Ming Chang, Abuja, Nigeria, 6 August 2007. Address of Trade Office available at "About ATEF, Embassies & Trade Offices of Africa Countries in Taiwan R.O.C.," Africa Taiwan Economic Forum official website, undated, http://www.africa.org.tw/introduction_english_2.asp?M = 2.

156. Interview between authors and Ambassador Jonathan Oluwole Coker, former Nigerian ambassador to China, Abuja, Nigeria, 6 August 2007.

157. "Nigeria Supports China's Anti-Secession Law: Joint Communiqué," FOCAC official website, 21 April 2005.

158. "African Countries Supporting China on the Adoption of the Anti-Secession Law," FOCAC official website, 22 March 2005.

159. Richard Lin, "About ATEF, Welcome Letter," Africa Taiwan Economic Forum official website, undated.

160. "About ATEF: ATEF Office," Africa Taiwan Economic Forum official website, undated.

161. News Release: "President Chen Addresses the Africa Day Celebration," Office of the President, Republic of China (Taiwan), official website, 28 April 2010, http://www.president.gov.tw/en/prog/news_release/
document_content.php?id = 1105499090&pre_id = 1105499090&
g_category_number = 145&category_number_2 = 145.

162. Large and Chien, 13.

163. Press Releases: "The 2010 Taiwan and Africa Environmental Leaders Meeting," ROC (Taiwan) Ministry of Foreign Affairs official website, 17 March 2010, http://www.mofa.gov.tw/webapp/fp.asp?xItem = 43888&ctnode = 1038.

164. In August the authors visited the Texray textile production facility outside Mbabane. 100,000 job figure from ROC vice president Vincent Siew press conference in Swaziland. Timothy Simelane, "Taiwan Pays Homage to SD's Support," *Swazi Observer*, 9 September 2008, http://www.president.gov.tw/2_special/2008vicepresi dent/english/international_news/01.jpg.

165. Simelane.

166. "Taiwan Medical Mission in Kingdom of Swaziland, History," "Taiwan Medical Mission in Kingdom of Swaziland, Faculty," Taiwan Medical Mission in Kingdom of Swaziland official website, undated. http://sites.google.com/site/tmmswazi land/mainpage/.

167. "Taiwan Medical Mission in Kingdom of Swaziland, Mission," Taiwan Medical Mission in Kingdom of Swaziland official website, undated.

168. Based on authors' interviews with Swazi government and royal family officials including Clifford S. Mamba, principal secretary, Sethabile E. J. Mdluli, under-secretary political, Ministry of Foreign Affairs and Trade, 20 August 2007, Phiwayinkosi E. Ginindza, chief executive officer, Swaziland Investment Promotion Authority, and Alma T. Andrade, new business manager, Tibiyo Taka Ngwane (Swazi King's personal fund), 21 August 2007.

169. Interviews between the authors and Phiwayinkosi E. Ginindza, chief executive officer, Swaziland Investment Promotion Authority, 21 August 2007.

170. *China Bulletin* 195 (25 July 1952), cited in Larkin, 220.

171. In 1949, Burhan, chairman of Xinjiang Province of the Kuomintang government, announced an uprising and accepted the CPC conditions of surrender. Burhan became the first chairman of the Xinjiang Provincial People's Government of new China, and later served as vice chairman of the National Committee of the Chinese People's Political Consultative Conference. "Burhan's Deep Love of Motherland," *People's Daily*, 18 December 2000, commemorating his 1989 death, reveals the extent of his CPC loyalty.

172. Larkin, 220, 234.

173. Mohamed Bin Huwaidin, *China's Relations with Arabia and the Gulf, 1949–1999* (New York: Routledge, 2002), 215.

174. Ogunsanwo, 33.

175. Bin Huwaidin, 214–15.

176. "Islamic Association of China Constitution," Zhongguo yisilan jiao xiehui zhangcheng, Islamic Association of China of China official website, 25 October 2006, http://www.chinaislam.net.cn/article/2006-10/20061025001300812.html.

177. In the 1950s, Libya (1951), Egypt (1953), Sudan (1956), Tunisia (1956), and Morocco (1956) became an independent bloc of Islamic North African countries.

178. Ogunsanwo, 43.

179. Shoujiang Mi and Jia You, *Islam in China* (Beijing : China Intercontinental Press, 2004), chap. 4-2, "The Formation of Islamic Organizations and Their Activities in China," 157–65.

180. Bin Huwaidin, 215. Huang Hua later became China's first permanent UN representative to in 1971 and served as China's foreign minister in 1976–1982.

181. "About the Summit," Islamic Summit Conference official website, undated, http://www.islamicsummit.org.sa/en/1.aspx.

182. "Premier Chou's Speech," *Peking Review* 17, 10 (8 March 1974): 6.

183. "Memorandum of Conversation: Nixon, Kissinger and Boumediene in the Oval Office," White House, National Security Advisor's Memoranda of Conversation, 11 April 1974, http://www.ford.utexas.edu/library/document/memcons/1552694.pdf.

184. "President Boumediene's Speech," *Peking Review* 17, 10 (8 March 1974): 6.

185. "The Organization of the Islamic Conference," PRC Ministry of Foreign Affairs official website, 15 November 2000.

186. "The Organization of the Islamic Conference."

187. "Al-Qaeda Vows Revenge on China After Riots," *Times of London*, 15 July 2009.

188. "Morocco Supports China's Tibet Policy, Beijing Olympics," *People's Daily*, 28 March 2008.

189. "Meeting Between Moroccan PM and Li Changchun," *Actualités & Revue de Presse Maroc*, 13 June 2008, http://actualites.marweb.com/maroc/politique/125.html.

190. "PM: Ethiopia Objects to Politicizing Olympics," *Xinhua*, 26 April 2008.

191. "Meles Receives Chinese Delegation," Ministry of Foreign Affairs of Ethiopia official website, 27 April 2008, http://mfa.gov.et/Press_Section/publication.php?Main_Page_Number = 4082.

192. "Chinese Deputy Minister Hails Excellent Ties with Comoros," *Al Watwan* (Comoros), 20 May 2008; "China Garners Broad International Support over Tibet Riots," *Xinhua*, 22 March 2008.

193. "Contact—Offices of Tibet," Tibetan Administration official website (government in exile), 24 September 2009, http://www.tibet.net/en/index.php?id = 86.

194. "Contact Us: Tibet Support Group Kenya," International Tibet Support Network official website, undated, http://www.tibetnetwork.org/node/395.

195. Kristen Zhang, "Chinese Tibetologists Brief Kenyan Lawmakers on Tibet," *Xinhua*, 27 August 2009. On 6 April 2009, for instance, Malawi's *Daily Times* newspaper ran a 12-page supplement on Tibet, which was actually a reprint of a white paper by the Information Office of the State Council, first published by *Xinhua* on 2 March 2009. "50 years of Democratic Reform in Tibet: Tibet an Inseparable Part of China," *Daily Times*, 6 April 2009. Original policy paper at http://news.xinhuanet .com/english/2009-03/02/content_10928003.htm.

196. Wei Tong and Kristen Zhang, "Chinese Tibetologists Visits to Kenya to Promote Cultural Exchanges," *China Radio International*, 26 August 2009.

197. "Important Issues—Worldwide Tibet Movement," Tibetan Administration official website (government in exile), undated, http://www.tibet.net/en/index .php?id = 84&rmenuid = 11.

198. "Mangosuthu Buthelezi's Weekly Newsletter to the Nation—China and Tibet," Inkatha Freedom Party official website, 28 March 2008, http://www.ifp.org.za/

Newsletters/080328wn.htm. Also see "Mangosuthu Buthelezi's Weekly Newsletter to the Nation," Inkatha Freedom Party official website, 11 May 2008, http://www.ifp .org.za/Newsletters/080511wn.htm. This meeting does not appear on the CPC-ID website list of foreign contacts.

199. "South Africa Bans Dalai Lama Trip," *BBC*, 23 March 2009; South African Friends of Tibet official website, 15 May 2009, http://www.saft.org.za/. Coetzee quote also available at http://www.jmlpress.com/OffenerBriefMotlanthe.html.

200. "De Lille slams Dalai Lama ban," *South African Press Association*, 22 March 2009.

201. "IFP: Statement by Mangosuthu Buthelezi, Inkatha Freedom Party President on His Online Letter," *Polity* (South Africa), 30 November 2009. Also see "Tibet Meeting Not Hostile Act Against China: Buthelezi," *South African Broadcasting Company* (SABC), 14 November 2009.

202. "Wang Zhaoguo Meets with National Assembly Opposition Leader." Also see "Vice Chairman Wang Zhaoguo Leaves for Africa Visit."

203. IFP: Statement by Mangosuthu Buthelezi, Inkatha Freedom Party President on His Online Letter; Mario GR Oriani-Ambrosini, "Tibet and the Road to Chinese Democratization," *Business Day* (South Africa), 21 December 2009. It is also worth noting that Wang Zhaoguo, who in addition to his CPC post is vice chairman of the NPC Standing Committee, traveled to South Africa on an NPC delegation. This example underscores the close relationship between CPC and NPC political outreach in Africa. See "Wang Zhaoguo Meets with National Assembly Opposition Leader."

204. Mike Cohen, "South Africa's Manuel Backs Decision on Dalai Lama," *Bloomberg*, 26 March 2009.

205. South African Friends of Tibet official website.

206. Sanusha Naidu and Stephen Marks, "Kung Fu Diplomacy," *Pambazuka News*, 26 March 2009.

207. Lydia Polgreen, "Dalai Lama's Visa Request Is Denied by South Africa," *New York Times*, 4 October 2011.

208. "Chinese Diplomacy, Western Hypocrisy and the UN Human Rights Commission, IV. Africa," *Human Rights Watch* 9, 3 (March 1997): 7.

209. "Chinese Diplomacy, Western Hypocrisy and the UN Human Rights Commission."

210. As of the 2009–10, 2010–11 cycles. "Membership 2006–12," UN Human Rights Council official website, undated, http://www2.ohchr.org/english/bodies/ hrcouncil/past_current_members.htm.

Chapter 4. Trade Relations

1. Mao Yufeng, "China's Interests and Strategy in the Middle East and the Arab World," in *China and the Developing World: Beijing's Strategy for the Twenty-first Century*, ed. Joshua Eisenman, Eric Heginbotham, and Derek Mitchell (Armonk, N.Y.: Sharpe, 2007), 116.

2. Wei Liang-Tsai, *Peking Versus Taipei in Africa 1960–1978* (Taipei: Asia and World Institute, 1982), 41.

3. "About Us," All-China Federation of Industry and Commerce official website, undated, http://www.chinachamber.org.cn/publicfiles/business/htmlfiles/qleng/s2569/index.html. The CCPIT aims "to promote the development of economic and trade relations between China and other countries and regions around the world." Also see "Nature and Functions," China Council for the Promotion of International Trade official website, undated, http://english.ccpit.org/Contents/Channel_402/2006/0525/840/content_840.htm.

4. Bruce D. Larkin, *China and Africa, 1949–1970: The Foreign Policy of the People's Republic of China* (Berkeley: University of California Press, 1971), 106.

5. *Xinhua*, 25 April 1955, cited in Larkin, 89–90.

6. Larkin, 20–21.

7. Wei Liang-Tsai, *Peking Versus Taipei in Africa*, 42.

8. UN Bureau of Economic Affairs, *Economic Developments in the Middle East 1955–1956: Supplement to World Economic Survey, 1956* (New York: UN, 1957), 6, 23, 26.

9. Larkin, 90.

10. Ibid.

11. *Hung-ch'I* (Red Flag) (Peking: CPC Central Committee, 1 April 1961); Larkin, 92.

12. Larkin, 106.

13. Michael Chege, "Economic Relations Between Kenya and China, 1963–2007," in *U.S. and Chinese Engagement in Africa: Prospects for Improving U.S.-China-Africa Cooperation*, ed. Jennifer Cooke et al. (Washington, D.C.: CSIS, July 2008), 15–16. Also see "Bilateral Relations," Ministry of Foreign Affairs of the PRC official website, 12 October 2003, http://www.fmprc.gov.cn/eng/wjb/zzjg/fzs/gjlb/3014/default.htm.

14. IMF DOTS, 1964–68, China pages, 270.

15. Larkin, 106.

16. Wei Liang-Tsai, *Peking Versus Taipei in Africa*, 46.

17. Larkin, 93, 106–7.

18. Alexander Eckstein, *Communist China's Economic Growth and Foreign Trade* (New York: McGraw-Hill, 1966), 310, cited in Larkin, 93.

19. CIA, "People's Republic of China: International Trade Handbook," October 1976, 1.

20. Ibid., 3. These capital purchases were generally seen as an "ill-fated economic policy of importing expensive state-of-the-art industrial plants from the West and Japan with little concern for their vital upsteam linkages or downstream costs." Richard Baum, *China Watcher: Confessions of a Peking Tom* (Seattle: University of Washington Press, 2010), 281–82.

21. CIA, "People's Republic of China," 5, 1.

22. IMF DOTS 1969–1975, 46, 50. See also Algeria, Egypt, Libya, and Nigeria country pages.

23. Deng Xiaoping, "Speech by Chairman of the Delegation of the People's Republic of China at the Special Session of the UN General Assembly," 10 April 1974.

24. Baum, 108; U.S. Department of Commerce, International Trade Administration, "China's Economy and Foreign Trade, 1979–81," May 1982, 14.

25. Baum, 108.

26. Bates Gill and Jamie Riley, "The Tenuous Hold of China Inc. in Africa," *Washington Quarterly* (Summer 2007): 43–44.

27. U.S. Department of Commerce, "China's Economy and Foreign Trade, 1979–81," 13.

28. Deborah Brautigam, *The Dragon's Gift: The Real Story of China in Africa* (London: Oxford University Press, 2009), 74.

29. Jian-Ye Wang, "What Drives China's Growing Role in Africa?" IMF Working Paper 07/211, August 2007, 20.

30. Data from 1995–2009 available from Trade and Law Centre for Southern Africa (TRALAC), Stellenbosch, South Africa, http://www.tralac.org/cgi-bin/giga.cgi?cmd = cause_dir_news&cat = 1044&cause_id = 1694.

31. Etim Imisim, "ECOWAS Positions for $10bn Chinese Aid," *This Day* (Nigeria), 17 June 2008.

32. Rob Crilly, "Chinese Seek Resources, Profits in Africa," *USA Today*, 21 June 2005.

33. *Nightly Business Report*, 22 February 2005, http://www.pbs.org/nbr/site/onair/transcripts/050222t/

34. William Kistner, "Timber Trade Fuels Liberia's Misery," *San Jose Mercury News*, 10 August 2003. Also see Allan Thornton, "Chinese Involvement in African Illegal Logging and Timber Trade," Testimony, House Committee on International Relations, Subcommittee on Africa, Human Rights and International Operations, 28 June 2005.

35. Kristen Nelson, "China Leads Energy Use, BP Statistical Review for 2011 Shows Demand Growth Fastest in Nearly 40 Years," *Petroleum News*, 12 June 2011.

36. Interviews with Chinese merchants in Lagos Chinatown clothing market, 10 August 2007.

37. "Africa-China Trading Relationship," TRALAC, 2010, 1.

38. "Africa-China Trading Relationship—Update 2009," TRALAC, 2009.

39. "Largest Cargo Ship Docks in Dar es Salaam," *Daily News* (Tanzania), 16 February 2011.

40. "Chinese Exporters Destroying Country Textile Industry," *Vanguard* (Nigeria), 16 November 2008. Also see "Not All Charmed by China's Desperate Scramble for Africa," *Sunday Tribune* (South Africa), 2 September 2007.

41. Harry G. Broadman, *Africa's Silk Road: China and India's New Economic Frontier* (Washington, D.C.: World Bank, 2007), 293.

42. Themba Munalula, "Statistical Brief Issue No. 3, China's Special Preferential Tariff Africa," COMESA Secretariat, Division of Trade, Customs and Monetary

Affairs, Statistics Unit, July 2007, comstat.comesa.int/researchdocs/China%20Statisti cal%20Brief. pdf.

43. Broadman, 174, 176.

44. "Uganda International Trade Fair 1993 Opens in Kampala," *Xinhua*, 30 October 1993.

45. In 2011 COMESA included Burundi, Comoros, DRC, Djibouti, Egypt, Eritrea, Ethiopia, Kenya, Libya, Madagascar, Malawi, Mauritius, Rwanda, Seychelles, Sudan, Swaziland, Uganda, Zambia, and Zimbabwe. "About COMESA," COMESA official website, http://about.comesa.int/lang-en/overview/history-of-comesa. The COMESA treaty was ratified a year later in Lilongwe, Malawi, 8 December 1994. Andrew Ngone, "China's Cooperation and Engagement with Africa: A COMESA Perspective," Presentation at Experience Sharing Program on Development Between China and Africa, Beijing, 22 May 2008.

46. "COMESA Trade Show Attracts 18 States," *Xinhua*, 13 May 1999.

47. "Common Market for Eastern and Southern Africa—COMESA," PRC Ministry of Foreign Affairs official website, 25 April 2002, http://www.fmprc.gov.cn/eng/ gjhdq/dqzzywt/2633/2639/t15592.htm.

48. "China Reiterates Its Support to COMESA," Press Release: COMESA Official Website, 11 November 2005.

49. "Interview: COMESA Looks Forward to Cementing Ties with China." *People's Daily*, 17 March 2005.

50. Ibid.

51. "China Granting Tariff-Free Treatment to Some Goods Exported to China by the Least Developed Countries,"FOCAC official website, 18 January 2005. Participating African countries included Benin, Burundi, Cape Verde, the Central African Republic, Comoros, DRC, Djibouti, Eritrea, Ethiopia, Guinea, Guinea-Bissau, Lesotho, Liberia, Madagascar, Mali, Mauritania, Mozambique, Niger, Rwanda, Sierra Leone, Sudan, Tanzania, Togo, Uganda, and Zambia.

52. Deborah Brautigam, "The List of Zero-Tariff Products Is Now Here!" Blog, 13 April 2010, http://www.chinaafricarealstory.com/2010/04/list-of-zero-tariff-products- is-now.html.

53. Munalula.

54. Li Nuer, Song Ying, and Tichaona Chifamba, "Interview: Customs Union Shows Strong Political Determination of COMESA States," *Xinhua*, 7 June 2009; Li Nuer, Song Ying, and Tichaona Chifamba, "Interview: China Urged to Invest More in Africa's Manufacturing Sector," *Xinhua*, 6 June 2009.

55. Li Nuer and Song Ying, "Interview: COMESA Customs Union conducive to Sino-African Cooperation: China's Special Representative," *Xinhua*, 9 June 2009.

56. "COMESA Says African Countries Should Learn from China's Development Path," *People's Daily*, 29 June 2011.

57. In 2011 SADC included Angola, Botswana, the Democratic Republic of Congo, Lesotho, Madagascar, Malawi, Mauritius, Mozambique, Namibia, Seychelles,

South Africa, Swaziland, Tanzania, Zambia, and Zimbabwe. Originally known as the Southern African Development Coordination Conference, the organization was chartered in 1980.

58. "Communiqué of the 2002 SADC Consultative Conference: SADC Institutional Reform for Poverty Reduction Through Regional Integration," Department of International Relations and Cooperation, South Africa official website, 28–29 October 2002, http://www.dfa.gov.za/docs/2002/sadc1029.htm.

59. "SADC to Further Boost Relations with China, India," *People's Daily*, 16 August 2004.

60. "Chinese PM Congratulates Southern African Body on 25th Anniversary," *Xinhua*, 19 August 2005.

61. "SADC to Seek More Cooperation with China," *People's Daily*, 20 August 2005.

62. "China Appoints Permanent Representative to SADC," *Economist* (Namibia), 20 April 2007.

63. TRALAC, 2009, 2.

64. "SADC, China Meeting Cancelled," *Bizcommunity*, 20 May 2011; "Trade Fair to Boost SADC-China Ties," South Africa official website 26 April 2011, http://www .southafrica.info/global/brics/imexpo.htm.

65. "China to Increase Imports from SADC Countries, Says Vice Premier," *Xinhua*, 4 June 2011; "Hu Jintao Meets with SADC Rotating President Pohamba," PRC Embassy in Mauritius press release, 5 June 2011 http://mu.china-embassy.org/eng/ zgxw/t828840.htm.

66. In 2011 ECOWAS included Benin, Burkina Faso, Cape Verde, Gambia, Ghana, Guinea, Guinea-Bissau, Liberia, Mali, Niger, Nigeria, Senegal, Sierra Leone, and Togo. "The Economic Community of the West African States (ECOWAS)," PRC Embassy in Norway official website, 17 May 2004, http://no.china-embassy.org/eng/wjzc/gjdqwt/ dqzz/t110994.htm.

67. "Nigerian Acting President Elected ECOWAS Chairman," *People's Daily*, 17 February 2010.

68. Profile: Economic Community of West African States (ECOWAS), African Union official website, undated, http://www.africa-union.org/About_AU/Abrecs.htm #ecowas.

69. "Yearender: Africa-A Continent Stepping onto World Stage," *Xinhua*, 18 December 2006.

70. TRALAC 2009 data.

71. "Interview: Nigerien President Terms Beijing Summit an Opportunity to Review China-Africa Cooperation," *Xinhua*, 20 October 2006.

72. "First ECOWAS Business Forum Final Report: Harnessing Private Sector Energies for the Challenges of Integration," ECOWAS official document presented in Accra, Ghana, 29–31 October 2007, 5–6.

73. "China, West Africa Initiate Trade Forum for Stronger Economic Ties," *Xinhua*, 23 September 2008.

74. "ECOWAS Bank and China to Establish Markets to Boost Trade and Investment," ECOWAS press release, 24 April 2008.

75. "ECOWAS Positions for $10bn Chinese Aid."

76. China, West Africa Initiate Trade Forum for Stronger Economic Ties, "China-ECOWAS Economic & Trade Forum Held in Beijing," China Gezhouba (Group) Corporation official website, 23 September 2008, http://www.gzbgj.com/english/article.asp?id = 853; Mei Hua, "China-ECOWAS Economic and Trade Forum," Dongfeng Chengli Special Automotive Co. Ltd, official website, 26 September 2008, http://www.dfclw.com/en/clnews/carnews138.html.

77. "China, West Africa Initiate Trade Forum for Stronger Economic Ties."

78. "ECOWAS Bank and China to Establish Markets to Boost Trade and Investment."

79. "Vice Foreign Minister Zhai Jun Meets with ECOWAS Delegation," Ministry of Foreign Affairs of the PRC website, 20 June 2011, http://www.fmprc.gov.cn/eng/zxxx/t832787.htm.

"ECOWAS Invites China to Participate in Regional Trade Fair," ECOWAS Press Release, 24 June 2011.

Chapter 5. Investment and Assistance

1. John Wong and Sarah Chan, "China's Outward Direct Investment: Expanding Worldwide," *China: An International Journal* 1, 2 (September 2003): 279–81; UNCTAD, *Asian Foreign Direct Investment in Africa* (New York: UN, 2007), 54; Garth Shelton, "China and Africa: Building an Economic Partnership," *South African Journal of International Affairs* 8, 2 (Winter 2001): 113.

2. UNCTAD, *Asian FDI*, 54; Wong and Chan, 281.

3. "Programme for China-Africa Co-Operation in Economic and Social Development," 17 November 2000, www.fmprc.gov.cn/eng/wjdt/2649/t15777.htm.

4. "China's African Policy," 12 January 2006, www.fmprc.gov.cn/eng/zxxx/t230615.htm.

5. "Forum on China-Africa Cooperation Beijing Action Plan," 16 November 2006, www.fmprc.gov.cn/zflt/eng/zxxx/t280369.htm.

6. Raphael Kaplinsky and Mike Morris, "Chinese FDI in Sub-Saharan Africa: Engaging with Large Dragons," *European Journal of Development Research* 21, 4 (2009): 553.

7. Chen Zhimin and Jian Junbo, "Chinese Provinces as Foreign Policy Actors in Africa," South African Institute of International Affairs Occasional Paper 22 (January 2009), 10–13.

8. "China to Unveil Its Foreign Assistance Policy," *Ethiopian News Agency*, 19 April 2011.

9. Jing Gu, "China's Private Enterprises in Africa and the Implications for African Development," *European Journal of Development Research* 21, 4 (2009): 573–76.

10. For background on Huawei's ties to the military, see Brad Reese, "Cisco vs. Chinese Military Partner—Huawei Technologies," 21 January 2008, www.network world.com/community/print/24176. For examples of private sector investment in Africa, see Jian-Ye Wang, "What Drives China's Growing Role in Africa?" IMF Working Paper, August 2007, 18.

11. Harry G. Broadman, "China and India Go to Africa: New Deals in the Developing World," *Foreign Affairs* 87, 2 (March/April 2008): 98.

12. Chris Alden and Martyn Davies, "A Profile of the Operations of Chinese Multinationals in Africa," *South African Journal of International Affairs* 13, 1 (Summer/Autumn 2010): 90.

13. Shinn, "Chinese Involvement in African Conflict Zones," *China Brief* 9, 7 (2 April 2009): 7–10. For example, China's ambassador to the DRC, Wu Zexian, explained that investors and governments in most countries see the Congo as a place with a lot of problems and tend to stay away. China, on the other hand, sees it as a country with "huge potential" and is prepared to stay for the long term to tap into that potential. See Alex Perry, "China's New Focus on Africa," *Time*, 24 June 2010.

14. Wong and Chan, 284–85; Raphael Kaplinsky, Dorothy McCormick, and Mike Morris, "The Impact of China on Sub Saharan Africa," unpublished paper (April 2006), 14; Mario Biggeri and Marco Sanfilippo, "Understanding China's Move into Africa: An Empirical Analysis," *Journal of Chinese Economic and Business Studies* 7, 1 (February 2009): 36; Anthony Yah Baah and Herbert Jauch, eds., "Chinese Investments in Africa: A Labour Perspective," *African Labour Research Network* (May 2009): 43, www.fnv.nl/binary/report2009_chinese_investments_in_africa_tem7–2366 3.pdf; Deborah Bräutigam, *The Dragon's Gift: The Real Story of China in Africa* (Oxford: Oxford University Press, 2009), 62–65.

15. Deborah Bräutigam, "Close Encounters: Chinese Business Networks as Industrial Catalysts in Sub-Saharan Africa," *African Affairs* 102 (2003): 466–67.

16. U.S.-China Economic and Security Review Commission, "The 88 Queensway Group: A Case Study in Chinese Investors' Operations in Angola and Beyond," 10 July 2009.

17. Chris Alden, "What Is China Doing in Guinea?" *Guardian*, 19 October 2009.

18. Bates Gill and James Reilly, "The Tenuous Hold of China Inc. in Africa," *Washington Quarterly* 30, 3 (Summer 2007): 49–51. For a good analysis of working conditions and labor relations at Chinese companies in Africa, see Baah and Jauch, 66–70; Bräutigam, *The Dragon's Gift*, 299–306.

19. Chris Alden and Christopher R. Hughes, "Harmony and Discord in China's Africa Strategy: Some Implications for Foreign Policy," *China Quarterly* 199 (September 2009): 576–79; Chris Alden and Ana Cristina Alves, "China and Africa's Natural Resources: The Challenges and Implications for Development and Governance," SAIIA Occasional Paper 41, September 2009, 20–21. Yang Guang, Director of the

Institute of West Asian and African Studies at CASS, commented at an Africa-China-United States Trilateral Conference in Monrovia, Liberia, 24 February 2010, on CSR responsibilities of Chinese companies. Yang led the research team that visited 20 companies in Mali, Sudan, and Ethiopia. He argued that the companies followed good CSR principles, adding there is room for improvement.

20. Li Anshan, "What's to Be Done After the Fourth FOCAC?" *China Monitor* (November 2009): 8. For a good discussion of Chinese overseas CSR practices and a discussion of the situation in Zambia, see Chloe Yang, "Corporate Social Responsibility and China's Overseas Extractive Industry Operations: Achieving Sustainable Natural Resource Extraction," Foundation for Environmental Security and Sustainability, August 2008, 1–12, www.fess-global.org/issuebriefs/CSR_China.pdf; Zhang Zhongxiang, "Corporate Conscience," *Beijing Review* 53 (2 December 2010): 12–13.

21. Jian-Ye Wang, 11; Helmut Asche and Margot Schüller, *China's Engagement in Africa: Opportunities and Risks for Development* (Eschborn: GTZ, 2008), 27.

22. UNCTAD, *Asian FDI*, 19. This page contains a country-by-country listing of Chinese FDI at the end of 1990 and 2005. The figures seem excessively conservative. They show, for example, $351 million cumulative Chinese FDI for Sudan at the end of 2005. The head of Sudan's Investment Office told the authors in mid-2007 that China's FDI in Sudan had passed $5 billion.

23. "Strengthen China-Africa Cooperation for Mutual Benefit," speech by Premier Wen Jiabao before Second Conference of Chinese and African Entrepreneurs, 4 November 2006; China Ministry of Commerce, "The Economic and Trade Relations Between China and African Countries in 2006," *China Commerce Yearbook 2007*, 615; Jing Gu, 572. See text of Wen Jiabao speech at www.china.org.cn/world/2009–11/09/content_18849890.htm; UNCTAD, *Report 2010 South-South Cooperation: Africa and the New Forms of Development Partnership* (New York: UN, 2010), 84–86, www.unctad.org/en/docs/aldcafrica2010_en.pdf; State Council, "China-Africa Economic and Trade Cooperation," December 2010, http://english1.people.com.cn/90001/90777/90855/7240530.html; "China Vows to Increase Government Scholarships for African Students," *Xinhua*, 20 April 2011.

24. UNCTAD, *World Investment Report 2010: Investing in a Low-Carbon Economy* (Geneva: UN, 2010), 32–33.

25. Olu Ajakaiye et al., "Seizing Opportunities and Confronting the Challenges of China—Africa Investment Relations: Insights from AERC Scoping Studies," Policy Issues Paper 2, January 2009, 4.

26. During May/June 2011 discussions in Beijing with Chinese specialists on Africa, Shinn raised these discrepancies on numerous occasions. His Chinese interlocutors had no explanation, but agreed that $9.33 billion FDI at the end of 2009 significantly understates the actual total.

27. Harry G. Broadman, *Africa's Silk Road: China and India's New Economic Frontier* (Washington, D.C.: World Bank, 2007), 94–97; UNCTAD, *Report 2010*, 84; "China Surges to 5th Largest Global Investor," *Xinhua*, 6 September 2010.

28. State Council, "China-Africa Economic and Trade Cooperation 2010"; Broadman, *The Silk Road*, 96–97; UNCTAD, *Report 2010*, 84; African Center for Economic Transformation (ACET), *Looking East: A Guide to Engaging China for Africa's Policy-Makers* 2 (Accra, November 2009), 26; Walter Kerr, "The Role of Chinese Provinces in Advancing China-Africa Relations," unpublished paper, George Washington University, 10. The African Development Bank concluded in 2009 that Chinese FDI flows to Africa had reached $1.3 billion annually and were concentrated in resource-rich countries such as Angola, DRC, Nigeria, and Sudan. See Richard Schiere, "Impact of the Financial and Economic Crisis on China's Trade, Aid and Capital Inflows to Africa," Development Research Brief, 11, September 2009, 1.

29. Lucy Hornby, "China Tries to Wean Africa Investors Off State Loans," *Reuters*, 4 November 2009.

30. Deborah Bräutigam, *China's African Aid: Transatlantic Challenges* (Washington, D.C.: German Marshall Fund of the U.S., 2008), 15; "China-Africa Cooperation in Development Financing," *African Economist* 26, 60 (May–June 2007): 13–15; Bräutigam, *The Dragon's Gift*, 115–17.

31. "CAD-Fund," www.cdb.com.cn/english/Column.asp?ColumnId = 176; Bräutigam, *The Dragon's Gift*, 93–95.

32. "Chi Jianxin," *Africa-Asia Confidential* 2, 9 (July 2008): 9; Stephen Marks, "Another Way to Build a Foothold," *Pambazuka News*, 23 April 2009. See China-Africa Development Fund web site at www.cadfund.com/en/; Conversation between Shinn and Cai Jinniu, CADF senior executive director, Research and Development, Monrovia, Liberia, 25 February 2010; Nora Wittman, "The Scramble for Africa's Nuclear Resources," *New African* 507 (June 2011): 73.

33. David Lawder, "China Interested in IFC Toxic Asset Plan—Zoellick," *Reuters*, 5 October 2009; Victoria Ruan and J. R. Wu, "Chinese Bank Defends Record in Africa," *Wall Street Journal*, 8 March 2010.

34. Jian-Ye Wang, 16.

35. UNDP, "China Africa Business Council: Annual Progress Report 2006," www.undp.org.cn/monitordocs/43576.pdf. Also see www.hkbu.edu.hk/~cabc/; www.cabc.org.cn/english/introduce.asp.

36. China Ministry of Foreign Affairs, "Implementation of Follow-Up Actions of the Beijing Summit of the Forum on China-Africa Cooperation," May 2008, www.focac.org/eng/zxxx/t459449.htm.

37. Jing Gu, 580.

38. "New Think-Tank to Focus on Africa."

39. UNCTAD, *Asian FDI*, 56–57. Barry Sautman and Yan Hairong, "The Forest for the Trees: Trade, Investment and the China-in-Africa Discourse," *Pacific Affairs* 81, 1 (Spring 2008): 22–23.

40. ACET, 29–30; Lucy Corkin, "The Strategic Entry of China's Emerging Multinationals into Africa," *China Report* 43, 3 (2007): 313–16; Olu Ajakaiye, "China and Africa—Opportunities and Challenges," African Economic Research Consortium,

9–10, www.aercafrica.org/documents/china_africa_relations/Opportunities_and_ Chal lenges%20_Olu.pdf. According to a 2009 global study, Chinese FDI tends to move into countries rich in natural resources that have a record of poor institutions. See Ivar Kolstad and Arne Wiig, "What Determines Chinese Outward FDI?" CMI Working Paper, 2009, 3, 15–16, www.cmi.no/publications/file/3332-what-determines-chinese-outward-fdi.pdf.

41. ACET, 89. China has invested massively in oil in Sudan; the 50 percent figure for manufacturing is suspect. The 87 percent figure for Zambia, where China has a large investment in copper, is also questionable. For a detailed analysis of Chinese investment in ten African countries see Baah and Jauch and a summary on pp. 35–40.

42. Bao Pu, Renee Chiang, and Adi Ignatius, *Prisoner of the State: The Secret Journal of Zhao Ziyang* (New York: Simon and Schuster, 2009), 101, 277–78; Martyn J. Davies, "Special Economic Zones: China's Developmental Model Comes to Africa," in *China into Africa: Trade, Aid, and Influence*, ed. Robert Rotberg (Washington, D.C.: Brookings Institution Press, 2008), 138–40.

43. "Nation to Hike SEZ Spending in Africa," *China Daily*, 15 September 2010.

44. Phillip Giannecchini, "Chinese Special Economic Zones in Africa," *China Monitor* (September 2011): 10–14. For an analysis of SEZs and details on those in Zambia, Nigeria, Mauritius, and Ethiopia, see Deborah Bräutigam, Thomas Farole, and Tang Xiaoyang, "China's Investment in African Special Economic Zones: Prospects, Challenges and Opportunities," *Economic Premise* 5 (March 2010), 1–6; Loro Horta, "China Building Africa's Economic Infrastructure: SEZs and Railroads," *China Brief* 10, 15 (22 July 2010): 9–12; Comments by Ian Taylor on SEZs at panel session during African Studies Association meeting in Washington, 17 November 2011.

45. Vivian Foster, William Butterfield, Chuan Chen, and Nataliya Pushak, "Building Bridges: China's Growing Role as Infrastructure Financier for Sub-Saharan Africa" (Washington, D.C.: World Bank, 2008), 35–39. In a separate study, Bo King at Johns Hopkins University estimated Chinese investment in the oil sector in Sub-Saharan Africa in 1992–2009 at $13 billion, www.sais-jhu.edu/bin/m/h/Chinas-Energy-Strategy-in-Africa.pdf.

46. Trevor Houser, "The Roots of Chinese Oil Investment Abroad," *Asia Policy* 5 (January 2008): 156; Xin Ma and Philip Andrews-Speed, "The Overseas Activities of China's National Oil Companies: Rationale and Outlook," *Minerals and Energy* 21, 1 (March 2006): 21. For a useful analysis of China's energy policy in Africa, see Ricardo Soares de Oliveira, "Making Sense of Chinese Oil Investment in Africa," in *China Returns to Africa*, ed. Chris Alden et al. (London: Hurst, 2008), 83–109. For an analysis of China's strategy for energy security, see Surya Narain Yadav, *India, China and Africa: New Partnership in Energy Security* (New Delhi: Jnanada Prakashan, 2008), 117–56.

47. Michael Bristow, "China's Long March to Africa," *BBC*, 29 November 2007.

48. Deborah A. Bräutigam and Tang Xiaoyang, "China's Engagement in African Agriculture: 'Down to the Countryside'," *China Quarterly* 199 (September 2009):

696–97; Duncan Freeman, Jonathan Holslag, and Steffi Weil, "China's Foreign Farming Policy," *BICCS Asia Paper* 3, 9 (2008): 15–21. For more examples of Chinese agricultural investments in Africa, see ACET, 77.

49. Genet Mersha, "International Agricultural Land Deals Award Ethiopian Virgin Lands to Foreign Companies," 12 August 2009, 12–13, www.ethiomedia.com/adroit/ethiopian_virgin_lands_for_sale .pdf.

50. Vincent Castel and Abdul Kamara, "Foreign Investments in Africa's Agricultural Land: Implications for Rural Sector Development and Poverty Reduction," African Development Bank Development Research Brief 2, April 2009, 2–3.

51. Lorenzo Cotula, Sonja Vermeulen, Rebeca Leonard, and James Keeley, "Land Grab or Development Opportunity? Agricultural Investment and International Land Deals in Africa," FAO, IIED, and IFAD report (2009), 55, www.reliefweb.int/rw/rwb .nsf/db900sid/KHII-75EHR4/$File/full_re port.pdf.

52. Stephen Marks, "China and the Great Global Landgrab," *Pambazuka News*, 11 December 2008.

53. "China Says Not Pushing to Expand Farming Overseas," *Alibaba.com*, 4 March 2009.

54. Carl Rubinstein, "Speaking Freely: China's Eye on African Agriculture," *Asia Times*, 2 October 2009; Bräutigam, *The Dragon's Gift*, 253–72. Bräutigam reported on her blog on 16 April 2010 that there is no strong evidence for large Chinese-owned farms in Africa. Rather, China is pursuing an innovative model of combining aid and Chinese agribusiness.

55. Riaan Meyer and Chris Alden, "Banking on Africa: Chinese Financial Institutions and Africa," SAIIA China in Africa Policy Report 5, 2008, www.saiia.org.za/images/stories/pubs/chap/chap_rep_05_meyer _alden_20 0806.pdf; Chris Alden and Riaan Meyer, "Unveiling the Diversity of Chinese Finance in Africa," *Pambazuka News*, 11 February 2010.

56. UNCTAD, *Asian FDI*, 132.

57. Tan Wei, "Overseas Expansion," *Beijing Review* 50, 48 (29 November 2007): 33; Julia Werdigier and Joseph Kahn, "Barclays Increases Bid for ABN Amro," *New York Times*, 24 July 2007.

58. "Absa, Barclays to Advise China's Eximbank Clients on Africa Investment," *Market Watch* (South Africa), 23 October 2006.

59. Ni Yanshuo, "Banking on Greater Investment," *ChinAfrica* 2, 8 (August 2007): 13; Parmy Olson, "China Grabs a Slice of Africa," *Forbes.com*, 25 October 2007.

60. William Pesek, "China's Africa Dream Is Looking Less Nightmarish," *Bloomberg*, 30 October 2007.

61. "The China-Africa Business Connection: An Interview with the CEO of Standard Bank," *McKinsey Quarterly* (June 2010).

62. Tom Burgis, "China Ready to Invest in Africa Again," *Financial Times* (5 March 2009); "Standard Bank Sees Chinese Returning to Africa," *Reuters*, 10 September 2009.

63. See CCB web site, www.ccbjhb.com/ccbjhb.html. "FirstRand, China Construction Bank Enter Deal," *The Times* (South Africa), 30 July 2009; Zhuan Ti, "BOC Marks 10 Years in South Africa," *China Daily*, 9 August 2010, www.bankofchinalocations.com/south_africa/.

64. See remarks by Zambia's central bank governor, www.boz.zm/publishing/Speeches/GovernorRemarksAtBankofChina_10Years.pdf.

65. "Ecobank Partners with China," *Kenya Broadcasting Corporation*, 15 February 2010.

66. "China Union Pay Enlists Equity Bank," *East African*, 20 September 2010.

67. "Mozambique: New Bank Inaugurated," *allAfrica.com*, 16 June 2008.

68. 22 November 2010 email from Gad Wavomba, account manager for Arik Air International.

69. Peter Kragelund and Meine Pieter van Dijk, "China's Investments in Africa," in *The New Presence of China in Africa*, ed. Meine Pieter van Dijk (Amsterdam: Amsterdam University Press, 2009), 90–91. African Development Bank, "Chinese Trade and Investment Activities in Africa," *Policy Brief* 1, 4 (29 July 2010): 2.

70. "IFC Finances China Investment in Africa," Bretton Woods Project, 18 June 2010, www.brettonwoodsproject.org/print.shtml?cmd[884] = x-884–5664 42.

71. Jing Gu, 585.

72. "Why Chinese Companies Are Doing Well Despite Global Credit Crunch," *Ghana Business News*, 27 July 2009.

73. Wang Duanyong, "China's Overseas Foreign Direct Investment Risk: 2008–2009," SAIIA Occasional Paper 73, January 2011, 18–25.

74. ACET, 30–32.

75. State Council, "China-Africa Economic and Trade Cooperation 2010." For an explanation of investment in China through Mauritius, see www.milonline.com/companies/investment-in-china.html.

76. Sue van der Merwe, "Reflections on South Africa-China Bilateral Relations," 19 August 2008.

77. Craig Timberg, "Inventive South Africa Firms Thrive in Booming China," *Washington Post*, 11 February 2007.

78. Kerr, 14, 19.

79. "China in Africa—SABMiller," *Business Day* (South Africa), 8 July 2010.

80. Andrea Goldstein et al., *The Rise of China and India: What's in It for Africa?* (Paris: OECD, 2006), 86–87.

81. Law Yu Fai, *Chinese Foreign Aid* (Saarbrücken: Breitenbach, 1984), 61–66, 240.

82. Ai Ching-chu, "China's Economic and Technical Aid to Other Countries," *Peking Review* 7, 34 (21 August 1964): 14–16. For an overview of the historical development of Chinese aid to Africa, see Liu Haifang, "China's Development Cooperation with Africa: Historical and Cultural Perspectives," in *The Rise of China and India in Africa*, ed. Fantu Cheru and Cyril Obi (London: Zed Books, 2010), 54–58.

83. Because of the importance of these principles, they follow in full: (1) The Chinese Government always bases itself on the principle of equality and mutual benefit in providing aid to other countries. It never regards such aid as a kind of unilateral alms but as something mutual. (2) In providing aid to other countries, the Chinese Government strictly respects the sovereignty of the recipient countries, and never attaches any conditions or asks for any privileges. (3) China provides economic aid in the form of interest-free or low-interest loans and extends the time limit for repayment when necessary so as to lighten the burden of the recipient countries as far as possible. (4) In providing aid to other countries, the purpose of the Chinese Government is not to make the recipient countries dependent on China but to help them embark step by step on the road of self-reliance and independent economic development. (5) The Chinese Government tries its best to help the recipient countries build projects which require less investment while yielding quicker results, so that the recipient governments may increase their income and accumulate capital. (6) The Chinese Government provides the best-quality equipment and material of its own manufacture at international market prices. If the equipment and material provided by the Chinese Government are not up to the agreed specifications and quality, the Chinese Government undertakes to replace them. (7) In providing any technical assistance, the Chinese Government will see to it that the personnel of the recipient country fully master such technique. (8) The experts dispatched by China to help in construction in the recipient countries will have the same standard of living as the experts of the recipient country. The Chinese experts are not allowed to make any special demands or enjoy any special amenities. The principles are available in State Council, "China's Foreign Aid," April 2011, http://news.xinhuanet.com/english2010/china/2011-04/21/c_1383 9683.htm.

84. Bräutigam, *China's African Aid*, 37–38; Chris Alden, "Emerging Countries as New ODA Players in LDCs: The Case of China and Africa," *Gouvernance Mondiale* 1 (2007): 5.

85. Yuan Wu, *China and Africa* (Beijing: China International Press, 2006), 47–50.

86. Li Xiaoyun, "China's Foreign Aid and Aid to Africa: Overview," slides 4, 5, 2008 PowerPoint presentation available at www.oecd.org/dataoecd/27/7/40378067.pdf.

87. Bräutigam, *China's African Aid*, 8–9. For two other analyses of the evolution of Chinese aid policy, see Penny Davies, *China and the End of Poverty in Africa: Towards Mutual Benefit?* (Sundbyberg, Sweden: Diakonia, 2007), 36–39; V. Maurice Gountin, "China's Assistance to Africa, a Stone Bridge of Sino-African Relations," 2006 unpublished paper available at www.cctr.ust.hk/china-africa/papers/Gountin, Maurice.pdf.

88. George T. Yu, "Africa in Chinese Foreign Policy," *Asian Survey* 28, 8 (August 1988): 857–58; Ian Taylor, "China's Relations with Sub-Saharan Africa in the Post-Maoist Era, 1978–1999," in *Politics and Economics of Africa*, ed. Frank Columbus (Huntington, N.Y.: Nova Science, 2001), 90–91. Zhao's "Four Principles" are (1) In carrying out economic and technological cooperation with African countries, China

abides by the principles of unity and friendship, equality and mutual benefit, respects their sovereignty, does not interfere in their internal affairs, attaches no political conditions and asks for no privileges whatsoever. (2) In China's economic and technological cooperation with African countries, full play will be given to the strong points and potentials of both sides on the basis of their actual needs and possibilities, and efforts will be made to achieve good economic results with less investment, shorter construction cycles and quicker returns. (3) China's economic and technological cooperation with African countries takes a variety of forms suited to the local specific conditions, such as offering technical services, training technical and management personnel, engaging in scientific and technological exchanges, undertaking construction projects, and entering into cooperative production and joint ventures. With regard to the cooperative projects it undertakes, the Chinese side will see to it that the signed contracts are observed, the quality of work guaranteed and stress laid on friendship. The experts and technical personnel dispatched by the Chinese side do not ask for special treatment. (4) The purpose of China's economic and technological cooperation with African countries is to contribute to the enhancement of the self-reliant capabilities of both sides and promote the growth of the respective national economies by complementing and helping each other. See Xuetong Yan, "Sino-African Relations in the 1990s," *CSIS Africa Notes* 84 (19 April 1988): 4. Law Yu Fai concluded on page 313 that the "Four Principles" represented a concise restatement of the original "Eight Principles." They emphasized actual results and acknowledged earlier management failures.

89. Colin Legum interview with Gong Dafei, *Africa Report* (March–April 1983): 22.

90. Law Yu Fai, 240–50.

91. Yuan Wu, 50–51; Bräutigam, *China's African Aid*, 10. For an updated historical account of China's aid to Africa, see Bräutigam, *The Dragon's Gift*, 22–104.

92. Yuan Wu, 52–54.

93. Bräutigam, *China's African Aid*, 10–12.

94. "Programme for China-Africa Co-Operation in Economic and Social Development."

95. "China's African Policy"; "Forum on China-Africa Cooperation Beijing Action Plan."

96. Martyn Davies et al., "How China Delivers Development Assistance to Africa," monograph, Centre for Chinese Studies, University of Stellenbosch, February 2008, 4–5. The link between foreign aid and export promotion dates back to the early years of China's aid to Africa. See Alexandra Close, "Aid from the Aidless," *Far Eastern Economic Review* 49, 5 (29 July 1965): 215.

97. There are various explanations for China's reluctance to be more transparent with its foreign assistance figures. See Penny Davies, 49–51; Carol Lancaster, "The Chinese Aid System," Center for Global Development, June 2007, 2–3.

98. For 1954–1979, see CIA, "Communist Aid Activities in Non-Communist Less Developed Countries, 1979 and 1954–79," October 1980, 18–20. For 1970–1985, see

OECD, "The Aid Programme of China," Paris, March 1987, 18–19. For 1957–1996, see Deborah Bräutigam, *Chinese Aid and African Development: Exporting Green Revolution* (New York: St. Martin's, 1998), 45–46.

99. Martyn Davies, "How China Delivers," 1–2; Penny Davies, 51–52; Thomas Lum et al., "China's Foreign Aid Activities in Africa, Latin America, and Southeast Asia," Congressional Research Service, 25 February 2009, 1–2; Asche and Schüller, 37–39; Katharina Hofmann, "Challenges for International Development Cooperation: The Case of China," FES Briefing Paper 15, November 2006, 4.

100. "China's Foreign Aid 2011"; Deborah Bräutigam, "China's Foreign Aid in Africa: What Do We Know?" in *China into Africa: Trade, Aid, and Influence*, 200–201; "China, Africa and the International Aid Architecture," African Development Bank Working Paper 107 (April 2010), 17–25.

101. "China Helps Africa Where West Failed—State Official," *Reuters*, 18 October 2007; Carlos Oya, "Greater Africa-China Economic Cooperation: Will This Widen 'Policy Space'?" *Development Viewpoint* 4 (June 2008). For a good summary of Export Import Bank activities in Africa, see Todd Moss and Sarah Rose, "China Exim Bank and Africa: New Lending, New Challenges," *Center for Global Development Notes* (November 2006). Also see Bräutigam, *The Dragon's Gift*, 111–14, 140–48.

102. Penny Davies, 47–48.

103. Paul Hubbard, "Aiding Transparency: What We Can Learn About China Exim Bank's Concessional Loans," Center for Global Development Working Paper 126, September 2007, 7.

104. Comments by Zhao Changhui, Chief Country Risk Analyst, China Export Import Bank, in meeting with Shinn in Monrovia, Liberia, 24 February 2010.

105. Shinn/Eisenman meeting with Eduardo L. Severim Morais, Deputy Minister of Finance, in Luanda, 15 August 2007. For an explanation of the "Angola model" of Export Import Bank loans, see Asche and Schüller, 36–37 and Ana Cristina Alves, "The Oil Factor in Sino-Angolan Relations at the Start of the 21st Century," SAIIA Occasional Paper 55, February 2010, 11–12.

106. Shinn/Bräutigam email exchange 15 November 2011.

107. Bräutigam, *China's African Aid*, 20, and "China's Foreign Aid in Africa," 208–11. Research done by New York University's Wagner School includes the face value of concessional loans, government-sponsored investment, debt cancellation, and grants. As a result, its totals for Sub-Saharan Africa are very large, reaching $9 billion in 2006 and $18 billion in 2007. A researcher at the Chinese Academy of Social Sciences, Zhan Shiming, stated that over the past fifty years, China's provision of foreign aid to Africa has totaled $44.4 billion. See "Conference Convened on 'Sensitive Issues in Contemporary Sino-African Relations'," *Contemporary Chinese Thought* 40, 1 (Fall 2008): 30.

108. Lancaster, 3. One analysis stated Chinese aid to Sub-Saharan Africa increased from $400 million in 1998 to almost $1.5 billion in 2007. Gerald Schmitt, unpublished

paper, "Is Africa Turning East?" October 2007, www.businessenvironment.org/dyn/be/docs/160/Schmitt.pdf. Jian-Ye Wang of the IMF suggested that Chinese aid to Sub-Saharan Africa may have been $1 to $1.5 billion in both 2004 and 2005 (8). By contrast, aid flows averaged about $310 million annually in 1989–1992.

109. Jean-Raphaël Chaponnière, "Chinese Aid to Africa, Origins, Forms and Issues," in *The New Presence of China in Africa*, 66.

110. Bräutigam, *The Dragon's Gift*, 168–72, 317.

111. Schiere, 2. See also Jean Claude Berthelemy, "China's Engagement and Aid Effectiveness in Africa," African Development Bank Working Paper 129 (May 2011), 11–16.

112. See for example, Law Yu Fai, 209–38, for the various kinds of Chinese aid projects.

113. Li Anshan, "Chinese Medical Cooperation in Africa," Nordiska Afrikainstitutet Discussion Paper 52 (2011), 9–22; Law Yu Fai, 226–29; Drew Thompson, "China's Soft Power in Africa: From the 'Beijing Consensus' to Health Diplomacy," *China Brief* 5, 5 (3 October 2005): 1–4; Shinn, "Africa, China and Health Care," *Inside AISA* 3/4 (October/December 2006): 14–16. Chinese provinces are also occasionally paired with African countries for providing training programs and even small amounts of grant aid. See Chen Zhimin and Jian Junbo, 13.

114. For a description of early Chinese agricultural engagement in Africa, see Bräutigam and Tang Xiaoyang, 688–92.

115. Yuan Wu, 56–68; Law Yu Fai, 230–38. For a detailed discussion of Chinese agricultural engagement in West Africa, see Bräutigam, *Chinese Aid and African Development*, 61–138; Yahia M. Mahmoud, *Chinese Development Assistance and West Africa Agriculture: A Shifting Approach to Foreign Aid?* (Lund: Lund University, 2007).

116. A 2010 McKinsey report noted that China has fewer than 1,000 agricultural extension experts in Africa whose efforts are uncoordinated and unsystematic. Several Chinese agricultural experts told the authors Chinese agricultural programs have had a negligible impact. See Davis and Woetzel, 5.

117. Shinn/Eisenman meeting in Beijing on 10 January 2007 with a senior official of the China State Farms Agribusiness Corporation.

118. "Beijing Action Plan."

119. "Full Text of Wu Bangguo's Speech at the China-Africa Business Cooperation Conference in Cairo," *Xinhua*, 21 May 2007.

120. "Full Text of Chinese Premier's Speech at 4th Ministerial Conference of FOCAC," *Xinhua*, 8 November 2009. For background on the agriculture technology centers, see Bräutigam, *The Dragon's Gift*, 247–52.

121. "China, Africa Cooperate on Agriculture, Forum Shows," *China.org.cn*, 12 August 2010.

122. Chaponnière, 68. For a listing of Chinese-funded infrastructure projects by sector for 2001–2007, see Foster et al., 65–72.

123. Chaponnière, 72. There is fierce competition among Chinese companies seeking infrastructure projects in Africa. In some countries, multiple Chinese companies provide the only competition. While SOEs are implementing most of these projects, the number of private Chinese construction companies is growing rapidly. See Lucy Corkin, Christopher Burke, and Martyn Davies, "China's Role in the Development of Africa's Infrastructure," SAIS Working Paper in African Studies, April 2008, 6, 15.

124. Foster et al., 13, 19. For a study of Chinese construction companies in Africa, see Chuan Chen, Pi-Chu Chiu, Ryan J. Orr, and Andrea Goldstein, "An Empirical Analysis of Chinese Construction Firms' Entry into Africa," International Symposium on Advancement of Construction Management and Real Estate, Sydney, 8–13 August 2007, 451–63. In November 2006, the Centre for Chinese Studies at Stellenbosch University published case studies on Chinese infrastructure in Angola, Sierra Leone, Tanzania, and Zambia, "China's Interest and Activity in Africa's Construction Sectors," www.dfid.gov.uk/Documents/publications/chinese-investment-africa-full.pdf. For case studies on Tanzania and Zambia, see Christopher Burke, "China's Entry into Construction Industries in Africa: Tanzania and Zambia as Case Studies," *China Report* 43, 3 (July 2007): 323–36.

125. Foster et al., 16.

126. Nicole Brewer, "The New Great Walls: A Guide to China's Overseas Dam Industry," *International Rivers* (July 2008): 17.

127. Peter Bosshard, "China Dams the World," *World Policy Journal* 26, 4 (Winter 2009/2010): 43–51.

128. Foster et al., 17–18; Faraja Mgwabati, "Tazara, China Seal 51bn/-Deal," *Daily News* (Tanzania), 30 December 2009.

129. "Wired for Growth," *Africa-Asia Confidential* 1, 9 (July 2008): 3. This article contains an excellent summary of Chinese telecommunications activity in Africa as of mid-2008.

130. Garth Shelton, "China: Transport Network Partner for African Regional Integration?" *China Monitor* (March 2010): 4–9.

131. "China Sends 50 Volunteers to Ethiopia," *People's Daily*, 31 October 2006; "More Volunteers to Venture Abroad," *China Daily*, 6 September 2006; Bräutigam, *The Dragon's Gift*, 123–24.

132. "Volunteers Return Home from Africa," *China Daily*, 29 January 2008; "Youth Volunteers in Zimbabwe for Exchange Program," *Xinhua*, 25 January 2007; "20 Volunteers Wanted for Togo Program," *Shenzhen Daily*, 2 July 2009.

133. State Council, "China-Africa Economic and Trade Cooperation 2010."

134. Jing Gu, John Humphrey, and Dirk Messner, "Global Governance and Developing Countries: The Implications of the Rise of China," *World Development* 36, 2 (2008): 285; Gernot Pehnelt, "The Political Economy of China's Aid Policy in Africa," Jena Economic Research Paper 051, 2007, 8–9. African officials welcome Chinese loans that do not attach governance and economic policy reform conditions.

For an analysis of this issue see Pang Zhongying "China's Engagement with Africa: Approaches and Challenges," in *China Outside China: China in Africa*, ed. Luca Castellani et al. (Torino: CASCC, 2007), 34–36. Bräutigam, "China, Africa and the International Aid Architecture," 37–39. For China's impact on human rights, democracy, corruption, and Zimbabwe, see Bräutigam, *The Dragon's Gift*, 284–97.

135. Chinese aid to Africa increased in the post-Tiananmen era in an effort that some observers believe was designed to win over allies as China experienced criticism from the West and pressure grew from Taiwan for diplomatic recognition. African states helped block efforts by Western countries aimed at condemning China's human rights record at the UN. See Scarlett Cornelissen and Ian Taylor, "The Political Economy of China and Japan's Relationship with Africa: A Comparative Perspective," *Pacific Review* 13, 4 (2000): 621–22; Nuria Giralt, "Chinese Aid to Africa: A Foreign Policy Tool for Political Support." master's thesis, University of the Witwatersrand, 2007, 48–50.

136. Yang Guang, director-general of the Institute of West Asian and African Studies, Chinese Academy of Social Sciences, at the Africa-China-United States Trilateral Dialogue, Monrovia, Liberia, 24 February 2010.

137. Quoted in Antoaneta Bezlova, "U.S. Nervous About China's Growing Footprint Across Africa," *IPS*, 31 July 2009.

138. Bräutigam, "China's Foreign Aid in Africa," 204; Chaponnière, 71; Berthelemy, 16–17. For an updated analysis of tied aid, see Bräutigam, *The Dragon's Gift*, 148–53.

139. Hubbard, 225.

140. Bräutigam, *The Dragon's Gift*, 154–57.

141. Shinn/Eisenman meeting in Luanda on 15 August 2007 with Eduardo L. Severim Morais, Angola deputy minister of finance.

142. Penny Davies, 67. Another study of Chinese construction companies in Africa concluded that on average they employ an equal number of Chinese and local workers and overwhelmingly use Chinese nationals for managerial positions. See Chen et al., 460. One major study on Chinese investment in Africa expressed concern about the large numbers of Chinese workers. See Baah and Jauch, 43–44.

143. Barry Sautman and Yan Hairong, "Friends and Interests: China's Distinctive Links with Africa," *African Studies Review* 50, 3 (December 2007): 86.

144. Jian-Ye Wang, 26. Bräutigam, *The Dragon's Gift*, 184–88.

145. See, for example, the concerns of UK International Development Secretary Hilary Benn in an article by Chris McGreal, "Chinese Aid to Africa May Do More Harm Than Good, Warns Benn," *Guardian* (8 February 2007); World Bank President Paul Wolfowitz in Daniel Schearf, "China Defends Role in Africa Against World Bank President's Criticism," *VOA* (24 October 2006); and U.S. Treasury Secretary Henry Paulson in an article by Adam Wolfe, "Upcoming Summit Highlights Africa's Importance to China," *Power and Interest News Report* (3 November 2006).

146. Helmut Reisen and Sokhna Ndoye, "Prudent Versus Imprudent Lending to Africa After HIPC and MDRI," draft paper published by OECD Development Centre (October 2007), 29.

147. Helmut Reisen, "Is China Actually Helping Improve Debt Sustainability in Africa?" draft paper presented at a conference in Paris, 6–7 July 2007.

148. State Council, "China-Africa Economic and Trade Cooperation 2010."

149. "Beijing Action Plan"; "Implementation of Follow-Up Actions."

150. Martine Dahle Huse and Stephen L. Muyakwa, "China in Africa: Lending, Policy Space and Governance," Norwegian Agency for Development Cooperation (2008), 22–23. For a detailed case study of China's role in Zambia's debt, see 31–54. Ngaire Woods, "Whose Aid? Whose Influence? China, Emerging Donors and the Silent Revolution in Development Assistance," *International Affairs* 84, 6 (2008): 6.

151. Lin Cotterrell and Adele Harmer, "Diversity in Donorship: The Changing Landscape of Official Humanitarian Aid. Aid Donorship in Asia," Humanitarian Policy Group Background Paper, September 2005, 19.

152. OECD, "The Aid Programme of China," 14; Xue Mouhong, "Sino-African Technical Cooperation," *Asian Review* 5 (1991): 108–9.

153. OECD, "The Aid Programme of China," 14. Also see www.uncdf.org; www.unhcr.org and www.unfpa.org; Cotterrell and Harmer, 19.

154. OECD, "The Aid Programme of China," 14; UNIDO Annual Report 2008; Xue Mouhong, 109.

155. OECD, "The Aid Programme of China," 14; UNICEF Annual Report 2008.

156. See www.wfp.org; Cotterrell and Harmer, 19.

157. OECD, "The Aid Programme of China," 14; IFAD Annual Report 2008.

158. FAO press release from Rome, 25 March 2009.

159. See www.imf.org.

160. IMF press release 09/204, 9 June 2009.

161. OECD, "The Aid Programme of China," 14.

162. See www.worldbank.org; Harry Dunphy, "World Bank Gives More Clout to a Rising China," *Washington Post*, 26 April 2010.

163. Richard McGregor, "World Bank to Work with China in Africa," *Financial Times*, 18 December 2007.

164. Aki Ito and Sandrine Rastello, "World Bank Gives First Loan to Chinese Firm in Africa," *Bloomberg*, 23 April 2010.

165. www.theglobalfund.org/programs/country/?countryID = CHN&lang = en; www.theglobalfund.org/documents/pledges_contributions.xls.

166. Jack C. Chow, "Foreign Policy: China's Billion-Dollar Aid Appetite," *NPR*, 21 July 2010, www.npr.org/templates/story/story.php?storyId = 128664027.

167. See www.afdb.org; OECD, "The Aid Programme of China," 14; Martyn Davies et al., 25. Bräutigam, "China, Africa and the International Aid Architecture," 40–41.

168. Sara Van Hoeymissen, "Aid Within the China-Africa Partnership: Emergence of an Alternative to the NEPAD Development Paradigm?" *China Aktuell* 3 (2008): 102–29; Pang Zhongying, 49–50.

169. For useful evaluations of Chinese aid, see Penny Davies, 62–72; Bräutigam, "China's African Aid," 30–31; Joshua Kurlantzick, *Charm Offensive: How China's Soft Power Is Transforming the World* (New Haven, Conn.: Yale University Press, 2007), 171–74, 202–4; Bräutigam, "China's Foreign Aid in Africa," 212–13.

170. Comment by Rong Ying, vice president of CIIS, in Beijing meeting attended by Shinn, 2 June 2011.

171. The EU Parliament adopted a resolution in 2008 critical of China's loans to Africa and its unconditional aid. China reacted indignantly. See Jin Ling, "Aid to Africa: What Can the EU and China Learn from Each Other?" SAIIA Occasional Paper 56, March 2010.

172. Ali Zafar, 125.

Chapter 6. Military and Security Ties and Peacekeeping Missions

1. For a discussion of these doctrines, see Ralph L. Powell, "Maoist Military Doctrines," *Asian Survey* 8, 4 (April 1968): 246–56; George E. Taylor, "Lin Piao and the Third World," *Virginia Quarterly Review* 42, 1 (Winter 1966): 1–11.

2. For an account of the China-Africa security relationship that includes a summary of China's military relations with ten African countries since 2000, see Shinn, "Military and Security Relations: China, Africa, and the Rest of the World," in *China into Africa: Trade, Aid, and Influence*, ed. Robert I. Rotberg (Washington, D.C.: Brookings Institution Press, 2008), 155–96.

3. China State Council, "China's National Defense in 2010," 31 March 2011, www.china.org.cn/government/whitepaper/node_7114675.htm.

4. U.S. Office of the Secretary of Defense, *Annual Report to Congress: Military and Security Developments Involving the People's Republic of China 2010*, 15, www .defense.gov/pubs/pdfs/2010_CMPR_Final.pdf.

5. Jonathan Holslag, "China's New Security Strategy for Africa," *Parameters* 39, 2 (Summer 2009); 34.

6. China Ministry of Foreign Affairs, "China's Africa Policy," January 2006, 8–9, www.chinese-embassy.org.za/eng/zxxx/t230687.htm.

7. "Forum on China-Africa Cooperation Sharm El Sheikh Action Plan (2010–2012)," 12 November 2009, www.focac.org/eng/dsjbzjhy/hywj/t626387.htm; "Implementation of the Follow-up Actions of the Beijing Summit of the Forum on China-Africa Cooperation," 10 November 2009.

8. Kristen Gunness, "China's Military Diplomacy in an Era of Change," paper delivered at National Defense University, Washington, D.C., 20 June 2006, www .ndu.edu/inss/symposia/pacific2006/gunnesspaper.pdf. For an analysis of the command

and control structure of the PLA, see David Shambaugh, *Modernizing China's Military: Progress, Problems, and Prospects* (Berkeley: University of California Press, 2002), 108–83.

9. Shambaugh, 295–96; Comments by regional experts from China at conference sponsored by George Washington University and China Institute of International Studies, Beijing, 1–2 June 2011.

10. U.S. Department of the Army, "An Assessment of the Military Assistance Programs of the People's Republic of China," 15 November 1974, 3, Digital National Security Archive.

11. For a discussion of Chinese military support for liberation movements in Zimbabwe, Angola and Mozambique, see Layi Abegunrin, "Soviet and Chinese Military Involvement in Southern Africa," *Current Bibliography on African Affairs* 16, 3 (1983–1984): 195–206.

12. Alaba Ogunsanwo, *China's Policy in Africa, 1958–1971* (London: Cambridge University Press, 1974), 146–47, 172–73; text of the protocol for sending Chinese military experts to Ghana 283–84; names, specialty, and dates of service for the experts, 277. See Ian Taylor, *China and Africa: Engagement and Compromise* (London: Routledge, 2006), 94–95, 110–12; CIA, "What the Chinese Communists Are Up to in Black Africa," 23 March 1971, *Foreign Relations, 1969–1976*, E-5, Documents on Africa, 1969–1972.

13. He Wenping, "Moving Forward with the Time: The Evolution of China's African Policy," paper for Workshop on China-Africa Relations: Engaging the International Discourse, Hong Kong University of Science and Technology, 11–22 November, 2006, 5.

14. CIA, "What the Communists Are Up to in Black Africa"; Bruce Larkin, *China and Africa, 1949–1970: The Foreign Policy of the People's Republic of China* (Berkeley: University of California Press, 1971), 183–84.

15. U.S. Department of the Army, 15.

16. Joseph P. Smaldone, "Soviet and Chinese Military Aid and Arms Transfers to Africa: A Contextual Analysis," in *Soviet and Chinese Aid to African Nations*, ed. Warren Weinstein and Thomas H. Henriksen (New York: Praeger, 1980), 104–6.

17. Ibid., 104–5.

18. CIA, "Communist Aid Activities in Non-Communist Less Developed Countries, 1979 and 1954–79," October 1980, 16.

19. Ibid., 15.

20. Smaldone, 106.

21. Lillian Craig Harris, *China's Foreign Policy Toward the Third World* (New York: Praeger, 1985), 81–82.

22. Smaldone, 109.

23. CIA, "Communist Aid Activities," 40.

24. Eric Hyer, "China's Arms Merchants: Profits in Command," *China Quarterly* 132 (December 1992): 1102; Richard A. Bitzinger, "Arms to Go: Chinese Arms Sales to the Third World," *International Security* 17, 2 (Autumn 1992): 86.

25. Daniel L. Byman and Roger Cliff, *China's Arms Sales: Motivations and Implications* (Santa Monica, Calif.: Rand, 1999), 3–4.

26. U.S. Department of State Bureau of Intelligence and Research, "China's Policy Toward Sub-Saharan Africa," 20 August 1985, 3–4, Digital National Security Archive.

27. Ibid., 50–53; John F. Copper, "China's Military Assistance," in *Communist Nations' Military Assistance*, ed. John F. Copper and Daniel S. Papp (Boulder, Colo.: Westview, 1983), 113.

28. Arthur Waldron, ed., *China in Africa* (Washington, D.C.: Jamestown Foundation, 2008), 97–101.

29. Richard F. Grimmett, *Conventional Arms Transfers to Developing Nations, 1992–1999*, CRS Report for Congress (Washington, D.C., 18 August 2000), 55, 58, 68.

30. U.S. Department of State, *World Military Expenditures and Arms Transfers* (2003), 165–66, 187–89, www.state.gov/t/vci/rls/rpt/wmeat/1999_2000/.

31. Waldron, 97–101; Byman and Cliff, 49–53; Ian Taylor, *China's New Role in Africa* (Boulder, Colo.: Lynne Rienner, 2009), 121; Mark Curtis and Claire Hickson, "Arming and Alarming? Arms Exports, Peace and Security," in *The New Sinosphere: China in Africa*, ed. Leni Wild and David Mepham (London: Institute for Public Policy Research, 2006), 44.

32. Waldron, 102–3.

33. Meeting between authors and former chief of staff of the Ethiopian Defense Forces chief of staff, General Tsadkan Gebre-Tensae, Addis Ababa, 2 July 2007.

34. Kenneth W. Allen and Eric A. McVadon, "China's Foreign Military Relations," Stimson Center Report 32, October 1999, www.stimson.org/china/pdf/chinmil.pdf.

35. Susan M. Puska, "Resources, Security and Influence: The Role of the Military in China's Africa Strategy," *China Brief* 7, 11 (30 May 2007): 2; military attaché website in Beijing, www.bjmac.org/HTML/Regions.htm.

36. Puska, 2.

37. Email dated 16 December 2007 from Western defense attaché in Beijing who obtained information from the PLA.

38. Conversation between Shinn and an AFRICOM staff member, Garmisch, Germany, 14 November 2009.

39. "New Era for China's Military Diplomacy," *People's Daily*, 6 November 2002.

40. Puska, 2–3; Holslag, 28.

41. China State Council, "China's National Defense in 2008," January 2009; "China's National Defense in 2006," December 2006.

42. Ibid.

43. Puska, 3; "China's National Defense in 2010."

44. "China's National Defense in 2008," 81–82.

45. Curtis and Hikson, 39.

46. "Statement by Vice Foreign Minister Qiao Zonghuai at the Opening Ceremony of the UN Workshop on Small Arms and Light Weapons," 20 April 2005, www.mfa.gov.cn/eng/wjb/zzjg/jks/kjfywj/t192412.htm.

47. Briefing by Assistant Foreign Minister Zhai Jun on 26 October 2006, International Press Center prior to FOCAC Summit in Beijing.

48. Jiang Yu, comments at a press conference, 30 January 2007.

49. China provided arms to both Ethiopia and Eritrea during their war in 1998–2000. Although this was clearly a conflict situation, China presumably would argue that they are both sovereign states and what they do with weapons they purchase is their business.

50. Meetings in Beijing in January 2007 between authors and various Chinese officials; Byman and Cliff, 31–41; Curtis and Hikson, 37–41. For the official Chinese position, see "China's Endeavors for Arms Control, Disarmament and Non-Proliferation," 1 September 2005, www.chinadaily.com.cn/english/doc/2005–09/01/content_474248 .htm; "Statement by Vice Foreign Minister Qiao Zonghuai."

51. 12 January 2007 meeting in Beijing.

52. Curtis and Hikson, 39.

53. "China's Endeavors for Arms Control, Disarmament and Non-Proliferation"; China, "Position Paper of the People's Republic of China at the 65th Session of the United Nations General Assembly," 13 September 2010, section V, www.fmprc.gov.cn/ eng/zxxx/t751986.htm.

54. Ian Taylor, "The 'All-Weather Friend'? Sino-African Interaction in the Twenty-First Century," in *Africa in International Politics: External Involvement on the Continent*, ed. Ian Taylor and Paul Williams (London: Routledge, 2004), 95.

55. Richard A. Bitzinger, "China's Re-Emergence as an Arms Dealer: The Return of the King?" *China Brief* 9, 14 (9 July 2009): 7–8; Stockholm International Peace Research Institute (SIPRI) database; Andrei Chang, "Lock and Load in Africa Part Three," *UPI*, 31 December 2008; Andrei Chang, "China Expanding African Arms Sales," *UPI*, 26 January 2009; Waldron, 97–101; Serge Michel and Michel Beuret, *China Safari: On the Trail of Beijing's Expansion in Africa* (New York: Nation Books, 2009), 131–44.

56. "China's National Defense in 2008," 102.

57. Richard F. Grimmett, *Conventional Arms Transfers to Developing Nations, 2002–2009*, CRS Report for Congress (Washington, D.C.: CRS, 10 September 2010), 52–53, 57–58, 65, 67.

58. Ibid., 10; Bitzinger, "China's Re-Emergence as an Arms Dealer," 8. Curtis and Hickson argue that China's arms exports have to be seen in the context of "its appetite for Africa's natural resources," 40.

59. "France Says Finding Too Many Chinese Arms in Africa," *Reuters*, 14 December 2006.

60. "Military Ties to Help Africa Develop," *China Daily*, 22 May 2010.

61. "Cooperation Tops Visit of Defence Minister to China," *allafrica.com*, 30 July 2010.

62. Hilary Andersson, "China 'Is Fuelling War in Darfur'," *BBC*, 13 July 2008.

63. For detailed information on China's military transfers to Zimbabwe, see Taylor, *China's New Role in Africa*, 123–25; Allen and McVadon, 33.

64. Levi Tillemann, "Blowback from Zimbabwe: China's Faltering Strategy on Arms Exports," *China Brief* 8, 13 (18 June 2008): 7–9.

65. L. C. Russell Hsiao, "Chinese Soldiers and Arms Exports Embroiled in Zimbabwe's Electoral Impasse," *China Brief* 8, 9 (28 April 2008): 2.

66. A senior CPC official told Shinn during a meeting in Washington on 13 December 2008 that the shipment of arms to Zimbabwe illustrated total lack of coordination within the government.

67. "Arms from China's 'Ship of Shame' Reach Mugabe," *Sunday Herald*, 17 May 2008; U.S. Office of the Secretary of Defense, *Annual Report to Congress: Military Power of the People's Republic of China 2009*, 58. There have been detailed accounts of this embarrassing episode, including Samuel J. Spiegel and Philippe Le Billon, "China's Weapons Trade: From Ships of Shame to the Ethics of Global Resistance," *International Affairs* 85, 2 (March 2009): 323–34; Miles Larmer, "The Zimbabwe Shipment Campaign," *Review of African Political Economy* 35, 117 (September 2008): 486–93; Nicole Fritz, "People Power: How Civil Society Blocked an Arms Shipment for Zimbabwe," SAIIA Occasional Paper 36, July 2009, 1–12; Max du Plessis, "Chinese Arms Destined for Zimbabwe over South African Territory: The R2P Norm and the Role of Civil Society," *African Security Review* 17, 4 (December 2008): 17–29.

68. Paul Holton, "Case Study: Liberia, 1992–2006," SIPRI (2007), 11, 15–17, 23–25; Amnesty International, "People's Republic of China: Sustaining Conflict and Human Rights Abuses, The Flow of Arms Accelerates," June 2006, www.amnesty.org.hk/html/files/images/ASA1703006.pdf.

69. Paul Horton, "Case Study: Sierra Leone, 1997-present," SIPRI (2007), 5–7, 12–13, 16, 20–21; Eric G. Berman, "Re-Armament in Sierra Leone: One Year After the Lomé Peace Agreement," Small Arms Survey Occasional Paper 1, December 2000; Taylor, "The 'All-Weather Friend'?" 97.

70. "Press Conference by Chad's Foreign Minister," United Nations, New York, 26 February 2008, www.un.org/News/briefings/docs/2008/080226_Chad.doc.htm; Holslag, 25–26.

71. UN Security Council, "Report of the Monitoring Group on Somalia," 10 March 2010, 74–98.

72. Damien Fruchart, "Case Study: Rwanda, 1994–Present," SIPRI (2007), 5, 9–10, 13, 15–16.

73. Damien Fruchart, "Case Study: Democratic Republic of the Congo, 2003–2006," SIPRI (2007), 6–8.

74. Amnesty International, "People's Republic of China"; Michel and Beuret, 136–37.

75. Pieter D. Wezeman, "Case Study: Eritrea and Ethiopia, 2000–2001," SIPRI (2007), 3–6.

76. Meeting in Addis Ababa on 2 July 2007 between authors and former Chief of Staff of the Ethiopian Defense Forces, General Tsadkan Gebre-Tensae.

77. For an overview of China's role in Sudan during the Darfur conflict, see Shinn, "China and the Conflict in Darfur," *Brown Journal of World Affairs* 26, 1 (Fall/

Winter 2009): 85–100. For two accounts that look at the arms connection from a human rights standpoint, see Stephanie L. Kotecki, "The Human Rights Costs of China's Arms Sales to Sudan—A Violation of International Law on Two Fronts," *Pacific Rim Law and Policy Journal* 17, 1 (2008): 209–35; Amnesty International, "Sudan: Arms Continuing to Fuel Serious Human Rights Violations in Darfur," 8 May 2007, www.amnesty.org/en/library/info/AFR54/019/2007. See also Richard Cockett, *Sudan: Darfur and the Failure of an African State* (New Haven, Conn.: Yale University Press, 2010), 277–81.

78. Pieter D. Wezeman, "Case Study: Darfur, Sudan, 2004–2006," SIPRI (2007), 4; "Powder Keg—Unfettered Arms Flows Reflect Sudan's Instability," *Jane's Intelligence Review* (13 November 2009); Taylor, *China's New Role in Africa*, 120–23.

79. Small Arms Survey, "Supply and Demand: Arms Flows and Holdings in Sudan," *Sudan Issue Brief* 15 (December 2009): 1. For a detailed analysis of Chinese military transfers to Sudan beginning in the mid-1980s and technical assistance in developing a domestic arms industry, see Small Arms Survey, "Arms, Oil and Darfur: The Evolution of Relations Between China and Sudan," *Sudan Issue Brief* 7 (July 2007): 4–6. According to UN Comtrade statistics, Sudan reported in 2003–2008 imports of SALW, ammunition, and military weapons and parts from China valued at more than $43 million. During the same period, China reported exports to Sudan of less than $1 million. According to Sudan's reporting, most of it arrived in 2004 and 2005. See Mike Lewis, "Skirting the Law: Sudan's Post-CPA Arms Flows," Small Arms Survey HSBA Working Paper (September 2009), 23–26. Human Rights First also published a thorough account of China's military relationship with Sudan. See "Investing in Tragedy: China's Money, Arms, and Politics in Sudan," March 2008, 11–16, www.humanrights first.info/pdf/080311-cah-investing-in-tragedy-rep ort.pdf. While Human Rights First emphasized that Russia has historically been Sudan's largest supplier of major weapons systems, it added that "China today is Sudan's single largest known provider of small arms" (15).

80. Wezeman, "Case Study: Darfur," 5–8.

81. See the UN Panel of Experts report, UNSC document S/2009/562, 29 October 2009, 35–36.

82. Hilary Andersson, "China 'Is Fuelling War in Darfur'," *BBC* (13 July 2008).

83. Shinn, "China and the Conflict in Darfur," 92–94; Daniel Large, "China and the Changing Context of Development in Sudan," *Development* 50, 3 (2007): 59–60.

84. James Blitz, "China's Arm Sales to Sudan 'Exaggerated'," *Financial Times*, 23 February 2008.

85. Lindsay Holmwood and Christopher Bodeen, "China Denies Report That It Increased Small-Arms Sales to Sudan as Darfur Violence Escalated," *AP*, 14 March 2008.

86. For a summary of attacks on Chinese nationals, see Jerker Hellström, "China's Emerging Role in Africa: A Strategic Overview," Swedish Defence Research Agency, May 2009, 18; Shinn, "Chinese Involvement in African Conflict Zones," *China Brief* 9, 7 (2 April 2009): 7.

87. "Car Blast near Nigeria Oil Port," *BBC*, 30 April 2006; Katherine Houreld, "Will Chinese Oil Workers Be Next Target of Militants?" *South China Morning Post*, 6 March 2006; Shinn, "Chinese Involvement in African Conflict Zones," 9.

88. "Chinese Telecom Firm's Special Team Arrives in Nigeria on Hostage Rescue Mission," *Xinhua*, 9 January 2007; "Nigerian Militants Release Five Chinese Workers," *VOA* (18 January 2007); "Three Chinese Workers Freed in Nigeria," *AFP*, 11 May 2008; Cyril I. Obi, "Enter the Dragon? Chinese Oil Companies and Resistance in the Niger Delta," *Review of African Political Economy* 35, 117 (September 2008): 417–34.

89. Tom Burgis, "Militants Criticise China's Plants to Tap Nigerian Oil," *Financial Times*, 29 September 2009.

90. Arthur Bright, "Sudanese Oil Field Attack Threatens Peace Talks," *Christian Science Monitor*, 27 October 2007; Andrew McGregor, "Sudan's Oil Industry Faces Major Security Challenges," *Terrorism Monitor* 7, 16 (11 August 2008): 10.

91. "Darfur Rebel Leader Claims It Attacked Chinese-Run Oil Field," *AP*, 11 December 2007. "Sudan: What Can Militants Do, and What Can China Tolerate?" *Stratfor Global Intelligence*, 13 December 2007.

92. "China Seeks Safety Guarantees After Sudan Oilfield Attack," *AFP*, 13 December 2007.

93. "Chinese Oil Workers Kidnapped in Sudan's Kordofan," *Sudan Tribune*, 20 October 2008; "Four Chinese Workers Killed in Sudan, Foreign Ministry Confirms," *Xinhua*, 28 October 2008.

94. Heba Aly and Scott Baldauf, "Will Killing of Oil Workers Harden China's Darfur Policy?" *Christian Science Monitor*, 20 October 2008.

95. Jeffrey Gettleman, "Ethiopian Rebels Kill 70 at Chinese-Run Oil Field," *New York Times*, 25 April 2007; Tsegaye Tadesse, "Petronas and Sinopec in Ethiopia Exploration Talks," *Reuters*, 10 December 2007.

96. Shinn/Eisenman meeting with Chinese embassy official in Addis Ababa, 2 July 2007.

97. Alison Klayman, "Beijing Vows to Protect Chinese in Africa from Al-Qaida Threat," *VOA*, 14 July 2009; Tania Branigan, "China Urges Its Companies and Workers to Be on Guard After Al-Qaida Threat," *Guardian*, 15 July 2009; Abdul Hameed Bakier, "Jihadis Identify U.S. Plots Against China in Xinjiang and Africa," *Terrorism Monitor* 7, 21 (17 July 2009): 3–5; Chris Zambelis, "Xinjiang Crackdown and Changing Perceptions of China in the Islamic World?" *China Brief* 9, 16 (5 August 2009): 7.

98. "Somali Pirates Release Taiwanese Ship, Says U.S. Navy," *International Herald Tribune*, 5 November 2007.

99. Christopher D. Yung and Ross Rustici, *China's Out of Area Naval Operations: Case Studies, Trajectories, Obstacles, and Potential Solutions* (Washington, D.C.: National Defense University Press, December 2010), 14.

100. Gabe Collins and Andrew Erickson, "Implications of China's Military Evacuation of Citizens from Libya," *China Brief* 11, 4 (10 March 2011): 8–10.

101. Edward Cody, "China's Expansion Puts Workers in Harm's Way," *Washington Post*, 26 April 2007.

102. Comments to Shinn by Chinese African specialists during May/June 2011 visit to Beijing.

103. "Sailing to Strengthen Global Security," *China Daily*, 26 December 2008.

104. Bates Gill and Chin-Hao Huang, "China's Expanding Role in Peacekeeping," SIPRI Policy Paper 25, November 2009, 1. So far, China has not provided combat troops to UN peacekeeping operations.

105. Ibid., vii.

106. Ian Ransom, "UN's Ban Calls on China to Be Bigger Peacemaker," *Reuters*, 1 July 2008.

107. "Chinese President in the Spotlight over Sudan," *The Star* (Johannesburg), 1 February 2007.

108. Stefan Stähle, "China's Shifting Attitude Towards United Nations Peacekeeping Operations," *China Quarterly* 195 (September 2008): 639; Yin He, *China's Changing Policy on UN Peacekeeping Operations*, Asia Paper (Stockholm: Institute for Security and Development Policy, July 2007), 16–17; International Crisis Group, *China's Growing Role in UN Peacekeeping*, Asia Report 166 (Brussels: ICG, 17 April 2009), 3. For a solid analysis of the evolution of Chinese thinking on peacekeeping, see Pang Zhongying, "China's Changing Attitude to UN Peacekeeping," *International Peacekeeping* 12, 1 (Spring 2005): 87–104.

109. Wu Zhengyu and Ian Taylor, "From Refusal to Engagement: Chinese Contributions to Peacekeeping in Africa," *Journal of Contemporary African Studies* 29, 2 (April 2011): 140–47.

110. Shinn, "Military and Security Relations," 177. For a description of the kinds of military and police personnel China sends to peacekeeping missions, see Philippe D. Rogers, "China and United Nations Peacekeeping in Africa," *Naval War College Review* 60, 2 (Spring 2007): 76–77.

111. "China to Send Peacekeeping Troops to DR Congo Next Month," *AFP*, 10 February 2003.

112. Pang Zhongying, 88; Rogers, 79–80; "Position Paper of the PRC at the 65th Session of the UNGA," section III (1).

113. "China's National Defense in 2008," 71.

114. Forum on China-Africa Cooperation (FOCAC) Addis Ababa Action Plan (2004–2006); FOCAC Beijing Action Plan (2007–2009); FOCAC Sharm El Sheikh Action Plan (2010–2012).

115. For figures on Chinese contributions to UN missions, see www.un.org/en/peacekeeping/contributors/2011/may11_3.pdf; "Chinese Elected to Lead UN Peacekeeping Force in Western Sahara," *UN News Service*, 27 August 2007; Gill and Huang, 34; International Crisis Group, 7–8. For the kinds of activities engaged in by Chinese peacekeepers in the DRC, Liberia, South Sudan, and especially the Western Sahara, see Rogers, 80–87.

116. "Darfur Is Hostile Region for Chinese Troops-Rebel Commander," *Sudan Tribune*, 24 November 2007.

117. "Darfur JEM Vows to Not Attack Chinese Peacekeepers," *Sudan Tribune*, 27 November 2007.

118. "China Opposes Public Threat to Security of Chinese Peacekeepers in Darfur," *People's Daily*, 28 November 2007.

119. Sara Van Hoeymissen, "China's Support to Africa's Regional Security Architecture: Helping Africa to Settle Conflicts and Keep the Peace?" *China Monitor* (March 2010): 10–14. "China Gives $3.5 Million for AU Mission in Darfur," *UN Integrated Regional Information Networks*, 21 June 2006.

120. Kwesi Aning, "China and Africa: Towards a New Security Relationship," in *The Rise of China and India in Africa*, ed. Fantu Cheru and Cyril Obi (London: Zed Books, 2010), 149–51.

121. Rogers, 88–89; see also ICG, 14–15; Gill and Huang, 15–16.

122. Rogers, 90.

123. "China Celebrates Ancient Navigator's 600th Anniversary of Navigating World," *Xinhua*, 11 July 2005. In an analysis of early Chinese sea power, Jung-Pang Lo argued that as the Yuan inherited the Sung navy, the Ming inherited the Yuan navy, thus continuing the spirit and tradition of the Sung navy. He concluded: "From a defensive arm the navy developed into an instrument of aggression and political domination, and from the East China Sea the naval power of the Chinese advanced to the South China Seas and into the Indian Ocean." "The Emergence of China as a Sea Power During the Late Sung and Early Yuan Periods," *Far Eastern Quarterly* (pre-1986) 14, 4 (August 1955): 503.

124. George T. Yu, *China's Quest for National Security and Political Influence: The Indian Ocean Connection* (Seoul: Institute of Social Sciences, Seoul National University, April 1979), 9–13.

125. China State Council, "China's National Defense in 2006," 29 December 2006, www.fas.org/nuke/guide/china/doctrine/wp2006.html.

126. "China's National Defense in 2008," 31.

127. U.S. Office of Naval Intelligence, "The People's Liberation Army Navy: A Modern Navy with Chinese Characteristics," August 2009, 10–11, www.fas.org/irp/agency/oni/pla.navy.pdf.

128. Shinn, "Military and Security Relations," 182; Dennis Blair and Kenneth Lieberthal, "Smooth Sailing: The World's Shipping Lanes Are Safe," *Foreign Affairs* 86, 3 (May/June 2007): 7; Robert D. Kaplan, "The Geography of Chinese Power: How Far Can Beijing Reach on Land and at Sea?" *Foreign Affairs* 89, 3 (May/June 2010): 24.

129. Jacques de Lisle, "China Rising: Assessing China's Economic and Military Power," Foreign Policy Research Institute Conference Report (Philadelphia, 2007).

130. Zhang Wenmu, "Sea Power and China's Strategic Choices," *China Security* 2, 2 (Summer 2006): 17.

131. Antoine Halff, "Africa on My Mind: The Panda Menace," *The National Interest*, 90 (July/August 2007): 40; U.S. Joint Forces Command, "The Joint Operating Environment 2008," 27, www.jfcom.mil/newslink/storyarchive/2008/JOE2008.pdf;

Toshi Yoshihara and James R. Holmes, "China's Energy-Driven 'Soft Power'," *Orbis* 52, 1 (Winter 2008): 131.

132. "The People's Liberation Army Navy," 18–21; "Military and Security Developments Involving the People's Republic of China 2010," 2–3; Ronald O'Rourke, *China Naval Modernization: Implications for U.S. Navy Capabilities-Background and Issues for Congress* (Washington, D.C.: CRS, 22 April 2011), 41.

133. Robert D. Kaplan, "While U.S. Is Distracted, China Develops Sea Power," *Washington Post*, 26 September 2010.

134. "The People's Liberation Army Navy," 19; "Military and Security Developments Involving the People's Republic of China 2010," 48; O'Rourke, 24–26; Chris Buckley, "China Launches First Aircraft Carrier on Maiden Sea Trial," *Reuters,* 10 August 2011. In addition, see Nan Li and Christopher Weuve, "China's Aircraft Carrier Ambitions: An Update," *War College Review* 63, 1 (Winter 2010): 13–31; "China Confirms Construction of 'Secret' First Aircraft Carrier," *Global Post*, 8 June 2011.

135. Robert D. Kaplan, "Center Stage for the Twenty-First Century: Power Plays in the Indian Ocean," *Foreign Affairs* 88, 2 (March/April 2009): 22; Kaplan, "The Revenge of Geography," *Foreign Policy* (May/June 2009): 101. For additional information on the use of Indian Ocean ports by PLA navy ships, see Daniel J. Kostecka, "The Chinese Navy's Emerging Support Network in the Indian Ocean," *China Brief* 10, 15 (22 July 2010): 3–5. For analyses that tend to support Kaplan's argument, see Lyle J. Goldstein, "Cold Wars at Sea," *Armed Forces Journal* (April 2008): 17, 43; Jonathan Holslag, "Embracing Chinese Global Security Ambitions," *Washington Quarterly* 32, 3 (July 2009): 111–12. For a more theoretical analysis of China's intentions in the Indian Ocean, see David Walgreen, "China in the Indian Ocean Region: Lessons in PRC Grand Strategy," *Comparative Strategy* 25, 1 (2006): 55–73.

136. Gordon Arthur, "Into the Shade: China's Overseas Naval Operations," *Jane's Intelligence Review* 22, 4 (April 2010): 55; Jason J. Blazevic, "Defensive Realism in the Indian Ocean: Oil, Sea Lanes and the Security Dilemma," *China Security* 5, 3 (2009): 63–64.

137. Peter Howarth, *China's Rising Sea Power: The PLA Navy's Submarine Challenge* (London: Routledge, 2009), 41–42; see also David Lei, "China's New Multi-Faceted Maritime Strategy," *Orbis* 52, 1 (Winter 2008): 149–51.

138. "Military Expert: China Should Consider Land-Based Support Center Located in East Africa," *China Review News* (21 May 2009).

139. "China's Navy Mulls Push into Arabian Sea," *UPI*, 30 December 2009; Christopher Bodeen, "China Navy Official Says Overseas Base Needed," *AP*, 30 December 2009.

140. Richard Weitz, "Global Insights: China Tests Waters on First Overseas Naval Base," *World Politics Review* (5 January 2010).

141. Michael S. Chase and Andrew S. Erickson, "Changes in Beijing's Approach to Overseas Basing?" *China Brief* 9, 19 (24 September 2009), 8. For an analysis of African seaport capability, see Gordon S. Magenheim, "Chinese Influence on U.S.

Operational Access to African Seaports," *Joint Force Quarterly* 45 (2nd quarter 2007): 22–27. For an analysis of potential PLAN basing options in the Indian Ocean, see Daniel J. Kostecka, "Places and Bases: The Chinese Navy's Emerging Support Network in the Indian Ocean," *Naval War College Review* 64, 1 (Winter 2011): 59–78. During a meeting in Beijing on 3 June 2011 with five members of the Chinese Academy of Military Sciences, Shinn asked why China has not asked France or the United States for access to their military base in Djibouti for storage and supply in support of the Chinese ships engaged in the anti-piracy operation in the Gulf of Aden. They responded that it would look too much like a Chinese military base in Africa, contrary to Chinese policy. Instead, they said, China will contract commercially for the support its ships require. They added that China expects to increase its ship visits to Africa.

142. Mingjiang Li, "China's Gulf of Aden Expedition and Maritime Cooperation in East Asia," *China Brief* 9, 1 (12 January 2009): 5.

143. Kaufman, 3.

144. Stephen Chen and Greg Torode, "PLA Given Nod to Lead Anti-Piracy Operations," *South China Morning Post*, 22 September 2010.

145. Quoted in Zhang Quanyi, "China's Multi-Purpose Naval Mission," *UPI Asia*, 26 December 2008.

146. Ibid.

147. Eric Baculinao, "China Enters New Waters with Pirate Mission," *NBC News*, 26 December 2008.

148. Quoted in Richard Weitz, "Priorities and Challenges in China's Naval Deployments in the Horn of Africa," *China Brief* 9, 24 (3 December 2009): 12.

149. Richard Weitz, "Operation Somalia: China's First Expeditionary Force?" *China Security* 5, 1 (Winter 2009): 32–35. See also Andrew S. Erickson and Justin D. Mikolay, "Welcome China to the Fight Against Pirates," *Proceedings of the U.S. Naval Institute* 135, 3 (March 2009): 38–39. Citing China's emphasis on building an aircraft carrier and adding to its nuclear submarine fleet, the Indian navy has concluded that China "is set on the path to becoming a blue water force"; India Ministry of Defence, "Freedom to Use the Seas: India's Maritime Strategy" (2007), http://indiannavy.nicoin/maritime_strat.pdf.

150. "China Backs Fight Against Somali Piracy-UN Envoy," *Xinhua*, 25 August 2010.

151. Phil Stewart, "Attack Pirate Bosses on Land, Chinese General Says," *Reuters*, 19 May 2011. Shinn learned during May/June 2011 discussions in Beijing at the Foreign Ministry and state-affiliated think tanks that this statement was not coordinated with the Foreign Ministry and probably does not reflect broader Chinese policy.

152. Kaplan, "The Geography of Chinese Power."

153. Vijay Sakhuja, "Maritime Multilateralism: China's Strategy for the Indian Ocean," *China Brief* 9, 22 (4 November 2009): 14; Harsh V. Pant, "India in the Indian Ocean: Growing Mismatch Between Ambitions and Capabilities," *Pacific Affairs* 82, 2 (Summer 2009): 290–91; Sanjay Kumar, "China's Naval Strategy: Implications for

India," Institute of Peace and Conflict Studies, New Delhi, 2 March 2009, www.ipcs .org/print_article-details.php?recNo = 2845; Amit Kumar, "China's Island Strategy in the Indian Ocean: Breaching India's Sphere of Influence," 4 June 2010, www.observer india.com/cms/export/orfonline/modules/analysis/attachments/influence_125325133 5478.pdf; Kaplan, "Center Stage for the Twenty-First Century," 22–23.

154. Jonathan Holslag, "China, India and the Military Security Dilemma," *BICCS Background Paper* 3, 5 (2008): 14–16; Pant, 287, 291–94. For an analysis of China's view of Indian sea power, see James R. Holmes and Toshi Yoshihara, "China and the United States in the Indian Ocean: An Emerging Strategic Triangle?" *Naval War College Review* 61, 3 (Summer 2008): 51–56; Kaplan, "Center Stage for the Twenty-First Century," 27–28.

Chapter 7. Media, Education, and Cultural Relations and Ties with Chinese Communities in Africa

1. Xin Xin, "Xinhua News Agency in Africa," *Journal of African Media Studies* 1, 3 (2009): 363–64.

2. Guitier Battistella, "Xinhua: The World's Biggest Propaganda Agency," *Reporters Without Borders*, October 2005, 1. Also see "Brief Introduction," *Xinhua*, undated.

3. These regional divisions are the same as China's foreign ministry's. Thus Khartoum's Xinhua correspondent reports to Cairo, not Nairobi. Xinhua's Shao Jie has served in the Middle East and speaks Arabic. He is also a Hui Muslim. Interview with Shao Jie, Khartoum, 6 July 2010.

4. "Xinhua News Agency," China Culture.org, undated.

5. "Concept," *Xinhua*, 2000.

6. Battistella, 1; see also "Concept."

7. Anne-Marie Brady, "Treat Insiders and Outsiders Differently: The Use of Control of Foreigners in the PRC," *China Quarterly* 164 (December 2000): 949–50.

8. "Xinhua Insight: Chinese Mass Media Building Int'l Communication Capabilities," *Xinhua*, 31 December 2009.

9. "Concept."

10. "Xinhua Insight."

11. June Teufel, "China's Approach to Africa," *Far Eastern Economic Review* (3 October 1963): 469.

12. Emmanuel John Hevi, *The Dragon's Embrace: The Chinese Communists in Africa* (New York: Praeger, 1966), 106–7.

13. Ibid., 107.

14. Fritz Schatten, "Peking's Influence in Africa," *Military Review* 41, 8 (August 1961): 53.

15. Teufel, 444.

16. W. A. C. Adie, "Chinese Policy Towards Africa," in *The Soviet Bloc China and Africa*, ed. Sven Hamrell and Carl Gösta Widstrand (Uppsala: Scandinavian Institute of African Affairs, 1964), 55.

17. List combines branches noted in Teufel, 469, Hevi, 106, and Alaba Ogun-sanwo, *China's Policy in Africa 1958–1971* (London: Cambridge University Press, 1974), 76.

18. Kurt London, "Communism in Africa: The Role of China," *Problems of Communism* 11, 4 (1962): 26.

19. *People's Daily*, 10 December 1961, reprinted in London, 26.

20. Adie, 53.

21. Hevi, 106–7.

22. Xin Xin, *Xinhua News Agency in Africa*, 367, 370–71.

23. Ibid., 367–68, 370.

24. Ibid., 366, 370, 373.

25. "Brief Introduction."

26. Xin Xin, "A Developing Market in News: Xinhua News Agency and Chinese Newspapers," *Media Culture Society* 28, 1 (2006): 45–66, 60.

27. Xin Xin, *Xinhua News Agency in Africa*, 367–68.

28. Battistella, 2.

29. Interview with Xinhua correspondents Shao Jie in Khartoum, Sudan, 6 July 2007, and Dai Adai in Luanda, Angola, 16 August 2007.

30. Xin Xin, *Xinhua News Agency in Africa*, 367–68, 372.

31. "50 Years of Democratic Reform in Tibet," *Daily Times* (Malawi), 6 April 2009. Also see "50 Years of Democratic Reform in Tibet" *Xinhua*, 2 March 2009.

32. Xin Xin, *Xinhua News Agency in Africa*, 373.

33. Ibid., 368, 370–71, 373.

34. "China: Call for State Media to Expand Reporting," *Xinhua*, 2 September 2004; "Xinhua News Agency," *China Culture*.

35. "Innovations and Successes," *Xinhua*, 2000.

36. Sidney Rittenberg and Amanda Bennett, *The Man Who Stayed Behind* (New York: Simon & Schuster, 1994), 194.

37. Battistella, 4.

38. Shao Jie, Dai Adai, and Li Huailin, Lagos Bureau Chief, and Qiu Jun, Xinhua Correspondent Lagos, Nigeria, 9 August 2007. Also see Battistella, 3.

39. Shao Jie, Dai Adai, and Wu Yihong, editor-in-chief, Xinhua Regional Bureau for North Africa and the Middle East and nine Xinhua reporters and editors in Cairo, 14 July 2007.

40. Battistella, 5.

41. Hao Yalin, "Chinese Official Stresses Role of 'Propaganda' During Beijing Olympics," *Xinhua*, 31 January 2008.

42. Shao Jie.

43. "Xinhua President Meets Heads of Four African News Agencies," *Xinhua*, 13 June 2007.

44. China's Xinhua News Agency to Enhance Coverage of Africa," *Xinhua*, 17 August 2005.

45. African news agencies with ties to Xinhua include Ethiopian News Agency, Tanzanian Guardian News Group, Zambia News Agency, Agence Tunis-Afrique Presse (Tunisia), Namibia Press Agency, Bua News Agency (South Africa), Maghreb Arabe Presse (Morocco), Kenya News Agency, Guinea-Bissau State Radio and Television Corporation, Senegalese News Agency, Gabonese News Agency, Togolese News Agency, Beninese News Agency, and Central African Republic State Television.

46. "Tunisia-China: News Agencies Agree to Strengthen Cooperation," *Xinhua*, 23 April 2004. Also see "Chinese News Agency Xinhua to Promote Media Cooperation with Sierra Leone," *Xinhua*, 4 July 2005; "Xinhua Pledges to Continue Working with Local Media," *The Herald* (Harare), 26 August 2007.

47. "Cultural Exchange Plays Important Role in China-Africa Relationship," *People's Daily*, 5 November 2009. Also see "Kenyan Newspaper Signs Deal with Chinese News Agency," *Kenya Times*, 1 June 2010.

48. "Zimbabwe: Xinhua, New Ziana Sign Co-Operation Agreement," *The Herald* (Harare), 15 December 2009.

49. Examples of BuaNews-Xinhua stories include "Drinking Water Top Priority in China's New Plan," *BuaNews-Xinhua*, 27 November 2007; "Officials Detail Plans for Better Beijing Olympics," 24 January 2008; "Trading Blocs Seek New Partnership to Boost Exports," 23 June 2009.

50. Interview with Chen Ming, Xinhua Bureau Chief, and Ye Yuan, Southern Africa Correspondent, Xinhua News Agency in Johannesburg, South Africa, 17 August 2007.

51. "Chinese News Agency to Cooperate with Ethiopian, Tanzanian, Zambian Media," *Xinhua*, 12 June 2006.

52. Bivan Saluseki and Brighton Phiri, "Zambian Leader 'Totally Satisfied' with China's Generosity," *The Post* (Lusaka), 5 February 2007.

53. Zhao Shulan, "Reflections of China's Assistance to Zambia," in *Fifty Years of Sino-African Cooperation: Background, Progress & Significance*, ed. Liu Hongwu and Yang Jiemian (Kunming: Yunan University Press, 2009), 385–86.

54. Donal Brown, "African Press Wary of China's Growing Influence," *New America Media*, 7 November 2006.

55. "African Press Delegation Visits China," *People's Daily*, 20 September 2006.

56. "African Journalists Conclude China Trip, More Media Delegations to Come," *Xinhua*, 11 August 2008.

57. "The 3rd Workshop for African Journalists Held in Beijing," FOCAC official website, 13 March 2006, http://www.fmprc.gov.cn/zflt/eng/zt/jzyxb/t240314.htm.

58. Xin Xin, *Xinhua News Agency in Africa*, 366.

59. Wu Yihong et al.

60. Shao Jie.

61. According to Li Huailin, Xinhua bought the land for its Lagos office from the Chinese Consulate on a neighboring plot. Visited July 2007.

62. Li Huailin and Qiu Jun.

63. Dai Adi.

64. Li Huailin and Qiu Jun; interview with Roy Chang, editor, *West Africa United Business Weekly* (Lagos), 9 August 2007; see *West Africa United Business Weekly* (Lagos), 8 August 2007.

65. "Forum on China-Africa Cooperation Sharm El Sheik Action Plan, 2010–2012," FOCAC official website, 12 November 2009, http://www.focac.org/eng/zxxx/t626387.htm.

66. China hosts symposium for African media officials. "During the workshop, expenses of accommodation and transportation for African participants will be borne by the Chinese side." Noted in "Application Form for 3rd Workshop for African Journalists," FOCAC official website, undated.

67. "This Day Foreign Editor Attends Workshop for African Journalists Held in China," Chinese Embassy in South Africa's official website, 30 December 2004, http://za.china-embassy.org/eng/znjl/t177580.htm#.

68. "Namibia: China a True African Friend," *New Era* (Windhoek), 26 October 2004. Interestingly, there appeared to be no Chinese reporting on the 2004 and 2005 workshops. In 2006, however, there were several reports and a webpage was set up. "The 3rd Workshop for African Journalists."

69. China's Xinhua news agency to enhance coverage of Africa.

70. "CPC Senior Official Meets African Press Official," *People's Daily*, 19 August 2005.

71. "The 3rd Workshop for African Journalists."

72. "Vice Foreign Minister Lu Guozeng Awards Certificates to African journalists," FOCAC official website, 16 March 2006.

73. Gideon Nkala, "Botswana: Journeying Across Unforgettable China," *Mmegi* (Gaborone), 27 June 2008.

74. Fidelis Munyoro, "Africa: Journalists Urged to Strengthen China-Africa Relations," *The Herald* (Harare), 4 June 2008.

75. "China, Africa to Intensify Press Exchange," PRC Government's official website, 10 October 2008, http://www.gov.cn/misc/2008-10/10/content_1117433.htm.

76. "Fifth Seminar for Africa Press Officials Starts in Beijing," *People's Daily*, 9 October 2008.

77. "China, Africa to Intensify Press Exchange."

78. "Press Seminar for African Officials Aims to Show 'A Real China,' Promote Press Communication," *CCTV*, 9 October 2008, http://www.cctv.com/english/20081009/104550.shtml.

79. "FOCAC Media Seminar 2009 Opens in Beijing," PRC Consulate in Kokata, India, website, 16 July 2009, http://kolkata.china-consulate.org/eng/zgbd/t574181.htm.

80. "Head of Press Officers from 19 African Countries Hoping to Boost Sino-African Media Exchange Visits and Cooperation," FOCAC official website, 1 July 2010.

81. "China Hosts Symposium for African Media Officials," *Xinhua*, 13 July 2011.

82. Nkala.

83. John K. Cooley, *East Wind over Africa: Red China's African Offensive* (New York: Walker, 1965), 77, 214–15.

84. Ibid., 214–15.

85. Teufel, 469.

86. Cooley, 215.

87. Ibid., 44, 88, 95, 131, 215.

88. Ibid., 3.

89. Ogunsanwo, 34.

90. Cooley, 40.

91. Tina Taylor, "Analysis: Chinese Influence on African Media," *BBC World Monitoring*, 7 December 2005.

92. Cooley, 29, 214.

93. George Yu, "Dragon in the Bush: Peking's Presence in Africa," *Asian Survey* 8, 12 (1968): 1023.

94. "History and Milestones: CRI English Service," China Radio International official website, undated, http://english.cri.cn/about/history.htm.

95. "History and Milestones."

96. "Overseas Activities—CRI English Service," China Radio International official website, undated, http://english.cri.cn/about/overseas.htm.

97. Taylor.

98. "Program Schedule for 91.9 FM in Nairobi," China Radio International official website, 9 January 2009, http://english.cri.cn/7146/2009/01/09/44s441997.htm.

99. Andy Sennitt, "Ni hao! Togo, China Sign Broadcasting Agreement," *republicoftogo official website, 18 July 2010.*

100. Deng-ker Lee, "Peking's Middle East Policy in the Post-Cold War Era," *Issues & Studies* 30, 8 (August 1994): 72.

101. Cooley, 220–21.

102. Teufel, 469.

103. Sandra Gillespie, "The Educational Exchanges and Cooperation Between China and Africa," Department of Foreign Affairs, State Education Commission, 18 April 1997, in Gillespie, *South-South Transfer: A Study of Sino-African Exchanges* (New York: Routledge, 2001), 247.

104. Ibid., 248.

105. Ibid., 248–49.

106. Kenneth King, "The Beijing China-Africa Summit of 2006: The New Pledges of Aid to Education in Africa," *China Report* 43 (30 July 2007): 342, http://chr.sagepub.com/cgi/content/abstract/43/3/337.

107. "China to Train 10,000 African Personnel in Three Years," *Xinhua*, 17 December 2003.

108. "Focus Is on Aid and Support for Africa," *Business Day* (South Africa), 1 October 2004. Also see "China to Train 10,000 African Personnel."

109. King, 341.

110. "Speech by Ambassador Liu Guijin at Seminar on China-Africa Relations held by ISS," PRC Embassy in South Africa official website, 30 December 2004, http://www.chinese-embassy.org.za/eng/znjl/t177587.htm.

111. King, 342.

112. Li Anshan, "China's New Policy Toward Africa," in *China into Africa: Trade, Aid, and Influence*, ed. Robert I. Rotberg (Washington, D.C.: Brookings Institution Press, 2008), 29.

113. "Forum on China-Africa Cooperation Beijing Action Plan, 2007–2009 (5.4.4)," PRC Embassy of Zimbabwe official website, 17 November 2006, http://www.chinaembassy.org.zw/eng/xwdt/t280603.htm. Also see King, 345.

114. "Cultural Exchange Plays Important Role."

115. "China-Africa Cooperation Aims to Build Africa's Capacity—Chinese Premier," *Xinhua*, 9 November 2009.

116. "Chinese Premier Announces Eight New Measures to Enhance Cooperation with Africa," *Xinhua*, 8 November 2009.

117. "China-Africa Cooperation Aims to Build Africa's Capacity."

118. "Fourth Ministerial Conference of FOCAC Concludes in Egypt," *Xinhua*, 10 November 2009.

119. Li Anshan, 29–30.

120. Ibid., 29–30.

121. Ibid., 30.

122. James Paradise, "China and International Harmony: The Role of Confucius Institutes in Bolstering Beijing's Soft Power," *Asian Survey* 49, 4 (2009): 651. The Confucius Institute Division is one part of Hanban. It also has an Examinations Division that develops Chinese proficiency tests, a Teaching Quality and Evaluation Division that selects Chinese language teaching materials, and a division that handles international exchanges and cooperation.

123. Lai Hongyi, "China's Cultural Diplomacy: Going for Soft Power," Singapore National University, East Asian Institute (EAI) Background Brief 308, 26 October 2006, 9, www.eai.nus.edu.sg/BB308.pdf.

124. Paradise, 651.

125. "President Hu Jintao visits Nairobi Confucius Institute," Chinese Government official website, 30 April 2006, http://www.gov.cn/english/2006-04/30/content_271487.htm.

126. Lai Hongyi, 9.

127. Ibid., 10. Also see Paradise, 651.

128. "Standard Model for Confucius Institute," China Radio International official website, 19 May 2007, http://english.cri.cn/4026/2007/05/19/1361@228917.htm.

129. "President Hu Jintao visits Nairobi Confucius Institute."

130. "Confucius Institute Set Up in Kenya," Chinese Government official website, 26 January 2006, http://www.gov.cn/misc/2006-01/26/content_172553.htm.

131. "Confucius Institute Bridges Friendship Between China and Africa," China Radio International official website, 17 February 2009.

132. Ibid.

133. Interviews at Kenyatta University's Confucius Institute, 29 July 2010.

134. In October 2011 the Hanban updated the number of Confucious Insitutes; see "Kongzi xueyuan," *Baidu*, undated. http://baike.baidu.com/view/44373.html. Even among official Chinese reports there remains confusion about the size and location of some Confucius Institutes. In July 2010 during meetings at the institute at Kenyatta University officials said there were 17 operating in Africa.

135. Shanglin Luan, "Egypt, China Sign Document on Setting Up Confucius Institute," Chinese Government official website, 26 September 2006, http://www.gov.cn/misc/2006-09/26/content_398574.htm.

136. "Egypt, China Sign Agreement to Establish Confucius Institute," Chinese Government official website, 20 November 2006, http://www.gov.cn/misc/2006-11/20/content_447157.htm; interview with Counselor Chen Mingjian and First Secretary Zhang Jianwei, Chinese Embassy, Cairo, 15 July 2007; "Confucius Institute Debuts Chinese-Language Class in Cairo University," *CCTV*, 19 March 2008, http://www.cctv.com/english/20080319/101691.shtml.

137. "Confucius Institute Tablet Awarded to Egyptian University," *CCTV*, 31 May 2007.

138. "Confucius Institute Unveiled in Egypt's Suez Canal University," *People's Daily*, 2 April 2008.

139. "The Confucius Institute at the Suez Canal University Opens the First Chinese Course in Egypt for Staff from Chinese Enterprises," Hanban official website, 5 January 2010, http://english.hanban.edu.cn/content.php?id=5306.

140. "Confucius Institutes South Africa," Confucius Institutes Online, undated, http://college.chinese.cn/en/node_3830.htm.

141. "Confucius Institute at Stellenbosch University, South Africa," Xiamen University official website, 2 April 2009, http://ice.xmu.edu.cn/english/showconfucius.aspx?news_id=1710&class_code=B&class_subcode=B2.

142. The authors visited Stellenbosch's CCS in August 2007 and met with its researchers and associates.

143. "Confucius Institute," Stellenbosch University Centre for Chinese Studies official website, undated, http://www.ccs.org.za/?cat=50.

144. "China and the Democratic Republic of Congo: Partners in Development?" *China Monitor* (Stellenbosch) (October 2008): 16, www.ccs.org.za/?p=1455.

145. "The Fourth Confucius Institute Conference Held—The Cooperated Confucius Institute Between OUC and the U.S. Cited for Its Achievements," Open University of China official website, 11 December 2009, http://en.crtvu.edu.cn/news/180/180. *Also see* "The 2008 Beijing Olympics," *China Monitor* (Stellenbosch) (May 2007): 20.

146. Teufel, 469.

147. Adie, 61.

148. Ogunsanwo, 85.

149. Cooley, 221.

150. David Holley, "Torture of African Students Alleged Chinese Police Accused of Stripping Youths Held 5 Days," *Los Angeles Times*, 3 January 1989. Interviews with students at the Hopkins-Nanjing Center (class of 1989) confirmed the accuracy of this account in December 2009.

151. Interviews with African students in Nanjing, January 2007, March, December 2009.

152. Interviews with African students conducted at Zhejiang Normal University, July 2009.

153. "Forum on China-Africa Cooperation Addis Ababa Action Plan, 2004–2006," *Xinhua*, 19 October 2006. Also see "China-Africa Youth Festival Opens in Beijing," FOCAC official website, 23 August 2004.

154. "Wen Jiabao Attends the Opening Ceremony of the 3rd China-Africa Youth Festival in Beijing," PRC Embassy in the Republic of Croatia website, 14 August 2009, http://hr.chineseembassy.org/eng/zxxx/t579243.htm.

155. The U.S., for instance, began its rapprochement with China when the U.S. ambassador met with his Chinese counterpart at a Hungarian fashion show and China pushed relations forward with a subsequent invitation for the U.S. National Ping-Pong Team to visit China in 1972. Patrick Tyler, *A Great Wall: Six Presidents and China: An Investigative History* (New York: Public Affairs, 2000), 75.

156. "Cultural Exchange Between China and Africa," *China.org.cn*, 10 December 2003, http://french.china.org.cn/english/features/China-Africa/82031.htm.

157. Ogunsanwo, 32, 34–35.

158. Ibid., 35.

159. Ibid., 36, 34.

160. Wang Yunze, "Increasingly Active Sino-African Nongovernmental Exchanges," Chinese People's Association for Friendship with Foreign Countries official website, undated, http://www.cpaffc.org.cn/yszz/detaile.php?id = 192&subid = 321.

161. As of November 2009, Hunan had established such ties with 53 other international cities and regions, "Hunan Concluded Sister Cities Relationship with 54 International Cities," Hunan Provincial Government official website, 15 November 2009, http://www.enghunan.gov.cn/Goverment/govNews/200911/t20091115_180358 .htm.

162. Wang Yunze.

163. "Forum on China-Africa Cooperation Addis Ababa Action Plan, 2004–2006."

164. "Cultural Exchange Between China and Africa."

165. "Cultural Exchange Plays Important Role in China-Africa Relationship."

166. Al-min Ciroma, "Second Chinese Film Week Holds in Jos This Week," *Leadership* (Abuja) (7 June 2008), http://allafrica.com/stories/200806070114.html.

167. "Cultural Exchange Plays Important Role in China-Africa Relationship."

168. Ibid.

169. Howard French and Lydia Polgreen, "Entrepreneurs from China Flourish in Africa," *New York Times*, 18 August 2007.

170. Interview with Huawei employees in Addis Ababa, Ethiopia, 3 July 2007.

171. Interview with Chinese workers and restaurant owner in Addis Ababa, Ethiopia, 3 July 2007.

172. "More on Chinese Workers Return After Equatorial Guinea Strike Clash," *South China Morning Post* (Hong Kong), 5 April 2008.

173. Interviews with Mesfin Gebre Yes, Board Member, Ethiopian Arbitration & Conciliation Center, Addis Ababa, Ethiopia, 3 July 2007, and Ali Abdulla Ali, Professor, Khartoum University, Economic Advisor to the Khartoum Stock Exchange, Khatoum, Sudan, 9 July 2007.

174. Kelvin Kachingwe, "Zambia: Controversial Chinese Firm Given Another Copper Mine," *Inter Press Service*, 2 June 2009.

175. Dickson Jere, "Anti-Chinese Sentiments High in Zambia Ahead of Hu's Visit," *Agence France-Presse*, 1 February 2007.

176. "Unrest in DR Congo After TP Mazembe Lose to Inter Milan," *BBC*, 18 December 2010.

177. Estimate from Chen Ming and Ye Yuan and corroborated by Dr. Charlie SB Huang, Member of Parliament, ANC, Cape Town, South Africa, 29 August 2007. In June 2008 BBC estimated that there were approximately 200,000 Chinese in South Africa. "S. Africa Chinese 'Become Black'," *BBC*, 18 June 2008.

178. Malia Politzer, "China and Africa: Stronger Economic Ties Means More Migration," *Migration Information Source*, August 2008, http://www.migrationinformation.org/Feature/display.cfm?ID = 690.

179. Chen Ming and Ye Yuan and Charlie Huang.

180. Ibid.

181. Ibid. Also see "Members of Parliament: Mr. Huang Shiaan-Bin," Parliament of the Republic of South Africa official website, undated, http://www.parliament.gov.za/live/content.php?Item_ID = 184&MemberID = 620.

182. "(Huaren jingying) Huang Shihao: zai zuru wangguo chicha fengyun," *Sohu.com*, 24 May 2006.

183. "Members of Parliament: Mrs. Chen Sherry Su-Huei," Parliament of the Republic of South Africa official website, undated, http://www.parliament.gov.za/live/content.php?Item_ID = 184&MemberID = 937.

184. Peter Gastow, "Triad Societies and Chinese Organised Crime in South Africa," Institute for Security Studies (South Africa) Occasional Paper 48, 2001, http://www.iss.co.za/Pubs/Papers/48/48.html.

185. Irvin Kinnes, "Structural Changes and Growth in Gang Activities," in Kinnes, *From Urban Street Gangs to Criminal Empires: The Changing Face of Gangs in the Western Cape*, Monograph 48 (Pretoria: Institute for Security Studies, June 2000).

186. Interview with Pan Feng, Economic and Commercial Officer, Embassy of China in Nigeria, 7 August 2007.

187. "China's Consulate Asks Chinese to Pay Attention to Security" (Zong lingguan jingqing zhongguogongmin zhuyi anquan), *West Africa United Business Weekly* (8 August 2007).

188. Interviews with Wang Baoting, Manager, Yafei Eastern International Trading Ltd., and Ren Guangming, Doctor Lagos Chinatown Health Clinic Chinatown Lagos, Nigeria, 10 August 2007.

189. Interview with Ndubisi Obiorah, Executive Director, Centre for Law and Social Action and Felix Morka, Executive Director, Social and Economic Rights Action Center, Lagos, 10 August 2007.

190. Wang Baoting and Ren Guangming, witnessed in August 2007.

191. Interviews and visits with African residents in Hong Kong and Guangzhou, December 2007, March 2008.

192. Ivan Zhai, "Some Struggle, Others Thrive in African Oasis," *South China Morning Post* (Hong Kong), 17 July 2009.

193. Tom Mackenzie and Mitch Moxley, "China's 'Little Africa' Is Under Pressure," *Global Post*, 23 February 2009.

194. "Africans Protest in China over Death of Nigerian," *This Day* (Lagos), 17 July 2009.

195. Mackenzie and Moxley.

196. Melinda Lui, "Beijing Vice: A Brutal Bust Reveals the Strong Arm of the Chinese Law," *Newsweek*, 25 September 2007.

197. Meaghan Brady, "The Scarlet Leader: How Oscar Mbeben Made His Name in Nanjing," *Map Magazine* (Nanjing) 59 (January 2007).

Chapter 8. China's Relations with North Africa and the Sahel

1. For an explanation of Egypt's reasons for recognizing the PRC and Beijing's reaction, see Mon'im Nasser-Eddine, *Arab-Chinese Relations 1950–1971* (Beirut: Arab Institute for Research and Publishing, 1972), 104–12. For the tactics by China to establish relations, see Xiaohong Liu, *Chinese Ambassadors: The Rise of Diplomatic Professionalism Since 1949* (Seattle: University of Washington Press, 2001), 60–61; Joseph E. Khalili, *Communist China's Interaction with the Arab Nationalists Since the Bandung Conference* (New York: Exposition Press, 1970), 98–99.

2. Much has been written on the early Sino-Egyptian relationship. See, for example, Nasser-Eddine, 46–55, 120–33; Bruce D. Larkin, *China and Africa, 1949–1970: The Foreign Policy of the People's Republic of China* (Berkeley: University of California Press, 1971), 17–26; Nigel Disney, "China and the Middle East," *MERIP Reports* 63 (December 1977): 4–7; Alan Hutchison, *China's African Revolution* (London: Hutchinson, 1975), 15–18; Vidya Prakash Dutt, *China and the World: An Analysis of Communist China's Foreign Policy* (New York: Praeger, 1966), 158–61; Malcolm H. Kerr, "The Middle East and China," in *Policies Toward China: Views from Six Continents*, ed. A. M. Halpern (New York: McGraw-Hill, 1965), 437–48; Yitzhak Shichor, *The Middle East in China's Foreign Policy 1949–1977* (Cambridge: Cambridge University Press, 1979), 27–33, 45–51, 97–101; John Franklin Copper, *China's Foreign Aid* (Lexington, Mass.: Lexington Books, 1976), 71–73.

3. Joseph E. Khalili, "Communist China and the United Arab Republic," *Asian Survey* 10, 4 (April 1970), 313, 317; Nasser-Eddine, 132–88, 203–32, 240–57.

4. CIA, "Chinese Communist Activities in Africa," 10, declassified study dated 30 April 1965, Declassified Documents Reference System.

5. Donald W. Klein, "Peking's Diplomats in Africa," *Current Scene* 2, 36 (1 July 1964): 4; Richard Lowenthal, "China" in *Africa and the Communist World*, ed. Zbigniew Brzezinski (Stanford, Calif.: Stanford University Press, 1963), 152.

6. Nasser-Eddine, 262–88.

7. Egypt Ministry of Foreign Affairs, "China-Africa in the 21st Century," presented at a conference in Pretoria, South Africa, 16–17 October 2006.

8. Aly El-Hefny, "Unlimited Potential for Egypt-China Cooperation," in *China Comes to Africa*, ed. Kinfe Abraham (Addis Ababa: Ethiopian International Institute for Peace and Development, 2005), 260; Shinn, "Military and Security Relations: China, Africa, and the Rest of the World," in *China into Africa: Trade, Aid, and Influence*, ed. Robert I. Rotberg (Washington, D.C.: Brookings Institution Press, 2008), 180.

9. Shinn, "Military and Security Relations," 165–66.

10. Li Shaoxian and Tang Zhichao, "China and the Middle East," *Contemporary International Relations* 17, 1 (January–February 2007): 24.

11. "China-Africa Relations Advance to New State in 2006," *Xinhua*, 7 December 2006.

12. Shinn/Eisenman meeting in Cairo on 17 July 2007 with Magdy M. Amer, Deputy Assistant Minister for East Asia, Egyptian Ministry of Foreign Affairs.

13. Shinn/Eisenman meeting with professor, Cairo University, 15 July 2007.

14. Shinn/Eisenman meeting with senior official, Ministry of Trade and Industry, 17 July 2007.

15. Miria Pigato, *Strengthening China's and India's Trade and Investment Ties to the Middle East and North Africa* (Washington, D.C.: World Bank, 2009), 92; Alaa Shahine, "Egypt to Offer Opportunities to China Sovereign Fund," *Bloomberg*, 15 June 2010; Ben Leung, "China's Egypt, Africa Investments," *Bikya Masr*, 10 August 2010.

16. All trade statistics in the four regional chapters come from IMF, *Direction of Trade Statistics Yearbook 2010* (Washington, D.C.: IMF, 2010) and the IMF online database. We use only import statistics for African countries and China.

17. Shinn, "North African Revolutions and Protests Challenge Chinese Diplomacy," *China Brief* 11, 6 (8 April 2011): 3.

18. For an account of Chinese assistance to the Algerian revolutionary movement, see Edmond Taylor, "The Chinese Invasion of North Africa," *The Reporter* 21, 4 (17 September 1959): 33, 36. In 1960, Algeria formally asked China for 90 military instructors, causing deep concern in France, Morocco, Tunisia, and the United States, which feared it might be dragged into the conflict through NATO responsibilities. Matthew Connelly, *A Diplomatic Revolution: Algeria's Fight for Independence and the Origins of the Post-Cold War Era* (Oxford: Oxford University Press, 2002), 231–32.

19. Disney, 7; Marc Aicardi de Saint-Paul, "La Chine et l'Afrique: Entre engage-ment et intérêt," *Géopolitique Africaine* 14 (2004); Joseph E. Khalili, "Sino-Arab Rela-tions," *Asian Survey* 8, 8 (August 1968): 683–87. For a detailed case study of China's relations with Algeria from 1954 to 1962, see G. P. Deshpande and H. K. Gupta, *United Front Against Imperialism: China's Foreign Policy in Africa* (Bombay: Somaiya Publications, 1986), 52–82. See also Fritz Schatten, *Communism in Africa* (New York: Praeger, 1966), 198–203; Copper, 74; CIA, "Chinese Communist Activities in Africa," 8; Connelly, 226–27.

20. Xiaohong Liu, 79–88.

21. "Algerian International Relations," *U.S. National Intelligence Estimate 62–71*, 31 July 1971, www.history.state/gov/historicaldocuments/frus1969–76ve05p2/d27.

22. "At Banquet Welcoming President Boumediene" and "Joint Communiqué," *Peking Review* 17, 10 (8 March 1974): 6–11.

23. Chris Zambelis, "China's Inroads into North Africa: An Assessment of Sino-Algerian Relations," *China Brief* 10, 1 (7 January 2010): 13.

24. Ibid., 10–12.

25. Ibid., 11; Jane Macartney, "Al-Qaeda Targets China," *The Times* (London), 15 July 2009.

26. Li Shaoxian and Tang Zhichao, 24.

27. "Algeria, China Sign Nuclear Accords," *Reuters*, 25 March 2008; Pigato, 91; Khalid Hilal, "China's Relations with North Africa," *China Monitor* (May 2010): 5.

28. Shinn, "North African Revolutions," 3.

29. Edmond Taylor, 32; Khalili, *Communist China's Interaction with the Arab Nationalists*, 112–13.

30. Larkin, 174–76; Schatten, 191.

31. Xiaohong Liu, 85; André Pautard, "Le Gouvernement de Pékin et les États du Maghreb," *Le Mois en Afrique* (June 1966): 68–69; Adie, 14; Alaba Ogunsanwo, *China's Policy in Africa 1958–1971* (London: Cambridge University Press, 1974), 29–30; CIA, "Chinese Communist Activities in Africa," 12.

32. "Special Report: Li Changchun Visits Five Countries," *Xinhua*, 25 March 2008; China Ministry of Foreign Affairs, "Hu Jintao Meets with Moroccan Prime Minster Jettou," 25 April 2006, http://jm.china-embassy.org/eng/xwt/t250008.htm; Xu Song and Li Shijia, "Wen Jiabao Meets Leaders from Eight African Countries," *Xin-hua*, 6 November 2006.

33. "Morocco Supports China's Tibet Policy, Beijing Olympics," *Xinhua*, 28 March 2008.

34. "Moroccan Foreign Minister Praises China's African Policy," *Xinhua*, 29 July 2009.

35. China Ministry of Foreign Affairs, "Morocco's Prime Minister Meets with Yang Jiechi," 13 January 2010, www.china-un.ch/eng/xwdt/t651401.htm.

36. Khalili, *Communist China's Interaction with the Arab Nationalists*, 118.

37. Larkin, 134–35; Ogunsanwo, 189–92.

38. CIA, "Communist Aid to Less Developed Countries of the Free World, 1977," November 1978, 15; China Ministry of Foreign Affairs, "Bilateral Relations: Tunisia," 25 August 2003, www.fmprc.gov.cn/eng/wjb/zzjg/xybfs/gjlb/2893/default.htm.

39. Pautard, 69; "China, Tunisia Sign Eight Cooperation Accords," *Xinhua*, 21 June 2004; "Visiting Chinese Commander, Tunisian PM Agree to Boost Defence Ties," *Xinhua*, 29 November 2005.

40. "Tunisian President, Chinese FM Talk Over Co-op," *Xinhua*, 19 May 2010.

41. "Tunisian-Chinese Trade and Investment Forum Held in Tunis," *Tunisia Online*, 8 June 2009; "China and Tunisia Look to Boost Cooperation Ties," *Xinhua*, 25 November 2009.

42. Shinn, "North African Revolutions," 3.

43. Wei Liang-Tsai, *Peking Versus Taipei in Africa 1960–1978* (Taipei: Asia and World Institute, 1982), 26; Khalili, *Communist China's Interaction with the Arab Nationalists*, 111.

44. China Ministry of Foreign Affairs, "Bilateral Relations: Libya," 25 August 2003, www.fmprc.gov.cn/eng/wjb/zzjg/xybfs/gjlb/2848/default.htm; "Taiwan and Libya to Revitalize Links," *Taipei Times*, 19 January 2006; "China Demands Libya Cease Official Ties with Taiwan," *Xinhua*, 11 May 2006; Yitzhak Shichor, "Libya Cautions China: Economics Is No Substitute to Politics," *China Brief* 9, 24 (3 December 2009): 6–7.

45. "Taiwan Appoints Representative to Libya," *Taiwan Central News Agency*, 21 February 2008.

46. "The Brother Leader Addresses the Students of Oxford University on Africa in the 21st Century," 16 May 2007, http://algadafi.org/html-english/P_oxford.htm.

47. "Musa Kusa told 'Middle East': Reject Resettlement of Chinese in Africa," *Sharq al-Awsat* (10 November 2009); Shichor, "Libya Cautions China," 5–6.

48. Remarks by Li Guofu, senior CIIS research fellow, 1 June 2011, in Beijing during a meeting attended by Shinn; Shichor, "Libya Cautions China," 6.

49. Shinn, "North African Revolutions," 3–4; Andrew Higgins, "China Stands by Its Ally in Oil," *Washington Post*, 23 June 2011.

50. Michael Wines, "Secret Bid to Arm Qaddafi Sheds Light on Tensions in China Government," *New York Times*, 11 September 2011.

51. Simon Denyer and Leila Fadel, "Libya's New Leader Calls for Reconciliation," *Washington Post*, 12 September 2011; "China Welcomes Early Establishment of Interim Government in Libya," *Xinhua*, 13 September 2011.

52. Ogunsanwo, 92–93, 216–19, 244–45; Hutchison, 97–98; Colin Legum, "Africa and China: Symbolism and Substance," in *Policies Toward China: Views from Six Continents*, 421; Dick Wilson, "China's Economic Relations with Africa," *Race* 5, 4 (April 1964): 67; CIA, "Communist China's Presence in Africa," 6; China Ministry of Foreign Affairs, "Bilateral Relations: Mali," 12 October 2003, www.fmprc.gov.cn/eng/wjb/zzjg/fzs/gjlb/3034/default.htm; John K. Cooley, *East Wind over Africa: Red*

China's African Offensive (New York: Walker, 1965), 146–51; CIA, "Chinese Communist Activities in Africa," 6–7.

53. Yahia M. Mahmoud, *Chinese Development Assistance and West African Agriculture: A Shifting Approach to Foreign Aid?* (Lund: Lund University, 2007), 134–35.

54. Abdrahamane Sanogo, "Les Relations économiques de la Chine et du Mali," African Economic Research Consortium Study Report, January 2008, 13–16, 24–27; Françoise Bourdarias, "Chinese Migrants and Society in Mali: Local Constructions of Globalization," *African and Asian Studies* 9, 3 (2010): 269–85.

55. Wei Liang-Tsai, 132–35, 340–41; Ogunsanwo, 224–25, 247–48; Wolfgang Bartke, *China's Economic Aid* (London: Hurst, 1975), 135; China Ministry of Foreign Affairs, "Bilateral Relations: Mauritania," 25 August 2003, www.fmprc.gov.cn/eng/wjb/zzjg/xybfs/gjlb/2853/default.htm; "L'Idylle sino-mauritanienne," *Jeune Afrique* 47, 2392 (12–18 November 2006): 50–51; CIA, "Communist Aid, 1977," 14.

56. "China, Mauritania to Expand Cooperation," *Xinhua*, 4 November 2006; "Sudan, China to Build $630 Mln Mauritania Railway," *Reuters*, 5 August 2007; "China's Company to Secure Long-term Iron Ore Supply from Mauritania," *Arab Steel*, 15 August 2007; Mahmoud, 132–33.

57. Cooley, 183; Wei Liang-Tsai, 183–84.

58. Keith Somerville, *Foreign Military Intervention in Africa* (New York: St. Martin's 1990), 61.

59. Wei Liang-Tsai, 184–85, 354–55; Wolfgang Bartke, *The Agreements of the People's Republic of China with Foreign Countries 1949–1990* (Munich: K.G. Saur, 1992), 32.

60. Bartke, *The Agreements of the People's Republic of China*, 32.

61. "China Severs Ties with Chad over Taiwan," *Deutsche Presse-Agentur*, 16 August 1997.

62. Peter Rosenblum, "Pipeline Politics in Chad," *Current History* (May 2000), 197.

63. "PRC Threats Led to Break with Chad," *Taiwan News*, 7 August 2006; China Ministry of Foreign Affairs, "Chinese and Chadian Governments Have Decided to Resume Diplomatic Relations at Ambassadorial Level," 6 August 2006, www.fmprc.gov.cn/eng/zxxx/t266930.htm; Keith Bradsher, "Chad Dumps Taiwan for New Link to Beijing; Taipei Criticizes Change in Relations," *International Herald Tribune*, 8 August 2005; Paul-Simon Handy, "Chad: Wading Through a Domestic Political Crisis in a Turbulent Region," Institute for Security Studies Situation Report, 5 December 2007, 9.

64. Comments by former member of Chinese embassy staff in N'Djamena to Shinn in Beijing, 1 June 2011; Howard W. French and Lydia Polgreen, "China, Filling a Void, Drills for Riches in Chad," *New York Times*, 13 August 2007; "Chinese Premier Meets Visiting World Leaders 8 August," *Xinhua*, 8 August 2008; "Chad Chides China, Libya for Lack of Support in Rebel Offensive," *Radio France Internationale*, 12 May 2009; "Chad Signs $7.5 Bln Rail Deal with China's CCECC," *Reuters*, 14 March 2011.

65. Cooley, 178–80; Wei Liang-Tsai, 185–87, 359–61; Mohamed A. El-Khawas, "China's Changing Policies in Africa," *Issue: A Journal of Opinion* 3, 1 (Spring 1973), 26; Ghana, *Nkrumah's Deception of Africa*, 127–29.

66. China Ministry of Foreign Affairs, "Bilateral Relations: Niger," 12 October 2003, www.fmprc.gov.cn/eng/wjb/zzjg/fzs/gjlb/3054/default.htm; "China Suspends Relations with Niger," *Xinhua*, 31 July 1992.

67. "China's Hu Jintao Meets Niger's President, Hails Progress in Bilateral Ties," *Xinhua*, 6 November 2006; "Nigerien President Meets with Delegation of Chinese Communist Party," *Xinhua*, 7 September 2007.

68. "China, Niger Sign Economic, Technical Agreement Worth 5.3m Dollars," *Xinhua*, 7 November 2007; Will Ross, "Outcry over China-Niger Oil Deal," *BBC News*, 30 July 2008; Andrew McGregor, "Mining for Energy: China's Relations with Niger," *China Brief* 7, 18 (3 October 2007), 8; Yvonne Lee and David Winning, "CNNC Buys Stake in Niger Uranium Mine," *Wall Street Journal*, 26 January 2010. The $5 billion agreement between China and Niger occurred during the presidency of Mamadou Tandja and began oil production in 2012.

69. McGregor, 8–9.

70. Adam Nossiter, "After a Coup, Niger Resumes Business as Usual with China," *New York Times*, 24 April 2010.

71. Pierre Englebert, *Burkina Faso: Unsteady Statehood in West Africa* (Boulder, Colo.: Westview, 1998), 150; Wei Liang-Tsai, 146–47; Edmond Taylor, "French Africa," *The Reporter* 32, 6 (25 March 1965): 30.

72. Wei Liang-Tsai, 147–48; Bartke, *China's Economic Aid*, 69, 194 and *The Agreements of the People's Republic of China with Foreign Countries*, 18–19; CIA, "Communist Aid Activities, 1978," 27. Pierre Englebert, one of the world's leading authorities on Burkina Faso, also asserted that it severed relations with Taiwan partly to demonstrate Upper Volta's independence vis-à-vis Côte d'Ivoire. See *Burkina Faso*, 151; "Visit of Burkina Faso Head of State," *Xinhua*, 5 November 1984.

73. Englebert, 157; "Diplomatic Ties with Burkina Faso Suspended," *Xinhua*, 5 February 1994. It is not clear why Burkina Faso switched to Taiwan at this time. Dollar diplomacy may be the answer. Shinn was U.S. ambassador to Burkina Faso from 1987 through 1990. He had regular contact with the Chinese ambassador. There was no indication during this period of problems in the PRC-Burkina Faso relationship.

Chapter 9. China's Relations with East Africa,
the Horn, and the Indian Ocean Islands

1. Joseph E. Khalili, *Communist China's Interaction with the Arab Nationalists Since the Bandung Conference* (New York: Exposition Press, 1970), 110–11.

2. Peter Adwok Nyaba, "An Appraisal of Contemporary China-Sudan Relations," in *Afro-Chinese Relations: Past, Present and Future*, ed. Kwesi Kwaa Prah (Cape Town: CASAS, 2007), 294–95.

3. CIA, "Chinese Communist Activities in Africa," declassified study dated 30 April 1965, 14, Declassified Documents Reference System.

4. Alaba Ogunsanwo, *China's Policy in Africa, 1958–1971* (London: Cambridge University Press, 1974), 173–74, 236–37, 245–46; Daniel Large, "From Non-Intervention to Constructive Engagement? China's Evolving Relations with Sudan," in *China Returns to Africa: A Rising Power and a Continent Embrace*, ed. Chris Alden, Daniel Large, and Ricardo Soares de Oliveira (London: Hurst, 2008), 276–77; Ali Abdalla Ali, *The Sudanese-Chinese Relations: Before and After Oil* (Khartoum: Sudan Currency, 2006), 11–43; John Franklin Copper, *China's Foreign Aid* (Lexington, Mass.: Lexington Books, 1976), 82–84; Sharath Srinivasan, "A Marriage Less Convenient: China, Sudan and Darfur," in *Crouching Tiger, Hidden Dragon? Africa and China*, ed. Kweku Ampiah and Sanusha Naidu (Scottsville, S.A.: University of KwaZulu-Natal Press, 2008), 58.

5. Ogunsanwo, 246–47; Nigel Disney, "China and the Middle East," *MERIP Reports* 63 (December 1977): 10–11; Alan Hutchison, *China's African Revolution* (London: Hutchinson, 1975), 171–72; see 221–22, for a description of a Chinese medical team in southern Sudan in 1972; Cecil Eprile, *War and Peace in the Sudan 1955–1972* (London: David and Charles, 1974), 122–23.

6. Ali, 52–54; Large, "From Non-Intervention to Constructive Engagement?" 276–80; Meeting 9 July 2007 in Khartoum between Shinn/Eisenman and Ali Yousif Ahmed, director of protocol in the Foreign Ministry and former ambassador to China; "China Invests 6 Billion Dollars in Sudan's Oil," *Sudan Tribune*, 6 November 2007. Another report puts Chinese investment in Sudan at $13.1 billion: Meine Pieter van Dijk, "The Political Impact of the Chinese in Sudan," in *The New Presence of China in Africa*, ed. van Dijk (Amsterdam: Amsterdam University Press, 2009), 144. For an analysis of engagement by China and other countries in the development of Sudan's oil, see Surya Narain Yadav, *India, China and Africa: New Partnership in Energy Security* (New Delhi: Jnanada Prakashan, 2008), 203–43.

7. Shinn, "Military and Security Relations: China, Africa, and the Rest of the World," in *China into Africa: Trade, AID, and Influence*, ed. Robert I. Rotberg (Washington, D.C.: Brookings Institution Press, 2008), 170–72. For a description of these facilities, see http://mic.sd/english/abouten.htm.

8. Daniel Large, "China and the Changing Context of Development in Sudan," *Development* 50, 3 (2007), 60–61; Richard Cockett, *Sudan: Darfur and the Failure of an African State* (New Haven, Conn.: Yale University Press, 2010), 272–77. For China's policy on Darfur, see Shinn, "China and the Conflict in Darfur," *Brown Journal of World Affairs* 16, 1 (Fall/Winter 2009): 85–100; Gaafar Karrar Ahmed, "The Chinese Stance on the Darfur Conflict," SAIIA Occasional Paper 67, September 2010. For an analysis by a Chinese official, see He Wenping, "The Darfur Issue: A New Test for China's Africa Policy," in *The Rise of China and India in Africa*, ed. Fantu Cheru and Cyril Obi (London: Zed Books, 2010), 155–66.

9. "China Avoids Condemnation of ICC's Fresh Move Against Bashir," *Sudan Tribune*, 15 July 2010.

10. Shinn, "Chinese Involvement in African Conflict Zones," *China Brief* 9, 7 (2 April 2009): 9; Daniel Large, "China's Sudan Engagement: Changing Northern and Southern Political Trajectories in Peace and War," *China Quarterly* 199 (September 2009): 618–19; Abdel Mitaal Girshab, Executive Director, Institute for the Development of Civil Society, Sharg El Neil College, North Khartoum, commented at a public event in Washington on 16 September 2009 that the Chinese are hated in Darfur and have no interaction with civil society in Sudan.

11. Large, "China's Engagement," 616–17.

12. "While China Wins Vote at the UN African Countries Snub Beijing," 29 April 1999, www.tibet.com/Humanrights/unhrc99–1.html.

13. "China Defends Decision Not to Veto Darfur ICC Referral," *Sudan Tribune*, 10 November 2009.

14. "President of China Congratulates President Al Bashir on Election Success," *Sudan Vision*, 12 May 2010.

15. Meeting in Khartoum on 11 July 2007 with Shinn/Eisenman.

16. Ibid. For an analysis of Sudanese views of China, see Barry Sautman and Yan Hairong, "African Perspectives on China-Africa Links," *China Quarterly* 199 (September 2009): 754–57.

17. "China Favors Sudan's Unity But Will Respect Referendum Outcome: Envoy," *Sudan Tribune*, 7 July 2010. See statement on China's policy toward Sudan, "Position Paper of the People's Republic of China at the 65th Session of the United Nations General Assembly," 13 September 2010, section III (10), www.fmprc.gov.cn/eng/zxxx/t751986.htm.

18. "China Pledges to Boost Military Cooperation with Sudan," *Sudan Tribune*, 16 November 2011.

19. Environmental groups have taken China to task as one of the primary contractors of the Merowe Dam. These organizations argue that the project, which China did not design, displaces local residents and did not take adequate account of environmental issues. See Peter Bosshard, "China's Role in Financing African Infrastructure," May 2007, http://internationalrivers.org/files/ChinaEximBankAfrica.pdf; Ali Askouri, "China Investment Destroying African Communities: The Case of the Merowe Dam Sudan," PowerPoint presentation, 22 March 2007, www.wilsoncenter.org/events/docs/askouri_presentation/pdf.

20. Meeting in Khartoum 10 July 2007 between Shinn/Eisenman and Mustafa Osman Ismail, advisor to the president and former minister of foreign affairs.

21. Meeting in Khartoum 9 July 2007 between Shinn/Eisenman and UN official involved in implementing the CPA. A former Sudanese ambassador told the authors in Khartoum on 11 July that China is working hard at the community level in South Sudan building schools, hospitals, and power systems. A senior South Sudan official told the authors that China has earmarked a $300 million grant for the development of the South. See Large, "China's Sudan Engagement," 623–24; Tom Rafferty, "China's Doctrine of Non-Interference Challenged by Sudan's Referendum," *China Brief* 10, 25 (27 December 2010): 12.

22. Meeting in Khartoum 12 July 2007 between Shinn/Eisenman and the leader of one of South Sudan's opposition political parties.

23. "South Sudan Tries to Assure China on Oil Investments," *AFP*, 15 October 2010.

24. "China Helps Promote Peace, Development of North, South Sudan," *Xinhua*, 9 July 2011.

25. "China Grants South Sudan $31.5m for Development Projects," *Sudan Tribune*, 24 October 2011; "Chinese Firm Wins Contract for S. Sudan's New Capital," *Sudan Tribune*, 28 October 2011.

26. China Ministry of Foreign Affairs, "Bilateral Relations: Somalia," 12 October 2003, www.fmprc.gov.cn/eng/wjb/zzjg/fzs/gjlb/3089/default.htm; Saadia Touval, *Somali Nationalism: International Politics and the Drive for Unity in the Horn of Africa* (Cambridge, Mass.: Harvard University Press, 1963), 142–41, 176–77; Bruce D. Larkin, *China and Africa, 1949–1970: The Foreign Policy of the People's Republic of China* (Berkeley: University of California Press, 1971), 94, 142, 174–75; Ogunsanwo, 83, 121–22; John K. Cooley, *East Wind over Africa: Red China's African Offensive* (New York: Walker, 1965), 33.

27. Roy Lyons, "The USSR, China and the Horn of Africa," *Review of African Political Economy* 12 (May–August 1978): 15–16; Ozay Mehmet, "Effectiveness of Foreign Aid: The Case of Somalia," *Journal of Modern African Studies* 9, 1 (May 1971): 37.

28. CIA, "Communist Aid, 1977," 20.

29. Hutchison, 91.

30. Peter Bridges, *Safrika: An American Envoy* (Kent, Ohio: Kent State University Press, 2000), 85.

31. Thomas Ofcansky," National Security," in *Somalia: A Country Study*, ed. Helen Chapin Metz (Washington, D.C.: USGPO, 1993), 213; State Department, Bureau of Intelligence and Research, "China's Policy Toward Sub-Saharan Africa," 20 August 1985, 4.

32. "China Donates 16 Mln Dollars to Famine-Stricken Somalia," *Xinhua*, 22 August 2011.

33. Jonathan Holslag, "China's New Security Strategy for Africa," *Parameters* 39, 2 (Summer 2009): 30–31; "China Donates over 4 Million Dollars Worth of Aid for the AU Mission in Somalia," *Xinhua*, 24 December 2010.

34. Comments by Foreign Minister Yang Jiechi, 2 June 2011 meeting, Beijing, attended by Shinn; "China Vows to Promote Somali Peace Process," *Xinhua*, 3 October 2011.

35. Meeting between Shinn and Ahmed Abdisalam Aden, Somali TFG Deputy Prime Minister, Lund, Sweden, 18 October 2008; meeting between Shinn and TFG Foreign Minister, Ali Ahmed Jama Jangali, Lund, Sweden, 4 June 2010; meeting between Shinn and Kadir Abdirahman Mohamud, Special Envoy of the President of Puntland, Washington, 14 September 2011; "China Willing to Play Constructive Role in Peace Process in Somalia," *Xinhua*, 25 April 2011.

36. "Somaliland's Civil Aviation Minister Ali Mohamed (Waran Ade) Signed a Contract with a Chinese Firm," *Qarannews*, 28 January 2010.

37. Shinn notes from 26 March 2010 meeting with Somaliland officials at the Council on Foreign Relations, Washington, D.C.

38. "Somaliland Says Petro Trans to Extend Berbera Port," *Reuters*, 20 August 2011; Shinn meeting in Washington 16 September 2011 with Somaliland Foreign Minister Mohamed A. Omar.

39. CIA, "Chinese Communist Activities in Africa," 9.

40. Donald W. Klein, "Peking's Diplomats in Africa," *Current Scene* 2, 36 (1964): 5–6. For a good case study of the Sino-Tanzanian relationship, see Mwesiga Baregu, "The Three Faces of the Dragon: Tanzania-China Relations in Historical Perspective," in *Crouching Tiger, Hidden Dragon?* 152–66.

41. S. K. G., "China in Africa—I," *Africa Quarterly* (January–March 1965): 227–28.

42. Sunil K. Sahu, "China's Africa Policy: A Study of Sino-Tanzania Relations," *Institute for Defence Studies and Analyses Journal* 10, 1 (July–September 1977): 60–62; Parbati K. Sircar, "The Great Uhuru (Freedom) Railway: China's Link to Africa," *China Report* 14, 2 (1978): 17; Hutchison, 92–93, 254–62, 67. The text of the "Sino-Tanzanian Treaty of Friendship" is available in George T. Yu, *China's African Policy: A Study of Tanzania* (New York: Praeger, 1975), 165–66. A partial text of Nyerere's speech to a mass rally in Beijing during his 1965 visit to China can be found in Julius K. Nyerere, *Freedom and Unity: A Selection from Writings and Speeches 1952–65* (Dar es Salaam: Oxford University Press, 1966), 323–25. Nyerere emphasized that Tanzania offers the hand of friendship "to China as to America, Russia, Britain, and others." He went on to praise his "great, new friend" in China and called on the UN to accept the PRC as a member.

43. Shinn, "Military and Security Relations," 158; CIA, "Communist China's Presence in Africa," 20 June 1969, 5, www.state.gov/documents/organization/54521 .pdf. For a solid account of China-Tanzania military cooperation up to 1970, see George T. Yu, *China and Tanzania: A Study in Cooperative Interaction* (Berkeley: University of California Press, 1970), 62–66.

44. CIA, "Communist Aid to Less Developed Countries of Free World, 1976," August 1977, 19–20; CIA, "Communist Aid Activities in Non-Communist Less Developed Countries, 1978," September 1979, 5.

45. Ogunsanwo, 135–37; Hutchison, 252–54; Legum, 423–25; J. D. Armstrong, *Revolutionary Diplomacy: Chinese Foreign Policy and the United Front Doctrine* (Berkeley: University of California Press, 1977), 222–23; Cooley, 38–51; William Attwood, *The Reds and the Blacks* (New York: Harper and Row, 1967), 156; declassified Department of State circular cable 1394 dated 30 January 1964; CIA, "Chinese Communist Activities in Africa," 9. For detailed accounts of early Chinese aid to Tanzania, including the Friendship Textile Mill, Ubungo Farm Implement Factory, and Mbarali Farm, see Ogunsanwo, 197–213; Hutchison, 92–96; Larkin 93–98; Bartke, *China's Economic*

Aid, 66–67, 178–90; Copper, 97–101, 103–8; Yu, *China's African Policy*, 106–20; Ai Ping, "From Proletarian Internationalism to Mutual Development: China's Cooperation with Tanzania, 1965–95," in *Agencies in Foreign Aid: Comparing China, Sweden and the United States in Tanzania*, ed. Goran Hyden and Rwekaza Mukandala (New York: St. Martin's, 1999), 172–83. For a description and analysis of Chinese aid to Tanzania from the beginning through 2007, see Heidi Sandvand, "Friends and Interests: A Comparison of Chinese and Nordic Aid to Tanzania" (master's thesis, Norwegian University of Life Sciences, 2007), 68–71, 74–77, 79–80, 83–84, 80–112, www.umb.no/statisk/noragric/publications/master/2008_heidi_sa ndvand.pdf. For an analysis of the evolution of Chinese aid to Tanzania from the beginning until the late 1990s, see Menghua Zeng, "An Interactive Perspective of Chinese Aid Policy: A Case Study of Chinese Aid to Tanzania" (Ph.D. dissertation, University of Florida, 1999), 177–211.

46. Hutchison, 92, 265, 272–73; Armstrong, 232–33; Richard Gibson, *African Liberation Movements: Contemporary Struggles Against White Minority Rule* (London: Oxford University Press, 1972), 65–66; Chang Ya-chun, 21. Shinn was U.S. embassy liaison with representatives of African liberation movements in Tanzania while serving in Dar es Salaam in 1971–1972.

47. Sahu, 65–66; Copper, 97–101. The Tanzania-Zambia railway project has spawned a cottage industry of books and articles. The most comprehensive, recent book on the subject is Jamie Monson, *Africa's Freedom Railway: How a Chinese Development Project Changed Lives and Livelihoods in Tanzania* (Bloomington: Indiana University Press, 2009). Older works include Richard Hall and Hugh Peyman, *The Great Uhuru Railway: China's Showpiece in Africa* (London: Gollancz, 1976); Martin Bailey, *Freedom Railway: China and the Tanzania-Zambia Link* (London: Rex Collings, 1976); Kasuka S. Mutukwa, *Politics of the Tanzania-Zambia Railproject: A Study of Tanzania-China-Zambia Relations* (Washington, D.C.: University Press of America, 1977); George T. Yu, "Working on the Railroad: China and the Tanzania-Zambia Railway," *Asian Survey* 11, 11 (November 1971): 110–17; Ngila Mwase, "The Tanzania-Zambia Railway: The Chinese Loan and the Pre-Investment Analysis Revisited," *Journal of Modern African Studies* 21, 3 (September 1983): 435–543.

48. Monson, 5.

49. Troubled TAZARA Railway in $700m Debt," *This Day*, 5 March 2009. For an account by someone who made the trip by rail from Dar es Salaam to the Zambian Copper Belt, see Howard W. French, "The Next Empire?" *Atlantic* (May 2010): 59–62.

50. Faraja Mgwabati, "TAZARA, China Seal 51bn/-Deal," *Daily News*, 31 December 2009.

51. Li Baoping, "Sino-Tanzanian Relations and Political Development," in *Afro-Chinese Relations:*, ed. Kwesi Kwaa Prah, 130, 135.

52. Baregu, 156–57.

53. "Tanzania Keen to Cooperate with China for Common Development," *People's Daily Online*, 8 October 2000.

54. Centre for Chinese Studies, "Evaluating China's FOCAC Commitments to Africa and Mapping the Way Ahead," report for Rockefeller Foundation, January 2010, 104.

55. Johanna Jansson, Christopher Burke, and Tracy Hon, "Patterns of Chinese Investment, Aid and Trade in Tanzania," Centre for Chinese Studies, University of Stellenbosch, October 2009, 3, 7.

56. John J. Okumu, "Foreign Relations: Dilemmas of Independence and Development," in *Politics and Public Policy in Kenya and Tanzania*, ed. Joel D. Barkan (New York: Praeger, 1979), 243; Sarah McGregor, "Trade-Tanzania: Cheap Imitation Goods Are Flooding Markets," *Inter Press Service News Agency*, 20 August 2008; Palash Ghosh, "Tanzania's Expulsion of Chinese Traders from Dar es Salaam Underscores Resentment of Asians in Africa," *International Business Times*, 13 January 2011.

57. Jansson et al., 7.

58. Baregu, 158–60.

59. "Tanzania, China in $3bn Mining Deal," *The Citizen* (Dar es Salaam), 21 September 2011.

60. Jansson et al., 3; Centre for Chinese Studies, 108. Suzanne van Keulen, "China's Infrastructure Investment in Africa: Consequences for Economic Development—The Case of Tanzania," *China Monitor* (April 2010): 7.

61. China Ministry of Foreign Affairs, "Bilateral Relations: Tanzania," 12 October 2003; Centre for Chinese Studies, 117–18. For Chinese traditional medicine in Tanzania, see Elisabeth Hsu, "'The Medicine from China Has Rapid Effects': Chinese Medicine Patients in Tanzania," *Anthropology and Medicine* 9, 3 (2002): 291–313.

62. Van Keulen, 9.

63. Centre for Chinese Studies, 102.

64. Shinn, "Military and Security Relations," 180; China Ministry of Foreign Affairs, "Bilateral Relations: Uganda," 12 October 2003.

65. "China Signs $21.9m Deals," *Agence France Presse*, 15 February 2009.

66. "China, Tanzania Sign Loan Agreements on ICT, Air Transport Infrastructure," *Xinhua*, 16 April 2010.

67. Legum, 427–28. Dutt, *China and the World* (New York: Praeger, 1966), 293; CIA, "Chinese Communist Activities in Africa," 12.

68. Thomas P. Ofcansky, "National Security," in *Uganda: A Country Study*, ed. Rita M. Byrnes (Washington, D.C.: USGPO, December 1990), 217; Copper, 112–13.

69. Hutchison, 274.

70. Shinn, "Military and Security Relations," 172–73; China Ministry of Foreign Affairs, "Bilateral Relations: Uganda"; Centre for Chinese Studies, 126, 143–48.

71. Joyce Namutebi and Cyprian Musoke, "Chinese to Build New Presidential Office," *New Vision* (Kampala), 14 August 2008; David Mugabe, "Uganda: Made in China: Do We Get Value for Money?" *New Vision*, 17 June 2009; Centre for Chinese Studies, 129–32; Dorothy Nakaweesi, "China Tops List of Foreign Direct Investors," *Daily Monitor*, 9 July 2010.

72. Centre for Chinese Studies, 132–38.

73. "President Receives Chinese Delegation," *Uganda Media Centre*, 24 October 2011.

74. "China Eyes Uganda," *Guardian*, 12 March 2010; "Tullow in $2.9 Bn Uganda Deal with Total, CNOOC," *Reuters*, 30 March 2011.

75. "China Urges LRA to Cease Violence," *Xinhua*, 15 November 2011.

76. Geof Magga, "Uganda Head Lambasts Commonwealth and Commends China," *Afrik News*, 25 July 2010.

77. Mary Karugaba, "Twenty Nationals Face Death in China," *New Vision*, 14 August 2010.

78. Oginga Odinga, *Not Yet Uhuru: An Autobiography* (London: Heinemann, 1967), 190.

79. Ogunsanwo, 162–65, 188–89; Larkin, 135–39, 173–74, 204–5; Cooley, 61–67; Hutchison, 116–19, 151–53; Copper, 108–9; Michael Chege, "Economic Relations Between Kenya and China, 1963–2007," in *U.S. and Chinese Engagement in Africa*, ed. Jennifer Cooke (Washington, D.C.: CSIS, July 2008), 12–17. Jane Masta, "Chinese Investments in Kenya," in *Chinese Investments in Africa: A Labour Perspective*, ed. Anthony Yaw Baah and Herbert Jauch (Accra: African Labour Research Network, May 2009), 385–87, www.fnv.nl/binary/report2009_chinese_investments_in_africa_tcm7-23663.pdf; Attwood, 173, 240–43, 246–50. U.S. ambassador to Kenya William Attwood wrote that some of Kenyatta's associates were urging a break in diplomatic relations with China since it was obvious "that the Chinese Embassy was encouraging subversion against his government" (259). Attwood said Kenyatta preferred to keep the Chinese in the country where he could watch them. Odinga left KANU early in 1966 and formed an opposition party. According to Attwood (269), Kenyatta summoned the Soviet and Chinese ambassadors and warned them that Kenya would consider continuing to support Odinga's opposition party cause to sever diplomatic relations.

80. Chege, 15–20; China Ministry of Foreign Affairs, "Bilateral Relations: Kenya," 12 October 2003; Masta, 388–89.

81. Cathy Majtenyi, "Chinese Radio Begins Transmission in Kenya," *VOA News*, 27 January 2006; "Kibaki Jets Back with Goodies from China" *Kenya Presidential Press Service*, 4 May 2010; "Chinese Party Leaders Visit Kenya," *Kenya Presidential Press Service*, 3 June 2010; Shinn visit to Confucius Institute at Kenyatta University, 29 July 2010.

82. Chege, 20–24, 28–31; Masta, 390–94; Paul Kamau, "China's Impact on Kenya's Clothing Industry," in *Chinese and African Perspectives on China in Africa*, ed. Axel Harneit-Sievers, Stephen Marks, and Sanusha Naidu (Kampala: Pambazuka Press, 2010), 108–27; "Kenyans to Protest Chinese Involvement in Ethiopia's Gibe III Dam," *APANews*, 17 February 2011.

83. For a detailed analysis of Chinese FDI in Kenya, see Masta, 395–403; see also Jeffrey Gettleman, "Future Kenya Port Could Mar Pristine Land," *New York Times*, 12

January 2010; David Okwembah, "China's March in Kenya Upsets Local Firms," *Nation* (24 January 2010).

84. Peter Draper, Tsidiso Disenyana, and Gilberto Biacuana, "Chinese Investment in African Network Industries: Case Studies from the Democratic Republic of the Congo and Kenya," in *The Rise of China and India in Africa*, 115–18.

85. Donovan C. Chau, *Political Warfare in Sub-Saharan Africa: U.S. Capabilities and Chinese Operations in Ethiopia, Kenya, Nigeria, and South Africa* (Carlisle, Pa.: Strategic Studies Institute, March 2007), 27–37; Chege, 24–30. For an update on China-Kenya commercial cooperation, see the agreement between Kenya's minister for trade and China's vice minister of trade dated 12 July 2010, released by Kenya Ministry of Trade at www.trade.go.ke/index.php?option = com_content&task = view& id = 164&Itemid = 176.

86. Kimon Skordiles, *Kagnew: The Story of the Ethiopian Fighters in Korea* (Tokyo: Radiopress, 1954), 100–104. For an analysis of Ethio-Sino relations, see Gedion Gamora and K. Mathews, "Ethio-China Relations: Challenges and Prospects," in *Chinese and African Perspectives on China in Africa*, 92–107.

87. Liang-Tsai, *Peking Versus Taipei in Africa* (Taipei: Asia and World Institute, 1982), 229, 387; Ogunsanwo, 9, 37, 242; CIA, "Chinese Communist Activities in Africa," 12–13. Gordon Brook-Shepard described one of the early Chinese cultural visits to Addis Ababa. It played to packed houses, was attended by Emperor Haile Selassie, and won plaudits by turning over all profits to charity. See "Red Rivalry in the Black Continent," *The Reporter* 26, 2 (18 January 1962): 24.

88. Liang-Tsai, 230–32; Larkin, 177–78; Eugene K. Lawson, "China's Policy in Ethiopia and Angola," in *Chinese and Soviet Aid to African Nations*, ed. Warren Weinstein and Thomas H. Henriksen (New York: Praeger, 1980), 168–69. When Ethiopia finally recognized China in 1970, it extracted a promise that Beijing would terminate support for the ELF. See Hutchison, 166; Liang-Tsai, 233–34.

89. Cooley, 35.

90. Hutchison, 119–20; Cooley, 28–37.

91. Liang-Tsai, 235–36.

92. David A. Korn, *Ethiopia the United States and the Soviet Union* (Carbondale: Southern Illinois University Press, 1986), 18–19; Lawson, 177.

93. Kinfe Abraham, *Ethiopia from Empire to Federation* (Addis Ababa: EIIPD Press, 2001), 408–9; Korn, 100; Peter Both, *International Relations of Ethiopia* (Bloomington, Ind.: AuthorHouse, 2004), 125.

94. China Ministry of Foreign Affairs, "Bilateral Relations: Ethiopia," 12 October 2003; Addis Dilnesa, *China Comes to Africa* (Addis Ababa: Ethiopian International Institute for Peace and Development, 2005), 245.

95. Chau, 21–34; China Ministry of Foreign Affairs, "Bilateral Relations: Ethiopia"; Ethiopia Ministry of Foreign Affairs, "An Overview of the Bilateral Relations Between the Federal Democratic Republic of Ethiopia and the People's Republic of

China," September 2006. For example, Ethiopian Chief of Staff Samora Yenus met with PLA Chief of the General Staff Chen Bingde in 2010 when they pledged to establish closer relations between the two nation's armed forces. See "China, Ethiopia Vow to Build Closer Military Ties," *Xinhua*, 28 June 2010. Shinn, U.S. ambassador to Ethiopia in 1996–1999, believes that while Ethiopia had generally good relations with both the United States and China during this period, many leaders were more comfortable dealing with the Chinese than with the Americans. They preferred the Chinese approach to bilateral relations and were ideologically closer to the Chinese way of thinking. China was important to Ethiopia, especially because it sold large quantities of arms, but did not have the global influence of the United States as the world's only superpower.

96. Michael Malakata, "China Accused of Jamming TV, Websites in Ethiopia," *Computerworld*, 29 June 2011.

97. "Connecting Both Sides," interview with Ethiopian ambassador to China, *Chinafrica* 2, 7 (July 2007): 10.

98. "Meles Disgruntled with Chinese Firm," *Addis Fortune*, 21 November 2004.

99. Toh Han Shih, "Ethiopia Dam Blot on China's Record," *South China Morning Post*, 7 June 2010.

100. Karby Leggett, "Staking a Claim: China Flexes Economic Muscle Throughout Burgeoning Africa," *Wall Street Journal*, 29 March 2005.

101. Comment made to Shinn in Addis Ababa 30 July 2010 by senior foreign ministry official.

102. William Wallis, "Ethiopia Looks East to Slip Reins of Western Orthodoxy," *Financial Times*, 6 February 2007; Walta Information Service interview with Chinese ambassador to Ethiopia, Gu Xiaojie, Addis Ababa, 19 August 2008. ZTE is playing a major role in telecommunication upgrades. An American IT expert who evaluated a ZTE operating system commented to Shinn in Washington on 9 April 2010 that the technology is already out of date, probably because ZTE bid low to win the tender.

103. *Ethiopian News Agency*, 12 January 2010.

104. Shinn meeting in Addis Ababa, 28 June 2007 with about 50 members of the Ethiopia Chamber of Commerce.

105. Peter H. Gebre, "China in Ethiopia: Just-in-Time," in *China, Africa, and the African Diaspora: Perspectives*, ed. Sharon T. Freeman (Washington, D.C.: AASBEA, 2009), 165, 176–80.

106. Shinn/Eisenman meetings in Addis Ababa, 29 June 2007, with senior government official and another on 5 July 2007 with the managing editor of a leading private newspaper. For a brief case study of ZTE's entry into Ethiopia, see Gebre, 173–75.

107. Shinn/Eisenman meeting in Addis Ababa, 3 July 2007, with pro-American Ethiopian who worked for many years at the Africa Union; in Addis Ababa, 4 July 2007, with Ethiopian expert on country's trade with other countries; in Addis Ababa, 5 July 2007, with Zaid Wolde Gebriel, Director General, Ethiopian Roads Authority; Gebre, 169–72.

108. Shinn/Eisenman meeting in Addis Ababa, 3 July 2007, with Zhang Yuebang, chargé d'affaires of the Embassy of China; Gebre, 167–68; "The Core Principles of Ethiopia's Foreign Policy: Ethiopia-China," *A Week in the Horn*, 10 September 2010.

109. Meeting in Addis Ababa on 4 July 2007 with Mahdi Ahmed Gadid. For a study of Chinese investment in Ethiopia, see Asayehgn Desta, "Chinese Investment in Ethiopia: Developmental Opportunity or Deepening China's New Mercantilism?" 21 May 2009, www.tigraionline.com/chinese_investment_desta.html.

110. "Ethiopia Objects to Politicizing Olympics: PM," *Xinhua*, 26 April 2008.

111. "Prime Minister Meles on an Official Visit to China," *A Week in the Horn*, 19 August 2011.

112. "Ethiopia, China Sign Ethio-Djibouti Railway Construction Agreement," *Ethiopian News Agency*, 26 October 2011.

113. "Ethiopia, Somaliland, China to Sign Agreements on Gas, Oil, Logistic Deals," Ethiopian Ministry of Foreign Affairs website, 15 August 2011.

114. "Unholy Tri-partite Deal Between China, Ethiopia and Hargeisa Administration," ONLF press release, 24 August 2011; Peter Heinlein, "Ethiopian Forces, Rebels Clash in Ogaden Oil Exploration Region," *VOA*, 2 September 2011.

115. Shinn/Eisenman meeting in Addis Ababa, 4 July 2007, with Ethiopian expert on trade.

116. Martyn Davies et al., "How China Delivers Development Assistance to Africa," Centre for Chinese Studies, University of Stellenbosch, February 2008, 36. This document contains a case study on China's development program in Ethiopia, 32–37.

117. Tekeda Alemu, remarks, Foreign Affairs University, Beijing, 15 April 2010, www.mfa.gov.et/Press_Section/lecture.pdf.

118. Cooley, 26–28. Hutchison (232) argued that China's subsequent refusal to support the revolutionary struggle in French Somaliland was an indication that Beijing valued de Gaulle's independent foreign policy and 1964 recognition more than support for revolutionaries. By 1966, when France began to seek closer ties with the Soviet Union, China added French Somaliland to its list of countries engaging in an anti-imperialist struggle.

119. China Ministry of Foreign Affairs, "Bilateral Relations: Djibouti," 12 October 2003; "China's Top Political Advisor Meets Djibouti Party Leader," *Xinhua*, 1 July 2010.

120. Ismail Omar Guelleh, "Djibouti encore besoin de Moi," *Jeune Afrique* 2574 (9–15 May 2010): 28.

121. Dan Connell, *Against All Odds: A Chronicle of the Eritrean Revolution* (Trenton, N.J.: Red Sea Press, 1993), 78–81; Richard Sherman, *Eritrea: The Unfinished Revolution* (New York: Praeger, 1980), 156. Roy Lyons, "The USSR, China and the Horn of Africa," *Review of African Political Economy* 12 (May–August 1978): 10; Paul B. Henze, "Africa Communism," *Problems of Communism* 41, 1–2 (January 1992): 220. Suresh Kumar, "Globalization and China Economic Policies Towards Africa: Emerging China-Eritrea Bilateral Relations," *Eritrea Profile*, 14, 28 (13 June 2007), www

.africaindia.org/chafr.htm; Comments to Shinn by Robert Houdek, former U.S. ambassador to Eritrea, 3 February 2009.

122. China Ministry of Foreign Affairs, "Bilateral Relations: Eritrea," 12 October 2003; "Eritrean Air Force Chief, Chinese Military Delegation Discuss Ties," *Voice of the Broad Masses of Eritrea*, 7 August 2005; Efrem Habtetsion, "Shaebia Interview with the PRC Ambassador to Eritrea," *Shaebia*, 17 October 2010.

123. Comments by Robert Houdek to Shinn; "Security Council Should Act Prudently in Imposing Sanctions," *Xinhua*, 23 December 2009.

124. Eritrea Ministry of Information press release, 20 February 2010.

125. Interview with President Isaias Afwerki, *China Business Weekly Magazine*, 21 March 2007, www.shabait.com/cgi-bin/staging/exec/view.cgi?archive = 13&num = 6354.

126. Ogunsanwo, 35, 45, 269–70; Cooley, 78.

127. Vinaye Dey Ancharaz, "David V. Goliath: Mauritius Facing Up to China," African Economic Research Consortium, January 2008, 5, 21–22. See 33–35 for a complete list of agreements signed by Mauritius and China between 1969 and 2007 and 39–43 for a complete list of grants and loans offered by China between 1972 and 2006. Wolfgang Bartke, *The Agreements of the People's Republic of China with Foreign Countries 1949–1990* (Munich: K.G. Saur, 1992), 115.

128. China Ministry of Foreign Affairs, "Bilateral Relations: Mauritius," 12 October 2003; Vinaye Ancharaz, "Mauritius: Benefiting from China's Rise," *China Monitor* (April 2009): 5; Sarah Raine, "Sino-Mauritian Relations: The Geographical Perspective," *China Monitor* (April 2009): 10.

129. Raine, 11.

130. Xu Song and Li Shijia, "Wen Jiabao Meets Leaders from Eight African Countries," *Xinhua*, 6 November 2006; Ancharaz, "David V. Goliath," 7–10; Ancharaz, "Mauritius," 5–6.

131. Alec Russell, "Mauritius Offers Asia Gateway into Africa," *Financial Times*, 6 March 2008); Ancharaz, "David V. Goliath," 19–20. Ana Cristina Alves, "Chinese Economic and Trade Co-operation Zones in Africa: The Case of Mauritius," SAIIA Occasional Paper 74, January 2011, 9–13.

132. Stephen Marks and Sanusha Naidu, "Forging a New China-Africa Consensus?" *Pambazuka News*, 19 February 2009.

133. Liang-Tsai, 250–54, 365–67; Legum, 428–29; Cooley, 76–78; Bartke, *China's Economic Aid*, 128; State Department, "China's Policy Toward Sub-Saharan Africa," 5; CIA, "Communist Aid Activities in Non-Communist Less Developed Countries, 1978," September 1979, 26.

134. China Ministry of Foreign Affairs, "Bilateral Relations: Madagascar," 12 October 2003; China Ministry of Foreign Affairs, "Premier Wen Jibao Meets with the Madagascar President," 14 May 2004, www.fmprc.gov.cn/eng/wjb/zzjg/fzs/gjlb/3029/3031/t112520.htm; China Ministry of Foreign Affairs, "Senior CPC Official Visits Madagascar," 31 August 2006, www.gov.cn/english/2006–08/31/content_374616.htm;

"Chinese Premier Hails Sino-Madagascar Ties," *Xinhua*, 15 May 2007; Jean Razafin-dravonona et al., "Étude sur les échanges entre Chine et Madagascar," African Economic Research Consortium, January 2008, 11, www.aercafrica.org/documents/china_africa_relations/Madagasca r.pdf. For Chinese FDI in Madagascar, 15–19; for 1995–2006 trade relationship, 23–24, 27–30, 38–39.

135. "Madagascar dans le collier de Perles Chinois," *Pambazuka News* 196, 5 July 2011.

136. China Ministry of Foreign Affairs, "Bilateral Relations: Comoros," 12 October 2003; Liang-Tsai, 286–87; Cooley, 79; CIA, "Communist Aid, 1976," 20. For China's medical teams and anti-malaria assistance, see Li Anshan, "Chinese Medical Cooperation in Africa," Nordiska Afrikainstitutet Discussion Paper 52, 2011, 15–16.

137. "China's President Visits China's Guilin," *Xinhua*, 21 June 2003; "Comorian President Arrives in Beijing for China-Africa Summit," *Xinhua*, 31 October 2006; "Chinese Deputy Minister Hails Excellent Ties with Comoros," *Al Watwan*, 20 May 2008.

138. China Ministry of Foreign Affairs, "Bilateral Relations: Seychelles."

139. China Ministry of Foreign Affairs, "Bilateral Relations: Seychelles"; "Hu Jintao Holds Talks with Seychellois President Michel in Victoria," *Xinhua*, 10 February 2007; "Hu Jintao Meets with Foreign Leaders Attending the Opening Ceremony of Shanghai World Expo," 2 May 2010, www.fmprc.gov/cn/eng/zxxx/t689875.htm; Cooley, 79–80; Bartke, *The Agreements of the People's Republic of China with Foreign Countries*, 160–61; "Seychelles President Meets Chinese State Councilor on Relations," *China Economic Net*, 29 July 2010. The United States had an important air force tracking station on Mahe, the primary island in the chain, until 1996, closing it on the grounds that it was no longer required. The U.S. embassy that opened in 1976 closed for cost reasons the same year, sending a message to the Seychellois that Washington was only interested in the islands so long as they were useful for American military purposes. The U.S. ambassador in Mauritius is accredited to the Seychelles and a branch consular office in Victoria is staffed by Seychellois.

Chapter 10. China's Relations with West and Central Africa

1. William Attwood, *The Reds and the Blacks* (New York: Harper and Row, 1967), 67–75; Richard Lowenthal, "China," in *Africa and the Communist World*, ed. Zbigniew Brzezinski (Stanford, Calif.: Stanford University Press, 1963), 165–66; John K. Cooley, *East Wind over Africa: Red China's African Offensive* (New York: Walker, 1965), 141–42.

2. Alan Hutchison, *China's African Revolution* (London: Hutchinson, 1975), 53–57; Bruce Larkin, *China and Africa 1949–1970: The Foreign Policy of the People's Republic of China* (Berkeley: University of California Press, 1971), 39–40, 64, 93–94, 98; Vidya Prakash Dutt, *China and the World: An Analysis of Communist China's Foreign Policy* (New York: Praeger, 1966), 285–90. For the text of the 1960 Treaty of

Friendship between Guinea and the PRC and the 1960 Economic and Technical Cooperation Agreement, see Alaba Ogunsanwo, *China's Policy in Africa 1958–1971* (London: Cambridge University Press, 1974), 278–80 (for additional information on the early aid relationship, see 158–60, 213–16). See also Fritz Schatten, *Communism in Africa* (New York: Praeger, 1966), 194–97; John Franklin Copper, *China's Foreign Aid* (Lexington, Mass.: Lexington Books, 1976), 88–91; Janos Horvath, *Chinese Technology Transfer to the Third World* (New York: Praeger, 1976), 9, 16, 20, 42, 58–59; Wolfgang Bartke, *China's Economic Aid* (London: Hurst, 1975), 45, 116–20.

3. Alex Blake, "Peking's African Adventures," *Current Scene* 5, 15 (15 September 1967): 7–8. Chang Ya-chun, *Chinese Communist Activities in Africa-Policies and Challenges* (Taipei: World Anti-Communist League, April 1981), 21; Alan Hutchison, "China in Africa: A Record of Pragmatism and Conservatism," *Round Table* 65, 259 (July 1975): 267; Colin Legum, "Africa and China: Symbolism and Substance," in *Policies Toward China: Views from Six Continents*, ed. A. M. Halpern (New York: McGraw-Hill, 1965), 420–21.

4. CIA, "Communist China's Presence in Africa," 20 June 1969, 6, www.state.gov/documents/organization/54521.pdf; CIA, "Communist Aid Activities in Non-Communist Less Developed Countries, 1979 and 1954–1979," October 1980, 18.

5. China Ministry of Foreign Affairs, "Bilateral Relations: Guinea," 12 October 2003, www.fmprc.gov.cn/eng/wjb/zzjg/fzs/gjlb/3004/default.htm; CIA, "Communist Aid Activities in Non-Communist Less Developed Countries, 1978," September 1979, 4–5.

6. "China Said to Build 150-Bed Hospital, Three Schools in Guinean Capital," *Guinea News*, 15 May 2008.

7. Lydia Polgreen, "As Chinese Investment in Africa Drops, Hope Sinks," *New York Times*, 26 March 2009.

8. Daniel Balint-Kurti, "Guinea: Bought by Beijing," *World Today* 66, 3 (March 2010): 15–17.

9. Shai Oster, "China Fund's $7 Billion Deal with Guinea Draws Scrutiny," *Wall Street Journal*, 2 November 2009.

10. Loni Prinsloo, "Bellzone Inks Definitive Deal with Chinese Investor for Guinea Project," *Mining Weekly*, August 2010.

11. "China and Rio Tinto Complete Guinea Mining Deal," *BBC*, 29 July 2010.

12. "Guinea, China in Talks over Bauxite Mine, Refinery," *Globserver*, 2 September 2011.

13. Donald W. Klein, "Peking's Diplomats in Africa," *Current Scene* 2, 36 (1 July 1964): 4–5. For research that includes information on Chinese migrants who began arriving in Ghana in the 1950s, see Conal Guan-Yow Ho, "The 'Doing' and 'Undoing' of Community: Chinese Networks in Ghana," *China Aktuell* 3 (2008): 45–76. For a detailed account of China's strategy toward Ghana from 1957 through 1966, see David Edward Albright, "The Soviet Union, Communist China, and Ghana, 1955–1966" (Ph.D. dissertation, Columbia University, 1971).

14. Donovan C. Chau, "Assistance of a Different Kind Chinese Political Warfare, 1958–1966," *Comparative Strategy* 26, 2 (April–June 2007): 141–16; W. Scott Thompson, *Ghana's Foreign Policy 1957–1966* (Princeton, N.J.: Princeton University Press, 1969), 177, 256–300; Hutchison, *China's African Revolution*, 57–59, 98, 123–26; Ogunsanwo, 146–49. For the text of the 1961 Treaty of Friendship between China and Ghana see Ogunsanwo, 280–81; Larkin, 94, 131–33; Dutt, 290–92.

15. Alex Blake, "Peking's African Adventures," *Current Scene* 5, 15 (1967): 3; Pierre Mertens and Paul-F. Smets, *L'Afrique de Pékin* (Brussels: Mertens and Smets, 1966), 81–85; "Ghana Accuses Chinese of Arming Foes in Guinea," *New York Times*, 7 April 1966. In 1966 Ghana's Ministry of Information published two white papers: *Nkrumah's Subversion in Africa* and *Nkrumah's Deception of Africa*. They detail Soviet and Chinese military assistance, secret guerrilla training camps, and training provided by Russians, East Germans, and Chinese. They contain copies of alleged secret documents related to the training that provide strong evidence of Chinese involvement.

16. Hutchison, *China's African Revolution*, 126–28.

17. Ogunsanwo, 147.

18. China Ministry of Foreign Affairs, "Diplomatic Relations: Ghana," 12 October 2003, www.fmprc.gov.cn/eng/wjb/zzjg/fzs/gjlb/2999/default.htm; Anthony Yaw Baah, Kwabena Nyarko Otoo, and Edward Fokuoh Ampratwurm, "Chinese Investments in Ghana," in *Chinese Investments in Africa: A Labour Perspective*, ed. Anthony Yaw Baah and Herbert Jauch (Accra: African Labour Research Network, May 2009), 87–88, www.fnv.nl/binary/report2009_chinese _investments_in_africa_tem7–23663.pdf.

19. Isaac Idun-Arkhurst, "Ghana's Relations with China," SAIIA China in Africa Policy Report 3 (2008), 4.

20. Dela Tsikata, Ama Pokuaa Fenny, and Ernest Aryeetey, "China-Africa Relations: A Case Study of Ghana," study for African Economic Research Consortium, January 2008, 6, www.aercafrica.org/documents/china_africa_relations/Ghana.pdf .

21. Idun-Arkhurst, 17–23; Yaw Baah et al., 92–94. According to China's Department of Commerce, Chinese FDI in Ghana in 2007 included 316 projects valued at $219 million, ranking China fourth among investing countries: Wenran Jiang and Jing Jing, "Deepening Chinese Stakes in West Africa: The Case of Ghana," *China Brief* 10, 4 (18 February 2010): 4.

22. Wenran and Jing, 4.

23. Martyn Davies, Hannah Edinger, Nastasya Tay, and Sanusha Naidu, "How China Delivers Development Assistance to Africa," Centre for Chinese Studies, University of Stellenbosch, February 2008, 38–40, 44, www.ccs.org.za/downloads/DFID_ FA_Final.pdf.

24. Idun-Arkhurst, 6, 9–10; Davies et al., 42.

25. Shinn, "Military and Security Relations: China, Africa, and the Rest of the World," in *China into Africa: Trade, AID, and Influence*, ed. Robert I Rotberg (Washington, D.C.: Brookings Institution Press, 2008), 166–67.

26. "Ghana Warns Africa: Don't Become China's Colony," *Reuters* (21 June 2007).

27. Felix Dela Klutse, "Kufour Challenges African Economists," *Daily Guide* (10 October 2007).

28. Ghana Ministry of Information and National Orientation website, entry by ministry of fisheries, 15 May 2008, www.ghana.gov.gh/ghana/our_doors_are_opened_constructive_dialogue_ minister.jsp.

29. Micael Boateng, "Alleged Maltreatment, Bui Workers Want Govt. Intervention," *Ghanaian Chronicle*, 13 June 2008. The study by Yah Baah et al. contains a detailed list of complaints about Chinese labor practices in Ghana. Oliver Hensengerth, "Interaction of Chinese Institutions with Host Governments in Dam Construction: The Bui Dam in Ghana," German Development Institute Discussion Paper 3, 2011.

30. Jin Zhu, "China, Africa Force Farming Ties," *China Daily*, 12 August 2010.

31. Will Connors and Francis Kokutse, "Ghana, China Ink $15 Billion in Deals," *Wall Street Journal*, 23 September 2010.

32. Awudu Mahama, "$3Bn Chinese Loan in Danger," *Daily Guide*, 28 September 2011.

33. Idun-Arkhurst, 12–15; Yah Baah et al., 89–91. For an analysis of the Chinese community in Ghana, estimated at 2,000–6,000, see Conal Guan-Yow Ho, 46–76.

34. Larkin, 55. Beijing does not seem to have been engaged seriously in the Congo before independence. It did show interest in a small Marxist group known as the Parti du Peuple led by Makwambala, who later became president of the Congolese Society for Friendship with China: Lowenthal, 167; Dutt, 280–83. Gizenga, at the time Congo deputy premier, sent a letter dated 8 September 1960 to Beijing requesting volunteers, food, finances, and arms: Schatten, 211. According to Larkin, 181, China provided 1 million pounds to the Lumumba-Gizenga government within four days.

35. China Secretariat of the General Political Department, "The Congo Situation and Its Development," 17 January 1961, trans. in *The Politics of the Chinese Red Army*, ed. J. Chester Cheng (Stanford, Calif.: Hoover Institution, 1966), 181. A second, secret analysis several months later commented that China "is continually and resolutely disclosing the American aggressive plot and giving great support to the Congo people"; see Cheng, 400. The document is titled "The Present Situation in the Congo and the New Schemes of American Imperialism."

36. Larkin, 56–57; Lowenthal, 181–82; Dutt, 283–84; Ogunsanwo, 104; Devon Curtis, "Partner or Predator in the Heart of Africa: Chinese Engagement with the DRC," in *Crouching Tiger, Hidden Dragon? Africa and China*, ed. Kweku Ampiah and Sanusha Naidu (Scottsville, S.A.: University of KwaZulu-Natal Press, 2008), 90.

37. Hutchison, *China's African Revolution*, 110–14; Cooley, 106–11; Martens and Smets, 32–33.

38. Larkin, 71–74, 181–83; Legum, 407–8; Cooley, 112–22; Warren Weinstein, "Chinese Aid and Policy in Central Africa," in *Soviet and Chinese Aid to African Nations*, ed. Warren Weinstein and Thomas H. Henriksen (New York: Praeger, 1980), 146–48; Curtis, 90–91.

39. Warren Weinstein, "Chinese Policy in Central Africa: 1960–73," in *Chinese and Soviet Aid to Africa*, ed. Weinstein, 57–59, 73–75.

40. John F. Clark, "Foreign Policy Making in Central Africa: The Imperative of Regime Security in a New Context," in *African Foreign Policies: Power and Process*, ed. Gilbert M. Khadiagala and Terrence Lyons (Boulder, Colo.: Lynne Rienner, 2001), 75; Shinn, 157–61. President Gerald Ford in a 1975 meeting with Mao Zedong in Beijing requested Chinese help driving the Soviets out of Angola. Ford suggested assistance go to Angolan opposition groups through Mozambique. Mao responded that the question needed more study but Mozambique was unlikely to cooperate, and any aid should go though Zaire. Mao was comfortable with China's relationship with Zaire at that time. See declassified memorandum of conversation, 2 December 1975, Digital National Security Archive.

41. State Department, "China's Policy Toward Sub-Saharan Africa," declassified document, 20 August 1985, Digital National Security Archive, 5.

42. CIA, "Communist Aid Activities, 1978," 24.

43. Oye Ogunbadejo, *The International Politics of Africa's Strategic Minerals* (Westport, Conn.: Greenwood Press, 1985), 27.

44. Curtis, 93–96; China Ministry of Foreign Affairs, "Bilateral Relations: DRC," 12 October 2003; Centre for Chinese Studies, "Evaluating China's FOCAC Commitments to Africa and Mapping the Way Ahead," report for Rockefeller Foundation, January 2010, 43–44, www.ccs.org.za/wp-content/uploads/2010/03/ENGLISH-Evaluating-Chin as-FOCAC-comm itments-to-Africa-2010.pdf.

45. Johanna Jansson, Christopher Burke and Wenran Jiang, "Chinese Companies in the Extractive Industries of Gabon and the DRC: Perceptions of Transparency," Centre for Chinese Studies, University of Stellenbosch, August 2009, 29–30; Johanna Jansson, "Patterns of Chinese Investment, Aid and Trade in Central Africa (Cameroon, the DRC and Gabon)," Centre for Chinese Studies, University of Stellenbosch, August 2009, 14; Centre for Chinese Studies, "Evaluating," 61–62.

46. Jansson, Burke, and Wenran, 36–37; Michael Komesaroff, "China Eyes Congo's Treasures," *Far Eastern Economic Review*, 171, 3 (April 2008): 38–41; Jeffrey Herbst and Greg Mills, "Commodity Flux and China's Africa Strategy," *China Brief* 9, 2 (22 January 2009): 4–6; Johanna Jansson, "DRC: Chinese Investment in Katanga," *Pambazuka News* 476, 1 April 2010.

47. The text of the first agreement is available in French and the second in French and Chinese at www.ua.ac.be/main.aspx?c = .GRALACE&n = 65909. The DRC handled the negotiation of these agreements in secrecy and did not present them to the National Assembly until May 2008, provoking a heated discussion: Stefaan Marysse and Sara Geenen, "Win-Win or Unequal Exchange? The Case of the Sino-Congolese Cooperation Agreements," *Journal of Modern African Studies* 47, 3 (September 2009): 373; Centre for Chinese Studies, "Evaluating," 53–56. DRC Senator Eve Bazaiba Masudi commented to Shinn in Caux, Switzerland, on 20 July 2008, that the government had not provided legislators with details of the agreements.

48. For an excellent analysis of this deal, see Marysse and Geenen, 371–96. See also Jansson, Burke, and Wenran, 33–36; Richard Behar, "China-Africa," *Fast Company* (June 2008): 115–16; Hannah Edinger and Johanna Jansson, "China's 'Angola Model' Comes to the DRC," *China Monitor* 34 (October 2008): 4–6. Wenran Jiang, "Chinese Inroads in DR Congo: A Chinese 'Marshall Plan' or Business?" *China Brief* 9, 1 (12 January 2009): 8–11.

49. Global Witness, "China and Congo: Friends in Need," March 2011, www.globalwitness.org/sites/default/files/library/friends_in_ need_en_l r.pdf; Claude Kabemba, "The Dragon Is Not Green Enough: The Potential Environmental Impact of Chinese Investment in the DRC," in *Chinese and African Perspectives on China in Africa*, ed. Axel Harneit-Sievers, Stephen Marks, and Sanusha Naidu (Kampala: Pambazuka Press, 2010), 139–54.

50. Marysse and Geenen, 389–91.

51. Jansson, Burke, and Wenran, 37–43; Thierry Vircoulon, "La Chine, nouvel acteur de la reconstruction congolaise," *Afrique Contemporaine* 227, 3 (2008): 110–12. For a case study of Chinese involvement in the DRC telecommunications sector, see Peter Draper, Tsidiso Disenyana, and Gilberto Biacuana, "Chinese Investment in African Network Industries: Case Studies from the Democratic Republic of Congo and Kenya," in *The Rise of China and India in Africa*, ed. Fantu Cheru and Cyril Obi (London: Zed Books, 2010), 112–15.

52. Centre for Chinese Studies, "Evaluating," 47–48.

53. Jansson, Burke, and Wenran, 30–32; Marysse and Geenen, 377–79, 383–87.

54. Vircoulon, 114–15.

55. Curtis, 103. For an analysis of Chinese employment practices, see Xiaoyang Tang, "Bulldozer or Locomotive? The Impact of Chinese Enterprises on the Local Employment in Angola and the DRC," *Journal of Asian and African Studies* 45, 3 (2010): 360–62.

56. "Chinese Mining Operations in Katanga Democratic Republic of the Congo," Rights and Accountability in Development report, September 2009, 1–6, http://raid-uk.org/docs/ChinaAfrica/EXSUM%20ENG%20LR.pdf. For criticism of Chinese practices, see Gilbert Malemba N'Sakila, "The Chinese Presence in Lubumbashi, DRC," *China Monitor* 34 (October 2008): 7–10.

57. Weinstein, "Chinese Aid and Policy in Central Africa," 150–55; Weinstein, "Chinese Policy in Central Africa: 1960–73," 61–66; Larkin, 127–29; Ogunsanwo, 116–19; Cooley, 109–12; Claire Sterling, "Chou En-lai and the Watusi," *The Reporter* 30, 6 (12 March 1964): 22–24; CIA, "Chinese Communist Activities in Africa," 13–14; Tareq Y. Ismael, "The People's Republic of China and Africa," *Journal of Modern African Studies* 9, 4 (1971): 516–17. According to George B. N. Ayittey, China had a long association with the Tutsi in Burundi. He wrote that Tutsis received training in guerrilla warfare in China beginning in 1953: "Africa in the Postcommunist World," *Problems of Communism* 41, 1–2 (January–April 1992): 214. Warren Weinstein argued that "Chinese involvement in Burundian politics was equally opportunistic; it contributed to a worsening of Burundi's internal problems": "Chinese Aid and Policy in

Central Africa," 151. He added that China's interest in Burundi was primarily linked to support to anti-government dissidents in the Congo.

58. Weinstein, "Chinese Policy in Central Africa: 1960–73," 69–72.

59. China Ministry of Foreign Affairs, "Bilateral Relations: Burundi," 12 October 2003.

60. "Interview: Burundian PM: There Is New Dynamic in Relationship with China," *Xinhua*, 11 October 2007.

61. Ogunsanwo, 156–58. Wei Liang-Tsai, *Peking Versus Taipei in Africa 1960–1978* (Taipei: Asia and World Institute, 1982), 126–28; Nicolas Lang, "Les Chinois à Brazzaville," *Est et Ouest* 17, 343 (1–15 June 1965): 3. Congo-Brazzaville president Fulbert Youlou wrote a damning account of Chinese activities in Africa, *J'accuse la Chine* (Paris: Table Ronde, 1966). The text of the 1965 Sino-Congolese Friendship Treaty is contained in Ogunsanwo, 281–82.

62. CIA, "Chinese Communist Activities in Africa," 5.

63. Wei Liang-Tsai, 128–31; Ogunsanwo, 221–23, 232; Hutchison, *China's African Revolution*, 92–95; Cooley, 103, 114; Charles K. Ebinger, "External Intervention in Internal War: The Politics and Diplomacy of the Angolan Civil War," *Orbis* 20, 3 (Fall 1976): 680; Ismael, 516. CIA, "Communist Aid Activities, 1978," 5.

64. China Ministry of Foreign Affairs, "Bilateral Relations: Congo," 12 October 2003; Jean-Christophe Boungou Bazika, "Les Relations économiques de la Chine avec la République du Congo," February 2008, 3–12, www.aercafrica.org/documents/china_africa_relations/Congo.pdf ; State Department, "China's Policy Toward Sub-Saharan Africa," 5.

65. Wei Liang-Tsai, 180–83. Mertens and Smets, 77–79; Larkin, 129–30; Hutchison, *China's African Revolution*, 120–22; Ogunsanwo, 162, 185–86; Cooley, 182–83. Daniel Nelson argued that internal military matters motivated the coup by General Bokassa; it had little or nothing to do with Chinese activities in the CAR: "Sino-African Relationship: Renewing an Ancient Contact," *East Asian Review* 4, 1 (1977): 75. Larkin, Ogunsanwo, and Hutchison agreed with this assessment; all three acknowledged Chinese subversion in several other African countries.

66. China Ministry of Foreign Affairs, "Bilateral Relations: CAR," 12 October 2003.

67. "More Countries Express Support for China's Handling of Lhasa Riots," *Xinhua*, 28 March 2008.

68. Weinstein, "Chinese Aid and Policy in Central Africa," 148–50; Wei Liang-Tsai, 178–79, 358–59; Weinstein, "Chinese Policy in Central Africa: 1960–73," 59–60, 72–73; Larkin, 87, 183; Cooley, 110–11.

69. China Ministry of Foreign Affairs, "Bilateral Relations: Rwanda," 12 October 2003; State Department, "China's Policy Toward Sub-Saharan Africa," 5. For background on the Chinese-built cement factory, see Yuan Wu, *China and Africa* (Beijing: China Intercontinental Press, 2006), 52.

70. "$8 Million Foreign Affairs Complex Plan Launched," *New Times*, 22 December 2006; John Gahamanyi and Alex Ngarambe, "Star Africa Media in Regional Expansion Drive," *New Times*, 24 July 2009.

71. Copper, 147–49. In contrast to China's steady pursuit of Equatorial Guinea, the United States closed its embassy on Malabo in 1995 for cost-cutting reasons and only reopened it in 2003 under pressure from American oil companies that had developed most of the oil production.

72. China Ministry of Foreign Affairs, "Bilateral Relations: Equatorial Guinea," 12 October 2003; Mario Esteban, "A Silent Invasion? African Views on the Growing Presence in Africa: The Case of Equatorial Guinea," *African and Asian Studies* 9, 3 (2010): 246.

73. For a thorough analysis of China's activities in Equatorial Guinea, see Mario Esteban, "The Chinese *Amigo*: Implications for the Development of Equatorial Guinea," *China Quarterly* 199 (September 2009): 667–85.

74. Ulrich, Jacoby, "Getting Together," *Finance and Development* 44, 2 (June 2007); Esteban, "The Chinese *Amigo*," 670–74. Journalist Richard Behar concluded (118) following a visit to Equatorial Guinea in 2008 that "China is systematically challenging the American oil giants here—locking in exploration or supply contracts, winning rights to new oil fields, doing massive infrastructure development, even stepping up military supplies."

75. "Not Working Out," *Africa-Asia Confidential* 1, 6 (April 2008): 6.

76. Mario Esteban, "A Silent Invasion?" 235.

77. Legum, 422, 430–31; Cooley, 151–52; Wei Liang-Tsai, 136–38, 387.

78. Ogunsanwo, 233–37, 243; Larkin, 178, 186; Hutchison, *China's African Revolution*, 156–60; Nelson, 77–78; Victor Nwaozichi Chibundu, *Nigeria-China Foreign Relations 1960–1999* (Ibadan: Spectrum, 2000), 6–7; Sharath Srinivasan, "A 'Rising Great Power' Embraces Africa: Nigeria-China Relations," in *Gulliver's Troubles: Nigeria's Foreign Policy After the Cold War*, ed. Adekeye Adebajo and Abdul Raufu Mustapha (Scottsville, S.A.: University of KwaZulu-Natal Press, 2008), 337. Ogunsanwo, Larkin, and Hutchison generally agree that China did not provide direct support to Biafra, but did allow weapons it had given to Tanzania to reach Biafra. Ndubisi Obiaga added: "Although there is not sufficient evidence to back the allegation that the Chinese supplied arms to the Biafrans, this was widely believed at the time. Chinese military assistance was said to have been channeled through Tanzania and the enclave. Peking had also offered to train the Biafran forces in guerrilla tactics and supply them with arms and sabotage equipment through an additional route—the underground network of Union des Population du Cameroun": *The Politics of Humanitarian Organizations Intervention* (Lanham, Md.: University Press of America, 2004), 22. A CIA report concluded that "although Peking has been replacing Chinese arms given to Biafra by Tanzania, it has shown little interest in assuming a more direct involvement in the Nigerian civil war": "Communist China's Presence in Africa," 20 June 1969, 8,

www.state.gov/documents/organization/54521.pdf. Gregory Mthembu-Salter argued that China supplied Biafra with small quantities of light arms: "Elephants, Ants and Superpowers: Nigeria's Relations with China," SAIIA Occasional Paper 42, September 2009, 6.

79. Alaba Ogunsanwo, "A Tale of Two Giants: Nigeria and China," in *Crouching Tiger, Hidden Dragon?*, 195.

80. Ogunsanwo, 243; Wei Liang-Tsai, 138–39; Mthembu-Salter, 6–10; Srinivasan, 338, 343–44; China Ministry of Foreign Affairs, "Bilateral Relations: Nigeria," 12 October 2003. The following analyses offer a Nigerian perspective on China-Nigerian relations: Pat Utomi, "China and Nigeria," in *U.S. and Chinese Engagement in Africa*, ed. Jennifer Cooke (Washington, D.C.: Center for Strategic and International Studies, July 2008), 49–58; Bukar Bukarambe, "Nigeria-China Relations: The Unacknowledged Sino-Dynamics," *African Journal of International Affairs and Development* 7, 2 (2002): 27–49; Nigerian Institute of International Affairs, *Nigeria and China: Bilateral Ties in a New World Order* (Lagos: Nigerian Institute, 2005). For a review of high level exchange visits in 1960–1998 see Chibundu, 12–16; for the Nigeria-China Friendship Association see 63–68.

81. Srinivasan, 340.

82. Chibundu, 43–46.

83. Ibid., 46–54.

84. Ibid. 33–41; Edwin Ikhuoria, "The Impact of Chinese Imports on Nigerian Traders," in *Chinese and African Perspectives on China in Africa*, 128–38.

85. An internal paper by the Nigerian Ministry of Foreign Affairs dated 1 October 2006 detailed Chinese investment in the country. Most of it was in telecommunications (Shanghai-Bell Alcatel, ZTE, and Huawei), hydropower, oil and gas, and miscellaneous manufacturing. For an analysis of Chinese FDI in Nigeria and its impact on the country, see Evelyn Atomre, Joel Odigie, James Eustace, and Wilson Onemolease, "Chinese Investments in Nigeria," in *Chinese Investments in Africa: A Labour Perspective*, 336–37, 343–64. For Chinese economic interests in Nigeria, see Abiodun Alao, "Banking in Nigeria and Chinese Economic Diplomacy in Africa," SAIIA Occasional Paper 65, July 2010, 9–11.

86. "Chinese Agency Reviews Sino-Nigeria Trade, Political Ties," *Xinhua*, 26 April 2006; Srinivasan, 341–42.

87. Bjørn Brandtzaeg, "Common Cause Different Approaches: China and Norway in Nigeria," Econ Pöyry Research Report 2008–014, February 2008, 11–13, http://eittransparency.org/files/publication_file/RR-2008-014%20BJB%20Common%20cause%20different%20approaches.pdf. For Chinese oil investment in Nigeria, see Mthembu-Salter, 11–14.

88. Alec Russell and Matthew Green, "Africa's Response: Big Push to Be More Assertive," *Financial Times*, 23 January 2008; "Acting President Jonathan Sets Out His Plans," *Africa Confidential* 51, 4 (19 February 2010): 6. For an analysis of activity by Asian state oil companies in Nigeria, see Lillian Wong, "Asian National Oil Companies

in Nigeria," in *Thirst for African Oil*, ed. Alex Vines, Lillian Wong, Markus Weimer, and Indira Campos, Chatham House Report, August 2009, 5–28.

89. E. Olawale Ogunkola et al. "China-Nigeria Economic Relations," February 2008, 4–5, www.aercafrica.org/documents/china_africa_relations/Nigeria.p df.

90. "Nigeria: China Investments in the Country Hits N888 Billion," *allafrica.com*, 27 October 2009.

91. L. C. Russell Hsiao, "China's African Inroads Shaken by Regional Political Uncertainties," *China Brief* 8, 21 (7 November 2008): 2; Mthembu-Salter, 15–16.

92. Brandtzaeg, 10; Ogunsanwo, "A Tale of Two Giants," 200. Representatives of the Taiwan Trade Office in Abuja told Shinn/Eisenman on 6 August 2007 that there were 600 Chinese companies in Nigeria: Mthembu-Salter, 14–21.

93. Mthembu-Salter, 21–23.

94. Shinn, 167–68.

95. "Nigeria, China Sign Pact to Replace Faulty Satellite by 2011," *Xinhua* (25 March 2009).

96. Atomre et al., 341.

97. Abiodun Alao, "Chinese Business Interests and Banking in Nigeria," SAIIA Policy Briefing 20, July 2010, 3–4.

98. "Nigeria, China Sign $23b Oil Deal," *BBC*, 14 May 2010; Debra Bräutigam, "China's $28.5 Billion Deal in Nigeria: How Real Is It?" blog, 17 May 2010.

99. Sunday Williams, "China Plans U.S. $20 Billion Investment in Country's Infrastructure," *Daily Trust* (Nigeria), 20 September 2010.

100. Dulue Mbachu, "Nigerian Resources: Changing the Playing Field." *South African Journal of International Affairs* 13, 1 (Summer/Autumn 2006): 80–81. Ogunkola, 11–12. Ogunsanwo, "A Tale of Two Giants," 196–98. In a meeting with Shinn/Eisenman in Abuja on 7 August 2007, Issa Aremu, acting general secretary of the National Union of Textiles, Garment and Tailoring Workers of Nigeria, was especially critical about the impact of Chinese textile imports on Nigerian textile production. He said the union also urged Nigeria to complain to the WTO that China is counterfeiting Nigerian textile designs, placing a "made in Nigeria" label on them, and selling them in Nigeria. In a meeting with Shinn/Eisenman in Abuja on 8 August 2007, Ochi C. Achinivu, director of trade, Federal Ministry of Commerce and Industry, complained about counterfeit Chinese textiles on the market. He also thought China might be dumping good quality shoes on the Nigerian market. He said Nigeria will not be in a position to take cases to the WTO until it has created a Trade and Investment Commission. P. M. Chun, executive director, United Nigerian Textiles PLC, repeated the concerns about Chinese textiles in a meeting with Shinn/Eisenman in Lagos on 9 August 2007. At its peak, the Nigerian textile industry employed 250,000 workers. For several reasons, including Chinese imports, he said the number of workers had dropped to 30,000 by 2007. For an analysis of Nigeria-China trade see Atomre et al., 337–41.

101. Sola Akinrinade and Olukoya Ogen, "Globalization and De-Industrialization: South-South Neo-Liberalism and the Collapse of the Nigerian Textile Industry,"

Global South 2, 2 (Fall 2008): 164–68. In August 2007, Shinn/Eisenman saw some of these textiles on sale in Chinatown in Lagos. In a separate article, Olukoya Ogen argued that Chinese "imperialism" in Nigeria is primarily driven by its quest for sources of energy and raw materials. He added that Nigeria's huge market is irresistible for the disposal of Chinese manufactured goods while Nigeria's poorly developed infrastructure offers rich opportunities for Chinese companies to obtain contracts: "Contemporary China-Nigeria Relations: Chinese Imperialism or South-South Mutual Partnership?" *China Aktuell* 3 (2008): 82–84. See also Ogunsanwo, "A Tale of Two Giants," 201–2.

102. Shinn/Eisenman meeting in Abuja on 5 August 2007 with Yaha Abdullahi Mohammed, Natural Link Ltd. For an analysis of China-Nigeria relations, see Ian Taylor, "China's Relations with Nigeria," *Round Table* 96, 392 (October 2007): 631–45. For an analysis of the China-Nigeria economic relationship, see Lemuel E. Odeh, "Sino-Nigeria Economic Relations 1990–2009," *African Renaissance* 7, 1 (2010): 43–56.

103. Shinn/Eisenman meeting in Abuja, 8 August 2007 with senior official, Ministry of Foreign Affairs.

104. Shinn/Eisenman meeting in Lagos, 9 August 2007 with a group of Nigerian scholars, Nigerian Institute of International Affairs.

105. Ogunsanwo, 53–54, 71–72, 172–73; Cooley, 99–103; Hutchison, *China's African Revolution*, 28–29. Lowenthal, 163–64, 173–74; Schatten, 203–10; Wei Liang-Tsai, 139–41. In addition, see Ghana Ministry of Information, *Nkrumah's Deception of Africa*, which implicates China in support of the UPC.

106. Ogunsanwo, 243–44. Writing in 1969, Soviet scholar A. Volghin said Cameroon provided an example of how Beijing combined extremism with pragmatism in its African policy. In the early 1960s, it urged the UPC to continue its struggle against the Ahidjo government at all costs. As China consolidated ties with other independent African countries, it started losing interest in the UPC: "Africa in Peking's Foreign Policy," *International Affairs* (September 1969): 30.

107. Wei Liang-Tsai, 142; China Ministry of Foreign Affairs, "Bilateral Relations: Cameroon,"12 October 2003.

108. Jansson, 7.

109. "China's Hu Jintao Meets Cameroonian President, Proposes Boosting Ties," *Xinhua*, 22 September 2003; "Chine-Cameroun: L'empire du milieu et l'Afrique en miniature," *Jeune Afrique* 47, 2392 (12–18 November 2006): 56–58. For details of Chinese aid to Cameroon, see Jansson, 7–8.

110. "China Donates CFA 532 Million to Cameroon's Armed Forces," *Cameroon Tribune*, 2 January 2007.

111. Wei Liang-Tsai, 131–32, 344–46; Ogunsanwo, 162, 185; Larkin, 130–31; CIA, "Chinese Communist Activities in Africa," 11; Cooley, 181–82; Hutchison, *China's African Revolution*, 122–23, notes the PRC blamed the United States for the break in relations by stirring up anti-China sentiment. For a detailed analysis of China's rice

cultivation scheme in Benin, see Law Yu Fai, *Chinese Foreign Aid: A Study of Its Nature and Goals to the Foreign Policy and World View of the People's Republic of China, 1950–1982* (Saarbrücken: Breitenbach, 1984), 269–85.

112. CIA, "Communist Aid Activities, 1978," 25.

113. China Ministry of Foreign Affairs, "Bilateral Relations: Benin," 12 October 2003.

114. Comment by Robert Neuwirth, a journalist who specializes in the world's alternative economy, at a conference attended by Shinn in Washington, 21 May 2010, on the informal economy in Africa.

115. Wei Liang-Tsai, 142–44, 348–50, 387; China Ministry of Foreign Affairs, "Bilateral Relations: Sierra Leone," 12 October 2003; "Sierra Leone: President Storms China," *Africa News*, 24 May 2009; CIA, "Communist Aid to Less Developed Countries of the Free World, 1977," 22.

116. Deborah Bräutigam, *Chinese Aid and African Development: Exporting Green Revolution* (London: Macmillan, 1998), 55–57, 211–13.

117. "Sierra Leone Signs Tripartite Agreement on Agricultural Assistance," *Standard Times*, 12 July 2006; "China, Sierra Leone Sign Cooperation Agreement on Economy, Technology," *Xinhua*, 19 January 2008.

118. Zhang Qi, "African Minerals in Funding Talks with Chinese Companies," *China Daily*, 4 June 2010; "Shandong Iron and Steel Pays US$1.5 Billion for Stake in African Minerals Project," *China Economic Review*, 14 July 2010.

119. "Sierra Leone Bans Timber Exports," *Reuters*, 15 January 2008.

120. CIA, "Chinese Communist Activities in Africa," 13.

121. Larkin, 143–44, 178, 185–86; Wei Liang-Tsai, 144–45, 338–40; Richard J. Payne and Cassandra R. Veney, "China's Post-Cold War African Policy," *Asian Survey* 38, 9 (September 1998): 872; CIA, "Communist Aid Activities, 1978," 26; China Ministry of Foreign Affairs, "Bilateral Relations: Senegal," 26 August 2003. The communiqué from Senegal's Ministry of Foreign Affairs dated 25 October 2005 that reestablished relations contains the following sentence: "The Government of the Republic of Senegal recognizes that there is only one China in the world, that the Government of the People's Republic of China is the sole legal representative of the Government of the whole of China and that Taiwan forms an integral part of Chinese territory." The letter dated 25 October 2005 to President Chen Shui-bian of Taiwan from President Abdoulaye Wade contains the following passages: "Today, the Government of Senegal has carried out a reassessment of our relations and deems it necessary to establish diplomatic relations with Beijing, with the consequences which necessarily ensue. However, I have made it clear to Beijing that Senegal intends to maintain economic, trade and cultural relations with the Taiwan authorities, should the latter so desire. I shall be consistent and loyal to our new partner as I have been with you. I do not consider it necessary to discuss the reasons for our choice. Perhaps General de Gaulle was right when he said: 'States have no friends. They have only interests'." The text of both documents is in *African Geopolitics* 23 (July-September 2006): 259–62.

122. "China, Senegal PMs Praise Growth of Ties Since Resumption of Relations," *Xinhua*, 26 April 2006.

123. "Senegal's President Says Restoration of Ties with China 'Correct' Decision," *Xinhua*, 4 November 2006. See Romain Dittgen, "From Isolation to Integration? A Study of Chinese Retailers in Dakar," SAIIA Occasional Paper 57, March 2010; Antoine Kernen, "Small and Medium-Sized Chinese Businesses in Mali and Senegal," *African and Asian Studies* 9, 3 (2010): 257–61.

124. Shinn notes from 28 September 2007 presentation by President Abdoulaye Wade at the CATO Institute, Washington. In a subsequent comment, Wade reiterated his concern about the time to get World Bank assistance: "I achieved more in my one hour meeting with Hu Jintao in an executive suite at my hotel in Berlin during the recent G8 meeting in Heiligendamm than I did during the entire, orchestrated meeting of world leaders at the summit—where African leaders were told little more than that G8 nations would respect existing commitments." Abdoulaye Wade, "Time for the West to Practise What It Preaches," *Financial Times*, 23 January 2008.

125. Liang-Tsai, 145–46. Bartke, *China's Economic Aid*, 68, 191; Ogunsanwo, 35, 269–70; China Ministry of Foreign Affairs, "Bilateral Relations: Togo," 12 October 2003.

126. Linn Axelsson and Nina Sylvanus, "Navigating Chinese Textile Networks: Women Traders in Accra and Lomé," in *The Rise of China and India in Africa*, 134–47.

127. Larkin, 133, 186; Ogunsanwo, 269–70; Liang-Tsai, 149–50; China Ministry of Foreign Affairs, "Bilateral Relations: Gabon," 12 October 2003; CIA, "Communist Aid Activities, 1978," 25; Ana Cristina Alves, "China and Gabon: A Growing Resource Partnership," SAIIA China in Africa Policy Report 4 (2008), 6–8.

128. Alves, 12–21.

129. "China's SINOPEC Provokes Conservation Uproar in Gabon," *AFX International Focus* (1 October 2006). Alves, 9–10; Jansson, 23–27, 39–41; Jansson et al., 16–19.

130. Jansson, "Chinese Investment in Gabon's Extractive Industries," *Pambazuka News*, 8 July 2010.

131. "Chinese Vice Premier Attends Funeral of Gabon's Late President Bongo," *Xinhua*, 16 June 2009.

132. "Hu Meets Foreign Leaders Ahead of Shanghai Expo," *Xinhua*, 29 April 2010.

133. "China to Send Agricultural Experts to Country," *FAO Africa News*, 18 January 2007; Javier Blas and Matthew Green, "Commodities: Feeding an Insatiable Appetite," *Financial Times*, 23 January 2008; Lydia Polgreen, "Pristine African Park Faces Development," *New York Times*, 22 February 2009; Douglas Yates, "French Puppet, Chinese Strings: Sino-Gabonese Relations," in *Crouching Tiger, Hidden Dragon?* 215–21.

134. Liang-Tsai, 150, 350–51; China Ministry of Foreign Affairs, "Bilateral Relations: Gambia," 26 August 2003; CIA, "Communist Aid, 1977," 21; Bräutigam, 58–60, 214–16.

135. Comment to Shinn by Barry Wells, U.S. ambassador to Gambia, Washington, D.C., 7 October 2009.

136. CIA, "Communist Aid, 1977," 22.

137. China Ministry of Foreign Affairs, "Bilateral Relations: Liberia," 26 August 2003; Liang-Tsai, 333–40; Yu Shiao-min, "Diplomatic Relations Established; Liberia, ROC Together Again," 5 October 1989, http://taiwanjournal.nat.gov.tw/ct.asp?xItem = 7005&CtNode = 118; Bräutigam, 57–58, 213–14.

138. China, "Bilateral Relations: Liberia."

139. China Ministry of Foreign Affairs, "China, Liberia Resume Diplomatic Ties," 13 October 2003, www.mfa.gov/cn/ce/ceee/eng/dtxw/t111878.htm; Alex Vines, "The Scramble for Resources: African Case Studies," *South African Journal of International Affairs* 13, 1 (Summer/Autumn 2006): 72.

140. Vines, 72–73.

141. "CDC Complains to UN, Others," *The Inquirer*, 19 September 2006; "China Slices Liberia's Debt," *The Analyst*, 3 November 2006.

142. James Butty, "Chinese President Signs Cooperation Agreements with Liberia," *VOA*, 7 February 2007; "Hu Jintao Holds Talks with Liberian President Johnson-Sirleaf," Chinese consulate in San Francisco, www.chinaconsulatesf.org/eng/xw/t295398.htm.

143. Francis Nyepon, managing partner of DUCOR Waste Management in Liberia, noted that Chinese investment threatens to surpass that of the United States and asked if the Liberian government has asked itself why China is engaging so extensively in Liberia. He wondered if Johnson-Sirleaf's anti-corruption campaign can cope with Chinese companies that are willing to bribe their way into lucrative contracts. He suggested Liberian policy-makers should study China's approach to Zimbabwe, Sudan, Angola, Zambia, and the DRC: "Is China Influence Growing at the Expense of America's?" *The Analyst*, 10 December 2007.

144. China Embassy website in Monrovia, http://lr.china-embassy.org/eng/sghdh zxxx/t625132.htm.

145. Rong Yan, "Chinese Vice-President Meets Liberian Counterpart 10 July," *Xinhua*, 10 July 2009.

146. "Helping Liberia Escape Conflict Timber: The Role of the International Community—China and Europe," *Forest Trends* 5 (June 2006).

147. All three made the remarks at the Kendeja Resort outside Monrovia on 24 February 2010. In a separate conversation with Shinn on 25 February, Sylvester M. Grigsby, deputy minister for international cooperation and economic integration in the Liberian Ministry of Foreign Affairs, added that China and the United States have a history of working cooperatively in Liberia.

148. Liang-Tsai, 150–51.

149. Ogunsanwo, 147, 172, 265; Cooley, 180, 207.

150. Liang-Tsai, 152. Drew Middleton," Ivory Coast Head Calls China Peril," *New York Times*, 10 April 1966; Edmond Taylor, "French Africa," *The Reporter* 32, 6 (25 March 1965): 30.

151. China Ministry of Foreign Affairs, "Bilateral Relations: Côte d'Ivoire," 12 October 2003.

152. François Lafargue, "La Chine: Stratégies d'influence en Côte d'Ivoire," *Monde Chinois* 8 (Summer/Autumn 2006): 42.

153. Ibid., 40, 47.

154. Cooley, 130–31; Richard Gibson, *African Liberation Movements: Contemporary Struggles against White Minority Rule* (London: Oxford University Press, 1972), 256–57; Ogunsanwo, 107, 179, 232–33, 239, 264.

155. China Ministry of Foreign Affairs, "Bilateral Relations: Guinea Bissau," 12 October 2003; Liang-Tsai, 148–49.

156. China, "Bilateral Relations: Guinea Bissau"; "Guinea Bissau: Rebuilding of Electricity Grid Brings New Opportunities for Economic Growth," *Macauhub*, 4 February 2008. As a result of internal conflict in the capital in 1998 the United States closed its embassy and never returned. The Chinese embassy is next door to the shuttered U.S. ambassador's residence. A *Washington Post* correspondent reported in 2008 that while the United States remains invisible, "China is making sure it has a showy, 'look-at-me' presence." Kevin Sullivan, "An Abandoned Oasis of American Comfort in Tiny Guinea-Bissau," *Washington Post*, 1 June 2008.

157. China Ministry of Foreign Affairs, "Bilateral Relations: São Tomé and Principe," 26 August 2003; Bartke, *The Agreements of the People's Republic of China*, 160; CIA, "Communist Aid Activities," 26. "Foreign Minister Meets São Tomé Officials," *Xinhua*, 16 January 1997; "China Suspends Diplomatic Relations; Blame Ties with Taiwan," *Xinhua*, 11 July 1997.

158. "Angola and São Tomé and Principe Gain Stature in China's Energy Policy," *Macauhub*, 24 August 2009.

159. "São Tomé and Principe: Chinese Businesspeople Analyze Possibility of Investing in the Archipelago," *Macauhub*, 18 March 2008.

160. "Changing Horses," *Africa-Asia Confidential* 1, 5 (March 2008): 5; Vasco Martins, "Aid for Legitimacy: São Tomé and Principe Hand in Hand with Taiwan," *IPRIS Viewpoints* (February 2011): 1–3.

161. China Ministry of Foreign Affairs, "Bilateral Relations: Cape Verde," 12 October 2003; Bartke, *The Agreements of the People's Republic of China*, 31.

162. Loro Horta, "The Changing Nature of Chinese Business in Africa: The Case of Cape Verde," *RSIS Commentaries*, 17 January 2008, www.rsis.edu.sg/publications/Perspective/RSIS0082008.pdf; Jørgen Carling and Heidi Østbø Haugen, "Mixed Fates of a Popular Minority: Chinese Migrants in Cape Verde," in *China Returns to Africa*, ed. Chris Alden, Daniel Large, and Ricardo Soares de Oliveira (London: Hurst, 2008), 320–21.

Chapter 11. China's Relations with Southern Africa

1. John K. Cooley, *East Wind over Africa: Red China's African Offensive* (New York: Walker, 1965), 94; John Franklin Copper, *China's Foreign Aid* (Lexington, Mass.:

Lexington Books, 1976), 101. For an overview of Sino-Zambian relations, see Dominik Kopinski and Andrzej Polus, "Sino-Zambian Relations: 'An All-Weather Friendship' Weathering the Storm," *Journal of Contemporary African Studies* 29, 2 (April 2011): 181–92.

2. Ian Taylor, *China and Africa: Engagement and Compromise* (London: Routledge, 2006), 164–66; Wolfgang Bartke, *China's Economic Aid* (London: Hurst, 1975), 72, 200–201; Bartke, *The Agreements of the People's Republic of China with Foreign Countries 1949–1990* (Munich: K.G. Saur, 1992), 217; Wei Liang-Tsai, *Peking Versus Taipei in Africa 1960–1978* (Taipei: Asia and World Institute, 1982), 242–43; Alan Hutchison, *China's African Revolution* (London: Hutchinson, 1975), 275–76; Alaba Ogunsanwo, *China's Policy in Africa 1958–1971* (London: Cambridge University Press, 1974), 208, 250–51.

3. Taylor, *China and Africa*, 167–68; Bartke, *The Agreements of the People's Republic of China*, 217. For a detailed account of Chinese aid to Zambia, see Inyambo Mwanawina, "China-Africa Economic Relations: The Case of Zambia," African Economic Research Consortium, 4 February 2008, 18–22, 26–28. Mwanawina documents Zambia's debt to China on 29, www.aercafrica.org/documents/china_africa_relations/Zambia.pdf. For another account of Chinese aid to Zambia and debt sustainability, see Martyn Davies, Hannah Edinger, Nastasya Tay, and Sanusha Naidu, "How China Delivers Development Assistance to Africa," Centre for Chinese Studies, University of Stellenbosch, February 2008, 47–50, www.ccs.org.za/downloads/DFID_FA_Final.pdf.

4. Taylor, *China and Africa*, 167–76; Bartke, *The Agreements of the People's Republic of China*, 217–18. A declassified 1985 State Department analysis said that since completion of the Tan-Zam railway in 1975 and Lusaka's acceptance of 12 Soviet MiG-21 fighters in 1979, Chinese aid to Zambia steadily declined: "China's Policy Toward Sub-Saharan Africa," 4.

5. Taylor, *China and Africa*, 176–80; China Ministry of Foreign Affairs, "Bilateral Relations: Zambia," 12 October 2003, www.fmprc.gov.cn/eng/wjb/zzjg/fzs/gjlb/3114/default.htm.

6. Anders Bastholm and Peter Kragelund, "State-Driven Chinese Investments in Zambia: Combining Strategic Interests and Profits," in *The New Presence of China in Africa*, ed. Meine Pieter van Dijk (Amsterdam: Amsterdam University Press, 2009), 127.

7. Chris McGreal, "Backlash as Cheap Chinese Labour and Products Follow Investment from Beijing," *The Guardian*, 5 February 2007; Muna Ndulo, "Chinese Investments in Africa: A Case Study of Zambia," in *Crouching Tiger, Hidden Dragon? Africa and China*, ed. Kweku Ampiah and Sanusha Naidu (Scottsville, S.A.: University of KwaZulu-Natal Press, 2008), 144; Sarah Raine, *China's African Challenges* (London: IISS, 2009), 138–39. Austin C. Muneku, "Chinese Investments in Zambia," in *Chinese Investments in Africa: A Labour Perspective*, ed. Anthony Yaw Baah and Herbert Jauch, African Labour Research Network (May 2009), 170. Aleksandra W. Gadzala, "From Formal-to-Informal-Sector Employment: Examining the Chinese Presence in Zambia," *Review of African Political Economy* 37, 123 (March 2010): 44.

8. "Zambian Party Delegation in China to Strengthen Economic Ties," *Xinhua*, 27 June 2005.

9. Raine, 139–41; Joseph J. Schatz, "Zambian Hopeful Takes a Swing at China," *Washington Post*, 25 September 2006; Robyn Dixon, "Africans Lash Out at Chinese Employers," *Los Angeles Times*, 6 October 2006; Paul Hare, "China and Zambia: The All-Weather Friendship Hits Stormy Weather," *China Brief* 7, 5 (7 March 2007): 7–9. Michael Sata documented his criticisms of Chinese practices in Zambia in a paper presented to the Harvard University Committee on Human Rights on 24 October 2007. See also Ching Kwan Lee, "Raw Encounters: Chinese Managers, African Workers and the Politics of Casualization in Africa's Chinese Enclaves," *China Quarterly* 199 (September 2009): 663–65.

10. Lydia Polgreen and Howard W. French, "China's Trade in Africa Carries a Price Tag," *New York Times*, 21 August 2007; "The Copper Clashes," *Africa-Asia Confidential* 1, 5 (March 2008): 6. For China's engagement with Zambia's mining sector, see Dan Haglund, "Regulating FDI in Weak African States: A Case Study of Chinese Copper Mining in Zambia," *Journal of Modern African Studies* 46, 4 (December 2008): 547–75. Haglund argues that the weak regulatory system in Zambia may allow Chinese investment to undermine local environmental, social, and fiscal regulation. For a study on Chinese investment in Zambia's mining sector, see Dan Haglund, "In It for the Long Term? Governance and Learning Among Chinese Investors in Zambia's Copper Sector," *China Quarterly* 199 (September 2009): 627–46. For a study of the Mulungushi Textile Factory, which Chinese investors tried to rehabilitate beginning in the late 1990s, see Andrew Brooks, "Spinning and Weaving Discontent: Labour Relations and the Production of Meaning at Zambia-China Mulungushi Textiles," *Journal of Southern African Studies* 36, 1 (March 2010): 113–32. Labor disputes, financial difficulties, and increased competition in global markets resulted in abandonment of the venture in 2006.

11. Peter Kragelund, "Part of the Disease or Part of the Cure? Chinese Investments in the Zambian Mining and Construction Sectors," *European Journal of Development Research* 21, 4 (September 2009): 648–51; Bastholm and Kragelund, 118, 124–33; Mwanawina, 7–14; Peter Kragelund, "Knocking on a Wide-Open Door: Chinese Investments in Africa," *Review of African Political Economy* 36, 122 (2009): 482–85; Yan Hairong and Barry Sautman, "Chinese Activities in Zambia: More than Just Mining," *China Monitor* (September 2009): 5; Gadzala, 52–55. For an analysis of the impact of Chinese investment on Zambia's economy and labor market, see Muneku, 173–195. For an analysis of Chinese investment in Zambia's copper sector from a Chinese perspective, see Pengtao Li, "The Myth and Reality of Chinese Investors: A Case Study of Chinese Investment in Zambia's Copper Industry," SAIIA Occasional Paper 62, May 2010; Fridah Zinyama, "Chinese Investments in Zambia Have Reached about $2bn—Mutati," *Post Newspapers*, 2 June 2010.

12. Muneku, 195. For an analysis of Chinese labor practices, see Gadzala, 50–52.

13. Kragelund, 487.

14. Ndulo, 142; Duncan Freeman, Jonathan Holslag, and Steffi Weil, "China's Foreign Farming Policy: Can Land Provide Security?" *BICCS Asia Paper* 3, 9 (2008): 17; Mwanawina, 14–18, 30–31, 36–37; Fredrick Mutesa, "China and Zambia: Between Development and Politics," in *The Rise of China and India in Africa*, ed. Fantu Cheru and Cyril Obi (London: Zed Books, 2010), 167–78. For a study of Chinese involvement in Zambian agriculture, see Yan Hairong and Barry Sautman, "Chinese Farms in Zambia: From Socialist to 'Agro-Imperialist' Engagement?" *African and Asian Studies* 9, 3 (2010): 307–33.

15. Barry Sautman and Yan Hairong, "African Perspectives on China-Africa Links," *China Quarterly* 199 (September 2009): 749–51; L. C. Russell Hsiao, "China's African Inroads Shaken by Regional Political Uncertainties," *China Brief* 8, 21 (7 November 2008): 2; "Zambia: We Are Not Against Chinese Investment-Sata," *Lusaka Times*, 16 January 2010. For a summary of China-Zambia military cooperation, see Shinn, "Military and Security Relations: China, Africa and the Rest of the World," in *China into Africa: Trade Aid, and Influence*, ed. Robert I. Rotberg (Washington, D.C.: Brookings Institution Press, 2008), 173.

16. "Unfair to Say China's Aid Leads to Africa's Corruption, Huge Debts: Zambian FM," *Xinhua*, 26 July 2010; Chilufya Chileshe, "Chinese Debt, Aid and Trade: Opportunity or Threat for Zambia?" SAIIA Occasional Paper 72, December 2010.

17. Chris Mfula, "Zambia Opposition Leader Says to Keep China Ties," *Reuters*, 16 September 2011.

18. "Obey Rules, Zambia's Sata Tells China," *Reuters*, 26 September 2011. At a 3 November 2011 conference at the Virginia Military Institute in Lexington, Virginia, attended by Shinn, Zambian ambassador to the United States Sheila Siwela commented that when President Sata found out how much China has invested in Zambia he moderated his negative approach. At the same time, he expects fair play from China and intends to change the rules so that Zambians benefit more from foreign investment.

19. Alexander Mutale, "Zambia's New President Sata Sets New Mining Rules for China," *Christian Science Monitor*, 28 September 2011; Elias Mbao, "Chinese Mine Reinstates Sacked Zambian Workers, Minister," *Africa Review*, 24 October 2011.

20. "'You'll Be Fired if You Refuse': Labor Abuses in Zambia's Chinese State-Owned Copper Mines," November 2011, www.hrw.org/sites/default/files/reports/zambia1111ForWebUpload.pd f.

21. Liang-Tsai, 280–82; Taylor, *China and Africa*, 182–83; Maitseo Bolaane, "China's Relations with Botswana: An Historical Perspective," in *Afro-Chinese Relations: Past, Present and Future*, ed. Kwesi Kwaa Prah (Cape Town: CASAS, 2007), 146–51.

22. Taylor, *China and Africa*, 182–88; Bolaane, 154–58; CIA, "Communist Aid to Less Developed Countries of the Free World, 1977," November 1978, 20; CIA, "Communist Aid Activities in Non-Communist Less Developed Countries, 1978," September 1979, 25.

23. Taylor, *China and Africa*, 182–88; Bolaane, 162–64.

24. Trywell Kalusopa, "Chinese Investments in Botswana," in *Chinese Investments in Africa*, 126, 143–44; Bolaane, 164–68. Surveys of nationals, especially opposition political figures, in Botswana concerning their attitude toward Chinese indicated they showed more hostility in other African countries. See Sautman and Hairong, 752–54.

25. Ni Siyi, "Chinese Vice Premier Huang Ju Holds Talks with Botswana President," *Xinhua*, 21 November 2005.

26. "China Must Not Repeat Colonisers' Mistakes," *The Reporter* (Gaborone), 8 November 2006. The Chinese ambassador in Botswana fired back to some of this criticism by noting the difficulties Chinese have in obtaining work permits and complaining that local media are biased against foreigners. "Work Permit Process Frustrates Chinese Envoy," *The Reporter*, 15 August 2008.

27. For a detailed analysis of Chinese investment in Botswana, see Kalusopa, 130–43.

28. Ding Ying, "Shifting Sino-African Ties," *Beijing Review* 53, 48 (2 December 2010): 10.

29. Kalusopa, 127–29.

30. Taylor, *China and Africa*, 106–12. Taylor concluded that "the relationship between Beijing and ZANU may be characterized as having been mutually exploitative and based on opportunism, rather than on any overwhelming ideological premises" (114); Cooley, 94–96; Liang-Tsai, 269–73; Jeremy Youde, "Why Look East? Zimbabwean Foreign Policy and China," *Africa Today* 53, 3 (Spring 2007): 7–8.

31. Taylor, *China and Africa*, 114–21; China Ministry of Foreign Affairs, "Bilateral Relations: Zimbabwe," 26 August 2003; Naome Chakanya and Nyasha Muchichwa, "Chinese Investments in Zimbabwe," in *Chinese Investments in Africa*, 239–40.

32. Taylor, *China and Africa*, 121–23.

33. Chakanya and Muchichwa, 240; John Blessing Karumbidza, "Win-Win Economic Cooperation: Can China Save Zimbabwe's Economy?" in *African Perspectives on China in Africa*, ed. Firoze Manji and Stephen Marks (Cape Town: Fahamu, 2007), 92–93. For an analysis of the "Look East" policy, see Heather Chingono, "Zimbabwe's 'Look East' Policy," *China Monitor* (November 2010): 4–8.

34. Lloyd Sachikonye, "Crouching Tiger, Hidden Agenda? Zimbabwe-China Relations," in *Crouching Tiger, Hidden Dragon?* 126–30; "China Now Zimbabwe's Top Investor," *The Herald*, 23 April 2007. The information on Chinese investment in Zimbabwe is conflicting. Chakanya and Muchichwa argue there was a significant decrease beginning in 2006 (245–47); see 346–54 for a detailed account of Chinese investment in Zimbabwe.

35. Khadija Sharife, "The Ties That Bind: China, Angola and Zimbabwe," *Pambazuka News*, 550, 29 September 2011.

36. Clemence Manyukwe, "Chinese Strike Diamond Riches," *Financial Gazette* (Harare), 21 October 2011.

37. Shinn, 173–75; Chakanya and Muchichwa, 254–55; Taylor, *China and Africa*, 108–10, 119–20.

38. Taylor, *China and Africa*, 123–26; Sachikonye, 134. The trade figures may not take into account considerable barter whereby Zimbabwe sends tobacco, beef, chrome, copper, and platinum to China to pay down loans.

39. Karumbidza, 100–101; Alex Bell, "ZCTU Warns Against Chinese Plunder of Zim," *SW Radio Africa*, 25 May 2011.

40. Tony Hawkins, "Design or Desperation: Trade and Investment in Post-Mugabe Zimbabwe," *African Analyst* 1 (third quarter 2006): 61–64; Chakanya and Muchichwa, 341–42, 349.

41. Alfred Chagonda and Walter Muchinguri, "China Blasts Sanctions," *The Herald*, 3 November 2004; Neil MacFarquhar, "2 Vetoes Quash U.N. Sanctions on Zimbabwe," *New York Times*, 12 July 2008; Stephanie Kleine-Ahlbrandt and Andrew Small, "Beijing Cools on Mugabe," *International Herald Tribune*, 3 May 2007; "President Mugabe Hails China's Continued Support for Zimbabwe," *Zimbabwean TV*, 19 July 2007; Youde, "Why Look East?" 10–11.

42. "Country, China Ties Get Timely Boost," *The Herald* (Harare), 25 April 2009.

43. "China Justifies Veto of Zimbabwe Sanctions," *Tianshannet*, 24 June 2009.

44. "Mugabe Thanks China for Steadfast Support," *AFP*, 11 August 2010.

45. Shinn meeting in Beijing on 2 June 2011 with Sun Baohong, deputy director-general for Africa, Ministry of Foreign Affairs.

46. Taylor, *China and Africa*, 93–97; Liang-Tsai, 264–68; Ogunsanwo, 172, 232–33, 270; Colin Legum, "Africa and China: Symbolism and Substance," in *Policies Toward China: Views from Six Continents*, ed. A. M. Halpern (New York: McGraw-Hill, 1965), 409–10; Cooley, 133–35; Bruce D. Larkin, *China and Africa, 1949–1970: The Foreign Policy of the People's Republic of China* (Berkeley: University of California Press, 1971), 189; Hutchison, 230–31, 241, 246.

47. Xiaohong Liu, 158–59; CIA, "Communist Aid Activities, 1978," 4, 23.

48. Taylor, *China and Africa*, 98–103; State Department, "China's Policy Toward Sub-Saharan Africa," 3.

49. Bartke, *The Agreements of the People's Republic of China with Foreign Countries*, 121–22.

50. China Ministry of Foreign Affairs, "Bilateral Relations: Mozambique," 26 August 2003.

51. Paula Cristina Roque, "China in Mozambique: A Cautious Approach," SAIIA Country Study Report 23, January 2009, 3.

52. Taylor, *China and Africa*, 103–5; China, Ministry of Foreign Affairs, "Joint Communiqué Between the People's Republic of China and the Republic of Mozambique," 8 February 2007; Johanna Jansson and Carine Kiala, "Patterns of Chinese Investment, Aid and Trade in Mozambique," Centre for Chinese Studies 6, www.ccs.org.za/wp-content/uploads/2009/11/CCS-Mozambique-Briefing-Paper-October-2009.pdf.

53. "Chinese Chamber of Commerce Set Up in Mozambique," *Xinhua*, 29 November 2007. "Mozambique Translates Labour Law into Chinese," *The News*, 9

October 2007; Centre for Chinese Studies, "Evaluating China's FOCAC Commitments to Africa and Mapping the Way Ahead," January 2010, 80–93.

54. Loro Horta, "The Zambezi Valley: China's First Agricultural Colony?" *Online Africa Policy Forum*, 9 June 2008; Southern African Regional Poverty Network, "Forestry in Zambezia: Chinese Takeaway," 19 June 2005, www.sarpn.org.za/documents/d0001753/index.php; "Hundreds of Containers of Illegal Logs Seized," Agencia de Informacao de Mocambique, 15 October 2007; Roque, 6–7, 10; Jansson and Kiala, 13–14. For a critical account of Chinese exploitation of Mozambique hardwoods, see Behar, 106–9; Daniel Ribeiro, "Disappearing Forests, Disappearing Hope: Mozambique," in *Chinese and African Perspectives on China in Africa*, ed. Axel Harneit-Sievers, Stephen Marks, and Sanusha Naidu (Kampala: Pambazuka Press, 2010), 155–62.

55. Roque, 4, 8.

56. "Mozambique to Start Building $2 Billion Dam in 2010," *Reuters*, 15 May 2009; Roque, 5; Jansson and Kiala, 8–12. For an analysis of Chinese investment in Mozambique, see Centre for Chinese Studies, "Evaluating China's FOCAC Commitments," 73–78; "China to Invest $13bn in Mozambique—Paper," *Reuters*, 27 August 2010.

57. Roque, 4–5. Jansson and Kiala, 4–7. Centre for Chinese Studies, "Evaluating China's FOCAC Commitments," 78–80.

58. Leighton G. Luke, "Mozambique President Visits China: New Finance Deals Signed," *Future Directions*, 17 August 2011.

59. Loro Horta, "The Dragon and the Mamba: China's Growing Presence in Mozambique," *China Brief* 11, 9 (20 May 2011): 12.

60. Taylor, *China and Africa*, 75–78. Eugene K. Lawson, "China's Policy in Ethiopia and Angola," in *Soviet and Chinese Aid to African Nations*, ed. Warren Weinstein and Thomas H. Henriksen (New York: Praeger, 1980), 169–74; Richard Gibson, *African Liberation Movements* (London: Oxford University Press, 1972), 224–25; Ogunsanwo, 106–7; Liang-Tsai, 259–62; Ana Cristina Alves, "The Oil Factor in Sino-Angolan Relations at the Start of the 21st Century," SAIIA Occasional Paper 55, February 2010, 5; Vete Willy Emmanuel, "Chinese Investments in Angola," in *Chinese Investments in Africa*, 366; Charles K. Ebinger, "External Intervention in Internal War: The Politics and Diplomacy of the Angolan Civil War," *Orbis* 20, 3 (Fall 1976): 681–82. For U.S. concerns over suspected Chinese support for Holden Roberto in the early 1960s, see Thomas J. Noer, *Black Liberation: The United States and White Rule in Africa, 1948–1968* (Columbia: University of Missouri Press, 1985), 109–11. In a 15 August 2007 meeting with Shinn/Eisenman, Paulo Jorge, MPLA secretary of the Political Bureau for International Affairs, explained that the MPLA sent a delegation to China in 1962. Jorge went in 1965, when China began to offer training and arms. Jorge added that 1974–1975 was the only period Chinese assistance to the MPLA totally stopped. For a pro-PRC account of assistance to the Angolan liberation groups, see Irene Gedalof, Steven Orlov and Herman Rosenfeld, "China and Angola," *New China* 3, 1 (Spring 1977): 31–35.

61. Taylor, *China and Africa*, 78–81; Lawson, 174–75; Liang-Tsai, 262–63; Ebinger, 689–92; Ian Taylor, "Mainland China-Angola Relations: Moving from Debacle to Détente," *Issues and Studies* 33, 9 (September 1997): 67–70; "China-Angola," *National Intelligence Bulletin*, 5 November 1975, 6; Digital National Security Archive; declassified memorandum of conversation between President Gerald Ford and Chairman Mao Zedong dated 2 December 1975, 13–16, Digital National Security Archive.

62. Taylor, *China and Africa*, 82–84. UNITA President Isaias Savakuva told Shinn/Eisenman in Luanda on 14 August 2007 that UNITA revived contact with China in 1976 and 1977. He recalled that the last Chinese shipment of arms to UNITA took place in 1978 rather than 1979. The shipment included SKS rifles and 75 mm cannon, and that this was UNITA's last significant contact with China. UNITA tried to reestablish contact with the Chinese in Lusaka in 1994, with no response.

63. Taylor, *China and Africa*, 84–88; State Department, "China's Policy Toward Sub-Saharan Africa," 3; Indira Campos and Alex Vines, "Angola and China: A Pragmatic Partnership," in *U.S. and Chinese Engagement in Africa*, ed. Jennifer Cooke (Washington, D.C.: CSIS, July 2008), 34. Paulo Jorge, MPLA secretary of the Political Bureau for International Affairs, commented to Shinn/Eisenman on 15 August 2007 in Luanda that the MPLA and CPC exchange visits annually, alternating between Beijing and Luanda.

64. Taylor, *China and Africa*, 88–90; China Ministry of Foreign Affairs, "Bilateral Relations: Angola," 26 August 2003; Bartke, *The Agreements of the People's Republic of China*, 6; Lucy Corkin, "All's Fair in Loans and War: The Development of China-Angola Relations," in *Crouching Tiger, Hidden Dragon?* 109.

65. Campos and Vines, "Angola and China," 39–40; Manuel Ennes Ferreira, "China in Angola: Just a Passion for Oil?" in *China Returns to Africa*, ed. Chris Alden, Daniel Large, and Ricardo Soares de Oliveira (London: Hurst, 2008), 302–4.

66. Shinn/Eisenman meeting in Luanda on 15 August 2007 with Eduardo L. Severim Morais, deputy minister of finance; Cecile de Comarmond, "China Lends Angola $15 bn But Creates Few Jobs," *AFP*, 6 March 2011; Campos and Vines, 35–39; Ferreira, 297–301; Corkin, "All's Fair in Loans and War," 109–13. Alves, "The Oil Factor," 12–14.

67. Campos and Vines, 40–42. There is a good discussion of Chinese investment in Angola in Ferreira, 304–8; Emílio Moreso Grión, "The Political Economy of Commercial Relations: China's Engagement in Angola," in *China in Africa*, ed. Garth le Pere (Midrand, S.A.: Institute for Global Dialogue, 2007), 150–53; Shinn conversation with U.S. Ambassador to Angola Dan Mozena, Washington, 7 October 2009; Alex Vines, Lillian Wong, Markus Weimer, and Indira Campos, "Thirst for African Oil: Asian National Oil Companies in Nigeria and Angola," Chatham House report, August 2009. For a review of China's oil sector involvement, see Ana Cristina Alves, "A Brief Analysis of China's Oil Interest in Angola," *China Monitor* (August 2010): 4–10; Lucy Corkin, "Uneasy Allies: China's Evolving Relations with Angola," *Journal of Contemporary African Studies* 29, 2 (April 2011): 174–75.

68. Corkin, "All's Fair in Loans and War," 116–17. For an analysis of Chinese investment in Angola, see Centre for Chinese Studies, "Evaluating China's FOCAC Commitments," 19–23; Emmanuel, 368–70.

69. Jim Polson and Edward Klump "Sinopec, CNOOC to Buy Marathon Stake in Angola Block," *Bloomberg*, 17 July 2009.

70. "Luanda Diversifies Its Portfolio," *Africa-Asia Confidential* 2, 11 (September 2009): 1; Alves, 21.

71. Yvonne Lee, "Sinopec to Acquire Angolan Oil Assets," *Wall Street Journal*, 29 March 2010.

72. The China International Fund Limited is a complex consortium of Chinese companies. An excellent case study, "The 88 Queensway Group," tries to untangle this complicated web: U.S.-China Economic and Security Review Commission, 10 July 2009, www.uscc.gov/The_88_Queensway_Group.pdf; Vines et al., 50–55. See also Khadija Sharife, "The Queensway Syndicate and the Africa Trade," *The Economist*, 13 August 2011, 21–23.

73. Ferreira, 297; Alves, 11–16; "Dongfeng-Nissan Auto Plant Opens in April," *Macauhub*, 12 March 2008; "The Trains Don't Run on Time," *Africa-Asia Confidential* 1, 9 (July): 7; "Angolan President Speaks Highly of China," *Xinhua*, 31 August 2008; Campos and Vines, "Angola and China," 46; Corkin, "All's Fair in Loans and War," 115. The Xinhua representative in Luanda in a 16 August 2007 meeting with Shinn/Eisenman said several of the delays in major infrastructure projects resulted from problems with two private Hong Kong companies that did not understand the local market and underbid the contract. For a review of Chinese infrastructure projects in Angola, see Centre for Chinese Studies, "Evaluating China's FOCAC Commitments," 27–32.

74. "China Funds US$1.2 Billion Project for Revival of Agriculture in Angola by 2010," *Macauhub*, 3 August 2009. For Chinese aid to Angola, see Carine Kiala, "China-Angola Aid Relations: Strategic Cooperation for Development?" *South African Journal of International Affairs* 17, 3 (December 2010): 313–31.

75. "Angola: Concern over Violence Against Chinese Nationals," *Radio Netherlands Worldwide*, 16 November 2009; Emmanuel, 367, 376–79; Ding Ying, 11.

76. Benoit Faucon and Sherry Su, "Hostility Toward Workers Cools Angola-China Relationship," *Wall Street Journal*, 10 August 2010; Jesse Salah Ovadia, "China in Africa: A 'Both/And' Approach to Development and Underdevelopment with Reference to Angola," *China Monitor* (August 2010): 13–14; Louise Redvers, "Cracks Show in China's Angola Partnership," *Asia Times*, 9 February 2011.

77. Shinn/Eisenman meetings in Luanda: 13 and 14 August 2007 with representatives of Western oil companies; 14 August 2007 with three Angolans in private sector; 15 August 2007 with Eduardo L. Severim Morais, Deputy Finance Minister, and with Manuel Correia de Barros, Deputy Chairman of the Executive Council of the Strategic Studies Center of Angola; 14 August 2007 with Abrahao P. S. Gourgel, Vice Minister of Industry; Corkin, "All's Fair in Loans and War," 117–19; Xiaoyang Tang,

"Bulldozer or Locomotive? The Impact of Chinese Enterprises on the Local Employment in Angola and the DRC," *Journal of Asian and African Studies* 45 (2010): 353–58.

78. For Sino-Angolan military cooperation, see Shinn, 165; Alves, 9.

79. "Angola, China Strengthen Military Cooperation," *Angola Press*, 26 May 2010.

80. Shinn/Eisenman meeting in Luanda on 14 August 2007 with Chinese Ambassador Zhang Beisan; Centre for Chinese Studies, 37.

81. Campos and Vines, "Angola and China," 44; Alves, 7; Centre for Chinese Studies, "Evaluating China's FOCAC Commitments," 35–36.

82. Shinn/Eisenman meetings in Luanda: 13 August 2007 with Manual Alves da Rocha, Academic Director of the Research Center, Catholic University; 15 August 2007 with Paulo Jorge, MPLA Secretary of the Political Bureau for International Affairs; Jose Pedro Benge, Executive Director and Administrative Counsel, Cabinet of the President of Sonangol; Eduardo L. Severim Morais, Deputy Minister of Finance; Manuel Correia de Barros, Deputy Chairman of the Executive Council of the Strategic Studies Center of Angola; Joaquim de Lemos, Director of Asia-Pacific Affairs, Ministry of Foreign Affairs and a manager of a western oil company. Elias Isaac in "The West's Retreat and China's Advance in Angola," *Chinese and African Perspectives on China in Africa*, 163–73, spells out how China filled the void in Angola.

83. Public comments by Joaquim David, Minister of Industry, in Washington on 9 May 2007 during "Angola Day." See remarks by Deputy Prime Minister Aguinaldo Jaime in Alec Russell and Matthew Green, "Africa's Response: Big Push to Be More Assertive," *Financial Times*, 23 January 2008). See also Vasco Martins, "Angola and China: Building Friendship Through Infrastructure," *IPRIS Viewpoints*, May 2011, 11–13.

84. "PM Says China Values Developing Friendly Relationship with Angola," *Xinhua*, 6 November 2006; "President dos Santos Ends Visit to Russia," *Angola Press Agency*, 1 November 2006.

85. Corkin, "Angola's Relations with China in the Context of the Economic Crisis," 4–5.

86. Chris Alden, "Solving South Africa's Chinese Puzzle: Democratic Foreign Policy-Making and the 'Two Chinas' Question," in *South Africa's Foreign Policy: Dilemmas of a New Democracy*, ed. Jim Broderick, Gary Burford, and Gordon Freer (Houndsmills: Palgrave, 2001), 119–20.

87. Gibson, 65–68, 74–76; Liang-Tsai, 273–75; CIA, "Communist Chinese Activities in Africa," 14; Cooley, 84–86; Sanusha Naidu, "Mutual Opportunities or Hidden Threats? South Africa's Relations with the People's Republic of China," in *Afro-Chinese Relations*, 179–80. Ian Taylor, "The Ambiguous Commitment: The People's Republic of China and the Anti-Apartheid Struggle in South Africa," *Journal of Contemporary African Studies* 18, 1 (2000): 91, 93–97. For a detailed discussion of the PAC and China, see Taylor, *China and Africa*, 130–32.

88. Liang-Tsai, 277; Ogunsanwo, 149–50, 272–73; Hutchison, 196–98; CIA, "Chinese Communist Activities in Africa," 14; Cooley, 87–88; Taylor, "The Ambiguous

Commitment," 92–93; Alden, "Solving South Africa's Chinese Puzzle," 122. For documentation of China's trade with the apartheid South African government between 1958 and 1963, see Jan S. Prybyla, "Pragmatic Marxism—Peking Style," *Challenge* 15 (November/December 1966): 12–14, 42.

89. Taylor, "The Ambiguous Commitment," 98–100; Taylor, *China and Africa*, 134–38; State Department, "China's Policy Towards Sub-Saharan Africa," 2.

90. Taylor, "The Ambiguous Commitment," 102–4; Alden, "Solving South Africa's Chinese Puzzle," 123; Taylor, *China and Africa*, 137–41; Garth Le Pere and Garth Shelton, *China, Africa and South Africa: South-South Co-operation in a Global Era* (Midrand, S.A.: Institute for Global Dialogue, 2007), 128; Naidu, 181–85.

91. Richard J. Payne and Cassandra R. Veney, "China's Post-Cold War African Policy," *Asian Survey* 38, 9 (1998): 874–78; Ian Taylor, "Africa's Place in the Diplomatic Competition Between Beijing and Taipei," *Issues and Studies* 34, 3 (March 1998): 127–29; Taylor, *China and Africa*, 142–48. Alden offers a useful analysis of the position of elements of South African society on the question of recognizing Beijing. For example, the labor union movement expressed concern over the implications of competing with significantly lower labor costs in the PRC. South African business was attracted by China's large market. The armament industry was interested in selling to China. See Alden, "Solving South Africa's Chinese Puzzle," 126, 130–33. On the issue of Taiwan's donations to the ANC election campaign, Garth Shelton estimates the contribution at $25 million and suggests that it was crucial for the ANC victory in 1994: "South Africa and China: A Strategic Partnership?" in *China Returns to Africa*, 259. See also Thulani Guliwe and Skhumbuzo Mkhonta, "Chinese Investments in South Africa," in *Chinese Investments in Africa*, 301–3. For a detailed account of South Africa's recognition of Beijing, see Dean Geldenhuys, "The Politics of South Africa's 'China Switch'," *Issues and Studies* 33, 7 (July 1997): 93–131.

92. Le Pere and Shelton, 139.

93. China Ministry of Foreign Affairs, "Bilateral Relations: South Africa," 12 October 2003; Christopher Burke et al., "Scoping Study on China's Relations with South Africa," January 2008, 7; Donovan C. Chau, "Political Warfare in Sub-Saharan Africa: U.S. Capabilities and Chinese Operations in Ethiopia, Kenya, Nigeria, and South Africa," March 2007, 44–45; Shelton, 260–61; Le Pere and Shelton, 139–41; Naidu, 185–87.

94. China Ministry of Foreign Affairs, "Bilateral Relations: South Africa"; Chau, 45–49; Shelton, 262–63; Le Pere and Shelton, 141–43.

95. Jan Hennop, "China, South Africa Sign Nuclear Cooperation Agreement," *AFP*, 21 June 2006.

96. Press release from the South Africa Presidency, 5 November 2006.

97. Remarks before South African Students Congress as reported by Alec Russell and Matthew Green, "Africa's Response: Big Push to Be More Assertive," *Financial Times*, 23 January 2008.

98. Transcript of Mbeki interview with *Financial Times* posted on South African government website, 12 April 2007. According to South African scholar Garth Shelton,

in a 22 August 2007 meeting in Johannesburg with Shinn/Eisenman, the Chinese were upset with Mbeki's initial statement and remained concerned even after his clarification.

99. Scott Bobb, "China Promises to Reduce Trade Imbalance with Africa," *VOA*, 7 February 2007.

100. Shinn, 169–70; Chau, 46–49; China Ministry of Foreign Affairs, "Bilateral Relations: South Africa"; Yao Yunzhu and Yang Guang, "China-South Africa Military Relations Further Expanded," *PLA Daily*, 21 October 2008; Andrei Chang, "China Eyes South African Weaponry," *UPI-Asia*, 12 January 2009.

101. "SA Signs Police Agreement with China," *Timeslive*, 30 July 2010.

102. Burke et al., "Scoping Study," 19–21; Shinn/Eisenman meeting 23 August 2007 with Counselor Wang Shi-Ting and First Secretary Li Gang, PRC embassy in Pretoria.

103. China Ministry of Foreign Affairs, "Bilateral Relations: South Africa"; Shinn/Eisenman meeting with Wang and Li.

104. "Xinhua, South Africa Discuss Stronger Media Cooperation," *Xinhua*, 17 September 2007; Shinn/Eisenman meeting on 17 August 2007 with Chen Ming, Xinhua Bureau Chief, and Ye Yuan, Xinhua southern Africa correspondent.

105. "The Centre for Chinese Studies," *African Connexion* (July 2007): 20.

106. Guliwe and Mkhonta, 311–16; Burke et al., 8–13.

107. Bheki Mpofu, "Chinese Buy Control of Wesizwe," *Business Day*, 25 May 2010.

108. Burke et al., 8; "Sinosteel Invests a Further US$440 Mln in South Africa," *China Knowledge*, 25 February 2008.

109. "South Africa, China Join Forces in Commercialization of Pebble Bed Nuclear Technology," *Power Group*, 30 March 2009.

110. David Fig, "Nuclear Energy Rethink? The Rise and Demise of South Africa's Pebble Bed Modular Reactor," Institute for Security Studies Paper 210, April 2010, 12–13.

111. Burke et al., 12; Guliwe and Mkhonta, 316–17.

112. Shelton, 270.

113. Burke et al., 13–15; Guliwe and Mkhonta, 303–11; "China, South Africa Pledge to Upgrade Strategic Partnership," *Xinhua*, 30 March 2010.

114. Shelton, 269.

115. Burke et al., 16–19; Le Pere and Shelton, 143–44; Taku Fundira, "South Africa: The China Textiles and Clothing Quota Failure?" *China Monitor* (February 2009): 10–12; Shinn/Eisenman meeting, 23 August 2007 in Pretoria with representatives of South Africa's Department of Trade and Industry; Shinn/Eisenman meeting, 29 August 2007 in Cape Town with Tony Ehrenreich, Director of the Confederation of South African Trade Unions. For labor relations of Chinese companies, see Guliwe and Mkhonta, 320–31.

116. Consensus from roundtable discussion with Shinn/Eisenman, 17 August 2007, on China-African relations at the South African Institute of International Affairs

in Johannesburg; Shinn/Eisenman meetings: with Chen Ming, Bureau Chief for Xinhua, and Ye Yuan, southern Africa correspondent for Xinhua in Johannesburg, 17 August 2007; 21 August 2007 with two members of the Chinese business community in Johannesburg; with Wang and Li; 24 August 2007 with representatives of the Taipei Liaison Office in Pretoria; 29 August 2007 in Cape Town with Charlie SB Huang, ANC Member of Parliament. For both history and analysis of the current Chinese community in South Africa, see Yoon Jung Park, *A Matter of Honour: Being Chinese in South Africa* (Auckland Park, S.A: Jacana Media, 2008).

117. Shelton, 272–73.

118. Shinn/Eisenman meeting 23 August 2007 in Pretoria with Isaac Mpho Mogotsi, Chief for Central and East Asia, and Fadl Nacerodien, Director for U.S. Affairs, South African Department of Foreign Affairs.

119. "Deputy President Jacob Zuma Concludes his Official Visit to the PRC," Presidency press release, 30 September 2004; "Chinese President Pledges to Enhance Cooperation with South Africa," *Xinhua*, 12 June 2008; "Jacob Zuma Assures Chinese Communist Party over Transition," *South African News Agency*, 13 June 2008.

120. Sanusha Naidu, "Consolidating a 'Look East' Policy Under President Zuma?" *Pambazuka News*, 21 May 2009.

121. Lee Labuschagne, "South Africa and China Sign Comprehensive Strategic Partnership," *Digital Journal*, 25 August 2010; Ethel Hazelhurst, "Analysis: China Deals Soar on Zuma Visit," *Business Report*, 29 August 2010.

122. Michael Martina, "China, S. Africa Ink $2.5 Billion in Deals in Dalai Lama's Shadow," *Reuters*, 29 September 2011; Emsie Ferreira, "Dalai Lama: China Sowing Fear and Lies," *Independent Online*, 8 October 2011.

123. Fakir Hassen, "We Are Not Dictated to by Other Countries: Zuma," *PTI* (Pretoria), 13 October 2011.

124. Remarks by Motlanthe, 30 March 2011, Council on Foreign Relations, Washington.

125. Ian Taylor, *China and Africa*, 153–54; Liang-Tsai, 278–80; Larkin, 189; Gibson, 123–25; CIA, "China's Policy Toward Sub-Saharan Africa," 3; Gregor Dobler, "Solidarity, Xenophobia and the Regulation of Chinese Businesses in Namibia," in *China Returns to Africa*, 238; Robin Sherbourne, "China's Growing Presence in Namibia," in *China in Africa*, 161–62.

126. Taylor, "Chinese Relations with Namibia," 154–58.

127. Ibid. 159–62; China. Ministry of Foreign Affairs, "Bilateral Relations: Namibia"; Dobler, "Solidarity, Xenophobia," 238–39; Sherbourne, 162, 164, 167; "Chinese to Promote Further Cooperation with Namibia—President Hu," *Xinhua*, 24 May 2006; Herbert Jauch and Iipumbu Sakaria, "Chinese Investments in Namibia," in *Chinese Investments in Africa*, 203–4.

128. Sherbourne, 164–67; Dobler, "Solidarity, Xenophobia," 240–41; China Ministry of Foreign Affairs, "Bilateral Relations: Namibia"; Taylor, "Chinese Relations

with Namibia," 162–63; "Chinese Ambassador Ends Fruitful Term," *New Era* (Windhoek), 5 October 2007; Chrispin Inambao, "Namibian, Chinese Trade Enjoys Rapid Growth," *Pambazuka News*, 27 January 2010.

129. "Chinese Visit Yields Millions," *New Era*, 7 February 2007; "Chinese President Makes Four-Point Proposal to Develop Ties with Namibia," *Xinhua*, 5 February 2007; Jauch and Sakaria, 205–6.

130. "Chinese Space Centre to Aid Namibian Development Efforts," *Africa: The Good News*, 11 August 2010.

131. "Issues at Rössing Uranium Mine, Namibia," 9 November 2008, www.wise-uranium.org/umoproe.html. For a review of Chinese investment in Namibia, see Jauch and Sakaria, 209–12; David Barboza and Michael Wines, "Mining Giant Scraps China Deal," *New York Times*, 5 June 2009.

132. Desie Heita, "China's Investments Offer Little Value," *New Era*, 26 March 2009. According to Christiane Doerner, Namibia's Ministry of Home Affairs has issued about 20,000 work permits for Chinese citizens. Some may not have come and others may have left. Jauch and Sakaria, 208–9.

133. "40,000 Chinese in Namibia," *Namibian*, 21 November 2006; "Chinese Confronted on Labour Abuse," *New Era*, 23 August 2006.

134. "Not Treating All Alike," editorial, *Republikein* (Windhoek), 18 August 2008.

135. Chamwe Kaira, "Namibia Bans Chinese Investment in Beauty Salons," *Bloomberg*, 22 February 2010.

136. Jo-Maré Duddy, "Business Grills President over Chinese," *Namibian*, 22 March 2011.

137. Sharon LaFraniere and John Grobler, "China Spreads Aid in Africa, with a Catch for Recipients," *New York Times*, 22 September 2009.

138. LaFraniere, "China Helps the Powerful in Namibia," *New York Times*, 20 November 2009.

139. Jauch and Sakaria, 213–29; Brigitte Weidlich, "Chinese Businesses 'Kill' Namibian Retail Outlets," *Namibian*, 21 October 2008.

140. "Chinese Businesses Under Scrutiny," *New Era*, 22 October 2008; Heita, "Chinese Investments Offer Little Value"; Servaas van de Bosch, "China in Africa—South-South Exploitation?" *IPS*, 21 May 2009.

141. Dobler, "Solidarity, Xenophobia," 246–55; Gregor Dobler, "Chinese Shops and the Formation of a Chinese-Expatriate Community in Namibia," *China Quarterly* 199 (September 2009): 707–27.

142. Legum, 412; Liang-Tsai, 284; Cooley, 89–90.

143. Taylor, "The 'Captive States' of Southern Africa and China," 84–86; Taylor, "China's Policies Towards Botswana, Lesotho, Swaziland and Malawi," 189–92; China Ministry of Foreign Affairs, "Bilateral Relations: Lesotho"; Bartke, *The Agreements of the People's Republic of China with Foreign Countries*, 109.

144. Taylor, "The 'Captive States' of Southern Africa and China," 86–89; Taylor, "China's Policies Towards Botswana, Lesotho, Swaziland and Malawi," 192–93.

145. Press release from PRC embassy in Lesotho dated 15 February 2006.

146. Figure from former U.S. embassy officer in Lesotho made to Shinn in Beijing, 27 May 2011.

147. "Lesotho: Anti-Chinese Resentment Flares," *IRIN*, 24 January 2008; "The Chinese Are Everywhere," *The Economist*, 5 August 2010.

148. Taylor, "China's Policies Towards Botswana, Lesotho, Swaziland and Malawi," 194–95; Liang-Tsai, 367–69; Larkin, 185; Ogunsanwo, 119, 149; Hutchison, 83–84; Richard Hall, *The High Price of Principles: Kaunda and the White South* (New York: Africana, 1969), 65. For a journalistic account of China's effort to obtain recognition by bribing Malawi officials, see Cooley, 96–98.

149. Taylor, "China's Policies Towards Botswana, Lesotho, Swaziland and Malawi," 195; "Second Ministerial Conference of China-Africa Cooperation Forum," *China View*, 3 October 2006.

150. "Yang Jiechi Chairs Opening Ceremony of Malawian Embassy in Beijing," *Xinhua*, 26 March 2008; Charles Kufa, "China Forces Malawi Not to Receive Taiwan Foreign Minister," *Nyasa Times*, 4 January 2008.

151. China Ministry of Foreign Affairs, "Chinese President Hu Jintao Holds Talks with his Malawian Counterpart Mutharika," 25 March 2008; "Chinese Premier Calls for Greater Cooperation with Malawi," *Xinhua*, 26 March 2008.

152. Deborah Nyangulu-Chipofya, "Windfall: K40bn from China," *Daily Times* (Lilongwe), 2 April 2008; Paliani Chinguwo, "Chinese Investments in Malawi," in *Chinese Investments in Africa*, 277–78; "Malawi: Beijing Preferred to Taiwan," *Radio Nederland Wereldomroep*, 25 June 2010. Claire Ngozo, "China Puts Its Mark on Malawi," *Guardian*, 7 May 2011.

153. "China, Malawi to Further Bilateral Ties," *Xinhua*, 8 April 2008.

154. Sam Banda, "Malawi Opens Door Wide to Chinese," *Africa News*, 16 May 2008.

155. Mu Dong and Liu Jinhai, "China Becomes Most Important Development Partner of Malawi," *Xinhua*, 28 December 2008; Chinguwo, 280.

156. Dickson Kashoti, "ZTE in US$25m Project in Malawi," *Daily Times*, 17 April 2009. "Remarks by Mr. Zhou Haihong, Chargé d'affaires of Embassy of China," Embassy web site, 12 August 2011.

157. For detailed trade information covering 2000 through 2006, see Chinguwo, 274–76.

158. "NGO Watching Chinese Involvement Closely," *Inter Press Service*, 27 May 2008.

159. Chinguwo, 284–95; Claire Ngozo, "China Puts Its Mark on Malawi"; "Malawi Still Overcast by July 20 Riots," *People's Daily*, 27 July 2011.

160. Taylor, "China's Policies Towards Botswana, Lesotho, Swaziland and Malawi," 194; Liang-Tsai, 372–74.

161. Cooley, 90–91; Larkin, 184; Legum, 412.

162. Shinn/Eisenman meeting in Mbabane, 20 August 2007, with Leonard Chao, Taiwan's ambassador to Swaziland. Chao estimated there were about 1,000 Chinese from the PRC and 100 from Taiwan living in Swaziland.

163. Shinn/Eisenman meeting in Mbabane. 20 August 2007, with Clifford Mamba, Principal Secretary in the Ministry of Foreign Affairs and Trade.

164. Shinn/Eisenman meeting in Mbabane with Mamba.

165. "Second Ministerial Conference of China-Africa Cooperation Forum," *China View*, 3 October 2006; "Ties Benefit African People Ministers," *China Daily*, 6 November 2006.

166. Shinn/Eisenman meeting in Mbabane, 21 August 2007, with Alma T. Andrade, New Business Manager, Tibiyo Taka Ngwane.

Chapter 12. Conclusion: Looking Forward

Epigraph: Bruce D. Larkin, "Emerging China's Effects on Third World Choice," in *China and the Third World: Champion or Challenger?* ed. Lillian Craig Harris and Robert L. Worden (Dover, Mass.: Auburn House, 1986), 116–17. Larkin is Professor Emeritus of Politics, University of California, Santa Cruz, and author of *China and Africa, 1949–1970*.

INDEX

ACKNOWLEDGMENTS

We would like to acknowledge the American Foreign Policy Council, particularly its president, Herman Pirchner, for his extensive support in both conceiving of and administering the grant funding for this project. We would also like to thank the Smith Richardson Foundation for its financial support and the advice and assistance of Allan Song. We are grateful for the help of the Chinese Association for International Understanding in Beijing. Without the support of these three organizations this project would not have been possible.

We would also like to recognize Richard Baum, Peiter Botteilier, Harry Harding, Eric Heginbotham, David M. Lampton, Derek J. Mitchell, Edward McCord, Michael O. Moore, Thomas I. Palley, David Shambaugh, Stephen Schlaikjer, Richard C. Thornton, and Anne F. Thurston for their insightful instructions on Chinese politics and economics; Edmond Keller, Michael Lofchie, and Daniel Posner, for their expert lessons in African politics and economics; Elizabeth Wood, Ilan Berman, Richard Harrison, Jeff Smith, and Annie Swingen for their collegial and administrative support; Alfred Romann for his expert editing; and the staff of the Charles E. Young Research Library at the University of California, Los Angeles, the staff of the Estelle and Melvin Gelman Library at The George Washington University, and the staff of the Ralph J. Bunche Library at the U.S. Department of State for their assistance and patience. We also would like to thank Deborah Bräutigam, Brian Chung, Jennifer Cooke, Lucy Corkin, Dai Fengning, Sebastian Grafe, Derek Grossman, Sanusha Naidu, Jeremy Roseman, Devin T. Stewart, Wang Duanyong, Wang Hongyi, and Wang Xudong for their encouragement.

Special thanks to George T. Yu for his excellent foreword and Bill Finan for skillfully shepherding the manuscript through the Penn Press publication process.

Lightning Source UK Ltd.
Milton Keynes UK
UKOW050748160612

194508UK00001B/22/P